AMERICAN SOCIOLOGY SERIES

KIMBALL YOUNG, GENERAL EDITOR

AMERICAN SOCIOLOGY SERIES

Edited by KIMBALL YOUNG

THE COMMUNITY AND SOCIETY
AN INTRODUCTION TO SOCIOLOGY
By LORAN D. OSBORN
Los Angeles Institute of Family Relations

and

MARTIN H. NEUMEYER
University of Southern California

CURRENT SOCIAL PROBLEMS
By JOHN M. GILLETTE
University of North Dakota

and

JAMES M. REINHARDT
University of Nebraska

AN INTRODUCTORY SOCIOLOGY
Revised Edition
By KIMBALL YOUNG
University of Wisconsin

SOURCE BOOK FOR SOCIOLOGY
By KIMBALL YOUNG
University of Wisconsin

JUVENILE PROBATION
By BELLE BOONE BEARD
Sweet Briar College

PERSONALITY ADJUSTMENT AND DOMESTIC DISCORD
By HARRIET R. MOWRER
Jewish Social Service Bureau, Chicago

SOCIAL AND CULTURAL DYNAMICS
(Three Volumes; Fourth Volume in Preparation)
By PITIRIM A. SOROKIN
Harvard University

ISOLATED COMMUNITIES
By OSCAR WALDEMAR JUNEK
Y.M.C.A. College, Chicago

AMERICAN SOCIOLOGY SERIES

AN INTRODUCTORY SOCIOLOGY

BY

KIMBALL YOUNG
University of Wisconsin

REVISED EDITION

AMERICAN BOOK COMPANY

NEW YORK · CINCINNATI · CHICAGO · BOSTON · ATLANTA

TO

MY DAUGHTER

HELEN ANN YOUNG

ACKNOWLEDGMENTS

Many persons have aided in the preparation of this book. The author first wishes to thank the following persons for reading and criticizing various chapters: E. A. Ross and J. L. Gillin, of the University of Wisconsin, S. A. Stouffer of the University of Chicago, J. E. Hulett of the University of Illinois, Arthur Katona of Bacone College, George Chandler of Principia College, W. A. Cornell of MacAlester College, and Charlotte Gower of Lingnan University. Hazen Carpenter of the Department of English at Carroll College, Fern McCoard, and Ruth Hill rendered valuable assistance in preparing the manuscript for the printer and in the task of proofreading. In anticipation of a revision many persons have offered a wide range of valuable suggestions although not all such friendly advice could be followed at this juncture. In particular, however, thanks are due Howard Becker, E. R. Mowrér, H. Ashley Weeks, A. E. Croft, G. F. Speiser, Harold Christensen, and O. W. Junek, who gave concrete suggestions, some of which have been incorporated in this revised edition.

Grateful acknowledgment is made to the following publishers and authors for permission to reprint material used in this book:

D. APPLETON-CENTURY COMPANY. *Principles of Sociology* (1920, 1930, 1938 editions), by E. A. Ross.

RICHARD G. BADGER. *Sex and Society*, by W. I. Thomas.

CAMBRIDGE UNIVERSITY PRESS. *Questions of the Day and of the Fray,* VIII.

F. S. CROFTS, INC. *Early Civilization,* by Alexander Goldenweiser; and *The Expansion of Rural Life,* by J. M. Williams.

THE JOHN DAY COMPANY. *The New Education in the Soviet Republic,* by A. P. Pinkevitch.

E. P. DUTTON AND COMPANY, INC. *Vision of India,* by Sidney Low.

HARCOURT, BRACE AND COMPANY, INC. *The Mentality of Apes,* by Wolfgang Köhler.

HARPER AND BROTHERS. *Social Mobility,* by P. A. Sorokin.

HARVARD UNIVERSITY PRESS. *Primitive Art,* by Franz Boas.

HENRY HOLT AND COMPANY. *Problems of Citizenship,* by Hayes Baker-Crothers and Ruth A. Hudnut; *Principles of Sociology,* by Frederick A. Bushee; *Comparative Religion,* by J. E. Carpenter; *Sociological Theory and Social Research,* by C. H. Cooley; *Political Economy,* by F. A. Walker; *Social Attitudes,* edited by K. Young.

HOUGHTON MIFFLIN COMPANY. *Familiar Letters of John Adams and His Wife Abigail Adams During the Revolution,* edited by Charles Francis Adams; *The Promised Land,* by Mary Antin.

JOURNAL OF THE ROYAL STATISTICAL SOCIETY. Selection from Volume LXIX.

CHARLES H. KERR. *Manifesto of the Communist Party,* by Karl Marx and Friedrich Engels.

ALFRED A. KNOPF, INC. *The Child in America,* by W. I. Thomas and Dorothy Swaine Thomas; *Danger Spots in World Population,* by Warren S. Thompson.

THE MACMILLAN COMPANY. *Religion and Business,* by Roger W. Babson; *Economics for the General Reader,* by Henry Clay; *Up from the Ape,* by E. A. Hooton; *The Phantom Public,* by Walter Lippmann; and *Social Origins and Social Continuities,* by Alfred M. Tozzer.

Acknowledgments

Massachusetts Agricultural College. *Mobilizing the Rural Community*, by E. L. Morgan.

McGraw-Hill Book Company, Inc. *Population Problems*, rev. ed., by Warren S. Thompson; and *Recent Social Trends in the United States*, Report of the President's Committee on Social Trends.

National Bureau of Economic Research, Inc. *International Migrations*, Volume II, by Walter F. Willcox.

The New Republic, Inc. Selection from *The New Republic*, Volume XLVI.

Oxford University Press. *Origin of Species*, by Charles Darwin.

Princeton University Press. *Heredity and Environment* (Fifth edition), by E. G. Conklin.

Real Estate Board and Guide. *Principles of City Land Values* (Fourth edition), by Richard M. Hurd.

School of Public Affairs, Princeton University, and Population Association of America. Figure from *Population Index*, April, 1938, Volume IV.

The Science Press. Selections from the following periodicals: *The Scientific Monthly*, Volumes XIX and XXXIV; and *Science*, Volumes XVIII and LIX.

Charles Scribner's Sons. *Reason in Religion*, Volume III in the series *The Life of Reason*, by George Santayana.

University of Chicago Press. *General Psychology* (Second edition), by Walter Hunter; *The Jack-Roller*, by Clifford R. Shaw; *The Mental Traits of Sex*, by Helen B. Thompson Woolley; and selection from *Publications of the American Sociological Society*, Volume VIII.

University of North Carolina Press. *Social Differentiation*, by C. C. North.

University of Southern California Press. *The Accommodative Process in Industry*, by Melvin J. Vincent.

The Viking Press, Inc. *Social Change*, by William Fielding Ogburn. Copyright 1922 by B. W. Huebsch, Inc.

CONTENTS

Introductory Note xiii
Selected Bibliography xviii

PART ONE

GROUPS, CULTURE, AND PERSONALITY

I. The Forms of Group Life 3
II. The Nature of Culture 18
III. How Culture Grows and Changes . . . 30
IV. The Expanding World of Interaction . . 57
V. Original Nature, Heredity, and Environ-
ment 89
VI. Personality 109

PART TWO

GEOGRAPHY, RACE, AND POPULATION

VII. Geography and Culture 137
VIII. Race 153
IX. Problems of World Population . . . 167
X. Differentials in Population . . . 186

PART THREE

SOCIETAL ORGANIZATION AND CULTURE

XI. The Family and Its Institutions . . . 215
XII. The Modern Family 231
XIII. Education and Its Institutions . . . 257
XIV. Religion 284
XV. Play and Art 304
XVI. Science and Philosophy 326

ix

x

Contents

PART FOUR

FUNDAMENTAL PROCESSES OF INTERACTION

CHAPTER		PAGE
XVII.	COMPETITION	349
XVIII.	CONFLICT	366
XIX.	CONFLICT (*Continued*)	383
XX.	CO-OPERATION	400
XXI.	AGE AND SEX DIFFERENTIATION . . .	416
XXII.	DIFFERENTIATION IN DIVISION OF LABOR AND IN LEADERSHIP	437
XXIII.	ACCOMMODATION	452
XXIV.	STRATIFICATION	473
XXV.	ASSIMILATION	495

PART FIVE

PHASES OF SOCIAL CONTROL

		PAGE
XXVI.	SOCIAL CONTROL	519
XXVII.	CONTROL IN ECONOMIC AND PROFESSIONAL RELATIONS	535
XXVIII.	SOCIAL CONTROL AND PERSONAL DEMORALIZATION	554
XXIX.	PROSPECTS OF CHANGE AND CONTROL .	575
GLOSSARY	. . . .	595
INDEX	. . . .	601

LIST OF FIGURES

FIGURE		PAGE
1.	Showing the continuity of attitudes from primary to secondary groups	10
2.	Showing opposition between primary and secondary groups when divided into we- and others-groups .	14
3.	Map showing Federal Reserve Banking Districts of the United States with areas of metropolitan newspaper circulation	74
4.	Showing the inheritance of dominant and recessive characters	93
5.	Showing sex as a Mendelian character	96

Contents

PAGE

FIGURE

6. Showing possible distribution of personality types . . 126
7. World population growth: 1650-1930 . . 168
8. Showing distribution of native white population of native parentage in Wisconsin for 1900 . 187
9. Showing distribution of population in the Province of Alberta, Canada, for 1911 . 188
10. Showing distribution of rural farm population by age and sex in the United States for 1930 . 189
11. Showing distribution of foreign-born population in the United States for 1920 and for 1930 . 190
12. Showing distribution of population by age and sex in the United States for 1930, and "medium" estimates for 1980 . 192
13. Diagram of interaction of pupils, teachers, and parents . 260
14. Showing distribution of occupations on the army scale of intelligence . 441
15. Showing distribution of population around an average of the cultural norms, thought of as mean or median, with the variants at either end . 556
16. Showing direction which behavior may take in the face of a crisis . 558

LIST OF TABLES

PAGE

TABLE

1. Showing permanence of primary and secondary associations . 12
2. Showing possible combinations arising in the second filial generation, F_2, following a cross between dominant tall yellow and recessive short green peas . 94
3. High and low population density for selected countries 175
4. Infant mortality in selected countries. Deaths under one year per 1,000 live births . 179
5. Average number of persons per family in selected communities, divided by broad occupational groups, 1930 . 234
6. Showing birthplace of persons in *Who's Who in America* for 1922-23 and the occupation of their fathers . 445

INTRODUCTORY NOTE

Broadly speaking, sociology deals with the behavior of men in groups. A *group* is any collection of two or more individuals who carry on social relations with each other. Group behavior depends not upon the mere presence of men together, but upon their interaction. This interaction takes three forms: person-to-person contact, person-to-group contact, and group-to-group contact. In stimulating each other and responding to each other, men develop common modes of thinking and acting. These we call customs, traditions, or folkways. More specifically, these include the regulations governing conduct and approved ways of acting, the manners and fashions of a group, and the whole range of social beliefs, values, conventions, social rituals, and techniques of living. The general term for these common and accepted ways of thinking and acting is *culture*. This term covers all the folkways which men have developed from living together in groups. Furthermore, culture comes down to us from the past. Each generation modifies or adds something to it and passes it on to the next generation.

Since group life depends on, or really consists in, interaction and contact, it is necessary to study the forms of such action or *social processes*. These are co-operation and opposition, the latter being divided into competition and conflict. From these develop other processes, such as the division of labor, the formation of social classes, the settlement of conflict by accommodation, and the merging of persons and groups of divergent cultures into a common group with a common culture, the change which we call assimilation.

The same interaction looked at from the angle of the individual determines what is called personality. *Personality* is that combination of ideas, attitudes, and habits which the individual develops as he plays his part within the boundaries of various groups: family, neighborhood, fraternity, trade union, merchants' association, political party, church body, and so on.

In the large sense, then, sociology deals with groups, with culture, with processes, and with personalities in interaction. Yet in practice sociology limits itself to a more narrow field. It is but one of the social sciences, although it has close relations with the others. Thus political science, which deals with the forms and functions of government, touches sociology at many points, especially in regard to social control. So, too, economics, which studies the means of production, distribution, and consumption of material goods, is related to sociology, especially in regard to the matters of co-operation, opposition, and differentiation, in reference to formation of social classes, and in regard to accommodation. Economic activity also has a place in family life, and is not unrelated to many other phases of culture: education, religion, recreation, and even philosophy.

Since the behavior of men in groups must be looked upon as a totality, we shall not hesitate to point out the relations of sociology to political science and economics when this is necessary or essential to an understanding of our subject. Yet, strictly speaking, sociology is concerned chiefly with *the study of the non-economic and non-political behavior of men, with particular reference to groups, their interrelations and basic processes, their culture, and to personality as it is influenced by social interaction.*

A word must be said about the relation of sociology to cultural anthropology. Cultural anthropology deals with the total culture of man: economic, political, and sociological. In a broad sense it becomes the unifying ground for all the special social sciences. Until very recently, however, much cultural anthropology has dealt with the archaeological deposits of dead cultures or has confined itself to the descriptive history of primitive peoples, leaving out of account the important matters of social processes and personality. But signs are everywhere apparent that modern cultural anthropology will more and more concern itself not only with archaeological finds and with living primitive peoples, but with all societies, both preliterate and civilized, and that moreover it will interest itself in the broader matters of processes and personalities.

Already cultural anthropology has profoundly influenced sociology, economics, and political science. In time parts of cultural anthropology and sociology may be united into one common discipline. Throughout the present volume the emphasis upon culture indicates clearly how these influences are already at work.

Something also may be said about the relation of sociology to history. History gives us an account of events, people, and culture in time and place. It is interested in the unique or isolated occurrence. Usually the historian is satisfied when he has collected, weighed, and recorded his evidence, and given us his best interpretation as to what the data mean. Sociology, like the other social sciences, is interested not in the isolated event so much as in the uniformity of certain events which furnish the basis for some generalizations or principles of behavior in society. Clearly history furnishes sociology with its basic materials.[1]

In practice, however, the line between history and the social sciences is not sharply drawn. Many historians go beyond their facts to offer general principles; and in this way they become for the time being sociologists, political scientists, or economists.

Finally, what is the relation of social psychology to sociology? Social psychology concerns the study of the individual in his person-to-person, person-to-group, and group-to-person relations. Its central theme is the manner in which the personality is built up. It draws upon physiological psychology for its material on the original motives for conduct, such as needs for food, mates, and survival. It also takes into account the mechanisms of organic action. But the personality emerges only as the individual is conditioned to the material and social world around him. Since this process of building the personality depends upon social interaction, social psychology must take into account groups, culture, and social processes. But its emphasis is always upon the individual as the unit, not upon the group or the culture, or upon the larger social processes. In other words if we wish to study groups, culture, and processes as units, we confine ourselves to sociology, political science, economics, or cultural anthropology. If we wish to study the individual as a member of a group and as a recipient and maker of culture, or as an element in the larger social process, then we approach the material from the angle of social psychology. For our purposes, therefore, we shall draw upon social psychology at many points in order to analyze and understand the behavior of man in society.

PLAN OF THIS BOOK

From this dual approach—sociological and social psychological —we shall undertake to examine some of the more important phases of social life. Our work is separated for convenience into five major divisions.

[1] The term *history* is here used in the sense of recorded event, not traditional academic history. A case record of a social welfare agency or a collection of population statistics from a census are in this sense "historical events." Obviously, however, traditional historical records of nations, classes, and societies constitute, for the present, most of the important data for the social sciences.

Introductory Note

PART ONE deals with groups, culture, and personality. The first three chapters sketch the dominant features of group life and culture. Then follows a chapter dealing with the expanding world of social contact from primary village life to the "world society." From this we go on to discuss the individual in the group, drawing largely upon biology and social psychology. These chapters are basic to all that follows.

PART TWO presents material on three important factors which underlie society and culture: geography, race, and population. But these do not affect man in society without reference to his culture, as we shall see.

PART THREE discusses organized group life or societal organization[2] and culture with particular reference to the family, education, play life, art, religion, science, and philosophy. While the emphasis in this section is upon the institutional phases of our material, the individual's rôle will not be neglected.

PART FOUR concerns itself with the fundamental forms of interaction or social processes, but these do not operate independently of each other nor of the culture of the particular society. The most obvious processes are co-operation and opposition, the latter divided, ordinarily, into competition and conflict. Out of these, in turn, develop other processes concerned with differentiation, accommodation, stratification, and assimilation.

The final division, PART FIVE, deals with social control, which is intimately bound up with societal organization and social processes. In our present world the rate of change and the problems of controlling the use of power are fundamental to the very existence of society itself. Nowhere is the challenge to social science greater than in regard to these matters.

CLASSROOM USE OF THIS BOOK

Since this volume is necessarily limited in the matter of illustrative material, at the close of each chapter selected references to other reading are provided. In order to make some of these concrete and illustrative data easily available, the author has prepared a *Source Book for Sociology* for collateral reading.

At the close of each chapter there are also a number of questions and exercises, and suggestions for class reports and longer

[2]The term *societal* refers to society as a whole, especially to its organized aspects, while *social* is a term indicating the interactional phases more particularly.

papers, designed to aid students in discussing the materials. The mere review questions are not very numerous; but obviously the teacher may devise any number of questions which will test his students' mastery of the material at the memory level. More valuable than mere recitation of facts is the use of questions and topics which will extend the students' knowledge and interpretation beyond the necessary limits of such a book as this.

Exhaustive bibliographies and references to source materials are so plentiful in the major textbooks and current periodicals in sociology and related fields that there is little occasion for duplicating these again. In the author's *Source Book for Sociology*, however, selected bibliographies are included at the close of respective chapters. In the present book such bibliographies are omitted, although in the class assignments certain references are cited from which the student or teacher may search further for additional materials in the preparation of reports or longer papers.

As an aid, however, to familiarizing the beginning student with the background materials, there follow at the close of this introduction about 150 titles of books which would make up a suitable working library in sociology for teaching purposes. Most of these references are to textbooks and collections of papers, but certain more fundamental monographic volumes are included. Many of the volumes listed contain ample bibliographies, both to books and to periodicals. These will assist the student and teacher in going further into the literature. No attempt at classification of this selected list is made, because of obvious overlappings and because most of these books are of general broader scope rather than particular studies. The titles usually indicate those books which cover the more specialized fields.

In addition to the selected bibliography of books, monographs, encyclopedias, and yearbooks, there is given a list of the principal journals which contain materials of interest to sociology. Again, this is not complete and is limited chiefly to publications in English. The address of the editorial office is added in some instances as an aid to possible communication. While not every college library will contain all these books and periodicals, the instructor and student will ordinarily find a sufficient number to aid him in his teaching or studying. The whole field of the social sciences is growing so rapidly that the student should be encouraged to make use of periodicals and new books at all times.

Introductory Note

SELECTED BIBLIOGRAPHY

BOOKS

Allport, F. H., *Institutional Behavior.* Chapel Hill: University of North Carolina Press, 1933.

Ballard, L. V., *Social Institutions.* New York: D. Appleton-Century Co., 1936.

Barnes, H. E., and Becker, Howard, *Social Thought from Lore to Science.* 2 vols. Boston: D. C. Heath and Co., 1938.

Blumenthal, Albert, *Small-Town Stuff.* Chicago: University of Chicago Press, 1932.

Boas, Franz, *The Mind of Primitive Man.* New York: The Macmillan Co., rev. ed., 1938.

Boettiger, Louis A. *Fundamentals of Sociology.* New York: The Ronald Press, 1938.

Breckinridge, Sophonisba P., *Women in the Twentieth Century; a Study of their Political, Social, and Economic Activities.* New York: McGraw-Hill Book Co., 1933.

Brunner, E. de S., and Kolb, J. H., *Rural Social Trends.* New York: McGraw-Hill Book Co., 1933.

Burke, Kenneth, *Permanence and Change.* New York: New Republic, 1935.

Carpenter, Niles, *The Sociology of City Life.* New York: Longmans, Green and Co., 1931.

Carr-Saunders, A. M, *World Population.* Oxford: The Clarendon Press, 1936.

Cavan, Ruth Shonle, *Suicide.* Chicago: University of Chicago Press, 1928.

Cooley, C. H., *Human Nature and the Social Order.* New York: Charles Scribner's Sons, rev. ed., 1922.

——, *Social Organization.* New York: Charles Scribner's Sons, 1909.

——, *Social Process.* New York: Charles Scribner's Sons, 1918.

——, *Sociological Theory and Social Research.* New York: Henry Holt and Co., 1930.

Cooley, C. H., Angell, R. C., and Carr, L. J., *Introductory Sociology.* New York: Charles Scribner's Sons, 1933.

Cowdrey, E. V., editor, *Human Biology and Racial Welfare.* New York: Paul B. Hoeber, Inc., 1930.

Cressey, Paul G., *The Taxi-Dance Hall.* Chicago: University of Chicago Press, 1932.

Davie, Maurice R., *Problems of City Life.* New York: John Wiley and Sons, 1932.

Davies, Stanley P., *Social Control of the Mentally Deficient.* New York: Thomas V. Crowell Co., 1930.

Davis, Jerome, *Contemporary Social Movements.* New York: D. Appleton-Century Co., 1930.

Davis, Jerome, Barnes, H. E., et al., *An Introduction to Sociology.* New York: D. C. Heath and Co., rev. ed., 1931.

Selected Bibliography

xix

Davis, Jerome, Barnes, H. E., et al., *Readings in Sociology.* New York: D. C. Heath and Co., 1927.

Dawson, C. A., and Gettys, W. E., *An Introduction to Sociology.* New York: The Ronald Press, rev. ed., 1935.

Dewey, John, *Democracy and Education.* New York: The Macmillan Co., 1916.

——, *Human Nature and Conduct.* New York: Henry Holt and Co., 1922.

Dollard, John, *Caste and Class in a Southern Town.* New Haven: Yale University Press, 1937.

——, *Criteria for the Life History.* New Haven: Yale University Press, 1935.

Duncan, H. G., *Backgrounds for Sociology.* Boston: Marshall Jones Co., 1931.

——, *Immigration and Assimilation.* Boston: D. C. Heath and Co., 1933.

Edwards, Lyford P., *The Natural History of Revolution.* Chicago: University of Chicago Press, 1927.

Elliott, Mabel A., and Merrill, F. E., *Social Disorganization.* New York: Harper and Brothers, 1934.

Ellwood, C. A., *A History of Social Philosophy.* New York: Prentice-Hall, 1938.

Eubank, E. E., *The Concepts of Sociology.* New York: D. C. Heath and Co., 1932.

Folsom, J. K., *Social Psychology.* New York: Harper and Brothers, 1931.

——, *The Family.* New York: John Wiley and Sons, 1934.

Frazier, E. Franklin, *The Negro Family in Chicago.* Chicago: University of Chicago Press, 1932.

Fry, C. Luther, *The Technique of Social Investigation.* New York: Harper and Brothers, 1934.

Gillette, J. M., and Reinhardt, J. M., *Current Social Problems.* New York: American Book Co., 1937.

Gillin, J. L., *Criminology and Penology.* New York: D. Appleton-Century Co., 2nd ed., 1935.

——, *Poverty and Dependency.* New York: D. Appleton-Century Co., 3rd ed., 1937.

——, *Social Pathology.* New York: D. Appleton-Century Co., 1933.

Gillin, J. L., and Blackmar, F. W., *Outlines of Sociology.* New York: The Macmillan Co., rev. ed., 1930.

Gist, Noel P., and Halbert, L. A., *Urban Society.* New York: Thomas Y. Crowell Co., 1933.

Goldenweiser, Alexander, *Anthropology.* New York: F. S. Crofts and Co., 1937.

Goodsell, Willystine, *A History of Marriage and the Family.* New York: The Macmillan Co., rev. ed., 1934.

Groves, E. R., *The American Family.* Philadelphia: J. B. Lippincott Co., 1934.

——, *Marriage.* New York: Henry Holt and Co., 1933.

Groves, E. R., and Ogburn, W. F., *American Marriage and Family Relationships.* New York: Henry Holt and Co., 1928.

Hankins, F. H., *Introduction to the Study of Society*. New York: The Macmillan Co., rev. ed., 1935.

Hiller, E. T., *The Strike*. Chicago: University of Chicago Press, 1928.

——, *Principles of Sociology*. New York: Harper and Brothers, 1933.

Hogben, Lancelot, *Genetic Principles in Medicine and Social Science*. New York: Alfred A. Knopf, 1932.

Hogben, Lancelot, editor, *Political Arithmetic: A Symposium of Population Studies*. New York: The Macmillan Co., 1938.

James, William, *The Varieties of Religious Experience*. New York: Longmans, Green and Co., 1902.

Johnson, Charles S., *The Negro in American Civilization*. New York: Henry Holt and Co., 1930.

Keppel, F. P., and Duffus, R. L., *The Arts in American Life*. New York: McGraw-Hill Book Co., 1933.

Kolb, J. H., and Brunner, E. de S., *A Study of Rural Society*. Boston: Houghton Mifflin Co., 1935.

Kroeber, A. L., *Anthropology*. New York: Harcourt, Brace and Co., rev. ed., 1933.

Kroeber, A. L., and Waterman, T. T., *Source Book in Anthropology*. New York: Harcourt, Brace and Co., 1931.

Lasswell, H. D., *Politics: Who Gets What, When, How*. New York: McGraw-Hill Book Co., 1936.

Lichtenberger, J. P., *Divorce*. New York: McGraw-Hill Book Co., 1931.

Linton, Ralph, *The Study of Man*. New York: D. Appleton-Century Co., 1936.

Lorimer, Frank, and Osborn, F., *Dynamics of Population*. New York: The Macmillan Co., 1934.

Lowie, R. H., *Primitive Religion*. New York: Boni and Liveright, 1924.

——, *Primitive Society*. New York: Boni and Liveright, 1920.

Lumley, F. E., *Principles of Sociology*. New York: McGraw-Hill Book Co., rev. ed., 1935.

Lynd, R. S., and Lynd, H. M., *Middletown*. New York: Harcourt, Brace and Co., 1929.

Lynd, R. S., and Lynd, H. M., *Middletown in Transition*. New York: Harcourt, Brace and Co., 1937.

MacIver, R. M., *Society: A Textbook of Sociology*. New York: Farrar and Rinehart, 1937.

MacKenzie, R. D., *The Metropolitan Community*. New York: McGraw-Hill Book Co., 1933.

Mannheim, Karl, *Ideology and Utopia* (transl. by L. Wirth and E. Sils). New York: Harcourt, Brace and Co., 1936.

Mead, Margaret, editor, *Cooperation and Competition among Primitive Peoples*. New York: McGraw-Hill Book Co., 1937.

Mowrer, E. R., *Family Disorganization*. Chicago: University of Chicago Press, 1927.

——, *The Family: Its Organization and Disorganization*. Chicago: University of Chicago Press, 1932.

Mowrer, E. R., and Mowrer, H. R., *Domestic Discord*. Chicago: University of Chicago Press, 1928.

Mowrer, Harriet R., *Personality Adjustment and Domestic Discord*. New York: American Book Co., 1935.

Muntz, E. E., *Urban Sociology*. New York: The Macmillan Co., 1938.

Murdock, George P., *Our Primitive Contemporaries*. New York: The Macmillan Co., 1934.

Murphy, G., Murphy, L. B., and Newcomb, T., *Experimental Social Psychology*. New York: Harper and Brothers, rev. ed., 1937.

North, C. C., *Social Differentiation*. Chapel Hill: University of North Carolina Press, 1926.

Ogburn, W. F., *Social Change*. New York: Viking Press, Inc., 1922.

Osborn, Loran D., and Neumeyer, Martin, *The Community and Society*. New York: American Book Co., 1933.

Park, R. E., and Burgess, E. W., *Introduction to the Science of Sociology*. Chicago: University of Chicago Press, rev. ed., 1924.

Pettit, Walter W., *Case Studies in Community Organization*. New York: D. Appleton-Century Co., 1928.

Pratt, J. B., *The Religious Consciousness*. New York: The Macmillan Co., 1920.

Queen, S. A., Bodenhafer, W. B., and Harper, E. B., *Social Organization and Disorganization*. New York: Thomas Y. Crowell Co., 1935.

Randall, J. H., Jr., *The Making of the Modern Mind*. New York: Houghton Mifflin Co., 1926.

Reckless, Walter C., *Vice in Chicago*. Chicago: University of Chicago Press, 1933.

Reckless, Walter C., and Smith, Mapheus, *Juvenile Delinquency*. New York: McGraw-Hill Book Co., 1932.

Reuter, E. B., and Hart, C. W., *Introduction to Sociology*. New York: McGraw-Hill Book Co., 1933.

Reuter, E. B., and Runner, J. R., *The Family*. New York: McGraw-Hill Book Co., 1931.

Rice, S. A., editor, *Methods in Social Science*. Chicago: University of Chicago Press, 1931.

——, editor, *Statistics in Social Studies*. Philadelphia: University of Pennsylvania Press, 1930.

Robinson, J. H., *The Mind in the Making*. New York: Harper and Brothers, 1921.

Ross, E. A., *Principles of Sociology*. New York: D. Appleton-Century Co., 3rd ed., 1938.

——, *Social Control*. New York: The Macmillan Co., 1901.

Sait, Una Bernard, *New Horizons for the Family*. New York: The Macmillan Co., 1938.

Schwesinger, Gladys C., *Heredity and Environment*. New York: The Macmillan Co., 1933.

Sorokin, Pitirim A., *Social Mobility*. New York: Harper and Brothers, 1927.

——, *Social and Cultural Dynamics*. 3 vols. New York: American Book Co., 1937.

Sorokin, Pitirim A., Zimmerman, Carle C., and Galpin, C. J., *A Systematic Source Book in Rural Sociology*. 3 vols. Minneapolis: University of Minnesota Press, 1930-1932.

Steiner, Jesse F., *The American Community in Action*. New York: Henry Holt and Co., 1928.

——, *Americans at Play*. New York: McGraw-Hill Book Co., 1933.

Sumner, W. G., *Folkways*. Boston: Ginn and Co., 1906.

Sumner, W. G., Keller, A. G., and Davie, M. R., *Science of Society*. 4 vols. New Haven: Yale University Press, 1927.

Sutherland, E. H., *Principles of Criminology*. Philadelphia: J. B. Lippincott Co., 1934.

Sutherland, R. L., and Woodward, J. L., *Introductory Sociology*. Philadelphia: J. B. Lippincott Co., 1937.

Sydenstricker, Edgar, *Health and Environment*. New York: McGraw-Hill Book Co., 1933.

Taft, D. R., *Human Migration*. New York: The Ronald Press, 1936.

Tawney, R. H., *Religion and the Rise of Capitalism*. New York: Harcourt, Brace and Co., 1926.

Thomas, W. I., *Primitive Behavior*. New York: McGraw-Hill Book Co., 1937.

——, *Sex and Society*. Boston: Richard G. Badger, 1907.

Thomas, W. I., and Znaniecki, F., *The Polish Peasant in Europe and America*. 2 vol. ed. New York: Alfred A. Knopf, 1927.

Thompson, Warren S., *Danger Spots in World Population*. New York: Alfred A. Knopf, 1929.

——, *Population Problems*. New York: McGraw-Hill Book Co., 2nd ed., 1935.

Thompson, Warren S., and Whelpton, P. K., *Population Trends in the United States*. New York: McGraw-Hill Book Co., 1933.

Thrasher, Frederic M., *The Gang*. Chicago: University of Chicago Press, 2nd rev. ed., 1936.

Todd, A. J., *Industry and Society*. New York: Henry Holt and Co., 1933.

——, *Theories of Social Progress*. New York: The Macmillan Co., 1918.

Veblen, Thorstein B., *The Theory of Business Enterprise*. New York: Charles Scribner's Sons, 1904.

——, *The Theory of the Leisure Class*. New York: The Macmillan Co., 1912.

von Wiese, Leopold, and Becker, Howard, *Systematic Sociology*. New York: John Wiley and Sons, 1932.

Wallas, Graham, *The Great Society*. New York: The Macmillan Co., 1914.

——, *Human Nature in Politics*. New York: F. S. Crofts and Co., 1921.

Waller, Willard, *The Family: A Dynamic Interpretation*. New York: The Cordon Co., 1938.

——, *The Sociology of Teaching*. New York: John Wiley and Sons, 1932.

Westermarck, Edward, *History of Human Marriage*. 3 vol. ed. New York: The Macmillan Co., 1921.

Willey, M. M., and Rice, S. A., *Communication Agencies and Social Life*. New York: McGraw-Hill Book Co., 1933.

Williams, J. M., *The Expansion of Rural Life*. New York: Alfred A. Knopf, 1926.
——, *Our Rural Heritage*. New York: Alfred A. Knopf, 1925.
Wirth, Louis, *The Ghetto*. Chicago: University of Chicago Press, 1928.
Wissler, Clark, *Man and Culture*. New York: Thomas Y. Crowell Co., 1923.
Wolman, Leo, and Peck, Gustav, *Labor in the National Life*. New York: McGraw-Hill Book Co., 1933.
Wood, Arthur Evans, *Community Problems*. New York: D. Appleton-Century Co., 1928.
Wood, Margaret M., *The Stranger*. New York: Columbia University Press, 1934.
Wooddy, C. H., *Growth of the Federal Government: 1915-1932*. New York: McGraw-Hill Book Co., 1934.
Woofter, T. J., Jr., *Races and Ethnic Groups in American Life*. New York: McGraw-Hill Book Co., 1933.
Woolston, Howard B., *Metropolis: A Study of Urban Communities*. New York: D. Appleton-Century Co., 1938.
Young, Kimball, *Source Book for Sociology*. New York: American Book Co., 1935.
——, *Source Book for Social Psychology*. New York: Crofts and Co., 1927.
Zimmerman, Carle C., *The Changing Community*. New York: Harper and Brothers, 1938.
Zorbaugh, Harvey, *The Gold Coast and Slum*. Chicago: University of Chicago Press, 1929.

Recent Social Trends in the United States. Report of President Hoover's Research Committee on Recent Social Trends. 2 vols. New York: McGraw-Hill Book Co., 1933.
Encyclopedia of the Social Sciences, edited by E. R. A. Seligman and Alvin Johnson. New York: The Macmillan Co., 1930-1934.
Encyclopedia Britannica. Fourteenth edition. Chicago: The Encyclopedia Britannica, Inc., 1929.
The American Year Book. New York: American Year Book Corporation, 229 West Forty-third St. (annual issue).
Social Work Year Book. New York: Russell Sage Foundation (biennial).
The Statesman's Year Book. London: Macmillan and Co. (annual).
Publications of the National Commission on Law Observance and Enforcement, especially the following: No. 6, *Report on the Child Offender in the Federal System of Justice;* No. 8, *Report on Criminal Procedure;* No. 9, *Report on Penal Institutions, Probation, and Parole;* No. 10, *Report on Crime and the Foreign Born;* No. 11, *Report on Lawlessness in Law Enforcement;* No. 12, *Report on the Cost of Crime;* No. 13, *Report on the Causes of Crime;* No. 14, *Report on Police*. Washington, D. C.: Government Printing Office, 1931.
Publications of the National Resources Committee, especially the following: report of the subcommittee on technology, *Technological Trends and National Policy*, 1937; report of the subcommittee on urbanism, *Our Cities,*

their Role in the National Economy, 1937; report of the subcommittee on population problems, *The Problems of a Changing Population,* 1938. Washington, D. C.: Government Printing Office.

Bulletins of the Social Science Research Council: report for the committee on personality and culture; No. 25, M. A. May and L. Doob, *Competition and Co-operation,* 1937; and the following research memoranda on the social aspects of the depression (all published in 1937); No. 27, T. Sellin on *Crime;* No. 29, S. A. Stouffer and P. F. Lazarsfeld on *The Family;* No. 31, D. Young, *Minority Peoples;* No. 32, J. F. Steiner, *Recreation;* No. 34, D. Sanderson on *Rural Life;* No. 36, S. D. Collins and C. Tibbitts on *Social Aspects of Health;* No. 38, R. C. White and M. K. White on *Social Aspects of Relief Policies;* and report for the committee on personality and culture; No. 41, T. Sellin, *Culture Conflict and Crime,* 1938. New York: Social Science Research Council, 230 Park Ave.

PERIODICALS

The American Anthropologist. American Anthropological Association. Treasurer: Cornelius Osgood, Peabody Museum, Yale University, New Haven, Conn.

The American Economic Review. American Economic Association. Executive Office: Northwestern University, Evanston, Ill.

The American Journal of Sociology. University of Chicago Press, Chicago.

The American Political Science Review. American Political Science Association. Editorial office: F. A. Ogg, 209 South Hall, University of Wisconsin, Madison.

American Sociological Review. American Sociological Society. Managing Editor: H. A. Phelps, University of Pittsburgh, Pittsburgh, Pa.

The Annals of the American Academy of Political and Social Science. Editorial office: 3457 Walnut Street, Philadelphia.

Eugenics Review. The Macmillan Co., 60 Fifth Ave., New York.

The Family. Family Welfare Association of America, 372 Broadway, Albany, N. Y.

The Journal of Abnormal and Social Psychology. Psychological Review Co., Eno Hall, Princeton, N. J.

The Journal of the American Statistical Association. Editorial office: 722 Woodward Bldg., Washington, D. C.

The Journal of Criminal Law and Criminology. American Institute of Criminal Law and Criminology, 357 E. Chicago Ave., Chicago.

The Journal of Educational Sociology. 42 Press Building, New York University, New York.

The Journal of Political Economy. University of Chicago Press, Chicago.

The Journal of Social Hygiene. American Social Hygiene Association, 50 W. Fiftieth St., New York.

Journal of Social Philosophy. Managing Editor: M. J. Aronson, College of the City of New York, Convent Avenue and 139th Street, New York.

The Journal of Social Psychology. The Journal Press, 2 Commercial St., Provincetown, Mass.

Selected Bibliography

The Journal of Social Work Process. Pennsylvania School of Social Work, University of Pennsylvania, Philadelphia.

Mental Hygiene. National Committee for Mental Hygiene, 50 W. Fiftieth St., New York.

Political Science Quarterly. Managing Editor: John A. Krout, Columbia University, New York.

Quarterly Review of Biology. Williams and Wilkins Co., Mt. Royal and Guilford Ave., Baltimore, Md.

Rural Sociology. Rural Sociological Society. Managing Editor: T. Lynn Smith, Louisiana State University, Baton Rouge, La.

School and Society. The Science Press, Grand Central Terminal, New York.

Scientific Monthly. The Science Press, Grand Central Terminal, New York.

Social Forces. Williams and Wilkins Co., Mt. Royal and Guilford Ave., Baltimore, Md.

Social Research. New School for Social Research, 66 West Twelfth Street, New York.

Social Service Review. University of Chicago Press, Chicago.

Social Work Technique. 3474 University Avenue, Los Angeles, Calif.

The Sociological Review. Le Play House Press, 35 Gordon Square, London, W.C. 1.

Sociology and Social Research. University of Southern California, Los Angeles.

Sociometry: A Journal of Inter-Personal Relations. Managing Editor: E. L. Horowitz, Post Office Box J, Beacon, N. Y.

The Survey. Survey Associates, Inc., 112 E. Nineteenth St., New York.

PART ONE

GROUPS, CULTURE, AND PERSONALITY

INTRODUCTION

PART ONE introduces the student to certain basic materials concerning groups, culture, and personality necessary for an understanding of the descriptive analysis that follows.

Group life and human life are synonymous. Men do not live alone and without contact with their fellows except in the imagination of story-tellers. The group is antecedent to the individual and persists after him in time. And at every point in the individual's career or life organization the impact of his fellows upon him is tremendous.

But groups are not biological entities; they are social and cultural in character. Man's social interactions produce common habits, attitudes, and ideas which become conventionalized into patterns that we call culture. Not only the mere presence of one's fellows, but also the way in which they act and think is important. How they act toward us, in turn, depends upon how they were trained by their parents and others.

This continuity of culture raises the problem of the manner in which culture grows and changes. Since the facts of cultural change necessarily intrude themselves at many points in our study, we must give attention to the general features of the change in this first division. So, too, we shall examine briefly the major features of our expanding world of interaction.

The personality is rooted in our biological makeup. So much emphasis, in fact, has been put upon the hereditary factors in behavior that we must re-examine some of the present facts and interpretations in regard to heredity in order to place the subject in a better perspective in relation to personality. Yet personality, although rooted in biological ancestry, is largely a product of the individual's interaction with his fellows as these contacts are affected by culture. The personality is made up of habits, attitudes, and ideas developed in the social and cultural world to which one is exposed. Both personality and culture are changing as the range of human interaction is expanded.

Note: For the exact meaning of the technical words used in this book, the student may consult the Glossary beginning on page 595.

CHAPTER I

THE FORMS OF GROUP LIFE

Man is a social being. He cannot long survive without contact with his fellows. By group life we mean the interaction of people with each other in terms of some common or like interests. Life in association varies greatly: a student has habits in a fraternity that are quite different from his habits in his own family; as a wage-earner a father has a wide range of contacts which have little or nothing to do with his home life; a married woman as member of a bridge club has functions which have little in common with her role as a wife and mother. And so it goes: each particular group sets the patterns of the thoughts and actions of its members.

PRE-HUMAN SOCIAL LIFE

Social life did not begin with man. It is found in many animal species. Among certain insects, such as the bees, ants, and termites, we find forms of group life in which there is a remarkable division of labor and organization. Some ant species keep "plant lice" or aphids in captivity, which they milk for purposes of securing food. The ants tend these plant lice carefully, moving them when they move, and seeing that other ants do not carry them off. Birds, too, show interesting features of life in association in their joint nest building, division of labor in seeking food, and in a wide variety of vocal gestures to indicate love, anger, or fear. And the higher animal forms, especially mammals, illustrate many aspects of social life, such as mutual care, protection, and co-operation.

Social Life among the Apes. When we come to a consideration of the monkeys and apes, we find social interaction so common that observations on monkeys and apes provide instructive foundations for understanding human social life, even without assuming a social instinct. Wolfgang Köhler in *The Mentality of Apes* (1927) brings out a large number of enlightening facts, among them the following:

3

A certain friendly interaction grows up among apes that have been confined together for any length of time. They feed together and co-operate in certain crude ways in securing food, as in building a rough pile of boxes from which to reach bananas suspended in the top of the cage. When one of their number is isolated from them, shut up in a nearby cage where they can still see and hear its cries, the remaining apes set up a great hubbub, yet curiously only so long as the isolated ape keeps up his wailing. Once he is silent, the other apes pay little or no attention to him, especially if he is also out of sight. When an isolated ape returns to the compound where his fellows are, his joy reaches a high pitch. Apes also show some capacity to care for each other in illness. So, too, they try to protect one of their members from punishment by the keepers, and often larger apes afford protection to weaker ones in times of danger.

Aside from sexual attraction, which naturally is a powerful biological foundation for social responses, certain comradeships develop which are not strictly sexual in character. Köhler remarks: "There are all grades of friendship and even qualitative colorings down to a small dis-like. . . . Rana, rejected over and over again by the bigger animals, took possession of little Konsul, and never tired of him till his death. Tschego and Grande formed a little group in themselves within the larger group, and the friendship between Chica and Tercera lasted through all the changes of time, Tercera always remaining the strong, helpful, 'giv-ing' half."

Also certain definite social gestures grow up. Apes use their hands, feet, eyes, and voice to indicate their emotions and to set up responses in others. While they do not possess true language in the human sense, they have worked out rather elaborate patterns of inter-stimulation and response which make for solidarity.

Another aspect of ape life in association is shown by their treatment of strangers. When a new ape is introduced into the compound, there is usually considerable antagonism or else avoidance of contact with the stranger. Köhler has described how difficult it is for the new ape to break into ape society. Gradually through play, mutual interest in feeding, and sex attraction, the newcomer may overcome the reserve of the others. Sometimes the new ape is set upon savagely, and even though in time it is tolerated, often it does not become thoroughly accepted. This treatment of the "stranger within the gates" shows in a negative way the solidarity which may be built up within a pre-human social group.[1]

Social life among human beings, of course, is infinitely more complex and diversified than among the lower animals, even

[1] Adapted from Wolfgang Köhler, *The Mentality of Apes*, rev. ed., 1927, p. 299.

among such highly developed forms as the apes. The habits which are learned in relation to other members of one's species are, in turn, taught to the new-born and the strangers of the group, thus establishing a continuity of habit or custom. The dependency of the infant on his group is itself beneficial since this transmission of habits makes it possible for him to short-cut the time needed to adapt himself to his society. This continuity of habits becomes the most important factor in human social life, making possible new learning as well as furnishing a foundation for adaptation to the environment. There is doubtless considerable continuity of habits from generation to generation among the lower forms, especially among the apes, although no one has studied the matter carefully. When this is done, we should know more about the origins of human social life than we do now.

FORMS OF HUMAN GROUPINGS

Social life among human beings takes on a variety of forms, some intimate and persistent in time, others temporary or less intimate. In order to understand man's behavior we must examine these in some detail.

Race, Society, and Community. People commonly think of *race* as one of the most inclusive human groups. Actually, race is a biological rather than a strictly sociological term, having to do with physical, not sociological matters. In popular speech, however, race is often confused with the more important concept of society. A *society* refers to the broadest grouping of people who have a certain common set of habits, ideas, and attitudes, or culture,[2] living in a definite territory, and often set off from other societies by certain attitudes of antagonism or difference. Within any society there exist all sorts of smaller groupings of men for more special social purposes.

The term *community* has been used in a wide variety of meanings. In its simplest sense it applies to a limited grouping of people of all ages having a more or less common culture and living in a definite region in which they find a geographical center for most of their common interests and habits. When men live in small groups as tribesmen or villagers, isolated by physical barriers and

[2] The nature of culture we shall examine in the next chapter. Here we shall be concerned with the forms of groups which tend to grow up within any given larger society.

differences in languages, customs, traditions, and laws, the community is virtually synonymous with society.

In current sociology the term *community* ordinarily refers to a locality grouping of people within a larger society, who carry on among themselves through subsidiary groups essential economic, political, educational, religious, and recreational activities. There is usually at the center a business and recreational district with stores, banks, warehouses, hotels, theaters, churches, lodge halls, city hall, and postoffice. Around this center one finds factory and residential sections extending outward to the open country. Such a community is not to be confused with the city, which has definite political boundaries. For example, the Chicago community extends to Oak Park, Maywood, Cicero, South Chicago, Evanston, and other suburban areas. There are also rural communities of varying size which, in turn, are related to others. (See Chapter IV.)

For our purposes we may distinguish between the *primary community* and the *secondary community*. The former is characterized chiefly by limited range of contact, by what we call primary groups, the latter by wide and often impersonal relations, by what we call secondary groups, and is, in fact, far less closely bound together. Put in another manner, we may say that the community represents a certain set of common patterns of behavior within which there exist a large number of smaller social units, subgroups, as they might be called, which give the definite tone or character to the community. This will be clearer as we examine these subgroupings.

Primary Groups. A fundamental structural division in associative life may be drawn between primary and secondary groups. The primary group is characterized by intimate face-to-face contacts and direct interaction, set up by common locality. The social stimuli are distinctly personal: voice, facial and other gestures, touch, smell, taste, and sight. These are the first groups into which the individual is inducted. The features of the primary group will be made clear if we note briefly certain of its more specific types.

The *family* is, in most societies, the first group into which the infant is introduced. It is made up of parents and children who live in a condition of social interplay. It originates in the sexual life of the mother and father, but as a social unit it may be thought of not merely as a two-party group of man and woman, but as parents and children, who have certain obligations toward each other. The family is the only social group in which the biological functions of procreation and nursing are integrated with the sociological aspects of behavior. In the family, moreover, the child acquires all his fundamental habits, those of bodily care, those of speech, those of right and wrong, those of obedience or disobedience. He learns submission to authority and practices rivalry and competition with his brothers and sisters. Affections and dislikes run deeply throughout the family. It is in this sense that the family is "primary" to all other groups.

The *play group* arises out of contact of the children whose families live near each other. It is more or less spontaneous in its formation, developing out of new situations not found in the family. In the first place, the children in the play group meet other children of like age. The pattern of parental authority is ordinarily not present. In these associations the child learns to give and take with other children. There may be quarrels and division, but there is also, as the child grows up, co-operation in games and teamwork. The child's play habits, however, are often influenced by his home training. For example, his aggressiveness or docility in the play group may well be a reflection of patterns he has acquired at home. For the most part, the play group affords him early training in meeting his equals, in learning to co-operate, and in struggling to express his own wishes—things not always learned or permitted in the family.

Another primary group is the *neighborhood,* where there is also direct face-to-face relationship. Neighborhoods are characterized by habits of lending and borrowing, barter, or even simple financial transactions, by the social control of gossip, and by face-to-face insistence on sticking to the moral codes. We must not, however, confuse the neighborhood with the primary community. As Kenyon L. Butterfield puts it:

"A neighborhood is simply a group of families living conveniently near together. . . . A true community is a social group that is more or less self-sufficing. It is big enough to have its own centers of interest—its trading center, its social center, its own church, its own schoolhouse, its own garage, its own library, and to possess such other institutions as the people of the community need. It is something more than a mere aggregation of families. There may be several neighborhoods in a community. A community is the smallest social unit that will hold together."[3]

[3]See introduction in E. L. Morgan, *Mobilizing the Rural Community,* Massachusetts Agricultural College, Extension Bulletin No. 9, 1918, p. 9.

Three other primary groups should be mentioned: the congeniality group, the comradeship, and the gang. The *congeniality group* is featured by a more or less conscious association of playmates based on common interests and habits. Such association usually develops within the matrix of the play life, but it is not confined to children. It appears wherever persons who find themselves frequently thrown together discover a sense of congeniality and friendliness in doing many things together. Usually, however, the congeniality group confines itself to leisure-time activities. It is informal in character. It affords an outlet for sympathetic and free relationships, sometimes regardless of race, religion, or politics. Often it does not even have a name, and it is not to be confused with the formal club. It persists only so long as the persons come into direct contact with each other.

The *comradeship* is an elemental form of association of but two persons built up from intimate face-to-face contact, and appears at all periods from childhood to old age. The pairing off may be between members of the same sex or it may cut across sex lines. It affords an expression for what W. I. Thomas calls "the desire for intimate response." It is not necessarily sexual in character. There is a common sharing of experiences, of heartaches and joys, a planning of life, an expression of ideals, ambitions, and desires, without fear of ridicule by unfriendly mouths. It affords a most free and untrammeled mutuality.

The childhood *gang* arises out of the play group. But in the course of contact with other play groups or gangs, or with expressions of adult authority—parents or police—the gang becomes integrated and formalized in a more permanent fashion. In this sense the gang takes on some of the features of more deliberately planned secondary groups. It is in its full development a kind of club, organized, however, by the members themselves and not by adults interested in providing recreation or education for youth. Because of this origin, it is usually classified as a primary group. In its conflict relations the gang typifies an organized group, much unlike the associations of comradeship, congeniality, and the usual play life.

These associations, family, play groups, neighborhood, congeniality groups, and gangs, represent the fundamental human associations. They are perhaps as old as the social life of man, and constitute together the primary community in its simplest form.

These groups are primary in several senses. They are the first groups in which the individual builds up his habits and attitudes. They are fundamental to the development of the social self, the moral sense, and give one the basic training in social solidarity and co-operation. On the other hand, they are not entirely free from rivalry and competition. There is always some difference of view and action. Self-assertion comes into play, although it is disciplined by the common sense of union.

Secondary Groups. Secondary groups are characterized by much more deliberate and conscious formation than are the primary forms. They represent almost entirely partial and specialized interests or needs. They are often called "special interest groups." They do not necessarily depend upon face-to-face contacts. Actually, direct relations are common but not absolutely essential. A scientific association may exist for years without the members ever meeting together in person. In many of their relations they use long-distance means of communication: the postal system, telephone, telegraph, radio, and the press. Secondary groups are illustrated by the nation, the political party, the religious body, the school groupings, various economic associations of employers or employees, all sorts of clubs, lodges, art and scientific societies, and philosophic "schools of thought."

Secondary groups usually outlast any given generation. Although they usually represent particular interests, these very interests or needs persist through time and often demand more organization than do the primary groups. There develop traditions, codes, special officers, and fixed methods of carrying on their functions, which we call social rituals and institutions. Some writers, in fact, classify secondary associations as institutional groups.

Most of the habits and attitudes built up in the primary group carry over to one's participation in secondary associations. Although Western society is more and more characterized by the growth of secondary associations, the primary contacts are not lost. We shall not here discuss in detail the variety of secondary groups, since in Part Three, where we deal with social organization, culture, and institutions, we shall examine some of them in considerable detail.

Impermanent Primary and Secondary Groups. In addition to these two broad classes of associational life, we must realize

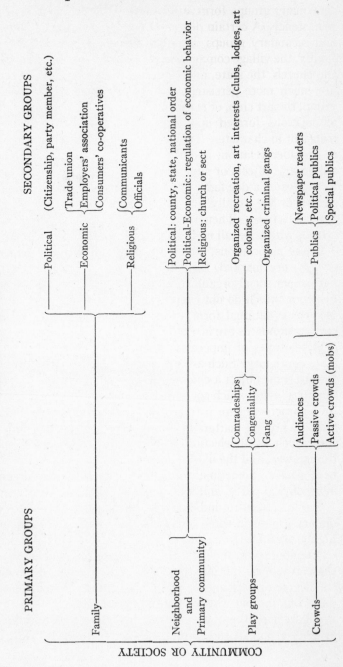

FIGURE 1

SHOWING THE CONTINUITY OF ATTITUDES FROM PRIMARY TO SECONDARY GROUPS. ONLY A FEW OF THE RELATIONS ARE INDICATED. OTHERS MAY EASILY BE FILLED IN.

PRIMARY GROUPS

SECONDARY GROUPS

Family

Political (Citizenship, party member, etc.)

Economic { Trade union / Employers' association / Consumers' co-operatives

Religious { Communicants / Officials

Neighborhood and Primary community

Political: county, state, national order

Political-Economic: regulation of economic behavior

Religious: church or sect

Play groups { Comradeships / Congeniality / Gang

Organized recreation, art interests (clubs, lodges, art colonies, etc.)

Organized criminal gangs

Crowds { Audiences / Passive crowds / Active crowds (mobs)

Publics { Newspaper readers / Political publics / Special publics

COMMUNITY OR SOCIETY

that many groups form and re-form without much continuity or persistence. A certain degree of permanence marks both primary and secondary groups, although some of these groups, like the family, the village community, on the primary side, and the school, the church, the state, and the economic order, on the secondary, are much more persistent than others, such as the congeniality group, the art club, or scientific body. Aside from these, there are associations formed upon certain occasions that are peculiarly transient in character. They depend on face-to-face and shoulder-to-shoulder relation, and they are usually formed around more temporary objects or situations. Such are street *crowds* that collect to watch a dog fight, or to listen to a soap-box orator. So, too, *audiences* are usually temporary and shifting, except perhaps in formal lectures. Then there are the more emotional temporary crowds which we call *mobs*, which are marked by violent behavior.

These associations, which we may call *primary impermanent groups,* are marked, then, by temporary character, by lack of permanent social organization, by a certain passing attention and behavior, which do not express themselves in any very highly ritualized or habitual form, except perhaps in the audience, where certain standards are insisted upon.

Other types of impermanent groupings do not depend on intimate contiguity. Such are the readers of newspapers who develop toward some object a common feeling of solidarity. The so-called "publics" with which social psychology is concerned are often of this character. There are many fluctuating, impermanent groupings built up around matters of public interest persisting only a short time, such as an election, a prize fight, a kidnaping episode, a foreign war, and the like. These we may call *secondary impermanent groups.* Sometimes, of course, a "public" gets organized, as in a political party, and then we have a definite secondary group.

Table 1, page 12, indicates the permanence of primary and secondary groups in three broad classifications: (*1*) permanent and highly organized; (*2*) rather permanent but partially organized; (*3*) temporary in time and slightly organized. Obviously some of these groupings fall into more than one category, depending upon the degree of permanence and organization. Permanence is obviously but another way of denoting continuity.

Figure 1 on the opposite page illustrates the continuity of the primary group attitudes and habits into secondary. Only a few of

TABLE 1

SHOWING PERMANENCE OF PRIMARY AND SECONDARY ASSOCIATIONS*

	PERMANENT AND HIGHLY ORGANIZED	RATHER PERMANENT BUT PARTIALLY ORGANIZED	TEMPORARY AND SLIGHTLY ORGANIZED
PRIMARY GROUPS:			
Family	*		
Play group			
Village community		*	(*)
Congeniality group	*		
Gang		*	
Street crowd	*	(*)	
Audience			*
Mob		(*)	*
			*
SECONDARY GROUPS:			
Educational	*		
Recreational	*		
Church	*	(*)	
State	*		
Economic group	*	(*)	
"Publics"		(*)	*

*Asterisks represent the modal or commonest feature of the specific association. The asterisks enclosed in parentheses represent the fact that in some associations there may appear at times features belonging to another category.

these relations are indicated, however, to avoid too much complication. Thus, the family members become citizens and adherents to a political party. They also become active in various economic and religious groups. So, too, play activities of a primary group sort lead to membership in more formal clubs, lodges, artistic societies, and the like.

The primary and secondary groups provide the individual with his fields of operation. He cannot live, in fact, without participation in some of these groups, although the primary types still furnish the fundamental attitudes, ideas, and habits of all the others.

We-Group and Others-Group. An important functional division of social groups is that between the "we-group" or "in-group" and the "others-group" or "out-group." This separation is found in all societies, primitive and modern.

The *we-group* is any association towards which we have a sense of solidarity, of loyalty, friendliness, and co-operation. It is characterized by the expressions "we belong," "we believe," "we feel," and "we act." Toward the other members of our group we have a definite sense of obligation, especially in time of a critical situation which would threaten them and us. We would protect them as they would protect us. Here we express our deepest sentiments of love and sympathy. We feel at home with those around us. We are familiar with their manner of acting and thinking, and the other members with our own. We understand their gestures. Their words are our words. Often enough the very term and accent are unique and themselves a badge of common membership. In short, our lives center largely around the in-groups to which we belong. The degree to which one's life centers in any particular we-group, of course, depends upon whether such a group fosters the major interests and satisfies the principal needs of the person.

The *others-group* is that association of persons toward which we feel a sense of disgust, dislike, competition, antagonism, fear, or even hatred. It is the group toward which one has no sense of loyalty, mutual aid, co-operation, or sympathy. Rather one is prejudiced against the members of the out-group. The family across the street is inferior to our own. Our neighborhood is better. One's race is much superior to another's. One's antagonisms, one's prejudices, one's hatreds are usually focused around the others-group. The trade union opposes the employers' associations. Toward members of the union, the individuals feel a sense of solidarity, helpfulness, and co-operation and loyalty. Toward the employer and especially toward the strike breaker, whom the union man dubs a "scab," there is intense bitterness. So, too, rival art groups criticize and ridicule the art of others. One religious organization is superior to another. Catholics cannot understand Protestants nor Protestants understand Catholics.

In ordinary times, and within the larger political community which we call the state, the attitudes toward others-groups are somewhat milder and more restrained than is the case in time of war, when another nation or state becomes for us the out-group. Then, all the violences of war, destruction, and death to the enemy come into play. In these cases it is even virtuous to plunder, enslave, or kill the members of an out-group.

This pattern of in-group *versus* out-group is a widespread feature of social organization wherever opposition comes into play. *Ethnocentrism* is the term often applied to the view that one's own group is the center of everything worth while. This is as common among civilized as it is among savage and barbaric peoples. All values are scaled to that of one's own group. The customs and

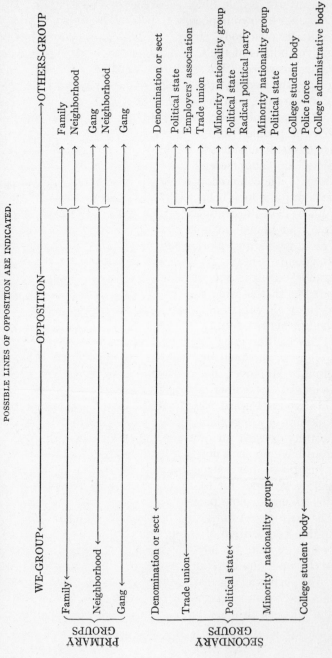

FIGURE 2

SHOWING OPPOSITION BETWEEN PRIMARY AND SECONDARY GROUPS WHEN DIVIDED INTO WE-GROUPS AND OTHERS-GROUPS. ONLY A FEW POSSIBLE LINES OF OPPOSITION ARE INDICATED.

folkways of people revolve around this opposition. Each group nourishes its own importance, believes itself superior to all others, exalts its own gods, and derides the gods of other tribes. The native Indians of the Caribbean islands when asked whence they came answered, "We alone are people." In many native languages the name of the tribe means "the people" or "men." All others are not men or people. They are inferior.

The ancient Hebrews divided the world into themselves, the "chosen people," and all others, "the gentiles." The Greeks referred to all outsiders as barbarians, which meant originally "babblers" or "stammerers," that is, people who could not speak Greek. The Chinese, upon whom most Western peoples still look with disdain, long held themselves superior to the Western world. An excellent illustration of ethnocentrism is found in a manual of education issued in China in 1896, in which this statement occurs: "How grand and glorious is the Empire of China, the middle kingdom! She is the largest and richest in the world. The grandest men in the world have all come from the middle empire."[4] In the same way the Western nations have long talked about their function in civilizing the world, or in bringing the light of highest culture to Africa and the Orient.

One caution must be noted. We do not assume that for every we-group to which one belongs, there is a corresponding out-group. Moreover, not every group in which one does not participate as a member is necessarily an out-group. There are outside groups toward which we are totally indifferent. The comradeship or congeniality group does not imply any attitudes of hostility toward an others-group, and many religious organizations have no such notion. The we-group *versus* others-group is a functional, not a structural relationship; and whether any association becomes for us an out-group depends on the relation of this group to some particular group of which we are a member. The attitudes of out-group *versus* in-group are fostered by opposition—competition or conflict. Where opposition arises, we find people dividing off into these opposing camps. The psychology of the we-group and the others-group is discussed in Chapter VI.

In concluding our discussion of group life, we must indicate certain interrelations between the we-group and the others-group, and between primary and secondary groups. Figure 2 shows a

---

[4]Quoted by W. G. Sumner in *Folkways*, 1906, p. 14.

two-dimensional relationship of these groups, reflecting also the community and wider society at the same time.

It illustrates how almost every primary and secondary group may, upon occasion, develop an oppositional relationship with some other group. It should be noted, too, that this opposition may extend from one group to another of different character. Thus economic groups often come into we-group—out-group contact with reference to the state; at other times the religious order may fall into opposition with the state or with the economic order.

Group Life, Participation, and Integration. The intensity, range, and nature of the individual's contacts with his fellows we may call *participation*. This differs in various groups to which he belongs. Thus participation occupies different degrees of a person's interests and energy, giving a kind of scale of interaction. During the early years, the person is bound up entirely with the family. Shortly, however, the play group and the wider neighborhood and primary community secure some of his attention and action. Gradually he comes into contact with the church, the school, and other secondary groupings, and his absorption in the family life, play group, and immediate neighborhood is dissipated. As he reaches late adolescence and adulthood, he finds himself taking part in any number of groups, none of which perhaps forms the center of his interest. Yet with most mature persons in our Western society, the founding of a family and the taking up of a particular vocation offer the chief foci of thought and activity.

We may, therefore, speak of more or less complete participation in any given group, ranging from those like the family and occupational groups which absorb much of our attention to those group associations which touch us only slightly, and in which our participation is distinctly segmental or partial.

Furthermore, since there are degrees of participation, it is possible for us to have a wide and varied range of partial or segmental activities, some of which may be quite contradictory to others and yet, because they do not converge, may be carried on rather independently. Thus a man's family life may be marked by sympathetic and kindly attitudes and habits, while his business contacts are marked by the severe and selfish methods of the jungle. Familiar to all of us are those men who have reached financial power through unscrupulous business dealings and yet find much public approval for their piety and contributions to church and charity.

Finally, one group may interrelate with another for some common purpose. Thus, a church organization may co-operate with a governmental institution like the juvenile court to foster and promote boys' clubs to prevent delinquency. Or an employers' association may link itself up with some phase of the educational order to promote a community enterprise.

Yet there is not only integration, but also opposition, as we have seen from discussing the relation of the in-group to the out-group. Conflict or competition becomes also a feature both of group activity and of the persons who are members of the group. In our discussion of social processes we shall see more detailed evidence of this whole matter of integration and difference. (See Part Four.)

CLASS ASSIGNMENTS

A. Further reading assignments:

1. K. Young, *Source Book for Sociology*, chap. I.

2. K. Young, *Source Book for Social Psychology*, chap. IV.

3. W. G. Sumner and A. G. Keller, *The Science of Society*, vol. I, chap. XV.

B. Questions and exercises:

1. Accepting a continuity in the social life of apes and man, what changes does this make in our conception of the relation of man to the animal kingdom?

2. Illustrate how the term *race* is confused with *society* in popular speech.

3. Is a democracy easier to maintain in a primary community than in one dominated by secondary groups? Discuss pro and con.

4. List the primary groups and secondary groups of which you have been or are now a member. How many of these groups are definitely oriented also toward out-groups?

C. Topics for class reports or longer written papers:

1. The likenesses and differences in the social life of apes and men. (Consult W. Köhler, *The Mentality of Apes*, 1927 ed.; S. Zuckerman, *Social Life of Monkeys and Apes*, 1932; R. M. and A. W. Yerkes, *The Great Apes*, 1929; W. N. and L. A. Kellogg, *The Ape and the Child*, 1933.)

2. The nature of society and group life. (Consult R. E. Park and E. W. Burgess, *Introduction to the Science of Sociology*, 1924 ed., chap. III; W. G. Sumner and A. G. Keller, *The Science of Society*, 1927, vol. I, chap. XV, and bibliographies; R. M. MacIver, *Society, a Textbook of Sociology*, 1937, chaps. VII-XVII.)

3. The nature of crowd and mob behavior. (Consult K. Young, *Source Book for Social Psychology*, 1927, chaps. XXII, XXIV; K. Young, *Social Psychology*, 1930, chaps. XX, XXI; R. T. LaPiere, *Collective Behavior*, 1938, chaps. XVII-XX.)

CHAPTER II

THE NATURE OF CULTURE

Our understanding of group life would remain incomplete were we to leave the matter as it is given in the previous chapter. Everywhere men living together have developed common ideas, attitudes, and habits without which they could not carry on. In the present chapter we shall examine these products of social living.

WHAT CULTURE IS

The word "culture" in popular parlance refers to good manners, proper etiquette, or to the refinements of taste in aesthetics. In the social sciences it means something far more fundamental than this.

Definition of Culture. Without the common ideas, attitudes, and habits which grow out of interaction, society would fall apart. Common thoughts and actions develop first of all around the basic needs for food, drink, clothes, shelter, and the requirements of societal organization and control. So, too, ideas emerge to explain man's place in the universe and his relations to the supernatural. These common or standardized ideas, attitudes, and habits the members of the group pass on to other individuals, to children born into the group, or to new members who get into the group in one way or another. This transmission of ways of thinking and doing runs through all society from the family and other primary groups to even the most loosely knit secondary types. This continuity of ideas, attitudes, and habits from one generation to the next is one of the outstanding features of man's life in society. Although the learning of the young animal is doubtless influenced by the teaching of the older animals, there is nothing among the lower forms, even the apes, to compare with the transference of human learned behavior from one generation to another, or from one group to another. These folkways, these continuous methods of handling problems and social situations, we call *culture*. Culture consists of the whole mass of learned behavior patterns of any group as they are received from a previous group or generation and as they are added to by this group, and then passed on to other groups or to the next generation. As John L. Myres says, "Culture, then, is what remains of men's past, working in their present, to shape their future," or, as the English anthropologist E. B. Tylor (1832–1917) defined it in the opening sentence of his *Primitive Culture* (1871), "Culture or civilization . . . is that complex whole which includes knowledge, belief, art, morals, law, custom, and any other capabilities and habits acquired by man as a member of society."

The meaning of culture will be clearer if we contrast the natural, physical environment of man as an animal, with the cultural world into which he as a human being is introduced and in which he passes his days. The natural environment is that found in the physical world of land, water, clouds, rain, wind, and the plant and animal kingdom—in short, everything that comes from the hand of nature. The cultural world is the creation of man himself as he has learned how to manage nature and himself throughout his entire existence. The English philosopher Herbert Spencer (1820–1903) distinguished between three types of environment: the inorganic world of physical and chemical elements, the organic world of plants and animals, and the super-organic world—the culture and societal order of man himself.

Culture is, therefore, a precipitate of man's social life, although the nature of association itself is profoundly affected by the culture of the time and place. Such primary groupings as the family, play group, and small community grow up everywhere regardless of culture. Yet as soon as common habits arise and become accepted by any number of persons, the forms of interaction or group life tend to become fixed and stable.

Nevertheless not all habits, ideas, and attitudes are determined by the culturized forms of association. It seems that certain universal features of social interaction arise regardless of culture. Thus, infantile attachment of child to mother, domination and submission, opposition to or love of another, and certain other basic psychological attitudes and habits seem to spring up wherever social intercourse takes place. These are called, for want of a better term, *personal-social* learning, in contrast to learning which is determined more distinctly by culture. This personal-social training depends on individual differences in physique, in intelligence, in temperament, and in emotions and feelings. Obviously even these precultural relations are affected at all points by culture. The difference between personal-social and cultural learning is really one of degree. Every society has a certain common culture, but within this society, as we have seen, there is a variety of smaller groupings, each of which has its own particular culture. Yet in both the wider society or community and the narrower associations, individual variation is always at work, resulting in modifications of the more standardized culture of the society or subgroup.

For convenience we may summarize the fundamental factors in culture as follows: (*1*) culture arises out of the *collectivity* or group in which man lives, especially as his actions there are affected (*2*) by his *basic needs* for food, drink, shelter, sexual activity, societal order, and his secondary needs for religious, artistic, and recreational expression. Furthermore, (*3*) these ways of thinking and doing become more or less *formalized* and (*4*) are *transmitted* both consciously and unconsciously from one group to another, thus (*5*) giving *continuity* to the culture itself.

Before we discuss the principal phases of culture, a word may be said about the relation of culture to civilization. Culture refers to the whole mass of man's learned behavior as this has become imbedded in his social life. Civilization refers usually to the complex cultures of the Orient and the Occident, dependent upon written language, and advanced technology, science, and philosophy.

CONTENT OF CULTURE

Although Part Three in particular deals with the interplay of groups, individuals, and culture, we must consider certain general features of culture as a background for our later discussion.

Units of Culture. The basic unit is the *culture trait*. This is the single combination of habits and ideas necessary to meet a given situation. For example, fire-making is a trait, expressible through the use of certain implements and the necessary skill. With the native it may be the device of rubbing sticks together; with civilized man it may involve the use of matches or some combination of steel and flint in the presence of an inflammable gas. So, too, polite salutations, modes of dress, and rites of magic illustrate single culture traits.

As a rule, however, traits do not exist independently of each other. They are combined into what is called the culture complex[1] or *culture pattern*. These patterns generally develop around some felt need or situation. Thus, the Ojibway Indians along Lake Superior built up a whole cycle of activities concerned with preserving their beds of wild rice, and of harvesting and preparing it for food. Likewise, totemism consists of a wide variety of traits having to do with ideas of descent from some animal ancestor, taboos on eating the totemic animal, magical conceptions of its power, festivals in its honor, and among some tribes, like those of our Northwest coast, a whole field of art. In our own society, common clusters of traits are found in political behavior like citizenship, voting, and jury service, or in family methods of dealing with recalcitrant children. In our complicated industrial and business organizations, there are literally hundreds of culture patterns having to do with the production, manufacturing, distribution, and consumption of material goods.

Various combinations of divergent cultural patterns, in turn, form even larger units of the total culture. Thus, among the North American Indians, patterns of maize culture were tied up with the making and use of pottery. There is no sound reason for this association of habits. Willow or grass baskets might be used for holding and cooking maize, as some Indian tribes do successfully cook their food in this way. So, too, as L. T. Hobhouse, the English philosopher (1864–1929), has shown, wife-purchase is connected with certain pastoral patterns, while it is not found among the hunting peoples which he studied. In our own society machine production is linked to capitalist ownership, but in Soviet Russia machine production is associated with collective ownership. Sometimes these linkages of culture patterns seem to have a certain logical basis in experience, as between impersonal relations fostered by factory labor and specialization, but many of them appear to result from the mere accidents of history.

While there are many kinds of culture patterns, it is clear that within this wide sweep of differences, there remain certain uniformities scattered throughout the whole range of societies. These we may call *universal patterns of culture*.

Universal Patterns. Cultural anthropology has often classi-

---

[1] Because the word "complex" has acquired a distinctive meaning in the psychology of personality, the author prefers the expression "culture pattern."

fied universal culture patterns into two major divisions: *material* and *non-material*. Under the former the tangible objects, such as houses and machines and the techniques of handling them, are included. Under the non-material are gathered all those intangibles of culture which are sometimes called the psychological patterns: language, systems of government, of property, of family organization, religious and magical practices, recreation, mythology, art, and science. Such a division may be misleading. We cannot neglect the psychological aspects of material culture, because without knowledge of techniques and skills, these concrete things could not be made or used. Some culture patterns have material counterparts or artifacts; others, such as a belief in a god or a scientific formula, exist within the subjective makeup of the individual. Both are equally parts of culture. Material and non-material culture traits are interlaced at every point. For purposes of description the division is useful, and we shall use it, bearing in mind, however, that even material traits have their psychological counterparts. In order to make clear the place of universal patterns of culture, let us mention them briefly as a background to our subsequent discussion.

Language is fundamental to any but the simplest forms of interaction. It may consist of silent gestures of hand and face, the so-called sign languages. It is found in vocal speech, and in more indirect form in writing and printing. Written language gave man a tremendous advantage since it made possible more permanent records of his total culture. It permitted more accurate recording of events, made possible the advancement of logical thinking, and altogether was an important turning point in the rise of more complex society.

While language rests upon organic vocal structure, words and their meanings themselves are the outgrowth of social intercourse. Each generation does not make up its language anew, but acquires it from the previous one. Language is a universal pattern basic to all other phases of culture, because without this means of communication, the use of other devices of culture would be limited indeed.

Without going into the ancient debate as to the relation of language and thought, it is clear that language as a composite of symbols is intimately bound up with thinking at every point. Higher thought cannot operate without symbols. Therefore, if the essence of culture rests in man's ideas and attitudes, language as the carrier and symbol of these becomes essential to the maintenance and continuity of culture itself. Objectively, language becomes a distinctive part of social-cultural reality. All persons, things, social situations, actions—everything that is thought or done, sooner or later gets a name, because without a name the use of these items is definitely restricted.

Language serves as a link between memory and present experience. With a name, experience can be stored for future reference. With a name, things, actions, and situations, or, put otherwise, features of culture, can be dealt with in thought, since the symbol is as good or even better than the object or situation itself in handling the preliminaries to the final overt action.[2]

Another universal culture pattern, or rather group of patterns, rests upon what the economists call the spontaneous wants of man for food, drink, clothing, and shelter. These are associated with *material traits*. Methods of food-gathering, hunting, fishing, tending domesticated animals, and the whole process of preparing foodstuffs for consumption may vary in technical devices with different cultures, but everywhere societies have worked out their own particular folkways. One of the outstanding characteristics of man in this matter is the development of tools and machines to aid him in satisfying these material wants. The tool is a direct device or instrument using man's own power to assist him in mastering nature. The machine, on the other hand, is a combination of tools driven by controlled power—either by human or by animal or more importantly by water, steam, electricity. These latter controlled forms of power are themselves harnessed by means of other machines.

The transportation of goods and services has given rise to a set of elaborate culture patterns. As communities and societies expand in numbers, surplus material goods may be bartered off to neighboring communities or societies. Thus *trade* and *commerce* arise and, in time, a host of *economic institutions* leading to complex financial and industrial organization.

The possession of goods and services themselves are expressed everywhere as forms of *property*, standardized and accepted within the particular community or society. In our own Western world,

[2] For a discussion of the relation of language and social-cultural reality see K. Young, *Social Psychology*, 1930, chap. XVI, and *Social Attitudes*, 1931, chap. V.

private property centers around material wealth, but in other societies, it may consist not at all in land or material goods, which may be communally owned, but chiefly in magical methods, in festival songs, or in the possession of some ceremonial object.

Man's association with his fellows gives rise to still other forms of culture. As the Biblical writer has it, "Man shall not live by bread alone." The reproductive functions lead to forms of sex control and *family* life, with a host of institutions such as marriage and guardianship.

Then, too, the demands for safety, regularity, preservation of peaceful relations within the in-group, and protection from enemies without lead to dominance by certain groups within the larger community or society for the welfare of the whole. In the tribe this power of social control often rests in the elderly men of the group. The elders, however, do not rule directly through their own whims so much as through the accepted rules of conduct which have grown up more or less unconsciously throughout the history of the particular society. These rules of moral behavior we call the *mores*. The mores have to do with social behavior that concerns the welfare of the group. They define what is right and what is wrong in conduct. Infraction of the mores is disastrous to group morale and safety and is punishable by various painful means—ranging from ridicule to banishment from the group or death. In our modern world, this same power expresses itself in the political state through its *laws* and officers of enforcement and in the whole range of moral codes supported by public opinion. (See Chapter XXVI on social control.)

Man, however, is not given over entirely to mere survival and to regulation of his family life or the general community. He also learns how to play and to create artistic articles and situations which please his fancy and enrich his life. *Recreation* and *art* are apparently as widespread and as deep in man's being as are the more material patterns and the demands for social control.

Not only play and art appear universally, but man seems everywhere to seek to understand, control, and explain the universe around him, not only that of common sense and everyday experience, but also the world of unseen and mysterious powers—the supernatural. Thus arise *religion* and *magic*.

The explanation of the events of the past and of the meaning of present experience is usually couched in *myths* and *legends*.

Myths and legends, sociologically considered, are not just pleasant stories collected for Christmas and birthday presents for boys and girls, but are the living and dynamic meanings which men give to the history of the universe and to themselves. They explain the past, the present, and often the future of man. Mythology is a form of both history and philosophy.

As man learned to manage the natural and social forces, *logic* and *science* developed, and these have greatly influenced the means of securing more efficiently man's material goods and social control. They have also affected the nature of mythology and philosophy.

Finally, the very processes of interaction, how men specialize in their work or fall into conflict, competition, or co-operation, how they make compromises with each other, and how they take on new ideas and actions—to mention only the most evident ones—all become the creatures of culture. Although it may well be that these processes and patterns grow up from interaction itself regardless of culture, and although it is clear that the rudiments of these interactional patterns are found in our pre-human relatives, as man has developed his social life, they become interlaced with standardized, accepted folkways. Hence the expression of these underlying psychological features of social interaction will vary with the culture of the time and place. (See Part Four.)

Since the various aspects of culture which concern sociology will be treated more fully in appropriate chapters, we need not give further details here. But a convenient summary of the outstanding universal patterns of culture may be offered as follows:

1. Patterns of communication: gestures and language.
2. Methods and objects for providing for man's physical welfare.
   a. Food-getting.
   b. Personal care.
   c. Shelter.
   d. Tools, instruments, and machines.
3. Means of travel and transportation of goods and services.
4. Exchange of goods and services: barter, trade, commerce, occupations.
5. Forms of property: real and personal.
6. The sex and family patterns.
   a. Marriage and divorce.
   b. Forms of kinship relation.
   c. Guardianship.
   d. Inheritance.

7. Societal controls and institutions of government.
   a. Mores.
   b. Public opinion.
   c. Organized state: laws and political officers.
8. Artistic expression: architecture, painting, sculpture, music, literature, dancing.
9. Recreational interests.
10. Religious and magical ideas and practices.
11. Science (in modern cultures).
12. Mythology and philosophy.
13. Patterns into which fundamental interactional processes are directed: forms of competition, conflict, co-operation, accommodation, assimilation, etc.

Ethos and Society. Those patterns of culture of a particular society which most distinguish it from other societies we call the *ethos* or societal character. William Graham Sumner (1840–1910), a pioneer American social scientist, in his well-known work *Folkways* (1906) defined ethos as "the totality of characteristic traits by which a group [*i.e.*, a society] is individualized and differentiated from others." Thus, Sparta and Athens, Judea, India, China, and contemporary industrialized capitalistic western Europe, or the United States, have their own distinctive patterns and values. Moreover, as Sumner says, "The ethos of one group furnishes the standpoint from which it criticizes the ways of any other group." Our own American culture seems dominated by a number of characteristic features, among them the following: (*1*) belief in individual material success and general national progress; (*2*) an amazing faith in universal literacy and education for all to solve our social and personal problems; (*3*) belief in the virtue of sheer size or bigness, witnessed in our eternal building of ever larger skyscrapers, larger industrial plants, bigger corporations, and larger school plants; (*4*) rapid movement through space, seen in increased mobility of our population and enhanced means of communication and transportation; (*5*) novelty or constant change to something new and more exciting, as in sensational news, exciting drama, speed racing, crazes and fads; and (*6*) sense of power or the craving for domination, especially in terms of physical bigness —the booster and the "bigger and better" spirit in almost every important feature of our public life.

In contrast to this, in the Orient, at least before Western culture and its values reached there in the nineteenth century, quite different patterns controlled men's thinking and acting. There was no belief in progress in our sense. Mere physical size had no special merit. Certainly no virtue inhered in rapid movement. Rather, calm deliberation and mental rumination of the scholar was the height of man's desires. In India, among large numbers of the population, instead of desire for personal material success and continued identification of the self with individuality, the fundamental desire expressed in religious form was desirelessness, a forgetting of self, the elimination of the wish to be somebody or something.

When two such contrasting cultures come into contact with each other, conflict is very likely to ensue if one group tries to impose its will upon the other. This, aggressive Western peoples have tried to do in the Orient, and have partially succeeded, only now to be confronted, in the words of the Arabian proverb, with their own chickens coming home to roost. The Orient is awakening under the stimulation of new culture patterns, and in time it may arise in power to crush the Western powers who first dared to push a new ethos upon an old one.

The ethos of any great body of people, therefore, becomes a clue to many matters of importance to sociology and the social sciences, especially those concerned with cultural change. The ethos is the heart of any culture, and in our contact with other societies, as in our analysis of our own or other cultures, we must adopt a relative and not an absolute view. Otherwise we shall never come to grips with the problems of the World Society, which lie about us on every hand.

TRANSMISSION OF CULTURE

Transmission refers to the means by which the older generation passes on the culture, or what is sometimes called the "social heritage," to the new and rising generation. It may also refer to the manner in which ideas, attitudes, and habits are passed from one person or his group to another person or group, regardless of age. These means of transmission we may conveniently classify as formal and informal. Although more detailed aspects of these will be treated in Chapter XIII on education, we must briefly note the more important phases of both at this point.

Informal Means of Transmission. Primary groups all pass on the "social heritage" (values, opinions, customs, moral codes, and the like) in an informal way in the process of daily intercourse. As

the periphery of the community expands, as specialization increases, and as secondary groups generally become more dominant,
the informal means of transmission through the printing press, the
radio, the drama, the motion picture, and the like increase in significance. Although the media of transmission are highly organized,
much of the material sent through them is of an informal nature.
The newspaper furnishes millions of readers not only news of the
world's events, but it also gives them ideas, opinions, values, which
the simpler, slower transmission in primary groups could not have
accomplished. Not only are the speed and uniformity of these impressions significant, but also new values and opinions are spread
over the world. Urban ideas and values reach the rural sections.
Revolutionary ideas from one country are carried to other countries
even without deliberate planning. The periodical and the book
create modern myths and legends. Universal literacy has not made
man less interested in gossip, in adventure, and in dreams of a different and wider world. Likewise, the motion picture and the
radio are constantly flooding us with new phrases, new ideas, new
song hits, pictures of fashion, reflections of antisocial or at least
divergent behavior, that are bound to influence the ideas, attitudes,
and actions of millions.

Formal Means of Transmission. Society has long since devised more formal, highly organized means of passing on its culture. In primitive communities this may be in the form of instruction by the elders and priests of the novices who are about to enter
the men's world of hunting, warfare, and marital responsibilities.
In the matter of mechanical skills, guilds of master workmen often
take over the apprentices, who learn the trade under their direction.
In the higher culture societies, formal educational institutions are
set up to assist in giving the rising generation their initiation into
the culture around them. The church has often played a part in
this formal instruction, since religious organizations are always
concerned that their devotees secure the correct dogma and practice. The school, as we shall see, not only contributes formal knowledge and skill; it also gives moral training which reflects the dominant culture. The school no less than the church is given over to
indoctrination, either conscious or unconscious. So, too, the state,
through its legal agencies, often serves as a transmitter of much of
the valuable culture which bears on political behavior. The state
also attempts through its correctional and penal institutions to

transmit the moral heritage to criminals and delinquents under its care.

In Western society, where the state has taken over most of the formal education, the power of the dominant political body to mold the population is enormously increased. This is clearly evident in the force of propaganda. While economic and church associations have long used propaganda as a formal but indirect method of persuasion, the state, since the World War, has at hand, through its police power to control such devices as the radio and the press, an effective means of transmitting ideas and attitudes to the citizens which those in power wish them to have.

The continuity through time of habits and practices, of beliefs and attitudes is highly important for man's social life. The culture into which the individual is inducted at birth makes up a very large section of his social environment. In truth, the group and its culture are antecedent to the individual. Throughout our discussion of societal organization, institutions, and processes, we shall see that the cultural factors are highly important. Yet, as we shall see, we cannot neglect the biological and psychological roots of man's behavior nor the influence of non-culturalized features of interaction.

CLASS ASSIGNMENTS

A. Further reading assignment:
   1. K. Young, *Source Book for Sociology*, chap. II.
   2. Clark Wissler, *Man and Culture*, 1923, chaps. IV, V.
   3. Ralph Linton, *The Study of Man*, 1936, chap. XVI.

B. Questions and exercises:
   1. Select some common culture pattern of our own society and divide it into its component culture traits.
   2. Illustrate some current myths and legends in our own American history.
   3. Contrast the ethos of America with that of contemporary Russia. In what ways is our own ethos changing?

C. Topics for class reports or longer written papers:
   1. Changing ethos of the Orient with particular reference to Japan, China, and India. (Consult H. A. Miller, *Beginnings of Tomorrow*, 1933, and bibliography therein; Maurice F. Parmalee, *Oriental and Occidental Culture*, 1928; E. R. Hughes, *The Invasion of China by the Western World*, 1938; H. M. Vinacke, *A History of the Far East in Modern Times*, 2nd rev. ed., 1936.)
   2. The relation of language and cultural reality. (Consult K. Young, *Social Attitudes*, 1931, chap. V, and bibliography; S. Chase, *The Tyranny of Words*, 1938.)

CHAPTER III

How Culture Grows and Changes

Social life is never static. Even in a tradition-ridden and isolated society individual differences make for slight changes. In this way even so-called stable societies show in time modifications in culture. Today, with easy travel and communication, with the whole world more or less bound up in economic if not political interdependence, change is rapid, striking, and accepted. Change is a part of the cultural atmosphere. It affects every phase of our social life.

In this chapter we shall discuss at the outset certain older theories of social evolution and social progress, then take up the factual data upon which present-day sociology and anthropology must rest their discussion of cultural change, and close with some reference to rates of change, especially in contemporary society.

THEORIES OF CULTURAL CHANGE AND PROGRESS

Primitive man seems to have had no notion of social growth or progress in our modern sense. The slight modifications made in his culture or societal organization were not connected in his mind with any general scheme of change. One of the earliest theories of social change held that man had decayed or fallen from a higher state. Early Greek society had the idea that man had degenerated from a Golden Age to an Age of Silver, through an Age of Bronze, to a very mundane Age of Iron.

Theories of Social Evolution and Progress. The theory of the Greek philosopher Heraclitus (c. 540–475 B.C.) that all the universe is in a state of eternal flux gave a firmer basis for the notion of change. But it does not necessarily imply direction. Empedocles (490–430 B.C.), another Greek, did have the idea of a gradual development in nature from less perfect to more perfect forms. And Aristotle (384–322 B.C.) made the first important classification of plants and animals arranged in some sort of natural scale. But for the most part the classic conceptions were static. Aside from the somewhat literary expression of the idea of development in *De Rerum Natura,* by the Roman poet Lucretius (c. 98–55 B.C.), we must wait until modern times for the concept of gradual evolution to become a central theme in biological and social studies. The idea that development goes on from simple to complex and perfect forms has its roots in two fields: biology and Christian theology.

Modern biological studies of evolutionary processes rest upon the work of several men. Carl Linnaeus (1707–1778), the Swedish biologist, gave us our modern system of classification of plants and animals. More important was the work of K. E. von Baer (1792–1876), the embryologist, who saw in the embryonic growth of the individual organism a recapitulation of the developmental stages of lower species, although he did not interpret this as really indicating a line of descent. Sir Charles Lyell (1797–1875), the English geologist, first worked out the stratification of fossil plants and animals in the earth's surface. Upon the background of this and other work, two men made the most important contributions to the theories of social evolution. One was Charles Darwin (1809–1882), the English biologist, whose epoch-making book *The Origin of Species* was published in 1859. The other was Herbert Spencer, who made evolution through the survival of the fittest one of the important keys to his theory of cosmic philosophy. Spencer saw in Darwin's doctrine of natural selection further support for his thesis. From Darwin and Spencer modern social scientists worked out various theories of social development. Before noting these theories, let us examine the idea of progress.

The classic idea of degeneration from a Golden Age took a different form in late Hebrew and Christian theology. The creation of man by fiat of God was followed in the Hebrew-Christian theology by the idea of redemption of man by a Messiah. Man may have fallen from a former high estate, but he was definitely on the way to a more perfect state or millennium in the future through the steps of salvation. There was here, of course, no notion of growth. It was all a divinely prearranged plan. But it did give men hope for a better condition in the future.

This idea of coming perfection found expression later in philosophic circles as men witnessed around them an increasing population and an expanding world of political and economic complexity. The Romanticists of the eighteenth century took up the idea of progress toward perfection and remade it along less theological and more mundane lines. They looked forward to a society in which justice, peace, and love would rule—the result of a steady and continuous improvement of man and society. The French scholar, Marquis de Condorcet (1743–1794), made a brilliant defense of the theory of perfectability of man. Another Frenchman, Auguste Comte (1798–1857), the inventor of the word *sociology,* gave us a more incisive theory of continuous cultural improvement. He maintained that differences in cultures depended on the rapidity with which various societies pass through a fixed order of change in three universal stages: the theological, the metaphysical, and the positive or scientific. The first was marked by superstition, fear, and crude culture; the second, by a tendency to philosophy but with no clear understanding of the nature of the world or of man and society; only the third, into which Europe was then passing, would give man his proper understanding and his proper place in the universe.

Cultural Evolution. In the last half of the nineteenth century these two notions of evolution and of progress toward perfection merged into the concept of social or cultural evolution. Herbert Spencer himself gave the chief impetus to the matter in anthropology and sociology. In his *Principles of Sociology* (1876–1896) he discussed the development of domestic, religious, and other institutions. Alexander Goldenweiser, an American anthropologist, summarizes Spencer's basic thesis in these words:

"In its bearing on social phenomena, the theory of evolution was to comprise the three following principles of development: that evolution is uniform, gradual and progressive, meaning by this that social forms and institutions pass everywhere and always through the same stages of development; that the transformations which they undergo are gradual, not sudden or cataclysmic; and that the changes implied in these transformations point in the direction of improvement from less perfect to more perfect adjustments, from lower to higher forms." [1]

Spencer worked out the main features of the evolutionary stages of development on the analogy of biological evolution and then set other persons to reading a vast literature from travelers, traders, and anthropologists in order to find data to support his

---

[1] A. Goldenweiser, *Early Civilization,* 1922, p. 21.

thesis. One has but to read him on the evolution of institutions to see how his evidence was collected: a trifle here, a bit there; this from a tribe in the sub-arctic, that from an African society, and so on; until an evolutionary mosaic was constructed to support his desired plan.

Other writers followed his lead. Lewis Henry Morgan (1818–1881), America's first important anthropologist, divided cultural advancement into three stages: savagery, barbarism, and civilization, each with distinctive characteristics and uniform throughout every society. Following suit, the economists built up such progressive economic states as hunting and fishing, pastoralism, agriculture, and machine industry. Students of the family explained marriage systems as beginning in primitive promiscuity with no regulations, leading on through polygyny or polyandry to the "perfect" monogamy of mid-Victorian England.

This scheme of step-wise upward progress became known as the unilinear theory of social evolution. Beginning in crude and simple form, institutions and forms of group life move ever upward by steady stages toward complexity and perfection.

This unilinear concept that culture advances slowly upward by small accretions persisted for several decades, with various writers working out their particular schemes to suit conscious or unconscious biases of their own.[2] One of these is the attempt to state social change in terms of cycles. Following somewhat the pattern of classic notions of regression of culture from a Golden Age to the present, philosophic historians have tried to chart the course of particular societies and their cultures from their inception through maturity to a final state of decay. A recent exponent of this theory is the German, Oswald Spengler, whose book *The Decline of the West* (transl. by C. F. Atkinson, 1926–28) traces the cycles of rise and fall of various Western societies. Sir W. M. Flinders Petrie, a brilliant English Egyptologist, in his book *The Revolution of Civilization* (1922 ed.) defends the theory of rise and decay on the basis of archaeological work in Egypt.

As soon as social scientists began to go not to books and theories, but to living peoples for their data, the whole unilinear theory broke down of its own weight. As more adequate material on the life and history of native tribes and civilized peoples came

[2]See, for example, C. A. Ellwood, *Cultural Evolution*, 1927. Ellwood finds that the parabola and not the straight line best suits his concept of cultural change.

to hand, and the whole culture of any society was seen in its dynamic relationships, the static concept of step-wise evolution gave way to an historical approach which would recognize in any given culture the influences of race, geography, invention, and previous culture. For example, the neat arrangement of economic development from hunting through pastoralism and agriculture to modern industrial society breaks down when we see that in some instances people moved directly from hunting to agriculture, or that often fishing, hunting, and rudimentary agriculture exist side by side, as among the eastern woodlands Indians of North America. Or again, in the family there is no evidence for a moral progress from sexual promiscuity to monogamy. Then, too, historically there are many evidences of sudden changes by revolution. The unilinear theories give little place for these cataclysmic changes in societal organization and in forms of control. Likewise they provide little or no place for cultural regression or decadence, no matter whether this decay be interpreted as the end of a definite cycle or merely as a transition to another set of culture patterns.

If simple evolution has fallen down, are we to assume that the social scientist has no concepts of cultural growth with which to work? In order to answer this question let us turn to see what the studies of actual societies and cultures reveal.

FACTORS IN CULTURAL GROWTH

Neither the static conception of the ancients nor the mystical principles of eternal progression ever upward and onward seem to give us an adequate picture of the dynamics of culture. Culture grows really by two means: invention of new culture traits, and the diffusion of traits. In order to understand these we must state certain fundamentals of the nature of man and of his relation to his environment.

Uniformity of Man's Reactions to the Environment. Although the simpler theories of social evolution must be abandoned, there are certain basic uniformities that must be taken into account in dealing with the growth of culture and society. Everywhere the mental life and the habits of men of all races are built up out of the same biological substructure. The native of Timbuctu or Australia is not so different from the civilized man of Paris, London, or Gopher Prairie as appearances might lead us to believe. The present view is summarized in the concept of "psychic unity." That is, everywhere the basic needs and the mental mechanisms of men are the same in spite of culture differences. Franz Boas, the American anthropologist, in his book *Primitive Art* (1927) remarks: "So far as my personal experience goes and so far as I feel competent to judge ethnographic data on the basis of this experience, the mental processes of man are the same everywhere, regardless of race and culture, and regardless of the apparent absurdity of beliefs and customs."

If this be so, how may we account for the endless variety of culture content which we find when we examine the lives of tribes and societies in detail? The answer to the variations in culture rests upon differences in geography and history. As we shall see, geography does not predetermine man's wants, but it sets certain limits upon the satisfactions of his basic needs. Peculiar problems arise from climate, soil, topography, and the nature of raw materials. The Eskimo do not hunt tigers nor do the Hottentots live in snow huts. The peoples of the plains of Asia or America face problems of climate, soil, and natural resources different from those of the torrid seacoasts of Africa or the East Indies. (See Chapter VII.)

History is, however, the more important factor in the building of culture. Once a device for meeting the environment or satisfying a need has been acquired, it is likely to persist and provide the groundwork for all subsequent development. In fact, invention, including accidental discovery, and diffusion, or borrowing, are the means by which culture grows.

Invention of Culture Traits. A distinction is sometimes drawn between invention and discovery. Invention is an active combination of devices or principles of action into some new form. Discovery is ordinarily thought to be a somewhat passive or accidental perception of existing relations of various elements. Actually invention and discovery are closely related. Discovery of new facts or relations in nature or society depends, for the most part, upon the invention of new methods of thinking or acting; invention, in turn, often rests upon some newly discovered facts. We shall use the term *invention* to cover both the creation of some new device or the discovery of some fact or principle.

Because in our society material inventions have made such a striking impression on culture, the ordinary man imagines that invention applies only to mechanical devices. But inventions cover both material and non-material phases of culture. The automobile and telephone seem highly significant. But so, too, are the Australian ballot, intelligence testing, and chain-store merchandizing.

Invention may be classified into two sorts: empirical and planned. Until the rise of modern science the bulk of inventions were of the former sort. Empirical invention grows largely out of trial-and-error attempts at improvement of some device already at hand or upon accidental discovery of some technique. Science has now provided us with the means of planning or directing and even predicting many of our inventions.

There is no point in trying to find out how inventions got started. This is to ask: How did culture originate? No one knows. But we may be sure that the early growth of culture was slow and blundering, and that inventions grew out of the slowly accumulating culture of the past. Today it is obvious that the elements in any invention are to be found in the pre-existing culture.

No matter how efficient the invention may be, it cannot survive unless it is fitted into a definite relation to the pre-existing culture. There is, in fact, a certain selective process going on at all times in reference to inventions in any society. If there are strong taboos against change, an invention may be dropped before being tried out. If, on the other hand, a society is receptive to inventions, they may effect profound changes. So, too, the use of an invention in the total culture is important. The Greeks invented the steam engine but limited its use to religious rituals. Their culture was not ready for its application to modes of transportation or machine production. Culture puts limits on inventions in other ways. Leonardo da Vinci (1452–1519) was certainly intellectually capable of inventing a successful flying machine, but he lacked the tools of modern mathematics and mechanics.

This raises the question of the stimulus to invention. The old proverb that "necessity is the mother of invention" requires qualification. Certainly recurrent need often induces inventions, but they may not be very efficient. Primitive man needed means to relieve pain and to counteract disease. And his magic was such a device, but only modern anaesthetics and medicines have met these requirements successfully. The long-continued use of old and ineffective ways of doing things is ample evidence that sheer necessity is not always the mother of efficient invention.

It is rather the cultural and social situation that makes invention possible. The existence of sufficient leisure for calm and deliberate examination of devices is important. Without doubt, "just monkeying around" with mechanical devices or ideas has brought about valuable new combinations. In trial-and-error invention, as in all trial-and-error learning, accidental combinations are often important. The false combinations may even suggest correct solutions later. Musing or daydreaming is not unimportant. Getting "hunches" or making guesses is perhaps at the outset as important as actual manipulation of physical objects or of social situations.

If it is the culture background that makes further invention possible, what relation has mental ability to invention? It is very easy to assume that inventions are the result of innate ability of a few chosen persons. As we shall see in Chapter V on heredity and environment, mentality itself is profoundly affected by culture. Nevertheless mental ability, formed as it is from hereditary backgrounds and environmental factors, varies considerably among individuals. There is no doubt that, given the proper cultural stimulus, the superior individuals will furnish the inventors. Yet what the superior person will do with his capacity depends on the society and its culture. It is hardly conceivable that the Negro genius of the jungle will become a great physicist. But he might well become a military leader or the inventor of a new religious ritual.

The inception and the direction of invention depends, therefore, upon culture as well as upon superior ability. This relation of culture to individual ability raises the familiar "great man theory of history." That is, does history make great men, or do great men make history? Confining ourselves only to the matter of invention, the particular direction of inventions and their nature is determined by culture. The great names in science and invention often mislead us into forgetting the slow accumulation of basic knowledge by less well-known men who made possible the more striking work of which the ordinary man hears. To the man in the street the story of Sir Isaac Newton (1642–1727) and the falling apple may suffice to describe the discovery of the law of gravitation; but to anyone else, his great contribution was the culmination of the work of dozens of others who had laid the foundation for his own important researches. The inventions of Thomas A. Edison

(1847–1931) in electricity would have been impossible without hundreds of researches in the century and a half before him.

Another important point in this connection is the duplication of inventions in our own Western society, especially since projected inventions have been made possible by the development of scientific methods. W. F. Ogburn in his book *Social Change* (1922) lists 148 rather major inventions and discoveries made independently by two or more persons in the fields of science and technology. We may cite only a few examples:

1. Discovery of the planet Neptune by Adams (1845), and Leverrier (1845).
2. Discovery of sun spots by Galileo (1611), Fabricus (1611), Scheiner (1611), and Harriott (1611).
3. Decimal fractions by Stevinus (1585), Bürgi (1592), and possibly by Beyer (1603), and Rüdolff (1530).
4. Logarithms by Bürgi (1620), and Napier-Briggs (1614).
5. Law of gases by Boyle (1662), and Marriotte (1676).
6. Isolation of nitrogen by Rutherford (1772), and Scheele (1773).
7. Photography by Daguerre-Niepce (1839), and Talbot (1839).
8. Telegraph by Henry (1831), Morse (1837), Cooke-Wheatstone (1837), and Steinheil (1837).
9. Phonograph by Edison (1877), and Cros (1877), and possibly by Scott.
10. Relation of micro-organisms to fermentation and putrefaction by Latour (1837), and Schwann (1837).
11. Theory of natural selection and variations by Charles Darwin (1858), and A. R. Wallace (1858).
12. Sewing machine by Thimmonier (1830), Howe (1846), and Hunt (1840).
13. Stereoscope by Wheatstone (1839), and Elliott (1840).
14. Reapers by Hussey (1833) and McCormick (1834).
15. Centrifugal pumps by Appold (1850), Gwynne (1850), and Bessemer (1850).[3]

It is apparent that inventions and discoveries do not depend so much upon one particular exceptional person as upon the nature of the culture out of which the new elements in the invention arise. If there were no superior persons available to make inventions, the rate of invention would be retarded; but since advances in invention depend so much upon minor accretions to the total body of knowledge, it is indeed doubtful whether any one particular inventor is essential at a given time. Yet society cannot afford to neglect those things which make the production of superior persons possi-

[3] See W. F. Ogburn, *Social Change*, pp. 90–102, for entire list.

ble: sound biological stock and ample educational and other social opportunities. Both are essential. Great men alone do not make inventions, but neither can culture as a body of knowledge produce them. Both factors must operate together.

Planned or projected invention in society is indeed recent. But projecting invention and discovery into the future has become a part of the culture pattern of modern science. The story of science is the story of planned invention and discovery. As science has built up a solid set of principles or laws in terms of mathematical logic, and as it has accumulated ever more precise and effective instruments of measurement, it has given man the means of directing the course of inventions. Yet this is not a simple matter of addition. One discovery or invention often has to wait on another. The photoelectric cell, long known to physics, was not perfected for practical use until the invention of a vacuum tube amplifier.

The planning of invention for the larger needs of the society has only begun. The method by which planned invention may be used is well illustrated in the case of the Liberty Motor developed for airplanes during the World War. William G. McAdoo, then Secretary of the Treasury, was charged by President Woodrow Wilson with the task of getting a satisfactory light-weight motor. McAdoo called in two consulting engineers, who were given a free hand. These men in turn employed three other experts from the automobile industry: one a specialist on carburetors, one on gases, the third on machine designing. Certain specifications were put before them, and with these in mind they set to work. With the help of still other scientifically trained persons they designed a new motor. Then the motor was constructed and later put through exacting experimental tests leading to certain minor modifications. Once the trial engine proved satisfactory, the manufacturers were put to work turning out these engines in large numbers for use in military operations.

The interrelation of inventions to each other is evident. The place of invention in the whole matrix of cultural change, however, can only be discussed after we have examined the major features of diffusion.

Diffusion of Culture Traits. Culture grows not only by invention but by diffusion. *Diffusion* is the borrowing and accepting of culture traits or patterns from other societies, groups, or individuals. Ordinarily we speak of diffusion as circulation of traits through space. In this sense it is not to be confused with transmission, which has to do with passing traits and patterns through time from generation to generation. Thus education is not identical with diffusion, but is an important part of transmission.

Culture traits may spread from one large society to another, from one national community to another, or from one region or smaller community to another, and from one class or group within a community to another. Thus Christianity spread from Europe and America to China and Japan. Much of the German higher educational system was borrowed by American universities. The use of irrigation spreads from one arid region to another. Fashions spread from the upper to the lower classes.

The methods of diffusion are direct or indirect. The former refers to direct contact of persons or groups. By indirect we refer to communication without personal or group contact. The first is illustrated by migration and colonization, by contact through war and trade, and by religious missionaries. The second is witnessed in the spread of printed materials, by the radio, and by the infiltration of ideas and goods by commerce carried on without personal contact. Indirect diffusion accompanies the development of secondary group organization. It is less personal and more objective in some ways, and has been a powerful factor in the rise of ever larger areas of interaction. (See Chapter IV.)

When people of divergent cultures come into contact by migration or colonization, even though one culture is more complex than the other, the diffusion usually takes on a reciprocal character. Thus the white man brought the American Indian the horse culture, the use of firearms, and many elements of the Christian religion which have worked their way into Indian culture. The Indian, in turn, passed over to the white man his maize culture and the growing and use of tobacco, tomatoes, squash, potatoes, and other plants. Indirect diffusion may not be reciprocal but it is likely to be.

Although not such evident factors, war and conquest have been important factors in diffusion. The march of the Roman legions spread Roman culture into the world around the Mediterranean and beyond. Not only political organization, but also economic organization and religion, have followed in the wake of war and conquest. Although formal as well as ordinary intercourse of nations is cut off by war, although isolation of each side from the other is

the avowed intention, diffusion still takes place. This is well illustrated by the World War, when the people of the Allied countries
and of the Central Powers were repeatedly told by their leaders
that the enemy were altogether evil and satanic, that nothing good
could come from contact with them. The citizens of these respective countries were warned to have no traffic of any kind with the
enemy or their ideas, customs, or products. Thus, in the hysteria of
the war, the Americans banned German music; German books were
suppressed although they had no direct bearing on the war; and
all things German were taboo. In the same manner the Germans
were forbidden any traffic with the Allies. It might be imagined
from this that no diffusion could take place. On the contrary a
good deal of transfer of culture occurred. Thus, all the devices
used by the enemy for killing people more effectively were adopted
as quickly as possible by the other side: poison gas, tanks, mines,
and long-range projectiles. So, too, methods of social control—
military rules for civilians, food rationing, censorship, and propaganda—were introduced on both sides.

It is now generally accepted that diffusion is more important
than invention in the total building of cultures. Of all the items in
any given culture, perhaps more are borrowed from other peoples
than are invented at home. Very often culture traits which are
thought to arise from the stimulation of geographical conditions, or
from crises, really come from other culture groups. Some anthropologists go so far as to lay down a kind of rule that other things
being equal, it is easier to borrow than to invent. Because of the
inertia of habit and the lack of originality in man, in the face of a
crisis it seems the more common practice to look around and find
some method already in use than to think up some entirely new
device for handling the situation.

It is clear upon slight observation, however, that various culture
traits and patterns diffuse at somewhat different rates. It is now a
well-accepted principle of cultural anthropology that material
traits spread much more quickly than those which have to do with
forms of the family, political organization, art, religion, or recreation. Natives, for example, soon adopt firearms, manufactured
weapons, tools, and cloth, at the same time retaining their language, kinship organization, native religion, and art.

Diffusion nearly always involves modification, large or small.
Rarely is any trait, unless it be of material character, accepted

by another people without some modification at their hands. Diffusion may go on in an informal and almost unconscious way, or it may be the result of a conscious attempt to foist an alien culture on another society. Diffusion by trade and migration is often of the first sort; that fostered by organized religion or by a conquering state usually takes on a more deliberate character.

There are also certain hindrances to diffusion, such as partial isolation and lack of means of transportation and communication, cultural isolation of various sorts, taboos on change, and taboos on foreign ideas and techniques. So, too, displacement of one pattern by another prevents the further spread of the pattern displaced. Thus the Orient, long cut off from Europe, did not receive the impact of Western changes in culture until the last 200 years. The taboos of one religion against another stop the missionary work of foreigners. Japan in the eighteenth century banished the Christian missionaries. The practice of coffee drinking is not likely to spread in a country like China, long addicted to tea. If fascism replaces representative democracy, the distribution and perhaps diffusion of the latter may shrink and the whole pattern lose ground. Various sorts of resistances to diffusion or invention arise out of the culture, even though there be no strong taboo against change. Once an industrial process is established, it costs money and a change of habits to cast it aside for one which logically is more efficient. As previously noted, the power of human inertia is perhaps more evident in matters of societal organization and art, religion, and the like than in material culture. The old ways, though obviously not perfect, are often preferred to the unknown.

The factors in the rate of diffusion may be summarized as follows: (*1*) availability of transportation and communication, including distance and barriers to travel, such as mountains or sea; (*2*) resistance to culture changes, such as taboo, sense of superiority, and general cultural inertia; (*3*) prestige of the diffused culture and its people; (*4*) conquest of one people by another; (*5*) migration, especially when *en masse,* as in the Teutonic invasions of the Roman Empire, or in modern immigration; (*6*) the need for some new element to meet a critical situation; and (*7*) adaptability of the recipients of the new culture, as in the ready adoption of Western industrialism by Japan.

Theories of Invention and Diffusion. Anthropology has seen the rise of different theories of the importance and relation of invention to diffusion. There are two principal "schools" of thought in this matter: the "diffusionists" and the "historical school." The British school of diffusionism headed by G. Elliot Smith, an English anatomist, contends that culture is essentially monogenetic.[4] That is to say, traits of culture are invented but once and then spread over the world. It is contended that since invention is unusual and is always related to the total culture, the chances of its duplication are so slight as to be unworthy of consideration. It is maintained, moreover, that in Egypt about 3000 B. C. the major elements of prehistoric world culture were invented: advanced agriculture, metallurgy, political organization of the state, kingship, priesthood, belief in life after death, mummification, use of monuments for the dead, writing, and many other elements. From this one center these are supposed to have spread to the Mediterranean world, to Mesopotamia, and thence eastward to India, to China, to Oceania, reaching even to far-off Peru and Mexico. Minor modifications of these major patterns were made locally. Later the Greeks began to modify what they had received, and modern civilization was begun.

This extreme diffusionism is opposed by the historical school in this country, in England, and on the Continent. For them culture must always be studied in its historical setting; and broad generalizations are, at best, dubious in cultural and social materials. Both invention and diffusion must be taken into account, but within the historical framework of the society in question. Unless there is positive evidence of diffusion, the historical school holds that the occurrence of identical or similar culture traits in widely separated areas, especially before the dawn of written history, indicates "independent invention." Among numerous examples may be mentioned the blow-gun of native Brazil and Malaya, the use of obsidian for mirrors by the Romans and by the Indians of Mexico and of British Columbia, sun-dried bricks in the Orient and in America, the number system of the Maya, including the use of zero, and the number system of Asiatic-European culture areas, the religious belief in impersonal supernatural powers in Africa, Oceania, and among the North American tribes.[5]

In short, the whole culture growth must be understood in terms

[4] The German diffusionists are less extreme in their views. For our purposes, their theories may be omitted.
[5] For a brief review of the controversy over diffusion and invention, see G. Elliot Smith, et al., *Culture: the Diffusion Controversy*, 1927.

of the historical background. For the historical school culture is the result of slow or rapid accumulation of traits, some arising from invention, some from diffusion. They give a place to geography and to individual differences in mental ability in reference to culture growth, but they do not separate these from the underlying folkways, which are largely the seed bed of future change.

With the general relation of invention and diffusion before us, let us first examine the matter of rates of change, and second the effects of these upon culture and the societal order.

REVOLUTION AND CHANGE

Cultural change depends, therefore, upon either invention or diffusion. So far as the effects upon the culture and the societal organization are concerned, it does not matter by which method; the shift occurs only as these new elements are integrated into the life of the people.

The introduction of new elements may be slow or rapid, and the extent or degree of change may well be influenced by the rate. In terms of rate, change has been classified as gradual or evolutionary (without implying universal unilinear stages) and abrupt or revolutionary. As we shall see, these terms are relative. There is no sharp line dividing evolution from revolution. The dramatic and striking character of the latter is often quite misleading when the larger historical process of change is taken into account. It is partially to see revolution in this larger perspective that we introduce this section here. Moreover, there are certain features of the whole relation of change to culture that are well brought out in analyzing revolution.

The term *revolution* has been used in various senses. The commonest refers to a sudden and violent political shift in the location of sovereignty or power within the state. The French and Russian revolutions were of this sort. In another sense, revolution means any rapid cultural change including not only political, but also economic, religious, and other elements. In this sense the Renaissance, the Protestant Reformation, and the so-called Industrial Revolution were revolutions. Certainly all these events have had profound effects upon the entire culture and societal order of the Western world. For our purposes, we shall confine ourselves to political revolution. This may be defined as a more or less sudden change, usually by forcible and violent overthrow of the existing political order, leading to the establishment of new forms of legal control. Overt violence, however, is not an essential feature of revolution, but sudden shift of political power is fundamental. The essential point is some new form of legality and sovereignty.

The Background of Political Revolution. The historical roots of political revolution may be discussed under four heads: (*1*) the desire for improvement of economic conditions; (*2*) the wish for higher social status or for political or religious equality; (*3*) the rise of leaders and minority groups who foster revolutionary ideas; and (*4*) the development of new social myths, that is, beliefs or ideas and attitudes looking to the revolution.

Economic factors, especially a growing discontent with the distribution of wealth, have been fundamental in most political revolutions of classic and modern history. In many instances this discontent has been connected with the problem of ownership of land. Among cultures dominated by agriculture, land hunger has been a crucial problem. The French peasants during the eighteenth century and the Russian peasants in the last century developed a craving for more and more land. The increase of taxes or rents and bad economic conditions following crop failures or decrease in market demand also increase dissatisfaction. Absentee ownership and luxurious living of the owners also add resentment. The peasants hate to see their landlords squandering wealth which they so painfully produce.

In much the same way, the city workers, in factory and shop, develop a bitter sense of injustice at the unequal distribution of wealth and the lack of economic opportunity. Under the factory system the laborer becomes a wage slave. He receives just what the labor market will supply in the way of money. He is haunted by the fear of loss of his job. And he sees only a blind alley ahead so far as advancement is concerned.

We must, however, utter a caution here. We must not imagine that it is the complete submergence of the peasant or the factory worker that makes for overthrow of government. This is a mistaken notion. When peasants, farmers, or city laborers are so reduced in economic status that they can scarcely keep "body and soul together," there is little likelihood of revolt. Abjection, complete discouragement, and resignation to one's fearful lot do not produce revolutionary action. Quite the contrary, it is necessary that there be a combination of hardship and sense of injustice with a relative improvement of conditions over the past. The peasants and city dwellers in pre-revolutionary France were better off than like classes elsewhere in Europe. In the case of both pre-revolutionary France and pre-revolutionary Russia, the peasants already owned one third of the land. The American colonies in 1776 were better governed than they had been in 1700. In spite of economic and industrial dislocation in Russia during the World War, the lot of the city factory workers and peasants was doubtless improved over the conditions 12 years before when the abortive revolution of 1905 took place. To be completely beaten down will not lead to revolt, but to resignation to the fates. In short, revolutions are not made by downtrodden masses who cannot and will not stand any more repression. As Lyford P. Edwards says, "The emotion which furnishes the driving power of revolution is hope, not despair."[6]

Connected with questions of land and wealth is the desire for *social status*. The poor peasant wishes to live like the rich peasant. The rich peasant becomes infected with the luxury virus of the landlord. The city worker wants to possess the comforts of his employer. The rich merchant or manufacturer desires to be knighted and to sit in parliament.

Closely linked with desire for social and economic position is the wish for *political rights*. Certainly in the Puritan, American, and French revolutions the demand for political participation by groups hitherto denied political privileges was a distinctive factor in stimulating discontent.

In some pre-revolutionary situations, religious inequality or denial of religious privileges has played an important rôle. This was true in seventeenth-century Europe. It was certainly one motive for the Puritan Revolution in England (1640–1660), although political and economic factors were also important.

Ideas of revolutionary sort also grow out of intellectual and scientific advances. In the case of England, the American colonies, and France in the seventeenth and eighteenth centuries, the emergence of modern science and philosophy, themselves dependent upon the renaissance of learning of the two centuries previous, must be reckoned with in interpreting the development of revolutionary ideas. The conception of natural law, the critical

[6]Lyford P. Edwards, *The Natural History of Revolution*, 1927, p. 35.

attitude toward religious institutions, the growing belief in individualism and democracy, and the undermining of the idea of divine right of kings were important.

From the soil of intellectual criticism coupled with growing discontent at actual conditions, there spring up *leaders* and *organized groups* concerned with fostering not only ideas but action. These minorities are frequently organized in secret and carry on their propaganda under cover. In the American Revolution, the local units of government often took over these functions. In the Russian Revolution, students organized propaganda societies two generations or more before the actual revolution, and their work was effective in building the background. Later more active organizations develop. As the revolution gets under way such minorities become political parties and prepare to seize the state.

These early intellectual leaders and agitators in many cases are not the same type as the active leaders, who carry forward the more violent agitation and manage the revolution once it is under way. The shift from one sort of leadership to another as the revolution draws near is itself an important feature of revolution. The early leaders are important in making vocal the wishes of the repressed classes. They help to build new ideas and attitudes. In other words, they help create a new social myth.

As we saw in the previous chapter, the *social myth* is basic to all social behavior. The ideas and attitudes which people carry about with them determine the kind of world they live in and not merely the material features of their environment. Unless men believe in their own folkways and institutions, unless they have faith in their own culture, they cannot carry on.

Thus, so long as the old and tried rules and the social myths of the old system remain intact, there is little likelihood of change, either gradual or revolutionary. The new social myth means that the desires, beliefs, attitudes, and habits of people who accept it have changed. It is "a new heaven and a new earth." The moderate intellectuals who begin to criticize the old social order also begin to fashion the new mythology, and the active, militant minority leaders who bring the revolution into being complete the process.

The new social myth is born when the intellectuals begin to describe the present order as "bad," "evil," "decadent," "corrupt," and so on. The rich are blamed for all ills. The redistribution of wealth is essential. These terms of opprobrium are caught up by others and carried on and become in time stereotypes to define the ruling class. Labels are used to distinguish the exploiting class from those who are their victims. In Roman history there were the Patricians and the Plebeians. In the mythology of modern revolutionary minorities the exploiters are often called "absentee owners," "capitalists," or "bourgeoisie." The exploited productive workers are called "workingmen," "wage slaves," or simply "the proletariat." The thinking classes are called "the intelligentsia," "highbrows," or the "intellectuals." This conception of a society fundamentally divided into antagonistic classes is highly important in the development of the revolutionary myth.

Yet the social myth is not only negative and critical. It is positive and constructive. It builds a picture of a world that will be far more just, honest, and delightful for all than the society now existent. A Utopian picture of the coming day is dangled before the oppressed groups. On the basis of this hope, they accept the picture as valid and begin to work for its realization.

As the revolutionary myth develops, those in power, the conservatives who wish to retain the *status quo*, also indulge in various devices to bolster up the old order. Too often in the past these efforts have been directed to suppression of freedom of assembly, of speech, and of writing. Sometimes, however, there is an effort to expand and foster the old myths and legends of the country and its heroes, so as to counteract the undermining forces moving in the opposite direction.

The Revolution Proper. The outbreak of the revolution itself is marked usually by four stages: (*1*) the concentration of attention upon one or at most a few closely related issues; (*2*) the outbreak of revolutionary action itself; (*3*) the reign of terror; and (*4*) the consolidation of the new political power.

The *issues* at stake become sharply divided. What H. A. Miller calls the "oppression psychosis" in the masses becomes more intense. They develop toward those in power open suspicion and hatred, and an itch for change in control. On the other hand, those in power lose confidence in their own cause. So long as the entire body of "repressors," as Lyford P. Edwards calls them, "believe firmly in themselves and in the righteousness of their actions, they cannot be overthrown by revolution."[7]

[7] Edwards, *op. cit.*, p. 60.

The *outbreak* of the revolution itself is often presaged by food shortage, strikes, lockouts, boycotting, and widespread disorder. The actual seizure of power may come in various ways. The popular notion, again, that angry mobs seize the arsenals and defeat the police and the army is frequently fiction. True enough, the ruling class finds itself unable often to cope with riots and public disturbances, but it is rather a matter of loss of will and technique than anything else. There is a piling up of obvious inefficiencies in the government. Stupid mistakes are made, silly orders issued, and last-minute promises of reform are made. But it is too late! The ruling class proves itself unable to manage its affairs, and at the outset the shift of power is to moderates and reformers who are at first also supported by more radical minorities.

This first shift in legal and political power to more moderate groups, if not universal, is certainly a rather common procedure. Shortly, however, there ensues a struggle for power among revolutionary factions. The moderates often become incapable of maintaining the public order. Their government, being made up of diverse elements and not bound together by any really consistent program, both temporizes with the conservatives of the old regime and tries to win and keep the support of the more radical groups which it fears. The class which has been dispossessed of wealth and political power plots to return. The more radical groups and their followers are dissatisfied with the first fruits of revolution. It is a time of open conflict. In such a period temporizing and mild measures will not do. There ensues a struggle between the moderates and the radicals for power. Autocratic force is necessary. A military regime is essential to preserve the gains already made and to carry forward the new ones. This calls for a dictatorship, for a swing to the radicals.

This is often a last desperate move on the part of the masses who support the revolution to get something done. The masses put their faith in determined and bold measures. They identify themselves, as always, with strength and power, because strength and power in a strong man give the weak man courage and a sense of power in himself.

The popular mind associates the shift to the left, to the radicals, with revolutionary mob activity and with the *reign of terror*. Both these forms of crowd behavior have been much exaggerated in the popular myths of revolution. From Dickens' *A Tale of Two*

Cities we have pictures of the storming of the Bastille and the operation of the guillotine. From popular accounts of the Russian Revolution we get distorted pictures of mob violence and of the Red Terror. Mob violence in revolutions is far less significant and far less bloody than most of us imagine.

The revolutionary reign of terror is but a deliberate expression of this new-found power. In terms of actual numbers killed it is probably a very humane affair. But in terms of its effect upon the public, both inside and outside the revolutionary country, it is almost unavoidably important and necessary if the revolution is to succeed. The purpose of the reign of terror is first of all to consolidate control in the hands of a new minority, and, secondly, to convince those outside the country that the revolution is genuine.

The reign of terror is generally concluded by the same forces that set it in motion. When the counter-revolutionary armies are defeated, when something approaching unification of power within the country is established, when malcontents are silenced, converted, or driven out, there is little need to continue the terror. Of course, as an event it lingers on in the myths and legends of the masses, and the threat of reinstating it is often effective for years in quelling organized opposition—witness Russia and Germany.

The final feature of the revolution, of course, is the *consolidation of political power*. The legal and governmental machinery is put into new hands. Interestingly enough, all revolutions produce their own particular rationalizations or explanations for this redistribution of power. The change is excused in terms of public welfare, on the grounds that the power of the owners and exploiters was being abused, and that this "new deal" was good for them as well as for the classes who are now in control. Thus the confiscation of property is made moral and legal by conscious and unconscious revision of the moral and legal codes.

Revolution, in short, runs a cycle of change a little more rapidly than in other cases, but the shift in culture and in forms of control is not essentially different from that under more gradual change. Before we can relate revolution to slower change, however, we must examine some features of the latter.

FACTORS IN EVOLUTIONARY CHANGE

The slower alterations in culture we have already examined in part in discussing invention and diffusion. The rate of diffusion under trade, missionary endeavor, and even in conquest and war is likely to be rather slow. Changes produced by borrowing or by invention do not ordinarily affect the totality of culture at once, but rather intrude themselves at particular points. We have noted the contrast of empirical and planned invention and said something of the place of the individual in the inventive process. There remain, however, some other features of slow change which should be mentioned, particularly the integration and selection of the new and the relation of material to non-material traits. We shall, moreover, choose our illustrations from modern society, in which the rate of change has been increased and new elements are being introduced on all fronts. This raises the problem of disorganization though it be of non-violent character. We shall close our chapter with a comment on the relation of change by revolution to change by evolution.

Interrelation Between the New and Old in Culture. Bearing in mind that so far as social effects are concerned it does not matter much whether the new element in a culture be invented or borrowed, we shall discuss the interplay of the new and the old in regard to cumulative, integrative, and reciprocal relations.[8]

The cumulative effects of new items are well illustrated in the gradual piling up of small changes in mechanical or non-material inventions. This is highly important in keeping up the trend of change and in building a foundation for still further improvements. Major changes are the results of a large number of separate introductions. The fundamental factors which made the automobile possible have a long history, reaching back to the physics and chemistry of gases, to discoveries and inventions in the field of electricity, and to the principles of mechanics. The more immediate background factors, said to be six in number (liquid gas engine, liquid gas container, running gear and mechanism, intermediate clutch, driving shaft, and carriage body), were finally put together in a new combination in the Selden patents that produced the first effective automobile.[9] In a similar way the steam locomotive, the modern battleship, the radio, the motion-picture machine, and dozens of other large culture traits are the outcome of hun-

[8] For excellent illustrations see W. F. Ogburn and S. C. Gilfillan, "The Influence of Invention and Discovery," chap. III, *Recent Social Trends*, pp. 158–66.
[9] See F. S. Chapin, *Cultural Change*, pp. 334–37, for a brief discussion of the invention of the automobile.

dreds of minor inventions and discoveries that are put together into novel forms.

A series of somewhat related new elements will have a more marked effect than single ones. The widespread introduction and popular use of the automobile, the motion picture, and the radio, all within a few decades, have influenced the home, the distribution of occupations, education, and other features of society.

The integration of new elements may be stated in another way. A new item in a culture produces a series of effects analogous to the putting of links of a chain together. For example, the automobile reduces the number of horses, which reduces the number of stables and the number of men engaged in handling horses, which produces problems of unemployment or shift in employment. The radio, in turn, may not only increase the speed and uniformity of news, but may also reduce the number of men engaged in the printing trades, which may, in turn, cut down the incidence of certain occupational diseases.

The causes and effects of new elements in a culture are often reciprocal. Thus the automobile may reduce the revenue of the railroads, and hence influence the consumption of coal. On the other hand, the automobile "causes" an extension of pipe lines for oil and increases the consumption of gasoline. The introduction of two items serving the same end, such as gas and electricity for household use, sets up a struggle for dominance. Such a competition itself serves a selective function.

Non-material changes must not be neglected. All sorts of social inventions have widespread effects. The juvenile court system set up in this country about 1899 has without doubt not only influenced the care and correction of young delinquents but has influenced the public attitudes toward the delinquent boy or girl, has led the schools to recognize misconduct among their pupils with a view to prevention of delinquency, and has doubtless affected parental control of children. It has also broadened the field of social work, and perhaps instilled new ideas into the minds of judges and attorneys.

Material and non-material changes influence each other. The invention of apartment houses affects the birth rate, but such dwellings are perhaps the result of a lowered birth rate in certain classes in the first instance. The non-material effects of mechanical inventions are of varying degrees and kinds. The use of the typewriter first changed the habits of clerks, who had formerly used pen and ink. Later it gave rise to a class of special opera-tives, mostly unmarried women. And the employment of daugh-ters as typists influenced the habits of the home: housework, con-trol of the income of children, and matters of freedom of mobility and social contact of the daughter.

Cultural Lag and Disorganization. In an isolated society change is almost imperceptible. We speak of such a society as static. When through invention and diffusion, many traits are rapidly introduced in a short period of time, we speak of such a changing society as dynamic. The two terms *static* and *dynamic* are relative. What may appear static to one group may not seem so to another. The intrusion of new elements not only goes on at varying rates in different societies, but within any society the rate of change in certain phases of the total culture may be different from that in others. The last 175 years have seen a tremendous burst of material inventions in western Europe and America which have altered the nature of material culture the world over. In sharp contrast corresponding changes in the non-material culture have been slow, halting, and ineffective. The new needs of people in the face of these rather sudden material changes have not been adequately satisfied. In other words, the previous integration of the major parts of a total culture has been lost.

This differential in the rate of change W. F. Ogburn has called "cultural lag," which he defines in these words:

"The thesis is that the various parts of modern culture are not chang-ing at the same rate, some parts are changing much more rapidly than others; and that since there is a correlation and interdependence of parts, a rapid change in one part of our culture requires readjustments through other changes in the various correlated parts of culture. . . . Where one part of culture changes first, through some discovery or invention, and occasions changes in some part of culture dependent upon it, there fre-quently is a delay in the changes occasioned in the dependent part of culture. The extent of this lag will vary according to the nature of the cultural material, but may exist for a considerable number of years, during which time there may be said to be a maladjustment." [10]

It is now generally accepted that many of our contemporary problems of society result from this lag in one part of our cul-ture in the face of changes in another. There is a wide range of

[10] W. F. Ogburn, *Social Change*, 1922, pp. 200–201.

new habits, attitudes, and ideas fostered by these material changes which society did not anticipate and for which there has been no preparation. This dislocation is largely a result of differentials in rates of change. In fact, *social disorganization* refers to the breakdown of the societal order to such an extent that the former controls are dissipated, the former close correlation of personality and culture is destroyed, and a certain chaos or disorder arises in which the old ways of doing have been lost and new ways not yet developed.

Probably no one doubts the advantages which have accrued to modern material culture: cutting down the severity of work and hours of labor, the increase in leisure for all classes, widespread education, mobility and travel, increased "animation" of life, extension of contacts, and a higher standard of living for millions. On the other hand many dislocations have arisen from the failure of the non-material culture, especially that connected with societal organization, to keep pace with these new material culture patterns. Mobility has broken down the neighborhood and primary community, loosened moral controls, and fostered certain types of crime. Changes in industrial production have caused technological unemployment, have destroyed the skilled trades, and put millions into the semi-skilled and unskilled classes who were never there before. High production and prosperity seem to fluctuate more violently than ever with business depressions, unemployment, and consequent hardship. The political order is marked with many dislocations: the continuance of outworn political units of voting, the restriction of residence for office holders, and the persistence of other governmental forms that belonged to the horse and wagon era, including the lack of adequately trained political personnel for technical work in a complex political society. The lag in laws and administration of justice and in the correction and care of dependents, defectives, delinquents, and criminals is self-evident. Coupled with these is the wide range of new forms of exploitation which need governmental regulations in order to protect the public. The hurry and rush of living today are thought to be responsible for the increase in insanity and in other forms of atypical behavior.

Relation of Revolution and Slow Change. Revolution itself is the product of slower-moving antecedent changes. Abuses arise and there develops a desire to overthrow the old order. But before this occurs the old is already passing out by a process of decay. Thus, while revolution involves the disintegration of one social order, it also involves "the reintegration of society along different and more efficient lines." Moreover, the changes brought about by the revolution are usually not so marked and divergent from the older order as is often imagined. For example, the Puritan, American, and French revolutions were but sharp turning points in the expansion of *laissez-faire* capitalism and in the rise of the nationalistic state dominated by the middle classes. These revolutions marked the triumph of the doctrines and practices of individualism, private profit taking, and political democracy— three items which characterize the capitalistic ethos of the Western world.

Nevertheless in the breakup of the old order, old attitudes and habits are destroyed and some new ones established. When the overt activities of the revolution are over, we find a great deal of merging of the old and the new. Thus, culturally considered, revolution is but an acceleration of change already under way.

CLASS ASSIGNMENTS

A. Further reading assignments:

1. K. Young, *Source Book for Sociology*, chap. III.

2. W. F. Ogburn and S. C. Gilfillan, "The Influence of Inventions and Discovery," chap. III, *Recent Social Trends*.

3. The following articles in the *Encyclopedia of the Social Sciences:* A. Goldenweiser, "Social Evolution," vol. V, pp. 656–62; A. L. Kroeber, "Diffusionism," *Ibid.*, pp. 139–42; W. F. Ogburn, "Social Change," vol. III, pp. 330–34; Carl Brinkmann, "Invention," vol. VIII, pp. 247–51; and Alfred Meusel, "Revolution and Counter-Revolution," vol. XIII, pp. 367–76.

B. Questions and exercises:

1. Why did the simple theories of unilinear or stage-wise cultural evolution break down?

2. How may we account for the rather frequent duplication of inventions? Cite recent illustrations.

3. In discussing modern social change why is it inconsequential whether we consider only the inventions made in a given community or those that are borrowed from elsewhere?

4. What is meant by cultural lag? Illustrate.

5. Develop a case study showing cultural lag and resultant dislocation between some material culture item or pattern and some non-material item or pattern.

6. Writing of revolution, Dale Yoder remarks, "The real revolution occurs

far below the surface of the social life." Explain the meaning of this statement.

7. Why are many Americans shocked by those who advocate violent revolutionary change when their own country was born of political revolution?

8. Name and discuss any new beliefs and ideas (social myths) now developing in the United States which may presage an economic or political revolution in the future.

C. Topics for class reports or longer written papers:

1. Critical report on early theories of unilinear cultural evolution with particular reference to Herbert Spencer and Lewis H. Morgan. (Consult Spencer's *Principles of Sociology,* 3 vols., 1876–1896; Morgan's *Ancient Society,* 1877; A. Goldenweiser, *Anthropology,* 1937, chaps. XXX, XXXI; articles by Goldenweiser and Kroeber cited above under A 3.)

2. Report on the controversy between the diffusionists and the historical school in anthropology. (Consult articles by Kroeber and Goldenweiser cited above under A 3 and bibliography.)

3. The Hitler revolution in Germany. (Consult Calvin B. Hoover, *Germany Enters the Third Reich,* 1934; Edgar A. Mowrer, *Germany Puts the Clock Back,* 1933; F. L. Schuman, *The Nazi Dictatorship,* 2nd ed., 1936; Stephan H. Roberts, *The House That Hitler Built,* 1938; and files of newspapers and periodicals.)

4. The factors in cultural change and cultural lag. (Consult W. F. Ogburn, *Social Change,* 1922; F. Stuart Chapin, *Cultural Change,* 1928; report of the National Resources Committee, *Technological Trends and National Policy,* 1937.)

5. The sociology of revolution. (Consult P. A. Sorokin, *The Sociology of Revolution,* 1925; L. P. Edwards, *The Natural History of Revolution,* 1927; C. Brinton, *The Anatomy of Revolution,* 1938.)

CHAPTER IV

THE EXPANDING WORLD OF INTERACTION

Against the background of group organization and culture, we must next examine the major changes in the nature and extent of social interaction in the modern world. These changes are characterized by the shift from the primary to the secondary community, with all that this means in the extension and modification of men's contacts with each other in our world today.

ISOLATION

As a first step in the discussion of the expansion of our social and cultural world we must examine the chief features of isolation. The early primary communities tended to be separated from others, giving rise to certain homogeneous and distinctive traits, physical and cultural.

Factors Fostering Isolation. *Isolation* means a limitation of the opportunity for stimulus and response. It grows out of a social situation which circumscribes the range of interaction. The limitations of contact or interaction depend chiefly on biological, psychological, geographical, and cultural factors. It is clear that races and sub-races are the products of an isolation which fosters inbreeding and little biological amalgamation with other races. The biological effects of isolation appear even today, as in Martha's Vineyard, an island off the coast of Massachusetts, where hereditary traits of deaf-mutism were apparently increased by long inbreeding of defective stock.

Other biological aspects of complete isolation appear in the so-called "feral men," those cases of untamed, wild individuals who are supposed to have grown up without the benefit of social contact. Kaspar Hauser of Germany, the Savage of Aveyron of France, the Wolf Children of India, and several other similar cases have been reported.

Kaspar Hauser (1812–1833) of Bavaria is said to have been placed in a dungeon by an Hungarian peasant, where he remained for years with few or no social contacts. When he appeared later in Nürnberg, in May, 1828, he was evidently bewildered by his surroundings. He knew but few words. He could not distinguish between statuary and living beings. His behavior was infantile and unsocial. While the records confirm the suspicion that he was slightly unbalanced, the boy was clearly the victim of long incarceration and isolation, and hence failed to develop into a normal social person. An autopsy showed his brain normal, but undeveloped. He is the object of much folk fiction, but his is perhaps one of the few fairly authentic cases on record.[1]

Many of these cases are largely legendary; others have the marks of myth-making. Some of these individuals were evidently low-grade mental deficients. Others were doubtless the victims of neglect and abuse. None of the reported individuals has been carefully studied. Until we have more objective evidence on these cases, we must be wary of reasoning about the nature of human behavior conditioned in a non-social environment.[2]

While we may dismiss most of the legends of feral men as nonsense, it is true that the low-grade feebleminded (idiots and imbeciles), the deaf, the mute, and the blind, all suffer from isolation as a result of the restriction of stimuli.

Geographical isolation coupled with culture makes for a distinctive society with its own ethos. India was long segregated by the protecting Himalayas from outside intrusions of culture, except periodically, until modern times, when she was invaded from the sea by European culture. China's own distinctive culture developed during her long isolation from the Western world. So, too, in modern Europe, British power was due in part to her maritime isolation, leading the poet Alfred Tennyson to write:

"God bless the narrow sea which keeps
........our Britain, whole within herself."

Cultural isolation arises where there is a strong we-group *versus* others-group feeling. Language differences make this distinction all the more evident, since language is a basic feature of any cul-

---

[1] See article "Hauser, Kaspar," *Encyclopedia Britannica,* 14th ed., vol. XI, p. 255.
[2] See R. E. Park and E. W. Burgess, *Introduction to the Science of Sociology,* 1924 ed., pp. 239–43, for summary of material, and bibliography, p. 276.

ture. F. Stuart Chapin cites an instance of this from central Europe:

"The Transylvania Saxons, although isolated from their German relatives for 700 years in the midst of a Hungarian population, have preserved the Teutonic traditions of the fatherland. They have clung stubbornly, tenaciously, blindly to each peculiarity of dress, language, and custom, knowing that every concession meant increased danger of assimilation into the surrounding Hungarian population. If they had been left on their native soil, and surrounded by friends and country-men, they would undoubtedly have changed as other nations have changed. Their isolated position and the peculiar circumstances of their surroundings have kept them what they originally were."[3]

Our own Southern mountain whites typify the same thing. Living for generations undisturbed by changes going on around them, these people have continued a culture which still reflects the seventeenth and early eighteenth centuries. Habits, attitudes, and ideas are those of the colonist and pioneer, and there is a general suspicion of the outside world.[4]

The Boers in South Africa kept up their Dutch culture in the face of a new environment. Olive Schreiner (c. 1855-1920) describes how they persisted in wearing their short velvet jackets, in the presence of uncomfortable heat, simply because they would not give up their European customs.

Other illustrations of cultural isolation are the ghetto of the Jew in European cities, where the Jewish culture, set off from contact with the Christian by custom or law, continued for centuries. Likewise all sorts of divergent sectarian groups who move into territory in order to be by themselves build up a distinctive primary community of their own with their entire culture distinctly centered in their religion. Such are the Mennonites, the Hutterites, the Doukhobors of Canada, the Molokans,[5] the Oneida Community, and the Mormons in Utah during their first generation or so in the Great Basin.

[3]Cited by F. S. Chapin, *An Introduction to the Study of Social Evolution,* 1919, p. 154, from Jane E. Gerard, *The Land Beyond the Forest,* 1888, pp. 31-34.
[4]See J. C. Campbell, *The Southern Highlander and His Homeland,* 1921; E. A. Ross, *World Drift,* 1928, chap. IV; also Percy Mackaye's *This Fine Pretty World,* 1924. For comparison see O. W. Junek, *Isolated Communities: A Study of a Labrador Fishing Village,* 1937.
[5]See Pauline Vislick Young, *The Pilgrims of Russian Town,* 1932, for study of a distinctive Russian colony in the heart of an American city, Los Angeles.

Certainly wherever social and material stimuli are restricted or lacking, the personality development will be influenced. Many cases of feeblemindedness assumed to be the result of hereditary factors may actually be cases of cultural and social isolation.[6]

Prisoners and delinquents locked up in institutions are cut off from normal contacts and often develop some of the features of the isolated person. So, too, such psychopathic cases as dementia praecox (schizophrenia) are marked by a retreat from the social world, the development of an internal world of fantasies, and ultimately a form of isolation. There are many normal persons of the so-called "shut-in" type who live in a decidedly confined world of interaction.

PRIMARY COMMUNITY

For centuries men lived in primary communities where face-to-face relations dominated. Most primitive people still live in just such communities, and until very recently peasant and rural people everywhere represented this sort of interactional pattern.

Isolation and the Primary Community. Cultural isolation, aided by the geographical situation, was common for centuries. Only gradually, as larger national states began to develop, did some of this isolation disappear. Thus, the unification of the Greek states in the face of invasion broke down some of their separateness, but not enough to save Greece from her more powerful enemies. Later, the Alexandrian and notably the Roman Empire unified the ancient world in regard to political, economic, religious, educational, and other phases of culture. In spite of this advancement, the break-up of the Roman Empire and the intrusion of the barbarian hordes threw Europe back upon more rudimentary organization for centuries, except for a few larger cities. It took the Renaissance, the Reformation, the rise of nationalism, and modern capitalistic commerce and industry with their stimulation of urban culture to wipe out the medieval societal organization, which in spite of the Roman Church and the remains of the Empire was dominated by the primary community.

Yet down to the first quarter of the nineteenth century in Great

[6]See M. H. Small, "On Some Psychical Relations of Society and Solitude," *Pedagogical Seminary*, 1900, vol. VII, pp. 45–50, on feral men. See Lightner Witmer, "Don: a Curable Case of Arrested Development, etc.," *Psychological Clinic*, 1920, vol. XIII, pp. 97–111. See also W. H. Burnham, *The Normal Mind*, 1924, pp. 570–96, for discussion of what he calls "pseudo feeblemindedness."

Britain, down to the last quarter of the same century in Germany and the United States, the primary community culture continued to mold the lives of the bulk of the population. Elsewhere the primary community continued important well into the present century, and even today, in spite of the rapid industrialization of the rest of Europe and other parts of America and the Orient—notably Japan—this primitive form of organization and culture plays an important part.

Isolation and Rural Primary Groups. This is not the place for an extended review of the culture of rural America, but we may note some of the outstanding features of rural communities as they have influenced American culture.

Rural communities vary widely in type, and the earlier and more prevalent ones were largely little worlds within themselves. In colonial and pioneer America, which set the pattern for much of our later American culture, the farmers produced their own goods, made most of their own utensils, clothes, etc., and perhaps sold their small excess produce to neighboring markets. The great part of their life centered in the farm and the village near by, where the storekeeper sold such things as sugar, salt, spices, molasses, and rum. In the village also were blacksmiths who supplied the farmers with tools or implements, carpenters who did some of the construction work, millers who ground the flour. There were also hatters, teachers, preachers, and, in the larger towns, printers.

The neighborhood was a dominant factor in the social life outside the family. Barn-raising, planting, and harvesting crops called for co-operation. Labor was not highly specialized except for the few skilled tradesmen noted. Most farmers themselves were literally jacks-of-all-trades and called upon the blacksmith, carpenter, miller, or painter only when their own time or capacity was limited.

As population grew, division of labor developed; the farmer marketed his produce in ever wider range; he used more and more machinery in place of hand labor; money economy became more important; and the community expanded outward to the more distant growing towns and cities, where he found a source of new ideas. Specialization in type of farming developed, and whole regions, in time, were given over to cotton or tobacco, or wheat, or fruit growing, and more recently, dairying and truck-gardening.

The Village and Town. The village and small town which grew up in the farming regions mark the first step in the breakdown of primary group isolation. While the primary group ideas, attitudes, and habits in family life are much the same, and while the neighborhood sense of solidarity remains strong, the village and town dweller experiences wider contacts than the farmer of the open country or farm village. The most important of these is that of the economic functions. The village and small town serve as trade centers for the rural hinterland. They become the focus for collection of farm produce for the outside market. The village and small town, therefore, are dependent on the rural hinterland, but they also reach out toward the cities and regions beyond.

Nevertheless, until rapid means of transportation and communication were introduced, with the consequent intrusion of urban culture into these rural and village areas, the small town and village community were not very different from the farming regions around. Contact for the most part was face-to-face in character. There was a strong sense of independence, on the one hand, and a kind of rural solidarity on the other. There was a strong conservatism and a distinct prejudice against new ideas and practices except perhaps those bearing directly upon economic techniques.

There were few outside diverting stimuli. The range of reaction was limited largely to the primary community. Contacts with the outside came through some reading of newspapers, perhaps, and through such institutions as the school, the political forum, and the church, although even these reflected the rural culture for the most part.

Recent Changes in the Primary Community. It is the intrusion of urban culture and the growing specialization of farming itself which have produced the major changes in the rural life of America in recent decades. These changes are indicative of what is going on elsewhere in the world. We can mention only the most important features of these changes here.[7]

For several decades down to 1920 there had been a steady expansion of world markets for agricultural goods, and a corresponding increase in prices and in the value of agricultural land. The

[7]See Edmund de S. Brunner and J. H. Kolb, *Rural Social Trends*, 1933, and the summary of this monograph in Chapter X, Report of the President's Research Committee: *Recent Social Trends*, 1933.

World War gave an exceptionally strong stimulus to further extension of farming, but the crash of prices afterward heralded the beginning of a long economic depression.

On the economic horizon there has been a steady increase in the number of tenant farmers. In 1890, 28.4 per cent of all farms were tenant operated; in 1930, 42.4 per cent. This increase is related to specialization in farm crops and to the intrusion into farming of business practices based on money economy. With the tremendous number of farms taken over by mortgage holders during the decades following 1921, there was bound to be a further increase in tenant farming. Such changes themselves mean a loosening of ancient attitudes of attachment to particular land and to the farm as a permanent home—all destructive of older attitudes and values of the rural dweller. Another matter has been the improvement in methods of marketing, in the growth of co-operatives among farmers, and in the extension of private business enterprise to handle farm products. Between 1915 and 1931, the number of farmers' co-operatives of all sorts rose from 5,424 to 11,950.

There are still 151,000 one and two-room schools in the United States, although there has been a steady movement toward school consolidation. So, too, of the 64,000 open-country churches in 1920, a decade later found four fifths of them still in operation. Evidently, educational changes lag behind some others. In a re-survey made in 1930 of 140 village-centered communities originally studied in 1924, of 513 neighborhood groupings, 118 had dropped out of existence and 24 new groupings had arisen. New special interest groupings, often with connections to larger organizations, like the Grange and the 4-H clubs, seem to be replacing the older spontaneous neighborhood groups.

The villages also show changes. Between 1910 and 1930 there was a steady increase in the population of villages of between 250 and 2,500 population. This has been most marked in the Far West and least in the Middle West. The villages seem to represent a mid-point in age and sex distributions between the open country and the larger cities. So, too, the village stands intermediate between the open country and the city as to trade, educational, religious, and recreational services. In some items, like grocery marketing and other immediate needs, the nearby village still is dominant, but items purchased only periodically and requiring a greater money outlay per unit are more frequently secured by mail order or from larger urban centers now easily accessible by motor.

In a recent study of 1,034 farm families in one Wisconsin county, it was found that most families traveled from four to six miles for groceries, farm machinery, some of their furniture, for dry goods, for local banking, for marketing their products, for high school, movies, church services, for social affairs, and for library service. The majority used mail-order houses for automobile tires, hardware, ready-to-wear clothes, and for certain dry goods.[8] Banking and larger marketing services of farmer and villager alike are generally dominated by the urban centers.

In spite of the continuation of many open-country schools and churches, there is a definite trend toward the village as an educational and religious center. The village schools secure more and better teachers; improvements and specialization of the course of study are apparent; and the village again stands between the open country and the larger urban world outside. Likewise, better educated pastors and more specialized church services are found in the villages.

In spite of these changes the primary community is still a powerful factor in Western society. The individualism of the American farmer, the time-worn methods of managing farm business, the conservatism in education, politics, and religion—these and other items all stand out in spite of the recent changes. This pull of the locality as a focus for strong we-group feelings will continue for a long time to influence changes in the relation of the primary to the secondary communities. Much of our social behavior still has its roots in the forms of social interaction of rural America. Some of our problems of political life are distinctly related to this. In all our cities the idea of political units within the city, particularly the practice of ward and precinct as voting districts, goes back to the notion of the village and the neighborhood as the political unit in early rural America. Again, the conflict between the farmer and the city man finds its roots in isolation and individualism, as they contrast with life in cities. This has ramifications in matters like farmer legislation, national prohibition, and the distribution of seats in the national House of Representatives and in the state legislatures. The antagonism of the rural population to the urban has still other implications in such matters as the support of state

[8] See Kolb and Brunner, *op. cit.*, p. 538.

and national education, the distribution of tax burdens, and even in matters of religion and social control.

While cities and wider secondary communities existed in ancient times, especially in the Graeco-Roman world, the city as a dominant feature of group life and culture is distinctly modern. Let us sketch some of the features, first, of the city, then of the region and the national state, and finally of the now emerging world community, or what Graham Wallas calls "The Great Society."

The modern city, in contrast to the rural neighborhood, village, or small town, is characterized by congestion of population and by secondary group organization.

Density of Population. Massing of people in a limited area is the most evident feature of the urban community. Wiechel, a German geographer, correlates density of population with occupations in an attempt to find the limits of urban life. Adopting a modified theory of cultural gradation, he holds that primitive hunting and fishing peoples have a density up to eight persons per square mile; those engaged in herding and forestry from eight to 26; in elementary agriculture from 26 to 64; in more advanced agriculture from 64 to 192; and in early industry from 192 to 256. Where agriculture and industry are combined, the density reaches to 381; but where industry predominates, it ranges from 381 to 512. From this point on we get varying densities. What Wiechel calls small cities have at their centers a density ranging from 2,560 to 5,120; centers of moderate cities reach to 12,800, while centers of large cities go to 25,600.[9] In some great cities the density is extreme. Shanghai, China, in 1925 had a density of 89,300 per square mile. Certain sections of cities show even greater concentration. The Borough of Manhattan, New York City, in 1920 reached the colossal figure of 104,200 persons per square mile.[10]

[9] See Mark Jefferson, "The Anthropography of Some Great Cities," *Bulletin American Geographical Society*, 1909, vol. XLI, pp. 542–44.

[10] While it is difficult to set a figure, Walter F. Willcox has proposed that urban territory be defined as that having more than 1,000 persons per square mile and in which there is practically no agriculture. Mark Jefferson would raise this to 10,000. The United States Census for 1930 includes as urban 28 unincorporated townships having a total population of 10,000 or more and a population density of 1,000 or more per square mile. See *Fifteenth Census, Population*, vol. I, p. 7. See also Willcox, "A Redefinition of 'City' in Terms of Density of Population," *The Urban Community* (ed. by E. W. Burgess), 1926, p. 119; Jefferson, *op. cit.*, p. 544.

Mere density alone, however, may be misleading, since there are some rural areas in China, India, and northern Europe which show a rather high concentration of population per square mile. It is the nature of the culture as well that is significant.

Machine and Commercial Culture. The growth of modern cities has depended chiefly on private industry and commerce demanding large quantities of both labor and capital. Economic specialization of function is perhaps the outstanding factor, but political, recreational, and even religious purposes have also aided the growth of cities.

This urban *structure of specialization* stands in contrast to the situation in the primary community, with its limited division of labor. Business, retail and wholesale, industry, transportation, and housing needs in our cities tend to be located in definite relationships reflecting the specialization of life. E. W. Burgess has worked out the theoretical picture of this urban structure by a series of zones. The first is the retail business, hotel, and downtown recreational center. In the second, just beyond this, one finds wholesale business and some light manufacturing, sometimes interspersed with cheap hotels and vice areas. The third is the rooming-house area proper—usually a section marked by rapid expansion outward from the center, leaving former higher-class residences to be given over to small apartments or rooming-house use. The fourth zone is made up of the tenements and slums, or working-class districts. The fifth zone is the high-class residential area, reaching often in our rapidly growing cities out into the suburbs. This structural layout varies in different cities depending on geographical and cultural factors, but everywhere it shows the variation which is introduced into the urban community by modern industry and business.[11] (See Chapter VII on geography.)

Population mobility is a definite factor related to this specialization. Population mobility refers to the actual movement in space of persons, not to social mobility, which has to do with changes in social status. This spatial movement is of three sorts: (*1*) the migration of people to the urban community, or away from it, to take up residence; (*2*) the changes in residence within the community itself; and (*3*) the daily movement of people within the community.

[11] See R. D. McKenzie, "The Rise of Metropolitan Communities," Chapter IX, *Recent Social Trends*, pp. 463–67, for data on changes in population and land values in various zones in selected American cities.

The cityward migration of population is evident throughout recent history. For example, New York City has increased 75 fold since 1800, Paris over five times, Budapest over 18, and Los Angeles shows the amazing increase of 3,300 fold. By no means all of this increase arises from migration. Much of it has come from excess of urban births over deaths, but the factor of migration is important, first, from rural sections of the country, and second, from foreign immigration. In the United States in 1800, four per cent of the population lived in cities of 8,000 and over; 100 years later about 32.9 per cent lived in towns or cities of over 8,000. In 1930, nearly 48 per cent lived in cities over 10,000. The strictly farm population constitutes about one fourth of all our people today.[12]

The urbanization of population tends to go on wherever we find intensive industrialism. In our own country not only are the cities growing, but the larger cities are also growing faster than the smaller ones. Between 1900 and 1930, the proportion of people living in cities over 500,000 increased from 10.7 per cent of the total to 17 per cent; the proportion in cities between 100,000 and 500,-000 rose from 8.1 to 12.6 per cent; the proportion in cities from 10,000 to 100,000 changed from 13 to 17.9 per cent. On the other hand, the proportion in cities of less than 10,000 has remained slightly over 8 per cent throughout the 30-year period.

Residential mobility has not been extensively studied, but it follows the spatial expansion of the city outward. It is plain that the rate of residential change is higher in hotel and rooming-house areas than in tenement sections, and higher in the latter than in districts farther out where people own their own homes. There is a definite inverse relationship between home ownership and residential mobility.[13]

Not only has the total population of urban areas grown rapidly, but also man's daily movement within the urban community areas is apparently increasing. Living in cities stimulates daily mobility through the concentration of activities in the business, industrial, and recreational zones.

[12] Before 1920 the U.S. census did not distinguish between rural farm and rural non-farm population. The present distinction is important since it gives us a measure of the actual number of farmers in the country and a fair approximation of the number of residents of villages and small towns who are not farmers.

[13] See K. Young, J. L. Gillin, and C. L. Dedrick, *The Madison Community*, 1934, chap. VII, for a discussion of this problem in a medium-sized city.

Daily movement is definitely related to this specialization and concentration of activities. Estimates showed that in Newark from 1912 to 1915 traffic increased three times as fast as did population. In London between 1911 and 1914 one count showed that traffic increased 6.4 times as fast as population. In St. Louis for the period 1913–1917 a similar study reported an increase in traffic nearly nine times as great as population growth. In 1860 a New York resident took an average of 43 rides a year in public conveyances; in 1890, 220; in 1924, 450. In the 20 years from 1902 to 1922 in London the population increased but 14 per cent, while the rides per person increased over 190 per cent.

The facts for the New York community are interesting in this connection. Manhattan constitutes obviously the heart of the city. Taking only the area below Fifty-ninth Street, it was shown that in 1924 there were 982,000 residents and transients remaining over night on any typical business day. On the same day, 1,959,700 persons came in and went out of this area. Of these nearly one half, or 43.8 per cent, came from areas north of Fifty-ninth Street; 38.1 per cent from Long Island; 16.1 per cent from New Jersey; and 2.0 per cent from Staten Island.[14] These figures are for more than a decade ago. Since then there has been an even greater concentration of business in the heart of Manhattan.

The study of regional planning made in New York some years ago[15] showed that at the present rate of increase auto traffic alone would become practically impossible unless drastic changes were made for handling this type of traffic. For example, in 1927 on the Boston Post Road, an important highway leading out of New York City, 1,500 automobiles passed a given point in one hour. If the present rate of increase in the use of the automobile were to continue, over 10,000 cars would pass the same point in an hour in 1965.

Many factors operate to make the problem of congestion serious. The process of growth itself is controlled, in part, by the nature of the land, its extent, use, and value. Street plans are also a factor. "The friction of space" becomes a genuine hindrance. Interestingly enough, devices to relieve urban congestion only make the problem more serious in the end. As Niles Carpenter says,

14 See *Regional Survey of New York and Its Environs,* vol. III, *Highway Traffic,* 1927, pp. 61–62.
15 *Op. cit.*

"The erection of high buildings lessens *congestion in density,* but increases *congestion in movement,* by vastly adding to the number of goods and passengers that must be moved into or out of, and within the area affected."[16]

Urban Personality. Urban specialization and concentration of function reflect themselves back into the life organization of the individual. The activities and interests are not focused or integrated around one or two groups but many. The family assumes less importance. The primary group neighborhood has practically disappeared from our great cities. A family may live in an apartment house and know no other of its families personally. Their friends may all be available to them through agencies of transportation or communication: telephone, telegraph, train, street car, motor car, or air lines. Closer associations like the church group are often dissipated in the city. In the village and town the neighborhood church was almost literally "just around the corner."

The relations of urban persons are thus much more of the touch-and-go variety. There exists only a wide range of partial integrations, involving not the whole personality but only special interests. Many contacts with one's fellows are marked by impersonality; economic relations are mediated through money and not in terms of personal relations of master and servant, or of apprentice and journeyman. So at play the individual pays for a seat at a baseball game or in a movie house. Although he may go with a friend or two, he is not dependent for his amusement upon close interaction with those around him but only upon the recreational devices which have been invented to amuse him directly. (See Chapter XV on recreation.)

The *social types* in the city are much more varied than in the country or village, where they are rather limited to farm owner, tenant farmer, farm laborer, and a few village types, such as general storekeeper, doctor, notary public, preacher, and teacher. The urban community, in contrast, sees many types. Noel P. Gist and L. A. Halbert in their book *Urban Society* (1933) list seven classes of urban social types, as follows:

(1) *Occupational,* including such obvious illustrations as the business executive, the realtor, the clerk, the waitress, the bookkeeper, the

---

[16] Carpenter, *The Sociology of City Life,* 1931, p. 127. Italics in original.

religious executive and leader, the whole range of various skilled and unskilled workers: clerks, bookkeepers, taxi drivers, and the more traditional skilled workmen; (2) the *political* types, illustrated by the political boss, the ward-heeler, the committeeman, and a host of municipal office holders who are political henchmen; (3) the *leisure-time* types, like the club man, the athletic sportsman, the debutante, the junior leaguers, the gambler, the gigolo, the charity-work volunteer, the uplifters; (4) the *social-pariah* types, the outcasts from our contemporary urban society—the hoboes, the homeless, the panhandlers, the prostitutes, the gangsters, bootleggers, beggars, and confidence men; (5) the *social reformers,* such as the political agitators, socialists, communists, pacifists, "muck-rakers," and the whole gamut of pious moral reformers; (6) the *bohemian* types—those persons who have broken from the conventional morality of the community, the intelligentsia, the artists, and the so-called "emancipated" persons who inhabit the artist colonies and transitional areas of our cities; and (7) various *language-group* types, that is, those who still identify themselves with foreign societies: the Jews, the Poles, the Italians, and so on. Among these latter, there are, in turn, a large number of social types again. Louis Wirth notes some of these among the Jews: the *Schlemiel,* the shiftless no-account who has, however, a strong sense of group solidarity; the *Luftmensch,* the Jewish hobo; the *Schacherjude,* the peddler; the *Groberjung,* the illiterate; the *Lodgenik,* the joiner; the *Kibitzer,* the genial joker and know-it-all; and the *Leptcheche,* the gossip.[17]

The wide range of stimuli and response permissible in the city makes for individuality, initiative, heightened animation, dynamic interest, restlessness, and for a certain superficiality.

While invention is perhaps accomplished without too great external distraction, very likely the increased sensitivity, the variation in situations, and the demands for further specialization in the city all stimulate the creation of new mechanical and social devices, facilitate art, and increase the itch for social change. Charles A. Beard, American political scientist and historian, has put the matter thus: "Noble virtues flourish in the country, but creative, inventive, and imaginative talents must have the facilities and stimulus of urbanism, certainly more or less, if they are to develop into great powers."[18] Yet in contrast to Beard it may be well to recall Goethe's aphorism that "talent develops itself in

---

[17]See Louis Wirth, "Jewish Types of Personality," in *The Urban Community,* 1929 (ed. by E. W. Burgess), pp. 106–12.

[18]Charles A. Beard, "The City's Place in Civilization," *Survey,* November 15, 1928, vol. LXI, p. 215.

solitude." Certainly the city affords stimulus to talent and invention because in the city tend to be centered such stimulating agencies as educational institutions and art colonies. Still the general run of life in the city may well be too distracting unless this stimulation for talent and invention be rather carefully directed. The city has also been the death of talent in many men and women who mistook its surface features for the more lasting requirements of accomplishment.

Not only this, but *mob-mindedness* is enhanced in our modern cities. The common stimuli of the press, the motion picture, the radio, and the demand for a certain conventionalization of public attitudes foster like-mindedness, common dead-level interests, and superficiality. Thus, while the city may stimulate variation, the cultural consequences of such deviations may be superficial.

In contrast to the rural personality, the city tends to foster verbal responses. So much of urban interaction depends on communication, often at a distance, and the extensive urban stimuli call for such a wide range of shallow information, that the language capacity of the city man is evident. The superiority of city school children over their country cousins in the verbal features of intelligence tests is perhaps rather a reflection of this difference than a mark of genuine difference in potential ability to handle actual situations in a rational manner. (On personality, see Chapter VI.)

The Dominance of City Culture. It is apparent everywhere not only that the city is growing in population at the expense of the country, but also that urban culture is rapidly disseminating itself in the rural areas. The growth of the city as the market for farm products and as a center of trade and financial control over the rural regions provides the economic background for this increasing dominance of the city. Along with rapid transportation, increased urban newspaper circulation in rural areas, and the coming of the motion picture and the radio has gone a diffusion to the country from the city of the whole complex of city attitudes, ideas, and habits.

Whether he likes it or not, the country dweller is rapidly falling under the spell of the city. Isolation is breaking down at every point. Some features of this we have already noted. Although it deals with the village rather than the open-country neighborhood, the following quotation from J. F. Steiner well summarizes the impress of urban life upon the primary community.

"In this emergence of the small town from its old isolation, nothing is more revealing than the efforts of the young people to escape from the thraldom of old traditions. The young people are naturally the storm center where the struggle between group practice and individual variation is being constantly waged. All local institutions and other means of control bring their influence to bear upon the rising generation, for unless the latter conform, the old continuity cannot be maintained. As long as access to the outside world remains difficult, the issue of this struggle is rarely in doubt. Here and there in the more benighted places, an exceptional individual may escape, but the rank and file of the young people fall ready victims to the social pressure to which they are subjected. It is true that today there is a decreasing number of communities sufficiently isolated to maintain absolute control. A generation ago, however, many hundreds of small towns were so situated that their traditional sway was seldom successfully challenged. The first inroads upon their power frequently came about in a seemingly accidental manner without any general recognition of the significance of the new innovations. Sometimes the disturbing leaven was a broadminded teacher or minister, the moving in of a progressive family, the coming of a railway, the building of good roads, the construction of a factory, the discovery of new sources of wealth, such as oil or coal, the use of automobiles, or some other factor that gave knowledge of the outside world or facilitated wider social contacts. Without such aid the first steps toward the emancipation of the young people would hardly have been possible. And this emancipation, it must be remembered, has gone forward very slowly except under the most favorable circumstances and rarely even today includes all areas of community life. . . ."[19]

Much has been written about the dangers to our whole culture and society from the overwhelming dominance of the city, and there has been considerable talk about decentralization of the city. Up to a certain point this has been possible. For example, electrical power permits the shifting of light machine-industry into suburban and even rural areas. So, too, increased facilities for travel have increased the growth of suburban centers around the larger cities. These changes do not mean less but more urban domination, since the fundamental urban culture still remains. Since the machine and modern commercial organization lie at the basis of urban life, we cannot escape the cultural changes implied in this life unless we drastically change the whole economic order. To give up this culture itself would likely mean a decrease in popu-

[19] From J. F. Steiner, "Village Mores in Transition," Chapter VII, *Social Attitudes*, (ed. by K. Young), 1931.

lation, a decline in standards of living, and a return to a pre-industrial life. There is no indication, at present, that we are headed in that direction. Yet in a time of economic depression naïve persons are very likely to advocate in all seriousness that the proper way to solve our economic problems is to "put people back on the farm." The overproduction of agricultural products in recent decades would seem an adequate answer to this suggestion. Others, like Ralph Borsodi, seriously suggest that urban dwellers live a combination urban and rural life, so that by raising and canning much of their own foodstuffs they would become economically more self-sufficient. This sounds fine in books, and it may work for a selected few; but as a general social program for millions of urban folk it is obviously out of the question.[20]

No, the machine and the city have come to stay, at least until there is a profound change in our forms of economic life. The problems raised by the city are to be faced in terms of the whole culture and not by any simple devices, no matter how plausible they may sound in a period of crisis. Rural isolation is over. The individualism of the American farmer may continue to handicap his adjustment to urban industrial culture, but in the end he must capitulate and adapt himself to the specialization and the commercial organization of agriculture. Unless he does this the whole matter of agricultural production may some day be taken out of his hands by corporations manned by experts and technicians who will raise our foodstuffs in the manner and spirit of modern factory production and not in the primitive way of the ancient rural community.

THE REGION

While the city typifies the secondary community in its fullest sense, there has developed along with it another spatial division which we call the *region* or section. Although it has been largely an economic unit, the region also has sociological and political implications which cannot be ignored.

The economic basis of regions in the United States, which we shall use as an example, rests upon geographic and cultural factors. The North Atlantic states early developed industry and agriculture; the South Atlantic states produced cotton and tobacco; the great mid-American region was given over to cereal crops and

[20] Ralph Borsodi, *Flight from the City*, 1933.

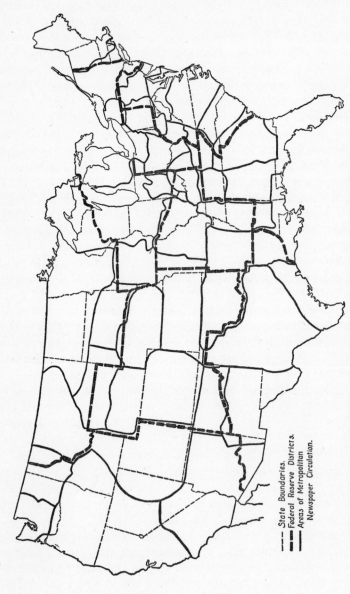

Fig. 3. Showing Federal Reserve Banking Districts of the United States. Overlapping these districts are shown areas of the circulation of metropolitan newspapers.

later in certain sections to heavy industry; the Far West was the home of the cattle and the sheep rancher. Both the Atlantic and North Pacific states developed fishing and lumbering, and California and Florida developed citrus fruit-growing and a recreational industry. These sections are only roughly delimited and time has changed many features, such as the disappearance of lumbering in New England, New York, Michigan, and Wisconsin, and the decline in cotton in the older Southern states.

Economic Regions. Although a region is first of all a geographic unit, it is more than that. It is the stage upon which a vast enterprise of economic, social, and even political life is played. There is always a center (usually a metropolitan community), a cluster of sub-centers, and a wide periphery inclosing the rural area. In our capitalistic culture it is the economic function which develops these centers and areas in the first place. As R. E. Park succinctly remarks, "Trade comes first but political and social institutions follow." The relation of the center to the supporting region is largely determined by the whole configuration of natural resources, agriculture, manufacturing, marketing, financial control, and transportation.

As illustrations we may refer to three sorts of regions, somewhat overlapping in area, but also somewhat distinct. The first is the Federal Reserve District, the second the wholesale trade area, and the third the area of metropolitan newspaper circulation—the latter a reflection of both economic and other social factors.

Figure 6 on the opposite page shows the Federal Reserve Districts of the United States. These districts were established largely on economic grounds. Political boundaries were ignored as unessential. The report to the United States Senate at the time the districts were set up states:

"Among the factors which governed the committee in determining the respective districts and the selection of the cities which have been chosen were: (1) the mercantile, industrial, and financial connections existing in each district, and the relations between the various portions of the district and the city selected for the location of the Federal Reserve Bank . . . , (2) the general geographical situation of the district, transportation lines, and the facilities for speedy communication between the Federal Reserve Bank and all portions of the district." [21]

[21] From 63rd Congress: 2nd Session, *Senate Document No. 485;* "Location of Federal Reserve Districts," p. 361.

Another criterion of major regions is the wholesale trade area. The United States Department of Commerce national survey of wholesale trade by counties for 1929 shows notable concentration of wholesale trade. Sixty-five per cent of the total trade was handled in eight states: New York, Illinois, Pennsylvania, California, Missouri, Ohio, Massachusetts, and Texas, in the order named. Within these states, 11 counties alone took care of 50 per cent of the grand total. An additional 12 per cent of the total business was handled by 13 additional counties. "Altogether 127 counties and independent cities in the United States, each with a business of $50,000,000 and over, contributed $57,644,485,002 or 83 per cent of the total volume of wholesale trade for the United States."[22]

The circulation of metropolitan newspapers to surrounding territories affords another, though somewhat imperfect, picture of regions. Taking Federal Reserve Banking centers and subcenters, a territory was assigned to each in which 50 per cent or more of the competing metropolitan papers came from that particular city. Only one paper was considered, and the data were taken from the Audit Bureau of Circulation.[23] On Figure 3, page 74, we have superimposed these newspaper circulation areas upon the Federal Banking Districts. Although the overlapping is not complete, the correspondence in areas is striking.

Metropolis and Region. The region, then, is characterized by a metropolitan center and a wider economic area which has also social, political, and other ramifications. The area of the metropolitan community is determined largely by the commuting of workers and retail buyers who move daily to and from the center. As the radius of the older village or local community was determined in large part by "the team-haul," that is, the distance a team could move a load of goods in one day, so the radius of the metropolis is the distance which may be traveled daily to and from the center by automobile or train. In the larger centers, like New York and Chicago, this may extend more than 50 miles, although the modal distance is perhaps between 20 and 40.[24] It is

[22]From *Wholesale Trade United States, Distribution Summary for U. S.,* U. S. Department of Commerce, Bureau of the Census, 15th Census of the United States, 1930, Washington, D. C., 1933, p. 42.
[23]See R. D. McKenzie, "The Rise of Metropolitan Communities," Chapter IX, *Recent Social Trends,* p. 453.
[24]*Op. cit.,* p. 457.

interesting in this connection to note that fully one half the people of this country live within an hour's automobile ride of a city of 100,000 or more.

The region around the metropolitan center is made up, first, of a zone of retail trading which may extend to 100 miles from the center; and the larger, less well-defined zone of wholesale trade and the general production and distribution area, of which the metropolis is the industrial, business, and financial focus. The central cities tend to foster a sectional consciousness not only in financiers and merchants but in the urban inhabitants, and especially in the people within the region who may come to the center not only for business purposes, but also for medical services, recreation, and education.

It is self-evident that political boundaries—city, county, and state—do not correspond to these newly developed secondary communities. Our political boundaries were, for the most part, laid out on irrational lines, and recent cultural changes have made their relative inflexibility more apparent than ever before.

The historic method of changing urban political boundaries to fit economic and social changes was by annexation of suburbs, but this method has limitations, and recent years have seen the rise of a variety of metropolitan political districts to handle water supply, sewage disposal, drainage, and recreation. These are largely administrative units, set up by state legislatures to care for the more obvious needs of the expanding urban community. Various proposals have been made for further expansion of this whole movement along more fundamental lines. Some even go so far as to suggest that our largest cities and their immediate environs be made into separate states. This is not likely to take place without great changes in our political ideas and practice. Hence the chief lines of political development seem rather to be in the direction of wider administrative districting. In matters of interstate public health, sewerage, and transportation, the federal government has taken over added duties. The whole interest of state and federal government in regard to the region is recent, and the changes already made have usually not been the result of long-time planning but are devices set up to meet more immediate emergencies. The Tennessee Valley Authority plan started in 1933 is really the first example of extensive combined federal and state planning for a particular region.

Historically, sectionalism in this country is not new.[25] It has had political, economic, and other cultural implications. The Civil War itself, of course, was a sectional conflict. Throughout our history political legislation has often revolved around these regional controversies: North *versus* South, industrial East against the agricultural Middle and Far West, rural *versus* urban. As various regions fall into new competitions or new alignments, we shall see new forms of political sectionalism growing up.

THE POLITICAL STATE AS A SECONDARY COMMUNITY

Although the study of government is the function of political science, we must note some of the important features of the national state as an extended secondary community. In the United States, the separate states themselves develop a certain we-group solidarity. Citizens identify themselves as belonging to the state, especially some of the older ones. Old Virginian families still count both politically and "socially," not only at home, but elsewhere in the South. Citizens of various states may develop a pride in their particular state government, as in the "progressivism" of Wisconsin. Or they may be proud of an excellent elementary-school system like that developed early in Massachusetts, or of a fine state university, as in Michigan. Or the climate becomes the focus of their pride in their state, as in California.

The National State. The nation, on the other hand, may and does take on all sorts of economic and other cultural control functions that make it distinctly a super-region set off from other nations. Its very existence with the sovereignty or power which its constituted authorities hold makes it a distinctive cultural unit in our modern world. The nation makes war and peace, sets up tariff walls, or enters into trade agreements with other nations, restricts immigration, and in general acts as the largest and most inclusive separate we-group which we have so far developed in the world today.

The rise of strong nationalism has been one characteristic of our Occidental ethos for several centuries. In spite of recent trends toward internationalism, the post-World War period has seen a marked recrudescence of intense nationalism. While edu-

[25] See Frederick Jackson Turner, *The Significance of Sections in American History* (ed. by Max Farrand), 1932, for papers on historical phases of regionalism.

cation, religious teaching, economic ideas and practices have long fostered political and cultural nationalism—by teaching patriotism, by connecting divine plans with the establishment of the nation, as many of our religious superpatriots have done, by advocating nationalistic economic independence—it is only in recent decades that national governments have so thoroughly supported conscious efforts to bend every phase of culture toward some particular nationalistic goal. Although Russia is on paper a communist state looking to a world-wide revolution which will overthrow both capitalism and nationalism, it is, in actual fact, a large federation of states with a distinctly Russian future at heart. Deliberate planning, not only in economics, but in education and in every other phase of mass impression is aimed at developing a new form of secondary community in which the dictatorship of the proletariat and a whole new culture based on the Marx-Lenin ideology will be brought about.

Modern means of transportation and communication, especially such devices for mass impression as the motion picture, radio, and newspaper, make this stimulation of nationalism more effective than it was in earlier times when travel and communication were slower and more restricted. Moreover, the mob-mindedness of the urban population, which may now easily infect the rural population as well, makes it possible to crystallize public opinion and stimulate action of whole nations in a way not possible in a period of more intense individualism, local and sectional rivalries, and the general inertia favored by cultural isolation.

Another and more consciously nationalistic program is that carried on by the Italian fascist government. The aim is to remake the ideas, attitudes, and habits of the Italian people to fit the fascist conceptions of the interplay of economics and politics. The fascists in Italy have not yet gone as far as the Russians in attempting to recast an entire culture. The more recent Hitler revolution in Germany is another strong nationalist movement, attempting to produce a thoroughly Teutonic ("Aryan") culture of a consciously planned type. Germany, in fact, has more background for this deliberate planning of nationalism than either Russia or Italy.[26]

[26]The following books discuss certain aspects of this problem: Samuel N. Harper, *Civic Training in Soviet Russia*, 1929; Samuel N. Harper, *Making Bolsheviks*, 1931; C. J. H. Hayes, *France: A Nation of Patriots*, 1930; Paul Kosok, *Modern Germany*, 1933; C. E. Merriam, *The Making of Citizens*, 1931; Herbert W. Schneider and Shepard B. Clough, *Making Fascists*, 1929.

This intense nationalism stimulates a strong we-group feeling, makes for solidarity in support of saber-rattling and war, even favors at times economic separatism, and altogether furnishes the individual citizen with a focus of his emotional attitudes, thereby tending to replace his attachments to the local community of an earlier day. Nevertheless, in spite of this strong nationalism, the influence of international contacts is not lost. A "world community" international in scope is not a mere phrase. Let us look at some of its sociological implications.

INTERNATIONALISM AND THE SECONDARY COMMUNITY

After a long period of nationalistic decline, during which the Christian church dominated Western culture, there came a rebirth of nationalism along with the rise of modern capitalism and the growth of Protestant religion. For some time there was a certain correspondence of political and economic life, when each state tried to control the economic organization in its own way. What is known as *mercantilism* in economics is actually a "political economy," in a literal sense. Under this system each nation tries to maintain its self-sufficiency on economic as well as on political grounds. The first period of colonial expansion was a part of this nationalistic economics. But modern commerce and the Industrial Revolution with their demands for new markets, both for goods and for capital, on the one hand, and for raw materials, on the other, undermined this narrow nationalistic economy. There arose in its place the doctrines of free trade and unhampered international economic relations along with notions of individualism in economic effort which escaped the boundaries of a particular state. The nations of western Europe at this time were just entering into a mad rush for colonies as outlets for goods and excess population, and as sources of raw materials. Modern Europe reached the Far East first in India. Later Japan and China were opened up for European trade and missionary activities. In more recent decades the whole African continent has been the object of European exploitation.

This expansion of Europe and America to Asia and Africa has broken down the barriers of isolation which for centuries separated these continents from the West. In spite of Kipling's famous line "East is East, and West is West, and never the twain shall meet," the Orient and the Occident have met on the world stage, on which every nation will sooner or later come to play a part. There is before us the possibility of a world-wide secondary community, "The Great Society," which offers challenging problems on every hand.[27] Some aspects of this wider community will be apparent in later discussions. (See Chapter IX on population.) We shall but sketch here some of the general implications of these expanding contacts.

Economic Expansion and World Contact. The interdependence of nations is apparent from slight knowledge of the world of trade and industry around us. Every day we purchase and use articles of food, dress, work, or play that come as raw materials or finished products from the wide world. In spite of all the recent talk of economic natic alism and self-sufficiency, it is evident to any but the political demagogue or the naïve superpatriot that the nation's business is the world's business.

A recent bulletin of the National Council for the Prevention of War (Washington, D. C.) lists 30 imported products upon which American industry is highly dependent. The same bulletin also lists 15 widespread industries and businesses which use these and other products: the automobile industry uses materials from 18 different countries; beauty shops need materials from 17; clothing manufacturers from 21; the electrical industry imports from 17 countries; the jewelry industry draws from 26 countries; radio alone from 18; the stationery-supplies industry from 24; and the telephone from 15 countries. In turn, the United States exports large amounts of coal, copper, gold, gypsum, lead, petroleum, phosphate rock, silver, and zinc among the minerals; meats, dairy products, apples, tobacco, and wheat from agriculture; lumber and hundreds of manufactured articles of slight or great importance: automobiles, electrical machinery, engines, firearms, hardware, farm machinery, sewing machines, cotton goods, motion pictures, and rubber products.

Just as one section or region of a great nation like ours or Russia is dependent on another in the national market, so in world economic relations there can be no isolation if we are to carry on modern industrial culture. The standard of living, the high spe-

[27] H. A. Miller in his *Beginnings of Tomorrow*, 1933, p. 11, uses the term "tertiary group" to refer to this world-wide community. He says, "Tertiary groups are intercultural or cosmopolitan."

cialization of occupations, and the extension of leisure time and educational interests in the past have all been tied up closely with these economic factors.

International Religious and Educational Contacts. The zeal of the missionary for new converts is nothing new. Christianity is distinctly a missionary religion, spreading as it did from its humble beginnings in the Near East to cover all of Europe, North and South America, and more recently deliberately diffusing to the Orient and to Africa. Buddhism, likewise of rather simple origin, spread over India, Indo-China, China, and Japan. So, too, Mohammedanism reached eastward to China and westward into Africa and southern Europe, often carrying its message by the sword rather than by more peaceful means.

The extent to which Christianity has spread is roughly indicated by the figures of membership in what are normally called non-Christian countries. One summary reports 7,000,000 Roman Catholics in Asia, 2,000,000 in Africa, and 1,500,000 in Oceania; 7,000,000 Protestants in Asia, 3,000,000 in Africa, and 6,000,000 in Oceania.[28] The spread of Mohammedanism in Africa is evident in the report of 44,000,000 of this faith there. Of the estimated 160,000,000 Mohammedans in Asia, nearly one half are to be found in India, where their influence extended long before aggressive Christianity reached that country.

Christianity has spread not only the Christian plan of salvation. Linked with it are other culture traits of education, politics, and economics that have affected non-Christians everywhere. Notions of economic individualism, of respect for women and children, and a stimulation of democratic and even socialistic ideas have followed in the wake of its formal and informal religious teaching. The Christian missionary schools have brought to Asia and Africa Western ideas of education for the masses, have taught children and adults the rudiments of learning that they would otherwise never have acquired. In short, this ferment, planted in the midst of alien cultures, has been a potent factor in undermining the older culture patterns. Christian standards of dress, consumption, and superiority foster trade in cotton goods, foodstuffs, firearms, and even sporting goods. Politically the ideas of democracy, of the importance of the common man, of the

[28]*The World Almanac and Book of Facts for 1938*, p. 431. Oceania, as used here, includes Australia and New Zealand, where European colonization has been large.

doctrines of equality and opportunity have unsettled ever larger sections of the populations of India, China, and more recently Africa. Consequent political unrest in these quarters is likely to disturb the world for some time to come.

The dominant Western powers had no intention originally of letting loose such ideas and attitudes of freedom and equality in Asia or Africa. They preferred to exploit these countries economically and religiously, but did not dream of the present repercussions upon world affairs. But nations, like individuals, cannot long eat their cake and have it too. Sooner or later, economic, political, and even religious reverberations were bound to disturb the old balance of power and to raise new questions of international relations.

International Political Contacts. No matter how strong the thesis of national isolation may be in the modern world, political states cannot exist without contacts with other nations. In the intense nationalistic period from the seventeenth century on to the present, the whole Western world witnessed a series of wars and treaties in which nations or combinations of nations sought to hold the balance of world power. Each nation operated as a strong in-group bargaining with other nations in an effort to preserve as much for itself and give as little to the other fellow as possible— very much in the manner of two rival feudal barons, or of rival capitalist entrepreneurs, or of rival criminal gangs in our modern American cities. There were individuals and groups, especially of a religious or socialistic sort, that advocated peace, that carried on a certain amount of education and propaganda in favor of more intelligent methods of settling international disputes, but down to the end of the nineteenth century most of these pacific movements had not greatly affected political practices of secret diplomacy and secret intrigue which made for international conflict.[29]

One of the first definite steps in the direction of more open and frank recognition of the rights of other nations or peoples in any controversy was the principle of arbitration laid down in the Treaty of Ghent (1814), which closed the War of 1812 between the United States and Great Britain. Shortly after that the Monroe Doctrine established our own form of peaceful protection over weaker American republics, thus preventing further European ag-

[29] See Jerome Davis, *Contemporary Social Movements,* 1930, pp. 753–59, 764–72, for a review of early peace movements.

grandizement in Latin America, and during the last 50 years various pan-American conferences have sought to cement closer friendship between this country and its neighbors to the south.

It was, however, the First Hague Conference, or more properly, the First International Peace Conference, held in 1899, that brought before the whole world the need of arbitration in place of war. This conference set up a tribunal which has, in the years since, settled 16 international disputes. In 1907 a Second International Peace Conference convened at The Hague, but proposals for a permanent court of international justice did not materialize. These were the only efforts which gave continuity of idea and practice in peaceful arbitration before the holocaust of the World War broke upon us, although in 1913 William Jennings Bryan (1860–1925) had worked out an elaborate treaty scheme looking to permanent peace between nations.

At the close of the World War, the League of Nations was set up. Woodrow Wilson (1856–1924), the chief sponsor for this organization, remarked that "the only way we can prevent the unspeakable thing [war] from happening again is that the nations of the world should unite and put an irresistible force behind peace and order." This he hoped to do "by means of a League of Nations."

The organization of the League of Nations consists of a league assembly meeting periodically, a permanent league council of selected persons, and a secretary-general. Attached to the League is a Permanent Court of International Justice, which sits at The Hague. It has considered a goodly number of cases.[30] There are also a number of international organizations sponsored by the League or related informally to it to study such international problems as trade, labor, the narcotic and drug traffic, white slavery, and others.

In the past few years peoples everywhere have lost faith in such forms of international organization. In 1935 Japan and Germany withdrew from the League of Nations, followed by Italy in 1937. The efficacy of this body today is highly dubious. The breakdown, largely for want of British support, of the League's

[30]The Permanent Court was set up by the League in 1920, the judges were elected in 1921, and on January 15, 1922, the Court held its first session. From then until the end of 1933 it handed down 21 judgments and issued 40 lesser orders, and in addition rendered 25 advisory opinions. See Manley O. Hudson, *The World Court: 1921–1934,* 1934.

economic boycott ("sanctions") to prevent Italy's conquest of Ethiopia, its impotence with respect to Japanese invasion of China and with regard to recent events in Spain, Austria, and Czechoslovakia, are all cases in point.[31]   The re-birth of aggressive nationalism, especially in Germany, Italy, and Japan, and even in so-called communistic Russia, serves to check peaceful practices among nations.   By 1939 the much-heralded Briand-Kellogg Peace Pact of 1928 for outlawing war was as dead as the dodo.

Nationalism versus Internationalism.   Even this short review will serve to remind us that the world today has moved into a form of interaction which no longer makes possible the isolation and self-sufficiency of any large body of people who have adopted present-day machine culture and all that it implies. "The Great Society" is, however, a recent emergence from the background of centuries of strong nationalistic sentiment. The modern economic order, which is at heart the most rationalistic, the most impersonal form of interaction yet developed, has made the wide world and all peoples its servant. Still, politically, religiously, educationally, and morally, the peoples of the world have not yet followed the implications of this change.[32]

The whole matter reduces itself to the change of various in-group—out-group relations and the fact that in some fields these relations have been altered more rapidly than in others. Modern industry, abetted by increasing facility of transportation and communication, is at odds with strong nationalistic sentiments and attachment to local gods of religion and morality. The matter rests upon identification. While the ordinary citizen may depend for many important material goods upon the wide world, he has not yet developed any highly emotionalized symbols in regard to these objects strong enough to counteract the expression of the more deeply imbedded culture traits of patriotism and faith in his own country. After all, the attachment to the soil, to the flag, to the external symbols of the national state are more immediate and

[31]The fact that the League of Nations and the Versailles Treaty of 1919 were linked together has doubtless been a handicap to the former, and sentiment in many nations, especially in Germany, is that France in particular used the League as a means of maintaining the *status quo* set up by the peace treaty itself. Recent events indicate the dissipation of this power device in international relations in Europe.

[32]See the incisive discussion of this problem in W. K. Wallace's books, *The Trend of History*, 1922, and *The Passing of Politics*, 1924.

more intimate than these new, remoter, and cold intellectual facts; *e.g.*, though the economic and social future of the American farmer is tied up with events in far-flung Argentina, Russia, or China, it is difficult for him to envisage the situation. To do so he must give up his individualism and his provincial attachment to his own region and his own nation. The economists may assure him that only in the freedom of world competition and easy passage of goods and services from one part of the world to another can a truly great international society grow up in which all will benefit. Yet such future Utopias seem remote indeed against the immediate appeal of the political demagogue who talks and writes that American standards of living must not sink to those of the peasant of Europe or Asia or who preaches the doctrine of economic and political self-sufficiency.

Looked at from another angle it is a question of narrower or wider morality. The age-old moral code of the we-group is to grab everything for one's own group, at any cost and with any device known to man. The newer morality maintains that in a world so interdependent as ours this narrow we-group standard must give way to another founded on economic realities of the widest exchange of goods, on the knowledge that nations are dependent for their continued existence, not only materially but otherwise, upon the live-and-let-live policy which undermines this more immediate morality. Arnold J. Toynbee, the British economist, puts the matter well in these words:

"So long as political obstacles to the world-wide circulation of people, goods and money are maintained by the policy of local sovereign states, the technical 'annihilation of distance' through the progressive mechanical inventions of Western science cannot yield anything like its full potential benefit to mankind.

.   .   .   .   .   .

"For practical purposes, it might be more profitable in the long run for goods and passengers to travel in ox-carts and coaches and sailing-ships and not to be stopped at the frontiers of local sovereign states, rather than to travel by railroad and motor-lorry and steamship and aeroplane in a world in which political frontiers are becoming less and less easy to pass." [33]

We may, in spite of such warnings, see a retreat from internationalism, in which nationalistic self-sufficiency will lead to

[33] Quoted from a mimeographed bulletin of National Council for the Prevention of War. Washington, D. C.

lower standards of living, to isolation of culture, and to renewed international conflict. Certainly until the world-wide community can produce for itself in the masses everywhere strong faith and emotionalized symbols, there is not much to hope for from super-state organizations like the League of Nations. Such new symbols and consequent super-state power would mean the loss of the ancient symbols and practices of political sovereignty, of religious and cultural superiority, and many of the values which peoples everywhere have held sacred for centuries. Whatever our pious wishes may be, in the face of danger to our own locality and especially to our own national existence, few people are ready or willing to support or to die for this more remote internationalism. Whether we can work out such a system of internationalism while still retaining the national state at all and the capitalist economic system so long associated with it, only the future can determine. It is a challenge, however, to anyone who sees that the international community does have a foundation in solid material traits that cannot be gainsaid.   (See Chapter XVIII.)

CLASS ASSIGNMENTS

A. Further reading assignment:

1. K. Young, *Source Book for Sociology,* chap. VI.

2. J. H. Randall, Sr., *A World Community,* chap. IV.

3. H. N. Brailsford, "Internationalism," *Encyclopedia of the Social Sciences,* vol. VIII, pp. 214–18.

B. Questions and exercises:

1. Illustrate isolation arising from (a) biological-psychological conditions within the individual; (b) geographical-cultural factors; (c) differences in language and culture regardless of geographical conditions.

2. What are the characteristics of the primary community?

3. What is meant by the expression, "the urban way of life"? What are the chief features of city life?

4. List and discuss the chief differences and likenesses in ideas, attitudes, and habits of the farmer and the city man.

5. What conditions keep the American farmer from fully absorbing the urban and world community culture around him?

6. Make up a list of the secondary groups to which you belong and indicate on a scale of five steps the degree to which you feel deep emotional attachment to these groups. (Use 1 as the most intense, 2 as intense, 3 as a midpoint, 4 as less intense than the median 3, and 5 as the least intense.) Compare your list with those of other members of the class.

7. Illustrate from daily interest in front-page news the fluctuating, shifting stimuli which reach the reader from the outside world. Contrast with the sort of stimuli likely to reach the isolated rural person from day to day.

8. Does the region really mean anything in the average person's existence unless he is directly connected with some business that concerns itself with the region?

9. What devices are used in the United States by governmental agencies deliberately to foster patriotism and national egotism?

10. What is meant by "The Great Society"? Illustrate.

11. What forces in this country are making for a wider appreciation of our international obligations?

C. Topics for class reports or longer written papers:

1. Studies in community isolation. (Consult O. W. Junek, *Isolated Communities*, 1937; G. B. Johnson, *Folk Culture on St. Helena Island, South Carolina*, 1930; C. A. Dawson, *Group Settlement, Ethnic Communities in Western Canada*, 1936, vol. VII of *Canadian Frontiers of Settlement*, ed. by W. A. Macintosh and W. L. G. Joerg.)

2. Studies in Amercian rural life. (Consult E. de S. Brunner and J. H. Kolb, *Rural Social Trends*, 1933; N. L. Sims, *Elements of Rural Sociology*, rev. ed., 1934; D. Sanderson, *The Rural Community*, 1932; C. C. Taylor, *Rural Sociology*, 1932; J. H. Kolb and E. de S. Brunner, *A Study of Rural Society*, 1935.)

3. National and regional planning in the United States. (Consult H. W. Odum and H. E. Moore, *American Regionalism*, 1938, and bibliography; H. W. Odum, *Southern Regions of the United States*, 1936; and various state and federal reports, especially those of the National Resources Committee. See p. 593 for additional references.)

4. Studies in city life. (Consult M. R. Davie, *Problems of City Life*, 1932; N. Carpenter, *The Sociology of City Life*, 1931; N. P. Gist and L. A. Halbert, *Urban Society*, 1933; H. B. Woolston, *Metropolis*, 1938; E. E. Muntz, *Urban Sociology*, 1938; *Our Cities, their Role in the National Economy*, 1937, report of the National Resources Committee.)

5. The controversy now going on in this country between those who advocate national self-sufficiency and those who stand for internationalism in economic, political, and other important relations. (See Samuel Crowther, *America Self-contained*, 1933; W. B. Donham, *American Ideals and International Idols*, 1933; Alvin H. Hansen, *Economic Stabilization in an Unbalanced World*, 1932; Ramsay Muir, *The Interdependent World and its Problems*, 1932; Parker T. Moon, *Imperialism and World Politics*, 1926; Jerome Frank, *Save America First*, 1938; and files of current periodicals such as *Foreign Affairs, Current History*, etc.)

CHAPTER V

ORIGINAL NATURE, HEREDITY, AND ENVIRONMENT

In no field of psychology or the social sciences has more nonsense been produced than that regarding original nature and the relation of heredity and environment. Popular misconceptions about these facts are carried over into serious books, articles, and into the classroom by many teachers. Behavior traits in others or in ourselves which we do not like, we blame on something called original nature or heredity. "Well, you might expect as much; he's just like his father, and you know there is bad blood in that family,"—so one person characterizes another who has done something which is not socially approved. Parents blame the "bad" behavior of their children on heredity, as do teachers, judges, juvenile officers, and statesmen. Privileged economic classes find support for their domination from such writers as Albert E. Wiggam. Crime, delinquency, insanity, poverty, even unemployment have been explained away by current popular and semi-scientific notions of biological heredity. Race and immigration problems are settled on assumptions of profound hereditary differences in races and nationalities by those who wish to believe in a new form of scientific predestination.

THE NATURE OF HEREDITY

In order to get a balanced view of the interrelations of heredity and environment, we must take up some of the important biological foundations of original nature and heredity.

Original Nature and Heredity. Properly speaking, original nature means the makeup, the combination of physical and behavior traits with which the human being begins life at birth. Human nature is sometimes considered as identical with original nature, but *human nature* is better used to cover those social and human traits which the individual develops in society.

Heredity refers to the "tendency of like to beget like," to the fact that any given generation resembles its ancestors in makeup, that likenesses between closely related families of organisms are, on the average, greater than between organisms more distantly related. That is, heredity has to do with those traits or structures which are carried over from parents to offspring by means of biological mechanisms. J. Arthur Thomson in his book *Heredity* (1907) writes, "Heredity is . . . a convenient term for the genetic relation between successive generations, and an inheritance includes all that the organism is, or has, to start with, in virtue of its hereditary relation."

Curiously, the word heredity has come to be used as if it were a force, power, or fate which moves an individual to do this, or not to do that. Words have a way of getting loose from their carefully defined meanings, and the term heredity, like the word instinct, has accumulated a great deal of meaning that the careful biologists never intended it to have.

Original nature is believed to be due to this something called heredity. And after birth another force called environment begins to operate on this inherited original nature to modify it, to control its expression, and to give it direction. *Environment* is thus defined as those forces or situations, or more strictly those stimuli, which reach and affect the human being from the outside.

Just as there are persons who hold that heredity is largely responsible for all our geniuses and inventors, or for all our criminals or fools, there are others who discount almost entirely the place of heredity and believe that environment is more important in social life. John B. Watson, best known for his behavioristic psychology, seems to believe that with the proper environment, one may make a child into almost any sort of genius or idiot one may wish. Many would-be reformers and dreamers of a social Utopia, or ideal society, believe strongly that the proper organization of environment would completely overhaul original nature and make children and adults into perfect beings only a little "lower than the angels." Naturally, they imagine that their own ideas rather closely conform to what this proper environment should be. Doubtless the truth of this whole matter lies somewhere between these extremes. Let us see what modern biology has to say about the matter.

The individual's biological heredity is fixed at the time of conception, that is, at the time when the male sperm fertilizes the female egg cell. Fertilization takes place when the sperm penetrates the egg, forming a new cell. The new cell divides and redivides, and by a continuation of this process the new individual comes into being. There is much specialization of the cells necessary for the formation of the different organs of the body. The reproductive cells proper remain unspecialized and are relatively independent of the somatic, or body cells, which make up the functioning organs of the body.

Mechanisms of Heredity. Heredity is believed to depend on certain units carried in the germ-plasm of the two sexes. In the reproduction of the race, these units are said to operate in a relatively fixed mathematical manner. We owe to two men the chief interest in this problem in our times. One of these was Sir Francis Galton (1822–1911), a cousin of the evolutionist, Charles Darwin. The other was Johann Mendel (1822–1884), an Austrian monk.

Using statistics, Galton developed two so-called "laws" of heredity. The first, the "law of ancestral inheritance," stated that an individual received one half his traits from his immediate parents, one fourth from his four grandparents, one eighth from his great grandparents, and so on backward in decreasing amounts from the more remote ancestors. The second, "the law of filial regression," maintained that the offspring are inclined to approach the average between the extremes of the parents. Thus, the children of one tall and one short parent tend to fall into a middle height, an average between the two parents, or the children of two short parents will tend to be taller than either parent.

In the light of later studies, both of these "laws" of Galton have been questioned, especially the first one. Yet Galton's enthusiasm stimulated important statistical studies in heredity. We owe to Mendel a greater debt for demonstrating by experiment certain basic principles of heredity now rather generally accepted. Mendel reported his findings in an obscure scientific paper in 1868. Unfortunately the importance of his discovery was lost to the world at that time. It was not until 1901 that Hugo de Vries, a Dutch scientist, working independently, came upon the same principles that had been worked out by Mendel. Moreover, it was de Vries who recovered from obscurity the significant work of Mendel.

In the years since the discovery by de Vries, much further research has been made on the mechanisms of heredity. Microscopic work has demonstrated that the germ-plasm itself is broken up into smaller units called *chromosomes,* and numerous investigations have been made into the operation of hereditary processes.

The chromosomes themselves are broken up into still smaller units called *genes,* perhaps no larger than organic molecules, which seem to be the ultimate determiners of heredity. There must be thousands of these genes in every cell. It is believed that the genes differ among themselves, but for each gene in the egg there is a corresponding gene in the sperm.

At the division of the chromosomes the genes divide, and the somatic cells derived from the fertilized egg "are precisely alike in the genes they contain." There seems little doubt that since the genes are divided hundreds of times in the building of the body, they are built up from the cytoplasm or energy-furnishing matter of the cells. *The genes are chemical substances and must be understood as such.* It is further assumed by the geneticists that the genes operate together in the production of traits and characteristics of the individual. In certain matings, some genes, however, apparently have a preference or dominance over others. This fact gave rise to the first law of Mendel, which he developed even before the nature of the germ-plasm itself was fully understood.

The Law of Dominance. If we cross two varieties of domestic fowl, say the Andalusian, one of which is pure white, the other a pure black, we shall find that the first hybrid generation, called the "first filial," or F_1, will be dark in color, a kind of bluish black. If the matter rested there, the naïve observer might conclude that the whiteness had disappeared altogether. One might naturally wonder what had become of this characteristic of one of the original pair.

Has some miracle taken place? If we cross the hybrids of the F_1 generation among themselves, we discover in the next generation that the pure whites appear again, in one quarter of the offspring. The other three fourths will still be dark, 25 per cent of them pure black, and 50 per cent of them bluish black, called "impure dominants." If the pure blacks are mated among themselves in the following generation, they will continue to produce all pure blacks thereafter. Likewise, if the pure whites are intermixed among themselves, they will produce only pure whites. The other 50 per cent, the bluish blacks, however, if mated among themselves, will continue to produce in each succeeding generation the ratio of one fourth pure blacks, one fourth pure whites, and one half the hybrids or bluish blacks.

This same principle holds for a large number of traits in different species. In peas, with which Mendel worked, tallness is dominant over dwarfness. So, too, yellow color is dominant over green. That character of one individual when mated in the second generation which covers over the corresponding character of the other individual is called the *dominant*. The trait "covered over" is termed *recessive*. Actually, of course, the basis for this condition rests in the chromosomes. Dominance or recessiveness depends upon whether the mature germ cell carries a double-determiner of the particular trait, one from each parent, or whether it carries but one. Those which carry a double-determiner are called *duplex*. Those which combine a dominant and recessive together, as in F_1 generation, are called *simplex* because only one of the dominant characteristics—in the case of Andalusian fowl, blackness—was carried in the germ-plasm. In the next generation, in the reassortment at mating, some of these dominants double up again, some of the recessives double up again, and some of the pairs reassort themselves like the impure dominants of F_1. Figure 4 illustrates the principle for one set of traits:

FIGURE 4

SHOWING THE INHERITANCE OF DOMINANT AND RECESSIVE CHARACTERS

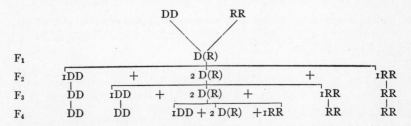

DD represents the pure dominant or duplex. RR represents the pure recessive. D(R) represents the impure dominant of the next generation, in which the recessive character is latent. This is the simplex generation. The numbers in each case represent the proportions of each generation. F_1, F_2, etc., refer to the respective filial generations.

The Law of Segregation. The second law is bound up with the first. It is now clear to us that the determiners of traits in almost all cases tend to separate out independently of each other at each new mating. Thus, although there are probably a distinct number of chromosomes for each species, these chromosomes carry an extremely large number of determiners. To use a simple illustration of merely two traits of a plant, say height and color, we should find that height separates out in the mixing independently of the separations carried on by the determiners of color, and the manner of separation rests upon the way in which the traits are linked together in the parent stocks. For example, suppose we cross certain varieties of tall yellow, tall green, short yellow, and short green peas. One set of pairs is represented in the male, the pollen; the other in the female ovules, as shown in Table 2.

TABLE 2

SHOWING POSSIBLE COMBINATIONS ARISING IN THE SECOND FILIAL GENERATION, F_2, FOLLOWING A CROSS BETWEEN DOMINANT TALL YELLOW AND RECESSIVE SHORT GREEN PEAS*

Pollen ♂	Ovules ♂			
	TALL YELLOW	TALL Green	Short YELLOW	Short Green
TALL YELLOW	TALL YELLOW TALL YELLOW	TALL Green TALL YELLOW	Short YELLOW TALL YELLOW	Short Green TALL YELLOW
TALL Green	TALL YELLOW TALL Green	TALL Green TALL Green	Short YELLOW TALL Green	Short Green TALL Green
Short YELLOW	TALL YELLOW Short YELLOW	TALL Green Short YELLOW	Short YELLOW Short YELLOW	Short Green Short YELLOW
Short Green	TALL YELLOW Short Green	TALL Green Short Green	Short YELLOW Short Green	Short Green Short Green

* *Characteristics printed in solid capitals represent dominance; those in lower case represent recessiveness. Thus, tallness and yellow color are dominant over shortness and green color, which are both recessives.*

Thus, in this second filial generation, F_2, we should get nine tall yellow combinations, or cases where both dominants exist in the same individuals. We should get three short yellows, of dominant yellow mixed with recessive shortness. We should get three tall greens, of dominant tallness mixed with recessive greenness. Finally we should have one short green or pure recessive for both height and color. Three or more pairs of characters behave in the same manner. That is, their genes assort independently in each crossing.

The principle of segregation of traits is important. It shows the complex number of factors which go into plant and animal reproduction. It also indicates that where there are a large number of determiners, the results of any given mixture are difficult to predict in any given individual. In certain cases, however, the genes are carried by the same chromosomes, and we have the so-called "law of linkage."

Sex Determination. The law of linkage can best be introduced by noting the discoveries in regard to the factors which determine sex. The determiner for sex is said to be carried by special sex chromosomes. In certain great groups of animals—mammals and insects especially—the occurrence of two of these chromosomes, called the X chromosomes, produces the female; the presence of but one produces the male. This means that the female is XX, the male XO. That is to say, there are two kinds of sperm cells, some which contain the X chromosome, some which do not. From any random or chance meeting of a sperm cell and an egg there may result an individual belonging to one or the other of two classes. If the sperm cell has an X, then the individual will be XX, since it is sure to receive one X from the egg. If the sperm is without an X, then the individual will have but one X. Those individuals with double X are female, those with single X are male. It is clear that, on the theory of chance, there will be an equal distribution of males and females. Figure 5 on page 96 indicates how this inheritance operates.

It has further been discovered that certain other determiners are linked to the sex chromosomes. As the sex-determining factor is carried over, these additional factors are carried along with it. In man, color blindness is linked with the sex chromosome. So, too, haemophilia, a condition marked by deficiency in the clotting power of the blood, follows the same pattern.

Modern Theory of Genetics. The principles of dominance, of independent segregation of the genes, and of linkage are basic to the theory of modern genetics or the science of heredity. T. H. Morgan refers to this independent sorting, which is the crux of the matter, as the *particulate theory of heredity*, meaning that we have to deal with particular units always in a state of flux. Since the number of genes in the higher animals is very great, and since the number of genetic factors going into the production of any trait is probably very large, this independence of the genes makes for great variability. In the shake-up at the time the sperm fertilizes the egg there is much shifting and mixing of the genes, making for divergence in the next generation. It means, as Morgan says,

FIGURE 5

SHOWING SEX AS A MENDELIAN CHARACTER[1]

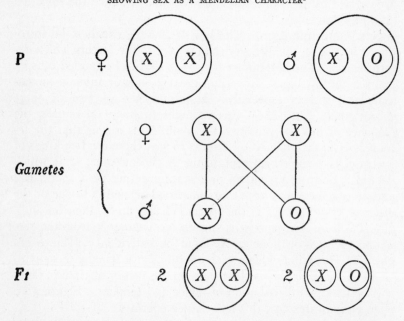

The female forms gametes all of which contain X chromosomes; the male forms two sorts of gametes, one half of which contain the X chromosome, the other half lacking it. All possible combinations of these gametes give 2:2 or 1:1 ratio of females to males. ♀ is a symbol for female; ♂, for male.

[1]Redrawn from Figure 58, E. G. Conklin, *Heredity and Environment*, 1930, 5th edition, p. 167.

two things: first, that mutations or changes may take place, and second, that in sorting and crossing, each unit is independent or separable from the others. There is no doubt that this stimulation of individual difference is one of the most important aspects of the mechanism and something of great importance for society. In this way nature not only produces individual differences, but through mutations affects the process of biological evolution itself.

While the careful workers in genetics understand this matter and realize the complexity of the genes in their interaction on one another in the production of the new individual, many psychologists and sociologists have accepted the older static theory of Mendelism and have unfortunately misapplied it to human problems.

HUMAN HEREDITY

One of the gravest of these errors concerns the alleged inheritance of intelligence by simple Mendelian form. This notion was made widespread by H. H. Goddard's work with the feebleminded and by the work of C. B. Davenport, A. W. Woods, and others on mental inheritance. Twenty years ago this notion had a wide vogue and is still accepted both by many serious scholars and by many popularizers. Goddard in his book *Feeblemindedness* (1915) held that a very large proportion of feeblemindedness was inherited in Mendelian fashion, contending that normal mentality is a dominant and feeblemindedness a recessive character.[2]

Inheritance of Defectiveness. In the literature of mental measurement and of social pathology one finds reports of family lines of defectives believed to demonstrate the doctrine of Mendelian heredity in the continuity of "bad" germ-plasm. Nearly every college student sooner or later hears about the Jukes, the Kallikaks, the Nam family, or the Hill Folk. The case of the Kallikaks is typical.

"One Martin Kallikak, a soldier in the American Revolution, met up with a feebleminded barmaid who had an illegitimate son, Martin Junior, from their relations. Martin Senior later married a normal woman and had a long line of satisfactory citizens. Martin Junior mixed with other feebleminded and from him came a line distinctly defective. The investigators discovered four hundred and eighty descendants of Martin Junior. One hundred and forty-three of these they said were conclusively feebleminded. Thirty-six were born illegitimate. Forty-one were known to be sexually immoral. Three were criminals. Three were epileptics. Twenty-four were confirmed alcoholics. Eighty-two died in infancy. Unfortunately the full history of the other branch of this family is not at hand, and we are assured that they are all upstanding people, which assurance is obviously doubtful. One psychologist writing

[2] See p. 549 of Goddard's *Feeblemindedness* for a chart illustrating this assumption.

of this says: 'The two branches of the family live in the same section of the state, although they are in ignorance of their relationship. Indeed in one instance a member of the abnormal line is in the employ of a descendant in the other line. Nothing could show more clearly than these two lines of descent the terrible hereditary importance of mental defects.' " [3]

When we discover the careless methods of collecting the information on this family, the classification of many distinctly antisocial acts as due to feeblemindedness or inherited criminality, and the lack of any adequate check-up on the social and physical environment of these families, we realize that there is little scientific validity in the conclusions drawn. While there were doubtless defective strains in this family, and while there may well have been inbreeding of near relatives, which would enhance these weaknesses, it must also be recalled that until we clear up the environmental situation and discount this, we are in no position to declare the Kallikaks the victims of bad heredity alone. Since on the assumption of Goddard only the mother of Martin Junior was feebleminded, it was necessary for Martin Junior, on Goddard's own interpretation of Mendel's theory—which we believe faulty—to marry into a distinctly feebleminded family in order to set this bad strain going.

This whole approach is a convenient solution of the inheritance of feeblemindedness, but like so many of these explanations it is too simple to match the facts. In the first place, it is a colossal assumption to hold that the normal mentality, on the one hand, and the feeblemindedness, on the other, are reducible to single Mendelian units, one dominant, the other recessive.

Intelligence, however, as the psychologists care to define it, is certainly no such single-unit affair.[4] In the first place, even the intelligence tests reveal a continuous, graded series of scores, quotients, or measures from superior through normal to defective. There is enormous overlapping of measures of defectives with nor-

---

[3] Walter Hunter, *General Psychology* (rev. ed., 1923), p. 58.
[4] Intelligence has been variously defined (*1*) as ability to reason from cause to effect, (*2*) as ability to do abstract thinking, that is, to form concepts and to use them in logical judgments, (*3*) as capacity to learn, (*4*) as capacity to manage one's own affairs with ordinary prudence. Certainly these definitions all imply cultural influences, and none of the methods of testing intelligence now in use has perfected any way to measure strictly biological or organic foundations of intelligence, whatever they may be.

mals; in fact, no sharp boundary exists except as arbitrarily set by the statisticians. If this gradation be true, how is it possible to fit simple Mendelian principles to the facts? Karl Pearson, in criticizing studies which defend such notions, wisely remarks: "No justification whatever can be derived from our data for talking of the mentally defective as lacking 'a factor necessary for full mental development,' or speaking of a 'unit character upon which normal development depends,' or of feeblemindedness as due to germ-plasm lacking a unique 'determiner.' All such descriptions are the work of theorists who have allowed theory wholly to outrun their knowledge and have dogmatized instead of setting quietly to work and measuring mental capacity of children segregated in special schools."[5]

This astounding misunderstanding of the nature of genetic theories of heredity rests on the fact that workers in other fields looking for some simple theories to explain their problems are misled when they apply such a static notion to the dynamics of social behavior. Even the out-and-out geneticists are critical of such ideas, while other biologists are daily introducing a number of new experiments into the study of heredity and growth which must be taken into account.

Complex Factors in Heredity. One of the first considerations known to every geneticist is the complexity of factors which go into any given trait or condition of the adult organism. W. E. Castle has cautioned us about this matter in his book *Genetics and Eugenics* (1916), wherein he points out that the differential factors of inheritance must be understood in terms of their effects in combination. Thus, Castle found that eight different factors may be involved in producing the coat color of rabbits. And C. B. Davenport tells us, for example, that there are at least four determiners for skin color among human beings.

While for certain purposes of study the genes may be considered units of a material sort, actually in the building of any organism they must be treated in terms of biochemistry. That is to say, they interact upon one another in determining, along with other factors, the growth and development of the organism. The genes are not some mystic force which like good fairies or bad demons arrange the organs of the body or manage behavior by

[5] Karl Pearson and G. Jaederholm, "Mendelism and the Problem of Mental Defect," *Questions of the Day and of the Fray*, No. viii, London, 1914, p. 36.

pulling strings like the producers of a puppet show. As H. S. Jennings well says:

"The genes . . . are simply chemicals that enter into a great number of complex reactions, the final upshot of which is to produce the completed body. The characters of the adult are no more present in the germ cells than is an automobile in the metallic ores out of which it is ultimately manufactured. To get the complete, normally acting organism, the proper materials are essential; but equally essential is it that they should interact properly with each other and with other things. *And the way they interact and what they produce depends on the conditions.*" [6]

The organism is made up of protoplasm of various kinds operating together in some sort of combination or pattern. This protoplasm develops from the original fertilized egg cell by the process of cell division, but the success or failure of this development depends on the correlation of genetic factors and the environment. Hereditary factors are not independent of environment, but are understandable only in their relations with environment.

Rise of Mutations. Students of genetics have shown that a large number of mutations or changes in species come about through the reproductive process. T. H. Morgan has produced over 200 such changes, great and small, in the common fruit fly, with which he has been experimenting during the past 20 years.

Many of these mutations are of a recessive character. Some are very slight and do not seem to persist. Others are rather marked and appear to persist indefinitely. These mutations occur rather more frequently than earlier biologists imagined possible. This new experimental evidence is important because it throws some light on the manner in which through the geologic ages changes in the species may have come about. Moreover, it shows definitely that no matter how pure or homogeneous a race or species may be at the outset, in the course of time, even without crossing with other species, it develops varied characteristics. Animal and plant breeders have long known this empirically. Once a new and desirable trait turns up, they select out the individuals who carry it and develop new types to serve their purposes. Seedless oranges, seedless grapes, dairy or beef stock, race horses or draft

[6] H. S. Jennings, "Heredity and Environment," *Scientific Monthly,* September, 1924, vol. XIX, p. 230. Italics in the original.

animals are all the result of mutations which have been retained by careful control of later breeding. Man has not yet dared to apply rigorously such methods to himself. At best he has tried by eliminating certain weak traits to prevent their reappearance in subsequent generations.

While the plant and animal breeders have to use trial and error methods, and while doubtless in the evolution of the species the unassisted natural factors made for great waste and slow change, recent experiments have demonstrated that by applying X-ray treatment to the germ cells, the rate of mutations can be profoundly altered. Germ cells have been exposed to X-ray treatment before fertilization. Sometimes monstrosities have been produced; at other times less marked mutations, though often in the nature of defects, have appeared. As one writer puts it, "The X-ray method has, therefore, a distinct advantage over the natural method, in that the geneticist can now produce gene mutations and breakages [in the chromosomes] at will, and in comparatively large numbers."[7] Likewise treatment with radium effects numerous mutations.

ENVIRONMENT AND DEVELOPMENT

Not only such extreme external factors as the X-ray treatment, but temperature changes, various mechanical forces, light, gravity, and centrifugal force all influence development. We cannot discuss these in detail, but mention may be made of illustrative studies.

Standard Environment and Development. A standardized, common environment plays an important part in normal development. There is reason to believe that the standardized environment in which the fertilized egg develops accounts in part, at least, for the regular and orderly physical features which we see in one generation after another. As C. M. Child has shown, alter these conditions and one is likely to get a different type of individual.[8] The following experiment on fish is in point:

"Stockard, exposing the eggs of a marine fish, *Fundulus*, to sea water with the addition of certain magnesium salts and of some other sub-

[7] J. T. Patterson, "X-rays and Somatic Mutations," *Journal of Heredity*, June 1925, vol. XX, p. 265.
[8] See C. M. Child, *Physiological Foundations of Behavior*, 1924.

stances, obtained developing young showing marked difference from the characteristics usually shown, notably the development of one-eyed fish. Sometimes this single eye was on one side of the head, giving a cyclopean form. It seems that in these fish the two eyes will develop in their usual places if the eggs are exposed to untreated sea water, but that various modifications of eye development and location appear if the sea water contains an unusual amount of certain magnesium salts. If, now, the sea water regularly contained larger amounts of these magnesium salts, should we not have these unusual forms of the eye as the usual characteristics of the species? In that case, by removing some of the magnesium salts we should obtain 'abnormal' forms bearing two eyes, one on each side of the head. *We cannot too strongly emphasize the fact that many of the so-called abnormalities are normal developments under particular conditions."* [9]

One popular notion in this connection is that drinking of alcoholic beverages injures the germ-plasm and thus affects the offspring. Stockard, Pearl, and others exposed guinea pigs, chickens, and other animals to large amounts of alcohol and found that there are injurious effects in the first few generations, but that the survivors of this severe treatment were little affected by alcohol. They argue that in the course of time the weak offspring of the alcoholic parents die off, leaving only strong stock to reproduce.

A caution should be made about trying to apply these findings to human beings. It must not be forgotten that Stockard's guinea pigs were alcoholized to a degree far greater than ever takes place with man. Karl Pearson and E. M. Elderton have gone so far as to show that parental alcoholism in human beings has no serious effect on the children. This is not to deny, of course, that in extreme cases alcoholic parents may produce defective children, but it must be recalled, too, that almost invariably alcoholism is likely to be associated with other factors such as disease, poor hygienic conditions, filth, poverty, and lack of normal social opportunities.

Endocrine Glands and Development. Recent studies of the endocrine, *i.e.*, the ductless, glands have shown that certain glands have much to do with growth. The chemical substances from the cells surrounding the sex glands proper evidently secrete substances which influence the development of the secondary sex features. If the male sex glands are removed, the male secondary

[9] W. D. Hoyt, "Some Aspects of the Relation of Species to their Environment," *Science*, n. s., 1923, vol. XVIII, pp. 432–34. Italics not in original.

sexual features do not develop. Likewise if the female sex organs are removed, there is no development of secondary female characteristics. So, too, the pituitary gland influences the sexual development. The thyroid, in turn, affects metabolism, heart action, and temperature. An interesting experiment of J. F. Gudernatsch may be mentioned.

He fed very young tadpoles pieces of thyroid gland. The tadpoles very quickly changed into frogs. In this way some mature frogs no larger than ordinary flies were produced. In contrast to this if they were fed on the thymus gland, they grew to be large, dark-colored tadpoles but did not change into frogs.[10]

The endocrine glands themselves are necessarily affected by the genes, but as they begin to function, they in turn affect development. Internal conditions, as well as external, always influence growth, even though the presence or absence of these factors in the organism depends on the genes themselves.

Oscar Riddle has made some rather interesting studies of the effects of disease upon sexual characteristics. Some years ago he reported observations on a female pigeon, a ring dove. This bird laid eleven eggs between January and April, 1914. A few months later she began to act like a male, increasing in weight, and even developing the crow of a male pigeon. After the last eggs were laid, a tubercular infection so severe as to destroy the female gland set in. It is known that tuberculosis sets up a condition which favors the development of maleness in birds, and which is "adverse to the development of the female sex." Forty-four months after the last eggs were laid, the pigeon died. An autopsy showed tubercular infection of the spleen, liver, and other organs. No female glands were found, but "two well-formed male glands in their normal position were present." In closing a report of this work, one writer says:

"The result clearly indicates that the hereditary basis of no bodily or mental characteristics may be considered as irrevocably fixed and uncontrollable, and that as one of the characteristics known to be hereditary and normally to be controlled through the so-called 'chromosomes' of the germ cell has been shown to be capable of reversal to the alternate form, it becomes wholly probable that all hereditary characteristics of every human being and of every organism are capable of reversal and

[10] J. F. Gudernatsch, "Feeding Experiments on Tadpoles, II," *American Journal of Anatomy*, 1914, vol. XV, pp. 431–80.

modification; and that the accomplishment of such modification and control is a matter which merely awaits the definitely directed efforts of investigation."[11]

Without going more extensively into the literature on this matter, it is clear that we must proceed cautiously in trying to analyze and explain complex social behavior in terms of simple biological theories of a past day. The biologists are coming to realize how important in growth such factors as gravitation, pressures, temperatures, chemical nature of media, glands, and disease are. In the face of these evidences, the psychologist and the social scientist dare not be dogmatic about human heredity.

Social and Cultural Factors in Development. Yet in dealing with social behavior much damage has been done by the easy assumptions about heredity. Two other pieces of evidence from studies on siblings (children of the same parents) reared in different foster homes and on twins living in different environments must be mentioned. Curiously enough the results tend to reflect, in part, the bias of the workers. L. M. Terman and Barbara Burks hold that heredity accounts for likenesses in foster-home siblings, while F. N. Freeman and K. Holzinger are much more cautious and attribute a great deal to environment.[12]

H. J. Müller and H. H. Newman have made beginnings in investigating the characteristics of identical twins reared apart as a test of this problem, and although so far they have reported only on ten pairs of such twins, their findings are suggestive.

Identical twins come from the same fertilized egg and hence should possess identical genes. Actually, they are not strictly identical, even in physical traits such as eye color, hair color, skin color, or fingerprints. Yet they are far more alike than normal siblings or non-identical twins. Newman says that they are about "90 per cent" identical.

With this closeness of physical features, the problem is to find pairs of identical twins who have been reared apart, and in this

[11] From "Change of Sex in Pigeons," *Science*, January 4, 1924, vol. LIX, Supplement, "Science News," p. xii, a review of Riddle's work.

[12] For papers by Terman, Burks, Freeman, and Holzinger on the influence of environment on foster children especially, see *Nature and Nurture: Their Influence upon Intelligence*, National Society for the Study of Education, Yearbook 1928. On twin differences, see K. J. Holzinger, "The Relative Effect of Nature and Nurture Influences on Twin Differences," *Journal of Educational Psychology*, 1929, vol. XX, pp. 241–48; N. D. M. Hirsch, *Twins: Heredity and Environment*, 1930; H. H. Newman, F. N. Freeman, and K. J. Holzinger, *Twins*, 1937.

manner to make some check on the influence of heredity and environment on the development of characteristics. Brief reports on Newman's study of his six pairs of identical twins raised in divergent environments follow:

"Case I. A pair of twin young women, one with very much more formal education than the other, but with a much more varied social experience, showed after twenty-odd years of separation the following condition: They were practically identical physically and in intelligence, but were extremely different in temperament—in personality.

"Case II. A pair of twin young women, one reared in London, England, and the other in a small Ontario town. They had about the same amount and kind of education. When tested, the colonial girl was very much more intelligent and in much better physical condition. In temperament—personality, they were extremely similar.

"Case III. Two twin young women separated over 20 years, reared in about the same social and physical conditions, but one had far more education than the other. Physically and temperamentally they were extraordinarily similar, but the more educated twin was strikingly more intelligent.

"Case IV. Two twin young men separated over 20 years, one reared in cities of some size, the other reared in country villages, both with high school education. The city boy was in much better physical condition and was slightly more intelligent. In temperament—personality, they were as utterly different as two persons chosen at random.

"Case V. Two twin girls, separated for 28 years, but visiting each other from time to time. One has always lived on a farm, the other has lived in a small town and has spent most of her time indoors. The farm girl stopped school after the grades, the town girl went through high school and has studied music for 20 years. These girls differ equally strongly in all three respects: physically, intellectually and temperamentally. They show the most pronounced effects of environmental differences of any of the pairs studied.

"Case VI. Twin girls, separated for 37 years, both married and with four and six children, respectively. One married a man who has always made a good deal of money, the other married a poor man. The life of one has been easy, that of the other very hard. Both nearly completed high school. There is very little difference between them in I. Q., only minor differences in temperament, but a very striking difference in physical condition. The twin who has had an easy life seems hardly over thirty while the one who has had a hard life seems eight or ten years older."[13]

[13] H. H. Newman, "Identical Twins," *Scientific Monthly*, February, 1932, vol. XXXIV, p. 171.

It is evident from these cases that there is just about as much difference in identical twins reared apart as among ordinary brothers and sisters or perhaps among non-related members of the population. This is striking evidence on the problem before us. Newman has already studied 50 pairs of identical twins reared together. He finds that the environment distinctly modifies some physical characters, such as weight and general health, but does not alter others, such as eye color, hair color, teeth, and features. More interesting for the sociologist, he finds that the environment profoundly modifies so-called "intelligence" and "personality." "In some cases the intelligence of a pair of separated twins was three times as different as the average of 50 pairs of twins reared together."

Additional light on this whole matter of heredity and environment has recently appeared from quite a different quarter. Mandel Sherman and Cora B. Key in a careful study of intelligence tests of isolated mountain children from Virginia have shown a definite correlation between standing in the tests and exposure of the children to culture. Those who lived in remote and inaccessible sections with little schooling and a low level of culture do distinctly less well in the tests than children with more schooling and in communities of higher culture. Moreover, it is apparent from their study that the effects of poor culture in the early years are not easily wiped out by later exposure to better opportunities.[14] So, too, the work of Hugh Gordon on London schoolchildren of migrant and underprivileged classes shows a definite correlation between ratings on intelligence tests and degree of schooling.[15]

Relation of Heredity and Environment. What, then, may we say about the relation of heredity to environment? It is clear that heredity is not some magic force operating independently of environment, but that the genes are organic chemical agents of some sort which, operating together in an internal environment, produce various traits, some of which, in turn, may be profoundly altered after birth, while others, like eye color, hair color, skin color, and facial features, vary little or not at all. We are coming to realize, furthermore, that many common features of physical makeup and of behavior must be understood not only because the

[14]Mandel Sherman and Cora B. Key, "The Intelligence of Isolated Mountain Children," *Child Development*, Dec., 1932, vol. III, pp. 279–90.
[15]Hugh Gordon, *Mental and Scholastic Tests Among Retarded Children: An inquiry into the effects of schooling on the various tests.* London: Board of Education, Educational Pamphlets, No. 44, 1923.

individuals have a common heredity, but also because they live in a standardized environment. No one would be so bold as to claim that heredity does not count in the development of the individual. It is rather that both heredity and environment correlate at every point in the production of the new individual. In the period of embryonic and foetal growth, environmental factors within the womb are important, pressures, temperature, gravity, and chemical influences playing a part. There is, of course, no evidence that ideas and attitudes of the mother will carry over to the child, as superstitious persons once believed, but the physiological environment of the womb is certainly important in development. After birth, physical and social environmental factors come more and more into play. Hence we must realize that the child and adult are the joint products of heredity and environment cooperating all along the line. As Leonard Carmichael puts it:

"The fact as it appears . . . is that no distinction can be expediently made at any given moment in the behavior of the individual, after the fertilized egg has once begun to develop, between that which is native and that which is acquired. The so-called hereditary factors can only be acquired in response to an environment, and likewise the so-called acquired factors can only be secured by a modification of already existing structure, which in the last analysis is hereditary structure. Facts too obvious to bear citation show that the somatic structures that can develop out of a fertilized egg are in some measure dependent upon the physical and chemical structure of the given germ itself. The characteristics which develop out of such a germ, nevertheless, are not *predetermined*. They are, on the contrary, *determined* by an environment acting upon the present nature of the individual at every stage of development from fertilization to death."[16]

[16]Leonard Carmichael, "Heredity and Environment: Are They Antithetical?" *Journal of Abnormal and Social Psychology,* October, 1925, vol. XX, p. 257.

Gladys C. Schwesinger, in *Heredity and Environment,* 1933, has reviewed the literature on the problem of heredity and environment in relation to intelligence and temperament. While she is critical of the static conception of heredity and environment in the minds of many workers, she still seems to consider the two, not as interrelated but as separate "forces" as evidenced by her "new approach," as follows: "Given a stated environment, how much variation will heredity permit for such and such a characteristic (among so and so individuals)? Or, given a stated heredity, how much variation could a given range of environment introduce for such and such a character?" (p. 459) Such a standpoint still fails, it seems, to take into account the interplay of environmental and hereditary factors within the organism—the intra-individual environment. It assumes that maturation is the result of heredity; and it fails to see that at all points there is an interplay of these inherited germinal structures and those which develop after conception.

With this point of view we can go ahead to study the nature of man's social life without becoming confused by any unwarranted notions about a sharply divided set of forces: heredity and environment. They are interdependent and not opposed to each other. The organization and unity of living things depends upon the interplay of internal chemical predispositions, and reactions to the environment. And the human being on the basis of this interaction of factors in prenatal life is made capable in varying degrees for postnatal adaptation to his social and material world.

CLASS ASSIGNMENTS

A. Further reading assignment:

1. K. Young, *Source Book for Sociology*, chap. IV.

2. *Encyclopedia of the Social Sciences*, articles as follows: A. Weinstein, "Heredity," vol. VII, pp. 328–35; Wilson D. Wallis, "Environmentalism," vol. V, pp. 561–66.

B. Questions and exercises:

1. What are the basic mechanisms of heredity?

2. Cite cases of present-day false notions about heredity in regard to insanity, crime, delinquency, and poverty.

3. Discuss, pro and con, the contention of H. H. Goddard that feeble-mindedness is a recessive unit trait.

4. Discuss, pro and con, Newman's observations on identical twins reared in divergent environments. Is this work crucial to the problem of heredity and environment? If so, why?

5. What are the limitations of the Sherman and Key study of mountain children so far as the matter of heredity goes?

C. Topics for class reports or longer written papers:

1. Critique of Galton's theories of inheritance of mental ability. (Consult G. R. Davies, *Social Environment*, 1917; Lester F. Ward, *Applied Sociology*, 1906, pp. 119–22; F. Galton, *Hereditary Genius*, 1892.)

2. Critique of modern genetics, and its implications for the understanding of human behavior. (Consult C. M. Child, *Physiological Foundations of Behavior*, 1924, and his chapter in *The Unconscious: A Symposium*, ed. by E. S. Dummer, 1927; G. E. Coghill, *Anatomy and the Problem of Behavior*, 1929; F. S. C. Northrop, *Science and First Principles*, 1931, especially chap. V; R. Goldschmidt, *Physiological Genetics*, 1938.)

3. The present status of the problem of heredity and environment in relation to intelligence and temperament. (Consult Gladys C. Schwesinger, *Heredity and Environment*, 1933, and bibliographies; H. H. Newman, F. N. Freeman, and K. J. Holzinger, *Twins: A Study of Heredity and Environment*, 1937.)

CHAPTER VI

PERSONALITY

The person plays his various parts upon the stage of life, and passes out at his last scene, leaving the drama in the hands of those who come after him. In this chapter we shall discuss the way in which society and culture prepare and fix the individual's part in this drama.

PSYCHOLOGICAL FOUNDATIONS

It is the business of physiology and psychology to describe and interpret the organic bases of behavior. For our purposes we need only survey the chief biological foundations of personality.

Structure of the Nervous System. While the whole organism is involved in the process of adaptation to its surroundings, it is the nervous system which has been developed for the special purpose of facilitating this adjustment. The nervous system consists of the *central* and the *autonomic* parts. The former system is made up of three divisions: the sensory; the motor or response; and the intermediate or middle sections—the brain proper and the spinal cord. The *sensory organs*, eyes, ears, taste and smell receptors, senses of touch, of muscular movement, equilibrium, and others, are specialized instruments developed to aid us in our contact with the world outside, or to give us a basis for awareness of movement within the organism. The *motor organs*, tendons, muscles, and glands, are concerned with responses to internal and external stimuli, in short, with adaptation. In his senses, muscles, and glands, and in the accompanying sensory and motor divisions of the nervous system, man is but little superior to his animal relatives. It is the higher development of the brain that sets him off even from the apes. This complex brain makes learning possible, including retention of past experiences, their association into new patterns, and all the higher mental processes—judgment, reasoning, and the formation of concepts.

In the development of man's culture and group life nothing is more important than the growth of the higher brain centers and the accompanying refinement of the response system, especially of vocal muscles and hand-eye co-ordination, so fundamental in the higher learning which makes culture and the societal order possible.[1]

The autonomic system is supplementary to the central, and controls the internal reactions of glands and smooth muscles. While the central nervous system is the structural foundation of the intellectual processes and learning, the autonomic system is important in reference to the basic organic needs and the expression of the emotions and feelings.

The *emotions* are fundamental mental states set up in the presence of situations that concern survival, sex, and all the basic demands of the individual which we are about to mention. Love, fear, and rage are three of the principal emotions. Closely associated with the emotions are the feelings of pleasantness and unpleasantness. These, too, have an organic foundation. They are largely dependent on general bodily reactions produced by tensions and the release of tensions. The emotions and feelings are not, however, purely the creatures of the autonomic system, since the central nervous system is also important. Certainly perception and memory processes dependent upon the central system have a part in emotional responses.[2]

Cycles of Activity. Basic organic activity falls into cycles. Human activity passes through a series of acts beginning with bodily needs and ending in the satisfaction of these by the receipt of adequate stimuli. We may describe this cycle under four heads: (*1*) need, requirement, or appetites and aversions built up in the form of tensions brought on by metabolic and other organic changes; (*2*) movement and restlessness of a preparatory sort looking to the satisfaction of these requirements; (*3*) the satisfaction of these needs upon receipt of the required stimulus or avoidance of noxious stimuli; and (*4*) a general pleasant relaxation of the organism following satisfaction of the needs.

Organic appetites or aversions are the driving or motivating forces of all fundamental activity. These forces are commonly re-

[1]See H. H. Bawden, "The Evolution of Behavior," *Psychological Review*, 1919, vol. XXVI, pp. 247–76. Reprinted in large part in K. Young, *Source Book for Social Psychology*, 1927, pp. 10–17.

[2]F. H. Allport, *Social Psychology*, 1924, chaps. II–IV, contains an excellent review of the organic basis of behavior.

ferred to as organic desires, wishes, instincts, instinctive tendencies, or original impulses. The wide controversy over instincts, wishes, or original tendencies need not detain us. At least, the infant's basic wants include those of feeding, drinking, bodily elimination, rest and sleep, vocalization, wide-ranging muscular activity, rudimentary sexual activity, the avoidance of painful and noxious stimuli, and a definite tendency to seek pleasant experience. Early writers added to their lists many more original instincts, including, among others, social and parental instincts and "instincts" for religious, artistic, and scientific expression. These more complex forms of behavior are acquired habits rather than true instincts.[3]

Anticipatory Behavior. The activity looking to the final satisfaction of our basic needs we call anticipatory behavior. At the outset this is largely gross overt movement, as seen in the baby's crying because it is hungry or cold, its mouth movements seeking its mother's breast, or its vocal expression, random activities, and restless trial and error responses. With the lower animals this restlessness takes the form of seeking food, sexual mates, or safety. In man, however, the incipient movements of this second stage in time become internalized. Through the mechanisms of learning, there are gradually built up mental habits to assist man in satisfying his fundamental wants. These wants in man, moreover, fall largely in the arena of his social contacts.

Learning is primarily the association of biological stimuli with new responses. The most familiar example is the training or conditioning of a dog to secrete saliva at the ringing of a bell. Most learning is not nearly so simple. We know from the work of L. Pavlov, the Russian physiologist, that a set of learned associations may be broken down by introducing still other stimuli, as when we overcome fear in a child by feeding him candy. Moreover, if we introduce a third set of associations, the pattern of this second learned action disappears, and the organism returns to the first conditioned response. For instance, a learned fear reaction that has been "cured" by some new associations reappears when some further new unpleasant fearsome stimulus appears. Our habits are largely built up by these processes of association. The stimuli appear in certain configurations, but the mechanism itself seems

[3] See K. Young, *Source Book for Social Psychology*, chap. VII, for a review of these problems.

fundamentally the formation of new associations in the higher brain centers.[4]

The Field of Thought. The control and reorganization of experience by means of association takes place within the individual. This is, in fact, the most important aspect of anticipatory behavior. In traditional psychology this is referred to as the mental, subjective, or intellectual process. In more static terms, this is the area of behavior known as intelligence. In the operation of this process, memory and imagination play the dominant parts. In other words, mental or intellectual processes rest upon our capacity to learn, or to profit by experience (the field of memory), and upon our ability to rearrange our past experiences and past thoughts (the field of imagination) in such a way as to aid us in adapting ourselves to present and future situations. That is, the effects of learned reactions are not lost, but remain as memories or habits which may be reorganized in order to control subsequent action. In this process, ideas play a fundamental part. An *idea* is a concept or abstraction from experience to which we have attached a name. The term covers a wide range of mental patterns: imagined objects or actions, qualities or relations of objects or actions, principles of logic or of conduct, opinions and beliefs, and a vast array of abstractions from experience covered by such terms as goodness, evil, truth, honesty, fidelity, loyalty, patriotism, and the like.

Attitudes also belong to the field of anticipatory behavior, but in contrast to ideas, *attitudes* are tendencies to act, associated with ideas in large part and often carrying with them feelings and emotions. In other words, attitudes are related to habits and, in fact, furnish the link between ideational processes and overt bodily habits themselves.

In the operation of the mental processes, language clearly has an important function. Since ideational processes are carried on largely in verbal terms, words act as the currency or symbols of thinking itself. The names of objects, situations, qualities, relations, and the like enable us to deal with our problems in thought in an ever widening range of possible actions—past, present, and future.

[4]The student will find valuable reviews of elementary psychology in R. S. Woodworth, *Psychology*, 1934 ed.; Gardner Murphy, *A Briefer General Psychology*, 1935; C. E. Skinner, editor, *Readings in Psychology*, 1935; J. F. Dashiell, *Fundamentals of General Psychology*, 1937; F. L. Ruch, *Psychology and Life*, 1937.

As a means of getting at certain features of anticipatory behavior, we must take note of two important types of thinking: logical, directed, or impersonal; and illogical, wishful, personal, or fantasy thinking.

Directed or *logical thinking* is an outgrowth of everyday contact with the physical and social world of events, where genuine cause and effect are apparent. The child associates events outside, enabling him later to prepare for their reappearance. He learns a relation, for example, between rain clouds and the preparation for a shower by donning overshoes and slicker, or he learns how to count, to make change at the store, and to follow complicated directions. Directed thought is evident in the development of all sorts of skills. It is the foundation of science and engineering. It is highly important in handling social relations, as in the management of people and in the development of rational devices of industry, business, and law.

Wishful or *fantasy thinking,* in contrast, develops from the fact that imagination itself offers us much satisfaction, even in reference to many fundamental wants. It is characterized by the failure to associate the symbol or word with the concrete object in such a way as to modify directly the external object. Thus, the child denied sweetmeats, daydreams of having all the candy he can eat, and up to a point of intense hunger such imaginative response may be pleasant and satisfying. Or the person may wish his enemy dead, and get considerable satisfaction from the thought, although nothing really happens to the enemy. Fantasy thinking is always personal. It is the world of dreams, daydreams, and free-flowing imagination, relatively unchecked by the logic of events outside.

People not only indulge in fantastic associations; they sometimes act upon them. The suspicious person not only imagines that others are talking behind his back, but he begins to treat the suspected person with distrust and hostility. As W. I. Thomas says, "If men define situations as real they are real in their consequences."

Obviously some wishful thinking is so unique, so remote from social reality, that it leads to complete isolation from society, as in the psychopathic patient in a mental hospital who imagines that he has billions in wealth, or that he is God or Caesar or Napoleon.

Yet all sorts of fantasy thought patterns get fully integrated to culture. Primitive magic often resembles very much the fantasy

of the insane patient, who if he had lived in a society favorable
to such thought, might actually have become a powerful medicine
man. It is very easy for us to ridicule primitive peoples for their
"queer" ideas and practices. But even with modern applied science
having so greatly changed our world today, there remains a great
deal of wishful thinking deeply rooted in our own culture. Our
worship of the words "loyalty," "nationality," "country," "freedom," "capitalism," the widespread belief in astrology and medical quackery, and the debasing of sound scientific ideas in the
minds of the masses—all show that fantasy thinking is powerful
among us.

Fantasy, moreover, plays a part in the creation of myths and
legends, so important in social control. Neurotics still report divine
messages, win large followings, and form new religious cults. Even
in our economic, political, and family life there is much of this
sort of thought, while art and recreation are largely the products
of fantasy thinking.[5]

This whole area of fantasy is as much a part of man's social life
as logic, or as tools and weapons used in everyday life. It is idle
to say that such thinking and acting are pathological, for what is
"pathological" depends on how behavior and thought are defined
in the culture of the time and place. Fantasy thinking is not only
natural, but it is evidently as essential to man's life as his more
directed logical thought and behavior.

Anticipatory Behavior and Acquired Motives. Not only does
the anticipatory system aid man in satisfying the basic needs of life
more adequately, but it aids him in modifying and adding to the
motives themselves. That is, not only are the responses changed,
but also the stimuli themselves are enormously extended.

This extension of the range of man's needs is distinctly the outgrowth of social interaction and culture. Even in such basic matters as hunger and thirst, culture adds much beyond mere physiological demand. Associated with eating and drinking are the
pleasures of companionship, or the demands of hard work and
sacrifice that others whom we love may eat. In the field of sex,
no matter what original nature may be, man has built up a system of family relations and has softened the vigor of his wants in
the face of sympathy and socialized love. Likewise, avoidance of

[5]See K. Young, *Social Psychology*, 1930, chap. XVI; *Social Attitudes* (ed. by
K. Young), 1931, chap. V; T. W. Arnold, *The Symbols of Government*, 1935.

pain and the demands for protection lead to social controls often far removed from the original needs of personal survival. Recreation, art, magic, religion, and science are all highly socialized additions to man's fundamental physiological needs. Finally the self or ego, with its insistence upon survival—even after death —its demands for expression and power over objects and other individuals, is an outgrowth of the need for food, shelter, and protection, for sexual expression, and for satisfaction of other elementary wants.

In short, in the process of learning, the individual not only comes to manage his physiological tensions, but he acquires many new needs and values which at the outset are secondary to immediate survival, but which in the end may even overshadow the latter. The Christian martyrs, the seekers after beauty or scientific discovery, and the citizen fired by patriotism to lay down his life for his country bespeak a departure from mere animal demands for life that one finds only in man himself.

Consummatory Response. Yet anticipatory behavior is only one step toward the closure of the cycle. There is the field of *consummatory,* or completed action. The untrained individual reacts pretty largely at the animal level. His responses follow directly upon receipt of the adequate stimulus for satisfying his basic wants, as in the hungry baby who seizes the mother's breast as soon as it is given him. At this level the duration between organic tension and its release is short. Through the building up of mental or anticipatory behavior, the period between organic need and consummation is extended, and the satisfactions are ordinarily more lasting. Thus, demands for food or sex may be extended in time. Better still, the goals or aims of a profession may take years to reach, and within this period of preparation there are hundreds of shorter cycles, all looking to the consummation of the larger one in securing professional standing.

The field of preparatory activity is normally directed toward the final complete response. Although mental life may be carried on for long periods for its own ends, it finally must and does relate to overt conduct.

When the consummation is reached, the organism falls into a state of pleasant relaxation, largely an emotional and feeling state. At the physiological level this may be rather short and biological in character. In the person long exposed to culture, this may well take on the highest pleasures of the aesthetic and moral life. Culture not only modifies and expands the character of our needs or desires, it not only assists us in the anticipatory field of preparation, but also it profoundly affects the nature of the final pleasure which comes from completed action itself.

Upon the basis of our physiological wants, or appetites and aversions, and in reference to the family and, later, other groups, the *social self* or personality is developed. Personality consists of the habits, attitudes, and ideas which are built up around both people and things. Our idea or conception of ourselves reflects our experience with others. In tracing the personality growth, we shall expose certain important mechanisms that arise out of social interaction: identification, projection, ambivalence, sublimation, compensation, and rationalization. So, too, we shall discover the importance of rôle, status, and what is called "social expectancy."

The Rise of the Personality. The mother is, in most cultures, the first person toward whom the infant is conditioned. It is perhaps safe to say that the mother is the most important person anyone will ever meet. It is she who sets the pattern of most of our ideas, habits, and attitudes. In the acts of nursing, bathing, clothing, and caring for the infant, the mother and child come into intimate contact, particularly involving the most rudimentary sense of touch, which underlies every other form of primary relations. These touch relationships are ordinarily closely linked with the emotion of love. Together touch and love are fundamental to adult love, sympathy, and co-operation.

Such elementary senses as taste and smell also enter into these first contacts. As sight and hearing are brought into play, they become associated with these more rudimentary experiences. The mother's odor, taste of the milk at her breast, color of hair, eyes, skin, shape of her mouth and form of her neck, bosom, arms, and hands, her posture, her walk, and her voice and facial gestures, all are powerful stimuli and are frequently and simultaneously associated with the pleasant activities of securing food, bodily care, relief from fatigue, and satisfaction of other basic wants. Not only are these pleasant physiological reactions associated with intimacy, but the mother extends her care to rocking the child while feeding, or swinging it gently to sleep, and offering it toys, and all sorts of objects not essential to the satisfaction of basic needs. The child quickly learns to expect this additional attention, and in time he cries not because he is hungry, or cold, or in pain, but because he craves the mother's comfort.

The mother, however, also imposes regularity of feeding and care and puts upon the child requirements of the social world from the day of birth. He must learn to manage his bodily and social needs along the lines laid down by her authority. A large part of this is a reflection of the culture. Yet there do develop ideas, attitudes, habits dependent on social-personal conditions—over-affection, undue anxiety, or perhaps conduct not approved by the outside culture.

The child likewise comes into contact with physical, material objects as well as social. He learns to avoid getting hurt, to shun fire, to select among the stimuli those which are beneficial and not harmful. Even here, the social impress is apparent, since the mother and others interpret his experience with the material world for him in terms of their own culture.

The mother, of course, is not the only person to whom the child is conditioned: father, brothers and sisters, and other relatives or servants also assist in defining the child's behavior for him. One of the fundamental mechanisms which comes into play in this whole matter is identification.

Identification has much in common with imitation. It is a learned reaction. The act of one person serves as the stimulus for another whose response is similar to the stimulus or act of the first person. Identification makes it possible for one person to take over or accept ideas, attitudes, or habits of another. Psychologically, this mechanism depends on imagination—on the capacity to develop within the internal subjective world the image of another. It is the basis of sympathy, and in it are mixed large elements of the emotion of love.

The responses of the mother and others in the family furnish the child with patterns for his own behavior. The picture of the mother in his imagination becomes an object which he seeks to imitate. Moreover, his own image of himself emerges from her reactions to him. He lives in her, and her responses to him get associated with his own feelings and reactions to her and to the objects which she brings to him. Both pleasant and unpleasant experiences with the mother may form a part of this image.

Thus, the child associates his own activities with the demands of others, and with their responses to his own conduct, building up a picture of what he should do in the presence of others. His own reactions are always carried on in reference to these others. C. H. Cooley (1864–1929) referred to this as "the reflected looking-glass self." E. S. Bogardus calls this man's "mirrored nature." These reflections of the ideas, attitudes, and habits of the family members are carried over to the child's later reactions. All through life we are constantly reacting in the manner laid down by our fellows in their *definition of the situation,* that is, their interpretation or meaning of the experience.

The manner, then, in which the individual defines the situation, that is, gives it meaning, will depend largely upon how those around him interpret the same for him. Obviously the child's acceptance of the definition of the situation by those in authority often implies a conflict with his own definitions, which follow his own more pleasant wishes for power, for love, and for having his own way. As we come into relations with the wider community and its numerous secondary groups, there often develops a wide division between our more personal wishes or definitions of the situation and the more utilitarian definitions of the community or its subgroups. A good deal of the struggle between the individual and the social order depends upon the conflict between his pleasure-seeking wishes and the group demands of conformity to the societal code.

Authority and Self-Image. Not only care and kindness come from the parents, but the demands of authority are early laid upon the child. The inhibition of action by disapproval is important in the growth of the self. While the mother begins the expression of power over the child, it is, in our society, usually the father who wields the final authority. Although our own culture more or less demands that the father praise the baby and show some outward marks of affection, as the child grows up the father takes over from the mother the task of discipline. But affection and love between father and child are as apparent as the child's fear of the paternal punishment. Out of this contact the child constructs the image of the father, which defines his own behavior in the presence of the father. In living with his parents, in fact, the child gradually builds up two rather divergent patterns. One is that of the father and mother as the givers of good things, as kind and loving. The other is that of stern parents who demand conformity which is unpleasant to the child, but which he must accept or suffer punishment at their hands. Thus arise two parental images which are in conflict with each other. The child is often confused in regard to his parents because of these divergent tendencies. On the one hand, he loves his parents and wishes to please them. On the other hand, he hates and fears them. The parental image, therefore, is really split in two, one representing the lovable object, the other symbolizing the parental power and authority. This division reflects a basic feature of all personality: ambivalence of thought and action.

Ambivalence is the simultaneous attractiveness and repulsiveness of an object, person, or action. Approach or withdrawal are elemental reactions to any stimulus. And our habits are built up along these same lines. Ambivalence is illustrated in the duality of love and hatred, of acceptance and disapproval by others, of "true" and "false" ideas. In the development of the self-image, the pleasant feelings and emotions toward certain sorts of conduct are set over against the unpleasant feelings and emotions toward other aspects of the same situation. Nowhere is this more evident than in the divided imagery in regard to the parents.

Identification obviously plays an important part in the action of approach and acceptance, since these involve sympathy and love. The tendency toward withdrawal or avoidance tends to unpleasant reactions—to set up fear and hatred. In this process another mechanism, projection, comes into play.

Projection has to do with thrusting outward upon some other person or object our own wishes, ideas, and attitudes. As the child suppresses his fear and hatred of the parents, our culture provides him with substitutes: Satan, evil people, or out-groups which he can hate. So, too, animism in religion, which attributes human qualities to nature, is a case of projection. It is seen in the person suspicious of others, who imagines that they talk about him behind his back. It is clearly brought out in the foisting upon children of thwarted ambitions of the parents, as when a man long desirous of being a musician but unable to study music forces his son or daughter to undertake a musical career.

Projection and identification therefore go together. Although largely unconscious, they are perfectly normal and essential features of interaction. They are especially important in the balancing of our ambivalent tendencies.

Identification and Rôle. The pattern or type of behavior which the child and adult builds up in terms of what others expect or demand of him we refer to as the *rôle*. It is clear, for example, that if a parent constantly tells Johnny he is "no good" or is a "black sheep" or, on the contrary, builds up in the boy an expectation of "good" conduct, the child will have to match these definitions. The rôle, therefore, is related to one's acceptance of the definition of the situation by others.

Each group sets up its definitions of situations and lays out various rôles for the members. The lad who swears like a pirate with his tough young friends is usually a different boy at home. This process begins in the family and other primary groups and continues throughout life. Primary groups still have the largest responsibility in setting the rôle of the individual. For example, whether a person takes a submissive or dominant attitude or whether he fully accepts the group definition or not later in life, may well depend upon fundamental training for his rôle in the family or in the play group.

It should be clear that there are really a number of selves or phases of personality, each of which reflects the groups of which one is a member. These selves are the result of social interaction. As William James, American philosopher (1842–1910), put it, "A man has as many selves as there are individuals who recognize him and carry an image of him in their mind." The self-image is but a composite of the reflected images of others.

To follow the patterns laid down for us by our fellows is universal. The fact of *social expectancy* is basic both to playing of rôles and to social control. In all groups apparently and in hundreds of common situations the expectation of others determines largely how we behave. The Chinese word for rude means "other than expected." The meaning of another's acts is linked up with this expected thought and action. Expectancy lies at the root of the sense of solidarity and participation itself. "We-feeling" is but another way of stating that the members think and react as their fellows expect them to do. The citizen as citizen must be patriotic or be cast out as traitor. The class-conscious proletarian has had built up for him ideas and attitudes which he must reflect if he is to remain in the party. Every group, class, profession, cult, and party with any strong sense of solidarity illustrates the same thing. The images of expectancy of what others will do and of what you will do yourself are important in the whole field of anticipatory behavior described above.

Status in the Group. Closely tied up with rôle is the status of the individual. Rôle and status have often been used almost interchangeably in sociology, but there is a difference. *Status* has to do with the position, the standing, of the individual within the group accorded him by his fellows. It does not imply high standing only, but position along the social scale. The rôle is what you do or do not do. It is concerned with activity. Status is the resultant place on the prestige scale. Then, too, since the attitudes of others are reflected back to us, we naturally assume the position which others give us.

A person may have a low status in one group and a high status in another. A major or colonel in an army in war time may, when peace is declared, become a subordinate in a banking house or profession. The whole matter of how rôle and status influence conduct and one's conception of one's self is illustrated in the story of Jimmy the Runt, a lad who, suffering from a physical inferiority leading to ridicule from his family and schoolmates, found a new rôle and a high status when as a member of a delinquent gang of somewhat older boys, he proved himself invaluable in getting through open transoms or squeezing into boxcars, thus opening the way for his pals to steal valuable property.

Two other mechanisms which must be noted appear in these early years and affect one's rôle and status. These are compensation and sublimation.

Compensation is the substitution of some other idea, attitude, or habit in the face of overpowering inability or incapacity to develop those one would really like. It is a means of overcoming some feeling or sense of inferiority. Sometimes this inadequacy is a matter of organic defect, as in the case of the crippled boy who becomes a star sports reporter. At other times the inferiority depends upon felt incapacity of an intellectual or emotional sort, as in the person dull in mathematics who takes up art in its place. The fundamental function of compensation is the preservation of the self from the feeling of inadequacy. It is an appeal from a court where one stands low to another where one stands high.

Unfortunately compensation has been used very loosely to cover all sorts of cases not properly distinguished from others. Thus Demosthenes is said to have suffered from a speech defect, and in overcoming this by practice in public speaking he became the greatest orator of his day. This is not compensation in the strict sense. If one plays a poor game of golf, tennis, or bridge, we do not speak of compensation when the person improves his playing. But the fat boy, dubbed "Butch" or "Tubby" because he cannot run or jump with others, secures his ego satisfactions by becoming the best scholar in the classroom. This is compensation.

Sublimation is another form of substitution where the new stimulus and response revolve around some object which is approved by our own society. Sublimation differs from other forms of substitution largely in this added factor of moral approval. In teaching the child primary group ideals and practices, the sublimation of the native responses and especially of the less moralized early attitudes is significant. For example, profanity is a substitute for fist work, but it is not recommended on moral grounds. On the other hand, innuendo, satire, and irony are often used and even accepted in polite circles in place of profanity or open attack. So, too, the spinster denied normal family and love life may secure intense satisfaction by taking up child welfare work, which is ethically appropriate in Western society. Sublimation is a highly important form of substitution because it carries societal sanction.

Preservation of the Ego by Excuse. Finally, we have to find excuses for our conduct. *Rationalization* is giving good and socially acceptable reasons for our conduct instead of the genuine ones, which are often unconscious and suppressed. Rationalization is always personal and subjective. Rationalization would "explain" our motives. Curiously enough, our fellows demand from us an explanation of any action which seems a bit off-color. Were we actually to tell the truth about the matter—if we knew this "truth" in the sense of motive—we should be met with hoots and groans.

The real motives for our conduct go back to the fundamental needs and those others which are early acquired. These are often quite completely suppressed through the process of social learning, so that as adults we have no exact idea why we do as we do.

At the outset the child does not resort to rationalizations. He does not wish to eat his spinach or cereal and says so, or simply refuses to eat it. An adult might say that it did not agree with him, or that he secured his vitamins or his carbohydrates in another form. When the child does not act to meet social approval of mother, father, and others, he is punished. If he does follow their instructions, the parents furnish the child with "reasons" for so doing. Thus, the eating of spinach is said to be "good" for one's health. Throughout the whole early training period, parents constantly furnish rationalizations for the child as a means of re-forming his habits and native reactions to conform with socially approved behavior. In adult life rationalizations are very common, and in the building of defenses of our conduct nothing is more important. Rationalization is a form of defense mechanism constructed to keep peace with ourselves and with our fellows.

Other Group Influences. While the home is literally the nursery of the personality, other primary groups also play a part in building up the individual's conception of himself and in widening the range of his rôle and changing the nature of his status. As we saw in Chapter I, play affords the child an opportunity for developing attitudes and habits of give and take from his equals rather different from those he had in the home dominated still by parental authority. In still another fashion the neighborhood and the primary community influence the growth of the personality. The group of elders outside the home often represents somewhat other conceptions of moral behavior, different status, and a wider range of thought and activity than are present in the closely knit home life. Through these groups, the child is introduced into the school, into the church, often into organized recreational and club life, into the economic system of trade and occupation, and finally as a citizen he participates in political life. Naturally, the child's responses to these groups will reflect, in part, his home background, and the parents and other family members will often by the verbal method partially prepare the child for contact with these other groups as he grows up.

No matter how diverse later secondary group contacts may be, the basic habits and attitudes acquired in the primary groups, especially the family, will not easily be dissipated. Where the family life itself is being modified as it is today in Western societies, certain of these early family influences are doubtless changed. We do not yet know what early nursery-school training will do for children. Nor do we know what happens when the.

child's training from early years tends to be taken over, or at least to be dominated by communist ideology and practice. But we may be sure that the early years will remain the basic period of personality building. The apparent, persistent effects of these early years lead at once to another important matter, that of types of personality.

Classifying people into types is an old habit and not different essentially from the classification of objects and events in nature. In spite of wide variations in personalities, the scientific study of behavior cannot avoid the problem of classification. Yet down to the present the matter has been by no means adequately handled.

Systems of Classification. The Greeks put men into four groups: the melancholic, the sanguine, the choleric, and the phlegmatic. Philosophers through the ages have made all sorts of attempts at this sort of thing. William James speaks of tough-minded and tender-minded individuals. More recently Dr. C. G. Jung, the Swiss psychoanalyst, has classified people into extroverts and introverts. At the moment this is the most widespread theory of types, at least in America.

The *extrovert* is characterized by interest in external matters. He lives within the social world of his fellows and the material world of objects rather than within himself. He is said to be illustrated by the business executive, political boss, the joiner, the Babbitts, and all other persons whose fundamental adaptation is toward the outside world. These are persons who live on the "outside of their heads." They tend to be realists and empiricists in philosophy. They are more impressed by action than by words and thought. In more pathological form the extrovert is seen in the patient who is said to settle his internal conflicts by "escape into reality."

The *introvert*, on the contrary, is dominated by his own subjective values, by a world built up from his rich fantasy life, which often tends to take on systematic form. He is inclined to avoid contact with his fellows and with those phases of the material universe which do not fit neatly into his self-made scheme. Introverts live on the "inside of their heads." In philosophy they run to elaborately worked out systems. They tend to be idealists. They want to fix up the universe in some rather water-tight scheme, in order to have a world safe from chaos, disorder, or uncertainty. To them thoughts tend to outweigh actions in importance. In the more pathological form the introvert is seen in the patient who is said to solve his difficulties by "escape from reality," that is, into the world of rich and highly personal fantasies.

Doubtless, the bulk of people fall between these extremes and may be called *ambiverts*, that is, persons who possess a mixture of both tendencies, inclining at times in one direction, at other times in the opposite.

An interesting attempt has been made by E. Kretschmer, a German psychiatrist, to correlate physique with these types of personality. On the basis of certain studies of both insane and normal individuals, he concludes that the stout or fat, which he calls the pyknic physique, is highly correlated with the extroverted personality. On the other hand, the slender, thin, asthenic build and the robust, athletic sort are correlated with the sensitive, egocentric introverts. While American investigations made to check Kretschmer's thesis do not altogether confirm his sharp divisions, there does seem to be some tendency for these physical body types to accompany these contrasted psychological characteristics.[6]

Figure 6, page 126, presents a theoretical distribution of types classified into introvert, ambivert, and extrovert. The curve is trimodal in form from the extreme of introversion to extreme extroversion, with ambiversion lying at the mid-point. The possible frequency is shown by the height of the curve. The bulk of the population is assumed to be ambiverted. Somewhat synonymous terms are given under the two major divisions. Also below the line on either side are listed possible occupational or social rôles determined in part, perhaps, by these personality differences. (See next section.)

Personality Type and Social Type. No matter how we classify personality types, they are not identical with the social rôle of the individual. Personality types are probably fixed once and for all in the earliest years of primary group participation and perhaps do not change much thereafter. The dominant social type or rôle of the person as an adult is largely the result of culture and social organization. W. I. Thomas and Florian Znaniecki in their *Polish Peasant in Europe and America* (1918–20) noted three

[6] See G. J. Mohr and R. H. Gundlach, "The Relation between Physique and Performance," *Journal of Experimental Psychology*, 1927, vol. X, pp. 117–57.

FIGURE 6

SHOWING POSSIBLE DISTRIBUTION OF PERSONALITY TYPES

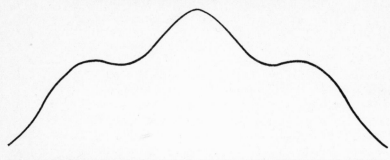

INTROVERT	AMBIVERT	EXTROVERT
Schizoid		Cycloid
(Asthenic or Athletic physique?)		(Pyknic physique?)
Dionysian		Appolonian
Tender-minded		Tough-minded
. . . .		. . . .
Logician		Business executives
Romantic writers		Political leaders
Mechanical engineers		Police officers
Surgeons		Salesmen
Systematizers of science		Empirical scientists

social types: Bohemian, Philistine, and creative. Following their suggestion E. W. Burgess has developed a number of distinctions between the personality type and the social type:

"Personality pattern [type] may be defined as the sum and integration of those traits which characterize the typical reactions of one person toward other persons. The personality pattern, according to our tentative hypothesis, is formed in infancy and early childhood through a conjunction of constitutional and experiential factors and persists with some modification and elaboration as a relatively constant factor through later childhood, youth, and maturity. It is determined, it should be noted, in the interaction between persons. . . .

"The term 'social type' does not refer to the mechanisms of personality reactions but to attitudes, values, and philosophy of life derived from copies presented by society. The rôle which a person assumes and to which he is assigned by society creates the social type. With Stanley, becoming 'a professional runaway,' 'a delinquent,' 'a criminal,' was taking on a rôle. His acceptance of the criminal code and the orientation of his ambitions to succeed in a criminal career have to do with attitudes and values and are elements that enter into the creation of a social type.

"The so-called permutations of personality are the abrupt and often revolutionary changes in social type, not in basic personality patterns. The transformation of Stanley from a criminal to a law-abiding citizen was a change in social type; his personality pattern remained the same. All similar conversions as from sinner to saint, radical to conservative, Democrat to Republican, dry to wet, or vice versa, are changes in social type, not in personality patterns. Our hypothesis is that personality patterns, since they are fixed in infancy and in early childhood, are likewise susceptible to reconditioning only in this same period. The conditioning of social types takes place in later experiences and may accordingly be reconditioned in youth and maturity."[7]

In our Western society, where money-making and political success are two principal values, the social types tend to develop around them: the salesman, the big-business executive, the politician, the conservative, or the radical. Yet social types may range over the whole world of action, so that, in a way, there are as many social types as there are major life interests. Edward Spranger, the German philosopher, in his book *Types of Men* (1928) really builds his system around social types in Burgess's sense of the term. Spranger has six fundamental types, which are constructed on corresponding interests: theoretic, economic, aesthetic, social, political, and religious. While we do not find these types in any pure state among living people, the classification may prove promising for further study of social rôle.

Attempts to classify personality and social behavior into types have been criticized, first, because the criteria are poorly set up; and second, because it is felt that personality, in spite of standardized cultural influences, is too unique a product to be fitted into any category. Up to the present most of the categories have been useful for description only. Certainly we must be cautious not to use them as explanatory principles until we know much more about the matter than we do at present. Yet if we expect personality studies and sociology to get beyond concrete description, we must attempt by comparison and analysis to reach behind variability for the more general and typical features of behavior. If this is impossible, then the fields of behavior cannot become the subject matter of anything but a "descriptive science."

[7] See Clifford R. Shaw, *The Jack-Roller*, 1930, pp. 193–94, where Burgess discusses this matter in reference to Stanley, a delinquent boy.

PERSONALITY AND GROUP PARTICIPATION

We must not neglect the relation of personality to other aspects of group life, particularly we-group and others-group interactions and the importance of moralization or the setting of group values. Finally the place of individual differences as they express themselves in group leadership must be noted.

Personality and Group Attitudes. Identification plays a large part in the development of a sense of loyalty, of solidarity, of we-feeling, of belonging together first in the family, play group, neighborhood, and in the primary community, and later in reference to a wide range of secondary groups. The whole notion of a collective or group consciousness, commonly accepted by certain earlier sociologists and social psychologists, has its roots in this amazing capacity of individuals to identify themselves with each other in view of their common interest, common culture, and common ancestry.[8]

Equally important, however, is the ambivalent set of ideas, attitudes, and habits built up in regard to the others-group. They range from opposition and mild dislike to strong disgust, fear, and even hatred in reference to members of the groups to which we do not belong. While identification builds up in-group solidarity, projection plays an equally important part in fixing our attitudes toward the out-group. Let us look more closely at how this is done.

We have seen that the individual may develop ambivalent reactions to any object, either personal or material. We saw that while the parents give the child much that pleases him, they also deny him many things and demand of him responses at the cost of his pain and displeasure. In reference to the latter he builds up a set of antagonistic reactions which, however, in the presence of the pleasanter associations and the power of the parents to inflict injury, he must suppress. These suppressed reactions are not lost. They remain within him to break out in other forms. Not only the parents produce antagonistic as well as sympathetic pleasant responses in the child, but brothers and sisters do the same, and often the intense rivalry of the children for power and for attention from the parents sets up even more intense op-

---

[8] Émile Durkheim, Gustave Le Bon, and other writers have made much of this. For a review see Chapter IV, "Social Psychology," *History and Prospects of the Social Sciences* (ed. by H. E. Barnes), 1926.

position among them, antagonisms often not so fully repressed as the opposition of the child to the parent.

We may well ask: What becomes of these suppressed attitudes? The nature of social organization and culture furnishes us a partial answer. As the child grows up, his play group may fall into competition and conflict with another, giving his opposition tendencies freer play. Furthermore, his suppressed dislike and hatred for his parents, his brothers and sisters, or other members of the household may be projected upon the members of the opposition play group, gang, or another group. Furthermore, the older family members themselves induct the child into these antagonistic attitudes by talk about the family across the street which is not "as good as ours," or about the neighborhood "over the tracks," where the children are dirty, the parents bootleggers, and generally not fit to associate with children and adults of our "better," "superior," neighborhood. Then we learn from the church and the home that our religious organization is superior to another, that Christians are better than heathens. In school, at church, and at home we learn not only the glories and superiorities of our country, but we learn to fear and dislike other nations. These attitudes are all founded upon fear, rivalry, jealousy, and opposition within the family and the primary groups. Later they are projected largely on to the out-groups.

The sense of nearness or remoteness in regard to other persons or groups is often called *social distance*. Toward members of our own congeniality group, our family, our comrades, our neighbors, our race, or our nation we feel intimate and friendly. Toward members of other families, communities, nations, and races we feel much more remote, much more distant, much less intimate or kindly. The degree of intensity of in-group *versus* out-group feeling may be measured along a scale of social distance.[9]

Integration of Personality. The balance or co-ordination of desires or tendencies—both native and acquired—within the person depends upon the nature of the group participation. In the early years the identification of the child with the parents and family situation is rather complete. As he grows up he identifies himself with his fellows in the groups to which he belongs. But as his group contacts reach outward, the intensity of the identifica-

[9] E. S. Bogardus and his students have done a great deal of work with this sort of measuring device. See his *Contemporary Sociology*, 1931.

tion decreases. The identification in the family circle is intimate and deeply emotional. The identification of the member with an international scientific association may be highly impersonal, intellectual, and but very slightly emotional, except perhaps as the membership enhances the ego. There is a kind of scale of identification from a deep and abiding sort with one's mother, father, or as an adult with one's mate and one's children, through the various primary and secondary groups to those rather illy defined publics or crowds of which we may be but temporary members. In the secondary groups our identification is likely to be largely to group symbols rather than to persons.

As we know, identification covers but half the process of integration. Man is not only filled with love, sympathy, and friendly reactions of approach and co-operation; he is also filled with hatred, dislike, and antagonistic reactions of withdrawal, or of competition and conflict. Once again the ideas, attitudes, and habits built up toward the others-group are important. Our integration or balance is accomplished by the interplay of these two sets of opposite patterns, such as love and hate, like and dislike, sympathy and disgust, approach and withdrawal, co-operation and competition or conflict. These dual patterns run throughout the social order at every point. They are reflected in culture because they exist in man and in his reactions with his fellows. We shall see them at work in various social situations as we carry forward our discussion.

Socialization and Moralization. *Socialization* is the interactional process by which the individual is taught his place in the social order. Since man cannot exist without society, every individual is socialized. Unfortunately sociology has not yet freed itself from ethics, and writers often use the term "socialization" to refer more especially to the building up of moral ideas, attitudes, and habits. This latter should be called more properly moralization.

An individual is always pulled between two opposite poles—a phase of ambivalence. One of these has to do with his own immediate pleasures, the satisfaction of his more elemental physiological wants and acquired personal desires. The other has to do with the moralized values and desires which man develops as he learns from his primary and secondary groups the objects and values which preserve society and give public approval. The first set of patterns, although affected by social interaction, is more rudimentary and often depends on personal-social rather than cultural conditioning. It leads to a personal, hedonistic (pleasure-seeking) definition of the situation.

The second set of patterns is laid down by the public demands for conformity, for ideas, attitudes, and habits that foster loyalty, group solidarity, and a useful rôle in the social order. The major institutions of the political state, of the economic order, of the church, and of the family furnish the individual with most of these utilitarian definitions of the situation.

Yet the person may resist the dominant moral forces of the community. Clearly the hedonistic definitions are not unaffected by interaction with other persons, but the purpose or object of this interaction is distinctly the wish for personal pleasure. The utilitarian, moral definitions are also influenced by other persons, of course, but in terms of group solidarity, preservation of societal values, and for the maintenance of the group or society even at the sacrifice of the more personal desires.

Group participation and personal integration fall into reciprocal relations. Certain groupings—comradeship, congeniality, criminalistic or orgiastic gangs, religious cults fostering intense emotionalism, or mobs—may afford the individual a chance to express his elementary personal desires rather fully. Or again the antagonism to the out-group, the hatred and even physical violence permitted with moral approval of the we-group, affords one a fine opportunity to express the more biological but pleasant desires of opposition. As we saw, the out-group offers us an object upon which to project the hatred and violence we would really like to wreak on members of our own in-groups. This is exactly what intense conflict does for us. War, laborer-employer disputes, religious controversy, even sports—all afford an opportunity to strike a balance between two otherwise opposite tendencies within us. (See Chapter XIX on conflict.) It is evident that the social order has grown up in reference to or out of these deeper patterns of the individual in interaction with his fellows.

In the process of moralization, myths and legends of the historical events and of the heroes of the group are brought to bear upon the child. These, along with *stereotypes*, or emotionalized words, help to define the situation along socially approved lines. In these matters, too, the primary groups set the patterns upon which most of the later moral control is built. (See Chapter XXVI on social control.)

Moral Views and Moral Action. One has but to open one's eyes and ears, however, to realize that men's professions of morality do not correspond any too closely with their moral actions. What men say, what they profess, is often at considerable variance with what they do. Verbal reactions seldom have to correlate perfectly with overt reaction, except in exact science and its applications. Verbal profession of moral codes will satisfy hundreds of situations where overt conduct is not demanded. Talk bulks so large in our world of interaction that it is little wonder that moral professions so often satisfy us. Formal ethics, of course, generally assumes that the most highly moral person "means what he says" and acts on what he professes.

The second matter concerns the strain within the personality set up by divergence between profession and practice. In a society like ours where Christian morality has a difficult time of it to match with business practices, where the making of money outweighs most other considerations, the verbal code is mostly a matter of mouthing a ritual or a phrase. The tolerance we show for the man who makes millions by dishonest stock manipulations, or by vice, gambling, and bootlegging indicates that in American society, at least, the true moral code is rather different from that taught by official religion and morals, or that found embodied in the law. In a society like ours there is actually less strain between belief and action than we imagine, the verbalisms of the higher morality to the contrary notwithstanding.

In this whole matter rationalization plays its part. When the action does not fit the profession, we consciously and unconsciously find excuses. Rationalizations usually come rather ready-made to us from our culture, and the simple mechanism of projection also lends its aid to lay the blame for our conduct on someone else, or on some phase of the situation. Even the man in the street who has picked up the mythology of modern science may "blame" his conduct on his disordered glands, on his "unconscious mind," or perhaps on "heredity."

Although moral codes differ in various societies, the strain between verbal profession and overt conduct is common everywhere. In closely knit religious communities with a simple economic order and direct primary group controls—such as were developed in

Europe and America after the Protestant Reformation—one often finds an amazingly high correlation between the culture norms of conduct and the daily conduct of the communicants. In a complex, highly diverse society like that in western Europe or America to-day, such integration of personality and social order is rare indeed.

Disintegration of Personality. While identification with one set of values and a group, on the one hand, and projection of antagonisms on to another group and its values on the other afford a balance or integration of our ambivalent trends and habits, disharmony within the personality may still arise. In these cases ideas, attitudes, and habits which are built up in reference to objects and values do not co-ordinate within the individual in such a way as to make for adequate adjustment. There are, of course, no perfectly balanced, adjusted persons in every situation, but most normal persons have worked out a sort of plan of action and thought which enables them to get along. Yet there remain many persons who are not able to strike any adequate sort of compromise, and hence fall into disorder.

Aside from the obviously deranged persons who are the object of study and treatment by psychiatry, the science of mental diseases, there are many persons who fail to work out a satisfactory adaptation to the social world around them. For example, a child from a broken home may suffer a nervous breakdown because he cannot adjust to changes brought about by death or desertion of one or both his parents. Or a woman may find a mental conflict in attempting to be a conventional wife and to engage in a profession. Then there are persons who have been exposed to divergent cultures. The immigrant from peasant Europe in the midst of industrial America often falls into this condition, or the Eurasian of mixed blood and culture who cannot find his place either as white man or yellow. (See Chapter XXV on assimilation for discussion of the "marginal man.")

Our interest in general features of behavior—a legitimate concern—may lead us to neglect the infinite variation in everyday behavior around us. In our discussion of personality, while we have rather emphasized the standardizing, conventional effects of one's fellows upon the personality, we must not forget individual differences. In the popular use of the word personality, the emphasis is more often on these unique variant factors than we realize. In a way, the common-sense conception of personality may be superior to our own, which, for scientific interests of generalization, over-stresses common or typical features. We shall discuss the influence of individual differences on personality in reference to social rôles and leadership in Chapters XXI and XXII on differentiation.

CLASS ASSIGNMENTS

A. Further reading assignment:

1. K. Young, *Source Book for Sociology*, chap. V.
2. Ralph Linton, *The Study of Man*, chap. XXVI.

B. Questions and exercises:

1. Why is the field of anticipatory behavior important in the study of personality? Illustrate.
2. What relation has language to thought?
3. Cite illustrations of logical, directed thinking, and of wishful, fantasy thinking.
4. Show how identification and projection operate together in child-parent relations.
5. Show how rôle and status are established (a) in the family, (b) on the playground, (c) in business or the professions.
6. Illustrate the principle of expectancy, (a) in mother-child relations, (b) in teacher-pupil interaction, (c) in relations of a nation to its citizens.
7. Is the distinction of Burgess et al. between personality type and social type valid? Does it assist us in dealing with personality and culture?
8. What factors in our society and culture aid the person in his integration? What factors tend to disintegrate him?

C. Topics for class reports or longer written papers:

1. The mechanism of learning with particular reference to social-cultural conditioning. (Consult K. Young, *Source Book for Social Psychology*, chap. X, and K. Young, *Social Psychology*, chaps. V, VI; J. K. Folsom, *Social Psychology*, 1931, chap. III; and especially G. Murphy, L. B. Murphy, and T. Newcomb, *Experimental Social Psychology*, rev. ed., 1937, chap. IV.)
2. The function of rationalization in social life. (Consult K. Young, *Source Book for Social Psychology*, chap. XII, and bibliography.)
3. The function of compensation and sublimation in determining rôle and status. (Consult K. Young, *Social Psychology*, chap. VII; Alfred Adler, *The Neurotic Constitution*, 1917; Alfred Adler, *Individual Psychology*, 1924; William Healy, Augusta F. Bronner, and Anna Mae Bowers, *The Structure and Meaning of Psychoanalysis*, 1930, pp. 248–53.)
4. The theory of introversion and extroversion. (Consult Gardner Murphy and Friedrich Jensen, *Approaches to Personality*, 1932, pp. 180–82; C. G. Jung, *Psychological Types*, 1923; P. M. Symonds, *Diagnosing Personality and Conduct*, 1931, chap. V, and bibliography.)
5. The nature of social traits and attitudes. (Consult Murphy, Murphy, and Newcomb, *op. cit.*, chap. XIII; G. W. Allport, *Personality*, 1937; R. Stagner, *Psychology of Personality*, 1937.)

PART TWO

GEOGRAPHY, RACE, AND POPULATION

INTRODUCTION

The purpose of PART TWO is to examine certain background factors of race, geography, and population. Race, although strictly the concern of biology, is pertinent to the present discussion because it is associated with culture concepts. Race relations are so closely linked up with prejudices and other features of culture that we must examine their foundations.

Man lives on the land, is affected by soil, topography, and climate. Yet geographical factors, rather than determining man's culture and societal organization, act to limit his food supply and his raw materials, and to modify his behavior. For this reason we must study the relations of geography to man and his culture.

So, too, man's social behavior is everywhere affected by his numbers, their increase or decrease, and by the distribution of the sexes, of the age classes, and by the relation of population to food supply. Many persons are anxious about the feebleminded outbreeding the normal and superior-minded people in our own society. Others are afraid that the lower classes will sweep away, in sheer numbers, the power now held by the upper classes. Still others would frighten us about the dangers of overpopulation in the face of a decreasing food supply. In like manner some of our leaders talk and write much of the dangers of restricting our birth rate lest we weaken our economic and political standing among the world powers through a decline in numbers. These problems are all so intimately bound up with our culture and societal organization that we must give them some attention.

CHAPTER VII

GEOGRAPHY AND CULTURE

Man's survival depends upon his adaptation both to his geographical and to his social-cultural environments. We have already sketched the chief features of the latter. (See Chapter II.) Here we shall deal with the geographic factors. These are traditionally classified into those of (*1*) the atmosphere; (*2*) the water; (*3*) the earth's surface, soil, and rocks; and (*4*) the living plants and animals. Before we attempt to correlate these factors with man's social life, we must review some ancient and still popular notions about the relation of geography to social life.

THEORIES THAT GEOGRAPHY DETERMINES SOCIETY

It is easy to assume that man's behavior is controlled by his physical environment. He is fundamentally dependent upon nature for his food, his water supply, and his shelter. He has had to take these things, at least down to recent industrial culture, largely where he could find them. Clearly he cannot long survive in a territory marked by little rainfall and sparse organic life, or marked by mountainous terrain, unless there are special adaptive devices. Nor can he get on well where there is too much rainfall and where the temperature rises to extreme heat or where it falls to excessive cold. These obvious limiting factors in the building of culture were not enough for earlier geographers, who wished to correlate culture and geography more closely.[1] Thus they believed that hot temperament goes with subtropical and tropical climates, or that the marvelous woodworking of our own northwest coast Indians developed out of the abundance of workable timber there, or that desert countries are conducive to religious mysticism, or that a paucity of fertile land in deserts or moun-

[1] See Franklin Thomas, *The Environmental Basis of Society,* 1925, for an excellent review of the theories of geographic determinism.

tains makes the population yearn for a democracy, whereas richer natural resources foster plutocracy and aristocracy.

The careful student of cultural history falls into no such particularism.[2] Instead he sees that geographic factors, while playing a part, cannot be considered apart from man's culture, and that geography serves as a limiting rather than as a predetermining condition. Furthermore, he realizes that it is material culture that most nearly reflects the geographical conditions. Even so, there are decided limitations due to culture. A few instances will make this clear.

The Eskimo represents a remarkable adaptation to a highly unfavorable environment, and if we knew only his culture, we might assume that all arctic inhabitants follow much the same patterns. Take housing: Is anything more natural than that he build snow huts from the bountiful material at hand? If we but glance across the Bering Sea to the Chuckchee of northeastern Siberia, in a similar climate, we find these people in winter months living not in snow houses but in large clumsy tents of hide stretched over heavy supports. Again, the Chuckchee use the domesticated reindeer for draft purposes, while the Eskimo use dogs to draw their sleds. The latter use the wild reindeer for food, hides, and bones but have not domesticated it. The Chuckchee apparently borrowed the use of the domesticated reindeer from their neighbors, the Tungus, living to the south of them. The Eskimo have not domesticated this convenient animal themselves nor learned how to do so from others.

Again, even though the northwest coast Indians have developed woodworking to a high art, why have not the northern California tribes, with equally ample woodlands, done the same? The answer lies not in the natural environment, but in the divergence in culture.

The American Southwest offers another striking contrast. The Hopi are intensive farmers; the Navajo do but little farming, living a pastoral life. The Hopi live in terraced sandstone houses; the Navajo in conical earth huts. The former possess high art in pottery making; the latter show very crude workmanship. The Hopi men do the weaving; the Navajo women handle the loom. The

[2] *Particularism*, prevalent fault of social science, refers to the habit of accounting for complex phenomena by simple and usually single or "particular" causes. See W. I. Thomas, *Source Book for Social Origins*, 1909, pp. 22–23, for a brilliant statement on this matter.

former are strictly monogamous; the latter permit polygyny. The family organization of the former has strong mother-in-law taboos and gives the maternal uncles great power over their sisters' sons, while the Navajo have no such rigid taboos nor the same form of organization. There are also marked differences in religious and magical practices. Finally, the Navajo, like the Plains Tribes, are warlike, while the Hopi have a more peaceful temper.

In a similar way, in the same sections of South Africa the Bushmen are seed-gatherers and hunters, live in crude windbreaks or caves, and use the bow and arrow. In contrast their neighbors, the Hottentots, are a pastoral people, living in mat-covered portable huts and using the spear as a principal weapon, although they have the bow and arrow. These tribes have many myths and other features of culture in common, but the striking differences in material traits cannot be gainsaid. Once more we have to seek the explanation in the history of their culture and not in the physical world in which they reside.

Another difference in culture within the same environment must be noted. The Digger Indians, living on the edge of the Great American Desert, considered the Rocky Mountain locust a particular delicacy. The locusts infest these areas periodically in great numbers, and the Indians took advantage of these occasions to drive them into brush enclosures, roast them, and have their fill. When the Mormon colonists settled the Great Basin beginning in 1847, they were greatly troubled during the first decade or two by veritable plagues of these insects, which ate up every living blade of grass, wheat, or corn. These white people did what they could to destroy the pests, but they were unable to bridge the cultural chasm between themselves and their Indian friends and bring themselves to take up a new dietary habit. Had their own food taboos been less severe, they, like the Indians, might actually have made something of a blessing out of what seemed to them a curse.

While the physical environment limits society and furnishes the "brick and mortar" for material traits especially, it cannot determine the form and content of the bulk of culture. Moreover, as man has advanced to more complex forms of culture, he has overridden the handicaps of the "natural landscape," putting in its place with increasing effectiveness the "cultural landscape." Not only has he changed the face of the earth itself, but he has overcome handicaps of poor soil by fertilization, provided more adequate water supply for crops through irrigation, insured himself against changes in temperature, and by the use of refrigeration in transporting and storing food stuffs has removed the barriers on seasonal foods. Culture history runs a sort of gamut from the more primitive societies, tied rather closely to their immediate physical environment, to modern society with little left in the life of the ordinary man, even in the realm of the physical forces, that has not been modified by his culture.

Nevertheless, the geographic forces are still operating, even in the face of man's cultural changes. We must bear in mind at all times, however, that society, its culture, and its physical environment are all bound together into a unity.

PRINCIPAL GEOGRAPHIC FEATURES

Man's residence is affected chiefly by two geographic features, location and natural resources. The former includes the land and water masses with their climate. The latter has to do with soils, mineral deposits, and the plant and animal life.

Climate. Some one has remarked that climate we have with us always, although weather changes from day to day. Under climate we include temperature, rainfall, wind movement, and the variations in amount of sunshine, but we shall discuss only the first two.

With respect to *temperature* the earth is traditionally divided into three zones, tropical, temperate, and arctic. Man's settlement of the earth has been limited by the conditions in these and by the seasonal variations. Primitives in relatively small numbers do manage to get on in the northern arctic regions. In the tropics, unless the humidity is too great, we find rather more populous primitive and higher culture peoples managing very well, but without doubt the most striking advances in the history of culture have taken place in subtropical and temperate zones. Down to the present the congestion of population seems most evident there. The location of the important large cities in the northern hemisphere illustrates this. They fall between the limits of average annual temperatures of 60° Fahrenheit (St. Louis, Lisbon, Genoa, Rome, Constantinople, Shanghai, Osaka, Kyoto) and 40° Fahrenheit (Quebec, Oslo, Stockholm, Leningrad). Along the central axis of this zone, 50° Fahrenheit, we find Chicago, New York, and Vienna.

Seasonal and daily variation in temperature is important. Extreme fluctuations in the seasons, of course, are wiped out in the averages, but in the tropics the variation is little from month to month or season to season. In the arctic the short summers and long winters make the adaptation in the latter much more difficult. It is in the temperate zones, where temperature changes with the seasons—but not too violently—that we find, for the most part, the largest congestion of population and the highest culture. Daily variation in temperature also seems important. Ellsworth Huntington, the geographer, states that human power is more efficient where the temperatures fluctuate somewhat noticeably from day to day. Uniformity of temperature produces low output of energy. He has also shown that daily variation in temperature stimulates energy output, that a fall in temperature is rather more stimulating than a rise, if the fall amounts to as much as four degrees.[3]

Rainfall obviously affects organic life. There are wide variations in the amount of precipitation in various regions. In the Great Basin west of the Rocky Mountains, the average annual rainfall is about 12 to 16 inches, in Wisconsin it is between 30 and 35 inches, and in Alabama between 55 and 60. The sharpest contrasts are found between such areas as tropical seacoast Brazil, where annual precipitation reaches 133 inches at the maximum, and parts of Java and India, where it is over 100 inches, and areas where rainfall is below 10 inches: central Australia, Tibet, parts of Mongolia, the Sahara, Nevada, and Arizona.

Temperature and rainfall together make for differences in types of agriculture and hence in man's social life. With rainfall adequate, wheat and corn grow best in the zone of mean annual temperature between 39° and 68° Fahrenheit; rice between 68° and 86°, while the date palm shows little or no growth below 64°. Important soil bacteria necessary to growth do not become active until soil temperature reaches 45° or more, and most crop plants do not grow below 42.8°.

If the temperature is torrid and the rainfall heavy, life may be difficult without unusual means of offsetting the climatic handicaps. In the same way, lack of moisture in hotter climates restricts man in even more definite manner. The distribution of man's habitations is limited by climate as well as by the nature of the

[3] Ellsworth Huntington, *Civilization and Climate*, 3rd ed., 1924, pp. 141, 142.

ground surfaces, 35 per cent of the land surface being arid, while
10 or 12 per cent gets so much rainfall that human habitation is
almost impossible.

Land Surfaces. Mountainous regions, plains, and river valleys affect the settlement of man differently.

Altitude definitely influences man's habitation. In Europe and
America there are few cities of any size at altitudes above 5,000
feet, except in the tropics, where altitude produces a cooler climate than along the seacoast. For example, from Mexico to
Chile, aside from certain seaports, the most important cities are
above 6,000 feet. Mexico City, with 1,000,000 people (1930), has
an altitude of 7,500 feet, and Quito, with 120,000 inhabitants, is
9,200 feet above the sea. In Asia there are many exceptions, but
unless sea winds moderate the temperature and humidity, life in
Asiatic cities is decidedly trying at certain hours of the day and at
certain seasons of the year.

In mountainous areas food production is often difficult. In
Switzerland grazing is possible on rather precipitous slopes, but
on most of the denuded mountains of China nothing will grow. In
Japan only 15 per cent of the land is under cultivation, 75 per
cent is mountainous, and the remaining area is either required for
non-agricultural purposes or is otherwise unfit for cultivation.

Where rainfall is moderate, as on the plains of the United States,
Argentina, and Russia, rich grain crops will grow. Where rainfall
is slighter and temperatures lower, as in the northernmost plains
regions of the northern hemisphere, there are found abundant
grasslands.

Even more fertile are the great river valleys, the Nile, the Eu-
phrates and Tigris, the Ganges, the Yellow River, the Dnieper, the
Volga, the Danube, the Rhine, the Rhone, the Elbe, and in North
America the whole internal basin drained by the Mississippi, Missouri, and Ohio rivers. Given sufficient cultural advance these
areas afford man a place of rich agriculture and a rapid expansion
of population.

Soil, its quality and nature, is a highly important factor. Good
soil teems with soil bacteria absolutely essential to plant life. The
types of soil will determine the sorts of crops. Sandy soil, for example, favors certain fruits and market gardening. Clay lands are
favorable to grasses and some grains. Loams, being intermediate
between the two, have the widest variations in use. Naturally land

utilization will be influenced by kinds of soil. Social life in the wheat areas is quite different from the life of the dairyman of New York or Wisconsin, or that of the market gardener of the Atlantic seaboard. The wheat farmer has an intensive period of preparation and planting, with a long stretch during the growing season when he has little to do, followed by strenuous harvesting. The dairy farmer has a constant problem of care of his cattle the year round, and certain seasonal work besides. The market gardener during the growing season is continuously busy, but like the fruit grower or wheat farmer has long periods of little farm activity.

It is evident that rural life in each of these areas will vary. The large wheat farms in America foster open-country neighborhoods, while dairy farming makes for smaller farm units. Fruit raising and market gardening go well with agricultural village life.

As long as plenty of free land is available, people are inclined to exploit nature unwisely, moving on to fresh land as the old is used up. This has been the familiar story, for example, in our own South, where the older cotton and tobacco soils have been exploited to such a degree that the cost of fertilizer necessary to make them productive is so great that the margin of profit is cut to a minimum.

This "destructive occupation" of the land, as Jean Brunhes, the French geographer, calls it, is an important factor in the relation of man to food supply in many sections. As cheaper fertilizers and improved methods of farming are developed, this misuse of land may disappear, but only in recent decades in our country have we realized the problem in terms of food supply and population.

The relation between poor land and poor culture conditions is certainly evident in our own society. In many regions it is only the educational, political, economic, religious, and social forces outside these communities that have helped to raise them to higher levels. Nothing they could have done themselves on their own slim economic base would have helped them up.[4] The contrast of the rich loam belt of central Illinois, yielding 35 to 43 bushels of corn per acre, with that of the pale gray clay of the southern sections of the same state, producing but 19 to 25 bushels, is a striking example. Per capita wealth, value of farm land per acre, percentage of urban population, school attendance beyond compulsory age

[4] I refer to the various programs to help the poor mountaineer of the South, the dweller on poor cut-over lands in northern Michigan and northern Wisconsin, and people living on the margins of desert land in the Far West.

limit, ratio of eminent men per 100,000 population, and other criteria of advanced culture are all higher in the former than in the latter section.[5]

Man's destruction of forests has been a serious factor in many regions, not only in wastage of timber but also in subsequent economic loss by erosion and by failure to replant the areas. The classic example of ignorant deforestation is the large mountainous area of China, now barren of all vegetation and useless for growing timber and, even more important, offering no ground-cover for snow or for retention of moisture. European practice has been more intelligent in this matter. In the United States we have been woefully extravagant of our timber resources in the past, but are slowly learning our lesson.

Mineral Resources. When man learned to smelt copper and especially iron ores and fashion more effective tools, weapons, and instruments, he made one of the great forward steps in culture. Down to this time he had chiefly used stone and bone. These durable and malleable metals were greatly superior to the earlier materials. Yet with the necessary techniques of combining iron and coal not yet discovered, iron did not dominate earlier material culture as it does today. The highest cultures of antiquity—Egypt, Babylonia, India, China, Greece, and Rome—all developed in areas with little iron ore.

The production of iron and coal together in the last century and a half, which revolutionized material culture, brought far-reaching effects on all other aspects of behavior as well. Nearly 80 per cent of the known iron ore deposits and an equal percentage of coal are found in rather narrowly defined sections of western Europe and the United States. Sixty-nine per cent of the world's coal is found in this country alone. It is the occurrence of coal and iron in fairly close proximity that makes them important in modern life. Unless the two are found together, heavy industry is not likely to develop. South America, for example, has considerable iron but no coal.

The use of these two resources together in new ways had to depend on other changes in culture: the making of improvements in smelting, the inventions of power machinery and the steam engine, and finally the applications of science in the modern use of steel for construction purposes never dreamed of before. This is an excellent demonstration that natural resources mean nothing till man

[5] See Ellsworth Huntington's discussion in J. Davis, H. E. Barnes et al., *Introduction to Sociology*, 1931, pp. 207–215.

is prepared by culture to use them. The American Indians who roamed over the coal deposits of the Alleghenies or hunted through the iron ranges in the upper Great Lakes country had no use for coal and iron. It took the diffusion of modern industrialism from England to America to bring about the exploitation of these materials.

The importance of coal and iron for modern industry and commerce and hence for modern culture is self evident. The political implications are also apparent; countries rich in these minerals are today at a distinct advantage over others which have little or none of them. During recent decades the world's economic and hence political struggles have revolved around coal and iron. As Walter S. Tower remarks, "Coal is the basis of modern economic strength, because it is the main and still the most convenient source of mechanical power."[6]

Besides coal and the older and still important water power, oil has an important place as a source of power in our world. The increases in the production of petroleum in this country alone since 1860 are astounding. In 1859 it was 2,000 barrels; in 1860 it sprang to 500,000; by 1861 to 2,113,609. By 1880 it had reached 26,286,123 barrels. At the turn of the century it was 63,620,529 barrels. It more than doubled in the next five years. By 1915 it had reached 281,104,104; by 1922 it had doubled again, and in 1929 it exceeded 1,007,000,000 barrels. In 1932 production fell to 785,000,000; but rose to a new high of 1,098,000,000 in 1936.

Oil has become a factor in international economics and politics. With the United States producing nearly 70 per cent of the world's supply, Great Britain, Germany, and other western European nations have had to depend largely on us or on other foreign fields. Since the World War there has been a mad scramble for new oil fields, particularly in Asia. Because her coal production is declining, Great Britain is particularly interested in petroleum, and she has acquired important holdings abroad. Without this new source of power her economic and naval dominance can hardly be maintained.

All three of these—iron, coal, and petroleum—illustrate man's destructive exploitation of nature's resources. Man has always tended to be prodigal with those resources which fall easily into his hands. As supplies are exhausted these items become clearly

[6]Walter S. Tower, "The Coal Question," *Foreign Affairs*, 1923, vol. II, p. 100.

matters of international concern. They may easily be factors in the development of intense competition and conflict.

There are various less well-known mineral resources that are important in modern industrial societies: nitrates, potash, manganese, cobalt, platinum, to mention but a few. Although often the supply of these is limited, or although they may not exist in a country at all, they are important for its industrial life. This is true of tin, nickel, and cobalt, which are lacking or found in very limited quantities in the United States. The supply of these likewise will influence international relations by fostering competition and even open conflict.[7]

GEOGRAPHIC FACTORS IN SETTLEMENT AND MIGRATION

With this brief sketch of general geographic factors before us let us note certain combinations of these factors in more detail as they influence the settlement and movement of mankind. Movements of population are affected by ease or difficulty of transportation and communication by land, rivers, seas, and oceans. Settlements likewise may be cut off by the larger bodies of water until transportation is improved, or restricted by barriers like mountain ranges, deserts, or heavy jungle. We have already noted in Chapter IV the effects of geographic isolation on cultural development. So, too, we have noted some of the geographic factors in settlement. Let us examine some of these influences in more detail as they affect the location and growth of cities.

The Location of Cities. In addition to climate, location, and soil, the rise of cities is affected by the purpose of settlement. Cities may be military in nature, as were the outposts of the Roman legions along the Rhine or Danube. They may be trade centers or industrial localities where abundant natural resources make heavy industry possible. Other cities grow up where power, transportation, and cheap labor stimulate light industry. Still other cities serve chiefly religious, political, or educational purposes.

If we look at a large map of any city, we note at once that its structure and growth are first of all dependent on the physiographic nature of the site itself. Richard M. Hurd remarks:

"The first step in studying the ground plan of cities is to note the topographical faults which normally control the shape of cities, by inter-

[7] See C. K. Leith, *World Minerals and World Politics*, 1931, for a discussion of certain phases of this problem.

fering with their free growth in all directions from their points of origin. These are of two kinds: water surfaces, such as harbors, lakes, rivers, creeks, and swamps, or sharp variations from the normal city level, such as steep hills, deep hollows, and ravines."[8]

Where the country is flat, with no marshes or interfering contours, the natural tendency is for the city to grow outward in all directions, unless man-made factors such as highways, defense walls, and railroad trackage interfere. Topography gives the most obvious ground structure to a city. The towns and cities located on waterways must follow the lines of growth laid down by the water barriers. In the hill and valley type of topography, the valley tends to be the seat of easiest communication and of industrial and commercial locations, while residential sections evolve on the higher ground. If the hills be too steep, travel between homes and work is made difficult, so that even residential growth tends at the outset to follow the line of least resistance, other things being equal. The combination of a good harbor, hills, and valleys favors the growth of seaport cities.

Hurd summarizes the major influences of topography by saying that—

"Level land attracts business, moderate elevations attract residences, land below the normal level attracts transportation lines, and filled-in land is generally used for warehousing, manufacturing, and cheap tenements."[9]

Man-made Topography. While the "cultural landscape" is evident wherever man has lived any length of time, the city shows these influences most markedly. From the very outset the hand of man gives any town or city a direction of growth which ordinarily continues ever afterward. The longer man has been settled in a locality, the less the influence of the natural topography becomes and the more constantly important becomes his own handiwork. Man cuts down, or through, hills, drains and fills swamps, builds dykes, dredges river mouths and harbors, constructs canals, and otherwise alters the natural landscape. Many of the cities on the east side of the North Sea are absolutely dependent on dykes and dredging for their continuance. It is said that one reason why ancient Carthage declined in trade was the natural filling in of her

[8] From Richard M. Hurd, *Principles of City Land Values*, 4th ed., 1924, p. 33.
[9] *Op. cit.*, p. 36.

harbor from the sea in a time when there was no known human way to prevent it.

The most obvious and the basic culture factor in man's building a city is the general location in respect to lines of communication and transportation. Modern cities tend to grow up on trade lines, and trade tends to follow the lines of least resistance. Men float their goods down streams to remote markets. Land routes along valleys, over low passes in mountains, by way of a chain of oases in a desert—all represent man's efforts to overcome nature's hindrances with the least expenditure of energy and time. Wherever there is a break in this flow, cities are likely to arise: where the sea trade must be transferred to river travel, where the river trade goes over to land travel, or where there is a break in land travel due to topography, political barriers, or other factors. Utica, New York, was built at the crossroads of travel north and south. Paris, France, grew up where trade lines north and south met the Seine river. C. H. Cooley puts it thus: "Population and wealth tend to gather wherever there is a break in transportation."

The site or specific locality where the city grows up soon develops a structure or form with the layout of streets playing the most important part. As Walter Geisler points out, when a city is founded, the streets are laid out with respect to natural topography, and the best available land is taken for retail stores and for residential purposes. The ground plan is thus settled more or less once and for all. Thenceforth streets become an obstructive element in city development. Streets constitute the lanes of traffic back and forth through the city. Cities with narrow or winding streets like Boston, Massachusetts, and Bridgeport, Connecticut, or cities with many diagonal streets like Worcester, Massachusetts, or Madison, Wisconsin, produce unusually bad traffic problems in this age of the automobile.

Unless hindered by natural topography the city tends to develop in a rectangular or radial fashion. Where the streets are laid out with regularity, in squares or rectangles, the city's growth is restricted usually to the direction determined by two main intersecting streets or thoroughfares. There are some distinct advantages and some disadvantages in the rectangular form. It allows the plotting of lots of about equal size, makes easy the division of the city into administrative districts, and permits of more adequate police or military control in case of a crisis. The disadvantages of rectangular blocks are those of population movement. There are no advantageous main thoroughfares to facilitate circulation between the center and the periphery, although within the center itself movement may be easy.

The radial plan arises where there is a natural center at the end of a number of converging thoroughfares. As the city grows, it tends to follow these major traffic lanes, producing the star-shaped cities like Tokio, Nürnberg, and the older sections of London. This is perhaps the most natural form of development.

Sometimes we find a combination of rectangular and radial patterns. Often there were originally a number of highways leading to the village or town, and as the city grew it was laid out in regular rectangular form superimposed on this system of highways. Broadway in New York was an old turnpike road which became a main artery of traffic from the north. Washington, D. C., was deliberately planned to combine the radial with the rectangular scheme.

There are two directions in which a city may grow. One of these is the axial. The other is the central or radial. The rectangular arrangement tends to foster development along certain axes, often at right angles to each other. The radial, or central form, tends to grow outward along the major streets in a star or fan shape. Hurd believes that the need for diagonal or radial streets depends upon the size and shape of the city's site. Narrow cities like New York or Boston do not need them; but they are of great utility in cities which spread out over level areas, such as Chicago, Cleveland, Buffalo, or Detroit.

It sometimes happens that streets are developed around certain sections of cities as walls have been torn down, moats filled in, or parks cut up. One does not see this sort of thing in the United States. In many European cities certain streets are an outgrowth of the natural evolution of the city. This is true of Paris, where there are at least four sets of circular streets which arose as old walls were torn down and new ones farther away were built, only in time to be razed and turned to streets themselves. The beautiful Ringstrasse in Vienna was cut out of a series of public parks which, in turn, had replaced older fortifications.

While the streets provide the basic ground structure to a city, railroad lines also contribute to it. For example, in Chicago, rail lines have tended to break up and isolate certain districts from others, although for the most part the lines have followed either the lake shore or the Chicago River and its branches. In South Bend, Indiana, and in Syracuse, New York, the chief railway line once traversed important main streets, greatly hindering other traffic. Wholesale trade areas and more particularly industrial sites call for much trackage, and in these areas, slums or disintegrated neighborhoods are likely to develop. Often railroad tracks located on the outskirts of a city later become a barrier to further growth as the city extends its boundaries.

Parks, squares, and open spaces scattered throughout a city have been called the "lungs" of the city since these areas are places where fresher air, more sunlight, and natural topography are available. Cities vary a great deal in the ratio of park space to population density. In New York City in 1925 there was one acre of park for every 577 persons, but only one acre for every 1130 persons in Manhattan proper. It is not only a matter of statistical averages. The real problem is the ratio of parks to congestion. What a city needs is a widespread network of parks and open spaces. Too frequently parks are found in the areas occupied by wealthy classes with few children, while congested slum areas often have no parks at all. The matter is not only the distribution of the "breathing spaces" on the purely physical health side; parks also mean recreational facilities for children who have no backyards and no opportunities for adequate play. The pressure of population growth in our American cities has been so great, the desire for rich profits from real-estate ventures so overpowering, and the strength of public sentiment so weak, that we have failed to strike a reasonable balance in the matter. Later we awaken to the problem and find that the creation of parks and open spaces can be done only at a terrific financial burden upon the taxpayers. One of the purposes of city and regional planning is not only to develop a zoning system of land in terms of further economic developments but to plan for parks, streets, and residential areas in terms of maximum use by the whole public.

Our survey of the city in reference to geography and culture serves to demonstrate in some detail how the hand of man everywhere changes nature, and how culture comes more and more to override the natural forces of land and water.

This is not, however, to gainsay the ultimate checks which nature puts upon man. The limitation of minerals is evident. There are definite limits to arable land. There are large areas that are not habitable without too great cost of time and human effort, in spite of the modern machine. Thus, the population of the world must face the geographical, that is, natural forces on which it depends, no matter how marvelous the inventions and discoveries of modern science prove to be.

CLASS ASSIGNMENTS

A. Further reading assignment:

1. K. Young, *Source Book for Sociology*, chap. VII.
2. R. H. Lowie, *Culture and Ethnology*, chap. III.
3. F. H. Hankins, *An Introduction to the Study of Society*, rev. ed., chap. VI.

B. Questions and exercises:

1. What is meant by "particularism"? Illustrate from theories of geographical influences on man.
2. What does E. A. Ross mean by stating in his *Principles of Sociology*, 1938, p. 87, "As civilization develops . . . ideas, dogmas and doctrines play a greater rôle, climate and scene a lesser rôle."
3. What modern inventions are tending to offset the uncomfortable effects of high temperatures?
4. Show how the type of agriculture influences the form of social life.
5. Should the government spend money on education, public health, and good roads for families living on sub-marginal (economically deficient) farms? Discuss pro and con.
6. Discuss the place of governmental control in restraining undue exploitation of natural resources. What "right" has the political state to attempt to conserve natural resources?
7. Distinguish between the "natural landscape" and the "cultural landscape."
8. What factors, geographic and cultural, in general, influence the growth of cities?
9. Prepare an outline map of your own community and show how its settlement and growth have been affected (a) by strictly geographic factors, and (b) by culture, especially by such matters as transportation, industry, business, and "non-material" factors.

C. Topics for class reports or longer written papers:

1. Critical review of the discussion about the geographic influences on history and culture. (Consult among others Lucien Febvre, *A Geographical Introduction to History*, 1925; Ellen C. Semple, *Influences of Geographic Environment*, 1911; Ellsworth Huntington, *Civilization and Climate*, 1924 ed.; E. G. Dexter, *Weather Influences*, 1904; R. H. Lowie, *Culture and Ethnology*, 1917, chap. III; H. J. Mackinder, *Democratic Ideals and Reality*,

1919; W. L. Bunting, *Where Geography and History Meet*, 1925; A. P. Brigham, *Geographic Influences in American History*, 1903.)

2. The problem of world minerals in relation to the dominant capitalist economic order and the present nationalism. (Consult among others C. K. Leith, *World Minerals and World Politics*, 1931; J. W. Furness, L. M. Jones, and F. H. Blumenthal, "Mineral Raw Materials: Survey of Commerce and Sources in Major Industrial Countries," *Trade Promotion Series*, No. 76, U. S. Department of Commerce, 1929; George O. Smith, *Raw Materials and their Effect upon International Relations*, Carnegie Endowment for International Peace, No. 226, 1927; Walter H. Voskuil, *Minerals in Modern Industry*, 1930.)

3. Critical review of the importance of coal, iron, and steel in relation to modern culture. (Consult among others Robert Bruere, *The Coming of Coal*, 1922; E. C. Eckel, *Coal, Iron, and War*, 1920; James Fairgrieve, *Geography and World Power*, 1927; C. K. Leith, *op. cit.;* George O. Smith, *op. cit.;* Robert P. Arnot, *The Politics of Oil*, 1924; Francis Delaisi, *Oil—Its Influence on Politics*, transl. by C. Leonard Leese, 1922; Louis Fischer, *Oil Imperialism*, 1926; W. T. Thom, *Petroleum and Coal: The Keys to the Future*, 1929; Pierre l'Espagnol de la Tramerye, *The World Struggle for Oil*, transl. by C. Leonard Leese, 1924; R. H. Whitbeck and Olive J. Thomas, *The Geographic Factor: Its Rôle in Life and Civilization*, 1932, chaps. IX, X, XI, and bibliographies.)

4. The struggle for governmental control of natural resources in the United States: (a) as to economic values in such a policy; (b) as a reflection of changing public viewpoint regarding extreme individualism *versus* societal interests. (Consult, among others, Charles R. Van Hise, *Conservation of Our Natural Resources*, rev. by Loomis Havemeyer, 1930; H. H. Barrows, "A National Plan and Policy for the Control and Use of Water Resources," in *Geographic Aspects of International Relations*, edited by C. C. Colby, 1938; reports by the National Resources Committee and of various state planning commissions; and pertinent titles above.)

CHAPTER VIII

RACE

Properly speaking, the racial history of mankind is the subject matter of physical anthropology. In this chapter we shall be concerned chiefly with the description of the living races from the standpoint of their physical and mental characteristics.

NATURE AND DISTRIBUTION OF RACES

There has been much loose talk about race. People speak of the Nordic race, or the Jewish race, or the German race. The Nordics really constitute a sub-race. The Jews are not racially homogeneous at all, but are a cultural group. The Germans represent a language group. The Nazi doctrine of an Aryan race is a myth (see p. 159). Popular beliefs confuse physical features, cultural traits, and narrower language and political differences.

Criteria of Race. Man (*Homo sapiens*) represents not several but only one animal species, and race, if it means anything at all, refers to physical characteristics held in common by a sub-species. It cannot apply to any other form of human association.

"A race is a great body of mankind having a majority of identical physical characters inherited from its common ancestors. The criteria by which race should be determined are heritable, non-adaptive features. In order to establish a type of any racial significance, it is absolutely essential that the individuals attributed to it show a certain homogeneity in the crucial physical features."[1]

The primary races are divided again into rather large and rather distinctive sub-races—usually the product of long inbreeding of one or two primary races in a region of relative isolation.

By what standard features are we to judge membership of any individual in a given race or sub-race? Again popular notions

[1] From E. A. Hooton, *Up from the Ape*, 1931, pp. 371, 372. By permission of The Macmillan Company, publishers.

have proved misleading. Color is perhaps the commonest standard of race for the man on the street, but this is clearly inadequate,
as we shall see.

Physical anthropology has developed a list of standards of
racial differences, some of them fairly discriminating, others of no
value. Among them are (*1*) *height,* which is so variable as to be
almost useless; (*2*) *weight* and *weight-height ratios,* which are
also of little use because so greatly affected by external factors;
(*3*) *head form,* or cephalic index, which is much better as a measure of sub-races than of distinctive races themselves; (*4*) *nasal
index,* and (*5*) *facial projection,* which are fairly good; (*6*) *skull
capacity,* which varies so widely as to be of slight value; (*7*) *hair
texture,* which is easily determined and seems most reliable and
valid; (*8*) *hairiness of body,* which is of moderate value; and
(*9*) *color of skin, eyes,* and *hair,* which are of varying usefulness.

These nine criteria are the most commonly used in distinguishing races and sub-races. Certain other traits, such as eyelid form
and ear form, may be used for detailed study of sub-races. Hair
texture and hairiness together, nasal index, and the cephalic index
are the three most frequently used. Certain of these criteria are
said to reflect the nearness of a race to its anthropoid ancestors.
Thus, the prognathism and broad nose of the Negroes is thought
to mark their primitive physical traits in contrast to the lack of
these in the white race. One must be wary of these attempts on the
part of white persons to find some physical features to bolster up
pride in their own race. Hairiness, which is a distinctly anthropoid
and mammalian trait, is most marked among the whites, while the
eversion of the lip, a distinctly human trait, is most marked among
the Negroes. As Hooton says, it is the *"combination,* rather than
any one or two peculiarities of physical features, which determines
the race."

Efforts have recently been made to develop other criteria of
races by means of blood chemistry, which reveals four types of
blood determined by the presence or absence of one or both of
two substances which affect agglutination. But no adequate cor-
relations have been found between peoples classified by blood-
types and those classified by the anatomical criteria of race.[2]

With the chief measures of racial distinctions at hand, is it at all

[2]See Allison Davis, "The Distribution of the Blood-Groups and its Bearing on the
Concept of Race," in *Political Arithmetic* (ed. by L. Hogben), 1938.

possible to classify the world's population into major races? If so, are these groups pure races, biologically speaking? The experts in this field have differed somewhat among themselves. Some writers give as many as five major races: black, yellow, brown, red, and white. Others, like A. L. Kroeber, give only three major racial stocks: Negroid or black, Caucasian or white, and Mongoloid or yellow.[3] Hooton gives three major races: white, black, and yellow-brown or Mongoloid, with a fourth, compounded of the other three in various degrees. Kroeber, likewise, has a place for certain large groups made up from varying mixtures of the three basic races, with some doubt as to just what the original connection with the major races was. Single characteristics do not serve to demark races, and variation in traits is evident everywhere. Let us sketch the principal features of the major races and sub-races.

The White Race. The white race, often miscalled the Caucasian, is distinguished by a very slight pigmentation, giving a light brown or olive or pale white color. The face is not prognathic, and the nose form is high and narrow to medium. The texture of the hair is fine or medium, the body hair usually abundant, and the hair form usually straight or wavy. The pelvic arch is very broad. The principal sub-races are five in number:

(1) The *Alpine* are short headed, broad faced, with dark, slightly coarse hair and dark eyes, slightly broad nose, skin color olive though sometimes white, and medium thick-set stature. Typical peoples are the Czechs, the Bavarians, the Russians, and southern Slavs.

(2) The *Armenoid* are broad headed, rather long faced, with brown eyes, dark, rather coarse hair, convex, high-bridged and rather narrow nose, skin color olive or brunette, hair abundant on head, face, and body, and stature like the Alpines. Typical peoples are the Armenians, Turks, Syrians, many Persians, and the Ashkenazim Jews, that is, those Jews found throughout most of eastern and northern Europe and in this country.

(3) The *Nordic* peoples are characterized by fine straight or wavy golden or blond hair, blue eyes, long head form, long face, long, high noses, and often a distinctive fold of skin over the eye. In stature they are tall, and the body build is slender. They are concentrated in Scandinavia and the Baltic regions and are rather common in England, Scotland, Normandy, the Netherlands, in the British colonies, and in this country. There are sporadic small Nordic groups elsewhere in Europe and in northwest Africa.

[3] See A. L. Kroeber, *Anthropology*, 1923, chap. III.

(4) The *Mediterranean* peoples are long headed with olive or pale white skin, very dark and usually wavy or curly hair, eyes black or dark brown, the face oval, nose narrow and moderately high. The stature is short, with tendency to obesity in middle and old age. Typical peoples are the southern Italians, southern French, the Spanish, the Portuguese, the Arabs, and the Egyptians.

(5) The *Ainu,* an almost extinct people of northern Japan, are not always classified in the white group, although most writers recognize distinctly white features. They are marked by abundance of black but wavy hair on the head, face, and body, brunette skin, medium or light brown eyes, rather short, medium-broad face, a low and somewhat broad nose, and short, stocky stature.

There are certain other groups within the white race representing ancient mixtures of various white sub-races, such as the *East Baltic* group, perhaps an Alpine-Nordic-Mongoloid mixture. These peoples live in the eastern Baltic and are rather common in Sweden and north Germany. The Finns, Esthonians, and some Russians fall in this grouping. Still another familiar mixture of sub-races is the *Keltic,* a Mediterranean-Nordic mixture, whom we know best as the Scotch Highlanders, the Welsh, the southern Irish, and the inhabitants of western France.

The Negroid Race. The Negroid or black race is characterized by a number of rather distinctive features. Among the most noticeable are the coarse, wiry, black, woolly, or frizzly hair, which is short on the head and sparsely distributed on the face and body; marked protrusion of the face; short, broad, or flat nose; black or dark brown skin; dark brown or black eyes; lips thick and everted. The head form is long, the stature variable, some groups being tall and others short. The various major groups are as follows:

(1) The *Negro* proper, who occupies tropical Africa, especially the west coast, the Sudan, and the Congo. (2) The *Melanesians,* or so-called *Oceanic Negroes,* differ somewhat from the true African Negroes. Their hair is rather more frizzly than woolly, the nose hooked and rather Semitic in form, lips less puffy and less everted than those of their African fellows. They have marked brow ridges. They are typified by the natives of New Guinea, the New Hebrides, New Caledonia, New Britain, and the Fiji Islands. (3) The *Negritos,* or *Pygmies,* are Negroid peoples found in central Africa, the Malay Peninsula, and in the Philippines. They are believed to be a more ancient sample of the black race. The nose form is very broad; the facial protrusion marked; and the hair growth in "spiral clumps." Moreover, they have an infantile body build, a short stature, and the forehead is noticeably bulged, with no brow ridges at all.

They tend to be broad headed, whereas both the true African Negro and the Melanesian peoples tend to be long headed.

There are also various racial mixtures usually classified with the Negroid peoples. One of these is the *Nilotic* group, living in the eastern Sudan and the lake region of Africa, perhaps a cross of Negroid and Hamitic, the latter a Mediterranean people of Egyptian origin. The natives of Tasmania, now extinct, were evidently a Negro-white mixture. So, too, the Australians are perhaps a white-Negroid, or white-Tasmanian mixture. The Bushmen and Hottentots of South Africa are believed by some to be a mixture of Negroid and Mongolian stocks.

The Mongoloid Race. The so-called yellow or Mongoloid race is widely distributed over Asia and the Americas. The most general characteristics are as follows: skin color yellow or yellowish-brown; hair coarse in texture, straight in form, and black in color. It is sparse on the face and body, but very long on the head. The eye form is quite commonly—though not universally—slanting, with the so-called Mongoloid fold. The face is very broad, the nose of medium breadth, with medium nasal index, the face slightly prognathic. There is wide variability in head form. The Mongolian races are usually of medium stature, but again with exceptions. The body build is rather squat, with broad shoulders, long trunk, short legs, and arms of medium length. This great racial group is usually divided into two major divisions:

(1) The *Mongols* proper follow closely the characteristics just noted. They are typified by the Tungus, Kalmucks, and Mongols, and in mixed form by the Chinese, especially the north Chinese, the Manchus, and the Koreans.

(2) The *American Indians* are usually classified as Mongoloid peoples, although they seem to possess certain other strains. They are yellow-brown or red-brown in skin color; the eyes are dark, face form broad and rather long with square jaws, nose form generally high bridged and convex. There is a slight tendency to protrusion of the face. The hair is straight, black, and very coarse, abundant and long on the head, but sparse on the face and body.

These people make up the native population of North and South America. There are wide variations among them, perhaps constituting fairly well marked sub-races. Some are long headed, others are round headed; while most of them are tall, some are short and stocky.

Certain composite racial groups may be mentioned. The *Dravidians* of southern India are perhaps a Mediterranean-Australian-Melanesian mixture. The *Indonesian-Malay* group is probably a mixture of Mediterranean with Mongolian stocks and a minor strain of Negroid blood. And the *Polynesians*—the Hawaiians, Tongans, Samoans, and others of the south Pacific—are apparently a cross between Mongolian and Mediterranean, with slight Melanesian influence added for good measure.

Pure Races Doubtful. It is apparent from this brief sketch that there is much overlapping, and that no combination of racial features distinctly marks off one group from another. While we must recall that it is a combination of physical traits which distinguishes one race from another, we must not forget that the combination of traits varies with every major race and sub-race. In the light of these facts, one wonders whether there is such a thing as a strictly "pure race." All the races belong to the same animal species, *Homo sapiens* (wise man), and properly speaking the so-called races are sub-species or varieties, although the differences between them are perhaps as marked as are distinguishing features of separate species in other animals.

This sort of technical problem need not detain us, but in any case we must be cautious in using the term *race*. There are probably no pure races at all in the sense that one race is distinctly marked off from another by a given and absolute set of criteria. At best, *these broad racial groups are convenient pigeonholes for classifying mankind as to physical traits only*.

MENTAL DIFFERENCES AMONG RACES

Turning aside from physical differences in race, we may ask if there are any mental differences in races which will enable us to classify them. When the European white man first came into extensive contact with the black and yellow races, it was only natural for him to feel superior in mentality and culture to the other races, whose customs seemed strange, often cruel, and at times positively ridiculous. White color meant superiority; dark skin denoted inferiority. Our current prejudices about the inferiority of other races have come down to us from white colonists, missionaries, traders, and travelers who have lived with these peoples. The bias about the mental inferiority of other races is itself a culture trait. It is no instinct. It is but an example of the white man's ethnocentrism. Such prejudices arise between peoples living in different countries although racially they come of the same stock.

The Nordic Myth. In western Europe this feeling was carried over into the post-Napoleonic period of intense nationalism. A French nobleman, Arthur, comte de Gobineau (1816–1882), wrote *The Inequality of Human Races* (1853), defending the thesis that the black races are very inferior to the white races and that the yellow races stand between the two. He contended that the European sub-races, which he falsely called "races," revealed very important differences. The Nordic, he said, was the superior white "race," the Alpine and Mediterranean were inferior. Today this book is thoroughly discredited by every competent anthropologist, but in its time it had a considerable vogue, especially in Germany.

After the establishment of the German Empire in 1871 came a great outburst of patriotism among the Germans for all things Teutonic. To support their belief in themselves and to impress others, many Germans began defending this now-called "Nordic" theory of superiority. Since the German population is not Nordic, but a mixture of Alpine and Nordic, and in some sections other European stocks, there was no sound biological basis for such a belief. But it was contended that the Teutonic culture was a Nordic product and that the leadership of Europe had been recruited from Nordic blood.[4] Since 1933 the Nazi regime has revived this social myth under the term "Aryanism" (as a device for social control), and contends that the Aryans, i.e., Germans, are a distinct race with special and superior capacities.

Outside of Germany this Nordic notion had little vogue until in this country, after the World War, certain writers began telling our older American citizens that our recent immigrants (since 1880) were injuring our pure Nordic stock. Madison Grant, a retired business man turned amateur paleontologist, published his *Passing of the Great Race* in 1916, a book which caught the popular fancy and led to a flood of books and articles all crying out for restrictive measures to prevent the dissipation of our better native stock. Then, too, the rise of Japan to world power following her defeat of Russia in 1904 stimulated fear of Oriental invasion, which the World War period enhanced, and Lothrop Stoddard's *The Rising Tide of Color* (1920) added fuel to the burning prejudices against other races. Moreover, various writers on population expressed fears that the colored

[4]See H. S. Chamberlain, *The Foundations of the Nineteenth Century*, 1899.

races would in time overwhelm the whites as the latter restricted their birth rates while the former were rapidly expanding their populations. (See Chapter IX.)

These beliefs caught the popular patriotic sympathy of the time and further increased the belief in white, especially Nordic, superiority in this country. While the same problem arose elsewhere, in South Africa and in the Asiatic seacoast regions where whites had settled, our American situation will serve as an example.

On the basis of these beliefs, sound or unsound, what has psychology to say on the matter of mentality of races? Are popular notions about inferiority sound? Are popular fears about overpopulation well founded? We shall deal with only the first of these questions here. The second we shall take up in Chapter IX bearing on population.

Tests of Intellectual Capacities. A common belief about primitive peoples is that they have wonderful sensory powers of sight, smell, hearing, etc., far in excess of those of the white man, but that they lack logical thinking capacity.

The first adequate tests of other races compared to whites were made about 1900 by two British psychologists, Charles S. Myers and William McDougall, when they measured the various senses of seeing, hearing, and the like among the inhabitants of the Torres Straits. Later, in our own country, R. S. Woodworth and F. G. Bruner tested a wide variety of pre-literates at the St. Louis Exposition in 1904. Since then still other investigations have been made on various native tribes. All this work showed primitives equal to whites in sensory and motor tests.

The intelligence tests developed since 1905 showed the black race inferior to the white in the higher mental processes, but it was after 1917, when group tests were developed, that a mass of new "evidence" was collected.

Nearly two million men from all parts of this country, from all occupational classes, and made up of first-generation Americans, American whites of long American ancestry, Negroes, and foreign-born, were given the army group tests: Alpha, a linguistic test, or Beta, a performance test. About the same time reports on similar tests applied to schoolchildren of various classes and races began to appear.

The various tests showed, for the most part, marked differences between the average scores of the whites when compared to the

Negroes, mulattoes, and American Indians. Most studies also showed the whites at least slightly superior to the Orientals, but not so markedly so as they were to the blacks. When applied to various sub-racial or nationality stocks in the white group itself, some rather sharp differences appeared. The native whites of British or north European backgrounds were superior to the foreign-born or children of foreign-born who came from southern and eastern Europe, with the possible exception of certain Jewish samples from eastern Europe.[5] While average differences were clear, the overlapping of the groups was marked in every instance.

These findings seemed to furnish scientific support to the contentions of such persons as Madison Grant, Lothrop Stoddard, and Albert E. Wiggam. It helped inflame popular prejudice against the colored races and against immigrant groups.

What the Tests Really Show. Certainly the tests show differences, but the basic question, however, remained: How are we to interpret these differences? Do they mean that we have discovered a method of determining biological racial differences superior to anything which the anatomist has worked out?

In answering this we must ask another question: What do the tests test? The assumption of the early testers in this country was that the mental tests measured something innate called intelligence; but it is clear to anyone but the most prejudiced that intelligence and the tests of intelligence all reflect the social and cultural milieu out of which they grow. Yet those psychologists who, following the lead of Sir Francis Galton, hold that intelligence reflects heredity, do not accept these cultural interpretations. While the controversy over the biological inheritance of intelligence continues, it should be clear that until the psychologist can control the factors of language, and past learning, that is, culture, he is not in a position to support the hereditary theory. As we saw in Chapter V, no one doubts that individuals differ in their capacity to learn, or that there is a slight percentage of the population which is physically and mentally atypical—the low-grade feebleminded. But this is a far cry from the wholesale notion that intelligence differences in races, as measured by the tests—themselves cultural products—rest chiefly upon hereditary grounds. Race, sociologi-

[5] For data on army testing see *Memoirs of the National Academy of Science,* vol. XV: *Psychological Examining in the United States Army,* ed. by R. M. Yerkes, 1921.

cally, means nothing without respect to culture; hence all so-called racial testing is really cultural testing. Recent work shows that differences among various groups of whites is quite as great as, or greater than, the differences in the average performance of various racial groups on the tests. Among the important factors are those of language, formal schooling, social and economic conditions, and attitudes toward speed or testing methods themselves.

Language is clearly a most important factor in intellectual activity. But all tests dependent upon language must take culture into account. Races or other groups are distinctly handicapped in taking tests framed in a language with which they are at best only partially familiar. Margaret Mead's study of Italian children in Hammonton, New Jersey, showed that there was a steady improvement in the test results in terms of the amount of English spoken in the homes of the children.[6]

Similar tests on Orientals show the same sort of results. The army tests of our immigrant men showed a distinct correlation between length of residence in this country and performance on the tests, which is another way of measuring familiarity with language and culture.[7]

The work of Mandel Sherman and Cora B. Key cited in Chapter V well shows the influence of culture.[8] If such conditions affect white American children, children of immigrants and of other races face the same sort of difficulty in reaching the norms of American children in the tests. The army test study also revealed that New York City Negroes almost equaled the scores of southern whites, but that the latter excelled the southern Negroes.[9]

Hundreds of examples could be given to show how completely many interpretations of the tests fail to take into account the cultural background of the persons tested. Even if formal schooling and occupational standing are equalized before testing various racial groups, there still remain other problems of culture.

Miss Velma Helmer at the University of Kansas undertook a study to expose this matter. She devised a test made up of items in the experience of the Indian tribes represented at Haskell

[6] Margaret Mead, "Group Intelligence Tests and Linguistic Disability among Italian Children," *School and Society*, April 16, 1927, vol. XXV, pp. 465–68.

[7] See *Memoirs of the National Academy of Sciences, op. cit.*

[8] See S. L. Pressey and J. B. Thomas, "A Study of Country Children in (*1*) a Good, and (*2*) a Poor Farming District," etc., *Journal of Applied Psychology*, 1919, vol. III, pp. 283–86, for a study showing how important cultural factors are.

[9] A. L. Kroeber, *Anthropology*, pp. 77–79.

Institute, an Indian school in Kansas. Otto Klineberg summarizes some features of her work as follows:

"The tests were modelled on the 'Best Answer' type, and other standard types, so that they cannot be said really to be alien to the white child in that sense, but they contained references to 'tepee' and 'hogun,' to Indian foodstuffs, religious ceremonies, social customs, etc., which were more familiar to Indian than to white children. On many of these tests, the white children were definitely inferior. This is obviously an unfair test of American white intelligence, but not more so than many other tests are of Negro or Indian or Italian intelligence."[10]

Thus a knowledge of the cultural differences and of the varying manner in which races value experience, should make us cautious about any easy notion of marked differences in mentality based on intelligence tests developed by white scholars.

Two other things may be mentioned briefly. One of these is the necessary *co-operation between the tester and those tested*. Fear, suspicion, strangeness, all prevent the persons tested from doing their best work.

Related to this factor is that of *motive*. Do the persons tested want to put forth their best efforts? This is highly important for successful and comparable results. The matter is related both to general culture and to the immediate test situation.

In present-day schools with the emphasis on rivalry, competition, good marks, and speed, paper and pencil tests given to pupils may easily arouse in them the desire to "shine" and to make the best possible records. With American Indians, with Negroes, or with foreign-born immigrant children, it may be difficult to secure their interest. Again it is hard to measure this matter, but it is highly important to recognize it. All the recent work on the relation of emotional attitudes to motivation leads to the belief that it is one of the most important single factors making for good performance in the tests, as it certainly is an important factor in ordinary school success, and for that matter in success in daily adult life in any occupation or profession. Without the drive, the will to try, little is accomplished anywhere. An illustration is in point:

A few years ago Otto Klineberg carried on rather extensive studies to discover how the factor of speed is reflected in the behavior of various

[10] From Otto Klineberg, "An Experimental Study of Speed and Other Factors in 'Racial' Differences." *Archives of Psychology*, No. 93, Jan., 1928, p. 15. Taken from Velma Helmer, *The American Indian and Mental Tests*. Unpublished M. A. thesis, University of Kansas, 1926.

racial groups in handling tests. Speed is so obviously correlated with various aspects of our daily lives that we find it hard to imagine any people, unless they be dull, who do not do things in a hurry. He gave a number of performance tests to white children aged about 7 to 16 years, and to American Indians and Negroes of about the same ages. Among the Indian groups studied were children from the Yakima tribe in the State of Washington, and from Haskell Institute; Negroes from New York City and from West Virginia were examined. The white children came from the same regions as the colored. Klineberg's purpose was to eliminate the language factor and to concentrate upon the problem of speed and accuracy. His results show distinctly that in speed the white children excel the Indians and Negroes, although interestingly enough those Indians and Negroes who had lived in more complex and urban cultures dominated by white notions of speed do better than their racial fellows who come from the rural South or from the reservations of the Far West. In other words, as the colored races take on the type of life which to the white person is "normal," they approach him in this "normal" trait of speed. It seems reasonably sound to conclude that environmental, that is, cultural, factors play a larger part in determining speed than does innate racial difference.

In the matter of accuracy there is no superiority of the whites over the colored races, and in some instances the colored boys and girls excelled the white children in this item. Klineberg also showed that there is little, if any, direct relation between proportion of white blood in mixed colored groups and their performance on the tests. Most of the attempts to correlate percentage of white blood in mixed races with test scores have been very badly controlled, and his results should make us skeptical of the usual material published on this matter. Until we control both the biological mixing and the culture of these mixed bloods, such studies mean little.[11]

Innate Ability and Race. We may now return to the question asked at the beginning of the present section: Are there any marked differences in mentality by which we may distinguish between the races or sub-races? Our rather brief review of a vast field of material answers with a rather decided, "No." While it may be extreme and presumptuous to say at this moment that all races are equal in all mental abilities, we can say with fair assurance that so far as carefully controlled studies go, there do not seem to be any marked differences in mentality between races, except as they are determined by culture and social experience, such as schooling, standards of behavior, motivation, attitudes of co-operation, and other matters which are learned and not biologically inherited.

[11] Summarized from Klineberg, *op. cit.*

Even where there are some differences in average performance, the overlapping is very great. Hence even in mental test findings it is clearly evident that variability is marked, and in mental as in physical traits no sharp and distinct lines may be drawn.

Using a simple theory of mental heredity, many have said that northern Negroes are superior to southern ones because the smarter Negroes come North, that urban children are smarter than rural children because only the duller people remain in the country, that the immigrant stock coming to America from 1880 to 1914 got increasingly worse, biologically. These differences seem clearly to reflect opportunity and culture rather than racial ability. As we have noted in Chapter V, the simple theories of biological inheritance adopted by the defenders of mental inheritance fall down in the face of the more dynamic view of the interrelation of heredity and environment from the moment of germination to maturity. The stickler for heredity and marked race differences is faced with the enormous task of explaining in his naïve biology some of the most complicated activities known to civilized man, some of which have been acquired only in the last few generations. Unless he wishes to believe in a very simple theory of inheritance of acquired characteristics, he must load upon the doctrine of biological heredity and upon mutation some amazing responsibilities.

It is not that differences in intelligence do not exist between races and sub-races. They do. The problem is what causes these differences. The evidence seems to point rather clearly to environmental factors rather than to strictly hereditary ones. For sociological purposes these facts of intelligence differences and social differences are highly important, but to attempt to account for them in terms of biological inheritance, or to use them for distinguishing between one race and another on biological grounds is presumptuous indeed.

CLASS ASSIGNMENTS

A. Further reading assignment:

1. K. Young, *Source Book for Sociology*, chap. VIII.
2. A. L. Kroeber, *Anthropology*, chaps. III, IV.
3. T. R. Garth, *Race Psychology*, chap. XIII.

B. Questions and exercises:

1. Why is the popular notion of race unscientific and unsatisfactory for our purposes? Illustrate popular misconceptions of race. Illustrate accurate conceptions.

2. What are the commonest and most easily accepted criteria of race? Why are the common-sense criteria so largely unscientific? Which criteria seem to be on the whole the best? Point out some of the difficulties in determining sharply between the major race stocks.

3. Are intelligence tests good measures of inherited racial differences? Discuss pro and con.

4. What makes it so difficult to determine the strictly biologically inherited factors in intelligence?

5. What are the cultural purposes (nationalistic, economic, religious, etc.) of the Nazi propaganda in defense of Aryanism? Cite illustrations of the Nazi doctrines on race. (See newspaper and periodical files; *e.g.*, see H. L. Childs, "The Nazi Primer," *Harper's Magazine*, Aug., 1938, vol. CLXXVII, pp. 240–47.)

C. Topics for class reports or longer written papers:

1. The development of prehistoric man. (Consult Sir Arthur Keith, *The Antiquity of Man*, rev. ed., 2 vols., 1928; E. A. Hooton, *Up from the Ape*, 1931; J. H. McGregor, "Human Origins and Early Man," chap. II in *General Anthropology*, ed. by F. Boas, 1938.)

2. Interrelations of race and culture. (Consult R. H. Lowie, *Culture and Ethnology*, 1917, chap. II; F. Boas, "Race," *Encyclopedia of the Social Sciences*, 1934, vol. XIII, pp. 25–36 and bibliography; R. Linton, *The Study of Man*, 1936, chap. II; A. Goldenweiser, *Anthropology*, 1937, chap. II; O. Klineberg, *Race Differences*, 1935.)

3. Recent studies in the measurement of Negro intelligence in this country. (Consult Garth, *Race Psychology*, 1931, and bibliography; O. Klineberg, *op. cit.*; *Psychological Abstracts;* and the summary articles which appear from time to time in the *Psychological Bulletin*.)

4. The recent findings concerning intelligence testing among Orientals and American Indians. (Consult same references as above.)

5. Critique of the Nordic hypothesis. (Consult F. H. Hankins, *The Racial Basis of Civilization*, 1927, and bibliography therein; J. Barzun, *Race, a Study in Modern Superstition*, 1937. See files of *Readers' Guide* for recent materials, especially in reference to the recent doctrine of Aryanism in Germany.)

CHAPTER IX

PROBLEMS OF WORLD POPULATION

There is a clear relationship between the size and composition of population and the nature of the societal order and culture. It is a commonplace today that the cultural changes in the last 175 years are more vast and far-reaching than corresponding changes in the previous 5,000 years. And rapid increase in population has been associated with these changes.

In this chapter two important features of population will be discussed: first, the relation of population to food supply and to modern industrial organization, and second, the different rates of population increase among the nations in recent decades. The first produces a problem of survival of peoples everywhere. The second concerns the "danger spots" of excessive population which may produce war and other conflict.

PRESSURE OF POPULATION ON THE FOOD SUPPLY

Population increase clearly depends on the excess of births over deaths. After centuries with but slight growth in numbers, the world began to witness an amazing increase. The marked increase in population began to be apparent in the eighteenth century, and in the nineteenth century it became even more imposing.

In 1650 the estimated population of the world was 465 millions. This had risen to 660 millions within the next 100 years, and to 1,098 millions by 1850. Estimates for 1938 put it well over 1,900 millions. Figure 7, page 168, shows a recent estimate of the population growth of the world since 1650. The increase in the white race alone is striking. The white population for the year 1000 A. D. is estimated at 30 millions. By 1800 this had risen to 210 millions; by 1915 the figure had grown to 645 millions. In other words, in 115 years the white race had increased 2.5 times as much as it had in the previous 800 years. Or take some figures nearer our own culture and nationality.　Great Britain in 1821 had 21 million people; in 1921 she had more than doubled this to 43 millions.　Similar increases in population have taken place elsewhere in the world, too, but not at such a marked rate.　Most of this tremendous increase in world population has come as the result of cutting down the death

FIGURE 7

WORLD POPULATION GROWTH, 1650–1930

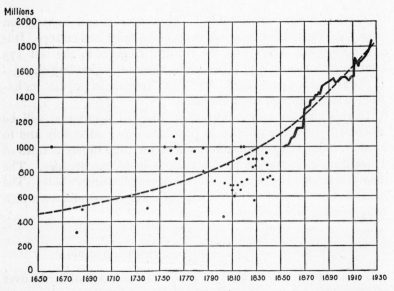

Contemporary estimates (dots and solid line) and present estimates (dash line) of world population at various times since 1650.[1]

rate, not by raising the birth rate.　This reduction in death rate was an outcome of medical science which accompanied the Industrial Revolution.　Infant mortality was reduced, and infectious and contagious diseases were controlled.　The consequent greater numbers were absorbed into the factories or became agricultural colonists, out to produce more food for the other millions of mouths.

Yet it is natural to ask: Can this rapid multiplication of peoples go on indefinitely until, in the words of one writer, there may be "standing room only"?　Are there no limits to the number of people that the world can support?　Let us see what the evidence is.

[1] From *International Migrations*, ed. by W. F. Willcox, 1931, vol. II, p. 79.

Theories of Population and Food Supply. The great changes in commercial and economic life and the rapid spread of political democracy in the eighteenth century sounded a note of optimism that found ready expression in the doctrine of social progress. This optimism found even more striking expression in the nineteenth century. (See Chapter III on cultural change.) Such men as the enthusiastic Marquis de Condorcet in France and William Godwin (1756–1836) in England typify the growing faith of the period in the steady march of mankind toward perfection. Once poverty, misery, vice, war, and crime were removed by proper social arrangements, all would be well. Godwin went so far as to say:

"Make men wise, and by that very operation you make them free. . . . There will be no war, no crime, no administration of justice as it is called, and no government. Besides this, there will be neither disease, anguish, melancholy, nor resentment. Every man will seek with effable ardor the good of all."[2]

On the other hand, there were some who were not so optimistic and who saw in war, poverty, and the sordid conditions of the peasants and city masses generally a challenge to this very faith in man's perfectibility. Thus arose two divergent schools of thought about the whole problem, one of optimism, one of pessimism. The controversy broke out in reference to population with the publication of an answer to Godwin by an English clergyman, Thomas R. Malthus (1766–1834), entitled *An Essay on the Principle of Population as It Affects the Future Improvement of Society*, etc. (1st ed. 1798). He contended that Godwin was wrong in blaming circumstances for our societal ills. It was original nature that was at fault. The sexual urges leading to reproduction tended to people the world more rapidly than man could increase his sustenance. Thus, in a time when romantic reformers were preaching doctrines of unlimited human progress, Malthus had quietly gone to work making calculations concerning the relation of food supply to population increase. He contended that there is a "constant tendency in all animated life to increase beyond the nourishment prepared for it"; that is, animal life is endowed with the capacity for rapid reproduction, but the food supply is restricted within definite limits. As he put it, "wherever . . . there is liberty, the

[2]Quoted by J. O. Hertzler, *Social Progress*, 1928, pp. 46–47.

power of increase is exerted, and the superabundant effects are repressed afterwards for want of room and nourishment." Applying this principle to human beings, he worked out the following formula: "Population, when unchecked, goes on doubling itself every twenty-five years, or increases in a geometric ratio." Food supply (which he calls "means of subsistence")[3] "under circumstances the most favorable to human industry, could not possibly be made to increase faster than in arithmetical ratio." In other words a population will increase every 25 years in the ratios of 1, 2, 4, 8, 16, 32, 64, and so on, while the food supply, at best, would increase in the ratios of 1, 2, 3, 4, etc. According to this computation, unless checked, in 200 years a population would stand, in reference to food, in the proportion of 256 to 9.

With this thesis before him, based as it was not on mere fantasy but on computations of population and food production of his time, he inquired as to the checks on population growth. These are of two sorts: positive and preventive. The *positive* checks are those of vice and misery growing out of poverty or want of food, such as disease, deterioration of morality, and want. The *preventive* checks are celibacy, deferment of marriage, and moral (that is, sexual) restraint, leading to reduction in the number of births.

No devices of political or economic organization or of emigration would stop the positive checks from operating, Malthus argued, except the moral checks upon the biological passions. This did not imply, so rationalized the pious Malthus, that God has not our welfare at heart, but rather that "natural and moral evil seems to be the instrument employed by the Deity in admonishing us to avoid any mode of conduct which is not suited to our being, and will consequently injure our happiness."[4] Although a strong moralist at heart, Malthus admirably expresses the doctrine of *laissez-faire* individualism in the political and economic fields. There is nothing that we can do about this struggle of the individual for food and shelter except to apply the principles of piety and self-restraint. His thesis of a *law* operating to restrict population was an expression of the eighteenth-century mechanistic concep-

---

[3] Malthus confuses the reader by identifying food supply and subsistence. At times he discusses what we today call "standard of living," which includes more than food. Elsewhere he uses "means of subsistence" to include only food.
[4] These quotations are from the 9th edition of his *Essay*.

tion of the universe presenting a determinism in nature which no one could escape.

Malthus apparently never heard of modern means of birth control, but defended sexual restraint as conducive both to high standards of living and to greater personal character as well. Many stupid accusations have been unjustly made against Malthus. He certainly did not advocate contraception as a means of gratifying personal desires without social responsibility. Above all else his writing was timely. It gave a needed dash of cold facts to the glowing enthusiasm of the Utopian dreamers of the time, who seemed so completely to ignore the natural and biological foundations of society.

The doctrine of progress and man's perfectibility might be easy to scotch, but it was hard to kill. Nineteenth-century enthusiasts arose on every hand to disagree with Malthus.[5] Significant expressions of optimism were found in the work of Karl Marx (1818–1883), who denied that population necessarily outran the food supply. He held that the problem of excessive population resulted from the exploitation of the masses by the capitalist class. Once the injustices of faulty distribution of wealth were remedied, there would be food enough for all. Henry George (1839–1897), best known for his theory of the single tax on land values, argued "that nowhere can want be properly attributed to the pressure of population against the power to procure subsistence in the then existing degree of human knowledge; that everywhere the vice and misery attributed to overpopulation can be traced to the warfare, tyranny, and oppression which prevent knowledge from being utilized and deny the security essential to production."[6] It was only a faulty economic and political order that "in the midst of wealth condemns man to want."

Throughout the nineteenth century, however, population continued to increase at a rapid rate. In spite of free land and increased industrial production with its call for laborers, poverty, misery, vice, crime, and hardship persisted. With a view to improving the conditions of the masses, there arose in England about 1880 a movement known as *Neo-Malthusianism*. It aimed to educate the masses to consciously cut down the number of births. These re-

[5]See Warren S. Thompson, *Population Problems,* 2nd ed., 1935, chap. III, for review and comments on these theories.
[6]Quoted by E. A. Ross, *Tests and Challenges in Sociology,* 1931, p. 8.

formers contended that the spread of contraceptive practices reducing the birth rate would lead to an improvement in health, in family life, and in the standards of living.

But the critics of birth control were not far behind. As birth rates did decline the cry of "race suicide" was heard. One of the most vocal exponents of large families and rapid increase of population was Theodore Roosevelt (1859–1919), who expressed the beliefs and attitudes of millions who saw in the declining birth rate a threat at man's very existence. They were particularly afraid that white supremacy might be the price of a Neo-Malthusian program.

In the face of these continued differences of opinion about population pressure, what view may we take today?

Population, Food Supply, and Culture. Without doubt population and food supply are related. But these are not the only factors to be taken into consideration in discussing the increase in world population. The densely crowded countries of northwestern Europe could not possibly support themselves from the food raised on their own land, but they furnish goods and services to other regions, which in turn provide them with foodstuffs and raw materials. Technological advances have provided work for millions in production, manufacturing, and distribution of these goods. So long as commerce between sections of the world can go on freely, large massing of population in industrial centers is not serious. Great Britain in the eighteenth and nineteenth centuries is a classic example of concentration of population and industrial service. Drawing upon remote regions for raw materials and foods, she became both the factory and the merchant of the world. Her own population increased rapidly, and the general conditions of living improved. Medical science made the cities more healthful, fewer mothers sacrificed themselves in childbirth, fewer babies died in the early months of life, and the whole condition of the people was bettered, without expansion in agricultural production proper in comparison to the increase in population.

In spite of the tremendous improvement in agricultural production, most of which recently has come from mechanical devices and not from improvement in natural fertility of land, in spite of the rising consciousness of the need to conserve forest and mineral resources, in spite of the possibility of synthetic foods produced by applied chemistry, and in spite of increased industrialization, there is no doubt that in many parts of the world population is still pressing on the means of subsistence: foods, timber, coal, iron, and oil. We saw in Chapter VII that land and climate distinctly limit the range of man's habitation. Of the total land surface of the earth little more than one third is available for raising food and other necessary articles of consumption. Yet the number of people which the world will support is, of course, definitely related to the standards of living. The earth would support at a bare subsistence level a great many more people than there are now.

When we translate the food supply of the world into equivalents in productive land, we find wide variation: first, in terms of productivity of the soil, and second, in standards of living. Warren S. Thompson has estimated that throughout the whole world there are 5.5 acres of agricultural land per person. This is a much larger area than is actually being used. The number of persons per acre varies enormously. In China, Thompson says, there are not less than 1.5 persons per acre of tilled land, about 2 in Java, and slightly more than 3 in Japan. In the United States in 1925 there were about 0.3 persons per acre of land in farm crops, and .125 persons per acre of total farm land. In other words, the United States has ten times as much tilled land per person as does Japan, nearly seven times as much as Java, and four or five times as much as China. When we take into account pasture and forest lands, the differences are still greater. What does this mean for future population possibilities?

Assuming no further technological advances and assuming that there are between 15.7 and 16.4 million square miles of productive land in the world, that this land is everywhere as fertile as that of this country, and that we expect the American standard of material comforts to prevail universally, it is evident that the world might support three or three and a half billion people. If the productive land could be used as intensively as much of the land in central, western, and northern Europe is now used, the world might well support a population of from four to five billions, at our standards of agricultural consumption. If, on the other hand, the world should be reduced to the lower levels of food consumption of the Japanese or the Chinese, the earth would support approximately ten billions.

High standards of living give a definite motive for consciously cutting down the birth rate. Certainly if the standards developed in this country and in northwestern Europe and her colonies, with all they imply for birth control, are diffused or spread to the Orient, to native Africa, and to South America, the growth of population is going to be very different from what it would be if the lower standards of these other regions should be forced upon Western societies. This raises the entire problem of the differences in population increase among the various nations and the meaning of these for world population problems.

DIFFERENTIAL RATES OF POPULATION GROWTH AMONG NATIONS

The people of the earth are not scattered uniformly over the various land masses, nor are all areas equally acceptable as places of residence. When these striking variations among the world regions become associated with nationalist ambitions, we have a clue to many of the most important population problems of today. In this section we shall examine certain facts about these variations in population, then examine the statistics of births and deaths, and close with an analysis of the "danger spots in world population."

Density of Population.   The people of the earth are not scattered evenly over the land surfaces, but tend to be concentrated in certain regions and not in others. Thus in Asia the wide steppes of Siberia, the large stretches of the Arabian, Mongolian, and Turkestan deserts, and the extensive mountainous areas in Manchukuo, in northern India, southwestern Tibet, and elsewhere make up at least half the land area of that continent. These regions support very few people. In contrast the rich river valleys of India and China support millions. Thus density of population must be taken into account, and concentration of people depends not on mere area alone but also on fertility of the soil, on natural resources, and on the type of the culture in the region.

The whole matter is clearly shown in Table 3, which gives the population per square mile for selected regions of the world, classified in terms of high and low density.

Not only does density vary among nations, but within any given country congestion occurs in certain sections. For example, in 1925 in highly industrialized Saxony there were 1,043 people per square mile; whereas the more rural East Prussia had but 161. In the United States, Rhode Island had a density of 644.3 per square mile in 1930, in contrast to Nevada, with 0.8 of a person per square mile. These differences in density reflect divergences in natural

TABLE 3

Countries of high density	Persons per square mile	Countries of low density	Persons per square mile
Belgium	705.0	Soviet Russia	20.0
England and Wales	680.0	Argentina	12.8
Italy	355.0	Australia	2.2
Japan	469.0	Union of South Africa	14.7
Java	817.5	United States	41.3
India	194.7	Canada	2.9

resources and their use, in division of labor, and in the whole culture complex of the respective regions. Where industry is highly developed, as in Belgium or England and Wales, so long as international trade is possible, a concentrated population may live. In other countries such concentration may be possible only as the standard of living is lowered. In Japan, industry and low standard of living go together. It is especially in areas like Italy, Japan, and China that the demand for expansion is most apparent. The pressure on the food supply and other means of support in these areas is terrific, and it is only natural that any number of political, economic, and sociological questions should arise. Various Western writers have warned us fully of these dangers. Warren S. Thompson introduces the argument in the preface to his book *Danger Spots in World Population* (1929) in these words:

". . . I have come to believe that the differential pressure of peoples on their resources is one of the important causes of friction between nations. The knowledge that such differentials exist is spreading rapidly in the world today. Furthermore, these differentials are increasing more rapidly today than ever before because changes in the rate of population growth are not the same in all lands. In some parts of the world, population growth is declining and will soon cease; in other parts of the world there is a large increase which is likely to continue for some decades; while in still other parts conditions are just shaping to inaugurate an increase. Now it so happens that the peoples who are already feeling keenly the need of new lands and resources are also the ones who are likely to have large increases for the next few decades. I cannot but believe that these differential pressures which will be more and more keenly felt in the near future will lead to efforts to secure lands and

[7] Based on most recent figures from various sources.

resources which can be used to relieve pressure where it is severe and thus equalize it in some measure.

"Will the efforts to equalize pressures result in war or will some other method of adjustment be found?"[8]

The whole matter comes down, therefore, to differences in the birth rates and death rates in various sections of the world. Modern science has cut down the death rate, but birth rates remain high in many areas. Let us look more closely at some of the facts.

Birth Rates. In discussing population growth it is necessary to distinguish between fecundity and fertility. *Fecundity* refers to the full potential or possible powers of reproduction in a population. That is, it is the potential birth rate if every woman of childbearing age—say the years 15 to 44—bore all the children she possibly could. Naturally fecundity is more dependent on the age and reproductive capacity of the female population than of the male. It has been estimated that normal women are capable of bearing an average of fifteen children. If such a high birth rate existed, the world population would increase enormously, unless checked by a high death rate.

Fertility refers to the actual rate of reproduction. It also is affected by age and other factors. Fertility is measured by the birth rate, but we must distinguish between the crude birth rates and the refined or specific rates. The crude birth rate is simply the number of births per 1,000 of population at a given period. Thus a population of 1,000,000 having 30,000 births in a year would have a crude birth rate of 30. The refined or specific birth rate is the births per 1,000 of women of childbearing age, usually figured from 15 to 44 years. The crude birth rate gives an estimate of the fertility of any population, but it leaves out of account matters in regard to age, sex, nativity composition, and various cultural factors.

For our purposes here the crude birth rates will reveal the changes in population growth in various countries. We do not know what the crude birth rate was before the nineteenth century. It probably exceeded 50 in most agricultural areas. Accurate statistics of birth rates in many parts of the world are not available. But let us look at some examples of changes in birth rates in selected countries where such facts are known. R. R.

---

[8]See also E. M. East, *Mankind at the Crossroads*, 1923, and Sir George Handley Knibbs, *The Shadow of the World's Future*, 1928.

Kuczynski thinks that the birth rate of the United States exceeded 50 in the years 1790 to 1820.[9] Other estimates place it at 35.[10]

At the opening of the last century, the crude birth rate in Finland was 35 per 1,000; in France, 31.4; in Sweden, 31.8; in Denmark, 29.5; in Norway, 32.7. The first available figures for England and Wales, for 1838–1842, give 31.6. Figures for other European countries are not available before the second half of the last century. But estimates for the Balkan states give 40 and better. Poland for 1898–1902 reported 43.7. The first figures for Russia, for 1866–1870, give 48.9. The figures for India are at best rough estimates, but for 1888–1892 the crude rate was 34.8, and for 1908–1912 it had risen to 38.4. For New Zealand, a typical pioneer country, the rate for 1868–1872 was 41.4; and for Australia, for the same period, it was 38.6.

Yet in recent decades in nearly all European countries, in the United States, and in the British possessions, the birth rates have declined rapidly. Kuczynski estimates for western and northern European countries that from 1841 to 1936 the birth rate fell from 31.9 to 17.0. It is generally agreed that the first sharp decline occurred in the 1880's, to be followed by an even sharper and more obvious decline during and after the World War. In the United States before 1929, our figures for the entire country are but estimates.[11] We know that the birth rate in 1920 was about one half what it was in 1820. In 1910 the crude rate of the United States was 26.6; for 1933 it was 16.6; for 1937, 17.0.

The specific birth rate within any nation is influenced by any number of factors, some biological, some cultural, the former including age, race, and nativity; the latter including such things as marital status, occupation, social class, religious affiliation, and type of community. These factors are important in regard to the social composition of any nation and will be discussed in the next chapter. For the world problem, the excess of births over deaths is the important factor. What has happened to the death rate?

Death Rate. Mortality may be measured by the crude death rate, which is the ratio between the number of individuals who die

[9]See his article "Births," *Encyclopedia of the Social Sciences,* vol. II, p. 569, also "The International Decline of Fertility," in *Political Arithmetic* (ed. by L. Hogben), 1938.

[10]E. B. Reuter, *Population Problems,* rev. ed., 1937, p. 222.

[11]In 1929 the entire country first came under the "registration area," *e.g.,* all states now report births according to federal regulations.

in a given interval of time and the median number of individuals alive during the interval, usually stated in thousands. Thus, a death rate of 12 means 12 deaths per 1,000 of the population. Specific death rates are computed for age, sex, and other factors.

Among primitive peoples both the birth rates and the mortality rates are high. And the births in many higher societies just about balance the deaths, so that the population remains practically stationary for generations. Figures from Hongkong, China, for 1909 show that 87 per cent of the children born there died under one year of age. From certain South African cities the death rate among the native (non-European) sections of the population is often two to three times that of the white population. Certainly in countries outside western Europe, the United States, Canada, New Zealand, Australia, and the scattered European colonies, until recently, high death rates have accompanied high birth rates. E. B. Reuter says that the present average death rate for the world is probably well above 25, but gives no data for his estimate.[12] Accurate figures are hard to get but in many regions the death rate remains high in spite of advances in medicine which have reduced infant mortality.

Yet recent decades have witnessed a rapid decline in the death rate. This trend has been going on in Europe for well over a century. There has been a similar decline in mortality in the United States, although adequate statistics for the entire country have been available only recently. The annual average in 1906–1910 for the registration area was 15 per 1,000. The death rate has fallen off considerably since then, except in 1918, when it was 18 because of an influenza epidemic. In 1920 it had dropped to 13; in 1930 to 11.8; in 1935 to 10.9. In 1937 it was 11.2.

While the principal decline in the death rates has occurred among Western nations, the phenomenon is world wide. Although the birth rate is also falling, it is evident that the mortality rates in many regions are falling somewhat faster.

Medical science has most strikingly influenced the death rate in the early years of life. A noteworthy decline in infant and child mortality is evident in every civilized country. Table 4 gives a few samples only.

The decline in child mortality is usually attributed to the following causes: (1) improvement in child care at home, especially

[12]See E. B. Reuter, *op. cit.*, p. 246.

TABLE 4

INFANT MORTALITY IN SELECTED COUNTRIES. DEATHS UNDER ONE YEAR
PER 1,000 LIVE BIRTHS[13]

Countries	1937 (Provisional)	Average rates for various approximate periods			
		1931–1935	1921–1925	1908–1912	1885–1895
New Zealand	31	32	43	61	88
Sweden	46	50	60	75	108
Switzerland	47	48	65	109	160
United States	54	59	74	...	...
England and Wales	58	62	76	112	148
Germany	64	74	122	170	207
France	65	73	95	123	168
Italy	110	105	126	147	190
Japan	117	120	159	159	155
Hungary	135	157	187	200	250
Rumania	178	182	209	...	205
Chile	241	248	265	314	...

in feeding and sanitation; (2) decrease in the number of children
born to the average mother, thus allowing for more adequate care
of those who are born; (3) improvement in medical care of children; and (4) the general improvement in economic status of
large sections of the population of the more advanced societies.
In regard to the second factor, various studies in France, in England, and in this country bear out the fact that infant mortality is
much lower in small-sized than in large-sized families. Lucien
March showed that in France the death rate during a given period
for first-born children in families of one or two offspring was 106
per 1,000 births; for first-born children in families of three to six
offspring, 221 per 1,000, and in families of seven or more, 265 per
1,000 births. The facts for England and this country are much
the same. As a British study on fertility states, when pregnancies
and births became too frequent, the risk of infant mortality "more
than counterbalanced the advantages" of the higher birth rate.[14]
Since small families reflect higher economic standards, it is evi-

[13]Data for 1885–1895 from Warren S. Thompson, *Population Problems*, 1930,
Table 50, p. 140; for 1908–1912, *ibid.*, rev. ed., 1935, Table 60, p. 182. Balance of
table from *Population Index*, July, 1938, vol. IV, Table 4, pp. 197–98. Computations are made on the basis of varying periods, so that in some instances only
approximate periods are covered. The sources give the precise dates in the more
extended tables. Data for the United States before 1922 are not complete. In 1900
for the registration area (ten states and selected cities) the infant mortality rate
was 165.4. In 1915, for the same states and cities, it had fallen to 99.8.

[14]*The Report on Fertility for 1911*, Part II, pp. l and li. Discussed in Thompson,
op. cit., p. 183.

dent that mortality is closely related to social and economic status. This, in turn, is a matter of standards of living. In countries where the bulk of the population lives near the bare subsistence level, the increase in population only adds to misery, poverty, and hardship, in spite of the medical care which may cut down the infant mortality.

The reduction in infant and child mortality has increased the expectation of life at birth. In 1935 in the United States the expectation of life at birth was 60.7 years for white males and 64.7 for white females. Any number of studies show that the real advances are made in cutting down deaths of infants and children under ten years of age. For ages above that, the death rates have not been reduced. In this country, in fact, the death rate of those above 55 years is actually increasing.

But the reduction of death in all ages the world over from the conquest of disease is an additional marvel. Malaria and yellow fever are being conquered, the bubonic plague has been practically wiped out, cholera occurs much less frequently than ever before, and such diseases as smallpox, diphtheria, measles, scarlet fever, and whooping cough are rapidly being eliminated so far as they seriously affect the death rate.

To repeat, the reduction in death rates in some countries, with no corresponding decline in the birth rates, leads to intensive population pressure, to desire for national expansion. In the Western world the reduction of both birth and death rates has been accompanied by rising standards of living and a general enrichment of the non-material phases of culture for the masses. Nothing like this has taken place in the Orient, in Africa, or in tropical Latin America, although the benefits of medicine have been more and more apparent in these latter regions.

Internationalism and Rates of Population Growth. Differences in rates of population growth among the nations complicate international relations. Rapid expansion of numbers is often associated with intense nationalism, with industrial and commercial competition, and with the desire for new land.

The principal grievance among the nations over the matter of land arises from the fact that northwestern European countries—chiefly Great Britain, France, and Holland—and the United States today control large areas of unused or underused lands which they will not permit other countries to settle and exploit.

The case of Japan is in point. The pressure of population there is severe. She is adding a million a year to her numbers. Industrially Japan is limited. Her situation is not like that of England in the last century. Japan lacks the natural resources for extensive industrialization, and her successful competition in foreign markets cannot be expanded much more without further ruthless exploitation of her working classes. Moreover, the death rate in that country, although still high, is likely to be reduced sharply by further application of medical science. What, then, remains for her to do? She must find new markets or expand her population into unused or underused lands or resort to a marked restriction of her own birth rate.

In much the same way Italy and the overpopulated Slavic countries of central Europe have little prospect of industrial growth and are blocked on every side from expansion into new, unused land.

In the light of these facts, what are some of the suggested solutions of the problem produced by these "danger spots" of excessive pressure of numbers? Among many solutions offered, we shall mention six: (1) emigration to other countries, (2) the postponement of the age of marriage, (3) the diffusion of the practice of birth control, (4) further advances in science which increase food supply, (5) peaceful international agreements looking to solution of problems arising in connection with the use of land, markets, raw materials, etc., and (6) the seizure by force of unused or underused land areas by those overpopulated nations which are powerful enough to effect it.

Emigration of excess population was common during the eighteenth and nineteenth centuries, when there were still new lands to colonize and when rising industrial countries like the United States called for cheap labor. Today this outlet is closed. Take the situation in Japan again. She cannot expand into Korea (Chosen), because the latter country is crowded and the Koreans live at a still lower level than do the Japanese. The same thing is true in Formosa. Much of Manchukuo and Siberia is cold and uninviting, and the former is limited in her resources, in spite of much popular talk to the contrary. On the other hand, the Philippines, Borneo, New Guinea, and Australia would give Japan room for expansion for perhaps 50 years.

Italy is in much the same situation. Like Japan she lacks the

natural resources for great industry. France and England doubtless will not permit Italy to expand greatly in Africa, though the
latter's conquest of Ethiopia (1936) was a move in that direction.
South America offers some outlet for emigration, but industrial
development and economic opportunities for large numbers in that
continent are still limited. Emigration from Italy to the United
States has virtually ceased because of our recent legislation.

Poland, Hungary, and Yugoslavia are also in an unfortunate
situation. Industrial expansion may do something for them, but
the limitations are obvious. What lands around them are available? Germany is crowded and is herself looking to the East for
additional land. Russia has her own expanding population and
is politically so powerful as to oppose movements in her direction.

Evidently, the prospect of emigration is slight. Moreover, such
a policy would only delay the solution of the ultimate problem. It
is well known that the relief of population pressure by emigration
does not prevent continued high rates of increase in the home
country; hence such a solution is temporary and in the present
world largely meaningless.

Postponement of the age of marriage has been practiced in some
countries faced with overpopulation. The classic example is Ireland in the last century. In spite of large emigration, recurrent
famine made life so hard there that the custom of deferring marriage became one means of restricting the size of families. There
seems to be some evidence of this method in Japan today, but it is
by no means a solution to the problem. Such a culture trait is not
likely to spread to large numbers. In India and Italy strong religious prejudice in favor of large families inhibits the development
of such a custom. This method, then, has distinct limitations, and
at best would only make the problem less serious.

As to the diffusion of birth-control practices, it must be realized
that the demand for expansion is psychological. As Thompson
puts it, "It is not *actual* pressure but *felt* pressure that creates the
international political problems arising from the differential birth
rates of nations." It rests in the social attitudes and beliefs of people, and not alone on the increasing number of mouths to be fed.
The people of Java are crowded upon each other too, but they lack
the nationalistic and industrial culture patterns of the Japanese or
Italians. Well-meant counsel of the advocates of birth control will
not accomplish much in the face of national ambitions. The social

beliefs and attitudes of these nations will have to change if they accept birth control.

There are some who firmly believe that the advantages of birth control, with all that it means for improving the quality of the population and for raising the standards of living, will soon become apparent to these overcrowded nations. But the diffusion into these countries of birth-control practices for large numbers is slow, and in the meantime the excessive population keeps growing.

Again culture is a powerful factor. In a country like China, where ancestor reverence remains strong, where children, especially boys, are at a premium as economic assets to protect old age against want, the propaganda for birth control falls on deaf ears. In Italy and the central Slavonic countries strong religious taboos prevent the spread of the practice of birth control among the masses. There is evidence that the upper economic classes in these countries do restrict the number of births, but this differential does not much affect the larger problem of rapid increase. (See Chapter X.)

The future of making synthetic foods by science lies in the lap of the gods. No one can safely predict what may be done to make foodstuffs cheaply by chemical methods. Furthermore, the growth of automatic machines may make it possible for us to manufacture goods at increasingly less expenditure of human energy. What a combination of cheap synthetic food and more leisure might do for the world's population no one knows. Still, without reference to these possible changes, we are confident today that with the widespread application of science, the earth could support at an average American standard of living nearly double its present population.

Peaceful international agreements regarding unused and underused lands and respecting a juster distribution of raw materials and of markets among the nations have been suggested in many quarters as a way out of the population dilemma. Yet the handicaps to this program are also obvious. We cannot think at present in terms of the world as a social unity. National boundaries and all they imply for prejudice and aggrandizement at the expense of others come into play. The world is not yet ready for a high common standard of living and a repression or sublimation of national ambitions in the interests of the world peace and unity. Until a more satisfactory international organization is effected, we may look for pressures of population as they accompany nationalistic enterprise and ambition to produce the situations from which international conflict arises.

There remains, then, the outlet of war. Many countries experiencing a rapid increase in population begin to feel that they are overcrowded, and have developed intensive nationalism and the desire for political and economic aggrandizement. And when this is true, international relations are pretty likely to blow up a storm. In fact, war remains one of the ways for these crowded nations to get what to them seems justice. Then, too, the suggestion to take up birth control in order to reduce their rate of population growth does not deflect them from the realization that all the world's best lands are already in the possession of powerful nations, who so far have not exploited them fully. Unless these other nations are willing to bargain peacefully to open their unused or underused lands for colonization or commercial exploitation, or to dispose of them outright by purchase to nations that feel the need for them, international conflict is likely to arise. Of course, if a nation does not feel strong enough to undertake recourse to arms, she may not attempt it, but the faith in national greatness, the myth of glory, and the desire for expansion are powerful stimuli to a people who may believe the gamble of war worth the cost in blood and suffering.

CLASS ASSIGNMENTS

A. Further reading assignment:

1. K. Young, *Source Book for Sociology*, chap. IX.

2. Jerome Davis, H. E. Barnes, et al., *Introduction to Sociology*, rev. ed., Book II, Part II, chap. III.

3. Warren S. Thompson, *Population Problems*, rev. ed., chaps. XXIII, XXVI.

B. Questions and exercises:

1. How rapidly has the world's population grown since 1750? How do you account for the same?

2. What factors have arisen in Western society since the time of Malthus which have changed the problem of food supply and population?

3. What were some of the chief nineteenth century theories of population?

4. How does population density reflect geographical factors and culture?

5. What does W. S. Thompson mean by "danger spots in world population"? Where are they located?

6. What factors bring on severe population pressure? How may they be remedied?

7. Contrast the biological and the social-psychological interpretations of population pressure. What constitutes the heart of the problem? Is it stress of mere sustenance or is it a matter of attitudes, that is, "felt" pressure, as Thompson puts it? What bearing have these matters on the quantity of the future world population? Illustrate the place of expansive nationalism in contemporary international conflict.

C. Topics for class reports or longer written papers:

1. Review of theories of population with particular reference to Malthus and his critics. (Consult Warren S. Thompson, *Population Problems*, rev. ed., chaps. II, III, and bibliography therein; A. B. Wolfe, *Readings in Social Problems*, 1916, chaps. I, II, VI; J. A. Field, *Essays on Population*, 1931, chaps. I, X; A. B. Wolfe, "Population Theory," article in *Encyclopedia of the Social Sciences*, vol. XII, pp. 248–54, and bibliography.)

2. Problems of world population pressure. (Consult Warren S. Thompson, *Danger Spots in World Population*, 1929, and his *Population Problems*, 1935; E. A. Ross, *Standing Room Only?*, 1927; E. M. East, *Mankind at the Crossroads*, 1923; Sir George Handley Knibbs, *The Shadow of the World's Future*, 1928; R. R. Kuczynski and A. B. Wolfe, article, "Population" in *Encyclopedia of the Social Sciences*, vol. XII, pp. 240–54; A. M. Carr-Saunders, *World Population*, 1936; B. N. Dell and G. F. Luthringer, *Population, Resources, and Trade*, 1938; C. C. Colby, editor, *Geographic Aspects of International Relations*, 1938, especially papers by Bowman, Hartshorne, and James.)

CHAPTER X

DIFFERENTIALS IN POPULATION

Not only are there important problems of population which concern the whole world and especially the various national units in relation to each other, but within particular societies the social composition of the population varies considerably according to biological and cultural factors. The differences in standards of living and rates of population growth between nations rest upon differences of this sort within the nations themselves. In the present chapter we shall examine the most important of these differences, first, as regards age and sex composition, and second, in reference to the selective factors in birth and death which affect the composition of the population. On the basis of this we shall go on to discuss the problems of controlling the quality of a population. Because the material is more satisfactory and because of our own interest, much of the discussion throughout this chapter will center around western Europe and this country.

SEX AND AGE DISTRIBUTIONS

There are certain problems of community life which reflect differences in the sex and age composition and which, in turn, are affected by such differences. If there is a disproportion of males over females, as was true in most pioneer communities, marriage rates will be affected, and such social practices as prostitution may flourish. If the proportion of children is high, the problem of education will certainly be different from what it would be if there are practically no children at all, as is true of certain sections of our large cities inhabited largely by adult males. Again, if the population has a disproportionate number of people in the older age groups, a host of conditions regarding support and status may arise, which would not be found if the population were younger. In this section we shall discuss several sample distributions as they play a part in the community life.

Population Differences in Communities. A growing community in this country during the last part of the nineteenth century typifies a rather normal condition as to age and sex distribution. The numbers of the sexes are about equal. There are many children born, but the infant mortality is high.

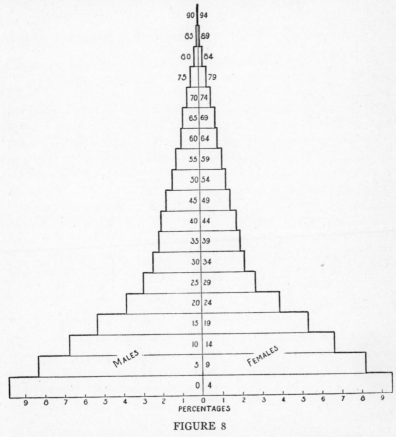

FIGURE 8

SHOWING DISTRIBUTION OF NATIVE WHITE POPULATION OF NATIVE PARENTAGE
BY AGE AND SEX IN WISCONSIN FOR 1900

The largest percentage of persons of both sexes is found in the lower age groups. As ages advance there are fewer and fewer individuals relative to the total population until the pyramid disappears in the small percentage of persons over 65 years of age. Figure 8 represents the native whites of native parentage for the state of Wisconsin in 1900.

In a pioneer community which has been settled rather rapidly we find quite a different situation. Figure 9, showing age and sex distribution for the province of Alberta, Canada, for 1911, is typical. Here we find a higher percentage of males, especially in the ages 20 to 35, and a small proportion of individuals under 19

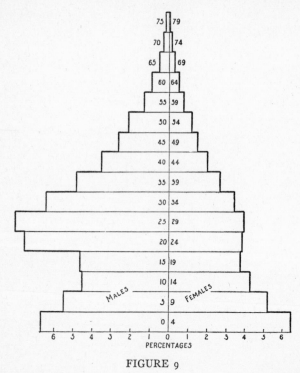

FIGURE 9

SHOWING DISTRIBUTION OF POPULATION BY AGE AND SEX IN THE PROVINCE OF
ALBERTA, CANADA, FOR 1911

years. This population is recruited by immigration rather than by births within the region. Family life is not as common as in a more "stable" population; community activities will be more masculine in tone; and the refinements of culture will be absent. There will be fewer churches, fewer schools, and perhaps little community solidarity. Social control will be of a different character under such circumstances.

The situation in the rural areas of a country that is gradually becoming more industrialized is well indicated in Figure 10, which gives the rural farm population of the United States for 1930. There is a high percentage of children, but the distinctive shrinkage in the age groups 20 to 29 shows clearly how the cities are draining the country districts of large numbers of young men and women. The American farm is already overcrowded. Agricultural produc-

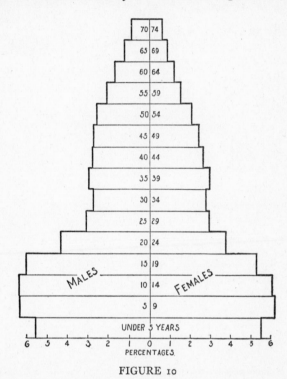

FIGURE 10

SHOWING DISTRIBUTION OF RURAL FARM POPULATION BY AGE AND SEX IN THE
UNITED STATES FOR 1930

tion exceeds our needs, and ambitious young people are following the call to the city as a way out of their economic problems.

A population may grow by natural excess of births over deaths or by immigration from the outside. Just as a pioneer country draws most of its population at first from the outside, a rapidly expanding industrial country, like the United States after 1880, may do the same thing. The excessive importation of foreign-born of adult age into a community produces problems of accommodation and assimilation which will not be found in one where the population is recruited from the births within the community. (See Chapters XXIII and XXV.) Figure 11 shows the distribution of the foreign-born in the United States for 1920 and for 1930. There is a high proportion of persons between the ages 20 and 44, a higher percentage of males than females in the years 25 to 50, and

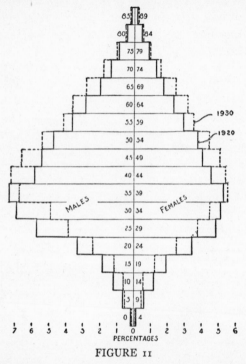

FIGURE 11

SHOWING DISTRIBUTION OF FOREIGN-BORN POPULATION BY AGE AND SEX IN THE
UNITED STATES FOR 1920 AND FOR 1930. THE FORMER IS IN SOLID LINES, THE
LATTER IN BROKEN LINES

a distinctly small ratio of children. The comparison of 1930 with 1920 is interesting. There is a decrease in the percentages of both sexes in all classes up to 30-35 years, due largely to the severe restriction of immigration following the 1924 legislation.[1] In contrast, the percentage of foreign-born in the upper age classes, 40 to 75, especially, has increased. By 1940 the decrease in percentage of the total will be more apparent in the age groups up to 45, with a corresponding relative increase in those over 45 years.

[1] In 1924 the first of a series of increasingly restrictive immigration laws was passed.

In our modern cities one finds all sorts of variations in community life: immigrants, first-generation Americans, native whites of upper income class whose ancestors arrived two or three generations earlier, mixtures of Americans and foreign-born in the transitional areas of the rooming-house sort, where young people gather who work in offices and in the nearby retail firms, and finally there are usually sections given over to transient men who live in cheap quarters, are highly mobile, and furnish a community or neighborhood pattern very different from that of the stable residential sections of the city. Each of these distinctive smaller communities within the larger urban community presents its own distinctive population. The immigrant neighborhood will have an excess of males from 20 to 44, will have fewer foreign-born children, but perhaps many children born of foreign parents. The first-generation American families are likely to keep up a high birth rate and to represent a rather typical population distribution. The native whites of higher income group will have fewer children because of birth control, and more persons in the upper age groups. The rooming-house areas will be filled with persons from 20 to 44 of both sexes. There will be few children, and relatively few people over 55 years. The highly transient male population of our urban "hobohemias" diverge most sharply from the usual form, with few persons under 20 years, with few females at any age, and with a concentration of men at ages 20–54.

It is clear that population reflects the nature of community life and problems, and that the age and sex composition of the population in turn sets the pattern of behavior in the community. The latter is nicely illustrated in the recent age changes in the United States.

Age Changes in the United States. Our population has been steadily growing older. The changes in the median age and in the proportion of the population in the various age groupings denote changes in societal organization and culture. In 1820 the median age of the population of the United States was 16.7 years; in 1930, it was 26.4 years. During these 110 years, the number of older people has increased at a faster rate than the total population, while the number of younger persons has increased more slowly. The age group 20 to 44 years has kept its relative position throughout the whole time.

While the aging of the population is not new, the rate at which this has gone on in recent years is striking. The census of 1930, for the first time in our history, showed a population in one five-year age group (30 to 34) a little smaller than the population in an older five-year group (35 to 39). In 1930 also there were fewer children in the age group under five years than in the age

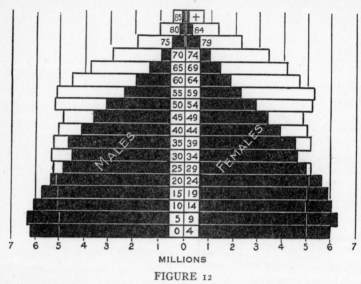

MILLIONS

FIGURE 12

SHOWING POPULATION OF THE UNITED STATES BY AGE AND SEX FOR 1930, IN BLACK RECTANGLES, AND ESTIMATED POPULATION FOR 1980, IN OUTLINE. THE LATTER DIS-TRIBUTION IS BASED ON "MEDIUM" ESTIMATES OF FERTILITY AND MORTALITY AND NO NET IMMIGRATION. From *Population Index*, April, 1938, vol. IV, No. 2.

group five to nine. In 1930 fewer children were born than in 1929—a noteworthy fact in a country long marked by a high birth rate. In contrast, the increase of elders is marked. In the age group 45 to 64 there was an increase of over 25 per cent between 1920 and 1930, and in those between 65 and 74 the increase was over one third.[2]

The National Resources Committee's report, *The Problems of a Changing Population* (1938), estimates our future population in terms of three hypotheses: (*1*) If our birth and death rates continue as at present—at "medium fertility and mortality rates" —and assuming no immigration, our population by 1980 will be

[2]See Warren S. Thompson and P. K. Whelpton, "The Population of the Nation," chap. I, *Recent Social Trends*, 1933, p. 27, for population pyramids illustrating this point.

153 million, which will give us about 2 million persons "at each year of age from birth to 60 years." Thus, the traditional pyramid would have become a rectangle! See Figure 12. (2) Assuming a net immigration of 100,000 persons per year from 1940 on, and assuming the "medium" birth and death rates, the "figure for 1980 is raised" to 158 million. (3) A "minimum estimate assumes a decline of about one third in the fertility of native white women from the 1930–34 level to 1980, with no accession of immigrants." In such a case we shall by 1955 have a population of 138 million, but see a decrease of 10 million during the 25 years following that peak.

In general, cities produce fewer children and have fewer old people than do rural sections. The larger the city, the greater is the difference. Then, too, most of our recent immigration has settled in our cities, a fact which increases the size of the middle age groups. There are also regional variations in these matters; to quote Thompson and Whelpton:

"To summarize the distribution of elders: they constitute the highest proportion of the population in older, rural states having a low rate of increase, and the lowest proportion in newer states and in those growing rapidly in urban population, California excepted."[3]

The reasons for these trends in age composition are largely immigration and the ratio of birth rates to death rates. The facts may be summarized as follows. First, from 1865 to 1900 the number of births increased rapidly. Large numbers of these people will be with us for two or three decades more. Second, immigration has contributed its greatest numbers to these very same age groups. Third, on the other hand, declining birth rates since 1900, and especially since 1920, have already influenced the number of younger persons in the total population. The consequences of such decline in birth rates are already apparent, not only in the United States, but also in Great Britain, France, Germany, and other "advanced" countries.

The effect upon education of this decline in the relative number of children is apparent. Our public elementary school enrollment actually decreased 886,954 from 1930 to 1936. During the next

---

[3]*Op. cit.*, p. 33. California is an exception because the climate attracts large numbers of older people. Thompson and Whelpton discuss in some detail the "causes" of these differences.

decade or so this effect will be felt right up into the senior high school. The number of young persons of senior high-school or college and university age has not reached the maximum, because births were increasing up to 1921, but by 1945–50 higher educational institutions should very definitely feel the effects of this restriction in the birth rate.

Of course, not all children are in school in this country; hence the immediate effect of this decline in the birth rate will not be very marked, because of the insistence on the part of the political state that all children attend school. But in time these changes in population will be noticeable, even if we should approximate universal education. Future planning for buildings and equipment may well consider these facts. The effects on family life are evident. The decrease in the number of children per family unit is but one aspect of profound changes in marital and household relations. We shall discuss these problems later. (See Chapters XII on the family and XIII on education.)

The second evident influence of these age trends is the marked increase in the number of older persons in the population. On the economic side the matter is serious. With the growing displacement of men by machines, with the constant temptation to replace older men with younger, with the talk that a man in industry is old at 40, there will emerge a serious problem of economic support for these classes. In 1930, 22.8 per cent of the population was over 45 years. In 1950 nearly 30 per cent will be above that age. Old age pensions may seem simple in 1938, when less than six per cent of the population is over 65. But what will it be in 1960, when the proportion of those over 65 will be perhaps as high as nine or ten per cent? The older dependents in our society will tend to replace the younger. In time orphan asylums may be made over into old folks' homes! So, too, in politics, economics, and social control generally, old age will wield an increasing effect, unless the young people deliberately drive their elders out. (See Chapter XIX on conflict.)

DIFFERENTIALS IN THE BIRTH AND DEATH RATE

The composition of the population will be affected by reproductive and lethal selection. The former, which refers to the birth rate, operates through such factors as economic status, occupation, place of residence, and religion. The latter, which has to do with the death rate, is influenced by such factors as disease, longevity of family strains, race and nativity, sex and marital condition, occupation, and place of residence.

Social Status, Occupation, and Birth Rates. One of the earliest studies to reveal the relation of economic status to fertility was published in 1899 by Jacques Bertillon (1851–1922), the French statistician and sociologist, who compared the birth rates of Paris, Berlin, Vienna, and London. The population of each city was divided into six classes according to economic condition. All cities showed a steady increase in the number of births as one passes from very rich to very poor sections. Although the death rate is higher in the latter than in the former, it is still clear that the poorer classes are reproducing themselves faster than are the wealthy.

Sir Arthur Newsholme and T. H. C. Stevenson, two British investigators, made a somewhat similar study of London for the year 1903. They divided the population into six groups according to the number of servants per 100 families. They summarize their findings in the following words:

"It will be observed that Groups 2, 3, 4, and 5, comprising 64.8 per cent of the total population of London, have a corrected total birth rate which only varied between 25.36 and 25.82. The two extreme groups show marked differences, the rich districts at one end of the scale having a corrected total birth rate of 20.45, and the very poor districts at the other end of the scale a corrected total birth rate of 31.56 per 1,000 of population. The former of these birth rates affects 9.7 per cent, the latter 25.4 per cent of the total population of London."[4]

Another study of the fertility of completed families in England and Wales showed much the same thing. On the basis of the 1911 census, marked differences were revealed in the number of children born to women in different social classes. For example, 100 women of the upper and middle classes who were over 45 years of age had borne 422 children, while 100 women of the unskilled class gave birth to 609 children. One hundred miners' wives had borne 684 children, and 100 farmers' wives, 632. By analyzing marriages and children in the order of fertility, it was further shown that the

[4] From Sir Arthur Newsholme and T. H. C. Stevenson, "The Decline of Human Fertility in the United Kingdom and Other Countries as Shown by Corrected Birth Rates," *Journal of the Royal Statistical Society*, March, 1906, vol. LXIX, pp. 34–87.

least fertile 25 per cent of marriages of completed families produced only 2.1 per cent of all births. On the other hand, the most fertile 25 per cent produced 52 per cent of all births. It is obvious that a larger proportion of the least fertile women belong to the upper and middle classes, while just the opposite is true of the most fertile. From this it is evident that here as elsewhere in Western society the upper classes are contributing a comparatively small ratio of people to the next generation.

Although France shows about the same situation as in the English-speaking countries, one exception should be mentioned. In France farmers appear to have relatively fewer children than elsewhere. The culture pattern of small families is linked to the desire for the retention of landed property in few enough hands to maintain the economic status of the family.

All the pre-war studies in Europe and this country show that as a rule farmers and peasants have the largest families, although in France this is not so. Next come the unskilled urban workers with large families. As we go up the economic ladder of income and social status, we find that the birth rate falls off steadily.

Since the World War even more marked changes in the birth rate have taken place. No very adequate studies of decreases in relation to occupation and social status, however, have been made. A few studies show a continuation toward further decline, except one recent investigation in Stockholm, Sweden, which indicates that in recent years the upper classes there are actually increasing, and at a slightly higher rate than the working classes.[5]

The relation of birth rates to occupation in this country is shown by Frank W. Notestein, who studied the size of several thousand families in the northern and western states. He found for this large sample that from 1890 to 1910 the proportion of childless and one-child families increased from 28 per cent to 39.4 per cent in the professional group, from 23.6 per cent to 39.4 per cent in the business group, from 22.1 per cent to 34.4 per cent in the skilled-labor group, from 16.8 per cent to 31.2 per cent in the unskilled-labor group, and from 17.8 per cent to 20.7 per cent in the farm-owner group.[6] It is very likely that

[5]See Karl Arvid Eden, "The Birth Rate Changes; Stockholm 'Upper' Classes more Fertile than the 'Lower'," *Eugenics Review*, 1929, vol. XX, pp. 258–66.
[6]Frank W. Notestein, "The Decrease in Size of Families from 1890 to 1910," *Quarterly Bulletin of the Milbank Memorial Fund*, Oct., 1931, vol. IX, no. 4, pp. 181–88. Summarized in *Recent Social Trends*, 1933, pp. 42–43.

the decline in the size of the family in all these groups has gone on since 1910, but no adequate study of the matter has been made.

The consumption habits of large numbers of the population, especially of the Western world, have risen steadily in the last few decades, related, of course, to the decline in both the birth rate and the death rate, especially among infants and children, and the general rise in standards of comfort, education, and the demands for leisure, intellectual and artistic stimulation, and other items of behavior long denied the lower economic classes. As R. M. MacIver, referring to the important British Report on the *Fertility of Marriage*, says, it "gives abundant evidence that fertility rates are directly and immediately responsive, not so much to economic status, as to the mode of life which is influenced by the type of occupation and by social factors other than wealth or poverty."[7]

While up to the present the upper classes have cut their birth rate more drastically than have the lower classes, present trends in Western countries indicate that the latter will cut theirs even more radically in the next few decades unless other changes come about. These classes have had a taste of the "better things of life" and are not going to give them up so easily.

If, then, these forms of economic and social practice spread from Western countries to the Orient and Africa, the whole population problem will take on a different hue. Many of the doubts and worries of the population experts will disappear. The "shadow of the world's future" may not be so dark as many imagine. (See the preceding chapter.)

Yet another shadow of overpopulation has appeared upon the horizon. This is associated with the recrudescence of intense nationalism in the fascist countries of Europe. As a phase of this movement, there has arisen again the cry for larger and larger populations, and propaganda for increased births is heard in Italy and Germany. For Germany at least the recent spurt (a rise from 14.7 in 1933 to 19.0 in 1936) can prove only temporary, for during the next 20 years the marriageable age groups there will reflect the sharp decline in the birth rate from 1922 to 1933.

[7]R. M. MacIver, *Population Problems in the United States and Canada*, ed. by Louis I. Dublin, 1926, p. 296.

Community and Religious Differences. There is an evident difference between rural and urban birth rates. P. K. Whelpton has shown for this country that as long ago as 1800 there were differences in number of children born to women of childbearing age according to whether the section was strictly agricultural, semi-industrial, or industrial. For example, in 1800 for the white population there were 1,000 children under five years of age per 1,000 women 16 to 44 years of age, for the country as a whole. For the agricultural states, the number of such children was 1,043; for the semi-industrial states, 962; and for the industrial states, 786. In 1920, for the agricultural states the number was 629, for the semi-industrial, 534, and for the industrial, 458.

The size of the community also reveals differences in the size of families. Warren S. Thompson's analysis of the data shows that in general "the smaller the community, the larger the family."[8] This seems to be true for native-born, foreign-born, and for all racial groups in our population. German studies reveal much the same sort of thing. For Prussia, 1911 to 1914, the urban population showed 178.9 births per 1,000 married women 15 to 45 years of age, while the rural districts showed 264.8. Over a period of 38 years, 1876 to 1914, the birth rate in rural Prussia declined 22 per cent, and that for the urban sections, 41 per cent.

Religious differences also influence the birth rate. Although we have no very clear evidence, certain studies in Germany have shown that Catholics have larger families than Protestants. But often the factors of rural or urban location were ignored, and it is somewhat difficult to tell how much of this difference was due to urbanization and how much to religious ideas and practices.

Yet even the Catholics, at least in this country, are following the trend toward smaller families. Thus, Stouffer's study of the "confinement rates" of 40,766 Catholic and non-Catholic urban families in Wisconsin for 1919–1933 showed that the fertility rates for the former were declining faster than those for the latter. He also found a like trend elsewhere in the United States.[8a]

With this review of certain important factors which affect the birth rate, let us examine those which influence the death rate.

Disease and the Death Rate. The expectation of life at birth has been greatly increased wherever medical science has reduced

[8]Warren S. Thompson, *Ratio of Children to Women in the United States, 1920.*
[8a]S. A. Stouffer, "Trends in the Fertility of Catholics and Non-Catholics," *American Journal of Sociology,* Sept., 1935, vol. XLI, pp. 143–66.

the infant death rate.   The life expectancy for the middle and upper age groupings has not been materially cut down.   Furthermore there seems to be little evidence for the belief that life expectancy in the middle and upper years will be increased, short of some striking discoveries in medicine.   The facts for the United States appear rather typical.   Trends in reduction of the death rate since 1870 in terms of age show definitely (*1*) that the death rate of children under five years of age did not decline materially until after 1900; (*2*) that the mortality rate of persons over five years but under middle life has moved downward; and (*3*) that the death rates for people in the upper age groupings has risen. The influence of disease on the death rate is related to age.

Some diseases are found chiefly in infancy and childhood, like diarrhea, whooping cough, measles, diphtheria, and scarlet fever. In addition, earliest infancy mortality is affected by congenital defects.   Other diseases, such as typhoid and pulmonary tuberculosis, attack middle life most frequently.   Adults in the later years are susceptible to pneumonia, cancer, diabetes, and to organic breakdown, such as nephritis and Bright's disease, and heart and circulatory disorders.

In the younger ages, then, the disasters of disease and death are related to poor living conditions, ignorant maternal care, and infectious and contagious diseases growing out of the environment.   In contrast, death in the later years seems related to organic breakdowns, which, in turn, may be due to damages from earlier infections or from congenital defects, that is, specifically inherited constitutional weaknesses, or to the nature of occupations and general environment.[9]

The trends in death rates from various diseases throw light on the whole matter of vitality.   Deaths from children's diseases, from tuberculosis, and from typhoid fever have declined rapidly in recent years, as adequate medical care, sanitation, and higher standards of living have become more common.   In contrast cancer, diabetes, cerebral hemorrhage, heart disorders, nephritis, and pneumonia are becoming more serious threats to life.   Since death from these diseases affects the upper age levels especially, it is clear that medical science has by no means found for us that "magic" which will increase the span of life, and not merely extend the life expectancy of infants and children.

[9]On the causes of death see Edgar Sydenstricker, "The Vitality of the American People," chap. XII, *Recent Social Trends*, pp. 614, 626–28.

As Thompson well puts it, "To maintain our present crude death rate of about 11, it is not sufficient to cut down still further the deaths in the earlier years of life, as we have been doing in the past; we must actually lengthen the span of life."[10]

Although the reduction in death rate is obviously largely due to cutting down the infant deaths from poor care and infectious diseases, we must not imagine the decline is entirely due to these causes. The campaign against tuberculosis has been effective, especially in cutting down mortality in ages above childhood. Louis I. Dublin's survey reports that the tuberculosis death rate in the United States in 1900 was 1.952 per 1,000 of the population. In 1926 it was 0.845 per 1,000.[11] In 1930, it was 0.68. This reduction of more than 64 per cent in 30 years is a remarkable record. Nevertheless, as Warren S. Thompson says, we must not overestimate the importance of this factor in the total problem of mortality. He points out that in this same period the reductions in infant and child deaths "were about twice as important" in the reduction of the general death rate as was the particular "saving from tuberculosis."[12]

Certain interesting matters are presented by these facts concerning disease and the death rate. First, the conquest of children's diseases and the improvement of sanitation have reduced infant and childhood mortality rates; these factors would soon give us a relatively stationary death rate for these ages. Yet the declining birth rate has greatly reduced the total number of babies born in any year. On the other hand, the death rate in the middle and upper years is increasing. Therefore, with a declining birth rate and a relatively stationary infant death rate, coupled with an increasing death rate in the upper age groupings, we ought to see a gradual increase in the total death rate, unless further medical discovery cuts the death rate for the upper age levels or we return to a higher birth rate again.[13]

Longevity and the Death Rate. The length of life itself seems to be influenced by family strains, that is, by heredity, but doubt-

[10]Thompson, *Population Problems,* rev. ed., 1935, p. 177.

[11]Louis I. Dublin, *Health and Wealth: A Survey of the Economics of World Health,* 1928.

[12]See Thompson, *Population Problems,* 1933, p. 149.

[13]See Warren S. Thompson and P. K. Whelpton, "The Population of the Nation," chap. I, *Recent Social Trends,* pp. 46–51, for a discussion of the future population of the United States as it is affected by these present trends.

less general standards of living and medical care also play an important part. Dublin has analyzed a large sample of American insurance records showing the duration of life of parents and brothers and sisters of insured persons.[14] He found a rough correlation between the longevity of parents and that of children. Raymond Pearl, the biologist, has also published data to show that life expectancy is related to parenthood, the long-lived parents giving their children a better chance of survival than short-lived ones.[15] In both these studies, however, differences in living conditions and culture were difficult to control; hence the results cannot be looked upon as absolutely final.

We have already noted that the death rate in the upper age groups is increasing and that it is natural to ask the question: Are we prolonging the lives of infants and children merely to have these people "peter out" in middle life? Does this reduction in infant mortality mean that we are breeding a race of physical inferiors and incompetents? As to whether improvements in medical care of infants and children have really influenced our racial vitality, Edgar Sydenstricker says:

"From the historical point of view there is no evidence that the decline in infant mortality is in any way associated with the increased death rate at older years. The entirely contrary fact is clearly evident: that the death rate at older ages was increasing long before any considerable reduction in infant or child mortality began to be manifested, and the downward trend in the death rate among persons 5–39 years of age has been fairly synchronous with the upward trend in mortality among persons over 50 years of age for as long a period as we have records in this country. At least, a causal relationship between interference with natural selection through death of infants and children and the increased mortality of older persons has not yet been demonstrated."[16]

The relation of longevity to mental incompetency is shown in studies of the mortality of the feebleminded. L. Pierce Clark and W. L. Stowell report the mortality of a large sample of feeble-

[14]Louis I. Dublin, "Heredity's Part in Determining Our Life Span," New York *Times*, June 8, 1930. See also Edgar Sydenstricker's critical comments on other studies, *Recent Social Trends*, pp. 615–16.

[15]Raymond Pearl, "Studies in Human Longevity, IV. The Inheritance of Longevity. Preliminary Report," *Human Biology*, May, 1931, vol. III, pp. 245–69.

[16]Edgar Sydenstricker, "The Vitality of the American People," chap. XII, *Recent Social Trends*, pp. 634–35.

minded children to be double that of normal children, and that of idiots and imbeciles to be six times that of normal children.[17] More recently a survey of deaths of morons, imbeciles, and idiots from Massachusetts institutions over a period of 14 years shows that for all ages the feebleminded have a higher death rate than "normals," especially, however, in the early, pre-reproductive years. The morons have a higher rate than the normals, and the imbeciles and idiots a much higher one than the morons. For example, at age 10, of 1,000 normal females born, there are 831 survivors. Among an equal number of morons, there are 722 survivors, while among equal numbers of imbeciles and idiots there are but 387 and 268 survivors respectively. This study showed further that while 54.2 per cent of all the females born survive the age of 60 years, but 22.5 per cent of the morons do, and but 18.5 per cent of the imbeciles and 5.2 per cent of the idiots. The differences are about the same among the males.[18]

The well-known family histories of the Jukes, the Kallikaks, and other congenital inferiors, of course, are always cited as sample proof of the seriousness of defective stocks. As was pointed out in Chapter V, scholars have not adequately taken the factors of physical and cultural environment into account in these cases. We need not gainsay defective physical and mental inheritance, but we must not ignore the factors of low economic status and inadequate cultural opportunities.

Race and Nativity and Survival. There is a lot of nonsense about differences in racial mortality. Wherever these differences appear they seem so closely bound up with economic status, with sanitation, and with medical care, that it is extremely difficult to segregate special racial factors. For this country and others, it is clear that the Negroes have a higher death rate than do the whites. For the United States, although the decline in Negro mortality has been evident, the death rate for this colored stock is half again as high as it is for the white. The life expectancy of Negro male industrial insurance policy-holders increased from 33 years in 1900 to 44 years in 1927. From birth to age ten, the life expectancy of

[17]L. Pierce Clark and William L. Stowell, "A Study of Mortality among 4,000 Feebleminded and Idiots," *New York Medical Journal*, 1913, vol. XCVII, pp. 276–78.

[18]Neil A. Dayton, Carl R. Doering, Margaret M. Hilferty, Helen C. Maher, and Helen H. Dolan, "Mortality and Expectation of Life in Mental Deficiency in Massachusetts—An Analysis of the Fourteen-year Period, 1917–1930," *New England Journal of Medicine*, March 17 and 24, 1932, vol. CCVI, pp. 550–70, 616–31.

Negroes is about 9 years lower for Negro males and 10 years lower for Negro females than for the same sexes in the white population. The Negro death rate in cities is higher than in rural sections, and higher in the North than in the South. Yet it is evident that the Negro is gradually moving toward the mortality rate of the whites of some generations ago. The greatest improvement in death rates with the Negro, as with the white, is apparently due to cutting down the infant and child mortality. A sound study by J. H. M. Knox and Grover F. Powers has shown that where Negro and white infants are given the same medical care and diet the differences in infant mortality between the races disappear.[19]

Nativity is also assumed to show differences in mortality. For our own country the death rate for foreign-born residents has fluctuated slightly, but because of the reduction of our immigrant influx with the resultant changes in their age composition, there is bound to be an increasing death rate among the foreign-born when the entire group is considered, since so many of them will be increasingly found in the upper age levels.

Edgar Sydenstricker has recently summarized trends in death rates for foreign-born, foreign stocks, and native whites from a study made by C. E. A. Winslow and P. L. Wang for six states for 1890–1920. He notes three principal sets of facts:

(1) There has been a decline in mortality for persons under 40 years of age, most marked for the foreign stock, less marked for the foreign-born, and least of all for the native whites. The greater decline in the first two seems definitely associated with improvements in public health, medical care, and standards of living. (2) For age groups 40–49 and 50–59 the mortality rate for foreign-born declined. On the other hand, the death rates for these age levels did not show any decrease for foreign stock or native whites. (3) The general mortality rate over 60 years has been increasing for all three groups, particularly for the native whites.[20]

Sex and Marital Status and Mortality. It is well known that the female foetus has a better chance for survival than the male, and apparently this difference persists throughout infancy and childhood. And adult women usually have a lower death rate than do men. Although during the childbearing years, the mortality rate

[19] J. H. M. Knox, Jr., and Grover F. Powers, "Effectiveness of Infant Welfare Clinics from a Medical Point of View," *Journal of American Medical Association,* March 11, 1922, vol. LXXVIII, no. 10, pp. 707–10.
[20] See Sydenstricker, *op. cit.,* pp. 642–44.

for women increases slightly, the rate is reduced again as soon as this period is over. Women seem less susceptible to diseases than men, and they are less exposed to occupational hazards.

In a study of deaths in various age classes in regard to sex and marital status, the French investigator Lucien March showed that in various European countries, married males have considerably lower death rates than single, widowed, or divorced men. In his study, married females between the ages of 20 and 39 had a somewhat higher rate than single women of comparable ages, but still lower than widowed or divorced. At other ages, married women have lower mortality rates than single, widowed, or divorced women.[21] Studies made in the United States show substantially the same thing, except that the difference in rate between married men and single men is even greater than that found in Europe.

Most of the facts of marital differences are not difficult to explain. Doubtless marriage acts as a selective agent. Only the more vigorous men tend to marry and take on marital responsibilities. There might be some such selection on the part of women, but in the past much less than among men. Secondly, greater regularity of living among the married, especially as it affects the men, is conducive to longevity. Thompson makes the point that on the whole marriage "apparently represents a better adaptation to life, physically and mentally, than does celibacy," this in spite of the fact that married women in the childbearing years have a higher mortality than single women of the same ages.

Occupational Mortality. A study of mortality from all causes at various age periods and average age at death of industrial policy-holders made by the Metropolitan Life Insurance Company for the years 1911–1913 showed wide variations in percentages of deaths at different age periods and in the average age at death. Farmers showed the highest percentage of deaths at 65 years or over (44.9 per cent). They had the highest average age at death, 58.5 years; bartenders the lowest percentage at 65 years or over, only 4 per cent; while clerks had the lowest average age at death, 36.5.

Other studies confirm the same facts. Workers in tin, lead, and copper mines and in steel mills have high mortality rates. Other

[21] Lucien March, "Some Researches Concerning the Factors of Mortality," *Journal of the Royal Statistical Society,* April, 1912, vol. LXXV, Part 5, pp. 505–38. See review in Thompson, *op. cit.,* p. 158.

occupations, such as preaching, teaching, and office work have very low risks. Day laborers, waiters, and many semi-skilled workers, who show a higher death rate than business men, professional groups, and the like, reflect not only occupational hazards, but standards of living, economic conditions, and general social status as well.

Urban-Rural Differences. There has long been a common opinion that it was much healthier and less hazardous to live in the country than in the city. Various studies made in the United States and Europe point out that rural death rates are lower than urban. However, some of the studies intended to prove this theory are useless because the rates for rural and urban sections are not standardized, and because the definition of "rural" and "urban" is not uniform.[22]

A recent study by Harold F. Dorn has thrown new and important light on this whole problem of rural and urban mortality. Although Dorn took figures for but one year, 1930, he analyzed the entire number of resident deaths for the state of Ohio, allocating the deaths to the last official residence of the individuals. Taking into account also age and sex distributions, his study reveals the following important facts. (1) Under 20 years of age, there are no significant differences in mortality between rural and urban areas, for either males or females. Between the ages 20 to 30 the rural mortality for both sexes is higher than that of the urban areas. After age 30 the urban death rates are slightly higher. (2) Analyzing the rural areas in terms of economic conditions, he shows definitely that the death rate fluctuates in different rural sections with the height of the economic status. In the poor agricultural and low-wealth rural sections of southeastern Ohio, the death rates are much higher than in the wealthier rural sections of the state. In fact these differences within the rural sections themselves are greater than the differences between the rural sections as a whole and the urban districts.[23]

This study by Dorn gives the first adequate material on the problem of rural-urban mortality rates which also takes into ac-

[22] Rural does not mean strictly farming. In the census of 1930 all places under 2,500 population were called rural. To list small cities of 2,500 as urban along with our great crowded industrial and commercial centers like New York, Chicago, and others, is to make difficult the comparison of figures. So, too, only in the last two censuses is a distinction drawn between rural non-farm and farm populations.

[23] Harold F. Dorn, *Mortality Rates for Ohio, 1930.* Ph. D. thesis, 1933. University of Wisconsin Library.

count such factors as age distribution and economic status. While one may not generalize for the United States on the basis of figures for one state, and from data for one year only, certainly the easy assumptions that rural mortality is lower than urban, that cities are less healthy than country sections, and that the urban districts are constantly draining the better stocks of people from the country must all be re-examined.

Other studies have shown that the death rates are highly correlated with *density* of population, especially in urban areas. In the congested slum areas of our cities the death rates are higher than in the less crowded residential sections. Once more, however, cultural and social factors are highly significant. The lower economic status of those living in the poorer quarters means low wages, poor food, larger families, poor sanitation, and less adequate medical care. Hence, in measuring density as related to death rate, we are also measuring death rate as related to economic status.

SELECTION AND QUALITY OF THE POPULATION

The possible improvement of population by biological means has been the topic of much discussion. Eugenics has been hailed by many as one method of bettering the quality of our stock and making possible a higher culture.

Selection Through Negative Eugenics. The term *eugenics* comes from a Greek word meaning nobility of birth. As developed under the leadership of Francis Galton, it is the science which deals with the influences which tend to improve the innate qualities of men and to develop them to the highest degree. So defined it covers both hereditary and environmental factors. Popularly, however, it has come to mean the improvement of racial stock by hereditary means, and the opposite term *euthenics* is sometimes used to refer to the betterment of man by changing his environment. Eugenics is conventionally divided into the "negative" and the "positive" phases. Negative eugenics aims to eliminate the unfit. Positive eugenics hopes to improve the stock by selective mating and reproduction among the fit.

One of the first problems of *negative eugenics* is to define and delimit the defectives. It is easy to determine the more obvious congenitally malformed, idiots, and imbeciles. All together these probably do not constitute one per cent of the total population. So far as the idiots and imbeciles go, they are so few in number and their fertility is so low that the public alarm raised about them is unwarranted. As to the morons and borderline feebleminded, much depends on the definition of intelligence as to whether we say there are one, two, or possibly three per cent of the population in this class.

Three principal methods of dealing with the problem of low-grade mentalities have been suggested: colonization, sterilization, and contraception.

Colonization is a program of segregating the feebleminded into colonies, where, living under supervision, they will be at least partially self-supporting. The sexes would be separated and reproduction prevented. In a competitive capitalistic society such a plan has to be supported by taxation. It is costly and inadequate for any but the lower-grade cases. Obviously, for the great mass of the feebleminded and dull normal people who perform useful work in our society other methods of handling will have to be devised.

Sterilization is a method of de-sexing individuals to prevent reproduction. This form of social control should be carefully restricted. In a democratic society, at least, the doctrine of individual rights is so deeply entrenched that we should be loath to abandon this in matters of such personal concern. There are many reformers who imagine that once we sterilize large numbers of our defectives we shall within a short period eliminate the problem of feeblemindedness. This easy assumption is open to considerable doubt, but the notion is widespread. As H. S. Jennings and others have pointed out, if inherited feeblemindedness be a group of recessive traits, then latent feeblemindedness is doubtless widespread among normal people. Therefore any measures to sterilize the known feebleminded can effect only a small reduction in the number of feebleminded in the next generation.[24]

Sterilization may well be used on the obviously low-grade feebleminded, but as a universal means of restricting the production of people of low mentality in the next generation the device is distinctly limited.

Contraception, or birth control, in one form or another has been long practiced by both primitive and advanced societies. The noticeable decline in the birth rate during recent decades in

[24] See H. S. Jennings, *Biological Foundations of Human Behavior,* 1930; and his article, "Eugenics" in *Encyclopedia of the Social Sciences,* vol. V, pp. 617–21,

western Europe and America can only mean that contraception is becoming increasingly widespread, not only in the upper income classes, but in the middle and even lower economic groups as well. There is no reason to believe that with clinical supervision even the high-grade feebleminded might not use contraceptive devices. With increasingly adequate and still rather simple means at hand, the removal of legal and theological bans on the establishment of birth-control clinics, the spread of birth-control information would soon show further effects on the birth rate, and doubtless in the very classes which the alarmists so fear. Since the mores and law both are changing in respect to this matter, eugenists may better support this movement than hope for too much from the more mechanical and more autocratic methods of colonization and sterilization.

Selection through Positive Eugenics. The purpose of positive eugenics is to foster the propagation of the abler and superior stocks in the population. Psychologically, negative eugenics takes on the form of a taboo and restriction of activity. Positive eugenics is quite the opposite. It tends to stimulate by education or propaganda action believed desirable.

Again the problem is not simple. The proponents of eugenics make much of the need for superior stock and of the danger of decay from excessive reproduction among the lower classes. Yet the middle and lower economic groups have been for a long time replenishing the upper classes. Even before our capitalistic competitive system arose, the upper classes doubtless tended to dissipate themselves and to be recruited from classes below them. Certainly this has been true throughout Grecian, Roman, and medieval history. In the light of this fact there are two major problems which the advocates of positive eugenics must face.

Who are the superior people who ought to reproduce themselves? This involves us at once in the age-long matter of heredity and environment. If "good" or superior stock is largely a matter of biological inheritance, we must devise better biological and psychological tests for determining and measuring this capacity than we have today. It is at present a fatuous argument to defend the theory of physical and mental superiority of the upper income classes in any given generation. A large fraction of our upper economic groups in this country are but two or three generations removed from European peasant or urban workers of lower economic status. The extremists of the hereditary doctrine want to have their cake and eat it too. One cannot make too much of the doctrine of sounder heredity among the well-to-do and at the same time reckon with declining birth rates in the upper economic groups, which groups are constantly replenished from below.

If, on the other hand, superiority is largely a matter of cultural opportunity, then the matter of producing sound stock is a matter of societal organization and social control rather than biological control. Enough has already been said to make clear how difficult it is to know who is superior. In our own society, with its emphasis on individualism and unlimited competition for wealth and monetary power, there are developed ideas, attitudes, and habits which if biologically inherited—they are not—might be considered in the long run of history unfortunate for society. We have put such emphasis on money-grabbing that our culture produces a great many unscrupulous individuals. As the Italian economist Achille Loria stated in 1912 to the First International Eugenics Congress, "The history of great fortunes goes to show that most often great patrimonies are created, not so much by supreme genius, as by shameful and iniquitous practices."[25]

The problem of deciding who the "good" and "superior" stock are is thus not easy to solve. The history of culture informs us at every point that the class in power always considers itself superior. Without doubt in our democratic, capitalistic society the business group would rank first, and from then on down the line the selection would be made of those who fit in best with the capitalist business ethos.

The second factor of importance in positive eugenics is reproduction. Will these "superior" stocks be as fertile as others? Education and propaganda, with perhaps some financial subsidy for those not able to carry the burden of larger families, are necessary. In a society dominated more and more by high standards of living and personal comfort, it may be difficult to devise adequate external rewards for eugenic reproduction.

Eugenics arose out of the belief that the control of heredity might improve the human stock, as the breeders of domestic animals have controlled and "improved" the stocks of our food-producing and draft animals. Yet the analogy between breeding domestic animals and the control of human reproduction is false.

[25] Papers communicated to the *First International Eugenics Congress*, p. 181.

It completely ignores societal organization and culture, or, put in psychological terms, the personality, with its habits, attitudes, beliefs, and values. To talk about "natural selection" in human beings as if it meant the same as "natural selection" in our flora and fauna is misleading nonsense of the worst sort.

The quality and quantity of modern populations in the Western world is so related to our industrial culture that we must note briefly the interplay of these on population. The present century has seen the machine constantly replacing the hand-worker. It is probable that the cutting down of the birth rate during the post-war years is not unrelated to this shift in our production system as well as to rising standards of living. This restriction will likely continue as work becomes scarcer and the means of birth control more widespread.

Yet the improvement in the machine and the rise in the stand-ard of living, meaning the development of ever new consumption habits in the masses, are the two key factors in the present eco-nomic order. The heyday of easy exploitation of foreign markets has apparently gone forever. In place of it has come, however, increased consumption at home. All this means that those born are not only more likely to survive, but also that chances are better for a fuller participation in the culture of their time, pro-vided that the masses may find work. Suggestions as to how to do this include devices to stimulate capital investment; but par-ticularly striking is the contention that a fuller utilization of our productive capacity coupled with a lowering of prices will enhance national wealth and improve our standards of life.[26]

If, then, we cut the birth rate of the less able and less efficient portions of the population through birth control and use steriliza-tion on the very inadequate, we should have in time a population of such quality that its participation in its culture will constantly lead to further improvements in standards of living and comfort and perhaps contribute something to that elusive state called human happiness.

CLASS ASSIGNMENTS

A. **Further reading assignment:**

  1. K. Young, *Source Book for Sociology*, chap. X.
  2. *The Problems of a Changing Population;* National Resources Com-

[26]See A. O. Dahlberg, *When Capital Goes on Strike*, 1938; and *Income and Economic Progress*, 1935. (Brookings Institution, Washington, D. C.)

mittee report on population problems, 1938: "Statement of the Committee on Population Problems," pp. 6–17, and chap. I, pp. 18–35.

B. Questions and exercises:

1. Illustrate the effects of culture (a) on age and sex distributions; (b) in reference to occupation and social status.

2. What cultural factors chiefly influence (a) the reduction in the birth rate; (b) the reduction of the death rate?

3. Why is there a decline in death rates in many countries today before there is a corresponding decline in the birth rate? What does this reveal as to diffusion of culture patterns and the relation of public health to birth control?

4. In the light of differential death rates in Western society in reference to infants, children, those of middle age, and those of old age, what, to your mind, are the pressing challenges of modern medicine?

5. As the middle and upper age groups increase relative to the younger age groups, what will likely be the effect on (a) competition for jobs; (b) conflict of age classes; and (c) social legislation for the aged?

6. What are the principal limitations (a) of negative eugenics; (b) of positive eugenics?

7. Karpinos (see end of paragraph 1 below), using an index of net reproduction in which 100 indicates that a population will just reproduce itself every 30 years, has estimated the net fertility rate for the white population of the United States (using 1930 figures) as 108. He has also computed certain variations in net reproductivity, as follows: for rural-farm population, the rate is 154; for rural non-farm (people living outside cities but who are not farmers), 129; and for urban dwellers, 84. Interpret these figures with respect to the sources of our future population, assuming no net gain from immigration.

C. Topics for class reports or longer written papers:

1. The decline in human fertility in terms of economic classes, locality, and the like. (Consult W. S. Thompson, *Population Problems*, rev. ed., 1935, chaps. VII, VIII, IX, and bibliography; F. Lorimer and F. Osborn, *Dynamics of Population*, 1934, Parts I, II, III and bibliography; E. B. Reuter, *Population Problems*, rev. ed., 1937, chap. XIV; Lancelot Hogben, editor, *Political Arithmetic: A Symposium of Population Studies*, 1938, chaps. III, IV; B. D. Karpinos, "The Differential True Rates of Growth of the White Population in the United States," etc., *American Journal of Sociology*, Sept., 1938, vol. XLIV, pp. 251–71.)

2. The history and present status of the eugenics movement. (Consult Paul Popenoe and R. H. Johnson, *Applied Eugenics*, 1918; H. S. Jennings, "Eugenics" in *Encyclopedia of the Social Sciences*, vol. V, pp. 617–21, and references therein; and *Encyclopedia Britannica*, 14th ed., vol. VIII; Raymond Pearl, *The Present Status of Eugenics*, 1928 [Sociological Press, Hanover, N. H.]; E. G. Conklin, *The Direction of Human Evolution*, 1923; and various issues of the periodicals *Eugenics Review, Journal of Heredity*, and others.)

3. The vitality of a population. (Consult Edgar Sydenstricker, *Health and Environment*, 1933, and his "The Vitality of the American People," chap. XII, *Recent Social Trends*, and bibliography.)

4. The fertility of families on relief. (Consult S. A. Stouffer and P. F. Lazarsfeld, *Research Memorandum on the Family in the Depression*, 1937; F. W. Notestein, "The Fertility of Populations Supported by Public Relief," *Milbank Memorial Fund Quarterly*, Jan., 1936, vol. XIV, pp. 37–49; H. C. Griffin and G. St. J. Perrott, "Urban Differential Fertility During the Depression," *ibid.*, Jan., 1937, vol. XV, pp. 75–89.)

PART THREE

SOCIETAL ORGANIZATION AND CULTURE

INTRODUCTION

As men living in groups find ways of satisfying their fundamental needs, there arise in society certain standard and more or less continuous forms or structures which make up a totality called *societal organization*. These structures are expressed in moral customs, institutions, laws—in short, the whole range of what William Graham Sumner called folkways or mores. Yet societal organization is never divorced from the culture of the time and place. The family, for example, has everywhere certain functions of reproduction and child care, but its particular function varies with different societies.

While the basic features of societal organization and culture were presented in Part One (Chapters I to VI), we shall, in PART THREE, go into more detail in reference to those phases of societal organization and culture which concern the family, education, religion, play life, art, science, and philosophy. The economic and political aspects of societal organization are the proper study of economics and of political science respectively and are not dealt with here except as economic and political matters bear directly upon our subject. Although we shall examine particularly the institutional features of societal organizations, including attention to social control, the more formal features of such regulation will be left to the final division of our book (Part Five).

CHAPTER XI

THE FAMILY AND ITS INSTITUTIONS

The family is everywhere the basic primary group and the natural matrix of personality. It is customarily an irreducible group involving two generations, parents and children. This group everywhere has recognition or sanction by the larger group—tribe or community. The *family* may be defined as a social group consisting of one or more men living with one or more women in the same household, and the children, at least during their early years, that have come from this union, or which by social custom, as with adoption, are connected with the family. It is essentially a social configuration of parents and children sanctioned by the larger society. There may, of course, be marriage without children. Although childless married couples usually set up for themselves the conventional household, and although many of their relations are not unlike those of parents, they do not represent a family in the strict sense.

The family sometimes consists of a father and mother and their married children and grandchildren living in the same household. This latter sort of group involving three or even four generations of near blood relatives is often called the "joint" family, in distinction to the smaller family of parents and children called "the marriage group."

The functions of the family vary greatly in different societies. In the light of much present-day anxiety about its changing functions in western Europe and America, it is well to bear in mind the divergent family patterns in other societies. For example, in some the men take their meals entirely outside the home; in others the family as an economic unit is decidedly subordinate; in others children are passed around under what seems to us a curious system of adoption; again, religious and ceremonial functions are in the hands of the family, as in early Rome or as is ancestor-worship in China.

In all this variety there appear some general features of family life. These we shall discuss under the following major headings: (*1*) parenthood, kinship, and social structure; (*2*) relations of the sexes within the family and outside; (*3*) changes in Western family life; (*4*) the economic functions of the members; (*5*) changes in the relations of men and women in the present-day family; (*6*) its functions in child training; and (*7*) its dissolution. The first two of these will be discussed in the present chapter, the rest in the chapter following.

PARENTHOOD, KINSHIP, AND SOCIAL STRUCTURE

The family is found in all societies. Certain theorists contend that originally there existed an undifferentiated horde of males and females living together more or less promiscuously. The children of these unions were considered the offspring of the whole group. This has been called "group marriage." Under such a system fatherhood would be difficult to determine, and the mother was believed to have the dominant rôle. Still other writers have held that the original family was made up of mother and children, the father playing a very indefinite and unimportant part. Actually, no such condition as these early theorists assumed has been found, even among peoples of the most rudimentary culture.[1]

The Family, the Basis of the Social Order. Everywhere the family consists ordinarily of father, mother, and children. Nowhere are mother and child alone recognized as a family. As Havelock Ellis remarks, the fundamental fact is "the desire of the parents for each other, the desire of each for the child, and the dependence of the child on its parents, rightly considered on both its parents, for even where there is no material need of a father, there is yet a spiritual need."[2] And as B. Malinowski says, "In all human societies the father is regarded by tradition as indispensable." This he calls *the principle of legitimacy*. In other words, in every society there is some form of regulation of family relations. Everywhere the child, in order to acquire status and obtain security, is recognized as a regular and legitimate member of the group. To be com-

---

[1] See R. H. Lowie, *Primitive Society*, 1920, chap. III, and his article "Marriage," *Encyclopedia of the Social Sciences*, vol. X, p. 150; also B. Malinowski's article "Marriage," *Encyclopedia Britannica*, 14th ed., vol. XIV.

[2] Havelock Ellis, "The Family," chap. IX, in *Whither Mankind* (ed. by C. A. Beard), 1928, p. 216.

plete, the family form requires both parents, and the husband serves as a "link" between the child and the rest of the community.[3] Although in some societies the function of the biological father is neglected, or even unknown, the children still have an approved rôle and status. Although fatherhood may be differently determined than in our society, some form of legality and marriage is essential. Illegitimacy is seldom given group sanction except in certain modern countries. In many primitive societies, as with ourselves, the disgrace of illegitimate birth is rectified by obligation of the presumptive father to marry the girl. In some societies, in fact, only after the first child is born, is the permanent family group set up. Nowhere is the family complete without father, mother, and child.

This social status is important not only within the family itself, but it connects the child to other groups in the community. This is neatly illustrated in certain primitive peoples, such as the Mentawei in the East Indies, among whom a child is adopted by the mother's father, and supported by her brothers until the genuine father, who up to this point has assumed no responsibility, formally takes the mother as his wife in middle life, adopts his own children, and gives them their final status in the society.[4] The Mentawei family, moreover, consists of at least three generations: grandparents, their children, and their children's children, bound together in a functioning unity. Here we see the "joint" family, within which the marriage group proper plays only a secondary part.

The family, rooted firmly in parent-child relations and centered in the household, has in many societies distinctive relationships with other groups outside, especially the clan and tribe. The clan is a larger kinship division than the family, but, in theory at least, a kinship group tracing descent in one parental line only and possessing important group functions. By "tribe" we refer simply to a particular primitive society. Thus, the individual has a dual relationship: one to the family, the other to larger, more extensive groups.

The Family and Lines of Descent. The matter hinges, obviously, upon the matter of descent, especially where lineage fol-

[3] See Malinowski's brilliant exposition of this matter in the symposium, *The New Generation* (ed. by V. F. Calverton and S. D. Schmalhausen), 1930, pp. 113–68.

[4] See E. M. Loeb, "Mentawei Social Organization," *American Anthropologist*, 1928, vol. XXX, pp. 408–33.

lows but one family line. Where, for example, descent is traced in the father's line, or is *patrilineal*, the child takes the father's family name, becomes associated formally with the paternal clan, and has little or no relation with the mother's family. The clan and the larger society build up various restrictions on marriage and other relations within these lines of descent. (See discussion of exogamy, page 224.)   It also determines the lines of relationship to members of the clan to which the individual belongs.

Where descent is counted in the female line—that is, *matrilineal*—quite different customs are found. Thus among the Hopi Indians of our own Southwest the maternal uncle of the boy takes charge of the boy's initiation into tribal practices and lore, leaving the father rather out of account. The latter, in turn, spends his time instructing the sons of his married sisters.

The *bilateral* family system does not permit the solidarity and continuity possible in a unilateral scheme. Here the adults come together without the restrictions and binding influences found in the unilateral cultures. In our own bilateral system, the children still take their father's family name. Although the bilateral system characterizes our Western industrial society, such arrangements are not unknown in primitive groups, as in the case of certain Indian tribes in the interior of Canada.

RELATIONS OF THE SEXES IN THE FAMILY AND OUTSIDE

In this section the relations of parents as adults are considered somewhat independently of their relations to their children. In these family interactions of adults, certain standards or group-accepted and group-expected patterns of action develop which we have called institutions. These serve to define and regulate the conduct of the parents to each other and to the children.

The Nature of Marriage. Sex relations and marriage must not be confused. Marriage is a group-sanctioned bond establishing the family relations, especially in reference to the offspring. Sex relations do not necessarily lead to marriage. Marriage in most cultures is not generally entered into for sentimental or romantic reasons. Sexual gratification is not the primary purpose of marriage, but rather the legitimacy of the offspring and their care and training through the early years. As B. Malinowski remarks, "Marriage on the whole is rather a contract for the production and

maintenance of children than an authorization of sexual intercourse."[5] In our own culture the sexual and romantic phases of
marriage may become more important with the decline in the birth
rate and the disappearance of economic and related functions from
the family. (See Chapter XII on the modern family.)

In most societies, marriage is a secular, not a religious contract.
Religious sanctions, true enough, are often added, but marriage is
not universally supported by religion. Where religion has a part,
as in Christianity, it no doubt serves to increase the emotional
bonds and to put more weight behind community sanctions.

Marriage, either secular or religious in form, carries with it
everywhere certain symbolism, certain subjective factors. It implies a welding of two lives together in reference to certain obligations and duties. In various parts of the world one finds symbolic
rites, such as the bride and groom eating out of a common bowl,
drinking from the same vessel, mixing clay or earth together from
two separate lots, as external witness of the union. In our own
society marriage symbolism is illustrated by the use of engagement
and wedding rings. Marriage, like entrance into the religious
congregation, means a new life for the couple, and cultures everywhere furnish various symbolic rituals to impress this fact upon
them.

Forms of Marriage. Marriage is the institution which determines the particular relation of parents to each other and to the
children. By the phrase "form of marriage" we mean really the
number of consorts or mates which a man or woman is permitted
by the particular society. Traditionally the chief forms of marriage are monogamy, polygamy (either polygyny or polyandry),
and so-called "group marriage." To these may be added the more
recent so-called "companionate" marriage.

Many attempts have been made to fit the forms of marriage into
some fixed system of social evolution, say from promiscuity
through polygyny to monogamy. It is now generally agreed that
there is no evidence for any definite stages in marriage forms. (See
Chapter III.)

Monogamy, the marriage of one man to one woman, is without
doubt the most widespread form of mating. It is generally agreed
that monogamy lends itself best to the basic function of the family—the bearing and training of children. Monogamy is the com-

[5] See his article "Marriage" in *Encyclopedia Britannica,* 14th ed., vol. XIV.

mon denominator of human marriage everywhere. The whole institution is founded on the fact that mating necessarily takes place between two persons only, and children are always considered by society as the offspring of one couple. As Malinowski says, "A form of marriage based on communism in sex, joint parenthood, domesticity, group-contract, and a promiscuous sacrament has never been described."[6]

Monogamy is found among the lowliest culture groups, such as the Andaman Islanders. It seems to be the common rule in simpler societies organized on the democratic principle and in which the ratio of the sexes is about the same. In Africa, while polygyny is rather widespread, many tribes, such as the Masai, are essentially monogamous. In our own Occidental society monogamy has been the prevailing form of marriage. Nevertheless, in cultures where monogamy has been common and usually accepted, other forms of marriage have been permitted. Even in Christian history polygyny was occasionally practiced.[7] In our Western society monogamy seems well adapted to the practices of *laissez-faire* economics and of political democracy. Freedom of mating and individual choice of occupation, residence, political affiliation, and religion are all linked together.

Polygyny is a type of marriage in which two or more women are legally mated to one man, the children being regarded as the legal descendants of the husband. This practice, so strange to most people of Western society, is often misunderstood. It is a mistake to assume that the institution arises from any marked sexual urges of the male, since sexual gratification is nowhere perfectly correlated with marriage, monogamous or otherwise. In most societies there is ample opportunity for sexual gratification outside conventional marriage. Nor is there any society in which polygyny is universal. Nowhere is there such a disproportion of the sexes as would permit every adult male to have two or more wives. We cannot speak accurately of a "polygynous society." Even where the hazards of life reduce the number of males, as with the Eskimo, we find only a small fraction of the adult population living in polygyny. Of the Eskimo it is reported that only five per cent of the married males in Greenland had more than one wife, and per-

[6]B. Malinowski, article "Marriage," *op. cit.*
[7]See Edward Westermarck, *The History of Human Marriage*, 5th ed., vol. III, pp. 50-51.

sons of wealth were limited to two wives. Jochelson reports about
six per cent of the men among the Koryak (a Siberian tribe) as
having two or more wives.[8] In Africa and in Asia certain families
report a large number of wives, but these cases apply only to individuals of wealth or political position. In short, even where
polygyny is widely accepted, monogamy remains the most common
form of marriage. Polygyny is really a form of multiple or inter-
rupted monogamy. In most instances, each household is separate,
and the husband rotates his attention among his wives. It is true,
of course, that in some societies there are joint households where
two or more wives and their children live together. In the latter
cases, naturally, the economics of the household will be different
from that where there are separate establishments.

Perhaps the most important stimulus to polygyny is economic
need. In Africa, for instance, additional wives are added to the
household as the husband demands more help in order to increase
his wealth. In the Trobriand Islands of Melanesia a chief's income derives from the annual endowments from the families of his
various wives.

Everywhere polygynous wives provide added prestige. Among
the Tupis of South America, prominent men kept several wives for
their prestige value, as well as for domestic service and labor in the
fields. The same thing is true in Madagascar, in large sections of
Africa, and among the Kai of New Guinea. Often the first wife
urges the husband to take a second and a third or even more wives,
each new one lightening the burden of the others, adding to the
economic benefits, and improving the social status of the husband.
Also, the first wife frequently retains a certain dominance and favoritism over the other wives, who are secondary in status to her.
In any case polygyny tends to reflect wealth and rank at the expense of the husband-wife relationship stressed in more strictly
monogamous societies.

Economic factors may also limit polygyny. In/parts of Africa,
where the bride price is very high, even bigamy is out of the question for the average man. Among the Kirgiz, a Siberian tribe now
converted to Mohammedanism, a man can scarcely ever afford to
buy a second wife, and rarely does so unless the first wife is barren.
Another cultural factor limiting polygyny is the matter of resi-

---

[8] See R. H. Lowie, *Primitive Society*, 1920, pp. 41, 43. This was the situation at
the time these tribes first began to have contacts with the white man.

dence. Where the matrilocal system is in vogue, that is, where the husband settles with the wife's family, plural marriages are impossible without the permission of the first wife's family, unless the sororate is practiced. (See page 226.) Thus, matrilocal societies like the Zuni and Hopi are strictly monogamous. There are a few isolated cases, like the Yukaghir of Siberia, where the matrilocal system was modified to permit the husband to live as son-in-law for part of the year with one wife's family and the remainder with another.

There is nothing essentially degrading in primitive polygyny. Within the framework of certain culture patterns, this system of marriage seems to prove satisfactory. And it must never be forgotten that although polygyny is permitted in the mores or in law, the great majority of marriages are monogamous.

In *polyandry* several men are legally bound to one woman. This is the least common of the forms of marriage, there being apparently but four or five localities in which it is found: in the Arctic, among certain, not all, Eskimo tribes; in central Asia, especially Tibet; occasionally among the Bahima of Africa; among the Nayars of southwest India; and—best known—among the Todas of southern India. None of these societies represents the simplest cultures, and it is difficult to make a case for the correlation of polyandry with a rudimentary stage of cultural evolution.

Polyandry, like polygyny, shows interesting variations. Among the Eskimo and Todas it is related to female infanticide. In Tibet the system is of the fraternal sort, that is, several brothers share a wife in common. Among the Nayars the wife lives apart from her husbands, who cohabit with her by arrangements among themselves. Descent is traced in the maternal line, but paternity is always fixed, the girl naming one or other of her husbands as the father who is obliged to provide for the child. Among the Todas, paternity is determined by the so-called "bow and arrow" ceremony, a ritual to establish paternity. All children born after the ceremony belong to the particular man who performs it. Paternity is allocated to another husband only if he, in turn, goes through the ritual. At times husbands long dead have been called the father of children because no other husband has performed the requisite ceremony.

The so-called *companionate marriage* is a suggested form of marital relationship which is not expected ordinarily to lead to children and the family life traditionally associated with marriage.[9] With no responsibilities for children, it is further suggested that such marriages might be dissolved by mutual consent. If, however, children are born to a couple who have entered such a contract, the marriage is then considered as binding as any other.

Marriage Prohibitions. As we have already noted, no society permits absolute free choice of mates. Close degrees of blood relationship, age differences, class differences, and wider kinship relations limit this choice.

The *incest taboo* is without doubt the most universal restriction on mating. It is directed chiefly to prevent sex relations between parent and child, and between brother and sister. It often reaches out to more remote blood relatives. The few historical instances of sanctioned incest, as among the ruling families of ancient Egypt, Peru, and Ireland, are not the result of primitive conditions and ideas, but rest upon a form of sophistication coupled with belief in divine powers which would be dissipated by marriage outside the royal line.

While such incest taboos are universal, it does not follow that the taboo derives from an instinct as do hunger, thirst, and sex drives. The taboo is a rather constant and expected result arising from the very nature of the social interaction between parents and children and among the children themselves.[10] Yet the very depth of the taboo itself is some indication that the rules are broken. Social workers, psychiatrists, lawyers, clergymen, and others dealing with more intimate family problems realize that incest is not unknown in present-day society.

Exogamy is the type of union in which a person marries someone outside his own group, whether that group be family, clan, village, or other social unit. The opposite type of union, in which a man mates within his group, is called *endogamy*.

---

[9] This expression was perhaps first used by M. M. Knight, but was made popular by Judge Ben Lindsey in his book *The Companionate Marriage*, 1927. Traditionally married couples who have no offspring still constitute a family because their *intention* is to have children. In the "companionate marriage" there is no intention to have children.

[10] L. H. Hobhouse, R. H. Lowie, and others hold incest taboos to be instinctive. Tozzer and others deny this. Present-day social psychology, indicating the tremendous power of early conditioning with its powerful taboos, is sufficient to explain the matter. Certainly where parents and children are separated, or where brothers and sisters grow up in separate households without intimate knowledge of each other and of their blood relationship, there is no evidence of the display of such an "instinct."

Tribal endogamy is almost universal. In the more rudimentary societies it is a natural outcome of isolation and strong in-group solidarity. Moreover, within the tribe or larger society where a clan system develops, or where professional or aristocratic ranks or economic status or a caste system arises, endogamy within these special groups is generally demanded. Religion plays an important rôle in fostering endogamy. In few major religions is marriage with outsiders sanctioned. Evident illustrations are Mohammedanism, Judaism, Christianity, and Hinduism.

Exogamy arises wherever groups of persons are believed sufficiently related to be forbidden to marry, with a consequent insistence on their mating in other groups within the wider community. It is found chiefly associated with wider kinship and clan relations. The most common example among primitive peoples occurs when the tribes are divided into two groupings, members of one being forbidden to marry within their own and obliged to seek their mates in the other. In our own bilateral system, formal exogamy is in little evidence. Aside from the incest taboos concerning sexual relationships within the immediate family or between close cousins, which are enforced by custom and law, people are not obliged to select their mates either within or without carefully determined limits.

Means of Securing a Mate. The literature on primitive marriage reveals a wide variety of methods of procuring a wife or a husband quite unknown to us. The popular notion of the most primitive method of getting a wife is the picture of the burly cave dweller who, after knocking a woman on the head, drags her off to his own camp site. This lurid picture is pure fiction so far as any living tribes are concerned.

There are, however, various methods of *wife-purchase*. Some of these are rather complicated and involve not only the prospective husband and bride, but the respective families in which sometimes a father begins accumulating a bride-price for his young son's future wife years in advance of the actual marriage. There are also forms of *dowry* in which the bride's family is required to pay the husband or the husband's family stipulated moneys or goods. This system existed in our own society until recently. It is still practiced in certain of the European countries.

Preferential mating is a term used to describe certain rules which limit the range of marriageable mates. We have already noted incest taboos, exogamy, and endogamy. Here we refer rather to cross-cousin marriage, the levirate, and the sororate.

Cross-cousin marriage is quite unknown in our Western society, but exists among the native tribes of Australia, in parts of Asia, and occasionally among our North American Indians. Cross cousins are cousins whose parents are brother and sister. In many tribes, so-called parallel or identical cousins, that is, those whose fathers are brothers, or whose mothers are sisters, are prevented from marrying by various kinship taboos. Cross-cousin marriage is of two sorts: a man may marry either the daughter of a mother's brother, or of a father's sister. The Kariera of Australia and some other tribes make cross-cousin marriage compulsory, while in other societies, as in the Fiji Islands, there is some provision for individual antipathy. Among the Todas, the Veddahs, and some others, marriage is prescribed whenever it is possible. The causes for this sort of mating are not known, but doubtless property and kinship play a part.[11]

The *levirate* provides that in remarriage one of the brothers of the deceased husband must marry his widow or often that her remarriage is limited to the husband's brothers. In some instances the widow may choose among several male relatives of the husband. In some cases such a choice is not obligatory. Among primitive peoples the levirate is more widespread than cross-cousin mating. Nearly half a century ago E. B. Tylor reported that one third of the tribes on which data were then available practiced this custom. It is extremely widespread among the North American Indians, and is common over all of Asia and Africa. Like other customs classified under the same name, the levirate is not everywhere identical. In some cases, the so-called "junior levirate" holds, where the remarriage of a widow is restricted to younger brothers of the dead husband. Naturally this system is easily tied with polygyny, as it was among the ancient Hebrews.[12] Property considerations are doubtless important factors in stimulating and keeping the levirate alive, especially where the system of a bride-price is common, since leaving a widow may necessitate returning the woman to her own family, and loss of her economic value. Still the economic motive is not the only one, and in some instances, it apparently has nothing to do with the levirate.

[11] For discussion of the theories, see R. H. Lowie, *Primitive Society*, 1920, pp. 29–32.
[12] On the levirate among the Hebrews see *Deuteronomy* 25:5–10; also *Genesis* 38.

In the *sororate* the wife's sister is supposed to marry the widower upon the death of the wife. Again, there are two sorts of mating possible. A man may be permitted to marry his wife's sisters during her lifetime, or he may be restricted to marriage with the dead wife's sister. The sororate, like the levirate, is widespread. In fact, the two systems go together in many societies. Like the levirate the degree of compulsion or expectancy differs with various groups.

Preparation for Marriage. The relations of the sexes before marriage differ in various societies. In some tribes prenuptial intercourse is not only permitted but often expected, but there is, as we have seen, no evidence of complete promiscuity in any society. Everywhere the incest taboos, class lines, age groupings, and other restrictions limit the relations of the sexes both before and after marriage. Although among the Trobrianders, the Samoans, and the Masai of Africa the older adolescents and young adults carry on sex relations before settling down to marriage, there are certain restrictions in terms of rank, age, and kinship. In some societies prenuptial relations are not supposed to lead to marriage. Among the Masai, for example, they are carried on by men and women of certain age classes until lawful matrimony is accomplished. From that time on, the former freedom is taboo.[13]

Among most peoples such premarital relations are decidedly preparatory to marriage. Among the Trobrianders, after various temporary liaisons, a young man and woman may decide to marry. Among many peasant peoples premarital intercourse is permissible after formal betrothal, and only after the girl becomes pregnant is the marriage consummated.

There is no uniformity in regard to premarital relations. In closely contiguous tribes, for instance, one group puts high value on chastity, while their neighbors consider it of no consequence at all. Some of the most lowly tribes, such as the Veddahs and other Negrito peoples, have as strong taboos against prenuptial sexual relations as are found in our own Christian society, where chastity is a high virtue. In the Christian culture the sense of sin and guilt associated with sex, colors not only all premarital contacts of persons, but profoundly influences subsequent marital relations as well. Christian marriage is so surrounded with religious sanctions that the whole matter of sexual adjustment may be very different

[13] See R. H. Lowie, *op. cit.*, pp. 50–51.

from that among other peoples, as Margaret Mead has shown in her book *Coming of Age in Samoa* (1928).

Among Christian peoples, however, rather striking differences often occur between theory and practice. Since the patriarchal system was carried over into Christianity, with all that it implies for male dominance and female submission, it was very easy for the so-called "double standard of morality" to arise. Thus in many Christian communities the unmarried male is permitted prenuptial sexual freedom, but only with women whom he would not marry. The marriageable women of the community, on the other hand, are held to strict Christian taboos on premarital sexuality. In such a society female virginity is rated high, but male continency is neither expected nor often desired, in spite of theological taboos.

Nowhere is prenuptial liberty considered a negation or a substitute for marriage. Where permitted, it is believed to be preparatory to matrimony and family life. Again it must be noted that sex life and marriage are not to be confused. So far as the latter is a matter of regulation, it is always pointed toward parenthood and the principle of legitimacy of offspring.

Other Forms of Sex Life Outside Marriage. In various societies we find customary provision for sexual relations outside the bonds of matrimony. *Concubinage* where practiced is a lawful form of cohabitation, differing from marriage because the concubine has a much lower social status than the husband and his proper wives. Children of such unions are not accorded equal rights of action or inheritance with those of the legal spouse. This system is often associated with polygyny, and at times it is difficult to distinguish between the concubine and the polygynous wife, especially where the latter has much lower status in the family and community than the first wife. Like polygyny, concubinage is usually restricted to a few persons of wealth and prominence.

Prostitution is distinctly limited in extent among primitive peoples. It is largely a product of more complex cultures. It seems to accompany urbanization, mobility of population, commercial life, and specialization of labor. In Christian societies it was a continuation of pagan customs carried over perhaps as a reaction against the severity of the official taboos on sexual freedom. Prostitution has always been a subsidiary form of sexual behavior, and doubtless it has had far less negative effect on the institution of marriage than has been popularly imagined. Today the whole system of commercialized prostitution seems to be disappearing from Western societies, as traditional taboos on prenuptial and extra-marital cohabitation disappear. Some people contend that the relaxation of the sexual codes which involve both husband and wife constitute a much more serious threat at the fundamentals of the traditional family than does prostitution. No one, however, can overlook the dangers of venereal infection which have so long been associated with prostitution. The serious consequences of these infections in regard to childbearing and marital happiness are well known.

Among some primitive societies, notably certain Eskimo, Siberian, and Oceanic tribes, we find the custom of *sexual hospitality*. Male guests visiting in a household are offered the host's wife as a temporary sexual partner. Yet custom throws about the practice various forms of restriction, and there is nothing here resembling promiscuity or so-called "sexual communism" in the popular sense. Sometimes the custom is a form of wife exchange, men agreeing that when on long trips these reciprocal rights will be accorded them as the demand arises.

Finally, in some societies, forms of sexual orgy are permissible in connection with religious or other ceremonials. These relations are highly temporary. They are hedged about with any number of taboos in terms of kinship and other groupings. Above all else they are not permitted to disturb the family and household arrangements. We need to re-emphasize the fact that parenthood and children are basic, and that all these extra-marital permissions do not change the "principle of legitimacy." Although children may result from these extra-marital episodes, the child is legitimate, that is, the legal husband is considered the father.

Position of Male and Female in the Family. The status and rôle of the parents are naturally greatly affected by the form of familial control and the method of tracing lineage. Patrilineal families are traditionally patriarchal, except in some of our urban families where the wife has assumed many prerogatives of control because of the husband's absence from the household.

In the patriarchal family the father is the dominant authority. In many societies his power is absolute in theory, as it was in the early Roman and Hebrew family systems. In Rome, say down to the third century B. C., the family consisted of the oldest living direct male ancestor, the patriarch, under whose control, as *pater familias,* his own children and grandchildren remained till his death. He might punish his children, sell them for slaves, banish them from the country, or execute them for grave offenses, although the latter power was usually modified or partially controlled by the law. No male member of his "joint" family had control over his property or his earnings, nor could he transmit his property to others so long as his father lived. So, too, the husband exercised complete control over his wife. As Cato commented, "The husband is the judge of his wife. If she has committed a fault, he punishes her; if she has drunk wine, he condemns her; if she has been guilty of adultery, he kills her."[14] Nevertheless the high reputation of the Roman matron is not pure mythology. Like the Grecian wife she had a good deal of domestic power and responsibility and seems to have been at once honored by, and subordinated to, her mate.

Matrilineal families tend, likewise, to be matriarchal in control. Yet the popular story books give a false view. Although in these societies the mother does exercise considerable power over the children, it is more often her family rather than herself that regulates family contacts. The case of the Hopi has already been noted, where the wife's brother has control over the children and undertakes their discipline and training.

Nowhere is there evidence that women rule either the household, the clan, or the tribe without regard to male power. The armchair theorists have made much of archaic female power, and the stories of the ancient Amazons may make good reading, but they are neither anthropology nor history. Even with the highly developed matriarchal system among the Iroquois Indians, the power of the women was everywhere hemmed in by complementary power of the men of the family and the clan.[15]

Three other important features of family life remain to be discussed: the dissolution of the family by divorce, the care of children, and the economic functions of the family. Since so many of our present-day problems relate to these, we shall discuss them in the next chapter in connection with the modern family of Western society.

[14] Quoted from *Quae Extant* by Willystine Goodsell, *The Family as a Social and Educational Institution,* 1915, pp. 116–17.
[15] See A. A. Goldenweiser, *Early Civilization,* 1922, chap. III.

CLASS ASSIGNMENTS

A. Further reading assignment:
1. K. Young, *Source Book for Sociology*, chap. XI.
2. E. R. Groves, *The American Family*, chaps. II, III, IV.
3. Ralph Linton, *The Study of Man*, chap. X.

B. Questions and exercises:
1. What is meant by saying that parenthood and the family are basic to all societal organization?
2. Distinguish between monogamy, polygyny, and polyandry. Show how the latter two are always limited in extent in any society unless very special circumstances arise. Name some of the unusual circumstances that favor polygyny or polyandry.
3. Does the "companionate marriage" constitute a family? Discuss.
4. Name and illustrate the types of prohibitions which limit and direct one's choice of a mate in our own society. Contrast with such prohibitions in primitive and in other civilized societies than our own.
5. What changes in the status of the wife and mother have taken place in recent decades in our own society? What effect has the declining birth rate had in this matter? (See Chapter X.)
6. What provision do we make for preparation for marital and family responsibilities? Suggest changes in our folkways which would improve these.

C. Topics for class reports or longer written papers:
1. The theories of social evolution applied to family organization and family institutions. (Consult R. H. Lowie, *Primitive Society*, 1920, chaps. II, III, IV, and bibliography; B. Malinowski, article "Marriage," *Encyclopedia Britannica*, 14th ed., vol. 14, and bibliography; Edward Westermarck, *The History of Human Marriage*, 3 vols., 5th ed., 1922, and bibliography; A. A. Goldenweiser, chap. V in *History and Prospects of the Social Sciences*, ed. by H. E. Barnes, 1926, and bibliography.)
2. The rise and nature of Mormon polygyny. (Consult M. R. Werner, *Brigham Young*, 1925, chap. VIII; W. A. Linn, *The Story of the Mormons*, 1902; Susan Ertz, *The Proselyte*, a novel, 1933.)
3. Contrasts in the sex mores of primitive and pre-literate peoples. (See Lowie, *op. cit.;* B. Malinowski, *Sex and Repression in Savage Society*, 1929; Margaret Mead, *Coming of Age in Samoa*, 1928, and her *Growing Up in New Guinea*, 1930, and her *Sex and Temperament in Three Primitive Societies*, 1935; Hortense Powdermaker, *Life in Lesu*, 1933.)

CHAPTER XII

THE MODERN FAMILY

Today the family in much of Europe, in America, and in the British Dominions is passing rapidly out of the patriarchal pattern into one in which the relations of wife to husband and of children to parents are profoundly altered; although under fascism the old patterns are being revived. Political and economic changes have played an important part in determining these relationships. Here we shall treat chiefly the American family and its problems.

CHANGES IN WESTERN FAMILY LIFE

Many influences have combined to produce the family patterns of contemporary Western society. The most important are those connected with Christianity, romanticism, the rise of individualism, and the Industrial Revolution.

Backgrounds of Western Family Life. The early Christian church was made up of small, devout bands of people who believed that the end of the world would soon be upon them. As this expected event failed to materialize and as the missionary zeal of the Christians converted ever larger numbers of pagans, the whole character of the church and its relation to the wider society changed. It borrowed everywhere from the culture around it, and by the third and fourth centuries it had become a dominating influence in Western society. Its principal effects upon family life were expressed in the doctrine of other-worldly asceticism, in the doctrine of sexual sin, and in the low regard for women. Asceticism would banish, if possible, sexual expression from man's social life. And in any event sex must be strictly controlled. The early Christian taboos against sex have come down to us today, including all sorts of notions about it being sinful, lewd, nasty, and debasing in character. Women were thought chiefly responsible for man's downfall in the first instance. Their rôle was at best to bear children and serve as housekeepers. Marriage, while not the highest state, was permitted; and the church made marriage one of the temporal sacraments—a concession to man's mortal nature, but withal a form of control to keep it within the bounds of the church. This view continued for centuries, until disturbed by romanticism, individualism, and economic changes.

Romanticism developed from the age of chivalry. Later it became connected with the doctrine of individualism. Romantic love, while it concerned only the aristocratic classes at first, did have the merit of refining the attitudes of men toward their women folk. The Renaissance, with its general enlightenment and criticism of tradition, influenced both theory and practice in regard to sex. But the Reformation, in turn, especially its Calvinistic branch, laid heavy taboos upon sexual freedom. As individualism developed and as eighteenth-century romanticism got under way, the position of women rose steadily, at least in theory, in spite of Calvinism and other Christian theology.

In practice the changes came slowly. Throughout the centuries, woman, high or low, was chiefly concerned with childbearing, child rearing, attention to her lord and master, and her contribution—among the middle and lower classes at least—to the economics of the household. The wife had no property rights of her own. In the law she was treated as a minor. She could not enter into a contract. Wages paid her went to her husband. She had no political duties such as voting or jury service.

The Industrial Revolution, beginning in England in the late eighteenth century, and on the continent and in America during the nineteenth, had a profound effect. With it went the gradual economic emancipation of woman from the father or the husband, the rise of political democracy with its final granting of the ballot to woman, the relaxation of the Christian taboos on sex for both men and women, and with the urbanization of population the decline of the household as a center of family economic life, and primary education. The weight of these factors in the total influence cannot be stated, but we may note some of them, first in the composition of the family, then in the economic life of the household, and finally changes in the status of wife, husband, and children in the family situation.

Size and Composition of American Family. Many people believe that the American family is rapidly disintegrating. No matter what may be happening to the economic and psychological structure of the family, and in spite of increasing divorce rates, the proportion of the American population 15 years of age and over that is married has been increasing steadily for some decades. In 1890, it was 55.3 per cent, in 1930, 60.5. Part of this increase is doubtless due to the increase in the numbers of the population of marriageable years. But taking this factor into account, the percentage married in 1930 was 57.6.

Not only is our married population increasing, but since 1890 the average age at which marriage occurs has been declining. In the age group 15–19, there were 15 per 1,000 more married persons in 1930 than for the comparable group in 1890, and 73 more per 1,000 for the age group 20–24 for the same years. Some writers believe the decade 1920–1930 marks a turning point. Hereafter we may see relatively less early marriage, although increasingly widespread knowledge of contraception makes early marriage less and less an economic risk so far as children are concerned.[1]

W. F. Ogburn has recently reported an analysis of the size of families in four types of American communities: sample farm, certain small towns of about 5,000 population, a group of cities between 50,000 and 150,000, and one metropolis, Chicago. Defining the family as made up of parents and children alone, or, if no children, of husband and wife or widowed persons,[2] his samples together gave an average size of unbroken families living at home as 3.67 persons in 1900, 3.58 in 1920, and 3.57 in 1930. The farm families actually increased in size three per cent in 30 years, those of small towns declined by like percentage, the medium-sized cities decreased four per cent, and those in the metropolis 11 per cent.

Contrasting Chicago with his farm sample, Ogburn shows that there were two and a half times as many unbroken families

---

[1]See W. F. Ogburn, "The Family and its Functions," chap. XIII, *Recent Social Trends,* p. 680.

[2]It should be noted that the statistical studies of family size and composition must always be interpreted from the definition of the family used. For example, the United States Bureau of the Census in 1930 defined a family as follows: "a group of persons, related either by blood or by marriage or adoption, who live together as one household, usually sharing the same table. Single persons living alone are counted as families, however, as are a few small groups of unrelated persons sharing the same living accommodations as 'partners'."

This is largely what other writers call a "household." In other studies, the natural biological family only is included, and in other instances still other definitions are used. See Mildred Parten, "A Statistical Analysis of the Modern Family," *Annals of the American Academy of Political and Social Science,* March, 1932, vol. CLX, pp. 29–31.

without children living at home in the metropolis as there were on the farms of his sample. In the former, however, only six per cent of husbands and wives living together had more than two children, while in the farming area, 35 per cent had more than two children. Furthermore, there are three and a half times as many families classified as "husband only" or "wife only" in Chicago as in the rural section. Wives living alone are five times as numerous in the metropolis as in the farming area. It must be noted also that in a metropolitan center there is a variety of cultural backgrounds to family life: immigrants, Negroes, residents of rooming houses, and more traditional families living in single dwellings. All these would vary greatly as to size. In rural America there is no doubt a far more nearly homogeneous family pattern.

Occupational status evidently affects family size, as the following table shows:

TABLE 5

AVERAGE NUMBER OF PERSONS PER FAMILY IN SELECTED COMMUNITIES, DIVIDED BY BROAD OCCUPATIONAL GROUPS, 1930[3]

Occupations	Average size
Professions	3.01
Clerical	3.04
Proprietary group (store owners, business managers, etc.)	3.25
Skilled	3.51
Semiskilled	3.47
Unskilled	3.91
Farm owners and farm renters	4.48
Farm laborers	4.32

Childless families present a special problem in our society. Where there are no children, the responsibilities and activities following marriage are quite different from those where there are. In 1930, for the four types of communities studied, 31 per cent of all unbroken families (with wives under 45 years old) had no children at all or none living at home. A similar analysis for 1900 gives 28 per cent of no-child families. There is a correlation with size of community. The percentages of no-child families in this sample were as follows: for the farm area, 18 per cent; small towns, 25 per cent; cities, 33 per cent; and in the metropolis, 49 per cent—practically one family in every two. The rural area actually shows a decrease of five per cent in no-child families since 1900, but the

[3] Table made up from data in Ogburn, op. cit., pp. 685–86.

small towns, cities, and the metropolis show an increase of eight
per cent, 14 per cent, and 30 per cent respectively.

Closely associated with changes in family size and in economic
functions of the household is the decline in the size of the family
dwelling. Guest bedrooms and the old-fashioned parlor are disappearing. And although the number of apartments is increasing,
the new apartments tend to be smaller per family unit. In Chicago
for 1913–1919, the average size of new apartments was 4.6 rooms,
for 1924–1928, 3.5 rooms. In New York City a similar report gave
the average size of new apartments in 1913 as 4.1 rooms; in 1928
it was 3.34.[4] Since 1929 figures are doubtless even more striking.
These alterations in the size of the family and its dwelling
are closely related to the changing functions of the family and
home in modern industrial society.

ECONOMIC FUNCTIONS OF THE FAMILY

The family has played an important part in the economic life of
most societies. Yet it would be a grave mistake to assume that
the form of the family and of marriage is determined solely by economic motives. True, the economic order in many societies is
closely linked to the family, but the cohesion of these culture patterns is not inevitable.

Where the household has an important economic function, we
usually find a certain sexual division of labor. The wife's activities
usually center in or near the household, the husband's in hunting,
fishing, caring for crops, or work in the factory.

We have already noted that such practices as polygyny and
bride-price reflect the economic worth of women. Inheritance systems are definitely related to the marriage system and the form of
the family. The disposition of property is relatively simple in the
ruder societies. The same division of labor which sets up the distinctive rights and duties of each partner while living determines
the allotment of the goods at the death of either spouse. A man
will inherit his father's or maternal uncle's or a brother's goods; a
wife, her mother's, her aunt's, or her sister's, depending on whether
it is a matrilineal or patrilineal system. A wife seldom inherits a
husband's property, nor does he inherit hers, since as R. H. Lowie

---

[4] For summary of data on this matter see R. D. McKenzie, "The Rise of Metropolitan Communities," chap. IX, *Recent Social Trends*, pp. 472–76.

points out, "according to a widespread primitive belief spouses form a temporary alliance with a pooling of interests; death dissolves the partnership, and the property held by either reverts to his or her kindred."[5] In European and American society, the dominance of the husband over the wife in matters of inheritance is largely a reflection of the patriarchal system of an earlier time. Only gradually have the property rights of the wife been partially equalized.

Recent Changes in American Family and Household. In pioneer and early rural America, the husband and wife shared a large number of economic responsibilities. The household was the center of many economic activities in which the wife played a definite rôle. Spinning, weaving, and making clothes long continued to be her duty, and even as machine industry replaced home manufacture, she made the clothes for the family. Then, too, she took charge of the curing of meat, of preserving vegetables and fruit for winter use, and usually had the care of the milk, eggs, and the garden produce. The household members were concerned with *making* a living rather than *earning* wages. Money economy had but a slight place in the scheme of things. The following extract from the diary of a New England farmer of a few generations ago states:

"My farm gave me and my whole family a good living on the produce of it and left me, one year with another, one hundred and fifty silver dollars, for I never spent more than ten dollars a year, which was for salt, nails, and the like. Nothing to eat, drink, or wear was bought, as my farm produced it all."[6]

Today the farmer, like the city worker, is concerned with earning a living. He has specialized in his crops. He sells his produce for cash, with which he must pay his taxes, pay his debts, buy clothes and much of his food. All these mean that even the farm household has been profoundly influenced by modern economic organization.

The *household* is usually considered to be all the persons living under one roof and may include relatives other than immediate kin, or servants, and lodgers. The average size of the American household in 1790 was 5.9 persons. In the four sorts of communities

[5] In article "Marriage," *Encyclopedia of the Social Sciences,* vol. 10, p. 149.
[6] Quoted by Lawrence K. Frank, "Social Changes and the Family," *The Annals,* etc., March, 1932, vol. CLX, p. 95.

studied by W. F. Ogburn, the average household in 1930 had 4.4 persons. Throughout recent decades the size of the household has been declining—a definite evidence of its loss of economic functions. But this shrinkage differs with the size of the community. Clearly the farm household has retained many economic activities now quite lost in the urban community. It is also interesting to note that the number of servants, lodgers, and boarders in a household declined from 63 per 100 households in 1900 to 44 (33 of whom were relatives) in 1930.[7]

The number of married women gainfully employed is a common measure of changes in the economic function of the household. In 1900 there were 769,000 married women at work; in 1910 there were 1,891,000; and in 1930 the figure had reached 3,071,000. In this 30-year period the total population had increased 66 per cent, the number of employed women 100 per cent, and the number of employed married women 300 per cent. Between 1920 and 1930 the number of married women working outside the home increased 60 per cent, while the total number of married women increased only 23 per cent. Formerly a great many gainfully employed married women had dependent spouses. Now there is an ever-increasing number of wives employed as additional wage earners. A recent study of 23,373 Chicago families showed that 17.6 per cent of the married women were employed. Of these one half also had wage-earning husbands. But there still remained 26,000,000 housewives in this country in 1930 who, though not listed in the census as employed, performed economic duties of no mean value.

Another evidence of changes in the American household is revealed in the duties performed by women at home. One study has shown that the amount of time spent in preparing meals and washing dishes is much less in the city than in the country.[8] Yet many changes have taken place in all households. In a study of 1,000 homes in 1930 it was shown that two thirds of the farm, three fourths of the village, and nine tenths of the city households used baker's bread only. The United States Census of Manufactures for 1929 shows that the per capita production of bakery goods made outside the home increased 27 per cent from 1919 to 1929, whereas

---

[7] See Ogburn, *op. cit.,* pp. 681–83.

[8] See Hildegard Kneeland, "Woman's Economic Contribution to the Home," *The Annals* etc., May, 1929, vol. CXLIII. Much of this is summarized by Ogburn, *op. cit.,* pp. 669–71. Other data from Miss Kneeland were supplied to Ogburn for his chapter, *op. cit.*

the per capita consumption of wheat both inside and outside the home actually decreased nearly 10 per cent.

Laundry work in city homes is also declining. Of the families studied in the above-noted sample, only 23 per cent of the city households did all their washing at home, while 70 per cent of the rural households did. Another study showed a contrast of 33 per cent of home laundry in the city and 88 per cent in the country. The manner in which disappearance of household functions leads to changes elsewhere is witnessed in the increase of 79 per cent between 1919 and 1929 in the number of wage earners in commercial laundering. There is ample evidence that cleaning and dyeing of clothes, cleaning furniture, renovating rugs and carpets are all disappearing from the modern American household. The number of cleaners and dyers in this country increased 220 per cent between 1919 and 1929. While some of these changes indicate a rising standard of living, doubtless the bulk of the change reflects the declining importance of these activities in the home.

In like fashion, refrigeration has made noticeable differences in home habits and has doubtless made cooking and serving meals simpler and perhaps healthier. As the Lynds point out in their community study, *Middletown* (1929), until the advent of modern refrigeration, most American families had a "winter diet" of heavy starches and meats, and a "summer diet" more largely confined to green vegetables, with a greater ratio of vitamins and roughage. Today almost all families may secure a better balanced diet at all seasons.

The industrial canning of fruits and vegetables, which doubled between 1919 and 1929, reflects another change in household occupations of women-folk. So, too, sewing of clothes at home has almost disappeared with the coming of ready-to-wear dresses and other clothes for women. The making of men's clothes at home disappeared long ago.

The use of power machinery to do what remains to be done in the home is related to a decline in the number of servants. Also the use of gas and electricity for the family needs has further changed the character of the household activities. Between 1920 and 1930 the number of household users of gas increased 41 per cent, while the number of families increased only 23 per cent. The domestic users of electricity increased 135 per cent during this same decade. The per capita production of such electrical devices for the home as toasters, grills, percolators, and waffle irons increased amazingly in the years 1920–1930. The number of vacuum cleaners per capita increased 20 per cent between 1919 and 1929; the number of electrical washing machines and ironers increased 65 per cent. While there is some decline in the rate of increase following the depression of 1930, this doubtless reflects a cyclical fluctuation.[9] This increase in the use of mechanical devices may help keep certain household functions alive by lessening the work of the housewife. It scarcely offsets the other losses in family economic functions.

The enormous increase in the number of restaurants and lunch rooms must represent a distinctive change in household activity. These increased 88 per cent between 1920 and 1930, while the urban population increased but 26 per cent, and the total population but 16 per cent. The number of persons engaged as waiters and waitresses increased 72 per cent in this decade. There may have been a decline in the number of boarding houses, but the rapid increase in restaurants can scarcely be explained by this decrease alone.

Most of the changes we have noted have gone on more rapidly in our cities than in the villages and rural sections. There are also distinct differences in the rates of change in various economic classes. As the Lynds have shown in *Middletown,* the business and professional classes take advantage of these opportunities to a greater extent than do the laboring groups. Yet, in spite of these differences in the rate of change, the character of the home life is everywhere greatly affected.

CHANGED RELATIONS OF MEN AND WOMEN

These external changes have their counterpart in the psychological attitudes and the more personal habits built up between husband and wife. The inferior position of woman in this man-made world we have already noted. This subordinate position meant that the woman was denied opportunities for emotional and intellectual growth. She remained in many ways little more than a "child-woman," as some one has called her.

Added to this inferiority are certain phases of the romantic marriage pattern common in Western society which help keep

[9] See R. S. Lynd, "The People as Consumers," chap. XVII, Table 15, *Recent Social Trends,* pp. 897–901.

woman in subjection. Romantic love in theory and practice rests
upon the picture of the dominant chivalrous male who sweeps
his beautiful woman off her feet, declares eternal love and fidelity
to her, and who puts her upon the pedestal of beauty, charm, and
delight, but refuses to accept her as an everyday equal in the work
of the world, a notion which puts her at a distinct disadvantage
today. So long as woman accepts this rôle and this status, she
must remain inferior to her mate. Changes of the last few decades
have altered this. Today women, both single and married, are getting into gainful occupations outside the home. They are receiving education equal to that of their brothers and husbands. They
have at last gained equal political and legal rights.

Yet everywhere in education, business, and politics it is difficult
for men who work with women to forget the traditional female
function, and it is only slowly that women themselves acquire a
feeling of independence and push their demands for genuine equality. In these outside relations many women want to retain their
former romantic rôle and still be accorded equality in economic
and political competition. They cannot long live in both the old
and the new world. They must either fall back into the former rôle,
or go on to a life which is integrated around more modern attitudes.

The Psychology of Husband-Wife Relations. The principal
social-psychological factors in this new pattern of family relations
touch companionship, stimulation to adequate activity commen-
surate with the demands of the social, economic, and political
world around them, mutual respect in a competitive world of industry or business, and finally the deeper relations of the love life.
Associated with these are the person's demand for security, for reassurance of his capacity, of his rôle and status, and the relation of
his sex functioning to self-assurance, confidence, and reassurance
from others. Let us look a bit more closely at these matters.

In previous societies, each mate had economic and educational
functions in the family, in addition to being the provider for or the
bearer of children, as the case might be. Today, with fewer children
and with the disappearance of economic and educational activities
from the home, the mates are more and more dependent on mutual
companionship and sexual attraction in order to keep them together. This comradeship must mean interstimulation for achievement in the outside world, and there must, perhaps, develop a
closer integration of occupation and the deeper sympathies of the

love life. Related with this must come also the respect and standing of the individual in the wider world outside, reflected back into the family life. It is largely in this way that the modern family group may be co-ordinated with the secondary groups outside the home.

There is an especially important interaction centering in the sex life. At the purely biological level this relation in man is not much removed from that of the anthropoids. Actually, however, sex functioning is everywhere profoundly influenced by culture. While in some societies rather little emphasis may be put on the more subtle features of the love life, there has grown up among certain classes the notion of mutual admiration, respect, and the intimate desire of each mate to please the craving of the other, not merely at the physical level, but in regard to all the finer, kindlier, and more sympathetic relations. As society removes from the family other functions, including the former heavy burdens of child-bearing and child training, these more intimate relations may come to play a greater part.

Every person has an intense craving for a sense of security. This is built up in the child in the stable structure of the family and is the psychological defense of Malinowski's "principle of legitimacy," as well as the *rationale* for consistent forms of home training for the child. Adults are no different. They carry over into later life the same needs for security. The pattern of security in the family finds one important expression in the rôle of the husband and father as provider, as professionally or occupationally successful in terms of what the culture sets down as an ideal. He also develops an image of himself as father of his children and as lover to his wife. When the relations with his wife, with his children, and with the wider world outside become unstable and insecure, these relations are reflected back into his own self-image. That his own self-assurance may grow and remain, he needs the reassurance of others, especially those intimate with him in the family. (See Chapter XXVIII on the effect of loss of occupation on attitudes.)

His self growth is also related to his sexual love. He may find in these intimacies his greatest stimulation to activity in the wider world as well as comfort from strain outside—in fact, a set of stabilizing factors not to be secured either in parenthood alone or in economic success outside.

In like manner the wife must find her security in the strength and companionship of the husband. If she has a profession, she will need not only the prestige afforded by her professional or business colleagues, but will require appreciation and understanding from her mate. If her work is cut off entirely from the rest of her life, it will remain a segment of her personality which she does not share with the man with whom she is otherwise most intimately connected.

So, too, the wife as mother and caretaker of her children develops a side of her self-image which will grow or diminish both in relation to the attitudes of the husband and of the children as well. If the family is marked by conflict, instability, and unpredictability, her own inner self cannot grow into a well-rounded structure.

Finally the sexual life of the wife must, like that of her husband, symbolize the deeper sympathies with her mate. It must be a source of comfort, release from stress, and a means of reassurance. Neither man nor woman can long continue to separate these more intimate relations from the rest of their lives and expect the sense of security, the balance of divergent desires, and the mutual interstimulation and response that are necessary for mental health.

It is easy to ask, What about the constancy of these relations? What have they to do with the changing size of family, with increase in the number of childless marriages, and with the problem of divorce?

So far as constancy goes, the older notion of marital contract enforced by outside coercion may in time give way to a realization that genuine constancy rests upon psychological factors. It is not to be denied that external pressure and social expectancy are important, but the fundamental demands for stability will develop out of these newer but more necessary intimate relations. If one spouse makes greater intellectual or professional progress than the other or develops too divergent habits and attitudes, inconstancy may appear. Where there are no children this may lead to other arrangements or to easy divorce. Where children are involved, the situation may be differently considered.

It is clear that in Western society, at least, the marriage pair, in the strict sense, become increasingly significant as the former family functions disappear. This change needs emphasis, since many writers on the family are still thinking largely of patterns of behavior that belong to an age which is rapidly passing away. Not to see and understand the newer relations in marriage is to fail to prepare for changes which are already at hand.

THE FAMILY AND CHILD TRAINING

The foundation of the "principle of legitimacy" is the bearing and rearing of children until they can assume their adult place in society. Traditionally the functions of the family in regard to the children concern reproduction, early care, training, and socialization of the child, including moral and religious instruction, and certain secondary functions related to play life, recreation, and preparation for vocation and citizenship. The parents' place in these functions varies in different societies.

Reproduction and Infant Care. Biologically the wife is always more intimately associated with procreation than the father. His part is momentary; hers continues not only through the period of pregnancy but also through months of nursing and years of subsequent care of the child. In some primitive societies the father's function in reproduction apparently is not known at all. But everywhere it is impossible to ignore the biological function of the mother.

Culture always lays down most of the patterns of the relations of mother and father to the child. We have already noted that in matriarchal and matrilocal societies, the wife's brothers often dominate the household much more than does the natural father. In patriarchal organizations the father and his family have a large part in child training.

In most primitive societies disease and unsanitary conditions take a heavy toll of both mothers and babies. It is only in recent times that applied science has reduced this tragic price which nature long demanded for reproduction, and we have already noted in Chapter X some of the implications of this change in infant mortality for population problems.

In present-day American family life we find changes in the relations of husband and wife in regard to the children, changes growing out of present economic conditions. In urban communities, particularly, the absence of the father from the home for long hours leaves to the wife nearly *all* the duties of child training and discipline, a condition not true of the earlier American family nor even now so true in rural America, where the father and children —at least those old enough to work—are in daily interaction. There is arising in urban family life a new sort of matriarchy in which the wife and mother is assuming a new rôle.[10]

Economic and Other Activities of Children in the Home. While reproduction and care of offspring are the central purpose of family life, the child is often considered an economic asset. Among peasant peoples everywhere children are put to work at early ages in the fields and in the household. Even in some pre-agricultural societies boys are often initiated early into fishing and hunting activities and girls into household duties. While child labor in our Western society was transferred from the farm to the factory in the first flush of capitalistic machine exploitation, in the last few decades there has been a steady decline in child labor in all the Western industrial nations. In the United States, for example, in 1880 the number of children gainfully employed was 16.8 per cent of the total number in the age group 10 to 15 years. The corresponding percentages for subsequent decades are as follows: 1890, 18.1; 1900, 18.2; 1910, 18.4; 1920, 8.5; and 1930, 4.7. Children, especially in adolescence, have had some work in nearly all societies; but naturally the conditions of labor in a factory or coal pit are not those of the open-country farm or the fishing or hunting activities of primitive groups. Standards of health, education, and child welfare today demand quite other behavior in these matters than was once taken for granted.

Religious and moral training of children has always been bound up with the home, and though formal religious education has reached into the earliest years, the family still furnishes the matrix of religious ideas, attitudes, and practices. We noted in Chapter VI on personality the importance of the early years in moral training. In the family the basic notions of God, of salvation, and of morality are laid before the child. Although the church and the school take over these training functions at increasingly early years, the influence of the mother and father, especially the for-

---

[10] A curious sidelight is thrown on this fact by the long years of unemployment following 1930, when many fathers found themselves at home for long periods. Social workers report the rise of marital problems growing out of the father's taking on functions of training and discipline which he had not formerly assumed. So, too, in many families wives were able to find some work outside the home, leaving to their unemployed husbands household duties which the latter had formerly little dreamed of assuming.

mer, seems to outweigh most of the effects which reach the child later in these fundamental religious and moral matters.[11]

The home also provides the first recreational patterns for the child, even though the play groups furnish important connections with the wider world outside. In earlier times the family as a unit frequently indulged in recreation together: games, picnics, family reunions. Today the individualized nature of recreation has tended to take this function almost entirely out of the home, although the radio and automobile have done something to re-unite the family for recreation.

As to education, the family training of the child in the earliest years is important to all his later formal learning. The interaction of parents and children is the background upon which most of the intellectual and emotional conditioning of the child takes place. In earlier societies the home furnished much of what is now in the hands of formal education. The nursery school, the kindergarten, and the primary schools have taken from the home many educational duties, as well as adding to the range of the child's training things which the home seldom gave. Yet in spite of great changes, the family still gives the child his basic training in social attitudes and habits. We must sketch a few of the fundamentals of these, since they are so important to adult participation in social life.

Psychology of Parent-Child Relations. Some of the features of the relation of parents to children we have already discussed in our treatment of personality (Chapter VI). There we indicated the rise of the self or ego, the importance of rôle and status, and the fact that the future adaptations to vocational, marital, religious, and political groups will be largely settled by the social conditioning of the earliest years. Since it is clear that the deeper motives of behavior are emotionally toned and that these motives are definitely tied up with early social interaction, we must mention five important features of childhood adaptation to the parents and family. These are (*1*) the sense of security, (*2*) companionship and growth of ideals, (*3*) power relations with reference to reality and authority, (*4*) freedom to grow intellectually, emotionally, and socially, leading to (*5*) the sense of responsibility and independence, that is, to the assumption of power itself.

Born as he is, helpless and incapable of managing his own be-

[11] See Hugh Hartshorne and Mark A. May, "Testing the Knowledge of Right and Wrong," *Religious Education Monograph*, No. 1, 1927, pp. 50–51.

havior, it is highly important that the child develop a *sense of security* out of his earliest social contacts in the family. The foundations of this sense of safety are laid first of all in the training in regular habits of feeding, sleeping, bodily care, and play. Consistency of training is essential because it provides the very stability that is necessary for further learning. It is basic to making the child's world both understandable and predictable. That is, he must learn that his contacts with mother, with father, with brothers and sisters, and with others fall into more or less comprehensible and regular patterns. One of the most serious faults in child-training is to play fast and loose with the child's emotions, so that he does not acquire any stable habits and attitudes.

The sense of security is particularly important in the matter of status. The child's position in regard to his parents and brothers and sisters is fundamental to all of his future relations in groups outside the home. Very often feelings of difference and inferiority arise in the home which may carry over to later life. The parents serve the very important function of setting before the child what W. I. Thomas aptly calls the "copies," or the ideals of action, with which he identifies himself. It is inevitable that he form in his own mind an image or conception of his parents from their treatment of him, and from their behavior generally. Thus, it is common for parents to talk about honesty, truthfulness, perseverance, and other virtues of our culture, but their overt conduct in these matters provides better "copies" than their verbalisms. The child early learns the meaning of Emerson's aphorism that "What you are sounds so loudly in my ears that I cannot hear what you say." Thus the self- or ego-ideal of the child, so important in defining a goal toward which to strive, will be affected by his contact with his parents at every point.

In order to provide adequate patterns, the child needs the *companionship* of his parents. If they are aloof, if they take on the stern patriarchal manner common in many cultures, the child will develop a rôle and ideal distinctly different from that which he gets if they try to meet him at the level of his own intelligence and emotional development. As the family pattern moves away from that of patriarchal dominance to that of mutual interaction, the rôle of the child and his position in the family will change.

The *power relations* with reference to social-cultural reality and authority also develop out of parent-child contacts. Habits of bodily care, of social relations, and of managing the material world are fundamental. Mother and father symbolize to the child forms of personal power, just as the inevitability of material objects forces him to reckon with impersonal power. The child's own wishes must give way in the face of demands for obedience and conformity to these powers external to him. The manner in which he learns how to get on with his family around him will be carried over to his interactions with school authorities, religious leaders, the police, and other agents of the organized state and morality. So, too, the manner in which the child learns to handle the material forces around him may bias his future interests and attitudes toward art, science, and religion. These first expressions of power arise from personal-social interactions, but very soon the cultural patterns of the wider community and its special groups come into play to modify these primary sub-cultural relations. (See Chapter VI.)

The over-domination of the parents may lead the child to a sense of rebellion, which though repressed or held back in childhood, will later express itself in resentment and resistance to other sorts of authority. There is a current theory that many revolutionaries are individuals who in their early years had an overdose of parental authority, followed by a later transference of resistance to other forms of power expression.[12]

Again, the child may so completely accept the dominance of parental authority that he remains emotionally linked to the parents throughout life at an infantile level, and thus will fail to develop an adequate sense of *independence* and *responsibility*. Normally, as the child grows up he transfers his affections to other persons; he learns to manage situations outside the home and family and with all this his intelligence, his emotions, and his social habits grow until he weans himself from the original dependence on the mother and other family members.

Fortunately, the demands of the material world around him direct the growth of the child's intelligence along important lines, so that somewhat independently of the family his intellectual learning continues. Yet in more intimate person-to-person relations with mother, father, and other family members, there is sometimes a tendency to keep the child and even adolescent at an early level of emotional attachment. Some parents simply will not

[12] See H. D. Lasswell, *Psychopathology and Politics*, 1930, especially chaps. VI–VIII.

permit their children to grow up emotionally and socially. They make them so dependent on them in the early years that later the children cannot make adequate emotional-social adaptations to other persons outside the parental family. In many cases, in spite of individualistic culture pattern, fundamental matters like choice of vocation, selection of love mate, adherence to religious body or political party are largely determined by direct parental influence. Such a child cannot develop into a normal, healthy, and responsible person. Until he does, he remains infantile or childish in his emotional-social life as an adult, handicapping his participation in adult groups.

The opportunity to grow up intellectually, emotionally, and socially results in the assumption of responsibility. This does not mean license but ordered living, in which independence of thought and action are coupled with ethical and other social obligations. Independence may give "rights," but these are always correlated with duties and responsibilities. If a parent remains too prominently in the thought and feeling of the children as they approach adulthood, the latter may fail to assume full adult obligations. For example, vocational choice should grow out of ability, talent, and abiding interest. But it may be the result of some projection of the parent upon the child. An ambition long harbored by the mother or father is often thrust upon the son or daughter, who is supposed to fulfill what the parent or parents could not have in the way of professional success. For the most part, such control of the child ends in inefficiency, unhappy life work, and often little satisfaction to the parents.

Another matter of great importance is the attainment of mature love life. As boys and girls come into puberty they usually learn about the other sex in a normal manner through school contacts, healthy recreation, and mutual regard. When parents constantly fear that "something will go wrong" with their adolescent children, when they refuse to let them discover many things for themselves perhaps by heartaches, injuries to pride, and defeat as well as by happy relations and success, the parents are likely to find in the end that their protected children are not able to assume the responsibility of adult mating and the establishment of an emotionally well-balanced family life, because they have not had a chance to grow away from the over-attachment of mother or father or from the fears laid upon them in their childhood by parents. Often, too, parents unwisely try to foist their political and economic views on their children, feeling that the children have turned away from them and their love, to take up with new and perhaps radical ideas and practices. Yet the independent and responsible child grown to adulthood may well be left to decide for himself in these matters.

In regard to religious attitudes and practices, many parents regret that their children do not follow the old ways, that they take up with some other religious organization, or that they leave the formal church entirely. The healthy-minded parent will give the child the fundamentals of religious attitudes and habits and will perhaps leave the other responsibilities to his church. In a world marked by individual choice in these matters, the parent can scarcely prevent his children from modifying many of the beliefs taught in his home.

When all is said and done, none of us can escape fully the impress of the parental patterns upon us, whether it be as to mating, choice of vocation, or participation in the economic, political, and religious order. The wise parent will know this; he will understand that the most subtle way to influence his child toward what seem to him good patterns or "copies" will be not only to instruct him, but better still, to act as sincerely as a parent in relation to these situations as he would have the child act. Example is always better than precept. The day-by-day unconscious relations between parent and child will leave their mark and will determine in basic ways the direction of the child's own life. It is only when the parental training itself has been emotionally infantile and false that unfortunate "copies" will be set before the child.

DISSOLUTION OF THE FAMILY

The family as a social group is dissolved by the death of one or both of the parents, by desertion, by voluntary separation, or by divorce. In the present section we shall discuss only the problem of divorce in its relation to the family.

Divorce. Although in a few societies marriage is a contract terminated only by death, nearly everywhere there is provision for the dissolution of this contract under special conditions. Where marriage is a religious rite or sacrament, divorce is often forbidden or is extremely difficult to obtain. Where the family is an economic unit and offspring are economically valuable, a sterile wife may be returned to her family. If a bride-price or dowry has been paid, this may be and often must be repaid to the husband or to his father or family representative. Impotence in the husband is often a cause for dissolution. Adultery is a widespread reason for divorce, although in societies dominated by patriarchal and masculine authority, adultery of the husband is often condoned, while with the wife it may not only be a reason for divorce but may even be considered to justify her death at the hands of her husband. Other grounds for divorce in some societies are economic insufficiency, bad temper, and insanity.

The presence of children almost everywhere acts as a deterrent to divorce, even though the customary or legal code permits easy dissolution. The tribe or state generally takes the view that the care of children is a primary demand of the family, a fact, of course, which we have emphasized as basic to the whole historical function of the family. In pre-capitalistic societies the care of children was something not so easily delegated to other agencies, as in classes or societies where the money economy dominates so many of our social relations as it does today. Where economic status permits adequate support, many present capitalistic societies permit divorce for a wide range of causes.

The inheritance of property and the economic use of children, as well as the demands of family functions proper, have all played their part in keeping the family intact. In a socialistic society in which the family as such has little economic function, these factors would play no part at all. Such is becoming increasingly the case in modern Russia.

Where divorce is easy, self-interest may still dictate a continuation of a somewhat unpleasant arrangement. If the wife and her children are an economic asset, or if outside social pressure in the form of status or good will is a factor, compromises may keep the family together.

As we all know, the divorce rate of the United States has been rising rather rapidly. In 1900 there were 20 divorces for every 10,000 married persons; in 1930 there were 36. In 1935 there was estimated to be one divorce for every 6.14 marriages.

There are regional differences in the divorce rate. New England and the north Atlantic states range between 12 and 24 divorces per 10,000 married persons, while the Mountain and Pacific states report 60 to 70. These differences reflect variations in divorce laws and in religious attitudes. Divorces in Catholic communities are much fewer than in Protestant sections.

These changes are reflected in another way. The percentage of total homes broken by divorce, separation, or annulment has increased from 6.7 per cent in 1900 to 9.8 per cent in 1930. These figures do not reveal the percentage of homes which are the result of remarriage of divorced persons. Much of this change, however, comes from dissolution of the families which have no children. Between 1900 and 1930 the percentage of broken homes with children as compared to all homes with children varied only from 10 to 9.2 per cent. In contrast, in 1930 the percentage of broken homes without children was 25.4 per cent, nearly three times as many as with children. Rural and town communities have a much lower percentage of broken homes with children than do cities. Moreover the cities show the most marked increase since 1900.[13] E. W. Burgess in a study of parent-child relationships reports that 23 per cent of the schoolchildren in his sample—largely from cities and of older parents—came from homes where the parents were not living together.[14] This included cases arising from divorce, separation, annulment, and death.

The legal grounds for divorce are usually not the "real" reasons. Various state laws provide for divorce on such grounds as adultery, sterility, impotence, desertion, cruelty, drunkenness, insanity, or non-support. The social-psychological reasons are often quite different: quarrels over money matters, incompatibility, sexual or otherwise, disputes over the training of children, and many subtle factors which the law does not and perhaps cannot take into account.

It is increasingly evident in this country that divorce is really granted on the grounds of mutual consent of the parties involved. While the ancient laws regarding recrimination, condonation, and collusion still stand, actual practice has departed from them except in rare instances. Divorce judges and attorneys everywhere are gradually coming to realize the futility of legal provisions which run counter to the mores and to changed public opinion regarding

[13] These figures are from the sample of communities studied by Ogburn, *op. cit.*, p. 689.

[14] See reference *op. cit.*, p. 674, to Burgess' report for the White House Conference on Child Health and Protection, "Function of Home Activities in the Education of the Child."

divorce. One trial judge put the common experience to the author in approximately these words:

When I came on the bench some years ago I was personally rather opposed to divorce in principle. As the years have gone by and I have talked to hundreds of couples seeking divorce, I am convinced that for the most part the courts can do nothing to bring back satisfactory relations to people who have lived together but now find, often after repeated attempts at reconciliation, that divorce is the one thing they desire in order to be rid of each other.[15]

The psychological effects of divorce on husband and wife may well be negative or beneficial, depending on the circumstances. Willard Waller in his book *The Old Love and the New* (1930) has ably discussed a number of cases of readjustment of divorcees. Among important matters is first the loss of companionship. Even though conflict has been frequent, the mere fact of living alone again may be a strain on the man or the woman. Of course, if there are children, whoever gets the custody of the children—usually the wife—has their companionship. Sometimes removal to a new locality is imperative and new friends must be made. Then there are those sensitive persons whose marital experience has so damaged their ego or self-image that they develop such a bitterness toward marriage and towards the opposite sex as to render future marriage and other satisfying emotional relations impossible. And there is the matter of normal sex life of divorced persons, a matter not always easy, and likely to lead to substitutions, such as heavy drinking, drugs, or to irregular and ordinarily unsatisfactory clandestine relations. There is little doubt that in many cases the need of sexual adjustment is a factor leading to early remarriage.

Remarriage itself is not a simple matter psychologically. It is not easy to clear oneself of the sense of guilt arising from separation from the former mate and children, if there be any, even though the "causal" conflicts were unbearable. Though a person may enjoy his new-found love in another marriage or liaison, he may feel that he has betrayed the old love. Then, too, in remarriage, no matter how emancipated from his first mating a person may feel

---

[15] See various studies on these present practices: N. P. Feinsinger and Kimball Young, "Recrimination and Related Doctrines in the Wisconsin Law of Divorce as Administered in Dane County," *Wisconsin Law Review*, vol. VI, June, 1931, pp. 195–216; N. P. Feinsinger, "Observations on Judicial Administration of the Divorce Law in Wisconsin," *Wisconsin Law Review*, vol. VIII, December, 1932, pp. 27–48.

himself to be, he may find himself in time making unfavorable comparisons between the new alliance and the former one. It is very easy to idealize the old marriage as time heals the wounds of past differences, especially if the present marital adjustments prove somewhat trying.

Divorce and Children. Divorce is likely to be an intense crisis for the children. The break-up of the home and family means a critical readaptation. Although quarreling, conflict, and desertion may have contributed to the break-up of the family, it has been throughout a group of intimately interacting persons. The sense of security both financial and personal may be lost, even though the conflict itself has become intolerable. Where the divorced parents cannot provide for the children, the state must take care of them. Foster homes or public institutions are the contemporary substitutes for the normal family when the state must make provision for the children of divorced parents. In the upper economic classes this outcome is unlikely.

Parents are sometimes stupid enough to use the children as weapons in their conflict with each other. This may go on within the family for years, with each parent using all the devices he has to get the child or children "to side with him." Often the children are at a complete loss to know where to stand. When the divorce is at hand, this emotional pulling back and forth of the child between the parents may become more acute, doubtless leaving emotional scars upon the child for years to come.[16]

Associated with divorce is the social stigma attached to children of divorced parents. Ridicule and censure easily produce a sense of difference and of inferiority on the part of children who, as we know, take up from those around them the very attitudes they apply to themselves. There is doubtless a distinctly healthy motive in most remarriages which will again give the children, even though but stepchildren, a status in the neighborhood and community.

It must be pointed out that culture standards will have much to do with this matter of ridicule, censure, and social non-acceptability of the divorced mate and the children. As divorce becomes ever more common than now and as it reaches into all classes of the population, much of the attendant shame should disappear. This is already evident in some of our classes. For example, the

---

[16] See the excellent discussion of this by Miriam Van Waters, *Parents on Probation*, 1927, chap. VI, "Who Is the Legal Owner of This Child?"

frequency of divorce in the Hollywood movie colony has built up a social tolerance that ought to make readjustment for both mates and children a little easier provided other factors do not interfere.[17]

There still remains the deeper problem of emotional attachment and security that is built up between parents and children. The loss of a father or a mother by divorce, like loss by death, may leave the child with a feeling of isolation that even the acceptance of divorce in the wider community may not make up to him. The whole problem of emotional-social development of the infant and child in relation to his parents or other guardians in the early years is accentuated in the situation of divorce. In spite of many expressions of opinion to the contrary, it is often a question whether or not some sort of marital compromise which will keep the family intact, at least while the children are growing up, is not for them at least a healthier situation than divorce and all that it entails. Yet an examination of many cases leads one to realize how difficult it is to generalize on this question when in every family there appear unique factors. The problem of emotional insecurity cannot be denied, and must be reckoned with in any sane discussion of family dissolution.

Remarriage is often fraught with difficulties for the step-children, especially when children born of the second marriage arrive and begin to play their rôles in the family drama. Favoritism, jealousy, and open conflict may result. Certainly not all remarriages involving stepchildren turn out badly, but the danger is there and must be taken into account as a further probability in the situation.

It should be apparent that divorce is not the cause of marital disturbance and change, but rather the reflection of changing culture norms. We are groping our way to new patterns of behavior in family life, and in doing so social strain and much personal suffering are involved. While divorce has been rather common in all cultures, in our own it is a doubly difficult problem, because it is related to a rapid shift in nearly all the basic institutions and culture patterns. So far we have not invented any social grouping other than the family which in a capitalistic society, at least, will better serve the fundamental function of rearing children. However, as agencies other than the home develop to provide care and

---

[17]Such "other factors" may be illustrated by the neurotic or unstable temperaments of parents and step-parents and undue publicity.

training in the early years, many of these intimate problems may not arise from marriage or divorce. Perhaps if we get away from attitudes of blame and ridicule in regard to marital difficulties and come to handle the problem as one for treatment and re-education, some of the difficulties will disappear. Present practices of marriage, family life, and easy divorce in Soviet Russia may also furnish the world with new patterns in which many of these problems, doubtless associated with our capitalist culture, may disappear. On the other hand, the reversion to traditional family patterns in fascist Italy and Germany may set up a movement which will offset the present tendencies toward small families, loss of many former family functions, and the general individualization of family life. Certainly it is difficult at this juncture to predict the future form of marriage and family life in our rapidly changing world.

CLASS ASSIGNMENTS

A. Further reading assignment:

1. K. Young, *Source Book for Sociology,* chap. XII.

2. W. F. Ogburn, "The Family and Its Functions," chap. XIII, in *Recent Social Trends.*

3. E. B. Reuter and Jessie R. Runner, *The Family,* chaps. XII, XV.

B. Questions and exercises:

1. What are the principal background factors which will enable us to understand family life in our culture?

2. Outline the principal factors in modern life which have changed the character of family functions: economic, religious, and in child training.

3. What relation is there between family size and the type of occupation of the father?

4. What are the principal demands of interaction between husband and wife today? How do they differ from those of parents 100 years ago?

5. Cite an instance, if you can, of conflict between older and younger generations in regard to child training which illustrates the older and the newer culture patterns of family life.

6. What are some of the most important items in sound childhood adaptation to parents and family?

7. Cite cases of child difficulties arising (a) out of loss of sense of security, and (b) from failure to develop sense of independence and responsibility.

8. How do you account for the increase in divorce in this country, especially since 1900?

9. Are the "legal causes" of divorce usually the genuine or "real" ones? If not, why not?

10. What are the principal problems of readjustment of the divorced parents in our society? What are these problems for the children?

C. Topics for class reports or longer written papers:

1. Trace the history of the modern European-American family from early Christian times to present industrial society. (Consult Willystine Goodsell, *The Family as Social and Educational Institution*, 1915; John Langdon Davies, *A Short History of Woman*, 1927.)

2. Family life and child rearing in "Middletown." (Consult R. S. and H. M. Lynd, *Middletown*, 1929, chaps. X, XI; and their *Middletown in Transition*, 1937, chaps. V, VI.)

3. Recent changes in family functions in the United States. (Consult W. F. Ogburn, "The Family and its Functions," chap. XIII, *Recent Social Trends*, and footnote bibliographies; also J. M. Gillette and J. M. Reinhardt, *Current Social Problems*, chap. XXII; see special issue on family, *American Sociological Review*, Oct., 1937, vol. II.)

4. The effects of economic depression on the American family, 1930-35. (Consult R. C. Angell, *The Family Encounters the Depression*, 1936; S. A. Stouffer and P. F. Lazarsfeld, *Research Memorandum on the Family in the Depression*, 1937.)

5. Report on current problems of child welfare in America. (Consult Gillette and Reinhardt, *Current Social Problems*, chaps. XXIII, XXIV, and bibliography; Una B. Sait, *New Horizons for the Family*, 1938, chaps. XI, XII; *The White House Conference, 1930*, 1931, and various special volumes for this conference; and pertinent publications of the Children's Bureau, U. S. Department of Labor, Washington, D. C.)

6. Marriage adjustment and maladjustment. (Consult E. R. Mowrer, *Domestic Discord*, 1928; H. R. Mowrer, *Personality Adjustment and Domestic Discord*, 1935; R. C. and F. W. Binkley, *What Is Right with Marriage*, 1929; W. Waller, *The Family: A Dynamic Interpretation*, 1938, chaps. XIII–XVIII; J. K. Folsom, editor, *Plan for Marriage*, 1938; Sait, *op. cit.*, chaps. XVIII–XX; B. J. Stern, editor, *The Family, Past and Present*, 1938, sec. 12.)

7. Report on Willard Waller, *The Old Love and the New*, 1930, as a picture of readjustment after divorce.

8. Report on parent-child adjustment in the home. (Consult Mary B. Sayles, *The Problem Child at Home*, 1928; Miriam Van Waters, *Parents on Probation*, 1927; Maude E. Watson, *Children and Their Parents*, 1932; E. B. Reuter and J. R. Runner, *The Family*, 1931, chaps. XI, XII, XV, XVI; *The Adolescent in the Family*, edited by E. W. Burgess, for the White House Conference, 1934; Stern, *op. cit.*, sec. 13.)

CHAPTER XIII

EDUCATION AND ITS INSTITUTIONS

Education is a part of the larger function of the transmission of culture. As the social order has become more complex, formal education has assumed an important place in the continuity as well as in the growth of culture itself. The purposes of education may have been altered as the cultural outlook itself has changed, but everywhere education assumes an important place in the life of the individual in fitting him for a place in his community.

Even primitive societies possess some sort of formal education, though many of the functions which we think of as "educational" fall to the family, the clan, the vocational guild, or the religious order. The fundamental purposes of primitive education may be summarized as follows: (*1*) instruction in verbal traditions—the folklore, the mythology, and history of the society; (*2*) training in essential manual skills of the material culture; and (*3*) instruction and practice in the moral customs, with particular reference to teaching the virtues and values of the society through talk, through ceremonials, through appeal to fear of supernatural powers, and through the presentation of situations demanding overt evidence of courage, perseverance, prowess, and endurance.

Formal education in anything like the modern manner did not appear until society had become highly complex, until secondary groups had increased the need of specialization, and especially not until writing had given man a means of preserving his culture in more objective form. All the great ancient civilizations—Egypt, Babylonia, India, Greece, and Rome—had systems of formal education. In all these it was confined to privileged and leisure classes, and much of what has now become a part of formal schooling was then left to other groups: family, religious, political, and economic. The rise of free education, stimulated by scientific research and by philosophic study unhampered by theological dogmas and the dead hand of the past, is an intriguing story which cannot detain us here. The spirit and practice of free inquiry stimulated by the Renaissance marked an important change in education, laying the foundation for the development of modern science, upon which so much of present-day culture rests.

Other events fostering the growth of modern education were the Protestant Reformation, the commercial and industrial changes since the fifteenth century especially, and the rise of political democracy. The contention of Martin Luther (1483–1546) and his followers that an individual could experience God directly without mediation of the formal church hierarchy, and the translation of the Bible into the vernacular tongues of western Europe favored elementary education of the masses in reading and writing. The demands of commerce and industry for literacy also aided in stimulating wider education of the growing middle classes. In time, as these advantages reached the masses, education increased their efficiency in labor, facilitated their participation in politics, especially through the agencies of education and propaganda, and stimulated a striking increase in consumption demands, particularly through advertising.

The rise of democratic nationalism put a more distinctive mark on modern education. The belief in universal literacy goes hand in hand with the belief in and practice of universal suffrage. In the democratic countries, especially Great Britain, the United States, and France, the abandonment of property qualifications for voting is correlated with the demand for compulsory elementary education. The argument runs that the responsible citizen is the enlightened citizen; and how may one be enlightened unless one can read! It is apparent enough today in democratic, fascist, and communistic states that literacy often makes the masses more subject to propaganda and dominance by the ruling classes, but the implication of this will be clearer in a later section of this chapter.

EDUCATION AND PRESENT-DAY SOCIETY

The place of education in an industrial society may be shown by an analysis of the contemporary American school and its relations to the community in which it finds itself. In a subsequent section we shall discuss some of the implications of education in other than democratic countries.

Rapid Expansion of Formal Education. Elementary education in the United States has been well entrenched, at least since the Civil War, resulting in a steady decline in illiteracy. Between 1880 and 1930 attendance in the elementary and secondary schools increased three and one half times, while for the same period the population increased two and one half times.

The most marked increases have been in secondary and higher education. In 1890 there were about 300,000 pupils in our secondary schools; by 1900, 630,048, and by 1930, 4,740,580, an increase of over 650 per cent in 30 years. In this same period the general population increased but 62 per cent. In 1900 there were 284,683 students in American universities, colleges, and teacher-training institutions. In 1930 the comparable figure was 1,178,-318, an increase of 314 per cent. Today approximately one person in every seven of college age is in college, and two thirds of the persons of high-school age are attending high school. Today about 25 per cent of the population and 80 per cent of all persons between 5 and 17 years of age are in school. In no other country in the world and at no other time in history has such a large percentage of the population been in school. It reflects both an amazing faith in education and a steadily rising standard of living.

The sex ratios among our school population also show interesting changes. Formerly females outnumbered males in secondary schools, and males outnumbered females in the higher institutions. In 1900, of the pupils in public secondary schools, 41.6 per cent were boys. By 1930 this had risen to 48.1 per cent. In colleges, the reverse tendency is evident. In 1900, only 34.6 per cent of college students were women; in 1930 this percentage had risen to 41.4, another evidence of the changing status of women in our society.

Still another proof of the place of education in our own society is the exceptional increase in school budgets. In 1900 the total expenditure for public elementary and secondary education was 214 millions of dollars; in 1930 this had risen to 2,316 millions, although some allowance should be made for the change in the value of the dollar over this 30-year period. Actual figures for total expenditures and value of all property of public elementary and secondary schools for the period 1900–1930 show that the total annual expenditures increased nearly 1,000 per cent, while the total value of school property increased nearly 750 per cent.[1]

[1] The data on enrollments and finances are conveniently summarized from appropriate governmental reports by C. H. Judd, "Education," chap. VII, *Recent Social Trends.*

While changes in Europe have not been so marked, education is as thoroughly accepted there. It is in Russia that the most remarkable changes in education have taken place. The attempt within a few years to stamp out illiteracy in this vast country has been one of many "wonders" of the Russian revolutionary government. So, too, the Orient is awakening to the need of mass education as well as special training for the upper classes and for professional personnel. It is evident everywhere that as science and industrialism spread and as emancipation of the masses from former traditions and customs becomes inevitable, education takes on an ever increasing importance.

Formal Education an Interactional Pattern. The school does not pass on all the culture of a given society, but only that section of it which is believed by the dominant groups of the community to be the proper function of formal education. Much is still left to the family, the church, the economic and other groups and institutions. As we shall see, formal schooling is gradually encroaching on these other areas.

Like other continuing groups, the school has evolved a separate set of culture patterns of its own to carry on its work. These involve the children, the teachers, and the adults of the community.

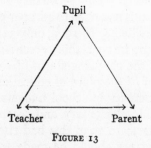

Pupil

Teacher   Parent

FIGURE 13

Diagram of interaction of pupils, teachers, and parents. The relations are reciprocal.

We may think of the entire configuration as represented in the triangular relation of pupils, teachers, and parents, including the adult community along with the latter. Figure 13 represents these reciprocal relations. In practice, of course, various combinations of relations arise: sometimes the pupils co-operate with teachers in reference to parents, sometimes parents and teachers co-operate regarding the children, or they may at other times fall into conflict. So, too, the children may develop opposition toward teachers and perhaps secure some help from the parents in the matter.

On the basis of this triangular relationship the function of the school in the community may be divided under three headings: (*1*) its purposes or policies as set down by the community; (*2*) its structure as a part of the organized state or other group; and (*3*) its internal organization for teaching proper.

The *purposes* of the school are determined by the dominant groups of the community; in America these are largely the business, the professional, and the religious elements. The community, through the organized state or church, sometimes through special groups like the wealthy classes, chooses *policy makers* or school boards and *executives,* who determine the general and specific objectives of education.

The school itself has *officials* to administer these policies, *teachers* to instruct and guide the pupils, *supervisors* to guide and correct the teachers, and finally a *definite group of pupils* who are given materials to learn or projects to work out. There are also disciplinary officers of the school to assist the teachers in impressing community authority on the pupils. These special officers enforce attendance of pupils, and if the latter fail to go to school, their parents are brought into conflict with the law.

Within the school itself there grows up a we-feeling, an in-group, with its own customs, traditions, and rules. Pupils, teachers, and other school officials, all assume various rôles and acquire status in this we-group, while the community outside has various relations, co-operative or antagonistic, to the school group.

Since the heart of education is the school itself, we may analyze its social relations under three headings: (*1*) teacher-pupil interaction; (*2*) pupil-to-pupil relations; and (*3*) teacher-parent relations.

Classroom Instruction and Teacher-Pupil Relations. The school provides the child, first, with the tools of further learning—reading, writing, spelling, arithmetic, grammar; second, with a content of cultural materials—science, history, literature; third, with certain manual skills, at least in some schools; and, fourth, with moral and social ideas, attitudes, and habits. This moral training is usually given informally by means of various institutional devices connected with formal instruction.

Classroom instruction is a matter of social interaction between pupils and teacher. While the materials of books and skills must be mastered, these do not exist without reference to personalities. Unfortunately much of our earlier educational psychology failed to recognize that all learning is essentially social; that it is not a matter of passive rote-memory but a dynamic process. If the social atmosphere of learning is not conducive to efficient work, if the teacher sets up emotional resistances in the pupils or fails to present the material in such a way that they can comprehend it, learning is retarded or made actually impossible.

The interactional pattern of teacher and pupil is borrowed first of all from the home. The teacher is a sort of substitute parent, and the school situation fosters the fundamental values of obedience, discipline, docility, regularity of attendance and of preparation, and perseverance, the roots of which lie in the home. Likewise, the teacher is a kind of preacher, not only as regards facts, but concerning moral and social matters as well. Centuries of religious dominance have left their mark on instructional practice. The lecture system is a clear case of the church manner of teaching, and even in the elementary and secondary schools the teacher often assumes the rôle of the exhorter, much in the preacher pattern. Even the physical set-up of the classroom, with its rows on rows of seats arranged before the teacher's desk, is borrowed from the church. The seats are but modified pews, and the desk the instructor's pulpit!

Teachers differ among themselves in personality makeup and hence in their appeal to the pupils. Although no one has made an adequate analysis of this matter, casual observation exposes various social types among teachers:

There is the "driver," with high-pressure methods, insistence on activity, punctuality, and obedience. Often the sheer energy and enthusiasm of this person makes him successful. There is the "Apollo," the athletic director or other teacher, who carries boys and girls along with him by reason of his physical attraction, his physical self-confidence, and his assumption of the hero rôle. It is easy for the boy or girl to identify himself with such a person. Another social type is the "sour grapes" spinster, male or female, who, disappointed in love, is touchy, exacting, and inclined to "take it out" on the pupils. Such a teacher is likely to be much upset by any moral infractions, especially those of a sexual character. Then there is the "angelic" type, the sweetdispositioned man or woman, who is all kindness, who is not exacting, and who is not infrequently the victim of pupil exploitation. One might multiply these social types to cover all sorts of teachers, but these illustrations indicate their rôle in the schoolroom.[2]

Another evidence of democratic primary group ideals is the belief that all children have equal ability to learn. While culture and opportunity have much to do with learning, this is not to gainsay individual variation in the speed and thoroughness of learning. Our schools still operate on the theory that learning can wipe out differences in information, skill, or talent. Connected with this is the continued faith in book learning. In spite of the laboratory, the workshop, and the project method, the printed page still holds the center of the educational stage. As William Graham Sumner remarks in his *Folkways*, "We ascribe to book learning power to form character, make good citizens, keep family mores pure, elevate morals, establish individual character, civilize barbarians, and cure social vice and disease."

Individual deviations are found not only in intelligence but also in emotional and social traits as well. Except in special cases, the schools have made little provision for these variations. As a result, the emotional interplay of pupil and teacher and of pupil and pupil is neglected or left to follow habitual patterns that may at times prove disastrous. A feeling of inferiority may greatly affect the child's learning; the teacher's mishandling of the matter may warp the child's personality and handicap not only his intellectual attainment, but may actually so condition him that his future social relations will continue to show the marks of his unhappy school life. Compensation for inferiority may lead the pupil to mischievous conduct, to showing off, to resistance to teacher authority, behavior which also affects the learning process. Physical handicaps among pupils are particularly likely to arouse ridicule and the sense of difference. The understanding teacher will know that such cases need careful handling so that the more serious features of the feeling of inferiority may not arise.

One of the features of our American school system which reflects the individualism and the competitive spirit of the economic and political order is the emphasis upon rivalry and individual at-

---

[2] I am indebted to one of my former students, Guy Hoover, for an interesting collection of case studies of various types of teachers based on his long experience as supervisor and superintendent.

tainment. Daily classroom procedure is frequently built around personal competition for grades and rivalry between groups within the class, these groups often being artificially chosen by the teacher, such as one row against another. Even the much lauded project method of teaching retains the essential characteristics of our individualistic ethos, even though it has other advantages in freeing the pupil from certain unnecessary routine and putting him into a form of competition with himself. It is usually still an *individual* and not a *group* project.

On the other hand, some of the so-called "progressive" schools provide collective projects in which the individual initiative is stimulated only with reference to the group aim. But on the whole the American belief in personal ambition and success, especially in making money, reverberates back into the classroom, where the child is put through a system of learning that continues to stimulate those habits and values that the adult community has found beneficial and which it believes will continue to yield the highest good, both personal and social.

The credit system is another institution which ramifies the American school from top to bottom. It is thoroughly supported by public sentiment. It is a social ritual set up to mark progress up the educational ladder and incidentally to give evidence of improved social status in a democratic society. The desire of the common man that his children acquire the hallmarks of aristocratic learning—such as Latin, mathematics, and literature—further keeps the system of credits and graduation diplomas alive. So long as the American communities worship medals and badges and clamor for academic degrees, we shall continue to establish educational prestige by conferring a few Latin phrases engrossed on sheepskin—the magic touch of learning.

Pupil-to-Pupil Relations and Education. Certain phases of pupil-to-pupil interaction have already been mentioned in reference to competition, rivalry, and individual differences. Other classroom situations, especially those of curricular activities, need comment.

Pupils build up distinctive patterns of action in the schoolroom itself. They assist each other in the learning process, the superior boy or girl often helping the duller or lazier pupils. It is unfortunate that little use has been made of the natural social interaction of pupils in the teaching process itself. Formal provision might easily be made in many instances for the pupils to teach each other. This would capitalize on haphazard and intermittent practices already going on.

Just as teachers themselves acquire social rôles, so do the pupils. There is the "teacher's pet," the athletic "hero," the "sissie," the "grind," the "grade getter," and the "clown." These grow out of classroom practices. Teachers, as well as the other pupils, are responsible for the development of these pupil types.

The play groupings of the neighborhood are carried over and extended at school. Organized recreation is simply an effort on the part of the school authorities and other organizations in the community to control and direct the play life of children. Regulations as to time and place of play and as to type of games simply reflect institutional growth.

Congeniality groups and clubs easily arise out of the pupil-to-pupil relations. The former develop out of school activities and are found at all ages from the elementary school through the university. Clubs, on the other hand, take on institutional features: a name, codes, rituals, officers, and special functions. While clubs spring up somewhat naturally out of the school situation, national and community organizations, such as the Hi-Y clubs, the 4-H clubs, the Girl and Boy Scouts, and others, assist the school authorities in managing play life and other extracurricular activities.

The primary groups of pupils, therefore, are not long left to carry on by themselves. In our increasingly complex society these more specialized secondary groups serve an invaluable function in helping to direct play activities into lines which prepare the boy or girl for later participation in other groups and in the community as a citizen.

Teacher and Parent Relations. We have already noted that the teacher assumes the rôle of a substitute parent in dealing out discipline and in exercising authority. The parents expect the teacher to assume such a responsibility. They frequently offer objections if they imagine that the school is failing to carry over this authority pattern. Parents are often really more concerned with the moral and social effects of education than with formal instruction, in spite of the fact that they hold dearly to the fetish of book learning.

The school, in turn, affects the daily routine of the family in many ways: the hours when parents must arise to get the children off to school; the hours when breakfast and luncheon must be served; trips which the parents must make on special occasions, such as school entertainments; and shopping tours for new garments for a school party or school drama. The family culture itself is affected. Instruction in cleanliness, brushing of teeth, proper diet, and even book knowledge reach back into the home, perhaps challenging parental ideas and habits and sometimes creating conflict between the children and the parents, especially where the parents have a culture different from the American culture which the child gets from the school. (See Chapter XXV on assimilation.)

In some communities the school organization itself has reached out to touch the home. We do not refer to adult education, which will be discussed later, but to such schemes as the visiting teacher movement. The visiting teacher is a specialized functionary who combines social case work and teaching, handling more difficult conduct cases or normal children who have trouble in adapting themselves to the school routine. She visits the parents, enlists their co-operation whenever she can, and assists the classroom teacher to understand the child's difficulties in the light of his whole personality. In this contact of school and home, the visiting teacher is able to solve many problems of family disorganization in situations in which no other social worker could legitimately take a hand. In more enlightened localities the visiting teacher is replacing the "truant officer," whose functions are largely those of school policeman.

Aside from the legal boards of education, the teachers and parents have built up organizations, such as the Parent-Teacher Associations, designed to bring about a better understanding between the teachers and the parents. The two chief differences between the school board and the Parent-Teacher Association are that the former is legally responsible and hence develops a more formalistic relation to the school situation and that in the latter the teachers have representation.

The place of the Parent-Teacher Association differs in various communities and in various sections of the same community. Often the teachers play too little part in these organizations, but this varies again with the locality. Much depends on leadership and on homogeneity of culture among the parents. In some towns and cities the organization tends to degenerate into a purely entertainment group for a few parents who wish to play cards and gossip. In more enlightened neighborhoods the organization has become a distinctly important factor in the control of the schools. In some of our smaller communities the Parent-Teacher Association is about the only general community organization of adults. Where there are church and lodge differences, or sharp economic differences between a few wealthy families and the rest of the town, such a general community agency may support not only school improvements but also may lead in dealing with broader community problems.

Teachers and the Community. Curiously enough, in spite of our faith in education, the teachers are seldom an integral part of the American community. The teacher's function is largely limited to instruction of the children. The teachers are treated casually, are seldom brought into close contact with the families of their pupils, and are often looked upon as nonentities.

Certain phases of our American educational system make for this condition. Nearly all elementary and two thirds of our secondary teachers are women, and doubtless the lower social standing of women generally reflects upon teachers. Mobility and early marriage also make for temporary relations between the members of the community and the teachers. School boards in most localities do not employ married women as teachers. Another factor is the insecure tenure of teachers. Lacking the advantages of group solidarity which would provide her with bargaining power, the teacher is always dealt with as an individual. When she gets into any difficulty, she has to fight her battle with the community and the school board single-handed. She can expect little aid and small comfort from her fellow teachers. As a well-known professor once wittily remarked: "Teachers are like a bag of rabbits. If someone thrusts in his hand to grab one, all the rest keep quiet."

These conditions combine to produce a sense of insecurity and inferiority on the part of the teachers themselves, doubtless keep more aggressive persons from continuing or from entering the profession, and help to feed the community stereotypes that teachers do not "amount to much" and that the schools are filled with "unsaleable men" and "unmarriageable women." Certainly, elementary and secondary teachers are lower in social standing than other people of corresponding education. Critics of American education seriously contend that this lowly position of the teacher is one cause of the ineffectiveness of our schools. In European countries, on the contrary, the teacher is a distinctive member of the community and merits a place of respect. There, however, our conditions of mobility and rapid turnover do not obtain.

Although the teacher usually has a low status and a restricted part in community affairs, the school boards frequently demand religious conformity from her. Protestant communities do not wish Catholic or Jewish personnel in the public schools; where the Catholics are in a majority, too many Protestants are undesirable. Membership in some Christian church is in the mores of most American communities, and teachers who do not conform are given little or no consideration—an illustration of the power of the mores in contrast to the legal code, which provides for "the free exercise" of religious faith.

In moral conduct the teacher must, for the most part, conform to the code of the most conservative groups in the community. Parents who themselves indulge in less traditional forms of action still demand that the teachers of their children shall exemplify the old and homelier virtues. In hundreds of American communities smoking, dancing, card playing, "keeping company with young men," and even bobbing the hair are taboo so far as the teachers are concerned.

In instructional materials conservative beliefs are also in the saddle. The recurrent controversy in American schools over the teaching of biological evolution and that concerning American history are the most striking instances of this. No textbook is likely to be selected which contains material that will offend the prejudices of any group in the community sufficiently well organized to protest. The American Legion, the Daughters of the American Revolution, the Ku Klux Klan, chambers of commerce, political, labor, and religious organizations—any of these or others like them may object to books or to teachers that they do not like. There is an orthodoxy in the schools not unlike that demanded by theology. The trial of John Thomas Scopes at Dayton, Tennessee, in 1925, for the teaching of evolution, and Mayor William Hale Thompson's attack on alleged "pro-British" American history books in Chicago schools in 1927–1928, are still fresh in our memories. It is not only in the lower schools that this taboo operates. Many colleges endowed by conservative churches restrict the teaching of science. Economic and political radicalism is also taboo in educational circles. There are few socialists or communists among teachers. The school tends to follow but not to lead the community in new thought and action.

The school has relations with other organizations in the community. We have already noted the connection of community recreational programs with the schools. The public library is an agency often called upon to furnish books, pamphlets, and periodicals for school purposes: debates, term projects, and general information. Our whole American public library system is correlated with our faith in democratic education. The school itself helps to make the community "library conscious."

Professionalism of Teachers. In spite of the low community status of the American teacher, there has been a marked trend toward professional preparation. The expenditure of public moneys for such training through normal schools and teachers colleges in 1900 was $2,786,123; in 1930 this had risen to $37,210,645. These funds do not include tuition and fees. Another measure is the increase in courses. A sample of 14 state normal schools showed a range in the number of courses in 1900 from 29 to 122; in 1930 for the same schools the number ranged from 35 to 723.

Professionalization is also illustrated in the large number of journals and technical societies which have grown up around teaching and research. William B. McCourtie in his book *Where and How to Sell Manuscripts* (1929) lists 91 educational journals, but this number is perhaps incomplete. Some of these periodicals are administrative and pedagogical in character; others bear on research. The development of national professional organizations gives rise to special magazines. *The American Year Book* (1932) notes 69 such groups, and invites the reader to "consult the U. S. Office of Education, at Washington, D. C." for the names of still others. These "associations" or "societies" range from the broad National Education Association, to the highly specialized "societies" for the fields of mathematics, chemistry, physics, biology, social sciences, and the humanities.

Rather different in purpose are the organizations of teachers to foster their professional solidarity. The isolation of teachers from community participation and their social and economic inferiority have led to attempts in some localities to build up teachers' unions, often affiliated with the American Federation of Labor. Yet the American tradition of individualism, the desire of the teachers to identify themselves with the bourgeois classes, and the belief of the teacher that he is somewhat set apart for a mission, has retarded this movement toward class consciousness.

College and university professors have a somewhat polite organization called The American Association of University Professors, set up in 1915, sometimes erroneously called the "Professors' Union." Loosely organized, with local chapters in various colleges and universities, it enlists a fair minority of teachers. It issues a regular journal which discusses educational matters, and it has within the last few years set up a sort of employment clearing house. Its principal purpose is to guard the citadel of academic freedom and of academic tenure. From time to time it has investigated cases of violation of tenure and freedom of teaching. Its reports reflect the liberal view of American higher education, but for the most part they have not led to the reinstatement of dismissed professors by administrators. Perhaps the publicity given these reports has improved the teaching conditions in the school concerned, while the threat of an investigation may in particular instances have restrained administrators from abuse of the principles of freedom and tenure.

NEW TRENDS IN EDUCATION

The wide-ranging changes in the social order and culture of the modern industrial world have slowly influenced the schools, although J. M. Williams is probably right in contending that for the most part the schools of the past have been a "repressive" and even a "reactionary influence" in America.[3] These newer developments have chiefly to do with changes in the school itself, development of formal education outside the traditional school, and the emergence of various sorts of adult education.

Recent Trends in Formal Education. This is not the place to discuss extensively the changes in formal school institutions and practices. We may mention, however, the growing interest in infant education demonstrated by the movement toward nursery schools, which enroll children from the age of two to primary-school age. These schools overlap the older kindergarten, but their work takes into account all phases of the child's life: nutritional, physical habits, and intellectual, emotional, and social growth. The nursery school aims at adult education designed to assist the

[3] See J. M. Williams, *Principles of Social Psychology*, 1923, p. 369.

home in child training. So far these schools, largely in the nature of "social experiments," have been confined to a few communities.[4] While it will be some time before this infant education will become tax-supported and widespread in character, it gives evidence that other agencies are taking over functions formerly belonging to the family.

There are a number of so-called "progressive schools" privately endowed or supported by tuition that are attempting to develop what is sometimes called "the child-centered school." Taking their cue largely from John Dewey and W. H. Kilpatrick, they believe that the child's own interests should determine the learning process, that coercion has little or no place in healthy education, that the adult should not impose his code or views upon the child, but that the latter should, with his fellow pupils, out of his "creative" capacities develop his own skills, knowledge, and values. Such a radical departure from traditional educational methods and organization is not likely to be widely adopted in the public or parochial schools of this country. (See final section, pages 277–282.)

Within the public schools themselves many changes have been made, especially those looking to a better correlation of the courses of study with the intellectual ability of the pupils, looking to increased vocational education in a society dominated by industry and business, looking more recently to provision for emotional and social training, quite aside from mere skill and knowledge. Associated with these changes has been a steady rise in the upper limit of the compulsory school age.

Vocational education has intruded itself into the older school curriculum in spite of much opposition from some school authorities and some groups in the community. One survey showed that comparing 35 Midwestern high schools for 1929–1930 with records for the same high schools in 1906–1911 and 1915–1918, there was a 700 per cent increase in the average number of courses in the industrial arts, including such items as manual training, automobile mechanics, and mechanical drawing. There was also a 500 per cent increase in courses in the household arts.[5] Between 1920 and 1930 there was a 200 per cent increase in the number of

[4] The Federal Bureau of Education listed 67 nursery schools in 1926 and 121 in 1928, located in 70 cities in 27 states. Many of these schools were short-lived. In 1930 the White House Conference on Child Health and Protection reported 169 separate nursery schools and 114 nursery schools connected with kindergartens.
[5] G. E. Van Dyke, "Trends in the Development of High School Offerings," *School Review*, Dec., 1931, vol. XXXIX, pp. 737–39.

pupils in vocational courses in schools which received federal aid under the Smith-Hughes Act and like legislation.

Night schools, which are largely vocational in character, are also on the increase. Federal reports show for cities of 10,000 population or more, between 1918 and 1930, that the number of cities offering this sort of education increased from 338 to 451, while the number of persons in the elementary branches in these schools increased 76 per cent, the number in high-school work, 90 per cent, and the number in vocational-school work proper, 97 per cent.

Colleges and universities are also offering special short courses and "institutes" in all sorts of matters, which to a medieval scholastic would seem definite evidence of fantasy thinking: police schools, farmers' institutes, "six-day schools" for sewage plant operators, three-day "institutes" for county-relief agents, two-weeks "courses" for rural ministers, and all sorts of academically stimulated conventions for special occupational groups, from cheesemakers to hardware merchants and dental surgeons. What is this but further evidence both of the profound faith in education, amounting almost to a fetish worship, and of the growing nexus between formal education and the "practical world" outside?

Then there are the extension and correspondence courses of our universities, which deliver formal education "right to your door." In this country in 1932 there were 28 theological seminaries, 44 state normal schools and teachers colleges, 82 colleges and universities, and 450 private correspondence schools, all offering courses by mail. One national organization, the National Home Study Council, with 36 private correspondence schools as members, lists 25,000 courses in every conceivable field of knowledge or skill which may be used by prospective students.[6]

Educational provision for defectives, delinquents, and feeble-minded will be noted in Chapter XXVIII.

Educational Devices Outside the Traditional School. The development of formal education outside public and parochial schools is a further indication of recent change. These are chiefly of three sorts: schools organized for private profit, various formal training devices developed by capitalist industry and business, and so-called "workers'" education.

The United States has seen no end of "schools" and "colleges" run for private gain to the owners. They touch all sorts of occu-

[6] See C. H. Judd, "Education," chap. VII, *Recent Social Trends*, p. 344.

pations: barbering, commercial subjects, training in manual skills, tap-dancing, radio announcing, dramatics, music, and even dentistry and medicine. They put on all the trappings and rituals of traditional education, with names, symbols of distinction, credits, scholarships, diplomas, and even try to develop a student *esprit de corps*. As private corporations, they may indulge in the American custom of enticing patrons by extensive and exaggerated advertisements of their wares.

Private industry and business have also gone in for formal instruction of employees in all sorts of ways. Large department stores have "regular" courses for salesmen, buyers, and clerks. Chain stores often have similar courses for prospective "managers," and even textbook publishers have short courses and "seminars" for their salesmen. Likewise some factories conduct courses in draftsmanship and mechanical skill for their workers, although the steady intrusion of the automatic machine and the increased simplification of industrial processes, as witnessed in the automobile industry, have reduced this need in many fields.

On the whole, however, commercial firms and industrial plants rather look askance at formal educational programs for their workers. Many doubt the economic value of this sort of vocational training, and they are even more skeptical of public vocational education. Most of the managers and employers seem to believe that "one learns to do by doing," and one prominent industrialist is reported to have gone so far as to remark that "practice work" as given in our public schools is immoral.

Through their leaders and organizations, workers themselves have attempted educational programs. In Europe some of these schemes have been in operation for decades, and many believe that the growth of labor and proletarian class consciousness is definitely related to such education. Like movements in this country have been sporadic and rather halfhearted. Organized trade-unions have ordinarily not supported these institutions. The rather feeble socialist parties have not done much better. However, the Rand School for Social Science, in New York City, founded in 1906, and Brookwood Labor College, in Katonah, New York, founded in 1921, have attempted to train labor leaders. The Manumit School of Brooklyn is an interesting and somewhat isolated case of "labor" education of an elementary sort, aimed not at the prospective leaders but at the workers themselves.

These inconsequential attempts at workers' education bespeak the essential weakness of organized labor in this country. Unless the laboring masses, under adequate leadership and with sufficient economic motivation, develop their own class feelings and philosophy of social change, we cannot expect them to go in for education of the workers on any extensive scale.

Other Adult Education. The development of folk schools or people's colleges in Denmark is an interesting instance of adult education which had much to do with the economic and social recovery of that country after its defeat at the hands of Prussia in 1866. Combining technical courses in farming and co-operative marketing with broader liberal education, these schools helped to revive the morale of the people, to improve standards of living, and to make the Danish people one of the most intelligent in the modern world. Nothing analogous to this has taken place in this country. For the most part, adult education has been a superficial outgrowth of women's literary clubs, lyceums, chautauquas, and forums. Since the World War the various adult education courses and lectures have revolved around current political and economic problems or around child training. The American Association for Adult Education was set up in 1925 to act as a central clearing house, to encourage adult educational programs, and to assist adult groups in making surveys of their local problems. The Parent-Teacher Association, the Child Study Association of America, the Foreign Policy Association, and similar organizations have also given attention to the development of adult education in the fields of their interests.

Adult education will doubtless loom larger on the cultural horizon in the future than it has in the past. The cry has gone up, "Why stop learning?" With increased hours of leisure, with rising standards of living, with a growing proportion of our population in the middle years of life, and with a conviction that political, economic, and other changes may be discussed and managed by the adult educational method, there may well be a new viewpoint in regard to the function of education in our society. When there are fewer and fewer children to enter the doors of our public schools, we may come to send many of their parents along to the same schools, perhaps at different hours, thus affording a new use for the buildings of which the founders of American education did not dream.

The relation of all education—for children and adults—must be examined in the light of two matters: contemporary theories of education, and the rise of new competitors of formal mass education—newspapers, magazines, books, motion pictures, and the radio. Since this last set of factors must be taken into account in educational theory, let us first examine the place of these devices in modern society.

COMPETITORS OF FORMAL EDUCATION

In the present chapter we have seen how formal education has constantly expanded its radius to take over the transmission of culture formerly left in the hands of the family, the skilled trade, the church, or other such group. Furthermore, many new features have been added to the school program. In spite of these changes, formal education must compete with other devices for mass impression, which in the end may prove more powerful than the school, unless some of them, at least, be tied more closely to the educational scheme itself.

The Printing Press and Mass Impression. Books are pouring from our American presses at the rate of about 10,000 titles a year. These books furnish, of course, material for formal education, but in addition the reading habits set up in school carry over to provide people a means of further acquisition of all sorts of knowledge, fantastic or objective, morally "good" or "bad," and aesthetically in good taste or in poor.

Perhaps more important than books are the magazines and newspapers. Periodicals have been increasing in number and circulation in recent decades. The largest single group, the monthly magazines, increased in number from 2,328 in 1900 to 3,804 in 1930. Although there is some decline in numbers of daily newspapers (from 2,514 in 1917 to 2,268 in 1931) and of the less common weekly and tri-weekly papers, the circulation of dailies has increased enormously. In 1929 the average total circulation of dailies per issue was over 42 million. The weeklies averaged nearly 19 million per issue.

This printed material—books, magazines, and newspapers— floods our people with a daily, monthly, and seasonal stream of words that cannot fail to leave their impression. Their competition with formal education is apparent. One may well ask if it is morally worth while to train millions to read and then discover that their interest does not rise above the tabloids and sensation-mongering news sheets, the mystery, love, or adventure story magazines, or the cheap, ephemeral "best sellers" among our books. This material is constantly providing myths, legends, and stereotypes for these millions that cannot but be reflected sooner or later in their political, economic, religious, and moral attitudes and behavior. The persistent reverence for the printed word as such is one of the reasons why propaganda and advertising are so effective in our world today.

New Agencies for Mass Stimulation. Today the motion picture and the radio are adding their influences to that of the printing press. It was estimated that on January 31, 1931, there were 22,731 motion-picture houses in the United States, with an aggregate seating capacity of over 11 million. Calculations as to weekly attendance vary from 77 million to 100 million. (See Chapter XV.) The radio has also become increasingly common. The federal census for 1930 reported 12,078,345 families owning radio sets, and careful estimates for 1938 give 26,666,500 families as owning at least one radio—not including automobile sets.

The effectiveness of the motion picture and the radio are not fully known, although some recent studies of the motion picture present suggestive data.[7] These new visual and verbal stimuli constantly confronting our people, old and young, cannot but influence their attitudes and habits.

Never before has the world seen such an array of agencies for mass impression. Oratory, formal teaching, religious exhortation at revivals, and all other methods of arousing large numbers of people with the same stimuli at the same time, pale into insignificance beside these mighty forces. Into whose hands the control of these devices falls will determine rather largely the direction in which our masses will go. Where there is a conflict of aims and content between formal education and these other agencies, one cannot predict which will prove the more powerful. In capitalistic United States, while formal education is predominantly state controlled, these other means of stimulation are, with few exceptions, in the hands of private enterprise out for profits. In other

[7] See monograph series, "Motion Pictures and Youth," the Payne Fund Studies under the direction of W. W. Charters, published by The Macmillan Company. Charter's summary, *Motion Pictures and Youth*, 1933, reviews the findings of this research group.

countries, notably Russia, Italy, and more recently Germany, the national state has taken over the control of these newer devices, combining them with the traditional educational system, in order to bend them completely to the ends of their particular political and economic systems.

The effectiveness of formal as against informal mass impression is a debatable issue. When we are presented with a combination of formal and informal methods of universal stimulation, especially under some ideal goal set by the ruling class, the whole question of cultural continuity, of propaganda, censorship, and education is put boldly before us. It raises the profound question of the conscious and unconscious direction of opinions, beliefs, and attitudes in relation to their ultimate effect upon overt conduct. The problems of indoctrination either by hit-or-miss methods or by conscious planning are before us.

Further, what new items either planned or unplanned may be introduced into culture by these methods of mass impression? The whole question of childhood, adolescent, and adult education as it relates to basic educational philosophies is involved. In our own country today certain "schools" of thought and practice offer us somewhat divergent views of the function of education and of conscious social planning. Let us see what these "schools" offer.

THE PLACE OF EDUCATION IN CONTEMPORARY SOCIETY

Under the impress of modern science, the older notion of the school as the passive carrier of culture from one generation to another has given way to a more dynamic view. This new standpoint leads us in two divergent directions. These we must examine, because not only the future of formal education but also that of our whole culture is bound up in them.

Progressive Education as Training to Think. Under the influence of John Dewey there has grown up a "school" of educational theory which places great faith in intellectual and emotional training of the child and the adult with a view to improving the worth of the common man, making him more intelligent about his world, and more able to cope with its innumerable problems. For Dewey the mind of man is but an instrument to aid him in adaptation to his environment, an idea born of biology and the machine age. When to this is added the democratic notion of the value of the common man, we get a standpoint which has had wide appeal in this country. Applied to the school this means that the child is the center of educational activity, that his growth as an intelligent unit in democratic society is the main concern. This growth implies the experimental and tentative method, because nothing is to be fixed and final in society. The child is to be trained to handle situations as they arise, but always with a reservation, since later some other situation may demand another solution.

The personality of the child grows out of his interests integrated with the democratic culture. There is in the literature of this group a healthy sprinkling of stereotypes of the "democratic ideal," of "the democratic way of life," of "personality," of "integration," and of the continued use of experimentation in handling personal and social problems. W. H. Kilpatrick, one of the most ardent of these educators, believes that the rising generation may be taught "to think that they can and will think for themselves, even ultimately, if they so decide, to the point of revising or rejecting what we now think."[8] There is great faith in "conscious control," in enthroning the "intelligence," and in setting up a "responsible criticism" of our society at any point where it seems advisable.

The school, therefore, is to become instead of the training ground the actual first stage in the process of remaking society. The wider society of which the school is a part should develop a planning, but not a "planned" method, never static or finished, but always dynamic and changing. In this the school will be an instrument of progress and not merely an institutional device for transmission of the old culture.

There is in all this a strong faith in the power of intelligence to solve our problems. Coupled with this, certain followers of Dewey hold a notion—not unlike that of Rousseau—that the child comes good and pure from nature, but that what he gets from culture makes or mars his future. That is, accepting something of the idea of the pure child of nature, unspoiled at the outset, they superimpose the further idea that the child may be trained to think out every situation so effectively that he can handle all the major social situations of the future in a rational manner. In this way, they connect the belief in rational thought and scientific method with the idea that nature furnishes us material favorable to these higher

[8]See W. H. Kilpatrick, "A Theory of Progressive Education to Fit the Times," *Progressive Education,* April, 1931, vol. VIII, pp. 287–93.

flights of development. While they give emotion a place as related to fundamental motives behind intelligence as a means to an end, they retain a firm belief in the power of trained reason to direct the deeper drives and emotions into ever more rational moral and socialized channels.

Thus for these theorists the common man still has his place. They contend that we need but widen the doors of educational opportunity, free him from the fetters of an outworn curriculum, and put the school into the social order as the first stage of actual living in society. When we have done so, they believe that we shall witness an emerging moral and social order, never fixed at any point, but always moving toward some new higher goal.

Education as Indoctrination. In contrast to this viewpoint, at least at many points, is one which supports the theory that the child is capable of much learning, that conditioning has wide possibilities, but that to ignore the place of fixed ideas and stereotyped beliefs as the foundation for social and personal action is to fly in the face of sound psychology and sociology. They hold that the imposition of ideas, beliefs, attitudes, and habits is natural and inevitable.

There is no standard body of doctrine in this "school" of educational theory. The individuals who have advocated indoctrination range from those like Ross L. Finney (1875–1934), who stood for the *status quo* and the more ancient virtues of primary group democracy, to such persons as George S. Counts, who has promoted the general proposition of indoctrination vigorously, and Fred J. Kelly, who has actually put a blue print of his project on paper for the world to see.

The people who stand for indoctrination accept many of the tenets of the Dewey "school," but they indicate that man has always had some sort of biased training, largely unconscious and unplanned, but nevertheless present in all culture. They doubt that we can have any education, formal or informal, which does not give witness to this. The very inculcation of the habits common to the group, of myths and legends of heroes and situations, the imposition of the basic ethos of any culture is a form of indoctrination. All that they ask is that we may today do this more deliberately and with reference to a planned society ahead.

Without doubt the courageous example of Russia, in particular, has stimulated the consideration of this doctrine in America. In his "Introduction" to A. P. Pinkevitch's *The New Education in the Soviet Republic* (1929), George S. Counts comments as follows:

"If the present experiment in Russia is allowed to work itself out, it will test the power of formal education in directing the course of social evolution. Russia has an educational program organized from top to bottom for the purpose of achieving a fairly definite objective; the building of a collective social order. . . ."

So, too, fascist Italy and, more recently, fascist Germany have given examples of the power of indoctrination consciously controlled by those in power. In all these countries the aim is the building of personality and a social order to fulfill the aims of the dominant group.

In reference to the United States, Counts believes that if we are not to be false to its promise we "must do more than simply perpetuate the democratic ideal of human relationships." The school must aid us by giving the child, by indoctrination, if you will, "a vision of a future America, immeasurably more just and noble and beautiful than the America of today."

Unfortunately, Counts does not as yet go beyond this promotional, revivalist stage. He has no specific plans except to arouse discussion, especially among the teachers. He himself deals in various stereotypes, not unlike those of his opponents: "educational task," "social obligation" of the school, and the "union of human reason, purpose, and will."

Fred J. Kelly, in contrast, goes further. For him the schools should assume responsibility in setting up our social, economic, and political goals:

There would be created a planning council made up of men from various fields of teaching, research, business, industry, agriculture, finance, and government. This council would formulate the fundamental principles, including, for democracy, such things as high quality of human stock, primacy of child welfare, supremacy of human over property rights, the crucial importance of law and its observance, and the inevitability and the implications of sound internationalism. This council would next work out the specifications for putting these principles into force. Some of these would find their way into the law; others would be a distinctive part of education. There would also be a conscious, controlled effort to develop an active preponderant opinion to support these plans and practices, including the needed prestige for this central council. Then to prevent too great formalism and loss of vitality, he would have a research section continuously revealing new facts and truth, and guiding the council in the constant revision of its policies.[9]

Interpretation. The first question which confronts us is this: Can the school rise higher than its source in the culture out of which it springs? Certainly the school is but a creature of the dominant culture of the dominant group of any society. In the past, with fundamental values pretty thoroughly accepted and social change slow in tempo, the school represented conservatism rather than change.

As to the struggle between training to solve problems and indoctrination, the differences do not appear so great as the proponents imagine. Truly indoctrination is the very essence of habit formation, so fundamental to Dewey's psychology. Even if we accept the optimistic theory of Kilpatrick, training to think is but another name for the ancient "mental discipline," which itself is but the indoctrination of logic. The question really concerns unconscious, hit-or-miss indoctrination, as against the conscious and deliberate sort. The examples of Russia, Italy, and Germany are but evidences that men in power in these countries have learned from modern science how to control mass impression to the end of building a new culture in a relatively short time. Believing as they must in the flexibility of human beings, they set out consciously to employ formal education and all the informal devices of books, magazines, newspapers, motion pictures, and radio to direct the ideas, attitudes, and habits of their followers along predetermined lines. They lay out a planned society, but none of them, admittedly, quite conceive their plans to be final.

In the end, therefore, the differences between the two "schools" are not great. Those who follow Dewey in their faith in education have their own "doctrines," based largely on a rationalized vision of an intelligent, democratic society. Their plans for achieving this may differ in detail, but are they not, like the others, looking to a future which will be happier and more just than the present? But to deny the place of "doctrines," "values," and "bias," to assume that man is essentially a reasonable creature, to forget the power of emotions in driving men to action, is to ignore the fundamentals of human behavior.

[9]See F. J. Kelly, "The Place of Education in Social-Economic Planning," *School and Society*, Oct. 29, 1932, vol. XXXVI, pp. 545–53.

It is clear that education and its institutions function with ever greater force in modern society. The faith in mass education has not abated. Yet its direction is being changed in harmony with the rise of new political and social organization. We have seen how education has more and more taken over many functions of the home, the shop, the business, the factory, and other community activities. We have seen that it has, however, competitors in the way of informal mass impression in the printing press, the motion picture, and the radio. It is also evident that these agencies may themselves become controlled by some central body or group who employ them and the more formal educational devices for directing the whole trend of social organization in the broad sense. In the end these means of culture continuity and cultural change become basic to everything else.

By the same token, education, formal and informal, as the transmitter and even inventor of culture, has an increasing part in the formation of the personality. If the transmission of culture is geared closely to the planned social order itself, the dominant groups of a given society can do much, if not everything, to form personalities—attitudes, values, and habits—along predetermined lines. The school therefore becomes in a sense the testing or "proving" ground for the basic sociological problem of the relation of the societal order to the personality and in regard to their reversible interaction. We still do not know whether there remains a residue of innate, biological factors which will limit the impress of culture and the societal order on the personality; but the wide variety of human conditioning seen in different societies leads us to believe that there is little that the human being is not capable of doing, within the limits of his basic capacity to learn and his biological urges to eat, drink, sleep, procreate, relax, and find a place for himself in his environment. If this be so, education, formal and informal, becomes the key to future society. (See Chapter XXIX.)

CLASS ASSIGNMENTS

A. Further reading assignment:
1. K. Young, *Source Book for Sociology*, chap. XIII.
2. Willard Waller, *The Sociology of Teaching*, chaps. II, IV.

B. Questions and exercises:
1. What do we mean by saying that the school represents an interactional pattern? Illustrate.

2. Give illustrations of social rituals in our public schools.

3. Illustrate how special interest groups in the community—patriotic, religious, or industrial and business—influence the schools.

4. How do you account for the rôle and status of the American public-school teacher in most communities? What might be done to alter the situation? Cite instances if you can.

5. What changes in school policy and practice will be likely to occur if our birth rate continues to decline? On what age groups will attention be concentrated during the next ten years?

6. Discuss pro and con the future development of adult education in America, especially as to the possibilities of its influence on economic and political life.

7. Discuss pro and con the question as to whether the political state should take over all means of mass impression and couple these with the traditional educational program.

8. Discuss "indoctrination" *versus* the "progressive" theory of education.

C. Topics for class reports or longer written papers:

1. Education among primitive peoples in contrast with major features of our own. (Consult W. D. Hambly, *Origins of Education Among Primitive Peoples*, 1926; W. I. Thomas, *Source Book for Social Origins*, 1909, part II and bibliography; Margaret Mead, "Education: Primitive," *Encyclopedia of the Social Sciences*, vol. V, pp. 399–403, and bibliography.)

2. The rise and success of "progressive" education in this country. (Consult H. O. Rugg and Ann Shumaker, *The Child-Centered School*, 1928; C. W. Washburne, *Better Schools*, 1928; Hughes Mearns, *Creative Youth*, 1926, and his *Creative Power*, 1929; J. W. Wrightstone, *Appraisal of Newer Practices in Selected Public Schools*, 1935; L. A. Cook, *Community Backgrounds of Education*, 1938, chap. XIX and bibliography; and the files of the journal *Progressive Education*.)

3. The rôle and status of the American teacher. (Consult Willard W. Waller, *The Sociology of Teaching*, 1932; Cook, *op. cit.*, chap. XVII.)

4. The theory of indoctrination and the various proposals related thereto. (Consult George S. Counts, *Dare the Schools Build a New Social Order?*, 1932, and his *The Soviet Challenge to America*, 1931.)

5. The theory of democratic education. (Consult W. H. Kilpatrick, *Education for a Changing Civilization*, 1926; W. H. Kilpatrick [ed.], *The Educational Frontier*, 1933; John Dewey, *Democracy and Education*, 1916, and his *Experience and Education*, 1938.)

6. Educational devices under the "New Deal"; *e.g.*, C.C.C., N.Y.A., etc. (Consult, for the CCC, the federal reports of the Director of Emergency Conservation Work; H. W. Oxley, *Education in the Civilian Conservation Corps Camps*, 1936; for the NYA, B. and E. K. Lindley, *A New Deal for Youth*, 1938; H. W. Bell, *A Study of How the Needs of Youth Are Met in Maryland*, 1938; H. P. Rainey, et al., *How Fare American Youth?*, 1937.)

CHAPTER XIV

RELIGION

The universality of religion gives ample proof that it is as deeply rooted in man's needs and in culture, as are economic, political, familial, educational, or other fundamental activities. As man learns to work, to control himself in the interests of his family or community, he also learns to worship. Yet when we look more closely at the matter, we find that religious beliefs and practices vary so widely among different societies that a common or general definition of religion is somewhat hard to find. *Religion* is frequently defined as man's belief in supernatural forces outside himself, which forces, he is convinced, influence human events. As a concrete experience, moreover, religion is accompanied by emotions and feelings, especially of fear, awe, or reverence. Actually, religious culture is more than this bare outline. In many societies it develops a wide range of institutions and a body of special officials, with forms of worship, ceremonies, sacred objects, tithes, pilgrimages, and the like. In the higher cultures it produces elaborate theologies to explain man's place in the universe. In many instances it has close connections with moral control and sets up a system of ethics with elaborate rules of conduct. Furthermore, the great religions of the world, Brahmanism, Buddhism, Judaism, Christianity, and Mohammedanism, are really the foci of elaborate culture systems that have dominated whole societies for centuries.

RELIGION IN CULTURE

Although our principal interest in this chapter is in the religious beliefs and practices of higher societies, especially our own, we must note briefly some phases of primitive religion as a background.

Primitive Religion. Primitive man finds himself confronted with forces in nature which he fears and does not understand. He speculates, and that is the beginning of philosophy. He puts forth a finger to investigate, and that is the beginning of science. He feels the emotion of awe, and that is the beginning of religion. Finally, bit by bit, he develops action patterns which seem to secure the desired adjustments in his environment and his relation to it. In these rudimentary patterns are the roots of all social institutions.

To the primitive, the various phases of life are not sharply subdivided as they are with us. Work and art, play and religion, magic and tool making—all are closely interwoven. Economic activities are often surrounded by non-economic rituals. Recurrent events which appear regularly in the life of the group, like birth, death, marriage, and seasonal changes, come to have special emotional significance, and ceremonies expressive of these emotions are developed and become part of the folkways.

Surrounded as he was by forces of nature and of other men, forces which he did not fully understand, primitive man did not distinguish in any logical way between natural and supernatural factors in behavior. They were interwoven in his daily life at every point. As R. R. Marett, the English anthropologist, remarks:

"The savage has no word for 'nature.' He does not abstractly distinguish between an order of uniform happenings and a higher order of miraculous happenings. He is merely concerned to mark and exploit the difference when presented in the concrete."[1]

In fact, it is difficult to distinguish primitive religion from the other phases of rudimentary culture. In particular, what we call magic overlaps with primitive religion on the one hand, and with naturalistic utilitarian behavior on the other.

Magic is invented or discovered in the same way that other techniques are invented or discovered. A certain act is performed either accidentally or because imagination suggests that it might be successful. If it seems to work, it is adopted as a rule of action. If it is discovered that friction produces heat, this may suggest fire. Thus the imagination furnishes a clue which proves valid in overt action. But again, imagination suggests that if I burn a wax effigy of my enemy, I will be doing harm to him. Or a barren woman among the Batak of Sumatra has a wooden image of a child

[1] R. R. Marett, *The Threshold of Religion*, 2nd ed., 1914, p. 109.

placed in her lap so that she may bear a child. If the intended victim actually does fall ill or if the woman conceives, the invention is successful. We call fire-making naturalistic or realistic because its action is fully explained by present-day physical science. We call effigy making magic because any success it may have is outside the scope of modern physical science.

Many writers have distinguished between religion and magic. One of the commonest distinctions holds that in religion the person uses such devices as prayer, entreaty, propitiation, and compromise in securing assistance from various supernatural forces. In magic, on the contrary, the person, following the formulae based on assumptions of inevitable cause and effect, really compels or coerces the supernatural powers in order to secure his own ends. It is said that the true religious participant comes before supernatural powers in awe and supplication, in humility, and even grovelling fear, while the magic worker has the self-assurance of the modern scientist, who is confident that with his instruments of control and his mathematical logic he can secure the wanted results. As a matter of fact, magic and religion are closely related among primitive peoples, and together they represent particular techniques for dealing with the problems of the society. Many of the devices of magic have given way to science in our own society, and religion in its turn has become increasingly more ethical among advanced peoples. The more elementary features have tended to disappear.

Primitive religion rests upon a belief in personal and impersonal powers which interfere in man's life. The belief in personal powers is called *animism*. It is illustrated by belief in spirits, ghosts, and demons which bring good or bad luck. Impersonal power, known by the name of *mana* (Melanesian), *orenda* (Iroquois), *manitou* (Algonquian), or other names, manifests itself in natural objects, through men, or through spirits or ghosts. These beliefs are expressed through all sorts of ceremonials, purification rites, use of sacred objects, shrines, and so on. There also grows up a body of special officials or priests who manage the religious life of the community. Religious symbolism is elaborate and is tied to primitive art on every hand. And primitive religion often plays an important part in societal control. In short, primitive religion offers man a means of dealing with superior forces, gives him an emotional outlet in times of great crises, and above all else serves to solidify the group into a unit. In terms of culture the savage's religious experience is as sacred and serious to him as our own religious emotions and habits are to us.

Turning to religious expression among more advanced societies, let us examine certain general features of the institutions and the special social rôles which have arisen within this area of experience.

General Features of Religious Expression. The institutional practices and formal theories which have grown up around religion are many. We shall note only a few: ceremonials, symbolism, sacred objects and buildings, theology, creed, and the church as an organization.

Ceremony or *ritual* is a standardized and accepted action directed toward some specific purpose or end. Rituals and ceremonies, of course, are not confined to religion. In religion it is a settled manner of entreating or controlling the supernatural powers in regard to some particular situation. Ordination, the sacraments, various forms of sacrifice and penance call for special rituals. In some churches, like the Greek or Roman Catholic, ceremonials are elaborate. In other churches, like those of the Quakers or Calvinists with their "bare kirk," ceremonials play a slight part in religious life. The importance of these things in the lives of the communicants depends largely upon their training. There seems to be a strong tendency for ceremonies and rituals to become so important in themselves that they lose their deeper meaning for the devotees. When ritual gets cut off from its genuine religious purpose, from its underlying symbolism, we may speak of over-ritualism or formalism.

Throughout religion *symbolism* plays an important part. Symbols are signs, substitutes, or representations of some object or situation. They may be verbal or tangible. The commonly recognized symbol assists the person to identify himself with his fellows. It promotes a sense of solidarity. Often it comes to stand not alone for the particular object or situation to which it was originally attached, but to the whole group and its culture. Thus, the cross stands for Christianity and the crescent for Mohammedanism. Sometimes a sect adopts distinctive clothes, as the Dunkards or Quakers, and these, in turn, serve as symbols. We must recall also that the symbol in the mind of the user is usually not approached intellectually but emotionally. For the religious worshiper, therefore, the object and its symbol are combined into an indivisible emotional experience that asserts itself whenever the situation calls for contact with the supernatural powers. The eucharist, for example, symbolizes for the Christian the supreme sacrifice of Jesus, and in this ritual the worshiper identifies himself intellectually and emotionally with one of the main tenets of his theology.

Associated with rituals and symbolism are all sorts of *sacred objects* which give external evidence of internal power. The Hebrew ark of the covenant and the phylactery; the Christian censer, bells, robes, surplice, candles, altar, and especially the cross are important in many religious exercises.

For their religious exercises people often repair to special localities: mountain tops, mineral springs, groves of trees, river banks, or seashores. Special *buildings* in which their exercises may be carried on are erected: the tabernacle of the ancient Hebrews, the temples of ancient Babylonia, Egypt, Greece, and Rome, and the cathedrals and churches of Christianity.

Theology is the systematic explanation which religious leaders work out to show man's relation to his god and to the universe. Often this includes some account of the origin of the world and of man, like the stories of creation in our own Bible. It presents the *creed* or body of beliefs and doctrines of the church. The written words become the sacred scriptures. In the more organized religious bodies, the creed often becomes highly elaborate, touching practically every phase of religion.

In a broad sense the *church* is (*1*) a body of devotees, (*2*) organized for religious purposes and developing as agencies for this, (*3*) rituals, (*4*) a hierarchy of officials and leaders, and (*5*) a body of doctrine and philosophy which ties the whole together into a more or less systematic unit. In common speech, too, the term *church* is sometimes used to mean a unity of common religious beliefs and practices, as when we speak of the Christian Church. At other times, the *church* refers to a more limited body of devout believers within this larger grouping, such as the Presbyterian or Methodist Church. These, properly speaking, are denominations.

The *sect* is a body of believers which grows up within the larger church or denomination. Certain persons, often few in number at first, begin to differ from the main ceremonials and creed of the parent organization. As a rule they do not think of themselves as outside their denomination. Only as they come into controversy and conflict with the ecclesiastical order of the original body, does the idea of separation arise. Often only after they have been excommunicated, do they gradually formulate their own creed, their own official hierarchy, and take on a distinctive name or "denomination" of their own. It was thus that many of the Protestant denominations arose. Judaism has at least two sects—the "orthodox" and the reformed. Mohammedanism shows the same sort of thing, with two major divisions and many smaller ones.

Special Social Rôles in Religion. In nearly all societies religious beliefs and practices give rise to distinctive social rôles. While these social types of religious personnel are not to be sharply distinguished from each other, they do tend to fall into two more general classes, the religious thinkers and mystics, and the executives. The former include the mystics proper, the prophets, and messiahs. The latter include the priests, formal teachers, many missionaries, and other executives. As to personality type, the former tend to be introverted, to indulge in rich fantasy life, to be interested in the substance or essence of supernatural contacts, and to interpret these experiences as divine communications. The latter tend to be extroverted, objective in attitude, and concerned with form rather than substance. Mystics are likely to be radical, innovators, and disturbers of the established order. Executives are generally, not always, conservative, and prefer the old and tried to the new. There is, in fact, a sort of recurrent struggle in religious groups between these two sorts of persons. Some would confine religious expression within rather definite limits set by symbols, rites, traditions, and established theology. Others would not unduly hamper religious experience by these established patterns of thought and action but would leave much to the individual's unique experience. Let us describe briefly some of the more common types.

The *priest* or *pastor* is a generalized group functionary carrying on the religious rituals and expounding theology. The hierarchy of the Roman Catholic Church, from the pope and cardinals at the top through the archbishops and bishops to the parish priests at the bottom, illustrates the rôle of the priestly class. They are the special persons to officiate at the church sacraments and to care for both spiritual and temporal affairs. The priest or pastor has a distinctive place in maintaining the morals of his parishioners.

Just as over-ritualism tends to make a church organization static and conservative, so a strong ecclesiastical body prevents innovations, and keeps the expression of religious life within the boundaries laid down by the official dogmas. Over-ritualism and a powerful priesthood tend to go hand in hand, as witness the history of religion in Babylonia, Egypt, Palestine, and the Roman Catholic Church.

Religious *teachers* or *philosophers* have played a distinct part in the rise of our great world religions. Jesus, St. Paul, Mohammed, Buddha, and Confucius are all familiar instances. These men secured a following by teaching religious and ethical principles. The *missionary* is a special teacher whose business it is to carry the message of some established religion to non-believers.

Mention must also be made of the *religious executive*, who may, as did St. Paul, combine within himself both missionary and organizer. In many Protestant churches where the priestly hierarchy is not developed or is practically non-existent, the affairs of the church organization are carried on by executives whose work combines that of priest or pastor with business management. So, too, as modern churches spread their functions to all sorts of tangential interests, such as club work, poor relief, recreation, and education, the executive type assumes an increasing importance.

The *mystic* plays a special part in religious growth. He identifies himself, or comes into union, with the God, or with the World-Spirit, or the Absolute—however the culture phrases the concepts. The mystic illustrates the place of the divergent person in a society who may initiate changes in culture. Mystics are sometimes epileptics, hysterics, or other pathological persons. Through their dreams, visions, and other unique mental experiences, they fully believe that they come into direct personal communication with divine powers.

The *prophet* is an important religious leader. While he may be a priest, more often he is a mystic. He serves as a mouthpiece for some divine power, issuing warnings, giving commands, and laying out plans for future events. He hears the voice of his god and passes on the word to man. The prophet's rôle, like that of the mystic, is set by the culture. Where there is a strong priestly hierarchy, as among the Ekoi of west Africa or in the Roman Catholic Church, there is little opportunity for these persons. In contrast, the religious transition set up by the Protestant Reformation stimulated a long line of mystics and prophets who have greatly influenced Protestant history.

The *messiah* is the divine leader or prophet who accepts supernatural attributes, who foretells some catastrophic end of the world, and often assumes the rôle of final judge. The messiah is the creature of the people themselves, who in a time of crisis look to him to save their society from disaster. The expectancy or anticipation of such a deliverer is well shown among the ancient Hebrews, who suffered severe hardships at the hands of their adversaries. The most outstanding of these was Jesus Christ. Yet he was but one of a long line of Jewish messiahs both before and since.

RELIGIOUS ORGANIZATIONS AND OTHER ORGANIZATIONS

Religion has long had intimate connections with other features of culture. Although in simpler societies this relationship is more obvious, the modern church has also reached out to other groups and institutions within the community. Although in many cases the political state has officially supported religion, in democracies official state religions have disappeared. Nevertheless, church leaders still wield political influence. In broader community activities the church has also become an important sponsor of various community organizations. In moral control, especially, and in education, the church has long played a dominant rôle. More recently it has developed recreational and social service features. And the relation of the church to the capitalist economic system must not be forgotten.

The Church and the Community. In the primary community of medieval Europe, the church was the focus of much of the life. In Protestant countries it continued to serve important functions, although where rival sects or rival denominations arose, the integrating benefits of religion and church organization were often lost in theological conflicts. In spite of the continuation of these divisive tendencies, the churches have served the community as the center not only of religious thought and action but also of moral standards as well. The primary-community church reflects the changes which have gone on in the wider world outside. The open-country churches, in this country, for example, are declining, while the village churches are becoming the center of both farm and village church activity. The rural and village church has added educational, recreational, and social-service activities to its roster of functions. For example, the National Catholic Welfare Conference has an active Rural Life Bureau, which has developed a program for rural and village sections covering economic, family, health, social, and educational problems as well as those of religion and worship.[2]

[2] See E. V. O'Hara, chapter VI, "The Rural Work of the Catholic Church," *Handbook of Rural Social Resources* (ed. by Henry Israel and Benson Y. Landis), 1926.

Various Protestant churches maintain organizations to deal specially with rural and village church problems, and in addition the home missions of various denominations take a hand with rural church work, although the latter sometimes foster competition rather than co-operation. In summarizing recent trends in rural churches in every section of the country E. de S. Brunner and J. H. Kolb point out the growth of co-operation among the churches, the decline in membership compared to total population, especially among Protestants, and note an apparent increased effectiveness of the church organizations and community programs in spite of a decline in membership, *i.e.*, among Protestants.[3]

Formerly the church in the city was also the focus of neighborhood and community life. The Catholic churches were particularly strong as neighborhood centers, because the membership was divided geographically into parishes in the same manner in which voting precincts or school districts are laid out. This gave the particular pastor a chance to serve the people, who were themselves neighbors to each other and who already had attitudes of solidarity growing out of common life. The Protestant parishes, for the most part, were never divided on geographic lines, with the result that members were drawn from widespread areas. But so long as the population remained fairly stationary, this handicap was overcome by the fact that the church buildings were located in the residential sections in which most of the members lived.

Today in our rapidly growing American cities the situation is quite different. Many church edifices are left stranded in the midst of retail or wholesale business districts or in cheap rooming-house areas just beyond the business section. The members are now scattered over extremely wide areas, and often are so remote from the home church that they drift away to other pastorates nearer by or give up their church affiliation entirely.

In other ways the city church is caught in the changes of life, especially in the growing emphasis upon secondary group organization. Sophisticated urban populations are skeptical of what organized religion has to offer. There is frequently a conflict within the church body itself as to whether it shall liberalize its dogma, take up social service and educational and recreational programs, or stick by the old and the tried at the cost of younger membership and at the cost of slow decay and perhaps final disappearance.

[3] See E. de S. Brunner and J. H. Kolb, *Rural Social Trends*, 1933, chap. VIII.

A survey of the situation reveals all shades of differences in the relation of the church to the urban community.[4] Again, the Catholic organizations seem to be more flexible than many of the Protestant. Many city churches are expanding their educational, recreational, and social-service agencies. Some of the features of this we shall discuss below. The occupational distribution of church workers reflects this change. There is a decided increase in paid workers in educational, recreational, and social-service branches.[5]

Two movements among the Protestant churches are noteworthy illustrations of the attempt to meet contemporary community problems, illustrated by the movement away from sectarian differences toward consolidation and co-operation. One of these takes the direction of federations of churches; the other finds its expression in the community church. An example of the former is the Federal Council of the Churches of Christ in America, consisting of 27 affiliated denominations with a combined membership of 24,000,000. The Council's objectives include the stimulation of fellowship and unity among the churches, encouragement of "devotional fellowship and mutual counsel" on religious matters, and co-operation in matters of moral welfare from the point of view of "the law of Christ in every relationship of life."

The *community church* is formed by the union of separate Protestant groups. Jesse F. Steiner describes the latter thus: "Strictly speaking, the term community church is applied to a church that has the whole community for its parish and is organized for the distinct purpose of ministering to the needs of all the people irrespective of their denominational preferences."[6] The community church often stimulates public forums, offers recreational facilities to boys and girls of the entire city, and undertakes preventive programs in the fields of health and delinquency. This is a far cry from the function of the church as the dispenser of dogma, or moral advice, and of unregulated charity.

Religion, Education, and Recreation. Formal teaching has long been the prerogative of organized religion. In Christian history, the church has played a decided part in education. The cathedral schools of the Middle Ages were used for religious and

---

[4] See H. Paul Douglass, *The Church in the Changing City*, 1927, for excellent case studies.

[5] See C. Luther Fry, "Changes in Religious Organizations," chap. XX, *Recent Social Trends*, p. 1031.

[6] Jesse F. Steiner, *Community Organization*, rev. ed., 1930, p. 290.

moral training, while Protestantism fostered elementary learning so that members might read the Bible.

The Sunday School was established in 1780 by an Englishman, Robert Raikes (1735–1811), with a view to more formal religious and moral education. The movement soon spread to America. In 1926 in the United States, 185,000 churches—about four fifths of the total—reported Sunday Schools, with more than 21,000,000 pupils, including both adults and children, an increase of 45 per cent since 1906.

More important than the Sunday School has been the continued rise of parochial schools, organized to fulfill the legal demands for formal schooling but offering the children of various churches religious and moral instruction not possible in public schools. From 1906 to 1926 the number of pupils in Catholic parochial schools increased by approximately one million, or virtually doubled, while the number in public elementary and secondary schools in this country increased at about one half this rate. The whole standpoint underlying this form of education is set forth in the "Encyclical on Education" (1930), by Pope Pius XI:

"It is necessary that all the teaching and whole organization of the school, and its teachers, syllabus and textbooks in every branch, be regulated by the Christian spirit, under the direction and maternal supervision of the Church; so that Religion may be in very truth the foundation and the crown of youth's entire training; and this in every grade of school, not only in the elementary but the intermediate and the higher institutions of learning as well." [7]

There is a certain conflict between the church and the democratic state implied in this whole standpoint. In 1922 the state of Oregon passed a law providing that after 1926 all parents must send their children to the public schools of that state. This law, in a test case, *Society of the Sisters of the Holy Names of Jesus and Mary* vs. *Pierce,* was found unconstitutional. The decision of the United States Supreme Court among other things said:

"As often heretofore pointed out, rights guaranteed by the Constitution may not be abridged by legislation which has no reasonable relation to some purpose within the competency of the state. The fundamental theory of liberty upon which all governments in this Union repose ex-

[7] See "The Pope's Encyclical on Education," *Current History,* March, 1930, vol. XXXI, p. 1101.

cludes any general power of the state to standardize its children by forcing them to accept instruction from public teachers only. The child is not the mere creature of the state; those who nurture him and direct his destiny have the right, coupled with the high duty, to recognize and prepare him for additional obligations."

Education still remains a family and religious prerogative in this country, in spite of the theory of public schooling for all. The long-standing culture trait of religious teaching is not abridged in our democracy, and we shall probably see the church continue to play an important part in formal education for a long time.

Closely related to more formal religious education has been the development of such organizations as the Young Men's Christian Association, the Knights of Columbus, and the Young Men's Hebrew Association. There are, in addition, vacation schools, clubs, and forums; and other devices are sponsored by the churches, in which more formal education is supplemented with opportunities for recreation or discussion of current moral, religious, and economic problems.

The Boy Scouts, Girl Scouts, Camp Fire Girls, and Girl Reserves, although not strictly religious in standpoint, have much in common with these other agencies. Their general purpose is to supplement the work of various groups such as the family, the church, and the school, chiefly through leisure-time activities, such as first aid, woodcraft, and athletics. They have developed summer camps and rather elaborate programs for the winter months in many of our cities.

It is significant that religious organizations are taking over many functions formerly located in the home, the neighborhood, and even in the school. Religious thought and activity are becoming again a *focus* for the integration of a host of separate activities. It is possible that the church may again become the nucleus of a large number of societal functions, even though some of its traditional supernaturalism shall have passed away.

Religion and the Mores. As we saw in Chapter II, the mores consist of the codes of social conduct which grow up in any community or society. The mores are the generally accepted and expected forms of conduct which are assumed to be necessary for group welfare. Religion has frequently been a powerful factor in lending emotional support to the moral code. The relation of religion to morality has been the subject of much controversy, both as to practice and as to theory. Some believe that religious experience is meaningless unless associated with approved social conduct. To others religion serves quite different purposes and need have no direct relation to moral action. Yet in all the great religions of civilized man there is a distinct intermingling of religion and morals. This is expressed in the religious support of taboos, in the effect on conduct of belief in a god, in the influence of a belief in future reward or punishment.

Taboo is a negative command, a restraint upon action. Taboos are the "Thou shalt nots" of society. They range over a wide variety of situations in which religious ideas play a part: childbirth, death, personal rank, sacred objects, and beliefs. It is possible by invoking taboos to extend the range of social control to almost any lengths, so long as the members of a group believe in such power. Notions of the clean and the unclean, of the sacred and the profane, ramify many cultures. If one is unlucky enough to handle a sacred or an unclean object, it may take elaborate rites of purification and penance to undo the consequences. The analogy between the supernatural power taboo and the force of electricity is evident. One becomes surcharged with this power and must do something to "decharge" himself. Like electricity, such force is beneficial when "properly" used, and dangerous when not.

Without doubt the *belief in a god* influences moral conduct. Even among the Ekoi of West Africa, where magic is so powerful and where spirits are used for antisocial ends, men believe in benign spirits who counteract the evil ones and aid man in more humane ways. And, for example, among the lowly Bushmen and Andaman Islanders the supreme being is thought to be the guardian of morality.

As the concept of an ethical god develops in many societies, this relation of god to morality becomes more important. By identifying himself with such a god an individual may modify his conduct. Among the Hebrews, Jehovah as a god of vengeance gradually emerges as a god of high moral qualities. In the religion of China, so marked by ethical tone, we find this comment in the Book of Rites:

"The object of all ceremonies is to bring down the spirits from above, even their ancestors; serving also to rectify the relations between ruler and minister, to maintain the generous feeling between father and son, and the harmony between elder and younger brother, to adjust the relations between high and low, and to give their proper places to husband and wife. The whole may be said to secure the blessings of Heaven."[8]

In Christian theology the struggle between the forces of God and the forces of Satan symbolizes the conflict within the individual between the moral and immoral, between righteousness and evil. Throughout Christian history the rôle of the gods and saints as standards for virtue is highly important. A personal deity becomes an ideal against which one may project his own conduct.

Any scheme of eternal reward or punishment for conduct here and now becomes a powerful aid to morality. Although the idea of continuity of life after death is rather widespread, not all groups have the notion of retribution or divine judgment. This idea came rather late in cultural development.

In many of the higher religions the belief in a final judgment with its terrible punishments for the evil and its glorious rewards for the virtuous is pictured in bold and striking manner. Without doubt, the fear of hell fire and damnation has been a factor in control of conduct for thousands. Associated with this have been developed systems of penance and absolution to remove or at least to lighten the burden of future punishment. As ideas of science permeate the masses, the notions of future existence change, and beyond doubt the fear of damnation is not the factor in conduct it once was.

The virtues of truth-telling, honesty, fair-dealing with others, conformity to sexual codes—in short, all the accepted details of moral conduct of the community or society—may become integrated with religious beliefs and practices. Today, with the disappearance of many of the ancient and primitive features of religion, the morality of fairer distribution of wealth, of sound and honest politics, of high community standards of health, conduct, and happiness become the religious ideals of the church.

Religion and the Economic Order. In primitive society nearly every feature of life is mixed with religion. This is clearly evident in economic life: food-gathering, hunting, fishing, herding, agriculture, trade, and barter. It is not always so apparent, however, that religion also plays a part in our more advanced capitalistic economics.

[8]Quoted in J. E. Carpenter, *Comparative Religion*, pp. 150–51.

Max Weber (1864–1920), the German sociologist, R. H. Tawney, the British economist, and others have shown a certain parallelism if not correlation between the development of Protestant ideas and practices and the rise of modern capitalism in western Europe and America.[9] The individualism of Protestantism goes hand in hand with the rise of nationalism and the change from the class system of the Middle Ages to the open class system of our own time. (See Chapter XXIV on stratification.) Secondly, the otherworldly asceticism of Catholicism, in which emphasis was put upon escape from this material world into contemplation of and preparation for the hereafter, gave way to what Weber aptly calls "worldly asceticism," in which, retaining the moral virtues of hard work, honesty, truthfulness, and steadfastness of purpose, the direction of activity is toward the affairs of this world as a preparation for the hereafter. Assuming a method of salvation, such as the Calvinistic doctrine of predestination or the Lutheran doctrine of grace, the individual must fulfill his rôle in this world of everyday affairs in order to demonstrate to God his membership in the Kingdom. Quite unlike St. Augustine's idea, therefore, the City of God is not up in the sky, but is transferred to the earth and demonstrated day by day by activity which is pleasing to the Divine Will. (See Chapter XVI.)

During the Middle Ages money-making was considered distinctly secondary to godly pursuits. Material culture was necessary to survival, but it was not the end of life by any means. By the sixteenth century money-making had assumed greater importance, and the profit system was well under way at the time of the Reformation. The dogmas of the new religious movement which we have just mentioned were not only in part an outcome of a rising philosophy which was influencing business and statecraft, but in turn gave further support to capitalistic endeavor. Thus hard work, sacrifice of present pleasures for future profits in a business, honesty in business dealings, and other homely virtues became the daily morality of the pious Protestants, especially the Calvinists, the Quakers, and the Separatists. The individual, having religious assurance of salvation, practiced these virtues as evidence of his godliness. While these new ideas and practices had to

[9] See Max Weber, *The Protestant Ethic and the Spirit of Capitalism* (transl. by Talcott Parsons), 1930; and R. H. Tawney, *Religion and the Rise of Capitalism*, 1926.

fight their way step by step against religious tradition, in time they won wide acceptance.[10]

Capitalism, Protestantism, and political democracy, bound together by certain accidents of history and certain similar ideologies, came to full bloom in America. Religious piety, individualism, the emphasis upon liberty or activity, the worship of material success coupled with unlimited natural resources, made America a living example of this combination of the repression of pleasure seeking and the direction of energy into hard work, success, and religious satisfactions. There is no better demonstration of the connection of business, religion, and certain moral virtues than is expressed in the words of Roger W. Babson:

"Statistics lead me to believe that the faith, industry, thrift, and enterprise in people are very largely due to religion . . . Where the people are irreligious, are found indifference, wastefulness, and extravagance. . . . Ninety-five per cent of the people who do not get along well materially owe their misfortune to lack of these religious qualities of faith, industry, courage, imagination, and thrift. This means that the real great work of the church today lies in reviving these great productive qualities in the souls of the masses."[11]

Where the church gets its support from the dominant capitalist class, it can hardly go far in differing in its economic views from those who pay its bills. Where the church, however, draws its support from the working classes, one may find improvement of economic conditions as one of the social aims of the pastor and congregation. The matter comes down to the leadership of the church. If the church, like traditional education, continues but to reflect the dominant economic and political views of those in power, it will consume much of its time and energy concocting excuses or rationalizations for the present economic and political order. On the contrary the church may stimulate broad economic and political reform and thus become a distinctive factor in social change. Which direction any denomination will take can only be determined in terms of the societal and cultural setting in which it finds itself.

[10] See Tawney, *op. cit.*, chapter IV.

[11] From Roger W. Babson, *Religion and Business*, 1921, pp. 97, 99. By permission of The Macmillan Company, publishers. See also André Siegfried, *America Comes of Age* (transl. by H. H. and Doris Hemming), 1927. In Russia today, many of these same worldly ascetic virtues are stressed without the religious overtone and without reference to private profit seeking.

RELIGION AND PERSONALITY

We have already noted that while culture always sets the general patterns of behavior in regard to man's needs, individual differences in biological makeup and in experience make for variations within these broad limits. This is nowhere more evident than in religious ideas and habits. We have also shown how the mystic, with his more nearly unique religious experience, stands in contrast to the priest, with his regimentation of religious expression in terms of the old and the accepted. The former stimulates religious change and stands often for personal righteousness; the latter supports ritualism, creed, and the established hierarchy. This sort of controversy has been common in almost all highly organized, institutionalized religions. What occurs with the exceptional mystic is common to large numbers of lay devotees whose religious experience extends beyond the boundaries of creed and theology. Not that they will set up a new sect or depart from the faith of their fathers, but their personal religious experience is somewhat different and perhaps larger than the formalized religion itself. As William James well said in his book *Varieties of Religious Experience* (1909), "In one sense, at least, personal religion will prove itself more fundamental than either theology or ecclesiasticism." A strong hierarchy and a long-established creed, however, tend to limit individual variation in these matters. In more flexible religious organizations, based in part on the theory of individualism, unique religious experience is more common. Still, no matter how formalized the religious organization may be, with its minutest details worked out, it cannot make provision for every religious need of the individual devotee.

Psychology of Religious Experience. Religion rests upon both a fundamental psychological need and upon long-standing culture. While the cultural features of religion may well change, there is no reason to assume that religion will disappear. The problem, then, is what function religious experience has in the life of the individual.

Aside from stimulating individual participation in various group situations, religious experience, at least in our Western culture, acts as an important balancing factor in personality. Such experience gives the person faced with difficulties, crises, or conflicts, surcease from worry and considerable faith in himself. If one believes in retribution hereafter, his conviction not only aids him in living up to the morals of his society, but it may assist him in carrying on in the face of defeats at the hands of those who abuse him. So, too, mystical experiences with the divine, no matter how they may be interpreted from a strictly scientific angle, give the individual a sense of participation in the universe which daily concern with material things scarcely affords.

In short, the mystic identification with power outside oneself may offset or balance the disappointments, heartaches, and pain of daily living, in which half measures, compromises, and self denials are common. It is easy for the critic of religion to point out that this sort of thing is "an escape from reality," a mass neurosis, or a mere "illusion," as Sigmund Freud argues in his book *Future of an Illusion* (1928).[12] In the light of cultural approval of religious experience and in the light of our broader definition of culture as psychological, such behavior cannot be considered "an escape" from something superior or better or real so much as a movement from one aspect of cultural reality to another. To deny the importance or significance of this other phase of reality is tantamount to denying the whole field of subjective thought and action based on personal wishes and fantasy. As Ruth Benedict puts it: "The world man actually lives in—in the sense of his inescapable necessities and the inevitable conditions of life—always bulks very small in relation to the world he makes for himself."[13]

In contrast, therefore, to the common-sense material world, we find a world based on fantasy or wishful thinking, particularly in religion, art, and play. This world helps to fulfill life, gives it a richer, more pleasing, and more personally satisfying meaning. That this world of experience will disappear even in the face of material changes seems at present unlikely.

Levels of Religious Experience. There is the further question of various levels of religious experience essential to satisfying

---

[12] It is our contention that cultural reality, as it may be called, is not something material nor made up out of biological reactions to food, drink, and sexual objects. It is at heart mental or psychological. It is a question of beliefs, attitudes, ideas, meanings. It exists in the minds of men. One cannot, therefore, with Freud, blandly dismiss religious experience as an unfortunate illusion without at the same time raising the problem as to whether art, philosophy, and most of the fundamentals of social organization and family life are not likewise "illusions." Faithfulness to a mate, loyalty to a country, or belief in a bank note can be shown by this logic to be illusions too. Even material culture disappears without the support of its subjective meaning.

[13] Ruth Benedict, "Magic," *Encyclopedia of the Social Sciences*, vol. X, p. 43.

the needs of people in any given society. Marked individualization of function in one society will foster variation in these levels,
which may not appear in another society in which like divergence
is not acceptable. In our own Western culture wide latitude is
permitted in religion. We may have standardized our economic
and political behavior, but in art and religion, at least, we permit flexibility. As will be maintained in discussing the relation of
the masses to standards of art set by sophisticated critics, so in
religious experience, the upper classes may easily fall into the error
of assuming that religious experience for all should conform to the
highly intellectualized forms suitable to themselves. No one is
prepared to say *what* kind of religious experience or church affiliation is *best* for people outside one's own social clique. This is a
matter of life organization, social status, and rôle, affected by a
host of factors touching on other phases of life: physical, economic, political, and familial. For example, some may easily object to the emotionalism of revivalistic churches, such as the Holy
Rollers or the Nazarenes. Such critics fail to understand the meaning of religious experience for the communicants of these sects. In
turn, members of the latter might well disdain the more thoroughly
rationalized, aesthetic, and intellectualistic views of the educated
Roman Catholic or Episcopalian. There is in our Western culture a
sort of scale of permissible religious experience running from the
extreme of emotionalism, sentimentalism, and fantasy to the
highly aesthetic, intellectualistic, or theological expressions suitable for educated minorities. Just where the individual in our society will find himself depends largely upon his own cultural background and upon his adult choice.

One may find his greatest satisfactions in contemplation of
otherworldliness; another may find it in contact with the world
in an effort to make it a more desirable place in which to live.
Certain religious groups favor the ethical, mundane interests, de-
parting considerably from more elementary supernaturalism.
They put little emphasis upon otherworldly interests and concentrate directly upon problems of social reform. Whether such a
field of activity, just because it is sponsored by a church and becomes slightly emotionalized, is religious in a strict sense, depends
on our definition. It is preferable to keep the definition of religion
within the narrower limits of an emotional, worshipful, or reverent
reaction to supernatural powers. If ethical concern, cut off from

concepts of a divine plan or will, becomes synonymous with religion, then religion must embrace such interests as communism, fascism, and liberalism. From one standpoint, so to broaden the definition of religion is to make the concept meaningless. Yet only the future trends in culture can determine what will be the accepted definition.

CLASS ASSIGNMENTS

A. Further reading assignment:

1. K. Young, *Source Book for Sociology,* chap. XIV.

2. C. Luther Fry, "Changes in Religious Organizations," chap. XX, *Recent Social Trends.*

3. *Encyclopedia of the Social Sciences,* articles as follows: Ruth Benedict, "Animism," vol. II, pp. 65–67; Ruth Benedict, "Magic," vol. X, pp. 39–44; and Alfred Bertholet, "Religion," vol. XIII, pp. 228–37.

B. Questions and exercises:

1. Make an outline indicating the principal organizational features of your own church or that of your family. Cover personnel, rituals, creed, and symbolism, and general community functions.

2. Illustrate by concrete instances the rôle of religion (a) in moral control, (b) in reference to business and industry, (c) in reference to art and recreation, and (d) in reference to education.

3. Illustrate by concrete case study the rôle of religion in the integration or balancing of the personality.

4. Has religion any place in an age of science? Discuss pro and con.

C. Topics for class reports or longer written papers:

1. The place of religion in rural and village communities. (Consult E. de S. Brunner et al., *American Agricultural Village,* 1927; M. N. Morse and E. de S. Brunner, *The Town and Country Church in the United States,* 1923.)

2. The rôle of religion in small and medium-sized cities. (Consult R. S. and H. M. Lynd, *Middletown,* 1929, chaps. XX–XXIII, and *Middletown in Transition,* 1937, chap VII; Albert Blumenthal, *Small-Town Stuff,* 1932.)

3. Changes in urban churches. (Consult H. Paul Douglass, *The Church in the Changing City,* 1927, *The St. Louis Church Survey,* 1924, and his *1,000 City Churches,* 1926.)

4. The place of fantasy thinking in religion and magic. (Consult Carveth Read, *The Origin of Man and of His Superstitions,* 1920; George C. Frazer, *The Golden Bough,* 1-volume ed., 1920; and K. Young, *Social Psychology,* chap. XVI.)

5. The relation of magic to science. (Consult Carveth Read, *The Origin of Man and of His Superstitions,* 1920; Lynn Thorndike, *The History of Magic and Experimental Science,* 2 vols., 1923.)

6. The place of the church in America during the depression, 1929–1935. (Consult S. C. Kincheloe, *Research Memorandum on Religion in the Depression,* Social Science Research Bulletin No. 33, 1937.)

CHAPTER XV

PLAY AND ART

Economic activity, political organization, family continuity, community controls, and transmission of culture represent fundamental needs of a utilitarian sort. But man has other needs and interests almost as strong: his religious expression, his play life, his artistic interests, and his concern with scientific and philosophic problems. These latter are not independent of the former but interlace themselves at many points with the more basic culture patterns. We have just discussed religion and magic. In the present chapter we shall discuss the place of play or recreation and of art in society. In the next chapter we shall consider science and philosophy.

GENERAL FEATURES OF PLAY

Play of some sort is universal in society, but what the child or the adult does in play varies greatly according to the culture. In discussing play we often use the terms *recreation, amusement,* and *leisure.* These terms have much in common, but some distinctions may well be drawn.

Definition of Play and Related Activities. *Play* means primarily free or active movement or exercise, specifically the free movements of the body and its limbs. Today, it is applied to any relatively untrammeled, pleasant form of muscular or mental action which does not concern securing a livelihood or the obligations and duties as parent, citizen, or member of the moral and religious order. Play may call for exertion and the expenditure of energy, but the aim is primarily to please oneself, to give rein to diversion and amusing behavior, overt or covert. *Recreation* means the act of re-creating the mental and muscular system or the state of being re-created through some refreshing, stimulating, and usually diverting form of activity. In a looser sense it refers to any pleasurable diversion, mental or muscular, and for our purposes may be considered synonymous with play life. *Leisure* refers primarily to the time which is not occupied by utilitarian pursuits, to freedom from necessary occupation. It is spare time. *Amusement* literally applies to gazing at or seeing spectacles. Actually there are many amusements which involve active participation of every member of the group. Amusement involves joyous and pleasant activity, often associated with wit and humor. Terms in common use, such as games, sports, gambling, festivals, hobbies, dancing, and story telling, refer to the types of play in which people indulge.

In our society we have usually distinguished between play and work. The latter is associated with useful activities and is linked up with obligations and duties, many of which are carefully restricted as to time and compensation. Distinctions are also often drawn between active and passive play. Active participation is said to involve muscular or mental exertion of the individual, directed toward the play end. Passive participation is assumed to consist largely in gazing at, hearing, or otherwise receiving sensory impressions from others who are performing for one's amusement or recreation. As a matter of fact, this distinction is meaningless as applied to many forms of play or recreation.

The Origin of Play. The traditional question, "Why do children play?" has been answered in various theories of play.

The first of these was developed by the German poet, Friedrich Schiller (1759–1805), and later taken up by the English philosopher, Herbert Spencer. They believed that play was the *expression of excess energy* developed in the growing child. While there may be some basis for this notion, children and grown-ups often continue to play when tired, and, moreover, a great deal of play does not consume much energy and yet is pursued with great delight by young and old. A second theory was developed by Karl Groos, a German, who holds that play is *preparatory to the later serious activities of life.* There is no doubt that a good deal of human play furnishes much training for future usefulness. The give-and-take attitudes in fair play, of rivalry, emulation, team cooperation, and group loyalty—all these have a place in later life, as does the muscular training. In their play children identify themselves with adult behavior. They adopt first one rôle and then another from copies set them by adults. Yet play is no more preparatory for later life than are the activities of one day preparatory for the next. The third theory connected play with the concept of recapitulation. The theory arose from the well-known biological fact that in embryonic and foetal growth, the child passes through various physical forms which resemble the biological stages reached by the lower animals. This repetition or recapitulation was assumed to go on after birth. Play life was assumed to repeat the cultural stages of the race. No serious student of child behavior today believes this theory.

These theories fail to take into account the social and cultural phases of play life. There is no doubt that spontaneous, pleasant, and somewhat aimless muscular activity is a distinctive biological and psychological manifestation in young children, evidently linked to the rhythms of physical activity common to all the higher animal forms. As the child grows up, contact with his fellows and the impress of culture give direction to these activities. Although the Manus children, according to Margaret Mead, are not provided with any cultural patterns of play, they still indulge in random and aimless activity.[1] In our own society from the earliest years children learn how and what to play from their older playmates and from the adults around them.

We cannot "explain" play without reference to social and cultural factors. The play life of military Rome and the European feudal society was tinged with the war and conflict spirit: gladiatorial games, chariot races, and the medieval tournaments. In a more pacific, industrialized, and commercial society the conflict phases are often sublimated into football or other games, and much more attention may be given to passive amusement. In pietistic, puritanical cultures, as we shall see, play life gets still another sort of interpretation.

THE FORMS OF PLAY LIFE

There are any number of classifications which might be made of play life. Without attempting to make our divisions necessarily logical, we may treat, first, those which follow a primary group pattern; second, those forms of play illustrated best by athletics or sports; third, gambling; and fourth, the more recently developed passive amusements, largely of a commercialized sort, like the radio and motion pictures. With this review before us, we shall discuss the broader matters of play and morality, and play as it influences the personality.

[1] Margaret Mead, *Growing Up in New Guinea*, 1930.

The Primary Group Forms of Play. In primitive societies play arose around family, clan, and tribal life. The festivals connected with religious and economic life often took on recreational and artistic features as well. In many primary community situations, either in primitive or in modern times, there is no such sharp line dividing play life from useful activity. Much labor of a collective sort, like fishing, hunting, barn-raising, planting, and harvesting, takes on festive features. A church or neighborhood sewing circle easily combines useful work with entertaining gossip. Even market days are not given over entirely to buying and selling. The mad rush to a bargain sale is a form of crowd behavior of a playful sort quite as much as a quest for lower prices. Many events symbolizing recurrent or occasional crises have recreational features: attendance at weddings, christenings, and funerals. Without doubt mass activities, like lynching bees, religious and speculative manias, and war, carry with them a great deal of emotion and pleasant satisfaction not unlike those secured from games or sports.

Aside from the connection of utilitarian action with play, there is in all primary communities a range of play patterns which stand by themselves to furnish recreation and amusement in leisure hours. Dancing, the drama, and much of art has this character. Folk music, festivals, and holidays provide an outlet. In medieval Europe the large number of holy days when work was taboo offered the peasants and townspeople an opportunity for relaxation. It is estimated that there were on the average about 115 holidays a year in medieval times. Although people were obliged to participate in religious ceremonials, these occasions served both a religious and a recreational function. Holidays which were originally holy, that is, sacred days associated with magical and religious rites, have today become secularized on every hand. In place of religion, patriotic holidays are the common thing.

In present American society, before the coming of the automobile and the breakdown of the neighborhood as our people have become more urbanized, play life retained much of its intimate character. In the winter months, dancing, sleigh riding, and neighborhood parties were common. In the summer time outdoor picnics, often sponsored by church or lodge, were the vogue.[2] So, too, congeniality groupings were common, and clubs of various sorts thrived on every hand. In spite of its vicious influence in

[2] See R. S. and H. M. Lynd, *Middletown*, 1929, chap. XVII, for description of some of these activities.

many cases, even the pre-prohibition saloon served as a center for entertainment and relaxation, for the working man in particular.

The decline of the primary community as the focus of people's activities and the increasing importance of secondary groups in our society have tended to destroy these traditional forms of recreation. As a result, churches, national recreational organizations, the public and parochial schools, and the business men's organizations have stimulated the growth of clubs designed to retain many of the intimate primary group features of play for boys and girls and for young men and women. Such are illustrated by the Y. M. C. A., the Boy and Girl Scouts, and the Camp Fire Girls. Many of these organizations aim to combine education, religion, and moral training with recreation.

Other clubs combine recreation with economic purposes. The growth of the business men's luncheon clubs is startling evidence of the felt need for some sort of surface friendliness in an economic order marked by keen individualistic competition. The Rotary, Kiwanis, and Lions—three of the most prominent—show the following growth: in 1917 together they had 389 local groups, with 6,839 members. In 1929, they could boast 38,700 local organizations, with a combined membership of 317,086. In the United States there are about 25 such national groups, most of them organized between 1917 and 1922 and today having a combined membership of approximately 500,000.

While the lodge is a combination of secret cult, financial organization, and club to stimulate sociability, there is no doubt that one of its strongest appeals is to the play interest of adult men and women. Fraternal orders are found in many Protestant communities. The ritualism which departed from religion in Protestantism returns to us in the secret lodge. The increased membership in fraternal orders in recent years is striking witness of the appeal of these forms of leisure-time organizations. In 1905 there were 9,796,000 members in insurance and non-insurance lodges; in 1930, there were 21,237,000.[3]

Parks and playgrounds have replaced the open-country play facilities for the country child, and supervised play provides the city boy and girl with better opportunities for recreation and leisure-time activities than they can find in gang life, which de-

[3] See Jesse F. Steiner, "Recreation and Leisure Time Activities," chapter XVIII, Recent Social Trends, p. 934.

velops when they are left to themselves. In 1930, 898 cities of 5,000 population or over reported 11,686 parks, containing over 308,000 acres. In 1935, another report gives 9,650 playgrounds located in 1,009 cities, which evidently does not include athletic fields, baseball diamonds, public bathing beaches, and the like.[4]

Community centers are also common. The community center is frankly an effort to recapture something of the older neighborhood solidarity so shattered by urban conditions. It attempts to stimulate recreational and educational programs of people within relatively circumscribed localities, chiefly in our cities. School buildings or church edifices are often used for this purpose. In 1930, the White House Conference on Child Health and Protection estimated between 8,000 and 10,000 community centers in this country, most of which are found in cities of over 5,000 population. This movement, like that of the playground and recreational associations, became crystallized into a national body with formal code, staff, annual conventions, and official publication. The work of these centers is carried on by both paid and volunteer workers, support coming from taxation and private philanthropy. They stimulate not only recreational activities, games, dramatics, and festivals, but also educational training from instruction in cooking and handicrafts to night classes in Americanization. (See Chapter XXV on assimilation.)

Athletics and Sports. Public spectacles of trained athletes to entertain the masses are as old as classic history. These might be gladiatorial contests, wrestling, boxing, racing, or various games using team organization.

In our own day commercial enterprise has capitalized upon American interest in all sorts of sports. Every year about 15 million Americans attend the baseball games of the two major leagues and of the Class AA minor leagues. It is estimated by Stuart Chase that 10 millions attend horse races every year. And other millions go in for witnessing prize fights, hockey matches, tennis and golf tournaments, to mention only the more evident commercialized sports.

Equally striking is the tremendous interest in college athletics. The importance of athletics in our educational system, especially our colleges, is apparent to everyone. The extracurricular activities of students from elementary school to the university have

[4] See *Social Work Year Book,* 1937, p. 408.

long run to play and recreation. In the Greek and Roman schools, of course, physical games were a distinctive part of the curriculum, but the medieval church, with its opposition to the expression of man's biological nature, suppressed all this sort of thing for centuries. Modern education, following the influence of romanticism and democracy, brought play back into the school.

Until recently school and especially college athletics were largely intramural in character. It was but a step from this to inter-school athletic contests. In recent decades college football has become in the United States a public festival, a sort of modern gladiatorial contest of 22 boys pushing, pulling, and mauling each other in order to entertain the spectators. Reports from the principal colleges showed that in 1921, for 49 colleges reporting, 1,504,000 people attended football games; in 1929, for the same schools, 3,617,000. Another report for 64 colleges shows that in 1921 the total gate receipts were $2,646,000, and in 1929, $9,032,000.[5]

The alleged "commercialization" of college football and its influence on the more serious purposes of education have been the subject of much comment. The fact that Knute Rockne (1888–1931) became a national hero is evidence enough that the remonstrances of faculty committees and of the trustees of educational foundations have not yet counteracted the mass enthusiasm for these public spectacles. So long as this enthusiasm continues, colleges are going to continue to hire $10,000- and $20,000-a-year coaches and to stimulate the college attendance of many boys who in other cultures would be on the battlefield, at the plow, or in earlier societies would engage in the exciting pursuit of big game.

Other Forms of Amusement. While athletics offer a form of vicarious recreation for large numbers of people, the drama in its various expressions has also long been of importance. This form of art furnishes both aesthetic satisfaction and relaxation or recreation for the audience. While tastes may differ as to what is "best" in the theater, the importance of this form of entertainment is evident in many societies.

The rapid development of the motion picture is one of the most striking events in recent decades. It is at once a medium of education, propaganda, news, and for the spread of fashion, as well as a form of amusement and recreation. The motion-picture theaters of this country will seat about 11 million persons at any

[5] Many of the facts cited here are summarized from J. F. Steiner, *op. cit.*

one show, and it is estimated that 77 million children and adults attend the movies every week, one seventh of whom are under 14 years of age.[6] In 1930 nearly 500 feature films with about 200 prints each were manufactured to meet the popular demand in this country alone.

The radio as a recreational instrument has leaped to prominence. In 1930, 40.3 per cent of the families in this country had radios (one for every 9.1 persons). By 1938, the number of radios, not including auto radios, had more than doubled since 1930. Nearly half a billion dollars was spent in radio equipment and broadcasting costs in 1930 alone. It is estimated that 50 million or more people listen in daily to the radio programs, which range from classical music and drama to jazz, and from burlesque humor to serious educational lectures. For the most part, the radio, like the motion picture, is geared to satisfy the lowest common denominator of taste in entertainment. Dependent as the radio usually is upon commercial advertisers, critics should not fail to recognize that the appeal must be chiefly to the mass of consumers, not to the intellectually and artistically superior ten per cent at the top of the social ladder. Like the motion picture, the radio furnishes more than entertainment. As we noted in Chapter XIII, it is a powerful weapon in propaganda and education.

Gambling as a Form of Play. *Gambling* may be defined as a game in which there is a deliberate wagering or staking of important or valuable considerations upon future events which—so far as the participants know—depend upon pure chance or luck. Games of chance are evidently as old as culture, and were often linked up with magic. Instruments of gambling were frequently used in divination.

Gambling games, such as are played with dice, cards, or roulette wheels, depending on the turn of events rather than skill, are widespread. The line between playing pure chance and other forms of action related to it is hard to draw. Betting and wagering on events not of a chance character are common: horse racing, cock-fighting, prize fighting, or any other sport may be the object of wagers. Men even bet on natural occurrences, such as weather changes. But these activities cannot be called gambling in the strict sense of the word.

[6]See Edgar Dale, *The Content of Motion Pictures,* etc., 1933. Estimates vary, but federal reports for 1935 gave the weekly attendance as 80 million.

The distinction between games of pure chance, wagering on various human or natural events, and speculations on the stock market is difficult to draw. While the capitalistic economic order is built on the theory and practice of rational calculations based on production and consumption demands, the persistence of taking chances on future market prices has been widespread throughout the centuries of capitalist economy—evidence again of the limitations of the rationality of business in the face of deeper-lying motives in man. The speculation manias which have been common in European-American society since the seventeenth century until the latest stock market boom of 1929 are really forms of mass gambling.

Around gambling, as around other recreational interests, a whole set of culture patterns develop which are important in directing its expression. Taboo or ostracism of players who load the dice, mark the cards, or "fix" the wheel of chance; insistence on payment of gambling debts, often in preference to commercial obligations; in some cases the legal sanction of gambling, as in public lotteries; in others where gambling is legally taboo, the development of a whole system of undercover organizations, as we see in our country with bookmakers and pools—these are but samples of the customs or laws developed to foster or to control this form of play.

PLAY, MORAL CONTROL, AND PERSONALITY

Play life not only bears upon utilitarian activities and upon art; it also has important bearing upon morals. This has taken both the form of repression of play and the more positive theory that play is fundamental to the building of character.

Play Life and Morality. The use of leisure time is not free of moral and religious implications. In some societies, notably those affected by Christian and especially the Puritanic, Calvinist theology, play and recreation have been looked upon as immoral. Just as the expression of the biological interests was taboo in all Christianity, Calvinism and pietism, in particular, took the stand that play was an immoral waste of time and energy, that it had its roots in evil design, and that it led man away from the religious and moral life demanded by the divine plan of salvation. Roman Catholicism has always been more tolerant of the play interests and other temporal foibles of man. Although occasional reformers like Girolamo Savonarola (1452–1498) and St. Bernard de Clair-vaux (1091–1153) would have restricted the recreational and artistic life of the communicants, the medieval church, for the most part, was more concerned with the major problem of proper sacra-mental evidence of membership in God's kingdom. While these temporal interests were not approved, they were considered venial, not mortal, sins. In the puritanical theory not only was the flesh a handicap to man, but man was also required to suppress and con-trol his more natural desires by useful work, sobriety, and thrift. All of these fitted into the developing capitalistic culture, which, in turn, gave added impetus to repressive measures not only to control but also to wipe out playtime activities. The restrictions on man's daily behavior in Geneva under Calvin and in the Cromwellian ré-gime in England are concrete evidence of this whole standpoint. The drama, carnivals, masques, fêtes, gambling, and other amuse-ments were suppressed. Sunday, a day which had long been one of both worship and relaxation in play, became such a sacred holiday that nothing but worship was permitted. The Puritan regulations of play or work on Sunday carried over to the American colonies and have persisted in this country longer than anywhere else. The shadow of the blue law is not yet removed from the American horizon.

In our society most reformers who look upon recreational activi-ties as sinful turn to the political state as a means of control, and just as they attempt to wipe out prostitution, liquor traffic, and gambling by legal fiat, they also attempt to regulate the motion pictures, the dance hall, and other forms of entertainment by legal repression. (See Chapter XXVI on social control.)

In the last few decades this severe standpoint has retreated into a more tolerant view, toward a conception that what we want is intelligent direction, not suppression, of play life. Many churches that formerly tabooed card playing, dancing, and musical enter-tainment do so no longer. Reform bodies that propose moralized recreational programs enlist more followers and usually obtain more financial support than those which advocate absolute taboos.

There is a return to the conception that play has a distinctive place in the normal life of man—something which the Greeks well understood. This idea has been a part of an important educa-tional theory since the time of Rousseau, and Progressive Educa-tion stresses it. Play is recognized as related to artistic creation.

Moreover, properly directed play is considered to be one of the basic devices for training in morality. Almost all community recreation programs have the moral purpose more or less consciously before them. Wherever tax-supported public recreation is found, it is defended on the grounds that it fosters good citizenship, prevents delinquency and crime, and prepares boys and girls for their future economic and familial rôles.

In some programs the moral features are stressed on nearly every hand. In others—less common—the morality is believed to grow normally out of group activity, out of team work, out of the unconscious development of moral attitudes and habits from participation in collective action with one's fellows. The latter indirect method of moral instruction, growing out of concrete social situations, is assumed to be in the end more effective than verbally linking some remote moral aim to sports, games, hobbies, and other forms of leisure-time activity.

Finally there remain two problems that bother the moralists about play life. One has to do with the alleged advantages of active as against passive participation. The other concerns the quality of play itself.

Obviously much of modern amusement and recreation is passive and vicarious in character. Millions sitting every season through the baseball or the football series, millions attending the movies or the legitimate drama, millions reading the comic strips or the best sellers, millions looking at horse races, going to prize fights, and other millions listening to phonographs, player pianos, orchestra and band concerts, lectures, and radios—all of these forms of entertainment do not for the most part call for active muscular and intellectual participation. On the other hand, there are other millions—or the same millions at other times—who dance, play golf, tennis, or baseball, swim, go hiking, or indulge in more active intellectual participation in card games or in solving cross-word puzzles, or go in for the creative arts and handicrafts as hobbies.

It is easy to say but hard to prove that the neurotic symptoms so current today would tend to disappear if all leisure and relaxation took on the more active form. A man may grow so neurotic over his golf stroke that all the alleged recreational benefits of the open air and muscular exercise are dissipated in bad temper and worry. Yet a balance of muscular and of sedentary recreation seems wise. The followers of Bernarr Macfadden are opposed by those who are convinced that excessive exercise is dangerous to health. The enthusiasts for vigorous exercise may overexert themselves, just as those who refrain from active play may suffer from ill-health as a result.

As to the quality of play, it is very easy for the economically superior classes to assume that all people should have the sort of recreation which belongs to their own class or status in society. One may regret the apparently cheap and tawdry leisure habits of others, but from the standpoint of mental health and social balance one cannot be too certain that any particular class standards will fit others. The projection on to others of our own class standards and habits of play often fails because we do not realize that play, like religion and art, is a matter of tastes and needs which may be quite different from our own. (See pages 323–24 on art standards.)

Play as a Balancing Factor in Personality. In the persons whose major life interests take on the characteristics of creative activity, their work produces deep satisfactions not unlike those which arise from play and recreation. For most people, however, necessitous occupation means drudgery and monotony, is looked upon as a mere means to money return, and does not integrate itself, as work, to their deeper motives and interests. While work for these people becomes in time a deep-seated habit which they could with difficulty lay aside permanently, most of them find a balance through leisure activity quite removed from their daily work.

One of the benefits is found in the release of muscular tensions. Much of our work today involves the finer muscle co-ordinations rather than those of the heavier muscle groups. Active games afford an opportunity to release muscular energy through the larger muscles in activity that is pleasing and exciting. Yet some people prefer more intellectual forms for the release of tensions, and still others like theirs at an emotional level. Individual variations are great, and one dare not lay down general rules.

There are psychological features of play which must not be neglected. Games for the most part are built on the pattern of hunting and doubtless afford in a sublimative way a deep-seated interest in new adventure and in exciting pursuit of game or goal. Perhaps every man desires deeply to make "his kill," whether it be in love making, in big game, in money at poker, or in a low score at golf. Another reason for stakes, wagers, and prizes in games and sports, or for the more honorific rewards of prestige, lies in the fact that these are tangible evidences of a successful "kill."

Another value in play lies in the ancient Greek notion of catharsis. The drama was said to give the spectators release from their own pent-up emotions and to act as an emotional but vicarious purgative. Doubtless a good deal of play and recreation gives just such release.

Laughter, wit, and humor have distinctive places in much of our amusement and recreation. The intense and serious purpose of the poker player or the golfer may afford satisfaction in the final successful issue, but much of our play carries with it the more spontaneous features of laughter and wit. The popularity of the theater in this connection is evident. From the highly sophisticated wit of the drawing room to the more Rabelaisian tone of the bar room there is a playful release of tensions not to be overlooked.

Play psychologically has its roots in fantasy thinking and acting. It is often a substitute for more utilitarian behavior. It affords an opportunity to forget the demands of the economic order, to escape the duties of citizen or parent, and to find, as an adult, release and recreation in a world of socially acceptable wishful thinking. The appeal of gambling is self-evident. Chance, in a sense, is the goddess of all fantasy, which belief rests on the desire to get something for nothing that will enhance the ego. And while the badges of ego expansion may vary with the culture, one of the most common cultural traits is some scheme or other for playing "Lady Luck." While the trend of rational, objective thought and action in much of our modern life runs counter to the luck interest, man still finds a place for its expression in play life, in art, and in religion.

The function of fantasy in lodge activities must be noted. One reason the fraternal order is so popular lies in the fact that the daily round of life in an industrial society is humdrum and drab. The ordinary man more and more tends to be reduced to the level of a mere robot. On lodge night, however, the ordinary shoe clerk or the third vice president of a bank may become for the time the Exalted Potentate of the Realm of the Mystic Knights of Akbar. The ritual, the costumes, and the official status afford him an opportunity to let loose his suppressed wishes for power—something which he cannot accomplish in our highly routine, mechanized, workaday world.

ART IN SOCIETY AND CULTURE

By *art* we refer to the aesthetic experience of man, to his interest in beauty. Artistic experience is denoted by pleasant emotions, attitudes, and ideas which are associated with the perception of line, form, color, sound, or words. In a material sense art serves no immediate purpose of survival. In a broader sense, art, like play and religion, seems to be essential to society. It gives satisfactions which do not always arise while one is providing for the basic physiological wants.

In our discussion we shall refer principally to the fine arts. By the fine arts we mean first, those of line, form, and color, including architecture, painting, sculpture, and the so-called decorative arts; second, the art of sound or music; and third, the art of words and sounds, or poetry and prose. There are three factors in all art: material, form, and meaning. The first concerns the medium in which the artist works: stone, wood, paints, clay, gold, steel, precious stones, the combinations of sounds or words. The second has to do with the structure of the product, designed in such a way as to give sensory pleasures in line, form, color, rhythms, or in the plot of a story. Meaning in art grows out of its association with other experience. Culture definitely influences the production and enjoyment of art. We shall briefly point out the foundations of art, its interrelations to other phases of culture, and then discuss the standards of artistic taste.

Foundations of Art. Clearly art is connected with the play impulse, and if we find the roots of play we possibly find those of art also. Like play, art is related to wishful thinking and the run of imagination beyond the immediate needs of survival. If play is something of an overt expression of fantasy life, as it evidently is as the child grows up, artistic expression itself may be thought of as but a further expression of this play put into more intellectualized and directed form. Certainly art lifts man above his cruder primary nature. It gives man a chance to seek perfection in some object outside himself, satisfies some craving or longing within him for a sense of completeness or wholeness, that is often not possible in the conflict and half-measures of daily social intercourse.

Art is not a mere "interlude" between periods of useful action. Neither is art "passive," while other parts of life are "active." It is easy to overemphasize the passive, escape notion, especially when we are overawed and overimpressed by the hurry and ceaseless activity that our material world demands of us.

In short, for the personality, art, like play, religion, philosophy, or creative science, may serve as a balance to an otherwise distraught and unintegrated life. It is not escape, but an extension of the individual's reality and behavior into a world created by imagination and enjoyed not alone by others. Art may have its origins in play and fantasy thinking, but it gets social acceptance and becomes an integral part of the culture. As with play and religion, art is not a neurotic illusion, not a drug to relieve the personality of its material obligations, but evidently a necessary part of our existence. (See Chapter XIV page 301, footnote 12, on cultural reality.)

Art and Material Culture. In the most rudimentary societies the struggle for survival was doubtless so intense that most of man's energy was used up in providing food, shelter, and clothing for himself and his family. Only as we get something in excess of these bare necessities have we time or disposition for play or artistic production. Yet there is no society today so elemental as not to have some forms of art. No matter how art originated in the race, it certainly must have made its appearance fairly early, along with the more utilitarian functions.

Pioneer America shows something of the lack of artistic development in the face of more immediate needs for survival. Not that our pioneers did not possess any art, but it was largely borrowed from elsewhere; and it is only as America has passed into a more stable and complex form of material culture that she has begun to develop her own art. Still the pioneer scorn of the fine arts remains; even today it is commonly believed that no "he-man" plays the piano or takes up other fine arts. The refinements of art are often said to be the province of women, children, and "weak" men incapable of worldly action. The men of our society are usually too busy making money or getting ahead professionally to look upon the creation or enjoyment of art as a vital part of their personal life organization.

Art is always affected by the stage of the material culture. In the days of handicrafts it had a distinctive place; artist and artisan worked together. In machine manufacture art must take on a different expression. There has been much nonsense written about the loss of art in the machine age, but the machine can destroy only an art not suited to its place. The machine cannot and has not done away with man's creative interests, nor with his inclination to put artistic flourishes on useful articles or to produce objects of beauty for the pleasure they afford in themselves.

At the outset the interest in the machine is largely that of ever-increased efficiency. Whenever decorative factors were introduced in the early factory products, they were likely to be added from the art of the past. Thus the highly colored decorations on early locomotives were heraldic arms, patriotic symbols, and local or national names in embellished style. So, too, modern architecture still carries with it many inappropriate applications from the Greek temples of 2,500 years ago.

The emergence of beauty of design in modern machinery comes only after the chief mechanical efficiencies are worked out. For example, the earlier designers of automobiles could not get away from the background of slowly moving wagons and stationary engines, because of what the psychologist calls the apperceptive mass of previous experience. It took time and experience to change to more effective devices for motor power and speed. In these developments the engineer and the artist have combined their talents. Such a man as the Russian designer, Alexis de Sakhnoffsky, could hardly have found a place in the American motor industry 20 years ago. Today work like his is combining beauty and utility in a really remarkable fashion. Art is not divorced from mechanical products, except where one lags behind the other, and where the interest is first in efficiency, as it is likely to be in an age dominated by applied science and concern with money-making.

What is evident as to modern vehicles may be said in reference to other products of the machine age from articles of daily use— razor sharpeners, typewriters, calculating machines, household devices—to buildings in which stone, concrete, brick, steel, and glass are put together in reference to lighting, heating, and the general purpose of the building. Frank Lloyd Wright, with his insistence that the building should suit its location, climate, material, and purpose, has stimulated the appreciation and practice of this newer art in architecture.

In short, machine products at first merely copied the products of the handicraftsman. Today the tendency is for the factory product to appear as if made by the machine, to bear, in other words, the hallmark of its age, a further evidence of the integration of practical industry and the arts.

Art and Religion. The English writer Jane Harrison points out in her book *Ancient Art and Ritual* (1913) that art and religious ritual grew out of practical situations, such as those concerned with planting, harvesting, and the solving of group crises. Gradually from these activities, ritualistic dancing and dialogue arose. For example, in the evolution of the Greek drama, the chorus represents a vestige of the time when there was no audience on one side and actors on the other, but the whole performance was a common social experience of the group.

Among many primitive peoples decorative symbols have magical and religious meaning. In the art of the Pueblo Indians three lines in a semicircle denote rain falling from clouds—a design which is used in their rain-making ceremonials. The sand drawings of the Navajo, the decorations of the Australian natives at their festivals, and the designs of many utilitarian objects possess a magical meaning to assist the hunter, the fisherman, or the horseman.

In the history of Christianity, art and religion are closely linked together. The beautiful images of the Christ, of the Virgin and Child, and of various saints represent some of the finest woodcarving or work in stone that we have in church art anywhere, and the whole range of painting and church architecture of the Middle Ages shows how artistic feeling and religious worship were intertwined. The expression of religious feeling in beautiful form is found almost the world over, sometimes in dancing and music, sometimes in religious drama, and in Oriental and Occidental cultures very definitely in sculpture, painting, and architecture.

Art and Moral Control. Art has a definite place in the mores and hence in social control. From Plato to the present there have been protests about the disastrous effects of sensuous art upon conduct. Plato was skeptical of any art which aroused the passions of men. This notion, modified by his followers and combined with certain taboos of Hebrew origin, became the basis in Christianity for the whole conception that the flesh of man is sinful and weak, and should be held in check by the spirit. Any forms of art which stimulate these sinful tendencies of mankind were taboo. Thus, while art played a part in medieval life, it was an art built around ideals of a perfect society, leaving the sensuous beauty of the human body, for example, quite out of consideration.

Renaissance and modern art returned to the classical conception of sensuous beauty, but the church and the moral reformers still resist and whenever possible censor those forms of art which appeal to the passions, on the assumption that such stimulation leads to overt conduct contrary to the moral codes of the society. Count Leo Tolstoy (1828–1910), the Russian novelist, attacked sensuous art on the ground that it deflected man from the serious social and ethical purposes of life. There are many people who still feel that he was correct.

Yet art largely reflects the society from which it springs. Music, drama, novels, pictures, sculpture, and architecture embody the values, ideals, and hopes of the people who produce them. They naturally serve to inculcate into the rising generation these same values. Until modern times this carry-over of ideals and values through art from one generation to another has been largely indirect and unconscious. Today, however, with propaganda developed to a scientific technique, art, like education, play, and religion, can be used consciously and deliberately as a part of a whole national plan to indoctrinate young and old with ideals and values considered sacred or moral by those in control. Thus, in Soviet Russia, art, like recreation and education, bears the stamp of communist ideas and is used to indoctrinate a whole people with selected and planned values.

Culture and Art Standards. Art standards reflect in large measure the accepted values or meanings of the particular culture in which we find them. The correct and proper in art, therefore, as in morals, is a matter of consensus and culture. This is well illustrated in the history of art. El Greco, the Spanish painter (c. 1542–1614), had little recognition in his time because other standards prevailed. In English literature the status of William Shakespeare (1564–1616) has varied with literary values since his time. Thus in the eighteenth century, when the classical couplet was in vogue and stereotyped drama and poetry the fashion, Shakespeare's style was viewed as incorrect. In the next century his work recovered its place. The importance of consensus is aptly illustrated in writing, painting, music, and sculpture today. To many, the work of James Joyce, Gertrude Stein, and other "moderns" is just so much jargon and verbal nonsense. To the "initiates" it is apparently highest art.[7] In the same way, cubism or futurism is meaningless to most laymen and to many critics. Often only the painter or sculptor retains the key to the intricate patterns of colliding lines, planes, and masses of color. In music we find much the same thing. Richard Wagner (1813–1883) was not widely understood or appreciated for years because his compositions ran counter to the musical traditions of his time. So, too, recent music has only gradually won popular acceptance. For example, the *Fire Bird* suite, by Igor Stravinsky, has been the subject of vehement controversy.

Still, if the essential thing in art is aesthetic enjoyment, not ideas and verbal communication, there is no reason why laymen will not come to accept this new art as standard and proper. In time, we may even see the work of the "great masters" of the past put away as the product of an unsophisticated and somewhat childish age. Who knows? Certainly the cultural standards of morality, religion, and art show curious variations. While it is difficult and dangerous to characterize whole cultural epochs, it is clear that much primitive art is marked by various sorts of symbolism and, from our point of view, by certain absurdities of dimension,[8] that fifth-century Athenian art possessed a certain cold beauty in contrast to the more decorative and somewhat gaudy art of later Greece and Rome, that medieval art avoided the sensuous with its emphasis on otherworldliness and theological conceptions, that the Renaissance rediscovered the sensuous beauty of classic art and expanded it, especially in painting, while modern art has been torn asunder in recent decades by controversies over light, color, and form, over the efforts to express so-called "pure ideas" or the essence of things in color and form only. To essay to judge which of these periods is superior to others is to fall afoul of our own particular cultural prejudices.

While there is a certain central theme of art in every culture, there is also within this cultural framework a place for individual initiative. Anything but the most superficial examination of European art and artists will show this. Ruth L. Bunzel has admi-

[7] See discussion of this in reference to the psychology of thought and language, K. Young, *Social Psychology*, Chapter XVI, and *Social Attitudes* (ed. by K. Young), 1931, Chapter V.

[8] See Ralph Linton, "Primitive Art," *The American Magazine of Art*, Jan., 1933, vol. XXV, pp. 17–24.

rably shown the place of individual divergence in primitive art in her volume *The Pueblo Potter, a Study of Creative Imagination in Primitive Art* (1929). Individual variation in art within the limits of any culture in the end brings about just those extreme departures from the older art which lead in time to new "schools." These latter, in turn, replace the old "schools" as the standards of art in the society.

Finally, we may ask, who, within any given society, sets the standards of taste or determines the direction of the consensus of which we have been speaking? Much of fine art in the past has been the art of the dominant classes, themselves a minority of the total population. Even in "the glory that was Greece and Rome," the slaves and lower classes had a different relation than did their masters to the art of the time. In serf and peasant Europe, the aristocratic and later the rich bourgeois classes patronized and enjoyed the higher arts. But it must not be imagined that the lower classes themselves did not have their artistic enjoyments, both in handicraft creations, in their folk dances, and in the drama or religious exercise. They did.

Art cannot be separated from the life around it. It is not an escape from life, but a part of it, and there is no such thing as pure aesthetics except in the minds of sophisticated specialists. Such rarefied notions exist only in people who themselves are remote from most of the life around them and who by means of money, political power, or intellectual rationalizations isolate themselves from others—an isolation which promotes snobbery.

If the masses today get their artistic enjoyment from the motion picture, from billboard and other advertising, from the so-called cheaper novels and other literature, or from jazz, we must realize that to them these values are as pleasant and as satisfying perhaps as Beethoven's *Fifth Symphony* or the novels of Marcel Proust are to a limited minority. While one must not gainsay the possible advantage of introducing all children to the opportunity for aesthetic creation on their own part, or to an understanding of the delights of "better" art, we must not forget that if art has a place in the individual life, it must touch that life at the vital point, that is, through the emotions and feelings. It can never do so in the purely intellectual sense, even for the critic and highly cultivated person, unless this intellectual concern is coupled with emotions and feelings. It is probably unwise to try to impose on the masses the higher and more logical foundations of aesthetics. These things, if they are to come at all, must grow slowly out of daily contact with good art, from creative education, and from other everyday actions of men and women in the world of economic, political, religious, recreational, and other social behavior. As Leo Stein well remarks:

"I have all my life been looking for some good reason why one *ought* to be interested in art, or should prefer good art to bad, but beyond such reasons as that art does less harm than alcohol or gambling, I have found no reason whatever within the limits of the usual discussions. What is commonly said, though often disguised in pseudo-profundities, is that the best people do so-and-so, and that every one should do the same. In short, the appeal is to authority."[9]

The appeal to authority is but the appeal to snobbery and prestige and has little inherent in it to catch the imagination of the man in the street, who as soon as he has heard the lecture on aesthetics, visited the art gallery, or listened to the symphony, is likely to sneak off to the first movie at hand, or to find himself a racy novel, or to enjoy an evening of modern ballroom dancing with his wife or sweetheart.

CLASS ASSIGNMENTS

A. **Further reading assignment:**
   1. K. Young, *Source Book for Sociology,* chap. XV.
   2. R. S. and H. M. Lynd, *Middletown,* chaps. XVII, XVIII, XIX, also their *Middletown in Transition,* chap. VII.
   3. I. Edman, *Human Traits and their Social Significance,* chap. XIII.

B. **Questions and exercises:**
   1. What is the function of play, for the individual, for society?
   2. How does play help to integrate the we-group feeling? Illustrate.
   3. Why is commercial recreation limited in the possibilities of stimulating group solidarity and we-feeling?
   4. What responsibility has the local community in stimulating and controlling leisure-time activities of its people?
   5. Discuss the relation of play to morality.
   6. Discuss the appeal of gambling.
   7. What is the function of art, for the individual, for society?
   8. Discuss, pro and con, the contention that machine production destroys art and aesthetic tastes.

[9]Leo Stein, "Art and the Frame," *The New Republic,* March 24, 1926, vol. XLVI, p. 143.

9. Discuss, pro and con, the point of view regarding art expressed by Leo Stein.

10. How do play and art aid in the integration of the personality? Illustrate.

C. Topics for longer reports or written papers:

1. Contemporary recreation programs. (Consult J. F. Steiner, *Americans at Play*, 1933; J. F. Steiner, "Recreation and Leisure Time Activities," chap. XVIII, *Recent Social Trends*. See also current files of *Recreation*, and the annual *Social Work Year Book.*)

2. The place of leisure in modern life. (Consult L. P. Jacks, *Education through Recreation*, 1932; and C. Delisle Burns, *Leisure in the Modern World*, 1932; H. L. May and D. Petgie, *Leisure and Its Use*, 1928; H. Lehman and P. L. Witty, *The Psychology of Play Activities*, 1927.)

3. Changes in leisure time activities during the depression, 1929–1935. (Consult J. F. Steiner, *Research Memorandum on Recreation in the Depression*, Social Science Research Council Bulletin No. 32, 1937; R. S. and H. M. Lynd, *Middletown in Transition*, chap. VII; Douglas Waples, *Research Memorandum on Social Aspects of Reading in the Depression*, Social Science Research Council Bulletin No. 37, 1937; Douglas Waples, *People and Print: Social Aspects of Reading in the Depression*, 1937; L. R. Wilson, *The Geography of Reading*, 1938.)

4. The relation of art to religion. (Consult Jane Harrison, *Ancient Art and Ritual*, 1913; George Santayana, *Poetry and Religion*, 1912; and various standard histories of art.)

5. The relation of art to morality. (Consult Havelock Ellis, *The Dance of Life*, 1923; Count Leo Tolstoy, *What Is Art?*, Eng. transl. 1898; Irwin Edman, *Human Traits and their Social Significance* and bibliography; George Santayana, *The Life of Reason*, vol. III: *Reason in Religion*, 1905.)

6. Art and the integration of the personality. (Consult Havelock Ellis, *The Dance of Life;* Hughes Mearns, *Creative Youth*, 1926, and his *Creative Power*, 1929.)

CHAPTER XVI

SCIENCE AND PHILOSOPHY

Throughout recent centuries man has developed a certain way of studying and interpreting the material and social world around him which we call science. *Science* is first a method of thinking based on logic and experimentation or controlled observation. It represents the highest development of objective thinking. It involves painstaking observation, tabulation, and analysis of carefully selected and defined facts or situations. Science is also the body of systematic knowledge or laws and principles which have developed from the application of logic and controlled observation. Science may be defined, then, as a body of systematic and verified knowledge stating in general terms the relationship between facts which have been exactly defined.

It is on the basis of these generalizations that man is able to foretell or predict and hence to control the forces around him. The chemist knows what will happen when he mixes a base with an acid, or when he breaks down water into hydrogen and oxygen. The physicist has worked out the laws of falling bodies, of electrical conduction, and so on. The biologist has given us important generalizations about heredity and has offered us hypotheses to explain the changes in species. Stated in a slightly different way, the aim of science is to discover genuine cause and effect relations in the universe which will enable man to predict and to control the forces around him for his own benefit.

Philosophy in its earliest form consisted of somewhat unsystematic comments about nature and man's behavior. The proverbs of the Bible, the moral tales of Aesop, and common-sense generalizations represent this "wisdom philosophy," as it has been called. More accurately, philosophy is a systematic and logical reflection on the universe in all its aspects, with a view to giving it general meaning. It attempts to establish principles applicable to all knowledge. Logic itself is an outcome of philosophy, and since science rests not only upon logic and experimentation but also upon a manner of viewing the world, it is clear that science and philosophy are closely related. For purposes of our discussion we shall take them up separately, trying to indicate something of their place in culture and society.

THE NATURE OF SCIENCE

The history of science in our society is the story of man's gradual emancipation from superstition and magic. It is a product of culture which has important bearings on nearly all other phases of culture.

Scientific Method. The manner in which scientific workers take up their problems and solve them differs with the situation, but in general the steps are those of formal logic, although they do not necessarily follow exactly the logical sequence. John Dewey's categories of logical thought will serve us as an introduction. He puts the steps in solving a problem as follows: (*1*) a felt difficulty; (*2*) the location and definition of this difficulty in time and place; (*3*) various suggestions for possible solutions; (*4*) development by logical thought or reasoning of the bearings of the most promising of these suggestions; and (*5*) the more careful observation of or experimentation with this suggestion, now an hypothesis, leading to its acceptance or rejection, that is, belief or disbelief, depending on whether or not it solves the problem set down in the first two stages of the analysis.

The history of science is largely an account of the manner in which men solved by these steps the difficulties or problems set before them by nature and society. But one illustration must serve our purpose here.

In 1781 Sir Frederick William Herschel (1738–1822) discovered the planet Uranus, and soon its orbit was observed and calculations made as to its future position, as was possible through then-known laws of astrophysics. By 1820, a number of unexplainable variations had been noted, and by 1840 these divergences from the expected, scientifically predicted course had become so great that it was evident that some unknown cosmic force was influencing this planet. How did the astronomers proceed? Did they assume that this force was something supernatural? Not at all. Following the theories of Copernicus and Newton, they assumed that the discrepancies were due to the attraction of another and yet undiscovered planet.

Independently of each other, two mathematicians, John Couch Adams (1819–1892) and Urbain Jean Joseph Leverrier (1811–1877), computed the probable course of the unknown planet, assuming that it was influencing the course of Uranus. When their computations were finished, John G. Galle (1812–1910), an astronomer, who had learned of their work, turned his telescope upon a certain spot in the heavens and there, at a certain time, he saw a new planet. The events followed the prediction to a nicety. And thus the new planet, since named Neptune, was discovered.

Science, therefore, is given over to framing pertinent questions, using measuring instruments to make controlled observations or experiments in reference thereto, leading in the end to prediction and control of the situation at hand. Its highest development is witnessed in the natural sciences: physics, chemistry, and biology.[1] They deal with events or situations in nature which are capable of being controlled. The social sciences deal with human events, which are much more difficult to observe under controlled conditions than are events studied by the natural sciences.

Science an Escape from Common Sense and Fantasy. Science has had a long and painful growth in human society. In our everyday experience, we do assign "causes" or "explanations" to events around us. Some of these are fairly accurate, others far afield. Common sense in some particulars is the forerunner of science; in some ways it is antagonistic to it. Thus, primitive man, through repeated connection of events, associated rain clouds with an oncoming storm, or, noting the recurrence of the seasons, prepared his land, planted his crops, and in due course harvested them. On the other hand, there were many features of natural phenomena that he misunderstood. Thus he believed that the sun traveled around the earth; that the moon gave us its own light; that potatoes must be planted in the dark of the moon; and that diseases were caused by evil magic.

The scientific temper is one of inquiry, of skepticism. It does not accept things on the basis of mere precedent or traditional authority. It discounts dogmatism. It questions every assertion, generalization, or principle that has not been scrutinized by its careful methods of examination. As the great scholastic Peter

---

[1] These three are the basic natural sciences. The more specialized sciences, such as biochemistry, astrophysics, bacteriology, geology, etc., rest upon them.

Mathematics, though commonly called a science, is strictly speaking the logic used by the sciences.

Abelard (1079–1142) put it, "By doubting we are led to inquire, and by inquiry we perceive the truth."

We owe to the ancient Egyptians, Babylonians, Hindoos, and especially the Greeks a great debt for evolving a means of checking common-sense observation and generalization. While the ancient Greeks did not develop the experimental method as we know it today, they did begin asking pertinent questions, checking the answers, not from prejudice and authority, but in the light of the situation and events at hand. From this they evolved the foundations of logic, which is absolutely essential to the scientific method.

Although experimentation was begun by the Greeks, as witness the work of Archimedes (c. 287–212 B. C.) with his study of the principles of floating bodies, it was only at the close of the Middle Ages and later that adequate experimental techniques began to emerge. Scientific advancement was long retarded, first, by the slow development of mathematics and lack of precise instruments of measurement; second, by the opposition to science offered by organized religion. We shall not go into the former; but we must take note of the latter, since it illustrates the interplay of institutions within a given society.

Factors Hindering and Fostering Science. The story of the struggle between science and organized religion was told by Andrew D. White (1832–1918) in his *History of the Warfare of Science with Theology* (1896). The student will do well to examine this book to learn of the long, hard road over which science has passed. The power of tradition, prejudice, and entrenched theology retarded its development on every hand. When Galileo was haled before the Court of Inquisition for his scientific work, the indictment set forth various charges:

". . . for holding as true the false doctrine taught by many—namely, that the sun is immovable in the center of the world and that the earth moves and also with a diurnal motion; . . . following the hypothesis of Copernicus, you include several propositions contrary to the true sense and authority of the Holy Scripture.

. . . .

"The proposition that the sun is the center of the world and immovable from its place is absurd philosophically, false and formally heretical because it is expressly contrary to the Holy Scriptures. . . ."

Since the scientific method demands freedom from bias and prejudice—in short, freedom of thinking—it is only natural that the traditional authority of the time should resent its growth. In the first place, science undid the Church's conception of the physical universe, substituting the Copernican system for the ancient Ptolemaic one. This reduced the earth to a mere speck in the total universe, and robbed man of much of his former conceit. Then in the nineteenth century Charles Darwin, with his evolutionary theory of man's origin from the lower animals, placed man himself in the natural order of things. Cultural anthropology supported this idea by its study of man's primitive relatives, who represented the social and cultural vestiges of an earlier state. Then, too, during the last 50 years psychologists have shown that man's mental life and behavior must be studied from the angle of biology and the natural sciences, so that today man and society are to be considered but parts of the total world of nature.

The struggle for freedom of science is still with us. The natural sciences, fortunately for us, are relatively free, except for some opposition from church organizations that reject the teaching of evolution or from special minority groups like the anti-vivisectionists, who object to experimentation on animals. The social sciences, on the other hand, as they challenge cultural traditions, have become the object of increasing criticism from conservative forces. Those who support the present order join hands to suppress studies in regard to our political, economic, and religious institutions. As William Graham Sumner put it in *Folkways*, any group in power is likely to demand an "orthodox" economics, politics, and sociology whenever they feel it essential to their survival. This is particularly evident in fascist and communist societies today and less consciously so in those controlled by capitalism.

SCIENCE AND THE INDIVIDUAL

So far as the individual is concerned, science influences him in two ways, first, as an occupation, and second, as it affects moral and social ideas, attitudes, and habits.

The Work of the Scientist. The scientist is not unlike the artist. His work is creative and exploratory, and stands in rather sharp contrast to the life work of the ordinary man, who does not rise above the expected duty and social rôle set him by his society.

The motivation prompting one to undertake scientific work, incidentally, may be desire for prestige, desire for some exciting adventure, or the acceptance of a challenge—in short, the same motives which lead other men to art, big game hunting, successful business or professional careers. In other words the emotional drive to science is no different from that in other fields. Only the objects of attention and means of accomplishment are different.

Science is a highly technical practice, requiring years of patient preparation and research to attain great results. So far as the personality of the scientist goes, his scientific work is often a rather definite compartment of himself, cut off from his other interests. The very pressure of logical thought and work is highly taxing and rather unnatural to man, who is so predominantly a "feeling" rather than a "thinking" individual.

This fact of high specialization, this intellectual isolation of scientific work from the rest of the personality, is not recognized by the non-scientific public. Sometimes even the scientist himself is misled by this because the public attributes to him general expert knowledge as well as special.[2] In other words, the scientist's wisdom is assumed to carry over to problems of which he is no more competent to speak than is the man in the street, or perhaps than is some other scholar who has not his prestige. Thus, Thomas A. Edison (1847–1931), himself a practical inventor rather than an experimental scientist, might discourse on any subject under heaven from religion and morals to diet, and be accepted as an authority by thousands, simply because he has acquired a great name with his fellow citizens. So, too, a great physicist may speak with "authority" on problems of religion, morals, and economics, and thousands accept his words at their face value because he is a famous scientist.

Such prestige usually does something to the scientist. To attribute power and knowledge to him enhances his own ego. To keep submitting problems of all kinds to a scientist will lead him in time to believe that he is an expert in these other fields as well as in his own. We have noted that science implies skepticism, freedom from prejudice, and a special method of handling problems. Curiously enough, many men of science, when they deal with matters outside their narrow specialty, neglect all three of these requisites. They believe and act like everyone else. They remain uncritical and expose the bias of their social class.

[2]See K. Young, "The Need of Integration of Attitudes Among Scientists," *Scientific Monthly*, vol. XVIII, March, 1924, pp. 291–305.

As experts in a limited area of knowledge, scientists are invaluable. As soothsayers on problems outside their own specialty, they easily confuse and befog the issue. By their very authoritarian pronouncements they may retard the slower growth of another science just emerging from guesswork. Because natural science *has* made the greatest contribution to date, we may expect mathematicians, physicists, chemists, and biologists to be consulted on all sorts of economic, political, and sociological problems. The disasters from this sort of thing should be too obvious to need illustration.

Effect of Science on Moral, Religious, and Other Attitudes. Measured by the circulation of religious as against scientific periodicals from 1900 to 1930, there is a steady decline in the influence of religion and a steady rise in scientific interest. In 1900 Protestant religious magazines had 4.69 per cent and popular scientific 1.02 per cent of the total magazine circulation. In 1930, the popular scientific journals had 3.73 per cent, while the religious had dropped to 0.83 per cent.[3] While this method of determining the relative place of science or religion in conduct and attitudes may be open to criticism, it does expose a changing interest of no mean importance. Doubtless courses in science in high school and college are filling people's heads with objective facts about man and nature as never before. We may well ask: What are we to expect from this intrusion of more objective thinking into the life of the ordinary man? We have just noted how difficult it is to "get science into the thought stream" of the scientist himself, so far as matters outside his specialty go. In the face of this difficulty with the scientist, how much more difficult will it be for the man on the street to grow more objective? In his daily contact with natural forms man is without doubt less superstitious today than formerly. The common man now rather thoroughly accepts the idea of order and regularity in nature. He is far less dominated in the twentieth century than were his ancestors by a belief in personal forces, demons, and spirits whose conduct man could not predict.

Yet are not these new interests but an expression of man's profound belief in science as the magical solution of problems, rather than the result of his working out a means of avoiding super-

[3]See Hornell Hart, "Changing Social Attitudes and Interests," chap. VIII, *Recent Social Trends,* pp. 390–92.

stitions and fears? In other words, is it not still an appeal to traditional authority? When it comes to handling our own intimate problems, how logical and scientific can anyone be? In matters of self-preservation, of ego expression, of love, hate, and sympathy, of patriotism and sense of solidarity toward the symbols of one's nation or one's economic order or one's religion—how objective, how free from bias are we? There are doubtless persons who apply logical reason to their own problems at times, but they are rare. To expect science to answer *all* personal and social problems seems at present to be asking too much of it. The very nature of our biological makeup and of our earliest conditioning makes such application of science difficult. Science is but one phase of thought and but one phase of behavior. It can scarcely organize or direct all life. It is but a tool of man in handling life; it is not life itself. It is disastrous to assume that science can take the place of art, religion, or philosophy. A world built solely on scientific lines would be a world of robots, capable of nothing but purely mechanical action, unfeeling and soulless.

On the other hand, changes in moral and religious attitudes and moral behavior are evident enough. Is science to blame for these? This question cannot be answered dogmatically. The question involves fundamental principles of learning and action. It concerns the relation of words to conduct. First, will reading or hearing of science and its skeptical analysis lead us to disbelieve in the values that developed out of the traditional culture? Second, how important is the prestige-value of the scientist himself in these matters? Does it make any difference "who's talking" or "who's writing"?

There is a certain correlation between words and action, especially if language is linked to emotions and feelings. This is clear in the moral training of the infant and child who is surrounded by an atmosphere of "don'ts" and "can'ts" by parents and others in the course of teaching him the moral order. Again, it depends upon who makes these comments. People with authority or prestige always count more than others in stimulating thought and action.

Doubtless when men of science analyze the traditional moral and religious institutions and action, and expose their origin, course, and meaning, readers or listeners may get ideas and attitudes that run counter to old beliefs. Yet it must not be forgotten that habits lie deeper in us than opinions and ideas, and that home training, religious instruction, and patriotic ideals from childhood are not so easily thrown aside later in life. Among our young people today there is a great deal more freedom of talk and discussion than there is freedom and novelty in action. This is especially likely to be true of college students, who learn from their teachers the pleasures of verbal analysis, opinion making and breaking, and who sometimes like to shock their parents and elders by apparent sophistication. Ideas from science do have their influences, but these are not nearly so powerful as some other items in our contemporary society.

It is the application of science through the machine, making possible mobility and new contacts; it is the congestion of people into cities; it is the increasing place of secondary groups which so emphasize impersonal contacts involving only a segment of one's total personality—these are the changes that have most profoundly affected moral and religious conduct. People are affected by what they get from science and its application in the newspapers, magazines, motion pictures, and radio. But they are doubtless more influenced by opportunities for escaping traditional social controls. Yet new forms of morality are arising, although in the meantime some chaos and without doubt a certain amount of personal demoralization is inevitable.

PHILOSOPHY AND CULTURE

There is no society which does not develop some explanation of the nature of the world and the universe. In primitive people, generally, this takes the form of myths and legends about creation and past history. In some cases moral stories representing ethical reflections are developed. Formal philosophy does not arise until complex culture is at hand, but it is an outgrowth of these beginnings.

Nature and Growth of Formal Philosophy. We may define formal philosophy as knowledge of phenomena explained by or resolved into causes and reasons, powers, laws, or principles. Although closely allied to science, which also deals with causes and effects, philosophy would give us a consistent and integrated picture of the entire universe.

Philosophy, both informal and formal, essays to give man some idea of the fundamental purposes and values of life. The question:

Why are things as they are as well as *how* they are, is one which man never tires of asking himself and his fellows. Man demands an explanation of the world in which he lives. Philosophy, along with religion and art, helps to give him the answer.

Formal philosophy is usually divided into four branches, themselves the outgrowth of questions asked about four fundamental matters: knowledge, nature of reality, rules of thinking, and morality. More technically these are called epistemology, metaphysics, logic, and ethics.

Epistemology asks the question: How can we know? It deals with the problems of knowledge. Most naïve persons imagine that we know things directly through the sense organs, but a little examination will show us that this is not so. Experience has much to do with the manner in which we know things, and since experience is affected by culture it is clear that *how* we know is a reflection of *what* we know.

Metaphysics inquires into the nature of reality. It asks, What is the essence or substance of things? Men have often held to some form of dualism, which separated material, sensory experiences from ideal or spiritual ones. The latter were often believed to be the more fundamental. Plato (c. 427–347 B. C.) contended that the ultimate reality lies behind the apparent, sensory one. He set the pattern of much of our philosophy since. Other philosophers held to a monistic theory that all things, in spite of apparent differences, rest upon a set of unified, common substances.

Logic is the set of rules of thought, of cause and effect, which men have developed from their experience—their observation of regularity in nature: movements within the solar system, the seasons, daily changes in the weather, birth, death, and all sorts of other physical and human events. Logic furnishes indispensable tools for scientific work, and without its elaboration into mathematics, modern science could not exist.

Ethics has to do with the study of man's moral relations to his fellows. Here again the Greeks were pre-eminent. It was Socrates (c. 470–400 B. C.), the teacher of Plato, who gave us perhaps the greatest impetus to the analysis of man's moral relations with his fellows.

This is not the place to trace the history of philosophy. Yet the philosophy of any society cannot be separated from the general culture in which it arises. It is quite as much a part of it as the economic system, the political order, the forms of the family, the educational system, art, recreation, or any other elements. It rests upon the culture and the psychology of the people. Let us look at two examples.

How Culture Influences Philosophy. The interrelation of culture and philosophy is well illustrated by Christian theology. Early Christian philosophy rested upon a fundamental belief in the great drama of salvation—itself the conflict of the forces of God and Satan. The world was made by God's hands, peopled by God's creatures. Adam and Eve, who through Satan's temptation sinned against God's order, brought sin and death into the world. Yet man was started on the long journey of redemption by divine aid, especially by the sacrifice of God's only begotten Son. In the end there would be salvation in Heaven for the faithful and damnation in Hell for those who continued to disobey the divine commands.

This whole conception rested upon a dualistic philosophy, originated in the Near East, probably in Persia, and elaborated by the early Christian fathers. The latter had been influenced by the followers of Plato, who had extended Plato's division of the world into sensory appearances and the real world of idea, thought, or spirit. St. Augustine (354–430), one of the greatest of the early churchmen, has given us perhaps the clearest notion of this whole picture. There were in the world two spirits, or as he called them "two cities": the city of Satan, with its corrupt artifices in whatever form—war, art, pagan philosophy—and the city of God, the seat of the righteous throughout the ages, the place of spirituality, divine love, and the Christian virtues. The philosopher George Santayana has put the contrast thus:

"All history was henceforth essentially nothing but the conflict between these two cities: two moralities, one natural, the other supernatural; two philosophies, one rational, the other revealed; two beauties, one corporeal, the other spiritual; two glories, one temporal, the other eternal; two institutions, one the world, the other the church."[4]

This struggle was to continue until the righteous were saved in God's kingdom, and the wicked engulfed in the fiery furnace of hell. This view of the world and of man was as real and genuine to the Middle Ages as our own material world is to us today. Man

---

[4] George Santayana, *The Life of Reason,* vol. III, *Reason in Religion,* 1905, pp. 95–96.

believed in heaven far away, the abode of the saints; and in a hell, a place of eternal punishment. One has but to observe the art and architecture of the period to realize how thoroughly men took this all for granted. Thus over the main portals of many of the great medieval cathedrals of Europe one may see carved in stone the last judgment, contrasting the glad faces of the saved with the misery of the damned, chained to Satan, who is taking them off to hell. And anyone who has seen Michelangelo's magnificent fresco of *The Last Judgment* in the Sistine Chapel in Rome must carry away an indelible picture of the final act in God's drama of salvation.

Preparation for the hereafter was theoretically the principal purpose of man's life in the Middle Ages. The sacraments of the church and the whole hierarchy of living priests and departed saints directed man's attention to the divine end. They were parts of an ordered plan. There was no growth in such a universe. There was no change and no place for forces not controlled by God.

The whole Christian philosophy is in effect but an elaboration of this. Thomas Aquinas (c. 1225–1274), the medieval scholastic, drawing upon Aristotle, elaborated and crystallized the whole Christian philosophy. And Dante (1265–1321) in his *Divine Comedy* put medieval theology into poetic form.

Five centuries later we find a very different ideology in Europe. During this time there had occurred a number of great crises which had shaken the foundations of the well-ordered universe of Dante and Thomas Aquinas. The Crusades and the commercial revolution had loosened men's attachment to locality and to attention to otherworldliness. The Renaissance, with its re-introduction of classical learning, had stimulated skepticism, new art, and emerging interest in science. The Reformation had split the Christian church of the West into two great rivals and had brought with it an anarchistic questioning spirit in regard to religion. Nationalism and gunpowder had blown the feudal order to pieces. Finally capitalism was getting its modern stride.

Beginning with Copernicus (1473–1543), Galileo (1564–1642), Kepler (1571–1630), Descartes (1596–1650), and Pascal (1623–1662), the advancement of mathematics and the physical sciences had been rapid. By the time we get to the late seventeenth century, mathematics and physics were ready for the great work of

Sir Isaac Newton (1642–1727), who drew together previous work and himself developed the binomial theorem, invented the calculus, and developed the principles of gravitation.

Newton gave the world a picture of a universe governed by regular laws of absolute cause and effect, of consistent forces, admitting no place for fantasy, of a thoroughgoing determinism, put into mathematical forms and measurable by the instruments of science.

His work became the key to the rise of a philosophy built around a universe which operated as a machine. Educated men applied this new notion to everything in the world, including ethics. The philosopher Baruch Spinoza (1632–1677) explained men's motives and passions in terms of geometrical formulae.

From this new science of material forces the eighteenth century blossomed out into the "Age of Reason," in which men, turning their backs on the Christian philosophy but not on a god, conceived of the universe as the creation of a divine force, or a god, who, having made the material universe and having set it in motion, left it to run by itself. This so-called Natural Religion, more commonly known as Deism, turned its back on the Christian drama of salvation. In the words of Voltaire (1694–1778):

"Every man of sense, every good man, ought to hold the Christian sect in horror. The great name of Deist . . . is the only name one ought to take. The only Gospel one ought to read is the great book of Nature, written by the hand of God and sealed with his seal."[5]

These conceptions of a mechanistic and atomistic world carried over into psychology, political science, and economics. In government, the individual citizen, freed from his class status in a feudal order, was the social or political atom in association with his fellows. In economics, Adam Smith (1723–1790) used the same notion in his defense of the individualistic doctrines of economic life. Man was a social unit, rational in makeup, capable of competition or co-operation with his fellows in terms of enlightened self-interest. Mental life was explained by the combination of atoms or units of experience through association, the basis alike of British associationism in psychology and present-day behaviorism. As David Hartley (1705–1757), the philosopher, put it, there was a demand to discover "the general laws of action" under "the

5 Quoted by J. H. Randall, Jr., *Making of the Modern Mind*, 1926, p. 292.

method of analysis and synthesis recommended and followed by Sir Isaac Newton."

For the time this doctrine of reason and of individualistic, social atomism fitted into the culture and found its defense on philosophical grounds in the hands of the natural sciences and the philosophy which grew out of them.

Nevertheless the forces of scientific observation and experiment soon began to undermine the Age of Reason. The culture trends in the Western world from the eighteenth century on have been so diverse that it is extremely difficult to characterize them by any simple formulae. Certainly two important factors, romanticism in art, literature, and philosophy and the rise of modern biology, are basic to the changes which occur down to the twentieth century, when the disturbing features of the recent developments in physics, chemistry, and mathematics have undermined our material conceptions.[6]

In this diverse development in all fields of knowledge, one outstanding feature is the conception that the world is not a static, finished product running on mathematical and material schedules, but is throughout in a state of flux, change, and growth.

Romanticism, first of all, placed its emphasis not on reason and deliberation, but on the emotions and feelings as factors in behavior. It gave a place for the emotional side of man, who was not merely a cold, calculating machine. Secondly, it stressed growth rather than mechanical ordering of the world. The best-known exponent of this newer view of nature and man was Jean Jacques Rousseau (1712–1778), who issued a clarion call to all to throw off the shackles of the Age of Reason and go back to natural behavior for the clue to our proper social and personal behavior. Intelligence, reason, obedience to institutions, and social conformity are all the result of an environment which is alien to natural man. His famous phrases are well known, "Everything is good as it comes from the hands of the author of nature; but everything degenerates in the hands of man." And again, "The whole sum of human wisdom consists in servile prejudices; our customs are nothing more than subjection, worry, and restraint." He felt that all restrictions on the individual crippled his natural growth. The child must be given free rein to his own powers, to his native inclinations. He defended the expression of the instinc-

[6] See A. S. Eddington, *The Nature of the Physical World*, 1930; Sir James Jeans, *The Mysterious Universe*, 1930, and other books of like character.

tive bases of behavior, believed that feelings and emotions were the best foundations of judgment. He even opposed complete subjection to habits. "The only habit which the child should be allowed to form is to contract no habit whatever."

Of course, Rousseau was not alone in placing emphasis on man's emotional nature. We must not forget such novelists in England as Laurence Sterne (1713–1768) and Samuel Richardson (1689–1761), with their sentimentalisms, and especially Henry Fielding (1707–1754), with his rather realistic men and women whose motives were certainly not the coldly calculating sort assumed by the Age of Reason. These men were hardly romanticists, but they did emphasize the emotions.

The influence of romanticism on philosophy was tremendous. We may note its effect in but four other major fields: religion, politics, education, and personal freedom.

The Protestant Reformation planted the seeds of individualism in its emphasis on personal relations with God, and of faith, not reason, as the basis of salvation. But the formalism of both Luther and Calvin crushed the extreme expression of these notions, and Calvinism, especially, rested upon grounds familiar to the rationalists.

It was the development of mystical faith as a foundation of religion, particularly in the hands of the Pietists like the Moravian Brethren, and later in the hands of George Fox (1624–1691) and the Quakers, that put emphasis again on the individual and his emotional experience. The Quaker doctrine of "inner light" supported essentially the doctrine of man as a creature of emotion and feeling, not of deliberation.

The philosophy of Immanuel Kant (1724–1804) helped give a more systematic discussion of the separation between rational thought and religious and moral beliefs. The material world of objects can be known by the reason; the essence of religion rests upon our faith, upon imaginative products which do not need the support of reason. Since we can never know things in themselves—but only their expression, Kant says, "I have, therefore, found it necessary to deny *knowledge* of *God, freedom,* and *immortality,* in order to find a place for *faith*."[7] It may seem a far cry from religious mysticism to Kant's philosophy, but actually his view

---

[7] Kant, *Critique of Pure Reason,* preface (transl. by Watson), quoted by A. K. Rogers, *A Student's History of Philosophy,* rev. ed., 1919, p. 436.

gained wide acceptance in the nineteenth century and aided in undermining rationalism.

So too, the revivalism of John Wesley (1703–1791) struck further blows at the citadel of rationalism. The outcropping of this emotionalism in American sectarianism after the Revolution, especially in the Ohio Valley and in Kentucky (c. 1798–1805), furnished the basis for much of our American Protestantism during the nineteenth century.

Thus, the logical defenses of Catholicism set up by Thomas Aquinas and his followers, the logic, divine plan, and foreordination of Calvin, and the logical support of Deism by Voltaire and others are dissipated by this newer spirit.[8]

In the political field, while rationalism had some part in furnishing the ideology of both the American and the French revolutions, Rousseau's ideas more profoundly supported revolution as a method of social change. If every man should follow the dictates of his own conscience in regard to religion and God, why not in regard to civil government? The excesses of the French Revolution, while not to be laid at the door of romanticism, certainly expressed something of the emotional fervor of Rousseau's standpoint, and the very crowds that enthroned the goddess of reason as the head of their new state religion probably did not realize that actually they were supplanting but one emotional faith with another under a slightly different name.

In regard to modern education, Rousseau has played a tremendously important part. The work of Johann Heinrich Pestalozzi (1746–1827), Friedrich Froebel (1782–1852), Horace Mann (1796–1859), and our own contemporary John Dewey have all been influenced by the notion that the emotions, feelings, and the natural desires of the individual are the important foundations upon which education must be built. As we noted in Chapter XIII, "freedom" and "self-expression" became the key words in learning for a whole school of modern educational theory.

Romanticism also played a large part in literature and in regard to personal freedom. The German writers of the so-called "Sturm und Drang," Johann Wolfgang von Goethe (1749–1832) and Friedrich Schiller (1759–1805), we know well, while the English

---

[8] The medieval philosophy of an absolutely co-ordinated universe under God's guidance was not as foreign in fundamental spirit to the "Newtonian world machine" of the Deists as they imagined.

poets, Samuel Taylor Coleridge (1772–1834), with his poem entitled "France: an Ode," and William Wordsworth (1770–1850), both in his early support of the French Revolution and later in his poems, illustrate the new view of man. Percy Bysshe Shelley (1792–1822) and Lord Byron (1788–1824) were even more radical in defense of personal liberty. The poets put into lyrical forms a philosophical view of nature interpreted in personal terms. Nature could not be completely understood by mere dissection and measured by the devices of rational science. Later our own Americans, Ralph Waldo Emerson (1802–1882), Henry David Thoreau (1817–1862), and Walt Whitman (1819–1892), wrote in defense of the revolt of the individual from the bonds of custom.

While romanticism profoundly influenced modern thinking, other forces were also at work developing the conception of a changing, growing world. History, adopting the critical method, began for the first time to get a clearer picture of the social changes of the past. To Georg Wilhelm Friedrich Hegel (1770–1831), the German philosopher, "Universal history is the exhibition of Spirit in the process of working out the knowledge of that which it is potentially." History expressed the steady ongoing process of universal becoming, of the march through time of the Absolute Spirit realizing itself in nature and in man. It was Karl Marx, the profoundest thinker of socialist philosophy, who made Hegel's idea the battlecry of radical social, political, and economic reform by linking it to the idea of economic determinism of history and the steady growth of power of the proletariat in their conflict with the privileged classes. (See Chapter XIX on conflict.)

In spite of Newtonian physics, even the material sciences began to consider problems of origins and growth in the physical and chemical world. The Marquis de Laplace (1749–1827) tried to explain the origin and development of the solar system, a matter which Newton had taken for granted. Later, geologists—notably Charles Lyell—studied the development of the earth and its plant and animal forms.

The Western scientific world was therefore well prepared for the publication of the *Origin of Species* by Charles Darwin in 1859, with its concept of biological evolution. This idea of growth and evolution seemed to support the idea of social progress—a notion which had grown in popularity through the eighteenth and nineteenth centuries. (See Chapter III.)

PHILOSOPHY AND THE INDIVIDUAL

Although formal philosophy is still largely the domain of the educated specialists, it must not be imagined for a moment that the standpoint and explanations of the formal philosophers do not have their effects on the masses of mankind.

Philosophy and Common Life. When people live in a world dominated by the ideology of a Thomas Aquinas or of a pious Deist like Newton, the rôle of the individual is very different than in a world swayed by the notions of personal liberty of a Rousseau. In the world of the first, the individual is swallowed up in the divine plan. His status both here and hereafter depends on his relationship in this complex order of the city of God. In the Age of Reason man was the creature of God, but was controlled by mechanistic forces, and rational thought gave the clue to action. In a world where men believe in emotions, feelings, and personal liberty, and where the doctrines of change, growth, and especially progress, are prominent, the individual becomes much more important. The simple order of the past is believed to give way to a better order in the future in which the individual will find an increasingly more adequate expression of himself.

The daily philosophy of the ordinary man, of course, is not dressed up in the garb of elaborate logic and words. It is a kind of practical guidebook, the contents of which are accumulated rather unconsciously from the culture around him. Nevertheless while his world views may not always be consistent, and while he may accept most of his interpretation ready made from the popular exponents of philosophy, he cannot get along without some sort of working philosophy. This is neatly illustrated today in the rising conflict between the philosophy of individualism, with its emphasis on personal ambition, on money-making, on the search for individual power, and the rather opposite but growing view that the group, the collectivity, is dominant over the individual, and that social justice and social welfare for all come ahead of personal greed and ambition. Many of our present problems of social control arise out of just this conflict. (See Chapter XXVII.)

Man's action always depends on premises about the world and his relation to it, and these premises, in turn, rest on a basic faith in their correctness. Although for most of us these premises and beliefs are largely unconscious, they always influence our major relations to our fellows. Thus while philosophy to the man on the street may seem the remote study of the cloistered professor, the work of the formal philosopher is pretty much that of rationalizing the beliefs and practices of the world of men around him. Philosophy is as much a part of culture as is the machine technique, political forms, religious practices, or the family organization.

It is also hard for us to realize that philosophy and science both represent principles that rest essentially on faith, and that what today seems final and satisfactory may in the future seem archaic and incomplete, as new vistas of the universe and man's place in it are revealed to us. Neither science nor philosophy offers us absolutely final answers. They but give us the most carefully developed principles of the universe that we have yet been able to attain. Perhaps religion can offer us the solace of an absolute answer, but certainly philosophy based on science alone cannot do so as yet.

Philosophy and Balanced World View. Philosophy has always left man some sort of answer to his longing for security. The medieval philosophy of Thomas Aquinas rested its case on God's divine law; and the Deists still believed in a God who made and set the clock of the universe going. And though mechanism and materialism seem for the nonce to offer man little in the way of solace and comfort, the philosophies of growth and change have given us the doctrine of progress and the notion of a social religion. We do not know what the future may give us, but evidently the common man will not long be held to a strictly materialistic philosophy of life, no matter how much at the moment this sort of concept may grip the minds of people and find its expression in a form of living which has no integration and no purpose. This is but a temporary phase, a transition, perhaps, to another form of life in which values other than personal freedom and self-expression are the keynote. We already see this at hand in the revolutionary changes of contemporary Europe and in the growing faith in more absolutistic philosophy at home.

The principle of integration of personality already noted in discussing religion and art holds also for philosophy. Philosophy should by its very nature offer mankind a center around which his life may be integrated. If science answers but a few of the problems of *how* the universe and mankind are governed by natural laws, it still scarcely answers the deeper problem *why*. It is for art and religion to add their bit to the making of a well-rounded philosophy which will give a broader meaning to our universe and our place in it. Until philosophy can find a place for art and religion as well as science, it cannot satisfy the craving of man for final answers and for certainty, and if formal philosophy cannot offer this solution, the man in the street will find it in some other form of philosophy, perhaps not so consistent, not so logical, but suitable to his daily needs. With art, religion, and philosophy let it be as Karl Marx said about the material goods of this world: May each "produce according to his powers and consume according to his needs."

CLASS ASSIGNMENTS

A. Further reading assignment:

1. K. Young, *Source Book for Sociology*, chap. XVI.
2. Irwin Edman, *Human Traits and their Social Significance*, chap. XIV.

B. Questions and exercises:

1. Illustrate the distinction between scientific thinking and fantasy thinking in the solution of a problem.
2. Discuss pro and con the influence of science on religious beliefs and on morality.
3. How does the culture of a time and place influence formal philosophy?
4. Show how the ordinary man is affected by the philosophy of his time.
5. Cite cases of the disturbing effects of scientific ideas on religious and moral views among persons you know. How were these conflicts settled?

C. Topics for class reports or longer written papers:

1. The outstanding steps in the growth of natural science since the Middle Ages, illustrating the conflict of science and theology. (Consult A. D. White, *History of the Warfare of Science with Theology*, 1896; John W. Draper, *History of the Intellectual Development of Europe*, 1861.)
2. The recent developments in scientific method in the social sciences, illustrated by concrete cases. (Consult *Methods in the Social Sciences*, ed. by S. A. Rice, 1929.)
3. Reports or written papers on selections from the following:
(a) The relation of Christian philosophy to medieval culture.
(b) The relation of Deism and natural science to the seventeenth and early eighteenth century culture.
(c) The interrelations of romanticism and political and literary culture of the late eighteenth and early nineteenth centuries.
(d) The effect of romanticism, the Industrial Revolution, and biological evolutionary theories on the belief in progress. (For these consult J. H. Randall, Jr., *The Making of the Modern Mind*, 1926, and bibliographies.)

—

PART FOUR

FUNDAMENTAL PROCESSES OF INTERACTION

Introduction

Part Four will discuss the forms of reaction among people which are fundamental to social life, and which as reactions modify and influence the relations of persons to each other and of groups to other groups. In analyzing special social processes we are but examining certain aspects of the larger and basic process of interaction itself.

The two fundamental forms of interaction are *opposition* and *co-operation*. The former is usually divided into *competition* and *conflict*. From opposition and co-operation springs *differentiation*, or the division of social labor in terms of rôle and status. Out of conflict comes *accommodation* or compromise, toleration, or some other kind of truce which strikes a working balance between contending groups or individuals. As a special outgrowth of accommodation and differentiation we have *stratification*, or the formation of society into castes, classes, or orders of status. But out of competition, conflict, and co-operation may also arise *assimilation*, or the merging of divergent groups or persons into a new and homogeneous grouping.

Social processes are distinctly related to societal organization. In fact, the study of social processes is but one manner of viewing society, while the analysis of the societal order and culture constitutes another way of looking at the same thing. One might with profit refer to the familiar analogy of function and structure. When we describe and analyze the processes, we are concerned with the social functions—the interactional patterns of individuals and groups. When we study societal organization and culture, we are dealing more especially with the structure of society. Truly, structure and function go hand in hand, and it is useless to attempt to treat one without reference to the other. As we shall see, co-operation, competition, conflict, and differentiation are all closely linked to the rise of order, and the processes of accommodation and assimilation but reflect another view of fundamental cultural and organizational phases of economic, political, and other social activities.

In addition to these special processes, cultural change itself may be considered as a social process, especially with reference to invention and diffusion. Because we considered change fundamental to our discussion of culture and the societal order, we discussed this in an earlier division. (See Chapter III.)

CHAPTER XVII

COMPETITION

Competition is an indirect form of opposition; conflict is direct. In the latter persons or groups thwart, injure, or destroy their rivals in order to secure the wanted object or goal. The former is literally a conjoint bidding for an object but differs from conflict in being primarily directed to securing the desired object and not necessarily in impeding or destroying the rival. The felt scarcity of something of value is said to be basic to both forms of opposition, and the rewards of struggle may be material goods, prestige, or personal vanity. But felt scarcity is no more fundamental to opposition than it is to co-operation, and culture plays a large part in determining the form of interaction which a group or person will adopt to secure the goal.[1] Here we shall consider competition. Conflict will be discussed in the two following chapters. Yet as a background to our treatment of both forms of opposition, we must note briefly certain biological aspects of the struggle for existence.

The Struggle for Existence in Nature. Opposition in one form or another is found throughout nature and human society. The limitations of space, food, and other factors essential to life make some form of opposing interaction inevitable. This tendency to opposition may be called the struggle for existence.

The struggle for existence is a much misunderstood expression. People often imagine it refers only to violent conflict between animals or men for food or mates. Charles Darwin, the naturalist, who made the term popular, showed clearly how it involved not only opposition—struggle and competition—but also a resulting interdependence of individuals and species and a balance of relations very broadly associated with co-operation and differentiation. Darwin himself stated:

[1]See Margaret Mead, *Cooperation and Competition among Primitive Peoples,* 1937; M. A. May and L. Doob, *Competition and Cooperation,* 1937.

"I use the term Struggle for Existence in a large and metaphorical sense, including dependence of one being on another, and including (which is more important) not only the life of the individual, but success in leaving progeny."[2]

Since animals tend to reproduce in geometric ratio, there is always a competition for food and space. As Thomas R. Malthus has shown, food is much more limited in its increase than animal reproduction. As Darwin put it:

"A struggle for existence inevitably follows from the high rate at which all organic beings tend to increase. Every being, which during its natural lifetime produces several eggs or seeds, must suffer destruction during some period of its life, and during some season or occasional year, otherwise, on the principal of geometrical increase, its numbers would quickly become so inordinately great that no country could support the product. Hence, as more individuals are produced than can possibly survive, there must in every case be a struggle for existence, either one individual with another of the same species, or with the individuals of distinct species, or with the physical conditions of life. It is the doctrine of Malthus applied with manifold force to the whole animal and vegetable kingdom; for in this case there can be no artificial increase of food, and no prudential restraint from marriage."[3]

The struggle for existence takes place in three directions: (1) in the struggle with members of one's own species; (2) in the struggle with one's foes or members of other species; and (3) in the struggle against physical conditions. The first is illustrated by competition for food among men, each seeking his own survival at the expense of others. The second is seen in the combat or conflict of the hawk and ermine, of the stag and the hounds, of the carnivorous against the herbivorous animals. The third is witnessed in the adverse climatic and geographic conditions against which the plant and animal species must wage their warfare.

The interdependence of individuals and species is best evidenced when they are not too closely related to each other in the scale of nature. Out of this interdependence is built up an established order and regularity.

[2] The full title of Darwin's volume is so expressive of his whole contribution that it should not be forgotten: *On the Origin of Species by Means of Natural Selection or the Preservation of Favoured Races in the Struggle for Life.* The quotation is from p. 58 of The World's Classics series.

[3] *Op. cit.,* p. 59. Malthus's doctrine of population and food supply profoundly influenced Darwin's viewpoint. (See Chapter IX.)

The struggle for survival, including competition and conflict, lies at the basis of much of our human social order, and it affects differentiation and division of labor, the formation of caste and class, the development of institutions and various forms of social control. But in discussing the features of oppositional action in mankind, we must not forget the co-operation which is ambivalent to this. Co-operation will be discussed in Chapter XX.

With this brief review of the broader aspects of struggle and competition in nature, let us examine more closely the sorts of competition which we find in human society.

FORMS OF COMPETITION

In this section we shall discuss the broader impersonal phases of competition, especially those concerned with economic, racial, cultural, and institutional fields. The more intimate, so-called "personal" competition will be discussed in the final section.

Economic Competition. Although economic competition is the special province of the economist, we must note the outstanding features of this type of competition, which looms so large in our own culture especially. We shall, moreover, indicate certain social psychological and cultural factors that are often neglected in the conventional treatment of economic competition.

Economic competition is rivalry and struggle in securing possession of those things classed as wealth. It is but one phase of the universal rivalry and struggle for goods, tangible or intangible. As traditional economic theory explains it, we have, on the one hand, a niggardly nature and, on the other, a population with an ever-increasing number of wants—wants which are insatiable in the light of nature's limited resources. This relation of wants to scarcity is basic to economic competition. The particular manner in which they are satisfied, and what men call wealth, vary in different cultures.

The traditional theory of competition is based on complete self-interest among buyers and sellers in regard to any article in any market. It operates on the principle that each man acts for himself alone, by himself solely, in exchange, to get the most he can from others while giving as little as he must himself. The following statement from F. A. Walker (1840–1897), an American economist, gives a notion of what may be called "pure" competition:

"The idea of competition is opposed to combination. . . . Men in this state act as freely and as independently as the minute particles of some fine, dry powder absolutely destitute of cohesion. . . . Competition is also opposed to custom. . . . Competition is opposed to sentiment. Whenever any economic agent does or forbears any thing under the influence of any sentiment other than the *desire of giving the least* and *gaining the most* he can in exchange, be that sentiment patriotism, or gratitude, or charity, or vanity, leading him to do any otherwise than as self-interest would prompt, in that case, also, the rule of competition is departed from."[4]

Such a view of competition clearly reflects the culture of extreme capitalistic enterprise. Other economists, however, recognize that competition even under capitalism depends on a give-and-take interaction. A. T. Hadley (1856–1930) held competition to be just what its name implies, "a concurrent *petition*" dependent on people doing "the best they can for somebody else, in order to induce him to enter into dealings with them."[5]

In bargaining, competition depends on the buyer and seller getting together in some sort of social relationship although gain may be their only motive. Out of the interaction of buying and selling some sort of service is afforded each and the wider society as well. Out of this interplay certain order and co-ordination of the social process arises. E. R. A. Seligman, another economist, notes five forms of competition:

(1) *Commodity competition,* which rests upon the fact of social choices. The buyer may go elsewhere if the seller holds his goods too dear, or if all such goods are too dear he may purchase a substitute. Every prospective purchaser is continually debating with himself whether to buy this commodity or that. Choice and judgment are always present in a competitive system. So, too, one agency of production may replace another because the buyers demand it. Producers are constantly on the alert to keep the purchaser coming to them for goods or services. Thus competition among the factors of production is an adjunct to commodity competition. This involves for absolute competition a fluidity of capital, labor, and materials, without let or hindrance. If this free flow is hindered by custom, law, or other economic causes, there is a limit to untrammeled competition. (2) *Competition of individuals* who produce some commodity or some factor in production. This is a form of personal competition in the economic field. The laborer improves his

[4]From F. A. Walker, *Political Economy,* 1887, p. 92. Italics not in original.
[5]A. T. Hadley, *The Relations Between Freedom and Responsibility,* 1903, p. 122.

efficiency and secures better wages. The manufacturer outdoes his rival and gains more profits. The business man by increased efficiency under-sells his competitor and secures greater dividends for his firm. (3) There is *market competition*, that is, not competition of individuals, but of markets one with another. One city is continually trying to outdo an-other as the dominant market for goods and services. Normal market competition again leads to reduced costs unless hindered by tariffs, legis-lation, or custom. (4) *Class competition* is an outcome of division of labor into groups of producers. We have not only laborers and capital-ists, but classes of each: unskilled and skilled laborers, and professions, some organized into associations or unions, others not; and of capitalists we have owners of agricultural, commercial, and industrial capital. Within these divisions there are minor subclasses of various sorts. (5) *National competition* is the rivalry of nations for trade. This in a sense is a wider phase of market competition but organized in terms of competition of one country with another.[6]

According to conventional economic theory, competition be-comes an organizing force within the community. If so-called "pure" competition exists at the level of dog eat dog and devil take the hindmost, of course, we have not order but anarchy. This method of securing dominance and wealth is in the end non-eco-nomical, since the rival is also consumer and producer of goods you may want. Carried to its logical conclusion "pure" competition would destroy society. The struggle for goods and services is a form of circular response—a form of give and take—and not the theoretical atomism of older economics. Actually, as competition works out, even in a society marked by *laissez faire* and individual-ism, interaction of buyer and seller puts limits on rivalrous, com-petitive behavior, and we have co-ordination and order developing. Thus out of these rivalrous relations, institutions arise in which co-operation has a place. It is evident again that competition and co-operation go together.

This interplay of competitive forces has given rise to four funda-mental economic institutions: private property, contract, profit making, and freedom of trade, or enterprise. *Private property* represents the control of the resources of society. *Contract* is the means of bringing persons, instruments, and materials together for operations associated with production, distribution, and consump-tion. These two serve as the mechanics of competition. *Profit*

[6] See E. R. A. Seligman, *Principles of Economics,* 1905, pp. 165–70.

taking is the lure or "bait," the "beacon and guide" which leads persons and corporations to produce and sell goods. The desire for profits, for making money, serves in our culture as a powerful psychological motive for accumulating wealth and hence prestige and power. The *freedom of trade* or enterprise is expressed in our individualism and *laissez-faire* attitudes and practices, and is important in the continual division of labor, making for efficiency and increased wealth. (See Chapter XXII on division of labor, Chapter XXIV on stratification, and Chapter XXVII on control in economic relations, for special aspects of economic competition in our society.)

Economic Competition and Societal Organization.   It should be evident that in discussing economic competition we cannot neglect societal organization and culture. The failure of the conventional economists of the nineteenth century and since to consider these factors is one of the glaring examples of what W. I. Thomas aptly calls "particularism," that is, the tendency to explain complex behavior in terms of simple principles and without reference to the historical factors of time and place. Let us look briefly into the matter.

Traditional economic competition grew up in a society still dominated by primary group organizations and the pre-machine age, in which individual face-to-face contact was the common form of economic interaction. Person-to-person relations were dominant. The merchant or manufacturer would keep one eye on the buyer, one on his rivals, and both eyes on his shop or plant. In such a situation personal competition was supreme. Individual effort was rewarded and self-interest seemed natural.

Then in a continent like America, with boundless resources ready for exploitation, individual effort and self-interest were richly rewarded. The existence of free land, mineral resources, and accessible water power developed our American attitudes of self-reliance, individuality, and an earnestness of purpose which are reflected in our present views of the importance of competition, even though most of the conditions making for these attitudes and habits have disappeared in the past few decades. The rise of manufacturing and world trade, first in England, with its rich coal and iron resources, and latterly in northwestern continental Europe, had already produced much the same ideology and practice elsewhere.

It was inevitable that the economic theorists, trying as they were to reduce man's economic behavior to a science analogous to Newtonian physics, should rationalize all this into a system in which competitive practices and the institutions of private property, contract, profit making, and *laissez-faire* freedom of action should be considered universal and eternal.

Several things have happened during recent times to alter this simple view. Such changes in the economic order itself as the rise of corporations and of monopolies, as the importance of banking, and as machine production and invention, are all-important. As Walton H. Hamilton puts it, "The presumptions which underlie competitive policy do not belong to a world of the machine process, the corporation, and quantity production."[7]

As our economic order has become more complex, banking comes to control all industry and business. Credit structure reaches beyond the local boundaries to the nation and then to the world outside. And out of all this has come that novel economic invention, the corporation or impersonal stock company, which replaces the individual merchant or manufacturer and the partnership.

In short, competition has shifted from the person-to-person sort to the competition of corporation with corporation, of market with market, of nation with nation. The whole struggle takes on an impersonal character which has no counterpart in the simple theories of competition which belonged to the pre-machine age. Money economy, specialization of labor, and impersonality of machine production replace the worth of personal service and the need of personal loyalty and face-to-face relations. The individual loses his personal primary group values and attitudes and becomes attached to those purchasable in the market, be they consumption goods, recreation, acquaintances, or what not. And this is but a reflection of changes in the whole economic order.

It ought to be clear from this that the old-fashioned competitive system of economics has broken down because it has largely outworn its usefulness. It belonged to a particular historical period, to a certain culture in time and place, but new cultural forms and new social organization bring new conditions. As a result the forms of rivalry and competition change. Among the most evident features of the whole development are monopoly, and the growing need of deliberate planning of the economic process, and the

[7]*Encyclopedia of the Social Sciences,* vol. IV, p. 145.

development along with this of forms of social control of economic activities which will conserve resources in men, capital, and materials and perhaps make for a more balanced societal order. (See Chapter XXVII.)

To summarize, then, we may say that competition does not exist alone and independently of other processes, especially those of a cohesive character such as co-operation. These two processes go together and cannot be separated. As the economist Henry Clay puts it:

"Competition tends to force us to struggle, fight, conflict with our neighbors; the desire to relieve ourselves from the pressure of competition compels us to combine, associate, co-operate with our neighbors. We associate with our competitors in one economic group, in order to compete more effectively with other groups."[8]

Racial and Cultural Competition. It should be clear from our discussion in Chapter IV of the widening contact and interaction in the modern world that divergent races and cultures have come into distinctive opposition to each other.

Strictly speaking, there is no racial competition or conflict. As we have said in Chapter VIII, for sociological analysis race is always associated with culture.

As was noted when discussing world population problems, standards of living and attitudes toward high birth rates profoundly influence the fertility of various races and sub-races. Throughout both pre-history and history, races have competed with each other for desirable territory in which to live. More fertile and vigorous peoples have pressed on less fertile and more docile peoples, both by direct conflict and by indirect pressure of competition. The rapid increase of Oriental populations, especially that of Japan, represents a form of competition in the Pacific basin with the populations of Australia, New Zealand, and other countries. The individuals do not yet feel this struggle particularly, but it is going on and in time may break out into open conflict in the form of war. Another illustration of a sub-racial competition is found in the rapid increase in numbers among the French Canadians, who are outstripping the English-speaking Canadians in natural growth. So, too, the Slavs of central Europe are competing with the peoples of Germanic stock, as the Italians are pressing on other Latin peo-

[8] From Henry Clay, *Economics for the General Reader*, 1920, p. 115. By permission of The Macmillan Company, publishers.

ples around them for food and land. The social implications of
this competition we have already discussed in relation to population. (See Chapter IX.)

Another cultural competition in the modern world lies in the field
of international economics. The competition of nation with nation
for trade has been common since about the beginning of the fifteenth century and is linked up with the whole development of *laissez-faire* economics and national competition discussed above. The
seeking of new routes to India following the capture of Constantinople by the Moslems in 1452, and the colonial expansion throughout the next four centuries in the Orient, Africa, and the Americas were bound up with the struggle for wider markets. Since then
the struggle has become increasingly intense, especially since the
World War.

A peculiar form of competition occurs wherever modern factory
products encroach upon the products of native handicrafts. In
America contact between the white men and the Indians led to the
loss of many of the arts and industries of the latter. This has also
been true in Africa and parts of the Orient and Oceania. Wherever
the cheaply made cloth, wooden or metal goods, and other products come into competition with the native goods, the latter tend
to suffer. This form of competition is very one-sided, and is a reflection of the rapid diffusion of material culture already noted in
Chapter III.

Competition in religion is illustrated in the struggle for converts between the Mohammedans and Christians, particularly in
Africa. Islamic faith is narrower, sterner, simpler, but more fa-
natical and concrete than Christianity, which is more abstruse,
more theoretical, more strict in its moral taboos, more opposed to
conflict and war.

Closely related to missionary activities among people of lower
cultures is the educational program. Education fostered by the
political state sometimes produces competing ideas and expecta-
tions on the part of the divergent culture group. In Africa and in
the United States it is evident that educating the Negro in the
higher occupations, only to shut the door of opportunity later, sets
up a form of irritation that will end in conflict. In South Africa
it is evident that sooner or later educated white men will be forced
to compete with like-trained natives. This threat of future competition is present in our own South. Both in Africa and in this

country the curtailment of funds for public education of the colored population may perhaps be an unconscious attempt to delay the ultimate day of this competition.

Finally competition is going on in the field of political organization and political philosophy. The Gandhi nationalistic movement in India was in competition and conflict with British rule. In the West we find the Russian political and economic philosophy gradually setting up competing ideas in people's minds in contrast to capitalistic practices in that and other countries. And fascism has come into the Western world since the World War, to offer still another competing set of ideas and practices. So, too, the internationalistic movement sponsored by the League of Nations represents a form of political philosophy that runs counter to extreme nationalism.

It is out of such competition as this that new political, economic, and social organizations are born. This competition at times may break out in open conflict or war, leading, in turn, to accommodations or compromises of various sorts. Or, in some instances, there may be a fusion of somewhat divergent ideas, as seems to be the case with the attempts of fascism to combine nationalism and certain features of socialism.

Institutional Competition. Strictly speaking, institutional competition is but a phase of cultural competition. *Institutions* are regular forms of ideas and actions which are centered around some recurrent needs of a particular society and are concerned largely with controlling and fostering means of adaptation.

Institutional competition may be conveniently divided into two areas: one within the wider institutional field, or intra-institutional; the other, between organizations of the major institutional fields, or inter-institutional.

There are distinct limitations to inter-institutional competition. The very division of social functions to satisfy the fundamental needs of material goods and food, of government, of religious experience, and so on, means that these basic areas of behavior are separated from each other by natural barriers, since they fulfill distinct functions. Nevertheless competition does arise between the major institutions.

In the history of Western society two major areas of such competition, occasionally leading to conflict, have been the early struggle between church and state for the dominance of government, and latterly, that between certain economic institutions and the state for power over the community.

During the Middle Ages the Roman Catholic Church carried on a long struggle for political dominance with the Holy Roman Empire. After the Church had established its supremacy for some centuries, the rising nationalistic states born out of the decadent Empire took up the struggle against the papacy, until in 1870, with the unification of modern Italy, the last "temporal" power of the Vatican was relinquished.

Today inter-institutional competition occurs between economic activities and the home and family, as witnessed in the decline of household activities and the emancipation of women from the home. So, too, recreational facilities are constantly competing with the home and the church for the domination of leisure time. There is also competition between business and industry and educational institutions for the time and attention of our young people. The study of competition among political institutions is the special province of political science, and we shall not treat the matter here. Competition between religious groups we have already discussed above. Certain phases of both political and religious struggle, however, will be discussed in the next chapter.

The field of education affords ample illustrations of institutional competition. In the elementary and secondary schools the newer subjects, often called "frills" by their opponents, such as art, music, and vocational courses, compete with the traditional courses for a place in the curriculum. There is also rivalry between the older conventional departments of teaching and supervision with the newer departments of education looking to vocational guidance, training of defectives, control of conduct cases, and the prevention of delinquency.

In the colleges and universities there is constant rivalry between different types of subject matter, forms of administration, and between teaching and research. The established curriculum, with its emphasis on languages, mathematics, and natural sciences, competes with social science and vocational subjects. The former entrenches itself with "required" courses, while the latter group attempts to make its material so attractive as to draw large bodies of students and thus to make the administration realize how "important" the demand for the "new" subjects is. Likewise, various professional schools enter into competition for students, although the movement to law, medicine, or engineering, to mention three, largely reflects the demands for these occupations outside.

The function of institutional competition in our own society is well summarized by E. A. Ross in these words:

"The competition for public favor between parties, sects, schools, universities, governments, manners, and ideals brings about the adaptation of institutions to popular wishes which characterizes democratic society. . . . As organizations and institutions compete, their line of development becomes subject to the general trend of opinion and feeling. With *status,* institutions make the character of their people; with *competition,* the people make the character of their institutions."[9]

COMPETITION AND PERSONALITY

Certain person-to-person features of competition will be discussed in more detail in Chapters XXI and XXII on differentiation. Here we shall discuss the place of so-called personal competition in personality organization.

Personal Competition. The expression "personal competition" is slightly misleading. We have defined competition as relatively impersonal striving of two or more persons for an object, as really a concurrent petition or bidding of rivals rather than an open person-to-person antagonism and struggle. In the literature of sociology, however, this expression *personal competition* refers to the individual rivalry for wealth, status, and power.

Personal competition rests upon the desire for some value which is scarce or believed to be scarce. Its more rudimentary form is seen in the spontaneous rivalry of persons when unaffected by any set standards of conduct, as witnessed in some situations in the family, the neighborhood, or children's play groups.

Even in rivalry, contact necessitates some mutual comprehension and sympathy with those about one. An individual cannot attempt to outstrip another unless he has in part identified himself with his rival. Without this sympathy and knowledge, he would not know how to outdo the other. C. H. Cooley has admirably discussed the social psychology of competition in the following words:

"It may be maintained that competition, when not unjust or destructive, promotes a broader social feeling. The free and open play of energy and purpose is calculated to arouse precisely that knowledge of

[9]E. A. Ross, *Principles of Sociology,* 2nd ed., 1930, p. 185. Italics in original.

others, and of the limitations which their life imposes upon ours, out of which a wholesome sympathy and sense of justice must spring. Competition involves contact and usually necessitates some degree of mutual comprehension. To succeed one must understand opposing forces, and understanding is the beginning of sympathy. Your competitor is one upon whom you must count, a factor in your life; unconsciously your imagination occupies itself with him, trying to make out his purposes and methods, interpreting his thoughts from his words and actions. If he turns out to be a person of your own sort, with desires, attachments, standards, powers, that you can appreciate, you will respect and perhaps admire him, no matter how much he may hinder you. Thus you will see life from a new point of view, and be correspondingly enlarged and delivered from your smaller self."[10]

For our present American society, at least, the following points in personal competition need attention: (*1*) its intensity; (*2*) its relation to personal restlessness, strain, and ambition; and (*3*) its relation to success. Closely allied to the latter is the relation of competition to leadership, to be discussed in Chapter XXII.

The *intensity of competition* refers to the relative amount of activity or energy used up in the process. The greater the degree of personal choice afforded an individual in a society, the greater the demand on his own initiative. In a society in which social rôle or status is relatively fixed, the opportunities for individual choice of social function are slight. In our own society, on the contrary, such choice is extremely wide, and there is consequently a more intense call on the reservoirs of energy.

This wide range of choice, moreover, reflects a condition of rapid transition in a society. Evidently it is only in societies with an open-class system and marked by rapid changes in material and non-material culture that such opportunities exist. As soon as we get more settled organization and acceptance of particular modes of behavior for particular people, the selective process of competition loses its force.

In our Western world the most dominant selective agencies are the cultural patterns which persist from the days of class organization. For example, such matters as family name and fortune play a decided part in limiting one's choice of competitive activity.

[10] C. H. Cooley, "Personal Competition: Its Place in the Social Order and Effect upon Individuals; with Some Considerations on Success," *Economic Studies,* April, 1899, vol. IV, No. 2. Reprinted in his *Sociological Theory and Social Research.* 1930, pp. 210–11.

Thus, generations of doctors and lawyers from the same family limit the professional selection of the sons. Or in another way, laws may restrict destructive and predatory competition of the "tooth and red claw" variety and make the competitors operate within certain rules of the game. Public opinion may develop a certain code of competitive conduct. This is seen when we get public exposure of unfair business methods. The fear of such exposure may serve to restrict the intensity of a cruder and what Cooley calls "lower, self-seeking" order of competition. In other words, these selective agencies imply a certain discipline. And so, too, public opinion may stimulate a higher, more ethical form of competition, looking to "emulation in service" in which high and long-range ideals replace more individual and selfish aims.

Competition is often associated with restlessness, ambition, and strain. The spirit or ethos of competition produces definite effects upon personal life organization. In a stabilized society marked by fixed status, by definitions of practically every life situation, mental conflict is not likely to be very prominent. There is an acceptance of one's lot in life. One knows no other. There can be no stimulus to get ahead or to change one's caste or class.

In contrast, in a society where opportunities for advancement abound and where the culture demands such advancement, there are animation and stimulation to activity that put a premium on the expenditure of energy. At the same time, such a society easily produces overstimulation. In our society, where there is a wide variety of choices, say of occupation, of mates, of locality, of political affiliation, of religious expression, and of recreation, it is easy for the individual to become confused. He gets a set of divergent images or ideals of what he may do, resulting in mental conflicts and strain. As Cooley again so aptly phrases it, "Opportunity seems to bring discontent . . . and thousands seek what only a few can gain."[11]

Likewise intense competition tends to foster insecurity. Where status is fixed, even though at a lowly level, at least one knows what to expect of life. Where the cultural atmosphere is surcharged with high ambitions, with stimulation "to keep up with the Joneses," failure to attain desired goals often leads to insecurity both in economic and in social status. This situation is more in evidence in the economic field than elsewhere in a period of

[11] *Op. cit.*, pp. 216–17.

financial and business depression. Yet even in prosperous times fear of the loss of the job and anxiety about present and future social position are the prices we pay for indulging in the game of intense competition.

It may well be that the apparently growing amount of nervous breakdown, of insanity, of crime, and of other forms of personal demoralization, is not unrelated to the wear and tear of such a competitive system as we have fostered in the Occidental world these last three or four centuries. Our materialistic, over-competitive spirit seems to have robbed us of certain values which make life richer and calmer.

Nevertheless competition also stimulates self-reliance, individuality, and a seriousness of purpose that makes for success. In Western countries, the man who makes money, the person who acquires large powers over property and goods, is lauded as successful. These persons form the élite in our capitalistic society.

In the professions of medicine, law, teaching, and engineering competition plays an important part in determining merit and success. The prestige standards of all these professions stimulate the urge to get ahead, to publish more and better research papers, to make a name for oneself. Yet the infection of the professions with the money-making ethos of the business world has likewise led to the belief that success in the professions and standing in the community are measured by fees collected and the ostentatious expenditure of money.

A word should be said about the relation of success to habits of work and to morality. There is no doubt that the success motive, as measured in material terms, sets the pattern of steadiness, of persistence, of regularity of daily behavior not found where more hedonistic (pleasure-seeking) practices are in vogue. In every group the standards of success imply a morality of conduct, that is, socialization in terms of what the group and the larger community demand. Sometimes, however, the morality of the smaller, more predatory groups runs counter to the morality of the wider community. In such cases rules of conduct, legal or moral, are laid upon the minority to bring them into line. Evidence of this will be apparent when we discuss social control in business and the professions in Chapter XXVII.

Competition implies a wide range of stimulation and response. It tends to free the individual from conformity to earlier patterns of behavior. It fosters inventiveness and innovation, in both material and non-material culture, and stimulates leadership on every side. We shall discuss leadership in Chapter XXII.

To summarize, we may say that personal competition or rivalry for status is found in many spontaneous groups. In our Western society in particular, however, following upon the commercial revolution of the fifteenth century, upon the discovery of new lands, and finally upon the Industrial Revolution of the last two centuries, there arose increased opportunity for personal competition. Under the philosophy of individualism and *laissez faire* fostered by the rise of democratic political institutions and by the rise of capitalistic exploitation, a person was free to move from class to class, from place to place, and from one occupation to another. This, in turn, stimulated innovations and fostered new forms of political and social activity, which made for more rapid social change. The world moved speedily from one type of material culture to another, and in time these changes also affected the non-material culture: beliefs, values, and all.

In time this rapid expansion of competition began to come to an end; that is, it gave rise to new forms of social control, legal and moral, which restricted in part the unlimited struggle. So far as the individual in our society is concerned, competition stimulates ambition, ego expansion, and expression of energy. Restlessness and seeking individual success become the patterns of behavior. But with growing restriction of these forms of outlet, there arises a tendency to instability and insecurity. The level of aspiration set down by the ideal of personal success is far above the level of achievement for a large section of the population. In such a situation the strain of competition begins to tell on many persons. This may give rise not only to compensatory aggressiveness leading often to more intense competition and even fostering conflict, but it may also stimulate forms of personal demoralization: vice, crime, suicide, and nervous disorders, which accompany the whole rapid shift in social organization and culture. (See Capter XXVIII.)

CLASS ASSIGNMENTS

A. **Further reading assignment:**

   1. K. Young, *Source Book for Sociology,* chap. XVII.

   2. R. E. Park and E. W. Burgess, *Introduction to the Science of Sociology,* chap. VIII.

3. Article by Walton H. Hamilton, "Competition," *Encyclopedia of the Social Sciences*, vol. IV, pp. 141–47.

B. Questions and exercises:

1. According to Malthus and Darwin, what are the basic "reasons" for the struggle for existence in nature? Do any of these factors operate to foster competition among human beings?

2. How did vast natural resources coupled with cultural factors stimulate *laissez-faire* competition during the past few centuries?

3. Show how the culture pattern of economic competition affects non-economic activities: recreational, religious, political, and familial.

4. Cite evidence from your own experience to show that struggle (either competition or conflict) plays a part in everyday life of family, church, school, and play as well as in the economic field.

5. What is the relation between political nationalism and competition between nations?

6. What forces are at work in the modern world which are modifying the former intensity of *laissez-faire* competition?

7. How does the stimulation of a high level of aspiration, *e.g.*, for personal success in money making, foster a sense of personal insecurity if there be a restriction of opportunity for achievement? Illustrate from the facts of the growing limitation on young people's getting ahead in business, the professions, or in skilled artisanship.

C. Topics for class reports or longer written papers:

1. The doctrine of individualism in European and American society since the fifteenth century. (Consult J. H. Randall, Jr., *The Making of the Modern Mind*, 1926, and bibliographies; R. H. Tawney, *Religion and the Rise of Capitalism*, 1926; John Stuart Mill, *On Liberty*, 1859; J. M. Keynes, *The End of Laissez-faire*, 1926; A. D. Lindsay, "Individualism," *Encyclopedia of the Social Sciences*, vol. VII, pp. 674–80, and bibliography.)

2. Cooley's treatment of personal competition. (Consult C. H. Cooley, "Personal Competition: Its Place in the Social Order and Effect upon Individuals; with Some Considerations on Success," *Economic Studies*, April, 1899, vol. IV, No. 2, reprinted in his *Sociological Theory and Social Research*, 1930, chap. IV; also Cooley, *Social Process*, 1918, chaps. VI-XIV.)

CHAPTER XVIII

CONFLICT

As we have already noted, co-operation and opposition are the basic forms of interaction out of which other processes arise. Opposition we divided into competition and conflict. In this chapter and the next we shall first examine the general nature of conflict; second, discuss the forms or types of conflict situation; third, show the function of conflict in the development of social organization; and finally, discuss certain relations of conflict to personality.

THE NATURE OF CONFLICT

Opposition, as noted in the previous chapter, grows out of felt scarcity of desirable goods or power necessary for survival. Self-interest or ego-expansion is the fundamental motive of behavior, and in the struggle for objects which make life possible and more tolerable, there is bound to be a clash of persons and groups. Scarcity and selfishness are the roots of struggle.

Characteristics of Conflict. When this struggle for a desired object is direct and personal, we call it *conflict*. When the struggle is indirect and impersonal, we call it *competition*. Although, under modern complex conditions, much competition is conscious, a large part of it remains unconscious. In conflict our opponents are on the ground. We know that they stand in the way of our getting what we want. Competition, moreover, tends to be continuous in time, while conflict is intermittent. The former is less violent in its emotional expression; the latter is likely to be highly exciting and intense, though not persistent over an extended period. In many situations competition and conflict are interrelated, the conflict pattern of behavior arising at critical points in competition.

At its most elementary level, conflict results in the elimination or annihilation of the opponent. In human society, of course, most conflict ends in some sort of compromise or accommodation or perhaps by assimilation or fusion of the two opposing elements. There is a cycle in the whole process somewhat as follows: (*1*) a felt need for some object which is limited in its supply; (*2*) struggle with others for this object; (*3*) the resolution of the conflict by annihilation or reduction of the opponent to ineffectiveness or by some form of accommodation or other method of adaptation. The structure of society is profoundly influenced by this balancing of forces in opposition, as we shall see.

TYPES OF CONFLICT SITUATIONS

Conflict finds its expression in all sorts of social situations, and no classification of types of conflict is entirely satisfactory. For purposes of descriptive analysis we shall in this section discuss conflict in terms of more conventional areas of social interaction, leaving the psychological features to be discussed later. We may classify the type situations as (*1*) industrial, (*2*) racial, (*3*) religious, (*4*) political, (*5*) inter-community and intra-community, (*6*) inter-class and intra-class, (*7*) sex and age conflict, and (*8*) conflict of intellectual or moral principles.[1]

Industrial Conflict. We shall discuss industrial conflict in the modern society from the angle of changes within the present capitalist order. The struggle aiming at the overthrow of private ownership of capital goods we shall handle as a phase of class conflict.

Industrial conflict concerns laborers on the one side, and owners and managers on the other. It is an outgrowth of capitalistic organization of industry and especially of the factory system. The outstanding features of this system in contrast to the pre-industrial, pre-capitalistic order are as follows: (*1*) capitalist ownership of the tools and machines of production, (*2*) specialization of labor, leading to loss of skilled trades and the substitution of the machine for human ingenuity and skill, (*3*) the wage system and the theory of *laissez-faire* individualism, which gives the owner or manager the "right to hire and fire" as he will, (*4*) the fluctuations of the business cycle, with periodic unemployment, against which no provision is made for the individual worker, (*5*) the determina-

---

[1] E. A. Ross in his *Principles of Sociology*, 3rd ed., 1938, chaps. XVIII–XXVII, presents one of the most adequate discussions in sociological literature of various areas of conflict. The interested student will do well to read these chapters for a fuller and somewhat different treatment of the conflict process. See also R. E. Park and E. W. Burgess, *Introduction to the Science of Sociology*, 1924, chap. IX.

tion, by owners, of the place and conditions of work, hours of labor, and not infrequently of housing and medical care. These conditions foster a form of domination sometimes tempered with a paternalism which itself may be distasteful to the workers.

In order to offset these conditions, laborers have attempted to organize among themselves and to have their agents act for them in bargaining with employers. The demands of organized labor concern chiefly (*1*) rates of pay, (*2*) hours of labor, including overtime wages, Sunday and night work, (*3*) conditions of discharge, (*4*) training and employment of apprentices, (*5*) conditions of work, such as removal of machine hazards, of dust, and of insanitary conditions, (*6*) determination that only members of the union shall work, that is, the recognition of the closed shop, and (*7*) various matters of shop discipline, rules, and fines. In the wider political arena labor has stood for freedom to organize, freedom of speech, the right to strike, and for free schooling.

Driven by the desire for profits, for increased production and sales, many employers adopt a position of antagonism toward any attempts on the part of labor to coerce them. They oppose the notion of collective bargaining, hiding behind the rationalization of individual choice to hire or discharge as they will. They deny the legal right of a third party, a union organization, to bargain with them over hours, wages, or working conditions. Especially they oppose any effort on the part of the union to say who shall and who shall not work in their plant. This notion rankles deep in men who themselves with their ancestors have been soaked for two centuries or more in the attitudes of the "acquisitive society," with all its trappings of private property, inviolate from others, and the attendant attitude that one may do as he pleases with what he owns.

The Strike as a Form of Industrial Conflict. The strike is a collective refusal to work, usually directed against the employer who refuses the union demands regarding wages, hours, and other conditions. It may also be directed against non-union workmen, against rival unions, the use of non-union-made goods, or the employment of objectionable foremen, or it may be called in sympathy with some other strike already at hand.

The strike rests upon the development of a strong we-group feeling among the workers. The trade union uses all the devices of the we-group to build up solidarity. There is a distinctive aim, a formal code, a hierarchy of officers and leaders, a whole range of symbols, badges, songs, and other paraphernalia common to an organized fighting group.

Because of the more obvious features of overt action of the strike itself, the public often gets the notion that it is unduly sudden and violent. Like a political revolution, the strike is the result of a long background of tensions. The rise and development of a strike well illustrates a cycle common in conflict. The process may be traced as follows: (*1*) a more or less extended period of unrest and emotional tensions between workers and employers—especially enhanced by the organization of the workers into unions; (*2*) failure of peaceful attempts to relieve strain by methods of collective bargaining or arbitration; (*3*) mobilization for direct action; (*4*) dismissal by employers of workers suspected of fostering the strike, use of labor spies, and use of other conflict devices to prevent the strike; (*5*) frequent beclouding of the issues by the rise of personal hostilities toward leaders or officials on either side; and (*6*) the strike itself. The strike, in turn, leads to (*7*) attempts to settle by various devices: conferences, arbitration by state or other outside body; (*8*) appeals from both factions to the wider public; and (*9*) the end of the strike by some means of accommodation. (See Chapter XXIII.)

The forms of coercion attempted by both sides of the strike illustrate the culture patterns which grow up around this sort of conflict. E. T. Hiller in his volume *The Strike, A Study in Collective Action* (1928) lists 13 methods of control which employers have been known to use. Not all of these are adopted in any given strike. They are the use of labor spies, "yellow dog" contracts (agreements with workers not to join unions), discrimination against members of the union, the use of legal delays in order to allow time to prepare for an impending strike, instigation of a premature strike in order to defeat and discredit the union, bribes to union officials, propaganda for workers and public to discredit the union, stimulation of fear panics in order to stampede the workers back to their jobs, use of the black list, eviction of workers and their families from company-owned houses, expulsion from the community, giving higher wages to strike-breakers, and the use of violent coercion.

The striking union, on its part, aside from refusal to work, uses sabotage (injury to machinery and goods), picketing, boycotting (refusal to buy goods produced by open-shop employers), violence toward strike-breakers—the "scabs" of labor—and appeals to the larger public for support of its cause.

The appeal to the wider public by both sides well illustrates the use of public opinion in conflict situations. The employers use the traditional stereotypes, myths, and legends about individualism, right to hire and fire as they please, and non-interference with private property rights. They particularly rationalize their stand by using the current satanic symbols of social revolution. Since the World War the most common of these in capitalist Europe and America has been the accusation that the strike is motivated, directed, and financially supported by the Communist Party of Soviet Russia. The stereotypes of bolshevism and revolution have been used in nearly every strike in this country and abroad since 1917. It is the old device of transference of emotion from the genuine issue to some non-applicable stereotype, myth, or legend. This appeal to fear of violent change is very effective, and many strikes have been lost by workers because they had no means to set up counteracting stereotypes, myths, and legends for the wider public against those used by the employers. Considerable public sentiment was aroused against organized labor in this country during the many strikes of 1936–38. Again the old symbols of fear and of subversive Russian communist influences among the workers were used by the groups who opposed these strikes—particularly against the C.I.O., since industrial unionism appears to many to be distinctly revolutionary in aim and tactics.

The press of this country in particular is often on the side of the capitalist owners, not because of direct bribery, as is sometimes believed by workers, but rather because the newspapers are themselves capitalist enterprises owned and manned by personnel who rather thoroughly accept the traditional practice of individual bargaining, private property, and the right of employers to hire and fire.

Nevertheless the strikers themselves also use the press to appeal to the wider public. They employ the stereotypes of hunger, hard working conditions, womanhood and children, patriotism, rights of citizenship, non-resistant suffering, and appeals to humanitarian sentiments. In our society, however, the strikers usually lack publicity and propaganda organizations to carry their message to the community or nation. In contrast the owners, with financial capital at their disposal, frequently have well-developed machinery of propaganda with which to put their side of the controversy before the public—by newspapers, periodicals, radio, and newsreels.

Racial Conflict. As we saw in Chapter VIII, the term *race* is meaningless in sociology without reference to culture and social organization. Race conflict is simply a form of direct opposition involving a wide range of cultural differences into which the symbols of race and color are injected. The background of race conflict lies in the breakdown of racial and cultural isolation. So long as racial or sub-racial groups remain isolated from each other, conflict does not arise. Even contact does not necessarily give rise to conflict. There must be mobility of races in such numbers into areas occupied by other races that their presence becomes a menace to the economic and political security of the older inhabitants. So long as there are only a few Negroes in a community, who do such menial work as cleaning or garbage removal, which no white man wishes to do, conflict is not likely to arise. When the Negroes come on in such numbers as to threaten the white men's jobs, conflict begins. The contact of Orientals and whites on our Pacific coast has followed the same pattern. When the Chinese were useful for doing the white man's laundry or cooking his meals, there was no trouble, but when thousands of Chinese were introduced into California by railroad contractors as cheap labor, conflict arose.

Mobility of large numbers and economic competition are the two outstanding causes of racial conflict. These in turn may be related to the spread of various ideas and practices among colored races. The factors stimulating race conflict may be summarized as follows: (*1*) contact and mobility of races in such numbers as to dislocate the political and economic equilibrium of certain regions; (*2*) the spread of exploitative capitalism into world areas; (*3*) the spread of nationalism, especially of the ideology of democracy among colored races; (*4*) spread of ideas of brotherhood of man by Christian missionaries; and (*5*) the rise of race consciousness, frequently associated with nationalistic ambitions.

Today particular danger spots of racial antagonism develop wherever divergent races and their cultures come into competition and conflict. These are found in the United States, in South Africa, in particular areas of Asia, and, especially important to us, in the islands of the Pacific wherever different races have come into contact. As we saw in Chapter IX, rapid increases in population in some of these areas make the conflict more severe.

The antagonistic contact of divergent races finds its expression in race prejudice. Prejudice is not instinctive or inherent. The word means what it says—pre-judging an individual, his race, or group before one really knows him or his group. The attitudes of bias are always emotional. Prejudice may be positive, that is, it may be extremely favorable, tending to a blind acceptance of something or somebody. Or it may be negative, that is, tending toward dislike, fear, and condemnation of somebody or something. It is in this latter sense that we more frequently use the term.

Prejudice is expressed in certain stereotypes, myths, and legends developed by one group about another group which is *thought of as a unit*. Thus, a Negro is not first Mr. George Johnson, with a certain background of experience which sets him off as an individual in our own society, but he is first of all to many of us a Negro, a colored man, and only incidentally and perhaps not at all a person in his own right. Frequently when a Negro commits a crime or otherwise gets into the public press, the headlines and story emphasize the fact that the man is a Negro and only very incidentally refer to him as an individual. That is, he is thought of first of all as a member of a race which is supposed to possess certain typical features that mark him off from all other races.

The stereotypes, myths, and legends about groups against which we are prejudiced serve to define our relations with them. For example, current stereotypes about the Negro in the minds of the white population cover such items as the following: "inferior mentality," "primitive morality," "emotionally highly unstable," given to "crimes of violence," to "occupational instability," or to "undue religious fanaticism." The Negro is said to be "lazy," "happy-go-lucky," "boisterous," "over-assertive" when he has any power, addicted "to carrying razors for purposes of fighting," has an "undue fondness for playing with dice," wears "gaudy clothes," and "cheap, flashy jewelry."

Prejudice therefore defines the situation out of which conflict develops. An illustration of this is found in Negro-white conflict in our own Northern cities in recent decades.

Following a period of disturbance and readjustment after the Civil War, the Negro-white relations of the South took on a form of caste organization which proved workable for several decades. Then followed an economic crisis which has precipitated the struggle into a new cycle. The principal features of this, particularly with reference to the struggle in the Northern states, were the following: (*1*) demand for cheap labor in Northern industry, especially that due to the shutting down of immigration from Europe and to the demands of the World War industry; (*2*) consequent rapid migration of large numbers of Negroes from the rural South; (*3*) expansion of colored residential sections into white residential areas, produced by demands for adequate housing of Negroes; (*4*) competition with whites for work, especially during the postwar years, when strikes were common because of wage cutting; (*5*) the use of the Negroes by unscrupulous politicians who controlled their votes by traditional devices of bribery, favoritism, and petty offices; (*6*) increased crime of Negroes, produced perhaps by political, economic, and general social crises; (*7*) demand for educational and recreational facilities for colored children; and (*8*) demand for other equal rights.

The use of violence in race relations is an old culture pattern in this country. In the South since the Civil War lynching has been a common device. It is an extra-judicial act, directed at the individual who has offended against the law or moral code. Its purpose is to "keep the nigger in his place." In the North, where more stable bi-racial adjustments have not been worked out, the conflict spreads to open warfare between whites and blacks. In this struggle the entire community may become involved. Individual malefactors on either side are soon lost sight of in the larger race riot. Race riots mark the breakdown of a former accommodation or indicate a failure to arrive at some working arrangement which will meet a present crisis.

Race conflict, then, is really a cultural conflict, centering around a racial group fighting for prestige and a higher status than that to which it has formerly been accustomed. In this sense, too, the ambition or struggle of races for recognition is not unlike that of serfs seeking to become peasants, of peasants seeking to improve their economic and political condition, or of immigrants desirous of citizenship and full participation in the life of their adopted country. But unlike the serf, peasant, or immigrant, the colored person usually cannot leap the barrier of race. Conflict and accommodation are therefore inevitable in this field until biological mixture is permitted in the law and the mores.

Religious Conflict. In our modern world, religious conflict has centered around the struggle for converts and power between some of the more aggressive world religious bodies, and around the struggle of sectarian groups within the framework of these larger religious groupings.

When religious bodies, large or small, are tied up with various non-religious institutions, e. g., economic, political, or educational, the power of the organization is enhanced, and the struggle between religious bodies becomes more intense. It is not only Christianity which many Oriental religious bodies resist or oppose, but it is the link-up of Christianity with capitalism, nationalism, and educational concepts foreign to the Orient. Thus, like racial conflict, religious conflict is likely to reflect a wider cultural conflict of which it is a part.

We have already noted the widespread struggle between Christian missionaries and the Mohammedans for conversion of the native peoples in Africa. (Chapter XVII.) Wherever the Christian missionary has gone, in fact, he has come into competition and conflict with native religious organizations, or with others which have been on the ground longer.

Within a large religious body like Christianity or Mohammedanism, the break-up of factions into opposing sects is usually marked by a bitterness and severity of struggle far in excess of the former opposition toward "the world" outside. Denominational and sectarian conflicts are well illustrated in our own country. The incipient conflict is reflected in the wide-ranging religious prejudices among Catholics, Protestants, and Jews. E. S. Bogardus, reporting his observations at a round-table discussion at a National Conference of Jews and Christians held at Los Angeles, California, in October, 1931, lists the following divisive factors among these three groups:

(1) Differences in church organizations, doctrines, and forms of worship; (2) differences in church traditions, and historical clashes; (3) the fact that each group believes it is the most important expression of religion in the world; (4) the fact that the members of each group tend to generalize more on the unfavorable reports about the other groups than on the favorable reports; (5) the fact that each reacts against proselyting on the part of the others; (6) the fact that racial prejudices tend to augment religious differences; (7) the fact that social, political, and occupational discriminations increase religious differences.[2]

[2] From *Source Book* for The National Seminar of Jews, Catholics, and Protestants held at Washington, D. C., March 7–9, 1932, p. 37.

The last two factors noted above indicate how racial, economic, and political factors interplay with religious prejudices themselves to enhance religious conflict. E. A. Ross well states that "The fewer the social, political, commercial, or professional advantages church membership bestows and the greater the spiritual advantages, the better will be the feeling among the churches."[3]

Religious conflict today is far less intense, contrasted to its fury and violence in earlier centuries. The Crusades against the non-Christian infidel in the Middle Ages were bloody enough, but they were mild compared to the violence and bitterness of the Thirty Years' War between Catholic and Protestant countries of Europe or to the cruelty of sectarian strife in the British Isles during the seventeenth century.

In many Protestant denominations the sectarian struggle takes on the character of a conflict between fundamentalism and modernism or between high church and low church ritualism. There is also a conflict between Christianity and various spiritualistic or therapeutic cults or churches, such as spiritualism and theosophy.

Political Conflict. While political strife is a special province of political science, certain phases of it have a wider bearing. Moreover, political conflict reveals important features of group struggle. We shall discuss political party conflict within the national boundaries and international conflict or war between rival political states.

Party politics can arise only within a political state which permits rival groups to struggle in non-violent fashion for the control of the government. Historically, political parties have their roots in fighting groups aiming by force or revolution to seize the state. Today they aim to control the state without disrupting its essential political structure. When any party plans to alter these accepted forms of government fundamentally, we have a revolutionary party. The successful issue of their efforts is a revolution. Here we are concerned with the struggle of rival groups for power within the constitutional forms of government itself, a form of legally approved intra-national conflict. There is no party conflict possible in communist Russia today or in fascist Italy, or Nazi Germany, since these states are not organized on multiple-party lines.

Voting is a form of "paper mobilization" of latent power of the masses. As Walter Lippmann says, "The justification of majority

[3]*Op. cit.*, 3rd ed., 1938, p. 306.

rule in politics is not to be found in its ethical superiority. It is to be found in the sheer necessity of finding a place in civilized society for the force which resides in the weight of numbers."[4] And as he further says, "Government consists of a body of officials, some elected, some appointed, who handle professionally, and in the first instance, problems which come to public opinion spasmodically and on appeal."[5]

Within the party itself, however, another struggle goes on between various factions aiming at control of party policies. Since at best party organization is loose and intermittent in effectiveness, inner cliques or "rings" develop, which furnish continuity between one campaign and the next. These political factions are usually more thoroughly organized than the party itself and often, like the well-known Tammany Hall of New York City, take on the nature of secret societies, with officials, a code, and a financial budget.

Through favoritism, bribery, graft, and election or appointment of their henchmen to political office, the "ring" or clique aims not only at the control of the larger party, but at the exploitation of governmental power for their own ends. The struggle of more honest political groups against these closely knit factions has been recurrent throughout American political history. The bitterness of this struggle resembles the bitterness of the sectarian struggle within the larger religious body. So, too, the frequent success of the "ring"—except for periodic reform waves of indignation and "political house-cleaning"—demonstrates the effectiveness of intimate in-group organization in any conflict situation. The clique not only defeats its less well-organized opponents within its own party, but it often manages the campaign of the party itself more effectively than the others, simply because it is groomed for fighting.

War or International Conflict. The most intensive form of conflict in the modern world is the struggle of nations for power. The national state is a fundamental we-group in modern society. One's own country represents many of the most precious values in life. It is the dominant power group under which other groups exist: family, school, church, economic organizations, and the like. The we-group sentiments of these smaller groups get entangled

[4] From Walter Lippmann, *The Phantom Public*, 1925, p. 58. By permission of The Macmillan Company, publishers. [5] *Ibid.*, p. 72.

at many points with national sentiments. Like all conflict, war has its roots in man's emotions and in his antagonistic interaction with his fellows. But as a form of conflict in our modern world it is to be understood in terms of its culture patterns.

The causes of war are population pressure, economic competition, desire for political power, and racial and cultural conflicts. Imperialism and militarism have grown up as patterns of conflict associated with the political state. The process of conflict in war will be made clear if we examine some of the social-psychological features, especially those connected with we-group solidarity, myths, and legends.

Warfare is connected with so many things held dear by our own group that during such a time solidarity and loyalty are at their highest pitch. On the other hand, hatred and fear of the enemy or out-group is in greatest evidence. A kind of religious zeal takes hold of peoples at war. As Clark Wissler remarks in his book *Man and Culture* (1923), "Deeply rooted in the complex of militarism is the ideal of duty and adoration." And as W. G. Sumner puts it in his volume *Folkways* (1906), in a time of warfare with another nation, "virtue consists in killing, plundering, and enslaving the outsiders."

Warfare, in short, is a culture pattern fastened on us first of all by the very nature of in-group *versus* out-group interaction. Second, groups constantly build up around war itself a number of fundamental values. If war becomes the common and accepted method of settling international differences, it may become the center of the national culture.

Many writers hold that the political state arose very largely by conquest through war of one group with another.[6] Certainly in the development of the great nations of the ancient world, such as Babylonia, Assyria, Egypt, the Athenian Empire, the Alexandrian Empire, and finally the Roman Empire, this was true. Later Charlemagne conquered different units which had split off from the Roman Empire and reunited them for a time under one government. The history of modern Europe shows centuries of warfare between various contending nations for power over the others.

Myths and Legend Fostering War. Nothing is more striking

[6] See Franz Oppenheimer, *The State,* transl. by John W. Gitterman, 1914. Compare with R. H. Lowie, *The Origin of the State,* 1927.

than the place of myth and legend in fostering and encouraging the culture pattern of war, even in time of peace. We saw in Chapter II that the myth is a part of the living belief or faith of a people. It is founded upon sound utility. Its purpose is to create social solidarity and willing obedience. It is extremely powerful in developing sanctions and approvals. Aside from their origin, the nature and function of the myth and the legend are much the same. Legends and myths romanticize and sentimentalize war, and take out its sting. Every child from the cradle is told stories of national heroes and national greatness. These are among some of the earliest impressions that reach him from family, neighborhood, and community groups. The American boy or girl is given stories of George Washington not only as first president but as war general: how he whipped the British, was kind to his troops at Valley Forge, how he crossed the Delaware in a rowboat in the dead of winter, and the like. In the same manner every war produces its heroes and heroic events: Sherman's march to the sea, Wellington's defeat of Napoleon at Waterloo, Joffre's saving of France at the Marne, and so on.

The motion picture has also assisted greatly in this whole matter. Beginning about 1924, a series of World War films appeared, built around fictional persons, but nevertheless very effective in developing the sentiments for war. Such films as *What Price Glory, The Big Parade,* and *Wings,* all served the purpose of making war attractive. Curiously enough, even films that aim to carry a pacifist message often fail to do so. *Journey's End, Sergeant Grischa,* and *All Quiet on the Western Front* do not necessarily develop antiwar sentiments in the ordinary man. Rather they make war, in spite of its gruesome character, a great adventure. The vicarious pleasure and satisfaction which the audience gets probably far outweighs their revulsion and intellectual opposition to the idea of war.

In addition to history and fiction, pictorial art and sculpture also furnish us much of our war culture. Art galleries, school walls, and homes often have pictures of heroes in war dress marching into a captured camp, storming a fortress, or receiving the sword of the defeated general. Our parks and museums are filled with "marble men on horseback"—generals, principally,—who brought us success in past wars. But the common soldier is not forgotten. No one knows how many Union and Confederate soldiers stand in the

public parks and cemeteries in our land to commemorate the fallen
heroes of the Civil War. And the doughboy of the World War
is scattered over the entire landscape, not only in parks and cemeteries but also along our highways, "lest we forget" his wonderful
sacrifices to "make the world safe for democracy." So, too, in our
public parks and squares everywhere one may see the symbols of
our power—captured cannon of our former enemies: British, Mexican, Spanish, German.

Closely linked with hero worship, we find the myths of national
greatness. The nation is personified and made to symbolize all that
we hold dear as a political state. In any crisis the state becomes the
dominant we-group, and patriotic sentiments and beliefs are simply aids to make that nation all-powerful in a time of struggle with
its enemies.

Besides the myths and legends of national greatness, there are
many symbols associated with the state—the flag and the map—
symbols of what Delaisi calls the "mysticism of the frontier,"
which must be protected and preserved. Then there are the songs
and the slogans of superiority: "Britannia Rules the Waves,"
"America for Americans," "Vive la France," "Deutschland,
Deutschland über Alles, über Alles in der Welt."

Of slogans in war time, of course, there is no end: "Save the
Union," "Hang Jeff Davis to a sour apple tree," "Make the world
safe for democracy," "Can the Kaiser." The words of our national
anthem appeal to a host of deep values:

> Praise the Pow'r that hath made and preserved us a nation!
> Then conquer we must, when our cause it is just.

Not only the words but the music itself gets into the very mar-
row of our beings, so that we can never shake it off. The beat of
the drums and the swing of the rhythm set off a pleasant, an expansive and an aggressive response.

The establishment of national holidays is another favorite device for enhancing the national sense of importance. Independence
Day in our country, Dominion Day in Canada, Bastille Day in
France are examples of days on which festivals and public ceremonies are held. Speakers recite the country's great exploits, laud
its heroes, and thus arouse emotional enthusiasm. In the recitation
of the deeds of the country, the auditors relive vicariously their
country's history. This vicarious experiencing of hardships and

success is one of the most important means of giving the necessary
continuity to the myth and legend of war. When the individual
takes part in imagination in his country's history, he makes this
history a part of himself. When a crisis like war comes along,
he is thus prepared to take up arms for his nation in order to preserve the values which have been implanted in him by this previous vicarious experience.

The power of this early training in hero-worship, in belief in
national greatness, through the use of myth, legend, symbols, and
stereotypes, is such that contrary ideas and emotions brought to
bear later upon the individual have little or no effect. Previous to
the World War one could hear German workmen of socialistic inclinations berate the imperialism of the ruling Junkers in Germany, declaring solemnly that they would not take up arms
against their fellow workmen in England, France, or Belgium in
the event of war. When in the summer of 1914 the war finally
came, these same men broke down in tears when refused military
duty to defend the Fatherland because they were not officially
called to the colors at once. The same thing was true in every
country involved. In France, for instance, the socialist Gustave
Hervé was a notorious *sans patrie* (man with no loyalty to his
country), who had for years belittled patriotism and nationalism as
implements of capitalistic exploitation. He carried on a constant
attack upon his country and upon capitalism through his *La Guerre
Sociale*. When the World War broke out in 1914 and he saw that
the life of his own France was in danger, he overthrew all his
previous ideas of international socialistic brotherhood and became
one of the most intense patriots. He changed the name of his paper
to *La Victoire* and made a sensational appeal to French laboring
classes of all shades in these striking words:

"Amis socialistes, amis syndicalistes, amis anarchistes, qui n'êtes pas
seulement l'avant-garde idealiste de l'humanité; mais qui êtes encore le
nerf et la conscience de l'armée française, la patrie est en danger!

La Patrie de la Révolution est en danger!"[7]

In much the same manner in the United States in 1917 most
pacifists who had been very loud in their condemnation of war

[7]"Socialist friends, syndicalist friends, anarchist friends, you who are not only the
idealistic vanguard of humanity, but who are also the force and conscience of
the French army, our country is in danger! The country of the Revolution is in
danger!" Quoted by H. D. Lasswell, *Propaganda Technique in the World War*,
1927, p. 55.

became almost over night ardent patriots, once the country had declared war on Germany. Their enthusiasm for peace was excelled only by their intense desire to crush the enemy. Only a few pacifists had the courage to hold out against these national sentiments. For this they were persecuted and even sent to prison. When the life of the political state—the largest and most important we-group in our experience—is threatened, we seldom have any sympathy for those among us who do not follow the herd. They appear as bad as or even worse than the enemies. In some ways they seem far more dangerous than the enemy, since if we permit them their freedom they may instill disobedience in others. We must not wonder at pacifists supporting war in wartime. They, like Hervé and the other European socialists, had been so deeply conditioned to patriotic responses to their country that in a time of crisis which might destroy their own country, their international good will disappeared. We could hardly expect otherwise in the light of their training and the important place which the national state plays in modern life.

It should be clear, then, that war is a conflict with many roots, political, economic, and religious. The costs in materials and especially in human life and suffering are enormous. Its disrupting effects upon the societal structure are evident to us all, particularly since the World War. Yet its effects have not all been negative or destructive. War has been a means of diffusing culture, it is a thrilling experience for the individual, and it often results in forms of accommodation and social organization that for the time produce an improved balance between conflicting countries.

Whether war as a form of conflict will be abolished, no one can say. Certainly since the World War we have seen the growth of even more intense nationalism than was evident before that holocaust. The continued expansion of Japan, the re-emergence of Germany as a world power, the extension of Italian influence in international affairs, and the evident strong nationalistic character of present-day Russia all show that the world has far to go before open conflict, or the threat of it, will not continue for a long time to come to play an important part in the larger social processes of international adjustment. At present we can at best foster international agreements which will restrict its expression and, better still, direct emerging international conflicts into channels of arbitration or other means of peaceful settlement.

CLASS ASSIGNMENTS

A. **Further reading assignments:**

1. K. Young, *Source Book for Sociology*, chap. XXI.

2. R. E. Park and E. W. Burgess, *Introduction to the Science of Sociology*, chap. IX, especially sections I, II A, and II B.

B. **Questions and exercises:**

1. Distinguish between conflict and competition. Illustrate.

2. List a number of conflict situations in which you have participated. Analyze one of these in terms of the crisis which produced it, the tensions which followed, and the subsequent struggle and its resolution.

3. Indicate by concrete example the relations of culture, societal organization, and type of conflict situation.

4. What are the chief items in employer-employee relations which foster conflict?

5. Define prejudice. Is it instinctive? How may it be prevented?

6. Analyze a case of race or religious prejudice which you know about, showing its cultural backgrounds, the myths and legends, and its expression in action.

7. Write out your emotional reactions and ideas after witnessing a motion picture of war. Did you like the picture? If so, why? If not, why not?

8. What factors in recent world history foster war? What factors tend to reduce its place in the world today?

C. **Topics for class reports or longer written papers:**

1. Negro-white conflicts in the United States since 1914. (Consult Park and Burgess, *op. cit.*, and bibliography; E. B. Reuter, *The American Race Problem*, 1927; Charles S. Johnson, *The Negro in America*, 1929; Herman Feldman, *Racial Factors in American Industry*, 1932.)

2. Party conflicts in democratic countries. (Consult C. A. Beard, *The American Party Battle*, 1928; Viva B. Boothe, *The Political Party as a Social Process*, 1923; A. N. Holcombe, *Political Parties of Today*, 1924; Frank R. Kent, *The Great Game of Politics*, rev. ed., 1930; C. E. Merriam and H. F. Gosnell, *The American Party System*, rev. ed., 1929; Robert Michels, *Political Parties*, transl. by Eden and Cedar Paul, 1915; Samuel P. Orth, *The Boss and the Machine*, 1919; and articles on "Political Parties," *Encyclopedia of the Social Sciences*, vol. XI, pp. 589–639, and bibliography.)

3. Conflict in the economic field, including use of labor spies, the sit-down strike, and the struggle between the C.I.O. and the A.F. of L. for dominance in unionism. (Consult W. E. Atkins and H. D. Lasswell, *Labor Attitudes and Labor Problems*, 1924; E. T. Hiller, *The Strike*, 1928, and bibliography; J. R. Walsh, *C.I.O. Industrial Unionism in Action*, 1937; L. Huberman, *The Labor Spy Racket*, 1937; L. MacDonald, *Labor Problems and the American Scene*, 1938.)

CHAPTER XIX

CONFLICT—*Continued*

In this chapter we shall complete our treatment of the forms of conflict, take up the broader problem of the relations of conflict to culture and to societal organization, and close with a discussion of conflict and personality.

OTHER FORMS OF CONFLICT

There remain for discussion those forms of conflict growing up out of the community situation, out of class, age, and sex contacts, and out of the struggle over impersonal ideas.

Inter-Community Conflicts. When the groups in opposition have as their focus the most dominant values of a community, we may speak of community conflict. It is illustrated by the clash between agriculture and industry, symbolized by the rural *versus* the urban community. It is seen in the larger struggle between primary group culture and secondary group culture.

The city has played a less important part in history than has the country. The bulk of the population has until recently lived on the land, and it is only natural that the dwellers on the soil should look askance at their city cousins. Thomas Jefferson (1743–1826) well expressed some of the feeling of the eighteenth century on this question when he said:

"The mobs of the great cities add just so much to the support of pure government as sores do to the strength of the human body. . . . Cultivators of the earth are the most valuable citizens. They are the most vigorous, the most dependent, the most virtuous, and they are tied to their country and wedded to its liberties by the most lasting bonds. . . ."[1]

Urban-rural conflict is largely a cultural struggle resulting from the breakdown of isolation and the interplay of new forces of cul-

[1] Quoted by C. A. Beard, "The City's Place in Civilization," *Survey*, Nov. 15, 1928, vol. LXI, p. 213.

ture with the old. The conflict is expressed on nearly all fronts, economic, political, religious, educational, and moral.

Among the more common economic factors which give rise to such conflict are: (*1*) belief of rural dwellers that city merchants aim to "gouge" them; (*2*) the economic power of city banks and loan companies which charge high rates of interest or commissions for lending money; (*3*) insufficient prices paid the farmer for his produce, and especially, the antagonism toward the middleman.

During periods of economic depression, farmers come into open conflict with the urban business interests. Their inability to pay their debts leads them to advocate cheap money, inflation, or other devices to raise prices. They may actually resort to violence, as they did during the depression following 1930, when armed crowds of farmers prevented sheriffs' sales of mortgaged goods, or when they actually invaded the courtrooms in Middle-Western county seats and tried to prevent legal judgment against their friends. It was in an effort to secure higher prices that the Farmers' Holiday Association was formed in the Middle West during the summer of 1933. The object was to withhold farm products from the market for 30 days in the hope of raising prices. On July 30, 1933, a strike was formally called. Farmers picketed roads leading into several cities, milk was dumped, and some violence against persons occurred. In some states the national guard was called out to quell the rioting.

As an expression of the resentment of the farmers against city merchants in their own regions, rural people have gone in for mail-order shopping with firms in the larger metropolitan centers. They have also developed agricultural co-operatives of various sorts, both for purchasing goods and for selling produce. The latter, of course, is aimed at the middleman rather than the retail merchant.

The rural dweller resents the heavy tax burden which he carries. Farmers frequently believe that rural areas are taxed to benefit the cities. Although this is not necessarily true, the stereotype again influences the behavior. As to local government, the country citizens often feel that they are not sufficiently well represented, although frequently the cities of a county have less political power in county government than have the rural sections.

For the most part, country people are more conservative in their religious and moral ideas than are city people. In the struggle of fundamentalism *versus* modernism, the rural church members tend to support the former, while the urban members incline to more liberal views. Simply because the city symbolizes the "world" and "sin," rural folks sometimes prefer their small, poorly manned open-country churches to better managed city churches which are easily accessible. The changing personal morality of the world outside is gradually encroaching upon the time-worn ideas and practices of country people. The rural young people, especially, are carrying this conflict directly into the homes of their parents.

In educational matters, too, the rural areas have been slow to fit the school system to a world of rapid communication and travel and to the modern economic and political order outside. The persistence of one- and two-room schoolhouses in some of our more enlightened states is but an evidence of the strong locality feeling which is aroused at every threat from the larger government to encroach on their traditional legal rights.

The rapid intrusion of urban culture into the country districts, however, is modifying the intensity of this conflict. If modern business methods are thrust into agriculture, many of the older customs of the farmer will disappear, his ideology will become urbanized, and while the conflict may not disappear, it will shift into the arena of industrial, business, or other economic conflict in which the locality features will not count.

Intra-community Conflicts. At times conflict of interests within the community may disrupt its equilibrium and destroy its solidarity. An employer-laborer conflict like a strike may temporarily disrupt a community. More often these community struggles represent factional fights of a different sort. One of the commonest is the antagonism which rends a community between the east-siders and the west-siders, or the north-siders against the south-siders. Many cities have grown largely by the merging of separate communities, and old rivalries appear later in the political and economic struggles within the community. For instance, a proposal to erect a municipal auditorium or a new high-school building may so arouse the fighting spirit of the citizens that the project will be lost in the bitterness of the debate as to where the building shall be located. Representation in the city council may be so unequal that one section of the city puts up a continuous fight until the city is more justly redistricted.

Sometimes a community is divided by religious differences. Occasionally the appearance of an intensive revival campaign, originally participated in by most of the Protestant churches, will end by splitting the town into warring camps of fundamentalists and modernists. Religious differences have led to conflict in the educational system over the employment of teachers of one denomination or another or the accusation that teachers were injecting religion into the schools.

Occasionally, a community has been divided over the management of the school system. School strikes in some of our American cities have on occasion led to intense bitterness and a destruction of community good will. Intra-community conflict like rivalry within the family needs to be limited and regulated in the interests of the group solidarity. Otherwise it will disrupt the entire group.

Class and Intra-Class Conflict. The *class struggle* implies the breakdown of a particular equilibrium which has grown up among the classes. Where one class—military, political, ecclesiastical, or economic—has come to dominate a society, the whole societal structure may be ordered in reference to this. But a crisis, like the Industrial Revolution, a new religion, or a war, may bring about tensions and unrest leading to an attempt by other classes to overthrow the dominance of the class at the top. The laity may demand from the dominant clergy more participation in the management of religious matters. This was partially the case with the Protestant Reformation. The whole Catholic theology and hierarchy rested upon the theory and practice of a dominant clergy and a submissive laity. This thesis Martin Luther and others challenged. The Industrial Revolution in Germany in the nineteenth century undermined the dominance of the landed gentry in favor of the rising bourgeois class. In our modern world, the most striking class conflict has been the economic and political struggle of the rising proletariat against the bourgeois capitalist class.

The intensity of class conflict, like other conflict, depends upon the range and depth of interests involved. One reason racial and international conflicts are so significant is that they involve basic culture patterns around which intense emotional values have grown up. So it is in class struggles. If a wide range of interests, economic, political, religious, familial, and moral, can be linked up with class struggle, it will become the all-absorbing form of opposition in any society.

This is precisely what the dogmas of Karl Marx and his communist followers do. Marx's theory of history holds for a universal and continuous struggle of the workers against exploitation by the owners of capital goods, every other important feature of culture being predetermined by the economic relations of workers and owners. He interpreted history in the ideology of the class struggle, which became the peg on which he hung all forms of conflict. Marx and his collaborator Friedrich Engels (1820–1895) say in their pamphlet *Manifesto of the Communist Party* (1848), "The history of all past society has consisted in the development of class antagonisms, antagonisms that assumed different forms at different epochs." This was expressed in history not only in economics but also in religion and politics. The modern period is marked by the attempt of the proletariat "to wrest, by degrees, all capital from the bourgeois, to centralize all instruments of production in the hands of the State, *i.e.*, of the proletariat organized as the ruling class."

Yet the aim of the class struggle, in the end, is a classless society, in which political power will give way to a true democracy of unselfish individualism. They say:

"When, in the course of development, class distinctions have disappeared, and all production has been concentrated in the hands of a vast association of the whole nation, the public power will lose its political character. Political power, properly so called, is merely the organized power of one class for oppressing another. If the proletariat during its contest with the bourgeoisie is compelled, by the force of circumstances, to organize itself as a class, if, by means of a revolution, it makes itself the ruling class, and, as such, sweeps away by force the old conditions of production, then it will, along with these conditions, have swept away the conditions for the existence of class antagonisms, and of classes generally, and will thereby have abolished its own supremacy as a class.

"In place of the old bourgeois society, with its classes and class antagonisms, we shall have an association, in which the free development of each is the condition for the free development of all."[2]

Thus, just as the foundations for international warfare are built up in every nation in terms of their own myths and legends of national greatness and destiny, so the communists have produced their myths and legends. Like all such ideologies they aim to explain the past and the present as a means of directing the future. The communists hope to enlist the workers of the world in one

[2] Karl Marx and Friedrich Engels, *Manifesto of the Communist Party*, transl. by Engels, Charles H. Kerr edition, 1917, p. 42.

grand class struggle to end all exploitation and class organization.

Intra-class conflict is a form of struggle between those who are members of a larger group and who accept some common premises of behavior. It is never so violent or destructive as inter-class conflict. Within the wide class of aristocracy, for example, there is always rivalry and conflict for status, jealousy for honors and privileges. Within the working classes there is struggle for jobs, status, and advancement. The interests of unskilled workers conflict with those of the skilled. So-called native American laborers have periodically opposed the demands of immigrant workers for a larger share of the jobs and the pay. Within the races themselves there is often an intense struggle for improvement. The mulatto is opposed by the pure black, who is jealous of the former's achievements. Within the sect or denomination the members may carry on an intense campaign for power. In short, intra-class conflict is but another term for factional fights within any we-group, which itself may be at odds with some other group.

Sex and Age Conflicts. In discussing differentiation later, in Chapter XXI, we shall see that age and sex differences play a part in setting the rôle and status of any population. Conflict of the sexes breaks out whenever the customary rôles are threatened. These customary relations naturally reflect the culture of the time and place. Problems of sex conflict in modern society have concerned themselves principally with political and economic rights. The chief points of the struggle of the sexes have been (*1*) for the ballot and for full participation in citizenship; (*2*) for full, equal property and contract rights; (*3*) for equal occupational opportunities; (*4*) for education; and (*5*) for common morality for both sexes.

Sex conflict is not likely to be as intense and as widespread as many other forms of conflict. First of all, the formation of strong we-groups in terms of sex can occur only within limited range. Women may organize a political party, a club, or possibly some occupational association. None of these reaches as deeply into basic interests as do the broader and more general industrial, racial, nationalistic, or class groupings involving both sexes. As E. A. Ross says, "Sex conflict is never grim and engulfing like conflicts between races or classes."[3] Men and women have too much in common in their respective functions in the family, in the church,

[3] E. A. Ross, *Principles of Sociology*, rev. ed., 1930, p. 196.

in the community, to allow the struggle to become all engrossing at the expense of these other attachments.

In both primitive and higher societies old age has tended to hold the reins of power. Yet as family, clan, class, and caste regulations break down in favor of an open-class system, young people strive to wrest power from their elders. The direction of age conflict depends upon the societal system and the culture. If the old men of a tribe hold the dominant control through knowledge and superior experience, a man must wait long before he falls heir to social power. In more complex societies, especially in times of rapid change, young men often have a chance to assume leadership. E. B. Gowin in his book *The Executive and His Control of Men* (1915) has shown that in modern history younger men have tended to assume control in times of crisis. Thus the Puritan Revolution in England (c. 1640–1660) was led by men whose average age was 42 years, while in calmer times English history has been guided by men well in the sixties or above. The dozen chief leaders of the French Revolution averaged 38 years of age, while the average age of French political officials and leaders in quieter times was about 59 years. The French revolutionary generals of 1793 were all young men, in contrast to the tradition-bound generals of the counter-revolutionary armies of England, Prussia, Spain, Italy, and Austria. Likewise our own American revolution was managed by men whose average age was under 40 years.

Marx was 29 years old and Engels 27 when they wrote the *Manifesto*. Many post-war revolutionary movements in Europe demonstrate the rôle of younger men in the agitation for change. Mussolini was 39 years old when his Black Shirts marched on Rome; and Hitler was 44 when he became dictator of Germany.

Not only in the arena of politics but also in economic life young men are constantly pressing on older men for control. In the history of great fortunes in this country, the rapid rise of relatively young men to positions of financial power is well known. In a rapidly expanding economic society like nineteenth-century America there was room for both youth and old age.

Nevertheless the increase of people in the middle and upper years due to changes in birth and death rates may foster age conflict. (See Chapter X on age changes.) Middle age and old age are likely to "sit tight" in their positions of power, and young men coming up the economic and political ladder may have to cool their heels for years before they secure these desirable places, unless in open conflict the elders are dislodged. J. B. S. Haldane, the British biologist, in his *Science in the Changing World* (1933), takes the view that the inflexibility of old age in positions of economic and political control is an important factor in retarding our solution of the pressing economic, political, and other social problems of the present. He reminds us that the average age of the British cabinet of 1932 was 57 years. None of the members was under 40 years, and nine of the 20 were over three score. The Hoover cabinet when it went out of office had an average age of 61 years, and the cabinet of Franklin D. Roosevelt at the time of its formation averaged 58 years.

Yet with the very changes which have increased the ratio of men in the middle years of life are associated cultural changes which require that a man must spend longer years than formerly in professional schooling before he is considered ready to assume leadership in medicine, law, teaching, engineering, or business. Then, too, age is not so absolutely correlated with conservatism as Haldane implies. Flexibility of viewpoint is rather the result of training than of years. Haldane tends to fall into the error of those who "explain" complex social and cultural factors in terms of biology rather than of psychology and sociology.

In any case age conflict, like sex conflict, is not likely to be so intense as are other forms which involve strong we-group *versus* others-group antagonisms. Age conflict would hardly prevent capitalist owners and leaders, no matter what their age differences, from sticking together against the revolutionary aims of communist or socialist labor. The struggle of age for power will tend to be confined within the particular we-group, be it racial, economic, political, or religious. The demands for the larger group solidarity against opposing groups will serve to limit the extent and intensity of age conflict itself. The struggle of age resembles the factional fights within a trade union, a sect, or a political clique, rather than the conflict between two strongly entrenched we-groups.

Conflict of Impersonal Ideas. The struggle for objective, impersonal principles is farthest removed from the direct, personal sort; yet it represents a cultural competition or conflict of great importance. It is best illustrated in the controversies of philosophy, and particularly in those of science. In theory, at least, these types of conflict are removed from the emotional and subjective attitudes of the individual. The arena of the conflict is supposed to be intellectual and impersonal. In all of them, of course, the personal feelings of the advocates may and do enter.

In the conflict of ideas, the person fights not for himself but for the objective principle. The ego is sacrificed on the altar of truth. The logic of the situation alone is supposed to determine the victor. The struggle of scientific findings must always end in complete victory for one or the other, given the same premises and methods from which the contest takes off. In this impersonal struggle there can be, theoretically, at least, no accommodation or assimilation. There can be only complete success or failure. Nevertheless, even in the world of philosophy and science, compromises do take place, especially in the form of suspension of hostilities until further facts are forthcoming. And in some cases two apparently contradictory principles are sometimes fused together into new ones which combine the evidently soundest features of the opposing ideas. Or even more striking, rather contradictory ideas are shown to be logically correct within the limits of their premises.[4]

This struggle in terms of principles, not personalities, has, however, two interesting implications. One concerns the use of this device in other sorts of conflict. The other has to do with the attempts to prevent the battle of impersonal ideas from taking place.

One source of strength in the Marxian argument of Nikolaii Lenin (1870–1924) lies in his contention that the whole communist philosophy is a matter of principles without respect to persons. Such a stand makes it possible to carry forward the revolutionary struggle in a long-time campaign unhindered by compromises or half measures. A group of revolutionaries who adopt a set of absolute principles assumed to be objective have the advantage of removing themselves from concern with mere individuals or groups who stand in their way. In their march to power they sweep everything and everybody aside. They do not hesitate to sacrifice themselves for the "cause," for it is divinely appointed.

[4] For example, the conflict of Darwinism and Lamarckianism or of heredity *versus* environment have led to certain new views on the problems of changes in the species. In modern physics, to mention another field, the dispute as to whether light consisted of particles or waves seems to be answered in terms of the mathematical premises and the form of experimentation. Both these theories now appear to be supported by sound experiment, depending on the standpoint from which the physicist approaches his problem. See Arthur H. Compton's review of this matter, "What Is Light?", *Sigma Xi Quarterly*, 1929, vol. XVII, pp. 14–33.

They have the fervor of the Christian martyrs who died for their religious principles.

The same thing applies to any fighting group. Let them but adopt the belief that their cause is absolute, divine, and cosmic in purpose, and their struggle will be all the more ruthless and uncompromising. Romain Rolland, the French novelist, has clearly pointed out the merciless character of the World War—"a war to end war." Such a struggle, he contended, was bound to be marked by extreme ruthlessness and persistence to the bitter end, simply because it was for an absolute principle larger than the personal interests of the combatants. For him an open war for material aggrandizement was likely to be much more humane and to end in an accommodation in which both sides get something out of the struggle.

The attempt to block the development of impersonal ideas and the inevitable struggle of these against traditional views has been admirably described by E. A. Ross in his *Principles of Sociology*, 3rd ed., 1938, in discussing the "conflict between the learned and the ignorant." He points out that the ignorant masses, especially under the leadership of rabble-rousers among the economic, political, or religious groups, are likely to thwart the efforts of the learned to promulgate their objective investigations and to confront tradition and custom with their findings, and thus to lay the foundation of a more sensible social order.

CONFLICT, CULTURE, AND THE SOCIETAL ORDER

It should be evident from the discussion just completed that conflict, like competition and co-operation, plays a distinctive part in setting up and in maintaining societal organization. We shall but draw together a few of the outstanding features, since the concrete details are already before us.

The Culture Patterns of Conflict. Although conflict is a universal process, it always takes place in a social situation affected by a particular culture. The form of conflict will be affected by the nature of the group and the individual interrelations. Where there is no class organization of society, there can be no class conflict. Where the economic order is simple in form and relatively non-exploitative, as in the Middle Ages, group economic conflicts are not likely to arise. In contrast, the Middle Ages was a period

when religious and political struggles occurred frequently, since
these two interests were the battleground of contending forces.
Family feuds are the order of the day in the primitive conditions of
our Southern mountaineers, but nothing of this sort exists in the
urban American family. Dueling was once a gentleman's way of
settling an insult. Today this mode of conflict is taboo.

Not only is the form of conflict modified by the particular societal order and the culture, but everywhere there arise regulations
to govern it. In the feud there are certain accepted methods for
killing the other fellow. Lynching follows a certain tradition.
Where the conflict is infrequent and where no adequate techniques
are worked out, more violent forms and unpredictable sorts of
conflict behavior arise, as in race riots. In war, of course, there
are all sorts of rules more or less agreed upon by the belligerents
during the interludes of peace. Litigation and the conflict of impersonal ideas have the most severe rules of all. The former are
those laid down by the law, which in theory is impersonal and just
to all. In the struggle of philosophic and scientific ideas the rules
are those of logic and scientific method. All personal interest of
a subjective sort is supposed to be absent.

Conflict and Societal Organization. While conflict as a form
of opposition is more violent and direct than competition, it is
not destructive of the societal structure. Some sociological writers
hold that conflict is always divisive and destructive of the "best"
society. This is not so. Conflict, like competition, is an inevitable
outgrowth of social interaction, resting as it does upon deep-seated
emotions and ego interests of the individual. It is in basic contrast
to co-operation and sympathy. Opposition and co-operation are
both fundamental to the societal order.

It is in conflict and competition that we-groups achieve unity
and solidarity. This they can do only by standing in a relationship
of opposition to some other group or principle. The very strength
of in-group loyalty and mutuality depends partly on the strength
of opposition toward some object outside the group.

Within the we-group also, from the family, neighborhood, primary community up into the wide range of secondary groupings,
rivalry as a form of conflict is inevitable and common. While the
person-to-person struggle for status tends to be regulated in the
interest of the larger good of the we-group, there is personal antagonism just the same.

There are two features of the conflict in relation to the societal organization which need special mention. These concern the intensity and the extent of conflict, and the advantages of sublimated conflict in a complex society.

The strength or *intensity of conflict* depends upon whether it is concentrated within narrow interests and centered in one or two groups or extended over a number of interests and many groups. As we noted in discussing racial, class, and other struggles, if conflict can be linked with a wide range of interests, it will be more intense, more lasting, and more fundamental. It is like the rivalries of the individual. If these concern his deepest drives, sex, hunger, and self-preservation, he will fight for them more vigorously than if they concern only highly tenuous matters like taste in art or fashion. One reason why sex and age conflicts are not likely to be so vigorous lies in the fact that there are too many counteractants in the social order to allow sharp and deep lines of cleavage to develop to the exclusion of other factors which unite the sex and age groupings.

Conflict ranges from the more violent, destructive sort, which is personally all-engrossing and bitter, like the feud, to that which is highly sublimated, regulated, and impersonal in character. As an expression of opposition, this *sublimated conflict*, like regulated competition, is preferable to the cruder and less moralized sort. In our complex society, with its extensive division of social labor and with its increasing domination by secondary group organization, the sublimated forms of opposition are much more effective. They preserve the order and solidarity which is so essential without disrupting the total balance and on-going activity of society. As Frederick A. Bushee puts it, "While division of labor is, in the first place, primarily a result of struggle, in its perfection it serves to attenuate conflict, because it makes the interference of individuals less direct. Even international or territorial division of labor, while not removing all causes of group conflict, must be recognized as a powerful force in the promotion of unity."[5]

Furthermore, conflict is in its very nature intermittent. It arises by virtue of some crisis or disturbance of interests. The sublimated and milder forms of conflict therefore are not so divisive of solidarity nor so consuming of energy. Still they make possible a somewhat more continuous opposition, which is essential to the

[5] Frederick A. Bushee, *Principles of Sociology*, 1923, p. 460.

putting forth of our best efforts in playing our various social rôles. What we want is not over-intense, violent, emotional conflict followed by apathy or defeat, but sufficient continuous stimulation through competition and sublimated conflict to keep us alert and efficient, and at just that heightened sense of difference that makes for dynamic living.

CONFLICT AND PERSONALITY

We are all profoundly affected by contact with others. Our training in mutual identification constantly tends to pull us in the direction set up by wishes of others. Still, by the expression of opposition, the demands of our own ego prevent this from going too far. Opposition sets up a sense of difference, a mental or social distance, which preserves us from the inroads of other personalities, until their demands are integrated with our own. Thus conflict sets up a kind of buffer between ourselves and others that preserves our integrity.

Furthermore conflict, with its strong emotional appeal, affords us a tremendous personal satisfaction. Even the struggle for impersonal ideas has emotionally a great value. There is in conflict a sort of catharsis, a freeing of pent-up emotions and repressions. This is one reason why fighting is so thrilling. Let us examine some of these features more closely as regards the identification of the individual with the symbols of the in-group and the out-group, and the integration of the personality in conflict itself. Since accommodation is the logical outcome of conflict, the personality aspects of resolving conflicts will be postponed until we have treated accommodation. Here we shall examine only the personality factors which appear during conflict proper.

Integration of the Person in Conflict. We have already noted many instances of the strength of conflict in terms of the breadth of the interests involved. For the personality this means that those conflicts which appeal to the person's deeper attitudes, ideas, and habits will influence him more than those conflicts which touch only superficial attitudes. Race, religion, the national state and its preservation, economic status, and community solidarity—these seem in our culture more important than class conflicts, or those of age, sex, or impersonal ideas of science and philosophy.

As we saw in Chapter VI, whenever one's ideas, attitudes, and habits are linked up with a strong in-group—out-group relation, there we get a balance or integration of personality. The whole function of conflict in relation to personality integration can best be illustrated by examining it in relation to war. Although war represents an extreme form of conflict, the relation developed between the person and the outside situation applies to other forms of conflict in a lesser degree.

Personal jealousies of a more intimate sort disappear in time of war. People are flooded with the suggestion of fellow feeling for all citizens of all classes. Members of the same household who may ordinarily be rivalrous for family power become amenable to reason and co-operate in the common project. Opposition, dislike, and hatred among neighbors, business rivals, and political opponents are forgotten in the face of the common enemy who threatens solidarity. All unite in a common cause. Everyone is full of patriotism, love of country, and good will toward one's fellow citizens. The man on the street may be taxed to the limit for support of the war. He willingly gives himself and his sons and daughters for war service. He is thrilled with religious fervor for the aims of his leaders. Slogans, myths, and legends sweep over him, and he identifies himself with the acts of brutality and the heroism of his fellows. He is like one reborn. He feels that he is performing great deeds. He is responsible, with his fellow citizens, for success of the venture.

Let us look now at the other side of this picture. What are the attitudes and habits developed toward the out-group, which serve as a balance to this thrill of patriotic love and co-operation with members of the national in-group? How does the individual integrate or correlate his intense hatred and fear of the enemy with his love and sympathy for his fellows? There is a strong desire to defeat and even to destroy the enemy. They contain only evil. Their leaders are satanic. Their national plans are thoroughly diabolical. As we look back calmly on the World War days, it is hard to understand the intensity of the hysteria which developed in this country toward Germany and Austria. In the same way the citizens of these latter countries blamed the Allies for all their troubles and had, from their own standpoint, equally valid reasons for fearing and hating their enemies. Each side drew up imposing lists of charges of demonism against the enemy: violation of international agreements regarding civilian private property, neutrality, indulgence in rape and cruelty to civilians, and so on.[6] No matter how ridiculous or absurd these charges may seem to others, to the patriots during war they are "facts" and "truth." So, too, cartoons, pictures of atrocities, movies, and all sorts of stories and public lectures were used to inflame the citizen against the enemy.

From the angle of the personality, love, sympathy, and kindlier attitudes are all directed toward the we-group and its ideals. The antagonistic emotions and attitudes of dislike, disgust, fear, and hatred are all drained off toward the members of the out-group and the values they symbolize. A balance or ambivalence of opposite emotions is struck, which is so well typified in all in-group *versus* out-group relations. There is no check on the unlimited hatred of a national enemy as there is ordinarily in we-group *versus* out-group relations. Rather one's fellows, all hating in the same manner, give open approval to extreme violence. As Ernst Lissauer, the German poet, put it in the "Hymn of Hate," the sentiments which are common to all strong in-groups in every war:

"We love as one, we hate as one.
We have one foe and one alone."

There is another emotional satisfaction in this experience. In our daily life we develop irritations and antagonistic attitudes toward other people in our own society. We dare not express our anger and hatred too openly or too fully to our in-group rivals or even to those out-group rivals who exist within the larger national framework. But when a war comes along we have an amazing opportunity to drain off our most vicious and unsocialized attitudes upon other national groups as objects of opposition and hatred. This transference of more personal hatreds and antagonisms to public objects is a psychological factor which critics of war too often neglect or do not understand.

Emotionally war gives us something else. One of man's deepest wishes is to express his emotions freely and without restraint. By the very ambivalence of hate and love just described we are able to accomplish just this, and at the same time. Such an integration of love and hatred is possible only in conflict, where the two opposite emotions are directed upon two simultaneous objects. Ordinarily at any given time we are supposed, because of social conditioning, to inhibit either our love or our anger. We express

[6]See H. D. Lasswell, *Propaganda Technique in the World War,* 1927, pp. 85–86.

either one or the other, not both at once. In war time we may experience both. Psychologically these two divergent trends probably interact in the organism to heighten the intensity of both.

Finally, one of man's deepest wishes is to get something for nothing emotionally. That is, he wishes to have a great emotional expansion without having to pay for it later by social disapproval and by self-inflicted punishment through his conscience. In a war situation, he has just this sort of experience. This is especially true of the ordinary citizen or the soldier under drill and instruction. Whether any such satisfaction comes from the actual killing of others in modern warfare is probably doubtful. Under primitive conditions it probably was true. Yet the heroism, the stimulation from adoring thousands, and all the social suggestion of one's fellow countrymen may make the actual killing seem holy and proper and absolve him from all personal blame.

This balance of hatred and love constitutes one of the important psychological advantages of all conflict. In the light of this profound effect upon the individual, the student of conflict must reckon with this fact in any attempts he may make to ameliorate or abolish conflict of any kind, including war. War in its cruelties seems unbelievably inhuman and brutal, in the effects of shell-shock, in crippled bodies, to say nothing of the loss of life and the suffering of noncombatants, or the economic and political disorder it produces. But when we see the power of cultural training on the one hand, and the balance of hate and love which goes with it, one wonders whether we shall ever escape war as a form of conflict. Certainly it is doubtful whether we can abolish conflict as a social process. The areas of conflict may change, but as a process it is as fundamental as co-operation and competition.

CLASS ASSIGNMENTS

A. Further reading assignment:

   1. K. Young, *Source Book for Sociology*, chap. XXII.

   2. R. E. Park and E. W. Burgess, *Introduction to the Science of Sociology*, chap. IX, especially sections II C, II D, and III.

B. Questions and exercises:

   1. What situations produce conflicts between communities? What ones allay them?

   2. Illustrate situations which produce intra-community conflicts.

   3. What are the basic appeals in the Marxian concepts of class struggle?

What factors in modern industrial society does the Marxian theory neglect or ignore?

4. What changes in the age composition of our population are stimulating age conflict? Note especially the significance of various programs for old-age security.

5. Why are age and sex conflicts likely to be less severe than those involving economic, religious, or political differences?

6. What kinds of conflict situations are disappearing from modern society and what kinds are on the increase? Account for these changes in terms of the larger changes within culture and societal organization.

7. Discuss the methods by which the individual settles those internal conflicts which largely reflect the social conflicts outside. Use some concrete instance of conflict as a basis for your discussion.

C. Topics for class reports or longer written papers:

1. Class conflict in the modern world. (Consult Karl Marx, *Kapital*, transl. by C. and E. Paul, 1928; Karl Marx and Friedrich Engels, *Manifesto of the Communist Party*, 1917 ed. by Charles H. Kerr; Louis Levine, *Syndicalism in France*, 2nd rev. ed., 1914; Paul F. Brissenden, *The I. W. W., A Study of American Syndicalism*, 1919, and bibliography; Nikolaii Lenin, *The State and Revolution*, 1924; Lewis L. Lorwin, *Labor and Internationalism*, 1929; the following articles in *Encyclopedia of the Social Sciences:* Morris Ginsberg, "Class Consciousness," vol. III, pp. 536–38, and Lewis L. Lorwin, "Class Struggle," vol. III, pp. 538–42, and bibliography; H. D. Lasswell, *World Politics and Personal Insecurity*, 1935.)

2. Conflict and the societal order. (Consult R. E. Park and E. W. Burgess, *Introduction to the Science of Sociology*, chap. IX, and bibliography; C. A. Dawson and W. E. Gettys, *Introduction to Sociology*, 1st ed., 1929, chap. X; N. J. Spykman, *The Social Theory of Georg Simmel*, 1925.)

CHAPTER XX

CO-OPERATION

As we have already noted in Chapter XVII, opposition and co-operation are basic though contrary (ambivalent) processes. They arise together whenever individuals come into contact. As A. W. Small (1854–1926) says in his *General Sociology* (1905), "Struggle and co-operation are correlates in every situation." Some writers would make struggle or opposition the fundamental social process. Others would make co-operation the basic process. There are also writers who use the term co-operation as a synonym for almost any social contact. For example, they contend that opponents in fighting must "co-operate" in order to exchange blows. In this sense traders must co-operate in order to exchange goods. Some writers even discuss organization of employers and workers to settle labor difficulties as a form of co-operation. This is rather a phase of accommodation. Obviously opposition (competition and conflict) and co-operation both arise in contact, but the term co-operation is meaningless if it is used in the broad general sense of any interaction. We must limit co-operation to a more specific meaning.

THE NATURE OF CO-OPERATION

Co-operation occurs in nature as well as in human society. A brief review of its place among plants and animals will serve as a basis for examining its place in human society. We shall discuss co-operation first as a form of mutual aid.

Mutual Aid in Nature. The interdependence set up between species is really a form of co-operation, although in nature this adaptation of species to species is not conscious in our human sense. This interdependence is often necessary to the survival of various species. Here the struggle for existence gives way to co-operation for maintaining life. Among plants and animals we may find veritable colonies built up for mutual support.

W. J. McGee, the naturalist (1853–1912), cites the case of how a mesquite springs up on a desert plain, how very shortly birds nest in its branches, and how they, in turn, drop the seeds of cacti which grow up and entwine with the mesquite. Grass seeds lodge around the roots and grow in the shelter of the mesquite and cacti. Still later, insects and rodents burrow into the sod and thus permit the scanty rains to water the plants, and so on, until a true community of plant and animal life is found. As McGee summarizes the matter: "A large part of the plants and animals of the desert dwell together in harmony and mutual helpfulness; . . . for their energies are directed not so much against one another as against the rigorous environmental conditions growing out of the dearth of water."[1]

This sort of co-operation is called *symbiosis* or *commensalism*. Symbiosis means literally "living together." One writer describes it as a "systematic, intimate, and laborious" partnership or as "systematic biological co-operation." Symbiosis among different species is found widely in nature and has been described by many writers in biology and sociology.[2]

The matter, however, goes further. What about mutual aid among members of the same species? Is the struggle and competition among members of the same species all that Charles Darwin and especially some of his followers implied? Certainly Darwin made clear the fact that struggle among members of the same and nearly related species is frequently more intense than the struggle between more remote species. In fact, according to him, interdependence arises as a rule only among the more distantly related animals. This statement may well be challenged so far as it concerns many species. Co-operation and mutual aid are distinct phases of the associative life among the animals. Co-operation goes, in fact, directly to the heart of gregariousness and sociability.

Among animals co-operation is found principally in sexual activity, feeding, in mutual protection, and in the care and training of the young. It is also evident in a certain crude division of labor in some species. Some aspects of this mutual aid among the animals we have already noted in discussing group life. (See Chapter I.) In short, co-operation and its related activities of sympathy and love as well as opposition and struggle are found in nature.

---

[1] Quoted by K. Young, *Social Psychology*, p. 16, from original article, W. J. McGee, "The Beginnings of Agriculture," *American Anthropologist*, vol. VIII, pp. 350–75.
[2] Some excellent examples from various writers are found in R. E. Park and E. W. Burgess, *Introduction to the Science of Sociology*, 1921, chap. III, pp. 169–72, 175–84.

Co-operation in Human Society. We need not posit an instinct of sociability or gregariousness in order to explain co-operation. The facts of interaction, especially in reference to the family alone, parent to parent, child to child, child to parent, furnish sufficient ground upon which to construct the co-operative social order which we find everywhere. Beyond the family, the neighborhood, the play group, and the whole set of secondary groups call for co-operation. *Human co-operation* is a form of interaction of two or more persons striving toward some goal or end which may be shared, either in material goods, in prestige, or in self-satisfaction.

The development of irrigation projects in the arid West is an excellent example of conscious co-operation. For instance, when the Mormons settled in the western valleys bordering on the Great Salt Lake Desert, it became absolutely necessary for them to co-operate in order to get water for their crops. Usually a group of farmers organized into an association or corporate body with the intention of developing a water system of their own. Water had to be drawn off the mountain streams by dams and canals and often brought long distances before it could be distributed over the parched land. Moreover, in the distribution of this limited water supply it was highly important that all co-operate in abiding by the rules laid down by the group. This illustrates C. H. Cooley's point that:

"Co-operation . . . arises when men see that they have a common interest, and have, at the same time, sufficient intelligence and self-control to seek this interest through united action: perceived unity of interest and the faculty of organization are the essential facts in intelligent combination."[3]

Co-operation is expressed along a scale from the unconscious, natural interaction found in the gregariousness of animals and man to the more deliberate and controlled co-operation of man at his rational level. The more or less spontaneous mutual protection found in gregariousness is seen in man or animals huddling together against the storm, in moving across a territory together, and in other sorts of mutual aid in which there is but a minimum of organization. From this we pass to those forms of mutual aid and co-operation in which some sort of order arises. The very

[3] C. H. Cooley, *Sociological Theory and Social Research.* 1930, p. 176.

process of interaction tends to develop division of labor and more efficient movement to the common aim, until we reach the carefully planned co-operation found in our complex social organization.

FORMS OF CO-OPERATION

The most obvious fields of conscious co-operation in our modern society concern economic and political behavior. But co-operation in the fields of religion and science is not to be neglected. The interplay of various processes and the culture of our society will be evident as we proceed. We cannot treat co-operation or any other fundamental social process without putting it in its proper cultural setting. Whatever may be the place of this basic process in nature, in human society culture patterns play a distinctive part in giving it direction and a place in the societal order.

Co-operation, like competition and conflict, is affected by social and cultural conditioning. The immediate motives for co-operation may be economic, such as saving money or securing better quality; or it may arise from the desire for self-satisfaction attendant upon prestige or control. Moreover, the existence of a social myth that co-operation is a sound device for survival is fundamental. In America we have been thoroughly indoctrinated with individualistic sentiment and with the belief in the importance of being efficient producers of economic goods. So, too, our consumption habits are highly individualized. As a result in both production and consumption we follow the private profit patterns and it takes a long time to build up by education and propaganda the democratic habits of co-operation.

Economic Co-operative Movements. Co-operation for economic welfare is one of the oldest forms of mutual assistance. Fishermen pulling on a net, hunters planning and executing together a successful kill, farm workers building homes and barns together, helping each other to prepare land and to plant and harvest crops are all evident examples. While such mutual aid need not imply communism in the distribution of wealth, it does involve motives and attitudes favorable to co-operation.

The economic co-operative movements of Western society have grown up within capitalism and not in opposition to it. They have been largely confined to attempts for reducing costs of production or to agencies for assisting the consumer to buy for less. The movement, which began nationally, has spread to international scope, following the ever-widening range of economic contact.

Medieval Europe presented a fairly well integrated and balanced organization of society, in which various forms of co-operation were worked out in connection with the economic order of the time. The Industrial Revolution of the eighteenth and early nineteenth centuries with its *laissez-faire* ideas and practices led to a loss of many of the culture traits of peasant life, such as common pasturage, rights of peasants to certain forest lands, and other community evidences of co-operation. The enclosure acts in Great Britain abolished many of these ancient practices for the rural dwellers there. But more important was the shift to urban and factory life, in which the individual wage earner was cut off from these older forms of co-operation, and in which he was reduced to unsanitary working conditions, to the periodic insecurity of unemployment, and to the loss of former communal support of his morale in times of stress. Although political suffrage was being extended, it hardly compensated for many of these losses.

Out of eighteenth-century romantic philosophy and the economic dislocation, agitation arose for a more fundamental organization of society by means of socialism or communism. Some advocated rather revolutionary change; others attempted to improve the conditions of the masses by changes within the capitalistic system itself.

About 1820 Robert Owen, an English reformer (1771–1858), began discussing the importance of planned co-operation as a basis for a new social and economic organization. He advocated self-sufficient economic and social groups within the community which would operate more efficiently along co-operative lines.

Although Owen and others stimulated radical ideas that were to flower later in more systematic communism, their conceptions did influence the working class co-operatives which were springing up at that time. The producers' co-operatives in England and on the continent, however, were confined largely to the handicrafts. The need for large capital for setting up factories and for purchasing raw materials prevented the workers from entering into co-operation in the field of factory production. In the United States we had a number of religious or idealistic groups which fostered some forms of co-operation or communism, like that set up at Oneida, New York, by John Humphrey Noyes (1811–1886).

Related to producers' co-operatives are organizations to establish credit for small producers. This sort of co-operative among farmers has been widespread in some European countries and, to a lesser extent, in the United States. It aims to provide funds for the purchase of seed, fertilizers, machinery, and for marketing goods. In urban communities such credit establishments are found in building and loan societies, and in some isolated instances labor unions have attempted general banking.

Curiously enough, industries and services which provide such universal necessities as fuel, light, power, transportation, and milk have scarcely been touched by co-operative movements, chiefly because of the large capital outlay necessary.

Consumers' co-operatives, for the most part, seem to have their origin among urban workers. In Great Britain, as early as 1767, funds were advanced through philanthropy to build mills for grinding wheat or to purchase consumption goods for the poor. In 1769, the Fenwick Weavers' Society, a friendly society of Scotland, agreed to buy food to be sold for the benefit of the members. The ideas of Robert Owen and others stimulated these co-operatives, and it is estimated that between 1830 and 1840 about 350 such societies sprang up in England, although most of them had disappeared by 1844.[4]

The first really successful effort of this sort was begun in Rochdale, England, in November, 1843, and the practice has spread widely under the title "The Rochdale Co-operative Movement." Following an unsuccessful strike, 28 flannel workers set up a co-operative store to purchase goods to be sold to the members at a modest profit. The following principles were developed:

1. Democracy and service are the aims, not profits.
2. Membership is open to all on equal terms.
3. Membership is obtainable through low-priced shares, usually payable in installments. Installments, in fact, may be deducted from dividends due.
4. One person may hold only a limited number of shares.
5. Each shareholder has one vote in the management regardless of the number of shares, and has equal voice in policies of management, etc.

[4] See W. H. Dawson, "Friendly Societies," *Encyclopedia of the Social Sciences,* vol. VI, pp. 494–98.

6. The surplus is the property of the members and is returned to them under various plans. Sometimes a portion is held in reserve; sometimes a part is devoted to education and social benefits to the members, including insurance; the remainder may be paid out as dividends proportionate not to the number of shares held but to the amount of purchases.

7. A fixed rate of interest usually of the legal minimum or less is paid on the shares.

The whole co-operative movement spread rapidly, and as early as 1869 the British Co-operative Union, a federation of various co-operatives, was established. This federation grew in importance and power, more than doubling its membership between 1901 and 1929. In the latter year more than 10 per cent of the population of Great Britain and Ireland belonged to some form of co-operative organization. The Federation fosters the establishment of wholesale firms and stimulates international co-operatives. Although in general these organizations have been non-political, certain conflicts with producers' co-operatives and with some trade-union organizations more or less forced certain political activities upon these consumers' organizations. The British Co-operative Party of 1917 proved to be abortive, and more recently the whole British co-operative movement has been riven by the introduction of political party interests.

Somewhat similar consumers' co-operatives have grown rapidly on the continent of Europe, especially in France, the Scandinavian countries, and, until recently, in Germany. In Russia the whole movement, which was once extensive, has been merged in the larger program of the Soviets. In the United States the development of co-operatives has been backward. In 1933 the Eastern States Co-operative League had about 13,000 members scattered in 24 local groups; and the Northern States Co-operative League reported 88 societies and about 50,000 members. Statistics for co-operative organizations in the United States are incomplete, but evidently there has been a steady growth during recent years. Estimates for 1936 report 6,500 local consumers' organizations with a membership of about two million families. But there is nothing to compare with the great co-operatives of Europe.

These organizations all follow a democratic principle of control: voting membership, often limited share holding, dividends in ratio to purchases, and subordination of the profit motive to the

common good, and in some instances agreement to buy only
through the organization. They all aim to eliminate the middleman—storekeeper, banker, and employer. Apparently co-operative devices have proved chiefly beneficial to those groups wherein
extreme thrift is essential, and clearly a period of economic distress fosters habits of co-operation.

Limitations of Economic Co-operation. The implications
of economic co-operatives can be understood only in reference to
various events on the national and international stage. As world
economic contacts expanded, it was only natural that the various
national co-operatives should take on international features. In
1895 the International Co-operative Alliance was founded to
foster an international movement, largely by education and propaganda. In spite of rivalries among various nationalist groups
reflecting religious, political, and other differences, and in spite
of opposition from socialist quarters, the international organization persisted until the World War and its chaotic aftermath.

The more serious handicaps to the extension of economic co-
operatives grow out of the lack of a sound social philosophy and
adequate motivation of aggressive attitudes. Without doubt the
socialist movement of the early twentieth century also retarded
the expansion of the co-operatives. The socialists maintain that
such organizations will ultimately fail because they attempt to
work within a capitalistic society, and hence will always reflect,
in spite of themselves, much of the capitalist theory and practice.
Moreover, argue the socialists, since capital goods are largely in
the hands of capitalist owners, the co-operatives will always face
difficulties in extending their efforts to the more basic industries
and services: utilities, fuel, iron, transportation, and extensive
distribution systems. Finally, they say, as most co-operatives are
non-political in character, they cannot hope to dominate any
society, since without the control of government there can be no
fundamental reorganization of society.

Co-operation restricted only to economic activities cannot profoundly influence the wider culture of any people. In a country
like the United States, still dominated by individualistic self-
interest, co-operation is often built up around self-interest, not
collective concern. This is well illustrated again and again in
agricultural producers' co-operatives, especially in the dairy, tobacco, and fruit industries. These associations get established in

difficult economic periods, but tend to break up as soon as private industry is able to pay slightly higher prices than the co-operative pools.[5] The consumers' organizations have had like difficulties.

The failure to develop aggressive programs among co-operatives rests upon both psychological and cultural factors. The very spirit of co-operation tends to be quiescent and pacific. If coercion has been developed, it has tended to be of non-violent sort. Moreover, the co-operatives of Western capitalistic society have, as their socialist critics well say, no fundamental political and economic plan for reorganization of society. In other words, they have no significant symbols around which a fighting morale of members may be built up.

In spite of the fact that there are between 70 and 80 million members in the economic co-operatives of 36 countries (and these organizations do stimulate self-help and co-operation among the producing classes), the whole movement is limited. Only as it touches politics, religion, education, recreation, art, and other fundamental patterns of culture can it become a really significant world movement.

Political Co-operation. We need not retrace the story of the extension of the political order in our modern world. We have already noted the widening range of men's peaceful interaction upon the world stage. (See Chapter IV.) The rise of nationalism was accompanied by a long period of international conflict and competition, in which peaceful political relations took on the nature of an armed truce rather than of planned co-operation. In spite of the disruptive aggressiveness of the World War, a world sentiment slowly emerged, largely out of the inevitable economic and non-political forms of interaction—religious, artistic, and scientific—which developed international features in spite of strong nationalism. The movement had two aspects; first, official treaties tabooing armed warfare, and the creation of The Hague Tribunal and the League of Nations; and second, the development of unofficial organizations fostering peace and international co-operation. But on the other hand nationalism, arising in part from post-war bitterness, has fostered international aggression and the hope of political gain by conquest. Until we change international economic relations, until profound cultural differences associated with religion and politics are wiped out or merged into

[5]See J. M. Williams, *The Expansion of Rural Life*, pp. 178–79.

a world-wide culture, we cannot expect a rapid acceptance of effective co-operation among the nations of the world today.

Again, there are those who believe that so long as nationalism exists, such co-operation is impossible. They advocate the overthrow of the nationalistic state everywhere and the substitution in its place of an international world state. In the light of strong post-war nationalism, this political fantasy seems a remote prospect. Yet, every effective attempt to foster good will, mutual aid, and understanding in the world as it actually exists today may well be a step forward to more effective political and economic co-operation in the future.

Church and Religious Co-operation. The divisive nature of the major religions of the world reflects the larger cultures of which they are a part. In the same manner the strong spirit of separateness, of we-group superiority which marks Christian denominations, is related to divergences in the wider culture of regions or nations. As the World Community has grown, as the barriers of prejudice and isolation have disappeared, certain tendencies toward co-operation have arisen. Such gatherings as world religious conferences, in which representatives of all the major religions have participated, are evidence of a growing awareness of common problems in religion in spite of differences of creed.

Within our own society, the recent decades have seen a tendency toward certain co-operative action among the churches. The organization of local ministerial associations is one example. And a federation for civic and religious programs, notably the Federal Council of the Churches of Christ, is another. (See Chapter XIV on religion.) Co-operation is more feasible among churches within the wider nationalist society than where church co-operation tries to reach beyond the national boundaries.

Co-operation through Science and Art. International co-operation has long been stimulated by the development of science and the arts. Certainly science knows no national boundaries. By its very nature it is as wide as humanity itself. Individual scientists have long communicated with each other in spite of nationalistic and theological barriers. During the last century any number of international scientific bodies grew up, first among the physical and latterly among the social sciences. Men of science, however, are not in a position to apply the principles of universality of science to more humdrum affairs of the marketplace, the church, and the political state. This is especially evident in times of international conflict, like the World War or the post-war revolutionary movements, when scientists often forget their objective scientific attitude and support their own governments. More seriously still they have at times prostituted their sciences in the interests of the dominant political and economic power. Because of the evident bearing of their fields on national polity, this has been more obvious in the social sciences than it has been in the natural sciences. The plight of social science and biology in Nazi Germany is a case in point.

This inability of scientists to apply their rational attitudes toward their specialties in the face of political crises illustrates in another way the partial integration of science into the life of the individual, in contrast to the deeper and more complete integration of the attitudes and habits bearing on political and economic survival in terms of the commonly accepted values. So it is in co-operation in science, art, and religion. It is easy to practice it until the more fundamental demands of national political and economic survival arise. In the face of such a crisis the international, humanitarian, and non-political aspects of science, art, and religion are likely to disappear, because they are still only superficially related to the deeper values for the individual.

Nevertheless, in spite of these handicaps, science is truly worldwide in scope and objective in purpose; and as the scientific attitude spreads to other fields, there may come an enhancement of international co-operation. Science may serve as an important leaven in the lump of prejudiced and narrow nationalism.

Art, likewise, has long been recognized as broader than the political state, although the history of art reflects regional and nationalist influences. Art in our modern world bespeaks broad cultural differences rather than narrow national ones. Still its close association with economic, political, and religious life tends to keep it from developing international features as rapidly as has been the case with science.

In fact, in the case of all three, religion, science, and art, the spread of wider extra-national co-operation is blocked by the deeper interests of an economic and political sort. Whenever a deep conflict for survival arises, these other more secondary features of our culture give way to the fundamental struggle with our enemies for our very existence. The spread of the ideas of

co-operation from these other areas of behavior into economic
and political fields comes slowly.   Only as the economic and political needs of mankind become international can we hope that
effective co-operation in these fields may arise.

Co-operation means mutual striving for a goal, certain rules to
insure better performance under co-operation than otherwise, an
approximate equal sharing of results, and usually some linkage of
such activity with other than the central aim.

Psychology of Co-operation.   While there is no instinct of
co-operation, it does grow up in all societies in one form or
another.   Yet for rudimentary mutual helpfulness to develop into
more deliberate form at least, people must first be directly motivated to seek a goal that may be shared.   Second, they must acquire some knowledge of the benefits of such activity; hence the
need for education to foster co-operation.   Third, they must get
a favorable attitude toward sharing both the work and the rewards involved.   And, finally, they need to equip themselves with
the necessary skills to make the co-operative plan go.[6]

We cannot have co-operation without the development of sympathy.   And sympathy, as we know, depends upon the capacity
of one individual to imagine himself in the place of another.   Co-
operation, therefore, rests upon the identification of one person
with another, looking toward the same common result.   The ego
or self expands to include others within itself.   The more selfish
impulses are inhibited or blocked in the demands of the situation
for mutual helpfulness.   There results from this a like-mindedness
or similarity of purpose and plans.

Co-operation by its very nature promotes teamwork, which involves co-ordination and integration of action.   As we advance in
the scale of differentiation and complexity of interaction, teamwork becomes increasingly more deliberate.   Co-operation is not
merely a matter of one individual adding his strength to another,
but it grows up from the very nature of group behavior.

Like opposition, co-operation arises from the orientation of the
individual to the we-group and to the out-group.   While competition, rivalry, and conflict may arise in the we-group, it is evident

[6]See M. A. May and L. Doob, *Competition and Cooperation*, 1937.

that the we-group could not persist were it not for co-operation. The solidarity of the in-group is expressed most strongly through mutual aid, helpfulness, and loyalty to the group-accepted symbols. Such co-operation is most in evidence when the we-group stands in sharp opposition toward some other body of persons, the out-group. As was noted in Chapter I, it is clear that the very strength of the in-group feeling of solidarity rests in part upon the fact that antagonistic feelings are directed toward some out-group. The intensity of the we-group feelings seems correlated with the intensity of antagonism to the others-group. The power of the oppositional attitudes to keep alive those of co-operation is neatly demonstrated in the following statement of J. M. Williams regarding a farmers' co-operative league in New York State:

"One of the psychological forces that has stimulated the growth of the League is the opposition it has encountered from milk companies and from the non-pooling co-operative association of dairy farmers. . . . The speakers at the annual convention *keep the hostile agencies before the farmers and so stimulate their loyalty to the League.*"[7]

Co-operation also imposes various forms of restraint upon the participant. The self cannot have its way entirely if it is working co-operatively with another self. If the self-assertive trends get too strong, the co-operation may easily cease and be replaced by struggle. Thus, co-operation always implies inhibition of certain impulses. As we advance to higher, that is, to more conscious and complex forms of co-operation, this matter becomes more evident. From the restraint so imposed there arises a moral strength which stands in contrast to the impulsiveness and lack of self-control found in uninhibited conflict. In the struggle of one group against another this is highly important, as it is, also, in controlling the relations of persons to each other within the group itself. So far as the relations of the in-group to the out-group go, such restraint favors what Williams very well calls "constructive resistance." The individual must curb his "unruly impulses," must learn to endure hardships, save money, restrict his sexual desires and other selfish wishes in order to preserve family ties and maintain community solidarity.[8]

In short, co-operation involves inhibition of untrained selfish impulses, rests upon the development of sympathy and the power of

[7] J. M. Williams, *The Expansion of Rural Life*, 1926, p. 180. Italics not in the original.
[8] See the discussion of this matter in J. M. Williams, *op. cit.*, p. 313.

identification, and promotes teamwork and we-group solidarity. The latter is often best stimulated if the inhibited impulses to opposition and struggle are projected upon some out-group that stands in contrast or opposition to our own in-group. Finally, co-operation through this very inhibiting mechanism fosters self-restraint and thus saves energy for the group purposes.

Certainly in modern societies co-operative groups seem to develop a we-group morale best where there is an opposing set of forces. Thus, propagandists for economic co-operatives in this country often advocate adherence to their organizations on the theory that they offer a threat of effective competition with capitalist business or industry. There is no doubt that the success of many co-operatives in Europe, especially in Scandinavia, rests upon just such competition with privately-owned enterprises. In other words, economic co-operatives are often successful only in a larger social system which permits private profit taking as well.

A word may be said about the effect, upon attitudes of co-operation, of a culture in which economic competition for private gain is abandoned. If the Russian communistic system works out, the individual private profit motive will disappear. Does this mean that competition will disappear and that co-operation will take its place? It is doubtful. Competition for status will go on, although social rank is determined by social rewards other than money making. As to co-operative attitudes, however, there is no doubt that concern with the survival of one's own soviet, with one's community, and finally with the Communist state—all stimulate co-operation. Whether these will be broader in scope than the co-operative attitudes in capitalistic countries is open to question. There seems no evidence that the present Russian system, for example, is any more likely to foster the kindlier and more sympathetic reactions of co-operation in regard to other nations or races than forces at work in capitalist countries. It must always be recalled that co-operation is counterbalanced by opposition, and that both are expressed within the framework of the various groups to which one belongs or toward which one has attitudes of like, approach, and participation, on the one hand, or ambivalent attitudes of dislike, withdrawal, and non-participation, on the other.

Other psychological features of co-operation are clearly evident in the individual's reactions to national and international problems. So long as men and women everywhere are tied to their own nation by habit and attitude, to the exclusion of interest in men and women of other nations, so long as national selfishness outweighs all other considerations, it is difficult to foster international co-operation. Just as economic co-operatives are handicapped by jealousies, international competition, and prejudice, so in the political field there must be a change of heart in the masses of mankind before effective international co-operation is possible. In a world dominated for centuries by local and nationalistic interests to the exclusion of friendly concern with outsiders, it is difficult to develop public opinion favorable to sane internationalism. Psychologically, it is important to shift the object of man's identification. Until he can sympathize with and live imaginatively in the attitudes and habits, i.e., in the culture, of people remote from him in space, it is difficult to expect him to give up his narrow local prejudices, especially if this involves any threat to his personal security.

Yet it must be borne in mind that the process of co-operation has much in common with the whole pattern of political democracy. Many defenders and advocates of economic co-operatives thoroughly believe that the principles laid down in their organizations as to ownership, control, and financial benefits furnish the only sane program which will enable political democracy itself to survive. The so-called co-operative commonwealth which many pacifistic socialists envisage is a theoretical projection of this dream. (See Chapter XXIX.) But whether modern democracies will develop along the lines of economic and other co-operative organizations lies within the lap of history. Certainly we must not neglect the place which both competition and conflict have in social life, for, unlike opposition, co-operation appears limited in its application outside the in-group.

Certainly the possibility of a strong nationalism which would foster certain permissible oppositional patterns within a larger world co-operative organization must not be overlooked. In any international scheme there is much to be said for keeping alive divergent cultures which would preserve a certain regional individuality and difference, and yet give the world a co-operative instrument to handle matters truly international in scope. The prospect of a world unity in which all the major features of culture and societal order were identical is neither pleasant nor perhaps desirable to contemplate. In view of the nature of man and of social interaction, it is doubtful whether a dead-level of naive co-operation would be possible. We must not forget that opposition, at its best sublimated and ethical in character, is the counterpart of co-operation. A world without both would be stupid indeed.

CLASS ASSIGNMENTS

A. **Further reading assignment:**

1. K. Young, *Source Book for Sociology,* chap. XVIII.
2. E. T. Hiller, *Principles of Sociology,* chaps. XI, XIII.

B. **Questions and exercises:**

1. Distinguish between co-operation and opposition. Show their relationship in reference to the we-group and the out-group, especially in reference to sense of solidarity and organization of effort. Is one more fundamental than the other?

2. In his *Principles of Sociology,* p. 269, rev. ed., E. A. Ross remarks, "A common task may be performed by *compulsory co-operation.*" Discuss the difficulties of compulsory co-operation not supported by attitudes and habits that are basic to voluntary co-operation.

3. What conditions at present stimulate or retard the growth of widespread and effective economic co-operatives in this country?

4. Discuss, pro and con, the possibility of building up international political and economic co-operation while still retaining the regional and national entities of culture.

5. What habits, attitudes, and ideas of the individual foster secondary group co-operation? Which ones hinder such co-operation?

C. **Topics for class reports or longer written papers:**

1. Mutual aid among the plants and animals. (Consult P. A. Kropotkin, *Mutual Aid,* 1902; and R. E. Park and E. W. Burgess, *Introduction to the Science of Sociology,* 1924 ed., chap. III and bibliography.)

2. Cultural variations in competition and co-operation. (Consult Margaret Mead, *Cooperation and Competition among Primitive Peoples,* 1937; and M. A. May and L. Doob, *Competition and Cooperation,* 1937.)

3. The European movements for economic co-operation. (Consult Elsie Glück et al. in article "Co-operation," *Encyclopedia of the Social Sciences,* vol. IV, pp. 359–99, and bibliography; Jerome Davis, *Contemporary Social Movements,* 1930, Book VI; *Report of the Inquiry on Cooperative Enterprise in Europe, 1937,* Washington, D. C., United States Government Printing Office, 1937; A. M. Carr-Saunders, P. S. Florence, R. Peers, et al., *Consumers' Co-operation in Great Britain,* 1938.)

4. Recent movements toward economic co-operatives in the United States, and difficulties in securing membership. (Consult *The Annals of the American Academy of Political and Social Science,* May, 1937, vol. CXLI: "Consumers' Cooperation"; B. B. Fowler, *Consumer Cooperation in America,* 1936; and Jacob Baker, *Cooperative Enterprise,* 1937.)

CHAPTER XXI

AGE AND SEX DIFFERENTIATION

Differentiation is the process of developing separate and distinctive functions or rôles for individuals and groups. The roots of differentiation rest in competition and co-operation. It is a normal and continuous outcome of interaction. In this and the next chapter we shall discuss differentiation as it concerns age, sex, mentality, and social and economic division of labor and leadership. Stratification, or the formation of classes, is a special phase of differentiation and accommodation which will be treated later. (See Chapter XXIV.)

Differentiation in regard to matters of age, sex, and mentality has been extensively studied by modern psychology. While we shall draw upon its findings, we must recall that for sociology and social psychology these individual differences have no meaning apart from man's culture and group participation.

All societies recognize age differences. In some, as among the ancient Incas, age classification was basic to the whole societal order. In this curious state socialism, the functions of every inhabitant—economic, marital, and political—were based upon age. The classification ran something like this:

1. At the beginning of life: "a babe in arms."
2. Later in infancy: "able to stand."
3. A fledgling: "under six."
4. From 6 to 8 years: a "bread receiver."
5. From 8 to 16 years: "one who needs light work."
6. From 16 to 20 years: a "cacao-picker."
7. From 20 to 25 years: "almost a man."
8. From 25 to 50 years: "able bodied," head of a family, and a taxpayer.
9. From 50 to 60 years: "half an old man."
10. From 60 years on: "an old man asleep."[1]

[1] See Alfred M. Tozzer, *Social Origins and Social Continuities,* 1925, p. 208.

AGE DIFFERENTIATION

There is bound to be divergence of activity because of differing ages. Adults have more physical strength and more experience than do adolescents. Youth has certainly considerable advantage over childhood, even though neither youth nor childhood has the capacity typical of maturity. In old age mental and physical powers decline, and dependence on others once more limits the range of social action. Yet everywhere these variations depend upon how the particular society handles and defines these age differences. For our purposes we may discuss age differentiation under four heads: infancy and childhood, adolescence or youth, maturity or adulthood, and old age.

Infancy and Childhood. In discussing the development of personality (Chapter VI) and in treating parent-child relations (Chapter XII), we have indicated some of the important factors in the development of the child's rôle and status which we need not repeat. Not only do the parents afford protection and care; they also instruct the child in the basic beliefs of their society. Religious ideas and practices, loyalties to tribe or nation, fundamental economic beliefs, notions of the beautiful, and forms of recreation are learned from the family and other primary groups.

Traditionally the central rôle of the child is that of dependency on and guardianship by older persons, and the years of such dependency and immaturity have been markedly prolonged in recent decades. As culture becomes enriched, as human life takes on more value, mankind extends the preparatory period before demanding adult responsibility. It might be held that the prolongation of the period of childhood and of the training of youth is a measure of advancement of any particular society.

Likewise the whole tendency in our society has been to move to a more humanitarian and kindlier view of children. The interests of the child have been increasingly more regarded. As Edward Westermarck, the great student of ethics and marriage, puts it, we have now arrived at the idea that "children . . . are in no respect the property of their parents; that the birth of children gives the parents no rights over them other than those which conduce to the children's happiness."[2]

[2]Quoted by C. C. North, *Social Differentiation*, 1926, p. 68, from Edward Westermarck, *History of Human Marriage*, 1st edition, p. 239.

The Rôle of Adolescence. As we have already noted, the break between various age periods is determined in part by culture as well as by birthdays. While some societies rather definitely recognize changes during puberty from childhood to sexual maturity by special ceremonials and changes in social status and rôle, other societies make no sharp division. Popular anthropology to the contrary, puberty ceremonies, even for the male adolescents, are by no means universal. And certainly the long period of preparation of youth for adulthood is relatively restricted to the higher cultures. C. C. North in his *Social Differentiation* (1926) goes so far as to remark, "All available evidence seems to indicate that primitive society gives little or no recognition to the period [of youth] as entitled to a social position distinct from that of maturity." As society has advanced in complexity and differentiation, there has been a tendency to extend the period before inducting the individual into the responsibilities of maturity. Training in education, religion, vocations, and in ideas of citizenship and morality are carried over to the adolescent by both formal and informal devices of education. In our society we have adopted the theory that such a period better prepares the individual for his full adult responsibilities.

In spite of wide cultural variations in treating the period of adolescence, there do remain certain basic physiological changes in the individual that furnish a biological foundation for a change in social rôle. The most noteworthy of these, of course, is the maturation of sex functioning and the coming of secondary sex characteristics to further distinguish the male from the female. Associated with these changes are increases in height and weight, changes in the ratio of muscles to skeleton, and others. There are wide variations in the age at which the individual passes through the pubertal changes, both within the same race and locality and between races. It may be that climate and diet as well as race are factors in these variations.

Connected with these sexual changes go differentiation in social rôles. Teamwork, co-operation, further moralization, and training for future vocation are expected in our society. So, too, in our society the separation of the sexes during youth was once accepted as right and proper. Today many of these barriers are breaking down. In other cultures sexual and other contacts of youth are quite as rigidly defined as in our own mores. In still other cultures there is a freedom in sexual and other mores which shocks the sensibilities of our own people.[3]

The law takes into account the changed situation in regard to youth in our culture. Whereas in earlier periods marriage, responsibility for crime, and occupational status were expected of the youth, our law definitely reflects the culture of the time in its increased recognition of the dependency of youth on the parents and on the state for support. Among other significant changes are (*1*) raising the age limits for marriage, (*2*) raising the age limits on full accountability for crimes, reflected in the changes of child welfare legislation dealing with juvenile delinquency, and (*3*) raising the upper age limit of compulsory education.

We have in our society a curious divergence in regard to youth. On the one hand we have thrown about them increasing protection by increasing the years of compulsory education, by preventing child labor, and by restricting early marriage. So, too, the continued emotional and financial dependence of children on parents is evident in a large number of families. Nowhere else in the world is there provided leisure and opportunity for education for young people, who in other societies would be taking up adult responsibilities. In contrast to this, our youth have greater freedom from parental control than formerly. Our adolescent boys and girls are more sophisticated and mature in many ways than their parents were in their youth. Opportunities for escaping from family, neighborhood, and community controls afford our young people forms of experience which their fathers and mothers often do not approve of or understand.

In our society today the rôle and status of youth, in short, are not clearly defined. The divergence between the adult theories and the actual practices of youth themselves, reflects a modern conflict of ages. (See Chapter XIX on age conflict.)

Adult Roles. Adulthood is marked by the assumption of full social responsibilities resting upon physical and mental vigor. The cultural definition of the situation determines how we look upon maturity. In every society the adult takes over functions not expected of children, youth, or old age. In a hunting society these

[3]See Margaret Mead, *Coming of Age in Samoa,* 1928; and her *Growing Up in New Guinea,* 1930. In the former territory, while there were certain restrictions as to kinship and rank, there was a great deal of sexual freedom allowed among young men and women. In contrast, the taboos among the Manus outdo even those of our Puritan ancestors.

adult functions will differ from those in a pastoral or fully developed agricultural society. The age at which the individual comes to maturity will be settled by factors intrinsic in the particular society.

Every tribe or state makes provision for the adult to take some place in the political control of his community. The age at which the person acquires full-fledged membership in the community varies in different societies. In our own, political majority is assumed when the person acquires voting privileges. In time of war the capacity to bear arms has in some countries become the standard of political responsibility. On the other hand, the capacity to hold office is assumed to go with age. In our country, while most local and state offices are open to any qualified voter 21 years or over, the holding of federal offices is restricted to narrower age limits. A person under 25 years of age cannot hold office as a Representative in the National Congress. One must be 30 years old to be eligible for the United States Senate, and 35 years or over to be eligible for the Presidency of the United States. Voting privileges, capacity to hold office, jury service, and obligation to bear arms are basic marks of adult political responsibility in our country. With these, of course, go all the obligations of the good citizen, which are stipulated, at least on the negative side, by the legal codes and mores regarding conduct, both private and public.

Marital responsibility in our culture is assumed when marriage takes place. If the individual marries before his political majority is reached, he nevertheless is not excused from his economic and other obligations to his family. When the parents do not fulfill their duties to the children, the state or public opinion or the mores step in to see that they do.

There are many other social rôles which go with adulthood. In the church a person may remain layman, or if the organization permits he may become lay preacher, vestryman, deacon, Sunday-School teacher, elder, priest, or pastor. Also there are financial obligations set up to support one's church. There are also various rôles in clubs, business and recreational, in fraternal orders, and in various special interest groups. There is a whole battery of character building and philanthropic community activities in which the alert and well socialized citizen will play a part: not merely in giving financial aid, but in lending his own services.

Old Age. A decline in physical and mental vigor leads to a gradual relinquishment of full social responsibilities. The external evidences of this decline are again difficult to determine. Individual variations are evident. One man at 50 may be far more vigorous than another, and some men at 60 have better health and more intellectual alertness than others ten years younger. There are few adequate studies of physical changes in old age. Old age is determined not only by physiological condition of muscles, glands, and brain. It is also a psychological and cultural matter. Where the old men of a tribe continue to wield great influence far into the years of physiological senility, old age in the cultural sense is delayed, no matter how feeble mentally or physically the individual may have become.

In some primitive societies old age carries with it a real distinction in rank or status. In many tribes the elders are the most powerful and revered members of the group. Goldenweiser remarks:

"While these [old men and in some cases old women] take a less active part in the everyday activities, their leadership in ceremonial and political matters is pronounced and they do everywhere constitute the great depositories of tradition, figuring as the mouthpiece, as it were, of the conservative *status quo*. They know the past, in fact, they know all there is to be known, and they see to it that this knowledge is passed on without much loss as well as without much addition. They are the great stabilizing fly-wheel of the civilizational mechanism."[4]

In a country like China, where ancestor worship has dominated family and community life for centuries, the power of old age over the social order is everywhere apparent. Deference to old age, to the patriarch of the family, the desire for sons to carry on the ancestor worship, the retarding influence of this practice on the rise of new ideas and new ways of life is self-evident to anyone who knows even a little of life in that part of the Orient.[5]

Throughout the history of our own European culture, old age has retained enormous power. Where the patriarchal family order holds, as in ancient Rome, the eldest male in the family retains control over all the others. It is true even today in the peasant areas of Europe. Where urbanization has taken place, where industry has developed, this reverence for old age has been modified. Nevertheless, positions of prestige still go to older men. Judicial, military,

[4] A. A. Goldenweiser, *Early Civilization*, 1922, p. 257.
[5] Pearl Buck's novel, *The Good Earth*, 1931, brings this whole Chinese practice before the reader in vivid fashion.

political, and economic leadership tends to remain in the hands of older men. The Franco-Prussian War (1870–71) was carried through by elderly military leaders. The King of Prussia was in his seventy-fourth year; Von Moltke, the leading Prussian general, was 71; Bismarck, the political master-mind, was in his fifty-sixth year. In the Russo-Japanese War we find the same phenomenon. All the prominent Japanese leaders—Prince Oyama, Nodzu, Yamagata, Kuroki, and Nogi—were 60 or over. The World War was directed largely by older leaders. At the outbreak of the war Kaiser Wilhelm II of Germany was 55; Clemenceau was 73; Lloyd George was 51; Sir Edward Grey was 52. Of the military figures Lord Kitchener, French, Haig, Joffre, Foch, Pershing, Von Kluck, Hindenburg, Emmich, Von Tirpitz would all be classed as relatively old men, most of them beyond 60 years.

However, with the increase in the number of people in the middle and older age groups we are likely to see a heightened conflict between older men and men in their prime. (See Chapter XIX.)

These cases of leadership and headship among older men, however, touch but a small fraction of the population in these later ages. We still have to face the fact that a large percentage of our old people become dependent on others for economic support. In our individualistic society in the past, the provisions for old age have rested upon efforts of the person himself and on his family. Only gradually as a new collectivist spirit grows are we coming to realize a certain responsibility of the community and state to provide care for old age through pensions and insurance.

In addition to provision for economic security, we are now beginning to recognize the need for adequate social-psychological support for the aged who have retired from active employment. Among other factors the following are important: (1) provision to keep them in good health, (2) pleasant social-emotional relations with friends and family, (3) adequate recreation or possession of interesting hobbies, (4) continuance, where they wish, of independence of residence and freedom of mobility, and (5) some form of "useful work-like activity"—not recreational in nature—which will contribute to their self-esteem. Obviously, how old folks react to their change in rôle and status reflects their own culture, and these points are predicated upon observations made of persons living in our essentially individualistic society.[6]

[6]See Christine M. Morgan, *The Attitudes and Adjustments of Recipients of Old Age Assistance in Upstate and Metropolitan New York*, 1937.

SEX DIFFERENTIATION

Sex differences also affect the nature of interaction and the social rôle and status. Throughout all societies one finds a double set of social functions associated with the two sexes. Naturally the most obvious of these is that connected with reproduction and the rearing of children. Sex also plays a part in the division of labor. It comes into play in relation to intellectual achievement, mechanical invention, aesthetic, religious, and other phases of social interaction. Almost all the major phases of social behavior have been or are now influenced by these differences. It must not be assumed, however, that all these divergent social functions grow directly and instinctively out of sex differences. In this area of differentiation, as in others, culture and societal organization play an important part. A large part of the traditional belief about differences between men and women are really rationalizations that have grown up in the course of cultural history. The chief areas of traditional sex differentiation are those bearing on parenthood and care of children, on economic and political activity, and on morality. Let us examine these first and then close this section with a review of some pertinent facts about physical and mental differences between men and women, in order to see whether there is a biological basis for these customary rôles of the sexes.

Differentiation in Parenthood and Child Care. Certain aspects of the divergent rôles of men and women in the family drama we have already discussed. (See Chapters XI and XII on the family.) Here we shall refer to some of these matters in a new setting in order to expose the process of sexual differentiation.

The obvious function of the female in childbearing sets her off at once from the male. Conception is for the male relatively incidental and temporary. It does not interfere with his physical activity in other matters. Not so with the woman. Conception to her means a marked change in physiological reactions. The period of gestation makes demands upon her strength. Her other activities are affected. And childbirth itself is not an easy crisis. While the meaning of childbearing is determined largely by the culture of the time and place, the more personal, intimate phases of the experience which underlie the cultural interpretation make for psychological differences between the male and female that perhaps can never be entirely bridged.

While both motherhood and fatherhood are essential rôles, the dominance of the male in most societies is self-evident, in spite of various armchair theories of matriarchal control. (See Chapter XI.) In early child care, however, the mother for the most part plays the leading part, but as the male child grows up he is in time taken over by the men of the group and inducted into male society. The girl is trained for her proper rôle by her mother.

The esteem which is given to women reflects the differentiation of the sexes in terms of power and authority. So far as physical strength goes, primitive women seem about equal to men. Yet they are seldom if ever accorded equal rights with the male members of their society. Women are not initiated into the secrets of the tribe. They are often segregated under severe taboos. Men and women have little in common by way of companionship. The men hunt, fish, work, and play together, while the women and children are almost a species apart. In some societies women are not even given credit for bearing children, but are thought mere vessels to carry the child before birth and to nourish it afterwards. They were denied souls by the early Chinese, and to give birth to a female child was almost a disgrace. In other societies, however, certain rights were given women, and as these rights are acquired the status of women is enhanced.

So far as family control in Western society is concerned, the patriarchal pattern has remained dominant. In classical and early Christian times the female was looked upon as distinctly inferior to the male. As we saw in discussing the development of family patterns in our own society, the Christians added the notion of original sin to the already current conception of woman's inferiority.

With the coming of the modern age, the respect of men for women has grown. As women have won a place in the world on their own merit, men have been obliged to give them status independent of sex. But the change has been slow. To this day men everywhere fall into the easy error of thinking that women are intellectually inferior to men, that their true function is childbearing, that they ought not to attempt higher education and the professions. Woman is said to be the helpmate and complement, not the equal, of the man. North says, "In the minds of a comparatively few only has woman come to be evaluated in terms of her own social worth, independently of her relation to some man."[7]

---

[7] North, *op. cit.*, p. 105.

Divergent Mores for the Sexes. The traditional morality applied to women in our society has been different from that applied to men. First of all, women are not expected to be so efficient as men and are often excused on all sorts of counts from participating in struggles and work which men find not only possible but stimulating. The male, having built up the pattern of fighting and pursuit, expends his energy freely. The female, with her pattern of more sedentary and more docile life, is hardly expected to cope with the same sort of situations as the male. Certainly our moral code is tempered to the woman. We forgive her or at least lighten the punishment of crimes committed by her against property. The woman shoplifter or forger is likely to get more lenient treatment by the courts than the man caught in a similar offense. We are not so lenient in the matter of sexual infractions. According to W. I. Thomas, the morality of the male is peculiarly related to business dealings, toward "society at large," especially toward other men. Women's morality is more personal in character, is to a greater degree a "morality of bodily habits," and childbearing becomes an important factor in matters of sexual morality.[8] While the "double standard" of sexual morality permits the male considerable freedom, chastity is, in many societies, a fundamental virtue of women. But her economic rôle is not neglected. The bride is supposed to be both chaste and capable of working. In our own middle-class society, in which the economic rôle of women is less important, the latter function does not seem so important as it does in peasant and primitive societies.

Sex and Economic Differentiation. As we noted in Chapter XII, the household has not only been the locus of childbearing and rearing, but also of important economic functions of the woman. The French anthropologist Charles Letourneau (1831–1902) quotes the old observation that "Woman was first a beast of burden, then a domestic animal, then a slave, then a servant, and last of all a minor." Though obviously exaggerated, this does summarize the traditional rôle of women in many societies, both primitive and modern. While observation of living primitive people shows that there is no rhyme or reason to the particular household duties which are allocated to one sex or the other, it seems reasonable to suppose that the first division of labor was an expression of sex contrast. War and the chase seem the more natural and obvious

[8] See W. I. Thomas, *Sex and Society*, 1907, Chapter V.

habits of the male, while sedentary occupations more easily become the female, who must remain near the primitive hearth in order to give personal attention to the young children. As W. I. Thomas puts it: "The primitive division of labor among the sexes was not in any sense an arrangement dictated by the men, but a habit into which both men and women fell, to begin with, through their difference of organization—a socially useful habit whose rightness no one questioned and whose origin no one thought of looking into."[9] Moreover, so accepted was this view that a man who did woman's work was looked upon with scorn and contempt, not alone by men but by women too. Modern peasant and farm households, until the introduction of industrial devices, were not greatly different from those of more primitive societies. It was not till the commercial and industrial changes of the modern world took women out of the home that their economic functions changed. The emancipation of women—both mothers and grown daughters—from the household economics illustrates again how culture patterns give the direction to social processes themselves. Recent industrial changes have affected the sex and economic rôle and status of women more profoundly than any other event in the history of mankind. The decline in the size of the family is largely a phase of these wider changes and, in turn, frees women from other home duties not strictly economic.

Women in increasing numbers have gone into vocations outside the home, giving them money wages of their own, freedom of residence, and stimulating changes in their personalities which influence other relations of the sexes as well. Some of these changes we have already discussed in Chapter XII.

In spite of great changes there remain many inequalities between the sexes as to rates of pay, hours of labor, control of working conditions, and types of work. Various surveys of wages for comparable work show that women usually earn less than men. As one federal report puts it, "Whether they are old or young, experienced or inexperienced, steady or intermittent workers, the women earn less than the men."[10]

The commoner defense of lower pay for women is that they are not as efficient as men, which is perhaps true in many cases, not

[9] W. I. Thomas, *op. cit.*, p. 140.
[10] *The Share of Wage-earning Women in Family Support*, Women's Bureau Bulletin No. 30, 1923, p. 18.

from less innate ability so much as from lack of adequate training. Then, too, they can often live on less than men, since most of them do not carry family responsibilities. Generalizations on these matters are likely to be false because of varying capacities and situations. In the whole public reaction to the newer economic rôle of women there is a curious paradox. On the one hand much so-called "social legislation" aimed at control of hours, wages, working conditions, and kinds of work for women rests upon the ancient premise of women as members of the "weaker sex." On the other hand, many advocates of women's complete equality with men, especially in economics and politics, demand that they be given the freedom allowed men to enter any vocation, to receive the same wages, and that they attain complete equality before the law. Doubtless this tendency to treat women at work like minors needing special legal protection is but a transition stage toward a different conception of the rôle of workers everywhere regardless of sex.

The Place of Women in Political Activity. Although in primitive society or in peasant and rural farm life women have had a distinctive part in household economics, in the wider community and political control until recently they have had little or no part at all. Even in matriarchal societies, though their community status was important, they nowhere had full control or even equality with men so far as many relations were concerned. The scattered examples of women in history who took part in political control—Cleopatra (69–30 B. C.), Lucrezia Borgia (1480–1519), Catherine de' Medici (1519–1589), Queen Elizabeth (1533–1603), or Catherine the Great (1729–1796)—are special cases, which, like some other exceptions, rather prove the rule.

It is curious that the eighteenth-century romanticists themselves had little place for women in their scheme, although such women as Mary Wollstonecraft (1759–1797), who was profoundly affected by revolutionary romanticism, played a distinctive part in her agitation for equality of the sexes politically and economically. No less a person than Jean Jacques Rousseau, who so greatly affected eighteenth and nineteenth-century thinking, wrote as follows on the education of women:

"The education of the women should always be relative to the men. To please, to be useful to us, to make us love and esteem them, to educate us when young, to take care of us when grown up, to advise, to console us, to render our lives easy and agreeable: these are the duties of women at all times and what they should be taught in their infancy."[11]

Certainly few of the founders of our own republic had any notions of women's political equality with men. That women at the time were not unaware of their changing importance is neatly illustrated in the well-known letter of Abigail Adams (1744–1818) of March 31, 1776, to her husband, John Adams (1735–1826), who was then attending the Continental Congress. Among other things she wrote:

"I long to hear you have declared an independency. And, by the way, in the new code of laws which I suppose it will be necessary for you to make, I desire you would remember the ladies and be more generous and favorable to them than your ancestors. Do not put such unlimited power into the hands of the husbands. Remember all men would be tyrants if they could. If particular care and attention is not paid to the ladies, we are determined to foment a rebellion and will not hold ourselves bound by any laws in which we have no voice or representation."[12]

As we know, little came of this entreaty and threat, but it is interesting to note that on July 2, 1776, New Jersey granted its women the right to vote, a provision which was rescinded in 1807.

This is not the place to retrace the story of women's struggle for a new rôle and status in the political arena of this and other Western countries. During the first half of the nineteenth century, Frances Wright (1795–1852) lectured on women's rights, while the Grimké sisters of South Carolina (Angelina Emily, 1805–1879, and Sarah Moore, 1792–1873) and Abigail Kelley (1810–1887) spoke and wrote against slavery and forced recognition of the right of women to discuss public questions.

It is a curious comment on masculine attitudes of the time to learn that the agitators against Negro slavery were split over the issue of permitting women to participate in their campaign of abolition. This unbelievable discrimination led Lucretia Mott (1793–1880), Elizabeth Cady Stanton (1815–1902)—both prominent leaders of women—to call the first women's rights convention at Seneca Falls, New York, in 1848. Other conventions followed, demanding political equality with men. The description of one of these conventions in the New York *Herald* for September 7,

[11] Quoted by H. Baker-Crothers and R. A. Hudnut, *Problems of Citizenship*, 1924, p. 168.
[12] *Familiar Letters of John Adams and His Wife Abigail Adams, During the Revolution*, 1876, pp. 149–50.

1853, reveals the attitudes and beliefs of the man-made world of that day:

"The assemblage of rampant women which convened at the Tabernacle yesterday was an interesting phase in the comic history of the Nineteenth Century . . . a gathering of unsexed women, unsexed in mind, all of them publicly propounding the doctrine that they should be allowed to step out of their appropriate sphere to the neglect of those duties which both human and divine law have assigned to them. Is the world to be depopulated?"[13]

The national crisis of the Civil War temporarily threw the agitation for women's rights into eclipse. Curiously the Fifteenth Amendment to the federal constitution, which provided the right to vote without reference to "race, color, or previous condition of servitude," did not include the word "sex." When American women naturally asked why they could not vote when the Negro man had been granted this privilege, the United States Supreme Court, in the case of *Minor* vs. *Happersett,* in October, 1874, handed down a decision that citizenship did not confer the right to vote.

Nevertheless, the right to vote was gradually granted women, first in school elections, later in other local elections, and finally in various states in all elections. From about 1896 to 1910 the movement was deflected into agitation for temperance and prohibition of the liquor trade, but during the second decade of this century the woman's suffrage movement was revived with vigor, and a large number of other states, especially in the West and Middle West, granted them the full ballot. In June, 1919, the nineteenth amendment to the constitution provided women full rights to vote.

Just as in business and industry the traditional rôle of woman as woman still plays a part, so in the political arena women are not yet integrated, as citizens, with their men folks. The continued existence of women's political organizations—leagues of women voters and the like—gives evidence that women, denied the equality which is legally theirs, must attempt by forming a bloc or pressure group to influence voting and legislation. Until these practices disappear, it is idle to deny that sex differences still play a part in politics.

In related matters of education and marriage, women have slowly gained equality with men. In 1836 Mt. Holyoke Seminary

[13] Quoted in Baker-Crothers and Hudnut, *op. cit.,* p. 174.

for Women was founded, in 1865 Vassar College was established, and in 1879 Radcliffe. Oberlin College, in Ohio, was the first college in America to adopt coeducation, throwing open its doors to both sexes in 1835. Many professional colleges have been loath to permit women to enroll. Women are not encouraged to enter law, medicine, or engineering, and some professional schools in these fields still bar women students.

Many of the changes in the marital and domestic relations of women we have discussed in Chapter XII, especially those concerning functions in the home, in regard to divorce, and as to freedom in relation to persons outside the family.

In the face of these changes, men have been forced to alter their own habits and attitudes toward women. The male in our society has been reluctant to relinquish his superiority and domination. On the other hand, in their anxiety to accomplish independence and equality, women have often gone to extremes. One of the common fallacies of the more extreme feminists has been their inclination to ape men in clothes, habits, and ideas. It is doubtful whether sex equality requires that differences in clothes, speech, interests, and habits should disappear. Women may well be given opportunities with men for professional work and participation in government not because they are women, but because they have ability. The sexual factor must be disentangled from the long-standing attitudes and habits of both men and women. There is no reason why women cannot develop independence in fields of their own choosing everywhere. What we need is not uniformity, but added variability and stimulation for social inventions which will prove more adequate to our needs. This we will not get if women merely imitate men in a narrow manner and do not really grow up emotionally and intellectually. As a basis for discovering whether women may reach the maturity of men, let us look at various studies of the physical and mental differences between the sexes. On the basis of these data we may be able to say more definitely what place sex may play in future social differentiation.

Physical Differences in the Sexes. Sheer physical differences between the sexes are obvious enough. Correlated with the primary sex characters essential to reproduction are the so-called "secondary" sex features, such as the particular distribution of hairiness of the male and female, the deeper voice of the male, and certain differences in bodily contours, although the wider pelvic arch and the development of the mammary glands in the female are definitely related to her childbearing and nursing. Just what function these secondary traits play in sex relations no one really knows. Much has been written about them, and it seems that among the animals they serve as more obvious external marks of sex differences and doubtless play a part in sex attraction and in the preliminary gestures of sexual activity. With man, affected everywhere as he is by his culture, they come to be associated with all sorts of adventitious things, dress, decoration, and ornamentation, as well as with sexual selection.

True enough, the male and female differ in physique and in sex functioning; yet some of the differences in physical contours probably rest on diet rather than on inherited qualities. Moreover, in sexuality there is evidence of marked overlapping between the male and the female. Everyone is bi-sexual in nature. There are not two distinct groups of traits, one male and the other female. And in social functions male and female rôles overlap at many points. Men by learning and perhaps partially by nature sometimes develop physical and social characteristics traditionally attributed to women, and many women develop so-called "masculine" traits. We all know docile, retiring men who marry dominant, aggressive women. And medical studies of the more intimate lives of married people reveal that in marital relations themselves the traditional rôles of pursuit and submission are not always followed.

Woman has long been referred to as "the weaker sex." Women cannot work so long nor run so far or so fast as men. They are often awkward in many kinds of muscular co-ordinations. They cannot play football, baseball, basketball, or golf as well as men.

It may be asked whether we have any sound evidence of absolute differences in this matter. One of the pioneer studies on the comparative motor and mental abilities of men and women was made by Helen B. Thompson (now Mrs. Woolley). She tested a number of men and women students at the University of Chicago. She found that in the tests of motor ability men outdid the women in most items. In precision of movement the men were but slightly better than women, and in the formation of new motor co-ordinations the women surpassed the men. Other studies have reported somewhat similar differences, but in all there is a great deal of overlapping between the sexes. Often the average differences are slight and statistically insignificant. Mrs. Woolley did not attribute these differences to innate causes, but she rather cautiously remarks, "While it is improbable that *all* the differences of the sexes with regard to physical strength can be attributed to persistent difference in training, it is certain that a large part of the difference is explicable on this ground."[14]

There is little doubt that culture plays a large part in these differences. In the 30 years since Mrs. Woolley's study, attitudes toward physical training for women have changed. One measure of this is seen in the improvement in the athletic records of women.[15]   Though men still excel women, the latter have made great gains. It must be remembered that even today the average boy gets much more physical practice than does his sister. Girls remain more docile, sedentary, less active than their brothers. The handicap of these early years of training in physical coordination and in the building up of strength cannot later be overcome. Expose boys and girls equally to the same physical regimen from early childhood on, and we shall not likely find much average difference. Until such an experiment is performed, people will still go about saying that the male is inherently stronger and muscularly more active than the female.

Mental Differences in Sex.   It is still a common notion that women lack the intellectual ability of men. This view is so deep in our culture that it is very difficult to eradicate it. Women are said to be more intuitive, more suggestible than men. Men are assumed to be more logical, more deliberate and rational. Woman is supposed to be highly emotional, more fickle in her interests, more personal in her vanities, and given to pretty behavior, while man is thought to be more stable emotionally, more impersonal, and concerned with objective, material matters. These differences are assumed to rest on inherited qualities.

What does modern psychology have to say about mental inequalities in relation to sex? Numerous studies do reveal some sex differences in mental abilities. Mrs. Woolley in the study mentioned above made comparative mental tests of the same group of persons to whom she gave the motor tests. We may summarize her more important findings as follows:

[14] Helen B. Thompson (Woolley), *The Mental Traits of Sex*, 1903, p. 178.
[15] See W. I. Thomas, *Sex and Society*, pp. 22–23. Compare with athletic records today. See *World Almanac and Book of Facts for 1938*, pp. 874, 876, 879, 880.

The differences in sense perceptions between men and women are slight, but show that sensory thresholds are somewhat lower for women; yet in sensory judgments in which movement plays a part, as in discrimination of lifted weights and of visual lines and areas, men are somewhat better. Regarding the so-called higher faculties, in Mrs. Woolley's subjects, women were "decidedly superior to men in memory." They seemed also more rapid in associative thinking, while men appeared superior in ingenuity. Regarding general information and intellectual interests there were no sex differences.

As to feelings and emotions there seem to be no sexual differences. "Social consciousness" seems more prominent in men, "religious consciousness" in women. The latter also possess a greater number of superstitions than do men. Certainly in these latter matters—social consciousness, religious faith, and superstitions—the cultural factors determine the differences. Mrs. Woolley's concluding statement is so apt that it is quoted in full: "The point to be emphasized as the outcome of this study is that, according to our present light, the psychological differences of sex seem to be largely due not to difference of average capacity, nor to difference in type of mental activity, *but to differences in the social influences brought to bear on the developing individual from early infancy to adult years*. The question of the future development of the intellectual life of women is one of social necessities and ideals, rather than of the inborn psychological characteristics of sex." [16]

Since Mrs. Woolley's study there have been many investigations of special mental traits such as perception, memory, associative thinking, logical reasoning, and the like. On the whole these studies confirm her findings. Women for the most part do better in memory tests and association, and less well in the logical processes, but the differences are slight.

When general intelligence tests were developed in this country after 1910, many investigations showing sex differences were made. The results tended to show that men were slightly superior to women on the average, and that they were also more variable. But it must be recalled that the tests are for the most part man made. They are also largely academic in character, that is, they bear on school materials. As we said in Chapter V in discussing heredity and environment, it is a highly dubious procedure to attribute most of the differences in general intelligence, as measured by the tests, to innate capacities. This applies to the problem of sex differences. As Havelock Ellis says in his book *Man and Woman* (1904 ed.), our present knowledge of men and women and of their differences

[16] Helen B. Thompson (Woolley), *op. cit.*, p. 189. Italics not in the original.

reflects not "what might be" or "what ought to be," but "what they actually are under the conditions of civilization."

Certainly we must give up the notion that men and women are distinct beings who never have understood and never will understand each other, and who therefore demand different kinds of treatment in our social world. There will continue to be, of course, the primary differences in the reproductive function, but, aside from this, culture will largely decide for us the sex differences in rôle and status.

Further confirmation of much of the discussion here will be found in Margaret Mead's book, *Sex and Temperament in Three Primitive Societies* (1935). Miss Mead investigated three tribes of New Guinea: the Arapesh, the Mundugumor, and the Tchambuli. Although these peoples live relatively near each other and have many cultural features in common, each tribe has a rather distinctive form of sex differentiation. The Arapesh have more or less standardized the personality (rôle and status) of both men and women into the sort which we would describe, against the background of our own culture, as "maternal, womanly, unmasculine." In sharp contrast, the Mundugumor have patterned the rôle and status of women as "actively masculine, virile," and lacking "any of the softening and mellowing characteristics" which people in our society traditionally label as "instinctively feminine." The Tchambuli have still another set of patterns. Their women have a definite position of family and community dominance. As persons they are happy, well-balanced emotionally, highly efficient, and moreover they largely determine sexual choice. The men are at odds with the opposite sex; they feel inferior, unwanted, and timid in love-making. They are so petty and unhappy as to give the outsider the appearance of emotional instability.

The fundamental explanation, therefore, of any differences between men and women, aside from the purely sexual, rests not upon the capacity of the brain or organism, but upon the direction of attention and training laid down in the society. The real variable is the individual, independent of sex or race. The traditional position of women results from lack of opportunity, failure of men to permit them to take part whole-heartedly in the culture, that is, from the isolation which prohibits them from developing their normal capacities. In this regard women are in a position analogous to that of children, the primitive races, and those in the lower economic strata of society. They are not what we call intellectual because they have not been taught how to handle the materials of knowledge. Until women are accorded equal opportunities with men on every hand, we cannot talk accurately about inherent mental or motor differences in the sexes. This whole matter is admirably put by W. I. Thomas in the following passage:

"The mind and the personality are largely built up by suggestions from the outside, and if the suggestions are limited and particular, so will be the mind. The world of modern intellectual life is in reality a white man's world. Few women . . . have ever entered this world in the fullest sense. To enter it in the fullest sense would be to be in it at every moment from the time of birth to the time of death, and to absorb it unconsciously and consciously, as the child absorbs language. When something like this happens, we shall be in a position to judge of the mental efficiency of women. . . . At present we seem justified in inferring that the differences in mental expression are no greater than they should be in view of the existing differences in opportunity."[17]

There may be some men who do not wish to see women inducted fully into the man's world. Those who oppose the advancement of women toward the full participation in the world of men should not hide behind outworn notions of innate biochemical or psychological differences. This only befuddles the issue by being essentially dishonest to both sexes.

In any case it will be some time before women are permitted full participation in the culture around them, and until then we shall see discriminations against them and hear the prophets of doom pronounce in serious tones about what will happen to the home and to children when women do get their equal chances with men.

It must be indicated, furthermore, that if women themselves wish this full participation in the culture around them, they (and men, too, for that matter) must give up many present-day attitudes and practices. If women wish to be treated as equals with men in business, school, or politics, they cannot expect in these situations the special deference, the polite chivalry, the protective treatment from men which traditionally are associated with

[17]W. I. Thomas, "The Mind of Woman and the Lower Races," *American Journal of Sociology*, January, 1907, vol. XII, p. 469. Reprinted in his *Sex and Society*, 1907, p. 312.

their sexual rôle. It is too often true that some of those women who talk glibly of equal rights and privileges themselves want the old-fashioned attentions of men—not only in love-making, but in many other relations quite removed from such.

CLASS ASSIGNMENTS

A. Further reading assignment:
1. K. Young, *Source Book for Sociology*, chap. XIX.
2. C. C. North, *Social Differentiation*, chaps. VI, VII.

B. Questions and exercises:
1. Define and illustrate differentiation.
2. Why must the discussion of individual differences reckon with culture? Illustrate.
3. How do you account for the extension of the period of youth in our society, in contrast to many primitive or peasant societies where the late adolescent is introduced into marriage and adult economic responsibiliites? Have we possibly overdone the matter?
4. Why has old age tended to hold the reins of social control? Is this control likely to continue? What influence has the aging of population on this?
5. Are traditional and present differences in the rôles of the sexes due to inherent or to acquired factors? In what rôles do organic factors play the most significant parts? In what rôles the least significant?
6. Outline the major steps in the emancipation of woman from dependence and social minority to her present relative equality with man in our society.
7. Outline the changes in male habits and attitudes that must necessarily accompany the maturation of women socially.

C. Topics for class reports or longer written papers:
1. Age classifications in primitive societies. (Consult R. H. Lowie, *Primitive Society*, 1920, chaps, X and XI, and bibliography.)
2. Changes in the rôle and status of the aged: recognition of senescence, old age assistance—economic and psychological, and possible contribution of the aged to society and culture. (Consult G. Stanley Hall, *Senescence*, 1922; I. M. Rubinow, *The Quest for Security*, 1934, Book IV; C. M. Morgan, *The Attitudes and Adjustments of Recipients of Old Age Assistance in Upstate and Metropolitan New York*, 1937; George Lawton, "The Study of Senescence," *American Journal of Sociology*, Sept., 1938, vol. XLIV, pp. 280–81.)
3. The changing rôle of women in Western society. (Consult W. I. Thomas, *Sex and Society*, 1907; R. Briffault, *The Mothers*, 1927, vol. III; Hayes Baker-Crothers and Ruth Allison Hudnut, *Problems of Citizenship*, 1924, chaps. XII–XVI, and bibliography; Lorine Pruette, *Women and Leisure*, 1924.)
4. Review of recent psychological findings concerning sex differences. (Consult Robert Sidney Ellis, *Psychology of Individual Differences*, 1928, and bibliography; Anne Anastasi, *Differential Psychology*, 1937; and current files of *Psychological Abstracts* as an introduction to the recent literature.)

CHAPTER XXII

DIFFERENTIATION IN DIVISION OF LABOR AND IN LEADERSHIP

Not only do age and sex play a part in social differentiation, but individual variability in mentality must also be taken into account. The dull find the competition for status or occupation severe. Able persons run ahead of their fellows in the race for prestige. The great majority of folks take a mediocre course because their mentality and social status decree it so. Individual variation in mental ability plays its part together with age and sex in the determination of social rôles. In this chapter we shall examine differentiation as it relates to the division of labor and to leadership.

THE DIVISION OF LABOR

In traditional economics the division of labor refers to the specialization of occupation. In a broader sense, the term applies to all social differentiation of activity. It is obviously related to the rise and continuance of social classes, or stratification. (See Chapter XXIV.) It is evidently basic to the setting up of social rôles or types within various occupational fields: business executives, entrepreneurs, salesmen, and laborers. Rôle is also exemplified in the functions of politicians, statesmen, teachers, administrators, magic workers, prophets, and priests. In fact, individuals in every major form of permanent grouping become differentiated among a number of special social types.

Economic Division of Labor. A society without economic specialization would be one in which each man worked for his own wants, and nobody for another's. Division of labor did not go very far in any society until men began to produce goods or services in such surplus that they could be exchanged for the goods or services of others. *Division of labor* is the specialization in work or service which is beneficial to one's self and others. As Henry Clay puts it in his *Economics for the General Reader* (1918), "From the point of view of the individual, division of labor means *specialization;* from the point of view of society it means *co-operation.*"

Some of the economic advantages of the division of labor are as follows. (*1*) It makes for certain types of occupation in particular *localities,* such as mining in Pennsylvania, shipping in New York City, or raising citrus fruits in Florida. (See Chapter IV.) (*2*) It permits selection of persons in terms of *capacity* to perform particular work. Both intelligence and temperament are important. (*3*) It facilitates the *acquisition of skill,* which means that the "jack of all trades" gives way to those who learn the requisite skill at the most advantageous rates of speed or accuracy. (*4*) It *increases efficiency* because it makes for concentration of attention upon single items in the total production and makes standardization of products possible at low costs. (*5*) It promotes the *factory system,* which allows the assembly of many workers and many machines under one management, makes supervision easier, allows concentration of raw materials at convenient points, and permits advantageous marketing.

The principal disadvantages of the division of labor, especially in our modern factory system, have been put down as follows. (*1*) There is a tendency for over-specialization to so concentrate attention and habits upon simple muscular acts that the *routine and monotony* of the work will destroy the incentive and interest of the worker and make him but a dull robot, tied to a machine that he neither owns nor loves. According to the critics, unpleasant, fatiguing, and disheartening work undermines the morale of the worker. In contrast, these critics point out that the artisan who made a total product—chair, house, pair of boots, piece of cloth, etc.—understood every step in the process, enjoyed himself in putting the material together, and had a genuine pleasure in seeing the finished product. The *machine dominates personality.* As Karl Marx so well pointed out, the machine—an objective, impersonal thing—controls the spirit, initiative, and freedom of the operator. The individual instead of being the end of the economic process becomes merely the means to production, becomes but an appendage to a monstrous system of machines that reduce him to a nonentity. (*2*) The use of the machine tends to *destroy skilled trades* and to substitute the semi-automatic or automatic machine, also leading in many cases to technological unemployment. (*3*) Over-specialization in a capitalist society tends to make the *workman* increasingly *dependent* upon the employer and the type of machine to which he is attached. This exposes him to the risk of unemployment when raw materials are lacking or when there is no market for the goods he helps to make.

Social Implications of Division of Labor. The most outstanding feature of the division of labor is not the separation of functions but the fact that it renders these functions interdependent in a society. Men in society find it advantageous to specialize in their work, only to find that this very specialization binds them to each other with powerful bonds of absolutely essential interaction. It is one of the curious turns of historical fate that the *laissez-faire* policy, which encouraged individualism, should in the end produce a societal structure so interdependent that the dislocation of any considerable part of it, say a key industry like coal mining or transportation, threatens the whole society. In other words, division of labor promotes not only separateness but also the integration of group life. It enhances competition within the circle of the trade or function, but is mutually beneficial for the total society. Clearly co-operation follows from specialization. The woodworker is dependent on the tool-maker for his axes, chisels, and hammers. The weaver is dependent on the shepherd for his wool, and both may require the services of the commercial trader or merchant to market their goods. As the machine age developed, and as the cost of multiple machines became excessive, the banker had to furnish money at interest for the entrepreneur who was willing to take the risk of putting up the factory or business.

Unfortunately the economist has concerned himself too much with the mere mechanics of this interdependence and this specialization. He has forgotten to take account of the social psychological features. As we saw in Chapter VI, interaction has a subjective phase, as well as an overt one of mere stimulus and response. The presence of others to whom we respond means that we have an internal or covert image of them which is associated with their overt behavior. We reflect or mirror these others in ourselves.

The division of labor and its resulting interdependence or co-operation sets up this imagery of interdependence. If one is dependent on another, one carries an image of that other in one's mind, resulting in a kind of like-mindedness in spite of divergence of external activity. As Auguste Comte well said, "It is ... the continuous redivision of our diverse human labors which mainly constitutes social solidarity and which becomes the elementary cause of the extension and increasing complexity of the social organism."[1]

Let us turn now to examine the possible relation of mental differences to division of labor, in economic occupations particularly.

Differences in Mentality and Occupations. The intelligence testing carried on with the American draft army during 1917–1918 threw a good deal of light on intelligence differences in various occupational groupings. Figure 14 shows the differences among various occupational groupings as they were revealed in the army tests. There is a difference in ability, running from unskilled laborers at one end of the scale to engineer officers at the other. Yet there is enormous overlapping. Take, for example, such a high group as mechanical engineers. At the lower end of the scale, this group overlaps about the upper 20 per cent of the laborer group, while at the upper end the mechanical engineers excel the average of all above them except the army chaplains and the engineer officers. Thus while on the average the unskilled and semiskilled have the lowest scores, the skilled and clerical trades the middle scores, and the executives and professional groups the highest, there exists throughout an enormous area of ability common to all.

This great overlapping of intellectual ability among various occupations lowers the statistical correlation between occupation and intelligence, as measured by the tests. Yet no one doubts that intelligence plays a large part in determining occupational rôle and success, although temperamental and emotional factors must be taken into account.

It is especially difficult to analyze the relation of emotional and temperamental traits to occupational choice. Yet recent investigations have thrown some light on the problem, and we may in time discover some really important things about the types of work people like or take up in terms of their dispositional differences. In a society like ours, where there is for most people a wide range of choices of vocation, such a discovery would have important bearings on social differentiation. In Chapter VI we discussed the differences between introverts and extroverts. These differences apparently appear in occupational selection.

While doubtless most people fall into the so-called ambivert

[1] Quoted by Durkheim, in *La division du travail social.* See Park and Burgess, *Introduction to the Science of Sociology,* p. 716.

FIGURE 14

Showing distribution of occupations on the army scale of intelligence

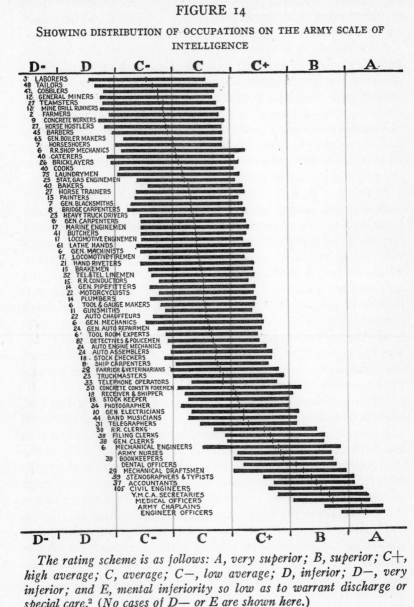

D-	D	C-	C	C+	B	A

The rating scheme is as follows: *A, very superior; B, superior; C+, high average; C, average; C—, low average; D, inferior; D—, very inferior; and E, mental inferiority so low as to warrant discharge or special care.[2] (No cases of D— or E are shown here.)*

[2]From *Army Mental Tests* (a pamphlet), 1918, p. 23.

class, certain studies of occupation suggest that choice of vocation is related to different temperamental and emotional characteristics which are called introversion and extroversion.

Max Freyd, in a study of "mechanically" minded and "socially" minded persons, held that the introvert is more inclined to mechanical interests, while the extrovert tends to be interested in dealing with people and social situations. He found that the socially inclined exceeded the mechanically minded in excitability, self-confidence, open-heartedness, talkativeness, neatness in dress, and in readiness to make friends. The mechanically minded were more self-conscious, conceited, careful of details in their work, and capable of finer co-ordination.[3]

Some years ago, G. W. T. H. Fleming made a study of the records of the mental hospital in the county of Dorset, England, covering a period of 40 years. While his classification was rough because of difficulties in earlier diagnoses especially, his reports tend to confirm these general beliefs. Among the various mental cases, engineers, students, bookkeepers, surgeons, dentists, chemists, soldiers, carpenters, stonemasons, bricklayers, and lawyers tended to fall into the introverted class. On the other hand, farmers, blacksmiths, shopkeepers, policemen, railwaymen, shepherds, merchants, managers, and business directors tended to fall into the extroverted group. There was considerable overlapping, but the differences appeared to be statistically significant in many of the occupational groupings.[4]

While such studies as these are tentative and inconclusive, they suggest that the choice of occupation is determined by emotional and temperamental interests quite as much as by intellectual ability. Of course, culture will play an important part. Where the dominant trends in a society favor particular types of activity, the culture itself sets the stage both for the development of temperamental qualities and for choice of occupation. In America today, dominated as it is by business interests and materialism, there is much indirect and direct pressure put upon our young people to go into business and money-making. The result may well be that we have developed what might be called an "extroverted" set of cul-

[3] See Max Freyd, "Introverts and Extroverts," *Psychological Review*, 1924, vol. XXXI, pp. 74–87.

[4] See G. W. T. H. Fleming, "Introverted and Extroverted Tendencies in Schizoid and Systonic States as Manifested by Vocation," *Journal of Mental Science*, April, 1927, vol. LXXIII, pp. 233–39.

ture patterns, in which the dominant values are those which look to externalities, to handling social situations for making money or acquiring prestige, but which neglect the more introspective arts of contemplation, of subjective literature, and other features of life which may have characterized other societies—the Oriental, for example.[5] This but illustrates again the interplay of psychological motivation and the culture of the time and place.

SOCIAL DIFFERENTIATION AND LEADERSHIP

Manifested in every group, even the intimate congeniality and comradeship associations, are dominance in some persons and a certain submissiveness and followership in others. In groups which have developed institutional features and have long-established culture patterns we usually find certain individuals with authority or power over others. The individual in authority is not, however, necessarily a leader. *Leadership* is a form of dominance and pace-setting which rests upon the interest and acceptance by the followers as well as upon the leader's ability to handle problems. Leadership depends on submissive attitudes and habits of control on the part of the followers. Power by virtue of the inherited position or by reason of some system of promotion up the scale of authority we speak of as *headship*. The boss of a prison chain-gang is not a leader. The president of a corporation, the head of a church, or an elected public official may likewise represent headship rather than genuine leadership. In a society in which there is open competition for rôle and status, headship and leadership often go together. In a caste or rigid class system this correlation may not occur.

Individual Differences and Leadership. Individual variation in the whole range of physical strength, intelligence, and temperament plays a part in leadership. In situations demanding cleverness, keen insight, and quick wit, a different sort of leader will be required than in a situation where brute strength is the essential quality demanded. F. W. Taussig in his *Inventors and Money Makers* (1915) points out how inventors furnish new ideas and new machines, but that business executives, in our culture, are necessary to market the inventions and put them to practical use.

[5] See Ruth Benedict, "Configuration of Culture in North America," *American Anthropologist,* January, 1932, vol. XXXIV, pp. 1–27, for an account of how the culture and the personality interact in primitive societies.

For the most part inventors seem to lack the ability to correlate their inventive work with the profit-making motive. E. B. Gowin in his *The Executive and His Control of Men* (1915) has shown that fire and police officials tend to be larger and stronger in physique than the average man. Where men have to impress other men in face-to-face contact, size and strength are frequently factors of importance in producing prestige and control. Other qualities, of course, are necessary in all of these cases.

Emotion and feeling may be distinctly important in the development of leadership in the arts. Yet emotional drive seems to be significant in executive leadership. In the latter form of leadership, intellectual cleverness alone often does not succeed in competition with less intellectual ability supported by emotional forcefulness. In any case leadership seems to call for efficient expenditure of energy on the issue at hand, forceful control of men or materials, emotional drive or persistence, and high intellectual ability.

Leadership grows not only out of exceptional talent or high intelligence, but at all times depends on the social situation and the culture. Nor are leaders persons with one universal set of traits in every case. We cannot talk about leadership in general, but rather of leadership in specific groups.

Situational Factors in Leadership. Where class organization is strong, leadership tends to go with status as a member of a particular caste or class, and submission and docility to go with membership in the lower ranks. In a democratic society where class lines are poorly drawn, leaders may arise from any group provided they follow the accepted patterns of the culture. In fact, leadership *must* follow the form of the social order and fit into the patterns of its expression laid down in the culture. Leadership is a combination of ability and opportunity. While variation in ability doubtless has some of its roots in biological differences, culture and crises will set the direction of its expression.

Without doubt crisis plays a part in the development of leadership. Confronted with a novel situation for which old devices—material or non-material—do not serve, there is set up an emotional and intellectual tension among members of the group. The leader, whether a mechanical inventor or a statesman, largely focuses these feelings and desires of his group upon a solution. Yet, as we have seen in Chapter III on cultural change, it seems rather clear that no matter how unusual a given leader may seem to his con-

temporaries, the stream of events is more powerful than the outstanding individual. This is not to belittle the leader, but to free
us from the bias that he can control events without reference to
societal organizations and culture.

Among these social situations affecting leadership are occupational and locality backgrounds of leaders. Any number of studies
have shown that leaders come from the better-educated classes
and from urban rather than rural sections. Stephan S. Visher examined the occupation and birthplace of persons included in the
1922–23 edition of *Who's Who in America* in an effort to study this
problem. Table 6 summarizes the pertinent data on the 18,400
persons included therein.

TABLE 6

SHOWING BIRTHPLACE OF PERSONS IN *WHO'S WHO IN AMERICA*
FOR 1922–23 AND THE OCCUPATION OF THEIR FATHERS

Birthplace	Per cent of total	Occupation of father	Per cent of total
Farms	25.9	Farmers	23.4
Villages and towns	24.5	Unskilled laborers	0.4
Small cities	24.8	Semiskilled and	
Large cities	20.6	skilled laborers	6.3
Suburban areas	4.1	Business men	35.3
		Clergymen	11.1
		Other professional men	23.2
		Men of leisure	0.3

Using the 1870 census as a basis (a fair estimate of the population for the period when most of these persons were born), Visher
shows that in proportion to population the cities contributed six
times as many persons as did the farm, villages nine times as many,
and the suburbs eleven times as many. Clergymen fathered 2,400
times as many notables as did the unskilled laborers, in proportion
to numbers. Today, doubtless the business classes, doctors, lawyers, and teachers contribute more than they did at that time, and
the fact remains that the professional and business classes together
still furnish many times their ratio of prominent men, when
prominence is measured on the basis of those who get into *Who's
Who in America*. Wealth alone is not the determining factor, since
clergymen and teachers are not known for high incomes. Doubtless cultural opportunity is the most important factor.[6]

[6] See Stephan S. Visher, "A Study of the Type of the Place of Birth and of the
Occupation of Fathers of Subjects of Sketches in *Who's Who in America*,"
American Journal of Sociology, March, 1925, vol. XXX, pp. 551–57.

Social Interaction and Leadership. Leadership is not static, but dynamic. Its traits are not fixed. They change as the confronting situation changes. Leadership rests, for the person, fundamentally on the expansion of the self-assertive or ego trends, although it is difficult to determine the factors which lie at the basis of ego-expansion or self-assertion.

The direction which ego organization takes is determined both by internal factors and by personal-social and cultural conditioning. Certainly family influences of domination or submission play a distinct part in the development of leadership. Aggressiveness in parents may serve as a stimulus for like behavior in the child. Parents encourage children to display themselves before others. They talk before them of their intelligence, of their qualities of leadership. Not only the strictly personal-social conditioning of children by parents and relatives, but also traditions of leadership in a family—the picture of long generations of successful men and women—affect the children. In our society social status afforded by wealth or professional prestige also plays a considerable part. On the other hand, a leader may arise in spite of repressive influences at home. His native impulses may be strong enough to offset the inferiority arising from the felt repression by parent, brother, sister, or others. For example, a child may develop a certain sense of being left out of things because of the over-attention showered on other children or for other reasons. So far as his own life organization is concerned, such a child may deal with this situation in one of two ways. He may retire into the background, ignoring his competitors and developing a sense of insufficiency, and daydream of being important. Or he may assume an aggressive, dominating attitude to gain attention and maintain his place as the center of the family, which attitude carries out his own fantasy of his continued importance. Such fantasies, in fact, may simply serve as internal stimuli to his aggressive actions. In the one case, the substitute responses remain covert or internal, that is, out of sight of social groups. In the other, they are openly expressed and become the basis for a new scheme of securing ego-expansion. This is probably what Alfred Adler means when he remarks that all persons have some sense of inferiority. With some the substitution remains hidden in the fantasies. In others it becomes overt in compensatory behavior.

Obviously not every overt compensation for inferiority develops into leadership. Other qualities are necessary—intelligence, sympathetic insight, capacity to handle other persons, and opportunity. To contend that all leadership arises as compensation would be to fall into the particularistic fallacy, that is, to attribute single "causes" to complex situations. Without doubt there is much sound leadership which represents genuine growth of personal power over men or situations. We do not yet know the psychology of great men, but the leadership of men like Washington, Lincoln, William James, and Einstein does not seem to be the result of compensation for feelings of inferiority. This belief may be open to question because we know so little of the internal lives of these men; yet they do stand in contrast with other leaders like Napoleon and Theodore Roosevelt, who seem to illustrate, at least in part, the overcoming of feelings of inadequacy.

Another important feature of interaction and leadership has to do with the relations of the leader to the masses who follow him. In large part the leader crystallizes the vague feelings and attitudes of the masses who are confronted with a situation they can not handle. They want something which they cannot define and hence cannot act on intelligently, because until we define situations our actions tend to be impulsive and usually ineffective. The leader offers his followers an object with which they may identify themselves. The phenomenal rise of Napoleon after the French Revolution, of Lenin in Russia, of Mussolini in Italy, or of Hitler in Germany well illustrates how the formation of definite programs accompanied by attractive symbols of strength and security attract the masses long weary of disaster, hardship, and especially uncertainty. They find in the leader and his platform an image that they can follow. So, too, in setting his rôle and in giving him status, they project upon him many qualities which they imagine a leader should have. Then by identification they again get these very qualities back into themselves with added dividends to their own personalities. This projection naturally reacts on the leader, who to be successful must assume these rôles and accept this status. In this sense all leaders are, in the words of Emerson, "representative men"; that is, for their devotees, they are symbols of great thought and power. Finally the leader as symbol affords a focus for feeling and acting together. Around him and his ideas they build up a pattern of response directed to an end and usually satisfying because it appears, at least, to bear fruits in action. In this way leaders become important factors in the process of social control.

Also the types of group and their culture will determine the objects around which leadership may grow up. An intellectual "society" does not foster military leadership, nor does a religious organization ordinarily stimulate scientific genius. Moreover, groups which face a crisis afford opportunities for the rise of leadership that will not occur where the going is smooth and uninterrupted.

In short, even the person who stands out from his fellows as leader is not separated from them except in degree. He has much in common with them in biological background, in his participation in social life, and in his culture. Still, he represents uniqueness and variability of thought and action, even within a particular society. While the culture and the group set the outlines of most of our thought and action, there remains the periphery of individual deviation. And this variation rests originally on biological differences from heredity, if you will, evident at birth and in the early years; it depends on maturation or physical growth, itself affected by endocrine balance; it is affected by personal-social conditioning, especially in the early years and perhaps chiefly by cultural factors; and finally, it depends on the particular interpretation which the individual himself gives to the mass of culture that pours in upon him.

Types of Leaders. While simple classifications are likely to be misleading in sociology and social psychology because of the complexity of our data, leaders have been conveniently put into two groups: the leader of men and controller of social situations, and the leader in the field of ideas. O. L. Schwarz in his book *General Types of Superior Men* (1916) calls the first sort the "man of action," the second the "man of thought."[7]

The first type of leader controls men and practical situations in business, politics, military activities, and the ritualistic and organized phases of religion. We may call this *executive* or *extrovert* leadership. The second controls ideas and imaginative productions, as in invention or scientific research, or non-material phenomena, as in art, religion, science, and philosophy. We may call this *nonexecutive* or *introvert* leadership.

[7]See K. Young, *Source Book for Social Psychology*, pp. 592–95, for pertinent selections from Schwarz.

We do not know how much to make of this possible connection of extroversion with one and introversion with the other. We constantly find the mechanism of substitution in both types, and in any detailed study of personality we must consider the entire history of the person himself and make an analysis of his whole experience. Certainly the person who deals with men is marked by a capacity to meet people in face-to-face situations and to adjust himself to them in the process of controlling them. He is able to determine their course of action, and yet he must be flexible enough to appreciate their own attitudes and ideas. The insight necessary to successful executive leadership, no doubt, requires a certain amount of introversion, or else the leader's identification with others would not be sufficient to enable him to control and direct them. In the intellectual leader, introverted traits are more apparent. Certainly the poet, the scientist, the artist, or the philosopher, who cuts himself off from the currents of action by living in a world created by his own imagination, is introverted. Nevertheless, extroverted traits are essential to enable the intellectual leader to have certain contacts with his fellows. Introversion and extroversion in their purest forms doubtless occur only in the neurotic or psychotic individuals. In all types of leadership there is sufficient balance of both to keep one within the bounds of certain social formulations. In other words many leaders are doubtless really ambiverts, possessing traits of both extroversion and introversion. (See Figure 6, Chapter VI, p. 126.)

Other classifications of leaders have been made. A. B. Wolfe in his volume *Conservatism, Radicalism, and the Scientific Method* (1923) has distinguished between the radical, the conservative, and the man of science. These men represent, in a sense, variations in social rôle. Wolfe shows that often the conservative and the radical are both emotional and highly biased in regard to the things they value most, while only the scientist, as scientist, retains his impartiality and impersonality.[8] Harold D. Lasswell in his book *Psychopathology and Politics* (1930), in discussing political leadership, has distinguished between the bureaucrat or administrator, the agitator, and the theorist. These again represent social rôles, based evidently upon rather distinctive personality characteristics. The *administrator* is characterized by habits

[8] The author has shown elsewhere that scientists are only impartial and objective minded in reference to their specialty. See K. Young, "The Need of Integration of Attitudes among Scientists," *Scientific Monthly*, 1924, vol. XVIII, pp. 291–305.

and attitudes of precision, orderliness, compulsions for system and for rigidity of action. The *agitator* is often marked by intense self-love, strong belief in verbal stimuli, great faith in magical or fantastic devices for reforming the world, and frequently a strong sense of being persecuted by others—itself a powerful motive for "fixing" things in the world so as to suit one's own conception of right and wrong. The *theorist* applies his energies toward making a more systematic analysis of the world, attempting thereby to formulate a consistent, logical picture of his world. Often he is interested in reform, but again he may desire to preserve the *status quo*. His essential interest, however, is in abstractions, in ideas, and in constructions of a rich but controlled imagination. Unlike the administrator, he is not bothered with concrete details of order and the daily round of duty.

These three types seldom occur in pure form, and persons frequently combine all three. Lasswell cites Herbert Hoover as essentially an administrator, the Old Testament prophets as agitators, and Karl Marx as a theorist. William Lloyd Garrison (1805–1879) was an agitator and administrator of ability. Nikolaii Lenin (1870–1924), on the other hand, and Thomas G. Masaryk (1850–1937) of Czechoslovakia represent a composite of all three.

Spranger's six types of men, theoretical, economic, aesthetic, social, political, and religious, might also serve as a classification of leaders. (See Chapter VI.) In fact, any classification of personality types or of social types for the general population may be used to describe the leaders of men, for after all the latter are but the symbols and representatives of the millions who stand behind them.

CLASS ASSIGNMENTS

A. Further reading assignment:
1. K. Young, *Source Book for Sociology*, chap. XX.
2. C. C. North, *Social Differentiation*, chap. IX.

B. Questions and exercises:
1. What does Clay, the economist, mean by stating that from the individual's point of view division of labor means "specialization," but from the point of view of society it means "co-operation"?
2. Cite cases in which intelligence or temperamental differences affect the social rôle of an individual.
3. Cite cases to show the differences in the social rôle of introverts and extroverts.

4. What are some of the broader societal effects of the economic division of labor?

5. Discuss, pro and con, the contention that machine specialization destroys the integration of the personality in regard to occupation.

6. What is a frequent classification of leaders as to social rôle? Illustrate.

7. Define introvert; extrovert. What relation have these personality types to the social rôles of leaders?

8. How may the nature of the crisis affect the rise of leadership?

9. How will the ethos of a society influence the type of leadership?

C. Topics for class reports or longer written papers:

1. Recent literature on individual differences in relation to economic and social status. (Consult Robert Sidney Ellis, *Psychology of Individual Differences*, 1928; Anne Anastasi, *Differential Psychology*, 1937; and bibliographies; also current files of *Psychological Abstracts* for references to more recent literature.)

2. The theory of personality types in reference to social rôle. (Consult Emil Kretschmer, *Physique and Temperament*, 1925, and his *The Psychology of Men of Genius*, 1931; C. G. Jung, *Psychological Types*, 1923; Gardner Murphy and F. Jensen, *Approaches to Personality*, 1932, and bibliography; and Gladys Schwesinger, *Heredity and Environment*, 1933, especially chaps. II and V, and bibliography.)

3. The social rôle of leadership: psychological and cultural phases. (Consult K. Young, *Source Book for Social Psychology*, chaps. XX and XXI and bibliography; H. D. Lasswell, *Psychopathology and Politics*, 1930, and bibliography; Paul Pigors, *Leadership or Domination*, 1935.)

CHAPTER XXIII

ACCOMMODATION

The social processes are not only continuous, but they vary with the nature of the interaction. As competition becomes direct and personal, it leads to conflict. But conflict by its very nature is intermittent, periodic, and cyclic. Man cannot go on fighting all the time. He must find food, shelter, mates, and satisfaction of other wants. Even though he again comes into conflict with his fellows, in the meantime some sort of working relation must be reached with those about him. If the persons or groups strike a truce but do not intermarry or fuse their cultures, we call this accommodation. If they intermarry and fuse their cultures, we speak of it as biological amalgamation and as cultural assimilation. In the present chapter we are concerned only with accommodation.

OPPOSITION AND ACCOMMODATION

Society is a vast array of groups and individuals constantly adapting and readapting themselves to each other and to their physical environment. Society is an interacting totality in a sort of moving equilibrium. In setting up this balance of forces accommodation plays an important part.

Nature of Accommodation. *Accommodation* is used to refer to a condition or state of being and to a process. As a condition it refers to the fact of equilibrium between individuals and groups which give them status, and which reveal the rules of the game which have been developed. The "proper" etiquette, the "agreements" developed between conflicting economic groups, and the techniques, traditions, and arrangements which define the relations of persons and groups are forms of accommodation. In other words, as a condition accommodation represents a *fait accompli.*

As a process accommodation has to do with the efforts of men to develop working arrangements among themselves in order to eliminate conflict and to make their relations more tolerable and less wasteful of energy. It concerns the movement toward the accommodated state. It is a means of resolving conflict without the complete destruction of the opponent. It is a working arrangement between rivalrous or conflicting groups which makes possible some form of interaction in which the identity of the respective groups is not lost. It takes place at a conscious but not necessarily rational level and for the most part is arrived at by formal and external regulations or arrangements. The definition by Melvin J. Vincent covers most of the essentials:

"Accommodation is that social process which brings about a conscious adjustment of conflict and which involves one or more, or all, of the following: some form of a gesture for peace, some consideration of the difficulties involved, some concession with respect to desired objects or ends, and some toleration of the proposed consequent status, in order to effect one or more of the following ends: (1) to soften or mitigate conflict between persons or groups so as to permit forces to work which will eventually bring about assimilation between the persons or groups; (2) to postpone overt conflict for definite periods of time; (3) to enable persons or groups widely separated by social distance to carry on life activities within close spatial distance, and this in the face of the antagonisms which may exist because of the barrier of social distance; (4) to forestall undesirable assimilation."[1]

Accommodation rests upon acceptance by both parties to the project. In other words a certain consensus grows up which permits the working arrangement to be carried on.

This balance of forces is expressed by the term *social distance*, which reveals the degree of sympathetic understanding, or the difference existing between persons or groups, or between a person and a group. As E. S. Bogardus well says, "It is the measure of latent or actual conflict. . . . It represents the inner spirit of social organization."[2] In other words, accommodation plays a distinctly important part in the development of the social order, in balancing antagonistic and competing interests. The relations may remain at this level, or they may be further changed by the still more intimate process of assimilation. (See Chapter XXV).

In spite of a balancing of antagonistic interests in order to secure social peace, there usually remain incipient or potential conflicts.

[1] Melvin J. Vincent, *The Accommodative Process in Industry,* 1930, p. 4.
[2] E. S. Bogardus, *Contemporary Sociology,* 1931, p. 328.

The very persistence of prejudices, myths, legends, and other culture traits of opposition and conflict as a part of the total accommodative residue is evidence of this. Some new crisis, some new situation for which the accommodation of the past is not prepared, is all that is usually needed to set aflame the latent conflict. For this very reason it is important that in the accommodative process provision be made for building up and strengthening those ideas, attitudes, and habits that foster the continuation of these accepted relations. In the event of a new crisis, these may limit the emotional extremity to which the new conflict will go. Some features of this point will be apparent as we discuss the forms of accommodation.

In a specific sense, accommodation deals only with those arrangements growing out of conflict. With this in mind, it is evident that the nature of the conflict, its background, its inception, and its course, will determine in large part the nature of the accommodation which results. As we have seen in Chapters XVIII and XIX, the direction and intensity of the conflict varies with the groups and the situations in which they find themselves with respect to each other. Where the conflict occurs between economic groupings, between nations, or between strongly organized religious groups which represent fundamental wants and interests with strong emotional identification of the members, the accommodative process will be different from that where it grows out of less intense and vital conflict.

FORMS OF ACCOMMODATION

For our purposes we shall analyze the *forms* of accommodation, regardless of the *areas* in which they arise. Our illustrations naturally develop out of the fields of conflict discussed in Chapters XVIII and XIX.

The accommodative process runs a course from those situations where there is direct power and coercion of one group over another to milder and more sublimated relationships which we find in conciliation, deliberation, and tolerant participation. There are clearly some differences to be drawn among these, and we shall follow a tentative classification as follows: (*1*) coercion and domination, (*2*) compromise, (*3*) conciliation, (*4*) toleration, and (*5*) conversion.

Coercion and Domination. *Coercion* is a type of accommodation in which action, thought, or social relationship is determined by restraint or the compulsion of force. Coercion always implies the existence of the weak and the strong in any conflict. It takes two forms, physical or direct, and psychological or indirect. The defeated party must accept the arrangements of relationship laid down by the stronger. Nevertheless, even these forms of forced conformity rest upon consensus within the community. Two excellent examples of coercion are found in slavery and in dictatorships or despotic control.

As we noted in earlier chapters, one way to settle a conflict is to annihilate the opponent. But this is the most primitive and socially the most costly outcome of conflict. Men learned that there were distinctive benefits to be gained by preserving the lives of their captives and putting them to work under an arrangement which gave them living and shelter but which did not permit them freedom of choice as to movement, occupation, or participation as citizens.

Thus, *slavery* is an accommodation to force, in which the basic social relation is one of subjection of slave to his master. A slave is one who is not free. There can be no slaves unless there are freemen. Slavery implies absence of political rights, compulsory labor, and property rights of the master in the slave. H. J. Nieboer in his book *Slavery as an Industrial System* (1910) defines a slave as "a man who is the property of another, politically and socially at a lower level than the mass of people, and performing compulsory labor."

Political dictatorships represent a form of coercive accommodation in which some strongly organized minority seizes the reins of power and inflicts its control upon whole populations. It is a mistake to imagine that despotism or dictatorship is never a welcome manner of settling conflicts. In a democracy like ours the ordinary person easily projects into slavery or dictatorship his own beliefs and attitudes. This simply confuses the interpretation of despotism. Political dictatorship usually arises in a time of crisis which involves a wide range of values and interests. Frequently the dictatorship is preceded by a long period of conflict between various special interest groups. The continued disorder often produces in the masses a desire for some strong hand at the helm which will bring peace and order. Napoleon Bonaparte (1769–

1821) was such a person. By a series of forced accommodations among warring elements growing out of the French Revolution he restabilized France. Benito Mussolini did the same thing for Italy in the post-war years. Adolf Hitler stopped the internal conflicts within Germany, brought about the long-sought union with Austria, and put up a solid national front to the outside world. Without a doubt the success of the Communist Party in Russia rests upon a similar solution of social crisis.

Force is used to settle other sorts of conflict than those of conquest and intra-national disorders. Coercion may arise in any situation where there is a sufficiently strong group on the one hand that has defeated or threatens to defeat another. In racial, industrial, and religious conflicts, it has been used over and over again. Even in the smaller primary groups of family, playground, and neighborhood, recalcitrant members are frequently forced to agree to activity which they dislike. The fundamental training in coercion and submission is, in fact, given in the primary group. The pattern is simply carried over later to the wider group contacts.

The socially disintegrative and "evil" effects of coercion in the modern world are apparent. Despotism and exploitation go hand in hand. Since coercion rests on force, it is very easy in the accommodative process for the dictator to confuse the use and abuse of this same power. Power, like jealousy, grows by what it feeds on. Force, too, breeds fraud. The masses and officials often develop all sorts of devices of petty graft or deceit for escaping the rigorous rules of conduct laid down by the dictator and his party. Outer conformity by no means implies inner conviction. Hypocrisy is an easy outgrowth of coercive measures.

Force defeats its own aims by building up force as a counteractant. The long ages during which the conflict patterns dominated the Western world demonstrated this once and for all. In the present highly differentiated society it is important to construct an order which fosters milder forms of conflict and hence milder forms of accommodation. As we saw in Chapter XVIII, the symbolism of war and open conflict carries over into subsequent peace times, thus serving as a germ from which will grow the next war or other open conflict.

Nevertheless coercion is not altogether useless. In times of great emergencies, in transitional periods when social change is taking place at a rate which produces disorder, the use of force may be necessary to preserve the whole structure from falling apart or to co-ordinate the societal order after a revolution. This is the rationalization of the Russian and fascist dictators, who stoutly maintain that their coercive measures are transitional in character.

Compromise and Arbitration. Unlike coercion, which follows from the distinctly unequal power of the two parties to the accommodation, *compromise* implies a certain degree of equality in bargaining power. It implies a condition of give and take. In this sense it is akin to barter and to higher forms of commerce, and thus comes close to some of the features of economic competition. Compromise we may define as a conscious method of settling a conflict in which all parties agree to renounce or reduce some of their demands in the interest of peace.

The readiness to compromise means that the parties to the situation are able to look upon their interests in a somewhat dispassionate, objective manner, at least up to the point of presenting their case to the other side in the form of negotiations. This capacity to objectify the situation is neatly recognized in wage and other industrial disputes where the conflict can be settled in terms of money. Agreement on wage rates, hours of work, sanitary conditions, and the like, represent for the conflicting groups factors in their relations which are considered somewhat distinct from their emotional attitudes.

In religious controversy, compromises can scarcely take this monetary form. Nevertheless, in agreements between warring sects, for example, each gives up some point of view in order to agree upon what are considered more fundamental matters. The whole trend to church consolidation today represents a form of compromise. (See Chapter XIV.)

In political matters, compromises often occur between fighting groups who find some common ground for agreement. The aphorism of Edmund Burke, the English statesman (1729-1797), is well known: "All government . . . is founded on compromise and barter. We balance inconveniences; we give and take;—we remit some rights, that we may enjoy others." The manner in which warring political groups reach agreements differs with the culture patterns of the particular government. In representative democracy this form of accommodation has been highly developed among political parties when they are about evenly matched as to voting power. Even in absolute monarchy or dictatorships the ruler must concede much to the interests and beliefs of his subjects. Still most of these latter practices grow up without formal conscious agreement and are not in the strict sense compromise. Strict compromise is a conscious modification and adoption of demands. Politically it is best illustrated in representative democracies where the party and parliamentary system have developed machinery for just this method of settling disputes and arriving at legislative action.

If we accept the theory that the state itself frequently owes its origin to the conquest of one community by another, we may well regard compromise as a factor in building up the political order, since the conquered, if not made slaves, would most likely be in a position to bargain for some rights, even against the conquerors.

Arbitration is a special device for bringing about compromise when the contending parties are unable themselves to end their struggle. The arbitrator is supposed to hear both sides and to render a decision which may or may not be binding on the contestants, depending upon the rules laid down beforehand. *Mediation,* closely related to arbitration, is the introduction of a neutral power into the situation whose efforts are bent to bring about an amicable settlement but without any agreed power to settle the conflict.

The use of a mediator or arbitrator has been common in industrial and religious disputes in our own society. Arbitration clearly differs from compromise by mutual agreement, but both methods have been found effective.

Where the wider community is concerned, as is usually the case in industrial disputes, the state may as arbitrator be also a party to negotiations in seeing that the public is not injured by the compromise agreements of two parties to an economic dispute. (See Chapter XXVII on social control.)

Critics have attacked the whole philosophy of compromise as weak and inefficient. The nineteenth-century school of economic and political liberalism tended to look upon compromise as the *sine qua non* of accommodation. The difficulty with compromise is that it encourages temporizing; it implies that the opposition has something to offer. Certainly there is much reason to oppose compromise and temporizing in the field of ideas and ideals. It is like putting scientific questions to a majority vote. As we noted previously, there is much to be said for the Marxian doctrinaries who have refused compromise and other forms of accommodation with other ideas and programs. It gives an objective tone to their struggles that aids them in gaining converts, especially in countries where compromises and half measures have failed.

Still, in a world of human beings, in which emotions and feelings and not ideas play such a large part, it seems idle to assume that compromise will not long continue to be an important method of settling conflict. There is no reason to abandon the position that the cultural and social world is one of balance and change, not some absolute entity in which there is but one course to follow. While there remains strain after compromise, while one does not have everything he wishes from it, it does have certain advantages in a world of temporizing. In our earliest social relations all of us learn to get along with half measures. To operate in the social world on the all-or-none principle is impossible. We soon discover it will not get us the things that we wish. In a world of contending wishes and interests and a limited supply of goods, material or otherwise, compromise seems inevitable.

Conciliation. Closely related to compromise is *conciliation*. It represents an attempt to reconcile the disputants as a means of bringing about an agreement. While in the industrial conflicts of modern capitalist society, arbitration is frequently linked with both mediation and conciliation, the standpoint is somewhat distinct in the latter.

In our modern industrial system certain forms of conciliation have grown up as a permanent program for settling disputes between owners and workers. Such organizations are variously called "works councils," "shop committees," and "company unions," which may or may not exist independently of trade unions. In these organizations representatives of the owners and the workers set up institutional devices for handling disputes as to wages, hours, and other working conditions. Again we see the culture patterns reflected in the processes themselves. Where the labor union movement, as in America, adopts the open conflict patterns, looking to agreements through compromise or coercion, the milder form of accommodation is scorned.

Conciliation has been used in religious disputes and even in racial conflicts. As elsewhere the strength of differences and attitudes of antagonism limit this means of accommodation. For conflicting races to adopt this method of settling their struggles would mean that they had already given up many of their distinctive ethnocentric ideas, their conceptions of absolute superiorities. Conciliation as a means of accommodation, then, depends upon the dissipation of the more violent antagonisms of the contestants. It implies a distinctive change of heart and a willingness to lay themselves open to assimilation.

Deliberation or discussion between the parties to a conflict is an essential ingredient of accommodation which arises out of compromise, arbitration, mediation, or conciliation. It means that the problems are faced in terms of ideas and objectivity. It implies a suspension of hostilities until matters of difference can be talked out. Deliberation as a means of settling disputes is distinctly linked to other culture patterns of any given society, particularly democracy, liberalism, and scientific attitude. It is important in giving rise to consensus of beliefs and opinions, so essential to an acceptance of any agreement which takes into account the demands and wishes of each party on any platform of comparative strength or equality. When the parties meet together to discuss their conflicts, the struggle is sublimated to the level of verbal give and take. The whole conflict is put forward in symbolic, not overt, terms. This permits the consideration of phases of the total situation, which would be lost in the less selective interaction of overt conflict.

Toleration and Participation. As we know, group life could not go on without participation of the members in common as well as in divergent action. As a means of settling conflict it is sometimes possible to bring the contending individuals and groups into such relations that they accept certain rules of behavior which make it possible for rather divergent interests to be carried forward without complete acceptance of each other's views or without formal or legal compromises being laid down. This we may call *toleration,* or better, *tolerant participation.* Toleration depends on the acceptance of the live-and-let-live policy. It implies appreciation of the views of the other fellow. It is a form of accommodation without formal agreement. It is sometimes not entirely conscious, growing up from long-standing practices of antagonistic interaction. It is well described by E. A. Ross as "regulated avoidance." The function of taboo in keeping groups or individuals apart is apparent here. It is common in class and caste systems, to be discussed in the next chapter. The following quotation well illustrates how the matter worked out between two opposing groups who resided within the same community, with many common views, but also with distinctive cultures and a definite disinclination to intermarriage and assimilation or fusion of cultures.

"It is curious to see how these two German races have existed side by side for over a hundred years without amalgamating, and this for no sort of antagonistic reason, for they live in perfect harmony, attending the same church, and conforming to the same regulations, but each people preserving its own individual costume and customs. The Saxons and Landlers have each their different parts of the church assigned to them, no Saxon woman would ever think of donning the fur cap of a Landler matron, while as little would the latter exchange her tight-fitting fur coat for the wide-hanging mantle worn by the other."[3]

What is called bi-racial accommodation is in large part another illustration of tolerant participation. Wherever races in any numbers come into contact with each other, the resulting conflict usually leads to some sort of accommodation if the divergent races are to continue to live in any sort of interaction. Only when biological amalgamation and assimilation take place, will this sort of arrangement disappear.

Negro-white relations in this country well illustrate bi-racial accommodation. The rise of the Negro from a low social status to a higher one is not unlike the changes which have taken place in history, with the emancipation of the serfs in Europe and their rise to the class of peasants, and later in urban Europe and America, their further emancipation to the rôle and status of wage earners in industry.

Although the process of Negro rise has been somewhat like that of serf, peasant, and wage earner, with the Negro the matter is complicated by the background of slavery and race prejudices. In a sense the Negro in this country represents a nationality group within a still larger group. (See Chapter XXV on assimilation.)

In recent years two major areas of bi-racial conflict have arisen. The first of these is the competition and conflict of Negroes and whites in urban localities involving labor competition, housing, voting, crime, and close race contact. This is chiefly confined to the Northern states. The second concerns the intrusion of Southern whites of lower economic status into occupations once in the hands of Negroes—domestic service, barbering, and unskilled labor.

[3]From Jane E. Gerard, *The Land Beyond the Forest*, 1888, pp. 96–97. Quoted by E. A. Ross, *Principles of Sociology*, 3rd ed., 1938, p. 330.

Unless there is assimilation, some sort of accommodation is necessary. Assimilation is impossible without the mixture of races. This racial mixture, which we may call *amalgamation,* does go on between whites and blacks in this country, but it is slow and relatively inconsequential, since the mulatto or mixed person is classified as a Negro and forced to take his place in the depressed groups. True, every year a few Negroes "pass" the color line, as it is put, but these small numbers can scarcely affect the process of accommodation or make for assimilation in the broader sense.

Various accommodative concrete devices have arisen out of Negro-white relations, some legal, some in the mores. "Jim Crow" cars for Negroes, the various "grandfather clauses" as a means of keeping the ballot from the Negro, community mores "to keep the nigger in his place," to restrict his economic advancement, to keep him from equal educational privileges with whites—these and others typify the form which the bi-racial accommodation has taken in the past.

No really rational and carefully planned form of accommodation has yet been worked out. Various leaders from both races have set up bi-racial committees to study the problem, which in some instances have tried to influence the course of law and public opinion. The Interracial Committee of Atlanta, Georgia, is one of the most effective of these groups, and the organization has played a part in directing public opinion on race questions into more intelligent channels. Following race riots or other racial conflict, local committees have sometimes grown up with quasi-legal status —often appointed by mayors or other officials—for the purpose of studying local racial problems and bringing in recommendations. This was done in Chicago and Detroit in the years following the World War, when large numbers of colored people moved in from the South and created industrial, political, and social problems of serious proportions. These committees have attempted to foster tolerant participation. The Chicago Commission on Race Relations in its report following the Chicago race riots of 1919 made fifty-nine specific recommendations directed to various public and private agencies and to the general public.

These covered among other points suggestions regarding (1) better police protection of colored groups, (2) improvement in recreational facilities for blacks and whites in the same sections of the city, (3) betterment of educational opportunities for the Negroes, (4) dissipation of false notions about the Negro race, especially through schools and public and private social agencies, (5) realization of community responsibility for violence of race riots, (6) removal of white prejudices about Negro mentality, criminality, and the like, (7) recognition by the colored population of their own prejudices, (8) betterment of labor conditions, (9) recognition by Negro workers of the problems regarding Negro labor unions, skilled trades, strike-breaking, and so on, (10) provision of adequate street car facilities for Negro passengers, (11) recognition of equal rights of Negroes with whites in restaurants, theaters, and stores, and (12) improvement in the honesty and accuracy of news stories of Negro-white relations and the avoidance of inflammatory accounts of conflicts.[4]

These recommendations represent, of course, an ideal of accommodation rather than an actuality. Particularly difficult to put into practice are: (*1*) those bearing on housing, where because of long-standing prejudices, it is difficult to hope that whites and blacks will live in the same neighborhood without some racial friction arising; (*2*) those bearing upon membership of Negroes in white unions, because of the prejudices against colored workers as inferior, as wage-cutters, and as strike-breakers; (*3*) those bearing on equality of treatment by employers; (*4*) those suggesting that Negro manual laborers learn the skilled trades, because there are so few opportunities for Negroes in the higher occupations; (*5*) those having to do with race pride among the Negroes, which is perfectly natural as a compensation for their felt inferiority; and finally, (*6*) those suggesting that the modern urban press do not continue to foster myths and legends about race friction, which in the light of the part the press plays as the principal myth-maker in our complex society is asking more than we may expect for some time to come.

The relations of immigrant groups to each other and especially to the dominant native citizens represent other areas of tolerant participation under forms of regulated avoidance and more or less specified contacts. The ghetto of the medieval town, the segregated districts of vice, and contemporary immigrant neighborhood illustrate spatial expression of this form of accommodation. (See Chapter XXV on assimilation.)

Other forms of conflict may be settled by somewhat the same sort of device. Sex conflicts may result in toleration and separation in which the respective spheres of each sex are more or less defined

[4] The full report and recommendations are published under the title, *The Negro in Chicago*, 1922. See pp. 640-51 for the specific recommendations.

by custom. Thus, the limitation on the occupation of women to certain fields and the social taboo on their participation in others is an illustration. Likewise age conflicts might conceivably result in the fixing of certain areas of behavior for the conflicting age groups, and in some societies age and sex classifications are firmly imbedded in the culture.

Regulated avoidance leads directly into the matter of social stratification, the fixing of class lines, which we shall discuss in the next chapter. But before closing our discussion of forms of accommodation we must look briefly at conversion, a somewhat special form of accommodation.

Conversion. Sometimes there is a sudden acceptance of the ideas and attitudes of an opposite group, which we call *conversion*. It usually involves a shift in attachment and loyalty from one group to another. In our society we witness it in adolescence, but it occurs in adult life also. Conversion is the one form of accommodation which cannot truly take place without strong emotional shift of object. Although conversion may not be permanent, while backsliding is not unknown, so long as it lasts it is effective, because there can remain little of the old life once the new is taken on. Not that psychologically the old life disappears entirely, but it must be suppressed into non-activity. This fact, of course, is always to be remembered: conversion is a formal defeat of one set of ideas, attitudes, and habits by another through the use of suppression. It is not a fusion but a transference, and like all substitutions, it involves some gains as well as losses. This is why conversion as a first step in accommodation is best followed by more adequate integration of opposing elements into a new whole. The conformity of the new standards must not only be at the outset voluntary, but in time must become "second nature" to the individual.

Conversion is best known in the field of religion and morals. It may take the form of a more quiescent personal revelation, communion with the divine, assurance of salvation, or it may take the form of a mass movement, such as we get in religious revivalism or religious mental epidemics. The form which it takes will depend upon the culture of the society. Whole sects have grown up out of revivalism and conversion practices which continue later as standard practices in the group.

Conversion is not necessarily confined to religion. It may take place in the field of economics and politics. We all know cases of conversion of persons from belief in representative democracy and *laissez-faire* capitalism to communism or fascism. Here as in religion the transference is accompanied by emotional as well as by intellectual change.

Conversion is directed more to individuals than to groups, although, as noted above, it may involve a large number of people. Unlike coercion, compromise, and even deliberation and participation, it is hardly a method by which a group may be consciously brought to agreement with another by ordinary conscious methods of accommodation. In this sense, conversion points toward a fuller and more complete assimilation later. This is not necessarily true of such processes as coercion and compromise.

PERSONALITY AND ACCOMMODATION

Accommodation grows out of or sets up interactions of domination and submission. Other subjective factors which accompany the accommodative process particularly are those of selection, balance, substitution, rejection, rationalization, and idealization. These personality reactions find their expression in accommodation as it develops out of conflict.

Domination and Submission in Accommodation. Georg Simmel has made an incisive analysis of dominance and submission, or superordination and subordination, in relation to conflict and accommodation.[5] We shall follow his classification and deal with the matter under three headings: submission or domination exercised by a person, by a group, or by an impersonal ideal or "principle higher than individuals."

In every social interaction there is a matching of ego power. Even in co-operation it is easy for rivalry to arise, as where persons strive to outdo others in the interest of the common good. In competition, and in its related process of differentiation, the struggle for goods or power, although relatively impersonal, implies an interaction in which conditions of superiority or inferiority arise. In conflict, this desire for dominance is all-important.

Submission to an individual implies that the group is completely under the control of one person. The group in this situation

[5] See Georg Simmel, "Superiority and Subordination as Subject-Matter of Sociology," transl. by A. W. Small, *American Journal of Sociology*, 1896, vol. II, pp. 167–89, 392–415.

may be viewed as a unity in reference to the dominant individual. There is identification of the members of the group to the individual as head or leader. The single unifying individual serves as a symbol for the accommodative relations of the others. The symbol of the sovereign in the political state is typical, and the division of powers is likely to foster a breakdown of the political solidarity, leading, in turn, to new conflicts and a new alignment of power.

When the domination is complete, as in the master-slave or absolute monarch and subjects relationships, it might be imagined that the latter had no freedom of action in reference to the former. This is not true. The master is not uncontrolled by his slave. The latter has at least a limited range of reciprocal relations. The master or monarch is himself bound by his commands to his slaves or subjects. In addition slaves or subjects set up whole areas of expectant attitudes toward the dominant person which he cannot very well ignore. As a Negro once remarked to R. E. Park, "We colored people always want our white folks to be superior." In instances of conversion the leader often plays an important part as the focus of subordination. In cases of arbitration or legal judgment the third person may acquire this sort of prestige.

If the domination takes the form of popular leadership in religious, economic, or political fields, the reciprocal obligations of the dominant person and his followers are even more apparent. As we have seen, the leader acquires power because he is given it by his followers; his prestige is an outgrowth both of identification of followers and their projection upon him of power and ability. Simmel quotes a German parliamentary leader as saying to his party, "I am your leader, therefore I must follow you." While the leader may crystallize and verbalize the feelings and wishes of the masses, he cannot escape their limiting influence upon him. Often he becomes the symbol of more than he really is. He not only acquires superior status, but he must follow the rôle which the followers set for him. This is what J. A. Spender, the English publicist, meant when he said that a public man, that is, the public's man, has no private life. He belongs to his followers, and if he fails to satisfy them, his days of leadership are likely to be numbered.

In all cases, therefore, of submission to an individual, there is interaction between him and his inferiors or followers. There is always a form of interaction and participation, even though it be circumscribed within the limits of political, economic, or religious despotism. As Simmel says, "Authority is a sociological product requiring the spontaneous and active participation of the subordinates." The particular direction which this interaction and participation takes will depend upon the form of accommodation laid down by the culture of the time and place. Consensus and acceptance set the pattern and the individuals fall into it very easily, unless disturbed by some crisis. Finally, the degree of identification of the individual to the dominant leader or master may touch only special areas of interaction, leaving him free for other forms of interaction elsewhere. Thus bureaucratic and militaristic Germany before the World War permitted a wide range of freedom in fields which did not touch upon political or military matters. In contrast today in Nazi Germany the political state demands conformity and submission to a dictator who has set up a wide range of social objects toward which submission is demanded and enforced.

Submission to a group is expressed in a number of situations. One of these is found where there is a gradation of groups holding power in pyramid fashion, crowned by a ruler or a small group at the top. Another is found in the subordination of the individual to the will of a majority. This finds its expression chiefly in primary or secondary communities, or in those special interest groups organized on the basis of individual voting power. This is the case where the individual is constrained to a line of action by the will of the majority which has outvoted him.

Majority power as the expression of some unitary group will rests in principle on the notion of the absolute sovereign power centered in one individual. This is symbolized and put in practice through the struggle of voting members of the group. The resolution of political party conflicts, of factional fights in labor unions, of sectarian struggles in religious disputes by this method has proved admirably adapted to a world dominated by growing individualism. In a world dominated by collectivist principles, this might not prove effective. In the latter complete unanimity may be demanded, and though the system of voting still continues in Russia, Italy, and Germany, it is very largely a political fiction kept up by a minority who have seized the reins of power and have kept something of a shell of former democratic practices. Actually their methods of control are those of coercion, of propaganda, and of persuasion by mass methods. (See Chapter **XXVI** on social control.)

Submission to an impersonal principle or ideal is the most objective form of accommodation. In theory these principles exist outside the person, and his absolute adherence to them is demanded by the logic of the situation. Yet the subordination to an objective principle influences the relations of persons who have this principle in common. Often power which at the outset grew out of everyday controls, such as the dominance of the father over the family, gets in time raised to a basic principle of social control, as in the doctrine of *pater familias* so common in classic times. The family patriarch himself becomes in time bound to this *idea,* or principle of domination, regardless of his personal feelings and attitudes toward his family members. Culture therefore acts on objective principle independent of personal wishes, settling the rôle and fixing the status of the individual or the group.

This type of arrangement is common throughout the whole societal structure. The process begins in those folkways which become the mores or moral codes. In more complex societies the law takes over many of these principles to control our economic, political, and familial relations: contract, property rights, citizenship, jury duty, taxation duties, inheritance, legitimacy, guardianship, etc. In addition, there still remain the moral codes which furnish us many imperatives outside the law.

Personal relations are theoretically controlled by these objective norms. The culture patterns determine the reciprocal relations of parent and child, of employer and employee, of citizen and judge in the court, of communicant and priest. Actually such rigidity is broken down at many points. Complete suppression of personal wishes, of emotions, of love, sympathy, and tolerance, even in the presence of wrongdoing or criminal acts, softens and modifies the operation of these objective codes.

In the accommodation that follows acceptance of an objective principle there are not any reciprocal relations in the ordinary social psychological sense. One must conform to the demands of cause and effect: the laws of nature are irrevocable and coercive. Wishful thinking out of harmony with these principles gets one nowhere. The authority of facts and ideals is external to personal whims. Acceptance in the end is inescapable. The absolute character of this sort of accommodation is evident; and as we said above, any group which can tie its cause to such an ideology, whether in the end it be logically defensible or not, has a distinct advantage over opponents who take a more temporizing, relativistic view of the objects for which they are struggling.

Clearly, since accommodation fixes the forms of relationship of groups in competition and especially in conflict, there is a direct bearing of accommodation on social control. Certain forms of control, in fact, are linked up distinctly with some of the forms of accommodation which we have used for illustration. We shall return to these later, in Chapter XXVI.

Resolution of Subjective Conflict. The manner in which the individual solves his inner conflicts falls into three general classes: (*1*) the rejection of one element or interest, usually by means of repression, and the selection of another, opposing one; (*2*) the splitting of the personality into two or more divisions, each looking toward some interest or object; (*3*) integration or balance of contending elements by some of the devices cited above.

The *selection* of one interest or trend out of many is a common method of settling inner conflict. If this struggle is the subjective reflection of a conflict within the group or among the groups to which one is attached, it means the giving up of some symbols of identification and the consequent attachment to others. The rejected interest is pushed out of mind, and the individual organizes his attitudes, ideas, and habits around the selected object of attention. Externally this means, too, that he must relinquish his membership in one group or the other, depending upon his decision.

In some instances the resolution of conflict by selection takes the form of conversion. For the individual this implies a rather complete suppression of one of the opposing objects of identification. He becomes—as a man reborn—entirely given over to the new group, its institutions, and its principles. Conversion is limited to those situations where such a reversal of ideas, attitudes, and habits will not be prevented. Religion, politics, and economic life permit it if there are no barriers like race, language, or perhaps sex to hinder it.

It is where the contending forces are more nearly balanced that the choice becomes difficult. In these cases a *split personality* may develop, although not necessarily of a pathological sort. Often the individual builds up a capacity to carry on rather contradictory thoughts and actions. If this contradictory behavior, moreover, gets connected with group interests of divergent sorts, but which nevertheless do not come into open conflict, the person may go on for years in this fashion. A delinquent or criminal identified with a gang may be a "good" provider and affectionate family man. A successful financier may be dishonest in business but a pillar of the church. When these conflicting claims for dominance in the person press hard upon him, he may suffer a mental breakdown or take to suicide, homicide, desertion, or other antisocial conduct.

When the individual has been exposed to two divergent cultures which stand in opposition, he is often particularly hard put to know which way to turn. A person with such a dual rôle and status has a "marginal" relation to two social-cultural worlds. Since he plays an important rôle in assimilation, we shall reserve our discussion of him until later. (See Chapter XXV.)

The most common resolution of conflict follows the external accommodation of contending forces outside. The individual identifies his wishes with the purposes of the group. When these are only partially satisfied, he represses those not fulfilled and perhaps projects on the opposing group the blame for his and his group's failure to get all that was wanted. That is, *rationalization* becomes an effective element in securing a balance of contending forces.

The more stable *integration* or balance of contending forces within the individual is found when the conflict is resolved in terms of current moral sanctions, or better, when the conflicts are settled in terms of an impersonal principle or ideal. This provides the highest form of morality and the most adequately balanced personality. More often people either select one course and reject another or else get along with a number of warring elements within themselves which in critical periods wrack them and waste their energy, but which in calmer times do not greatly disturb their daily life.

In any case opposition and accommodation are reflected back into the subjective life of man, and the external conflicts of groups find their counterpart in the inner struggle of men with themselves. Again the ambivalent trends of sympathy, love, and co-operation come into play to help us in this balancing process. If we were left to the mercies of conflict without these ambivalent trends, we probably could not get on at all. It is the very fact that we can love our fellow group members so intensely in a period of conflict like a war which makes it also possible to hate our enemies with equal vigor. The real problem, of course, is how to balance these trends when the intense struggle situation typified by international war or family feud or violent race or class conflict is not at hand. One appeal is to impersonal ideas and ideals around which we can integrate our conflict attitudes of dislike of evil or error on the one hand and our co-operative attitudes of love and righteousness on the other. Short of this the individual must adapt his inner life to the external accommodations which are provided him by the various groups to which he belongs. For the most part, short of annihilation of enemy or idea, or complete conversion to another form of life, the settlement of conflict is likely to be a matter of partial measures, leaving the individual open to future conflicts at any time the working balance is disturbed. It is only in assimilation that complete harmony can be secured.

CLASS ASSIGNMENTS

A. Further reading assignment:

1. K. Young, *Source Book for Sociology,* chap. XXIII.

2. R. E. Park and E. W. Burgess, *Introduction to the Science of Sociology,* chap. X.

3. E. B. Reuter and C. W. Hart, *Introduction to Sociology,* chap. XIII.

B. Questions and exercises:

1. Define accommodation. What relation has this process to opposition?

2. Define and illustrate social distance. As a concrete sample, the student should rearrange the following names of various nationalities in a numbered order-of-preference series, putting first the group toward which he feels most sympathy and friendliness, placing second the next group, and so on till for number 13 he places the nationality toward which he feels the least friendliness and the least sympathy: Mexican, Canadian, German, English, Japanese, Scandinavian, Chinese, Turkish, Italian, Russian, Dutch, French, Polish.

3. Select and write up a short case of accommodation from one of the following fields: industry, religion, politics, race. Show how the accommodation may well lay the foundation for a future conflict.

4. Under what circumstances are coercion and domination likely to prove effective forms of accommodation? Under what circumstances are they less satisfactory?

5. What are the advantages of "talking it out" between contestants or between conflicting groups?

6. Is submission to a principle morally preferable to submission to a group or person? Discuss, pro and con.

7. Cite a case illustrating how an individual has solved his inner conflicts. Show, if you can, how this subjective conflict reflects his interaction and group relations outside.

C. Topics for class reports or longer written papers:

1. Forms of accommodation in industry. (Consult Melvin J. Vincent, *The Accommodative Process in Industry*, 1930; articles in *Encyclopedia of the Social Sciences*, as follows: Carter Goodrich, "Industrial Arbitration," vol. II, pp. 153–57; B. M. Squires, "Industrial Conciliation," vol. IV, pp. 165–69; G. W. Guillebaud, "Industrial Relations Councils," vol. VII, pp. 717–22; Lois MacDonald, *Labor Problems and the American Scene*, 1938; C. R. Daugherty, *Labor Problems in American Industry*, 4th ed., 1938; and bibliographies cited in each.)

2. Forms of accommodation in race relations. (Consult Park and Burgess, *op. cit.*, and bibliography; C. S. Johnson, *The Negro in American Civilization*, 1930, and bibliography; Paul E. Baker, *Negro-White Adjustments*, 1934; John Dollard, *Caste and Class in a Southern Town*, 1937; B. Schrieke, *Alien Americans*, 1936; D. R. Taft, *Human Migration*, 1936; F. J. Brown and J. S. Roucek, editors, *Our Racial and National Minorities*, 1937.)

3. The contribution of Georg Simmel to the analysis of conflict and accommodation. (Consult Park and Burgess, *op. cit.*, chap. X, and N. J. Spykman, *The Social Theory of Georg Simmel*, 1925.)

4. Recent illustrations of accommodative relations of nations aimed at the reduction of war or the threat of war. (Consult F. L. Schuman, *International Politics—An Introduction to the Western State System*, 2nd ed., 1937; H. M. Vinacke, *International Organization*, 1934; F. H. Simonds and B. Emeny, *The Great Powers in World Politics*, rev. ed., 1937; see World Affairs Pamphlets published by Foreign Policy Association, 8 West 40th Street, New York.)

CHAPTER XXIV

Not only do factors of age, sex, and mentality influence the division of labor and the rôles which people take in any society, but groupings of people in terms of status or rank also come into every society which develops any complexity at all.

Stratification may be looked upon either as a process or as a condition. In discussing it as a process we are concerned with the manner in which classes or castes grow up. As a condition, the study of stratification becomes an analysis of the fixed rules and institutions which have developed around classes or castes. In this chapter, while we shall note some examples of stratification as a condition, our chief interest will be to study the formation of classes, especially in our own society.

PROCESS OF STRATIFICATION

The formation of systems of rank, classes, or castes is a process closely related to differentiation and accommodation. Some writers consider stratification as a special form of accommodation growing out of conflict only. Accommodation following conflict, however, is but one phase of stratification. Not all social strata develop in this way. The growth of economic, political, and religious privilege is often the result of gradual deposition of rights and powers that come out of the interaction of groups within any given society. Strictly speaking, in this latter respect stratification is rather a phase of differentiation than of accommodation.

Characteristics of Stratification. We may describe *stratification* as a process growing largely out of competition and conflict, leading to the formation of more or less fixed systems of class, rank, or caste within a community or society. Stratification is a fixing and acceptance of occupational, political, military, religious, or other rôles with their associated status. Common examples of

473

social strata are the castes of India, the aristocratic classes of Europe, and the more flexible class system of our own capitalistic society.

Stratification begins to arise as soon as some specialized function gets into the hands of a particular group within the larger society and as soon as such functions are accepted as right and proper by others. Until something beyond the rudimentary state of the family and the primary community is reached, we do not get much in the way of social strata, although we may already in these primary groups get differentiation of function in terms of sex, age, and mental ability. In other words, secondary groups with more specialized functions must arise before stratification can become complex.

Some writers hold that all rank, caste, or class systems arise from economic differences. Such a view is too narrow. Since it is power and prestige that men want, status may come from political, religious, or other differences. It all depends on the culture and its values.

Prestige is obviously an important factor in building up and in retaining social strata. Man has many of the characteristics of the peacock about him. He wants to exhibit himself as important in the eyes of his fellows. The desire to keep whatever prestige and status he has acquired is natural. If he performs an act that another cannot do, or do as well, he perceives his superiority, and once having performed an act it is usually easy to repeat it. But this first reaction is enhanced for him when he realizes that others think his performance was exceptional. Thanks, praise, or appreciation are accorded the successful person. Their acceptance is carried back to the individual through circular response, and he begins to believe himself as good as others believe him to be. In this way prestige arises and is maintained. Once this prestige is attributed not to the individual but to a group of individuals within the framework of the larger community, we get the foundations of a class system. And a group of individuals having acquired such prestige and power in regard to some function will be expected and prepared to continue them.

If a group has the power to coerce another group, they may set themselves up as the carriers of some special privilege which the others must accept. In time, in spite of irritation, the arrangement gets accepted. This is particularly true in the case of military conquest and resultant control. But not all stratification rests on direct coercion.

As social strata arise, certain rules or institutions develop. The special functions of the respective strata in regard to the total society are subject to regulations. Then other institutional devices are designed to protect the rights and privileges of the particular class. These may be caste systems, aristocracies, nobilities, knighthoods, or corporations, such as guilds or ecclesiastical orders. All sorts of external marks of difference and privilege—costumes, distinctive and exclusive behavior patterns—are developed. Once these divisions are established and the institutional and social control features set up around them, and once they are traditional or customary, the class principle is established. C. H. Cooley well summarized the fundamentals of the rank or status formation, when he said, "Fundamental to all study of classes are the two principles, of inheritance and of competition, according to which their membership is determined."[1] The beginnings of the principle rest upon competition and effectiveness of performance, but once the rank or status is fixed, it operates on what Cooley calls the "biological principle," that is, membership in the caste or class is determined not by efficiency and individual merit, but by birth into the class or caste.

Once the stratification has been set up, what features does it reveal? We have already noted the place of prestige. The psychology of class consciousness is marked by three additional features. In the first place there is within the caste or class itself a distinct sense of co-operation, mutual aid, common interests, and "consciousness of kind." It is a strong in-group. There are built up a set of common attitudes, habits, sentiments, and values upon which the members agree, which give them a basis for understanding each other, and upon which they may act in harmony. To belong to a caste or class is to know how to act in certain prescribed ways. It gives a fixity and a predictability to behavior which may be important in the smooth running of the social order.

A second feature is the sense of inferiority and submission which the members of one caste or class feel toward those in the class or caste above them. The lower strata usually admit the upper to be superior and better, to have rights and privileges which the lower do not possess. When this attitude or feeling of inferiority

[1] C. H. Cooley, *Social Organization*, 1909, p. 210.

is accepted as "right and proper" in the culture, there is not much likelihood that the social hierarchy will be disturbed. When it breaks down, the class system is in the process of disintegration and reorganization.

A third characteristic is the feeling of superiority of the caste or class toward the strata below them. The attitude of domination and superiority bolsters the individual in his position. If he feels inferior toward those above, he can hold those below him in contempt. This duality of feeling has its limits, since those at the bottom of the social ladder have no other class or caste upon whom they may look with disgust and disdain. The upper class or caste likewise may not need to develop any sense of inferiority to any other rank above them, although they may perhaps project some such feelings into the heavens and develop some sense of submission and inferiority toward God or abstract principles.

The fundamental factors influencing stratification may be summarized under the following headings: first, the heterogeneity of population, leading to specialization of function on the part of certain groups within the larger framework of the culture group or society. These we have already discussed. Second, the rate of social-cultural change is important. As the society becomes more and more complex, as the demands for meeting crises arise, as two societies are brought together by migration or conflict, as diffusion of culture introduces new elements, or as invention does the same thing, there may arise a re-shuffling of social strata leading to the breakdown of some arrangements and the rise of others. These we shall observe in the shift from feudal to modern Europe. As Cooley remarks, "A settled state of society is favorable, and change hostile, to the growth of caste, because it is necessary that functions should be continuous through several generations before the principle of inheritance can become fixed."[2] Third, related to the rate of social change, is the state of culture and communication. If the society is relatively isolated, if the level of culture is rather simple and enlightenment prevented or frowned upon by the upper ranks, there is not much likelihood that a rigid system of status will dissolve. If the system becomes well established, it may last for generations, even though it loses much of its social effectiveness. On the other hand, the intrusion of alien peoples or alien cultures may cause the social strata to fall apart.

[2] C. H. Cooley, *op. cit.*, p. 225.

CLASS AND CASTE SYSTEMS

There are any number of classifications of the forms of stratification. C. C. North in his *Social Differentiation* (1926) notes five classes of rank or status: personal and civil, economic, political, religious, and honorific. Certainly status, associated with economic differences, with occupation, with political power and military prowess, and with religious activity, is the fundamental cue to class or caste systems. More difficult is the attempt to distinguish clearly between class and caste. Once again cultural factors must be taken into account. We may well accept Cooley's idea that the core of the class system is the application of the principle of biological heredity to social status. If the principle of fixity of status is thoroughly established in family and class pedigrees, and if this fixity reaches into the most important areas of social interaction—economic, political, religious, and perhaps racial relations—we have caste. The word *caste* comes from the Portuguese *casta* meaning lineage. As applied to societal organization, family lineage is distinctly important. But often color or racial differences also play a part. The Hindu word for caste is *varna,* meaning color, and there is no doubt that in India and elsewhere color and racial differences have had some part in setting up caste lines. If the system of rank or status is more flexible, if the fixity does not ramify such a wide area of behavior, we get class systems. If, on the contrary, individual initiative, personal competition, and merit determine class status, and if the boundaries of class are constantly changing, we get an "open class" system, to use Cooley's term. The last is so important in our own society that we shall devote a special section to it. In the present section we shall note some of the features of class and caste in primitive societies, and then discuss class and caste as developed in India and in the Mediterranean civilizations.

Class and Caste in Primitive Societies. Class or caste systems among primitives are not extensive in native North and South America, although they were found in ancient Peru (see p. 416), in Mexico, and among certain tribes of less complex culture. In contrast, they are common in parts of Africa and Asia and are particularly highly developed in Polynesia.

Among many African tribes the rulers are looked upon as divine in origin and power. All others are commoners, and although some of these latter may be raised to social prestige by the rulers, such rank is not inheritable. In other sections of Africa, the caste system seems to rest upon conquest, as among the cattle-raising Wahuma of East Africa, who look down upon the horticultural Bantu, whom they govern.

It is in Polynesia that we find the richest flowering of caste among pre-literate peoples. The Maori nobility of New Zealand traced their descent through primogeniture back to the highest gods. Every man of distinction had to memorize his lineage so that upon occasion he could recite his pedigree.

In Samoa the caste system is for the most part like that of New Zealand but with local variations. There are five groups of freemen: chiefs, priests, landed gentry, large landholders, and commoners. But the gradations of rank within these castes are numerous. Complex forms of address and carefully detailed rituals are worked out to control the relations of the gradations to each other.

Among the American Indians the tribes of the northwest coast had three classes: nobles, commoners, and slaves. The latter were recruited by capture, and although ordinarily well treated, were liable to be put to death for sacrificial purposes or as an evidence of prestige in outdoing one's rivals at the great festivals. The commoners were freemen but had little wealth. Among the slaves and commoners there were no further castes of rank, but among the nobles there were many distinctions of status.

Caste in India. The Hindu caste system has been the object of much interest among Western peoples, and around it have grown up a wealth of legends and myths which often mislead the unwary. In actual practice it is more flexible, more dynamic, and less vicious than we imagine. Limitation of space forbids more than a cursory survey of its most prominent features.

Hindu tradition relates that the major divisions were established about 600 B. C. The ancient laws of Manu gave the four chief castes as follows: (*1*) the *Brahmans,* or priests, to whom were "assigned the duties of reading the Vedas (the sacred books), of teaching, of sacrificing, of assisting others to sacrifice, of giving alms if they be rich, and if indigent of receiving gifts"; (*2*) the military chieftains, or overlords, called the *Kshatriya,* whose duties were "to defend the people, to give alms, to sacrifice, to read the Veda, to shun the allurements of sensual gratification"; (*3*) the agriculturists, herdsmen, and traders, called the *Vaisya;* (*4*) the servile class, or *Sudra,* whose duty it is "to serve the before-mentioned classes without depreciating their worth."[3]

The four divisions, however, are but the skeleton of a highly complex system of castes and sub-castes. The census of India lists over 800 castes and sub-castes. When the local differences in sub-castes are taken into account, the number in fact reaches nearly 5,000. Castes and sub-castes are constantly forming and reforming by division or unification. When we come to study the system closely, we find not the static, stereotyped picture of fiction or popular legend, but a living, changing social organization. Although the Indian system of castes represents the most highly integrated and the most "self-conscious system" of social stratification that has arisen anywhere, its very dynamic character shows that while the regulations are severe and of long standing, the actuality of social practice cannot be defined within the narrow limits of simple description.

Caste or sub-caste, moreover, is not determined by any one standard. Castes are formed in terms of occupations, sectarian groups, races, tribes, and other associations of people with distinctive culture traits or social functions.

There are some broad general features which may be noted as fundamental to most of the caste relations. These are as follows: (1) descent through the caste and family lines determines caste membership; (2) intermarriage with members of other castes is forbidden; (3) occupations follow the caste lines; (4) social regulations regarding food and daily habits keep the castes apart; (5) religious ideas and practices are linked up with caste regulations and help to keep the system alive—there is great pressure exerted on the true Hindu not to join any other religious faith; and (6) severe social ostracism is invoked against all who "lose caste."

For people of Western culture, some of the regulations of caste seem extreme indeed. For example, a man may not sit down to eat with another who is not of the same caste. All meals must be prepared by one of his own caste, or by a Brahman. No man of inferior caste may touch the cooked rations of one of higher caste, or for that matter enter into the latter's culinary quarters. No water or other liquid, once contaminated by the touch of one of inferior caste, may be used. Tanks, rivers, and other larger bodies of water, however, are not considered capable of defilement.

[3] *Manu X,* pp. 88–90. Quoted in *Encyclopedia Britannica,* 11th ed., vol. V, pp. 466–67.

Articles of dry food—for instance, rice, wheat, etc.—are not made impure by passing through the hands of a man of lower caste, but they cannot be used if they become moistened or greased. There are also certain prohibited articles of diet, such as cow's flesh, pork, and fowls. Among the peoples of southern India, where the unclean castes are peculiarly offensive to the higher ranks, pollution may occur even without touching. For example, a Kaniyan causes pollution to a Brahman if he comes within 32 feet of him, and a Nayar is polluted at a distance of 24 feet.

The severity of social pressure on the man who has been put out of his caste is striking. When a Hindu is expelled from his caste, his friends, relatives, and fellow townspeople refuse to accept his hospitality; he is not invited to their houses; he cannot secure brides or bridegrooms for his children; his own married daughters scarcely dare visit him lest they also lose caste. His priest, barber, and washerman will not serve him, although this is becoming more difficult to enforce. Fellow members of his caste even decline to assist at a funeral of one of his household. And in certain instances, a man expelled from his caste is denied access to the public temples. With such a hold of the group codes upon the individual, it is no wonder that such a system persists even in the face of many forces which tend to disintegrate it.

Yet the caste system represents a remarkable scheme of societal organization. It is a form of accommodation and differentiation in which friction and strain are reduced to a minimum. Sidney Low in his book *Vision of India* (1906) writes:

"The crudities and cruelties of the caste system need not blind us to its other aspects. There is no doubt that it is the main cause of the fundamental stability and contentment by which Indian society has been braced up for centuries against the shocks of politics and the cataclysms of Nature. It provides every man with his place, his career, his occupation, his circle of friends. It makes him, at the outset, a member of a corporate body; it protects him through life from the canker of social jealousy and unfulfilled aspirations; it ensures him companionship and a sense of community with others in like case with himself. The caste organization is to the Hindu his club, his trade union, his benefit society, his philanthropic society. An Indian without caste, as things stand at present, is not quite easy to imagine."[4]

In the years since this was written, many changes have come

[4] Sidney Low, *Vision of India*, 1906, chap. XV, p. 263. Quoted in *Encyclopedia Britannica*, 11th ed., vol. V, p. 465.

over India. Although the caste system remains dominant, mention must be made of factors which are now undermining its hold on the population. Briefly these are the following. (*1*) The urbanization of population affords the person who has lost caste a chance to change his identity in a great city, to take up another occupation, and perhaps to marry outside. (*2*) Travel and mobility throw the castes together in situations that were not likely to arise before the coming of the railroad and the crowded conditions of large cities. (*3*) Schooling has helped to alter attitudes and ideas regarding caste, especially among those who have had a higher education. (*4*) The spread of nationalistic and democratic ideas has been a powerful ferment in India and has assisted in breaking down some features of the caste system. When democratic notions of equality become accepted, the anomaly of a caste system becomes apparent. (*5*) Christianity and other foreign religions doubtless have gradually had some effect upon attitudes and ideas regarding caste.

Yet the inertia of custom and habit is powerful. The village is still the heart of Hindu social structure, and the village is the seat of caste at its best. The conservatism of family life, seen especially in the continuation of child marriages and the low position of women, retards change. Likewise religion affords one of the most powerful supports of this system.

Class and Caste in Mediterranean Culture. Whether the Mediterranean culture in Babylonia, Egypt, Persia, Greece, and Rome developed the caste system depends on one's definition. But there was nothing as elaborate as that now developed in India. In Egypt, there were two upper classes, warriors and priests. Besides these there were various lesser classes of professionals and artisans, all relatively fixed. Babylonia, as early as the time of Hammurabi (c. 2250 B. C. or 1950 B. C.), had a pyramidal sort of feudal order in which class lines were strictly drawn. Mesopotamia, on the other hand, seems to have been fairly free of anything suggesting caste, while ancient Iran and Persia, from which the Aryan conquerors of India are thought to have come, had, according to legend, four castes—priests, warriors, agriculturists, and artificers. In Greece we find considerable variation. Sparta long retained what was in effect a caste system, with its division of the population into citizens, two intermediate castes, and Helots. In Athens, on the contrary, as she developed into a cosmopolitan state, the ancient caste lines disappeared.

In Rome the story is an interesting one of relatively fixed classes constantly being broken by changes in economic and political power and then re-established, until we get to the Empire, with its final crystallization of Roman society. With the gradual disappearance of the middle classes, the patricians formed a closed caste, and the masses were rather thoroughly subjugated under a severe economic and political régime from which the individual could not escape.

With the break-up of the Roman Empire following the barbarian invasions, society in western Europe was refashioned along somewhat different lines. The feudal order which emerged was a class system. There were the various gradations of the overlords, lesser lords, knights, burghers, guild members, freemen, and at the bottom serfs. These classes were never crystallized into a rigid caste scheme with religious sanction. For several centuries, however, western Europe was rather thoroughly under the domination of a class system in which status was relatively fixed, and shift from one class to another was difficult. Gradually economic and political changes began to operate, and the seeds were sown for a disintegration of the old order and the rise of modern "open classes."

OPEN CLASS SYSTEMS

At the close of the Middle Ages, emerging business and commerce based on money economy rather than on barter and household manufacturing gave rise to various new occupations which tended to form new classes. In this process, the trade and merchant guilds played important parts. An enterprising artisan or master workman might by increasing his business gradually rise in wealth and shift from lower to higher social status. The old limitations of aristocracy and birth began to break down. Wealth, not birth, was soon to determine social status. Furthermore, the rural classes could no longer be kept in the old framework. Opportunities for working in the cities gave the peasant and the serf a chance to escape the obligations to lord and master.

Rise of Open Classes. Two things in Western history finally brought about the shift to a more flexible class system. One of these was the discovery of America and the opening up of large areas of free land where people had almost unlimited opportunities to create wealth and obtain financial independence. The other was the coming of the factory system, which broke down the trade guilds, freed men and women everywhere from feudal class regulations, and brought about individualistic *laissez-faire* competition. As the factory system developed in the late eighteenth and early nineteenth centuries, the whole occupational structure changed. The factory workers were gradually forced into certain class-conscious groupings such as trade unions. The entrepreneurs, who took the risks of business enterprise, became increasingly important politically and socially as well as economically.

The United States affords an excellent example of the revamping of a class system. Under the stimulation of economic opportunity, first in the form of free land, second in the form of opportunities to exploit natural resources, and third in the opportunity to make money in the expanding fields of business and industry, large numbers of people rose steadily from lower economic status to positions of wealth. Competition and a certain kind of merit became the open sesame to the higher status. Wealth and not birth or education was the standard of rank.

An open class system is characterized by great mobility or movement of persons from one social level to another. In democratic countries like France, Great Britain and her colonies, and the United States, in which the political privileges are common to all, status is determined largely by occupation and wealth. The desire for wealth comes to dominate all classes.

In this connection, we must point out two features in present-day capitalistic society: first, the extent of change in occupations, in economic wealth, and in political power, and second, the manner in which the open class system is perpetuated.

Occupational Mobility. The degree to which sons follow their fathers' occupations is one measure of vocational shift. In the Indian caste system a vocational shift from father to son is impossible. During the Middle Ages there was very little if any such change from generation to generation. In our day there is a great deal. Summarizing 23 studies from various countries, P. A. Sorokin says that the maximum transmission of occupation from father to son is about 70 per cent, the minimum ranging from 3 to 10 per cent. The average index varies a great deal in different countries, ranging between 20 and 60 per cent. The trend today is toward a decrease in the carry-over occupations from fathers to sons. One study showed that 72 per cent of the grandfathers of those questioned had the same occupations as that of the great-grandfathers, only 38.9 per cent of the fathers had the same vocations as had the grandfathers, and only 10.6 per cent of those questioned had the same occupation as did their fathers.[5] Yet in vocations demanding special training and skill or the possession of great capital, and in those having marked social prestige, there is less change from generation to generation than in other occupations.

The significance of occupational mobility in our own time is revealed in another way by the shifting from occupation to occupation during the lifetime of individuals. One study undertaken by the Metropolitan Life Insurance Company showed that of wage earners among the policy-holders of this company, 58.5 per cent had another occupation at the time of their death than they had at the time their insurance policies were issued, although there is some variation among the vocations. Among the policy-holders the "professionals" had shifted their occupations in but 28.6 per cent of the cases.[6] A study of 407 University of Minnesota alumni showed that in from ten to fourteen years 57.5 per cent of them had changed their vocations: 39.5 per cent had changed once; 11.5 per cent twice; 5.6 per cent three times; 2.2 per cent four or more times. Sorokin thus reports studies in this country and in Europe:

"Other conditions being equal, first, within the same occupation the more qualified and better paid strata shift less intensively than the less qualified and more poorly paid groups; second, members of occupations which disappear shift more intensively than members of occupations which develop and prosper; third, unskilled labor is more mobile than skilled labor; business and professional groups (their higher strata) are likely to be still more stable even than the group of skilled labor. In a country where agriculture does not rapidly disappear, the occupational mobility of those engaged in agriculture is likely to be low; in a country where agriculture dies out, the shifting of agriculturists to other occupations is likely to be high."[7]

The process of social climbing in our Western society goes on, however, not by sudden jumping from the lower to the higher levels, except in extreme cases, but by a gradual movement up the social

[5] P. A. Sorokin in his *Social Mobility*, 1927, has brought together and interpreted a vast body of literature on the subject of occupational mobility. Many of the data in this section have been derived from this source.
[6] See Louis I. Dublin and R. J. Vane, "Shifting of Occupation among Wage Earners as Determined by Occupational History of Industrial Policyholders," *Monthly Labor Review*, April, 1924, vol. XVIII, pp. 732–40.
[7] P. A. Sorokin, *op. cit.*, pp. 426–27.

ladder. The various statistical studies made of the sources of occupation from which exceptional leaders and the higher professions are recruited all show this. (See Chapter XXII.)

While the likelihood for occupational advancement is not so great in Europe as in this country, there is still a good deal of such shifting there. In England the nobility is constantly being recruited from the business and professional classes, and in Germany, France, and other continental countries it is not impossible for boys of lower economic classes to rise to higher classes.

A study made by Otto Ammon tracing the changes in occupation of three generations of migrants from the rural sections to the city in Germany is interesting. It shows a distinct upward movement in social and occupational status. Rural immigrants into Karlsruhe distributed themselves as follows: 82 per cent in the lower classes, 14 per cent in the middle classes, and 4 per cent in the professional (educated) classes. Their sons, the second generation, distributed themselves in these three classes as follows: 41, 49, and 10 per cent each; their sons, the third generation, for the same three classes showed 40, 35, and 25 per cent. Thus between the first and second generation the decrease in position in the lower class was 50 per cent, with corresponding increases in the two upper classes. This continued until in the third generation, when one fourth of them were in the professional classes in contrast to the one sixteenth in these classes among their grandfathers.[8]

There is not only occupational ascent, there is also occupational descent. One study by H. C. Burdge of sample American data, cited by Sorokin, showed that 6.4 per cent of the children of professional men, 5.4 per cent of those of clericals, 7.6 per cent of the children of business men, 10.3 per cent of those of executives, and 7.4 per cent of those of officials became unskilled laborers. There is other evidence that descent down the occupational ladder is taking place in our own country. It is easy to account for this, in part, by individual differences of mental, emotional, and habitual sort. But in our own day, certain facts of the industrial order itself may enhance this. One of these is technological unemployment, which throws skilled and semiskilled artisans out of work. Another is the gradual closing of the doors of opportunity in the upper economic positions. In a crisis like the long business and industrial depression following 1930 such a descent down the occupational ladder is likely to be enhanced. In fact we may be

[8] See Sorokin, *op. cit.*, pp. 443–46, 450–51, for a summary of a vast amount of data on this whole matter.

entering a phase of occupational shifting which will not be upward but downward for thousands of persons.

In short, in capitalistic societies there has been marked circulation of individuals up and down the economic scale. For the most part, this movement has been in the direction of improvement of status from one generation to another. But it is quite possible that with the settling down of our economic order to slower rates of change there may actually be a reverse movement down the economic ladder.

Mobility in Political and Religious Power. Since the breakdown of the Middle Ages, say in the fifteenth century, down to the present, there has been a gradual loosening of class rule in the political field. The emergence of nationalism led within two centuries to the beginnings of democratic control. The circulation of persons up and down the political ladder—like the movement in occupations or wealth—is accelerated in periods of rapid social change or revolution. During the last century political changes in Great Britain and on the continent brought political power first into the hands of the middle classes and then into the hands of the lower classes. In the Scandinavian countries and in the Netherlands mild socialist parties came into control, with a consequent rise of a new élite. Russia of the Czars gave way to a dictatorship of the proletariat, begun by Lenin and Trotsky and carried forward by Stalin. Hungary, after a fling at Bolshevism, settled down to a dictatorship, supported by the middle class and landed aristocracy. The Ottoman Empire became a parliamentary government which brought about profound reforms under Kemal Pasha, a man of bourgeois origin. Republican Germany (1918–1933) saw the rise of a number of leaders of lowly origin such as Friedrich Ebert (1871–1925), the first president, the son of a saddle maker. After sixteen years as a republic, Germany swung over to a dictatorship, a combination of the old Junker party and the National Socialists, led by Adolf Hitler, a man of the common people. Italy after a period of quasi-socialistic parliamentary rule, went over to fascism under Mussolini, a journalist-socialist and former ardent radical. Thomas G. Masaryk, whose father was a poor artisan, became the leader of Czechoslovakia. In Spain, the overthrow of the monarchy brought a number of new leaders to the front. In the Orient, especially in China, Persia, Afghanistan, and Arabia, new blood infused itself into the ruling cliques.

These changes were accompanied by the descent of the former ruling classes. The dispossessed aristocracy of Russia, Germany, the former Austro-Hungarian Empire, of Greece, and more recently of Spain, migrated to other European countries or America, where they were forced often to take up menial tasks unless they were able to capitalize on their blue blood among those bourgeois classes who always hanker and yearn after nobility, even though it be dispossessed. In short, the open class system appeared in the field of politics, just as it did in the field of economics. Whether the future will see less of this mobility remains to be seen.

In the field of religious activity, much the same thing has taken place. Although during the history of the Roman Catholic Church certain families sometimes dominated the highest positions, it is nevertheless true that the Church has always provided ample opportunity for people of ability from the lower social classes. The Protestant Reformation made possible a greater chance for persons of lower status to rise in importance.

The Perpetuation of the Open Class System. The open class system which grew up throughout the last 300 years of economic, political, and religious individualism has become so established in our culture that it is difficult to alter except as the forms of social organization are modified gradually under changing economic and political conditions.

In our capitalistic culture the control of material things which wealth gives sets the standard for reverence and acceptance of this open class order. The individual is concerned with securing as much of this world's goods as he possibly can. John A. Hobson once remarked about Americans, that unlike the class member of England, who was satisfied, more or less, with his status, the American desires above everything else to have material things as good as his neighbors' or at least things that look as good. If one cannot have an eight-cylindered car, at least he hopes to have a four or a second-hand six. If one cannot have the latest high-powered, many-tubed radio set, he may secure from the mail-order houses one nearly as good in quality and one that certainly looks as good to the eye. To possess a home, to wear clothes that are in fashion even though of poor materials, to be able to attend motion pictures or to see baseball games or to play golf on municipal courses—just a little inferior to the exclusive private grounds—all these give evidence of the importance to us of material culture. The critic may say that it puts a premium on shabby quality and on cheapness, but since man is a peacock by nature and not altogether a rational judge of materials, appearances often count more than substance. When the industrial-commercial order has performed such miracles as to produce these material necessities and luxuries in great quantities at a low cost, it is little wonder that material possessions hold such a power over us and encourage the upward striving within the open class system.

This whole matter is related to the prestige which conspicuous consumption gives. Thorstein Veblen (1857–1929), American economist, pointed out the whole appeal of this matter in his classic volume *The Theory of the Leisure Class* (1912). To show off one's wealth by spending has set the pace for the whole development of what may be called the "consumer psychology" of America. This itch for more material goods reflects itself upon the demand for a higher standard of living on the part of those in the lower income brackets.

Our money-making theory influences the whole system of beliefs of the multitude. First, it directly influences the professional classes: doctors, lawyers, engineers, and teachers. These persons are all given specialized training built around the notion of individual merit and competition for ever higher and higher incomes. Furthermore, these professional classes, especially the first three, are largely dependent upon the rich for their own livelihood. Again it was Veblen, in his *Engineers and the Price System* (1919), who clearly pointed out the dependence of the engineering profession upon the wealthy capitalist, although there is no inherent connection between technical skill in production and the profit motive of private capitalism.

The belief in individualism and in the upward rise in the economic and social scale is reflected back into the whole ambition-complex of American culture. Every schoolchild is told from the cradle on that there are endless possibilities if he only works hard and gets a specialized education. The old myth of "log cabin to White House" is still with us, but equally powerful is the myth about progress from machine shop to the ownership of a thriving factory or a great building. The school teaches the child the individualist theory. The newspapers scream it at him. Such periodicals as The *American Magazine* carry stories every month of men who began on a few dollars and rose to wealth or at least to munificent salaries. So, too, the Horatio Alger sort of stories of the messenger boy who becomes a banking magnate, of the striving but poor inventor who escapes the wiles of the shrewd and dishonest promoter to become both famous and rich—these are a part of the social myth of individualism and ambition. The motion pictures, the radio, and other media of informal education carry the same message.

Finally, one of the most powerful factors fostering the continuation of the open class system is the circumstance that the individual aim in every case is not to raise his own class, but to pull himself up out of this class into the one higher. This is highly significant, since it means that any tendency for class solidarity to develop is always faced with the opposite desire of the most prominent and promising individuals to rise out of the class into the one above. Thus open classes, unlike castes and more rigid classes, do not develop the sense of solidarity to the point where the whole group is taken for granted and where the interests of one are identified with those of the other members. Because of this, strong we-group attitudes can hardly develop among the flexible classes. There are no fixed rules in the sense in which there are customary or legal regulations in the caste or class system. Of course there are codes which the individual must follow in order to make good in the upward climb to higher rank. Also in the open class system as it has developed in connection with modern capitalistic society, there is a certain impersonality about relations which was not evident in the caste or class organization. There is not that personal loyalty to other members of the class, there is not that personal sense of obligation to those above, nor quite the general class support to the sense of superiority toward those below one.

Thus within the open class system nothing is fixed; there is more variation and much more person-to-person play. The limitations on personal growth are broken down, and there is more interplay for divergent social behavior. Flexibility in the open-class system is one of its chief assets.

THE PLACE OF STRATIFICATION IN SOCIETAL ORGANIZATION

Some writers maintain that certain kinds of classes or grades of rank or status always arise whenever society develops complex patterns of interaction.

Theories of Stratification. Albion W. Small believed that there was in every society a tendency for three basic classes to develop: the privileged upper stratum, the middle classes, with some privileges but really dependent on the top class, and the underprivileged, those without property, influence, or adequate economic and political rights. Small held furthermore that these differences arose first in the economic field and only later found expression in the political. Once the process of stratification is begun, the dominant group attempts to fix the differences by setting up limitations and hedging in their prerogatives by means of feudal organizations, nobilities, aristocracies, or corporations. That is, there is a tendency to set up what he called the dynastic interest, or what Cooley called the biological principle of heredity applied to social phenomena.[9]

Karl Marx constructed in his socialistic writings a dual class organization of the exploiters and capitalists and of the proletariat. Marx well realized that within this dual division there were many subdivisions, and his purpose was essentially to develop, philosophically, a system that brought out the main contrast between these two classes in the struggle for power. (See discussion of Marxianism in Chapters XVI and XVIII.)

It is doubtful whether any simple two-fold, three-fold, or like grouping of classes or castes will do. But from the analysis of particular societies one may discover for such societies some convenient general shorthand classification of ranks. There are always dominant and subordinate groups. Whether these may be broken up into various subdivisions will depend upon the data and the purposes of description and analysis of the student.

One may ask the question, Are class differences desirable or commendable? Such a question involves moral evaluation of the process of stratification itself. Many writers with an ethical turn of mind have written critically of undue stratification. Gustav Schmoller, a well-known German economist and sociologist, believed that any class organization which developed dominance and exploitation might be harmful if not checked by other forms of social organization. He felt that in our capitalistic culture the wealthy and economically strong held in subjection the weaker classes and used the political state, whenever they dared, to retain

[9]See Albion W. Small, *General Sociology*, 1905, pp. 275–78.

this dominance. He believed that the development of constitutional and legal means of counterbalancing this domination of one class over all others was the only way to prevent one class from complete control.

E. A. Ross in the first edition of his *Principles of Sociology* (1920) p. 321, had this to say of stratification:

"Stratification is virtually a social disease which checks the natural sifting of human beings, clogs the rise of capables and the descent of incapables, benumbs the higher faculties of the masses, arrests the circulation of sympathy and, if not remedied, ends in the paralysis, perhaps the break-up, of the group."

In his revised edition of the same book, Ross points out the dangers of too fixed stratification and outlines among other devices for counteracting such tendencies in society the following means of equalizing opportunity:

(1) the development of a civic state in which all are treated with equal justice and right; (2) the development of personal freedom so far as it is compatible with the general social good; (3) the firm establishment in law of rights of personal and public character which shall not be alienated by any class interest; (4) the permission of the underprivileged to organize into unions or other associations bent on securing and holding their rights; (5) "the downward percolation of culture," that is, the diffusion of learning and knowledge to all classes; (6) the diffusion of economic opportunity to all; (7) the spread of the margin of leisure to more and more people who will not be denied relaxation and rest from weary toil; (8) the diffusion of educational opportunities to all; (9) the genuine democratization of government to prevent special privilege and encourage social legislation which will ameliorate the conditions surrounding the underprivileged; and finally, (10) the spread of social science, that is, the objective study of social conditions with the aim of social benefit to all.[10]

Both Schmoller and Ross are critical of any societal order in which gross inequalities exist. Their suggestions reflect their faith in democratic, political, and economic order to remedy the abuses of power which arise in a capitalistic society unless checked by some larger community plan of action. Cooley would essentially agree with them, for he has abundant faith in a well-run democracy. Perhaps none of them would deny the place of social classes or the fact that some sort of stratification tends to develop in any

[10] See E. A. Ross, *Principles of Sociology*, 3rd ed., 1938, chap. XXXVII.

but the most rudimentary society. But all three bespeak the faith of the nineteenth and early twentieth centuries in constitutional guarantees to alleviate the worst features of class domination.

The real problem before us is this: Can we have a complex social order without the formation of classes? Let us re-examine this matter briefly.

Stratification Inevitable in Complex Society. We have already discussed much evidence of the naturalness and social inevitability of stratification as a social process. It seems to develop in every culture group of any size beyond that of the most rudimentary type. Wherever division of labor arises, wherever it becomes evident that specialization of function is advantageous to the group, some sort of differentiation occurs. When this differentiation gets associated with family groups, with groups of artisans, with military men, with conquest, with commerce, or with dominant priesthood, the process of class and even caste organization is at hand. The interaction of those who perform the special functions with those who accept these functions sets the stage for social stratification. The persons who perform the functions build up special habits for doing the required acts. This gives them confidence and faith in their capacity. The others in the group see that the former know how to do the required acts and, in turn, attribute to them this power and capacity and thus come to expect them to perform these acts in the future. The prestige of the specialized group grows with the acceptance by others of these very functions as necessary. When this expectancy and prestige, on the one hand, and the habitual performance of the act on the part of a smaller group, on the other, are developed together and connected with the principle of heredity, the class or caste system is well established.

It seems clear that we can scarcely deny the inevitability of a class system of some sort. Just what form this will take depends on the economic and political direction of the particular society.

Two matters in connection with this must be noted. The thesis of Vilfredo Pareto, Italian economist (1848–1923), that every society has some sort of élite or dominant class seems well taken. Furthermore, he points out that there is in historical time always a circulation of this élite class, even though the changes may be very gradual indeed.[11]

[11] See G. H. Bousquet, *The Work of Vilfredo Pareto,* 1928. (Hanover, N. H. The Sociological Press.)

The other matter concerns the moral judgment as to what kind of stratification we prefer. There is much to be said for a flexible open class scheme, since it provides for circulation of individuals up and down the scale in terms of ability and interest. If we take the view that the growth of the individuality—that is, uniqueness and freedom of initiative—is a dominant value so long as it does not destroy the societal order, then we may contend that the open-class system affords a wider range of choice, a greater spread of stimuli, than any other so far developed. Such a continued individuality should enrich not only one's own life, but also perhaps the lives of others. This is the challenge which must be put to every economic and political organization that proposes to bind the individual to certain tasks or to force him into a certain framework rationalized in terms of some mystic collective good. This challenge in our own time must be put before both the fascist and the communist theories of dictatorship. There appears little choice between them in regard to the limitations placed upon individual initiative.

No matter how attractive the fascist or communist order may seem in the first flush of its re-formation of the economic and political culture of its group, sooner or later this problem of the inevitable limitation of individual choice will arise. Perhaps the wise leaders of the democratic capitalistic order will sense this fact in time to make those changes in their own economic and political households which will at once protect the individual from exploitation without curtailing his choice and initiative beyond the necessary limits of a stable societal order.

CLASS ASSIGNMENTS

A. Further reading assignment:

1. K. Young, *Source Book for Sociology*, chap. XXIV.

2. C. H. Cooley, R. C. Angell, and L. J. Carr, *Introductory Sociology*, chap. XX.

3. *Encyclopedia of the Social Sciences*, articles as follows: A. L. Kroeber, "Caste," vol. III, pp. 254–57; Paul Mombert, "Class," vol. III, pp. 531–36; Morris Ginsberg, "Class Consciousness," vol. III, pp. 536–38.

B. Questions and exercises:

1. Define stratification. What is the relationship of differentiation to stratification?

2. Distinguish by example between stratification as a phase of more or less fixed societal organization and stratification as a process.

3. Distinguish between caste, class, and open class systems.

4. What are the factors making for a shift from class to open class systems in western Europe and America? What conditions today are making for a reversal of this process?

5. Is democracy antithetical to classes?

6. Will recognition of individual differences in capacity destroy democracy?

7. Will the encouragement of the use of individual differences in ability prevent the formation of classes?

8. What is the function of class structure in a complex societal order?

C. Topics for class reports or longer written papers:

1. Class or caste systems in primitive societies. (Consult R. H. Lowie, *Primitive Society*, chaps. X, XI, XII, and bibliography; Gunnar Landtman, *The Inequality of the Social Classes*, 1938.)

2. The caste system in India. (Consult H. H. Risley, *The People of India*, 2nd ed., 1915; J. N. Bhattacharya, *Hindu Castes and Sects*, 1896; article, "Caste" in Hastings' *Encyclopedia of Religion and Ethics*, vol. III, pp. 230–39; see also bibliography from Kroeber's article "Caste" in *Encyclopedia of the Social Sciences*, vol. III, pp. 256–57.)

3. The open class system under capitalism. (Consult C. H. Cooley, *Social Organization*, Part IV; P. A. Sorokin, *Social Mobility*, and bibliography.)

4. Recent studies in the mobility of social classes. (Consult Sorokin, *op. cit.*; also P. E. Davidson and H. D. Anderson, *Occupational Mobility in an American Community*, 1937; E. L. Anderson, *We Americans: A Study of Cleavage in an American City*, 1937.)

CHAPTER XXV

ASSIMILATION

If we were to leave group-to-group, person-to-person, or person-to-group relations at the level of accommodation, the fusion of cultures could not go on. Assimilation involves more fundamental changes in the whole culture and corresponding changes in the person than the external relations agreed upon in accommodation.

THE NATURE OF ASSIMILATION

In a broad sense *assimilation* refers to the manner by which two or more cultures are merged. It means the common sharing and fusing of folkways and mores, of laws, and all the other features of two or more distinctive cultures by peoples who have come into direct relations with each other. We shall restrict our discussion to the process by which peoples of divergent racial and cultural heritages living in the same political state acquire a common culture sufficient to maintain national solidarity and independence. We may define assimilation as an interactional process by which persons and groups achieve the memories, sentiments, ideas, attitudes, and habits of other persons or groups and by sharing their experience become incorporated with them in a common cultural life of the nation.[1] It is a reciprocal process at all times resulting in a new combination of elements. We must leave out of account these larger phases of fusion and cultural interpenetration which do not involve the larger national community, for example those concerning age, sex, religion, and economic differences, unless they bear directly upon the problem at hand. Also the trends toward fusion of world cultures looking to a world community which may over-

[1] This political limitation is made clear in R. E. Park's article "Social Assimilation" in *Encyclopedia of the Social Sciences*, vol. II, pp. 281–83. Contrast this with the discussion in R. E. Park and E. W. Burgess, *Introduction to the Science of Sociology*, chap. XI, where the political aspect, though recognized, is not made the limiting factor.

ride the national state in some matters will not be discussed, since these relations will for a long time to come fall rather in the field of accommodation.

Accommodation, Assimilation, and Amalgamation. The differences between accommodation and assimilation will bring out important features of the latter. Both of them are related to cultural change, in which three factors are important: (*1*) the rate of change; (*2*) awareness of change; and (*3*) the nature of the interaction.

Accommodation is a form of adjustment in which many of the independent culture patterns of the contending groups are retained. Treaty agreements are reached only upon matters which have a common bearing and without which the conflict would continue. The adjustments are often made rather quickly, once a truce is declared, and in such a form as conversion the accommodation is often almost instantaneous. In contrast, in *assimilation* the whole change in ideas, attitudes, and habits takes place slowly. There is a gradual growth of common culture patterns out of the old elements. As Park and Burgess wrote, "If mutation is the symbol for accommodation, growth is the metaphor for assimilation."

The process of accommodation is largely conscious. The individuals and groups are aware of the fact that they are striking a balance of power in the interests of commonly accepted needs for such action. In assimilation the individuals and groups are at best quite unconscious of the slow fusion of ideas, attitudes, and habits that is taking place. Naturally there are critical periods, and often there do arise conflicts which necessitate accommodations. Accommodation is not infrequently the first step toward assimilation.

Assimilation is most complete where the contacts are of the primary sort. In the family, the play group, the neighborhood, and the primary community the fusion of new patterns is facilitated on every hand. Accommodation, in contrast, concerns secondary groups in large measure and may take place—and often does take place—without any close contact of the individuals. As we have seen, accommodation implies for the individual only a segment of his personality, only those ideas, attitudes, and habits which center around some special interest, such as a job, religion, or political concern. In assimilation the process reaches into the deeper and wider areas of personality, involving all the fundamental values and attitudes.

It is this intimate, personal, and direct setting for assimilation which makes biological *amalgamation* or intermarriage of divergent groups so important as the background for complete assimilation. When persons of divergent cultures intermarry, the family life is bound to be affected, and the growing children will be exposed to training from both cultures. This cannot but result in some integration of the respective elements into new ideas, attitudes, and habits, that is, into new culture patterns. Yet mere mixture of races will not produce assimilation. Intermarriage must itself be in the mores and the law to make it an effective foundation for assimilation. In this country there has been considerable racial crossing between whites and blacks, but there certainly is no complete assimilation in spite of much culture held in common. With our immigrant groups, most of whom have a common racial background, biological amalgamation is a definite indication of such fusion. It is an inevitable step in the completion of this process.[2] The very fact that male immigrants outnumber female immigrants, especially in the childbearing ages, creates a situation which favors marriage of foreign-born men with women of native or mixed parentage.

We are now ready to look more closely at the concrete factors which enter into the assimilative process. Since the United States was long ago aptly described as "The Melting Pot," we shall draw largely upon the abundant data from our own country, although references to other situations will be made as occasion demands.

Assimilation does not take place on all fronts with equal effectiveness or speed. It goes on much more easily at some points in culture contact than at others. Thus while assimilation may be evident in certain areas of interaction, isolation of the respective groups from each other may prevent it. The process itself will be influenced chiefly by these factors: (*1*) the racial characteristics; (*2*) the social heritage or culture of the immigrant; (*3*) the native culture and society into which he is introduced; and (*4*) certain personality clashes of members of both groups. For example, immigrants from the British Isles to the United States have so much in common with the native Americans that assimilation is easy. Those who come from northwestern continental Europe require more time than the British; yet they also have much in

[2] See T. J. Woofter, Jr., "The Status of Racial and Ethnic Groups," chap. XI, *Recent Social Trends*, pp. 598–600. See also Julius Drachsler, *Democracy and Assimilation*, 1920.

common with us. In contrast peoples of southern and eastern Europe who come to America possess many more divergent culture traits which retard the rate of assimilation and produce many social and personal problems.

Since the whole matter rests on reciprocal interactions between groups and persons, we shall discuss first those situations which hinder assimilation and then treat those which aid it. The factors of culture and the societal order will be emphasized at the outset. Later the personality aspects will be discussed.

SITUATIONS HINDERING ASSIMILATION

We shall discuss the hindrances to assimilation first, since they reveal the contrast of cultures and societal organization, which enters into the process at every point. On the basis of these retarding conditions, we shall be better able to examine and appraise the forces which make assimilation possible.

Nationality and Segregation. The unassimilated persons or groups in a country are obviously isolated from the native community. In Europe, because of migration and especially on account of military conquest, various communities with their own language and culture sometimes found themselves within the political boundaries of a state with which they had little in common. The partition of Poland by Russia, Austria, and Prussia in the eighteenth century and the whole conglomeration of cultures and sub-races in the old Austro-Hungarian Empire are cases in point. Most of these groups in time developed their own race and social consciousness in an effort to escape assimilation by their conquerors. We call them nationality groups. R. E. Park puts it thus:

"Under conditions of secondary contact, that is to say, conditions of individual liberty and individual competition characteristic of modern civilization, depressed racial groups tend to assume the form of nationalities. A nationality, in this narrower sense, may be defined as the racial group which has attained self-consciousness, no matter whether it has at the same time gained political independence or not."[3]

This development of separate nationalities inside the political state stimulated the movements for political independence apparent in nineteenth-century Europe. The isolation of the Jew

[3] R. E. Park, "Racial Assimilation in Secondary Groups," etc., *Publications of the American Sociological Society,* 1913, vol., VIII, p. 82.

from the Christian community throughout the medieval and modern periods of history is somewhat akin to this. The Jew has retained an amazing cultural solidarity in the face of terrific persecution at the hands of Christians. From time to time this solidarity has found its further expression in nationalistic hopes, the latest illustration being Zionism.

The Negro in this country has much in common with the depressed nationalities of Europe. Although he is partially assimilated in our American culture, he still remains outside the pale politically, and in many economic, religious, and other social matters. The Garvey movement was an attempt to foster the racial consciousness of the Negro and to load him with nationalistic hopes.

The American Indian makes up another sort of nationality minority within the United States. While many Indians are really mixed bloods, they are not fully assimilated into our culture. They represent a curious anomaly of being partially fused into American national life, yet retaining much political dependence upon the government, on the one hand, and much of their native culture, on the other.[4]

Clearly the rise of nationalities within other nations makes for conflict and results in accommodation. It is thus a handicap to assimilation and may even block it entirely. The whole matter is neatly illustrated in the attempt of Prince Bismarck (1815–1898) to stimulate the assimilation of the Poles into German culture. The forced introduction of the German language into the schools, the attempts to colonize Posen with German peasants from the Rhineland, the growing governmental restrictions regarding the Poles, coupled with the rising agitation for Polish nationalism, combined to defeat the whole scheme.[5]

It is not that official public agencies may not aid in assimilation, but, as we shall see in discussing Americanization, to force the process by external devices is often to defeat its very purpose.

Immigrant Heritages. The European immigrant peoples who have come to the United States have not fostered nationality senti-

---

[4]See Donald Young, *American Minority Peoples*, 1932, chap. VI, pp. 195–203; and F. A. McKenzie, "The Assimilation of the American Indian," *Publications of the American Sociological Society*, 1913, vol. VIII, pp. 37–48.

[5]See W. I. Thomas, "The Prussian-Polish Situation: An Experiment in Assimilation," *Publications of the American Sociological Society*, 1913, vol. VIII, pp. 84–100.

ments to the extent which we find them in Europe. Yet out of their first adjustments many influences retard assimilation.

Segregation into neighborhoods of their own is common among immigrants. This is natural and inevitable in view of our economic order and our native American attitudes. Most immigrants are in the lower economic strata and are forced to seek cheap housing. Then their own countrymen who have migrated ahead of them are the first to whom the newcomers turn for help and advice. Thus arose the immigrant sections of our cities: the ghetto, Dago Town, Little Sicily, Little Hungary, and so on.

These separate immigrant neighborhoods within the larger American community represent one of the chief hindrances to rapid assimilation from the angle of the immigrant. Here the immigrant continues to use his own language, to keep the same dietary habits and dress, to continue old-world family life and forms of social control.

Such agencies as the native-language press may aid in this isolation, especially when in news, editorials, and correspondence columns, the newspapers stimulate the readers to look homeward rather than toward America, especially in respect to family ties, religion, and community customs.

When strong nationalist sentiment exists in Europe, the government at home may actually encourage the immigrants to keep up contact with the homeland. The Italian fascist government has taken this course, and Irish nationalism of the last quarter of the nineteenth century was fostered in large part from this country. Nostalgia often covers over some of the very unpleasant features of the homeland which the migrant was once anxious to escape.

In many immigrant communities there also arise mutual aid societies of one sort or another which keep up the homeland solidarity. Some of these are economic organizations, for banking, purchase of goods, or transportation of relatives and friends from abroad. Some of them have a distinctly recreational and perhaps patriotic bent. So, too, the clergy often keep the immigrant aware of his native land. The use of home languages in the church services is particularly effective.

We may characterize the effects of spatial segregation and retention of immigrant heritages as follows. (1) They maintain a continuity with the old culture. (2) The immigrant sees the new country and its culture through the eyes of his own culture, especially reflected in the ideas and attitudes of relatives and friends already on the ground. Naturally the newcomer defers to the definition of the American situation offered him by his fellow countrymen already here. (*3*) This continuity of the old and the interpretation of the new through his fellow countrymen softens the severity of the change, but profoundly influences the process of assimilation itself. (*4*) It is only as the immigrant is introduced into more and more of the features of American culture, and especially as his children come into contact with the school, with agencies of recreation, with American family life and other intimate patterns that the effects of these earlier contacts wear off and assimilation really gets under way. But the immigrant is not alone responsible for the retardation of assimilation. Let us now see what situations in the native communities hinder it.

Reactions of Native Populations to Immigrants. The most striking features of the native reaction to the immigrant are avoidance and prejudice. The newly arrived immigrant in this country has always had to face the resistance of those whose ancestors arrived earlier. It is one of the paradoxes of history that in this country "native Americanism," as it was called before the Civil War, and "one-hundred percentism," as it was called during and after the World War, reflect in large measure the fear of loss of status by groups in the population whose own ancestry was immigrant.

This prejudice finds its most frequent expression in economic competition with the newcomers, who were thought to cut wages, to work longer hours, and otherwise to threaten to "do" the native Americans out of their jobs. Also many of the more recent immigrants are Roman Catholics, and the Protestant communities resent the intrusion of Catholics into their localities. Finally, the exploitation of the immigrants by unscrupulous politicians has made their participation in community and public affairs open to suspicion.

Out of these relations grow up certain accommodations which serve to prevent more open conflict and to give a basis for certain common relations, but which, in turn, retard assimilation. There are no feelings of intimacy, no like-mindedness, and the relations are largely those of an external sort. But accommodation is often the first step to assimilation. Whether further steps are taken depends on other situations. Let us see what they are.

SITUATIONS HELPING ASSIMILATION

Unless blocked by color differences, the accommodative relations which grow out of differences tend to give way in time to more sympathetic and intimate contacts, finally fusing the separate cultures into one. Certain groups and institutions are particularly favorable to assimilation. They lead to appreciation of the alien culture by the native residents and help to interpret their culture to the newcomers. In this section, we shall reverse the previous order and take up first those aids developed by the native population. Then we shall see what things the immigrant brings or develops which facilitate the process from his angle.

Factors in the Native Community Aiding Assimilation. Special institutions or agencies for helping the immigrant in the process of assimilation are of recent origin and even now touch only a fraction of his problems. Other institutions already at hand have long played a part in the process.

Without a doubt the school is the most important single help in assimilating foreigners and their children. It is the children of adult immigrants especially who make up the most important group in the assimilative process. Common language is absolutely essential for any adequate social participation, and the school furnishes to the immigrant child both this tool of communication and a world of culture along with it. The child not only learns English, but the history, geography, and literature closely bound up with the deeper values of American culture. He learns to share with American children in the myths and legends of our national heroes. He takes part in holiday festivals. The symbols of the United States: the flag, the map, the letters U. S. A., come to have emotional meaning for him. He is also inducted into patterns of regular attendance at school. The whole ritual of obedience, preparation and recitation of lessons, movement through the grades, and graduation as a symbol of status and achievement, becomes significant in his assimilation. He accepts the American fetish of education, which comes to be looked upon as the open road to economic, political, and social success.

Extracurricular contacts and recreation are perhaps next in importance to the public school in facilitating assimilation. On the playground he learns American slang, and he finds that intimacy with American children is possible without the intrusion of adult prejudice. In the give and take of play the children of foreign background learn not only American games, but also folkways and mores which will be useful to them as adults. They learn the place of individual initiative and independence of action. They discover that patriarchal family control has little place in the American community. They take on American attitudes toward law, morals, and success.

Organized recreation through clubs under the guidance of the school or of private agencies goes further. The very programs of athletics, drama, music, and art are often directed toward making the immigrant child America-conscious.

The American charity organizations are often the first groups with which the adult immigrant comes into contact. When out of work, ill, or unable to obtain aid from his own foreign friends and neighbors, he is forced to appeal to public or private relief agencies for help. Present-day charity is concerned, of course, not alone with material relief but with training its clients in self-sufficiency and responsibility. The immigrant often first learns from these organizations about American standards of health, American family standards of cleanliness and cooking, and our conception of the rôle and status of the husband, wife, and children in reference to each other. Legal aid societies prevent exploitation of the immigrant by sharpers of his own nationality, from abuse in work relations with American employers, and from loan sharks, who prey upon these groups.

Then, too, settlement houses and community centers are often located in immigrant neighborhoods with a view to aiding the immigrant in becoming adapted to American life. The work of Jane Addams at Hull House in Chicago is well known. This is only an outstanding example of similar organizations elsewhere.

Americanization. The crisis of the World War made Americans particularly aware of the fact that they had millions of immigrants and their children within their gates who were not yet assimilated. The demand arose for the public schools and private agencies to undertake a nation-wide program to stimulate this process. Americanization as a widespread, conscious program became the order of the day. Although this word had been applied to the matter of immigrant assimilation long before, it took on new meaning.

In the manner of the World War campaigns, so successful in

raising money and in mobilizing material forces and large bodies of men in military camps and in war-time industries, energetic leaders and organizations sprang up to throw their energies into the "drive" method of making all individuals "one-hundred per cent" Americans. It was in this way that the conscious plan called "Americanization" arose. The notion got abroad that Americanization would be easy, that it was a sort of conversion phenomenon, that the external marks of naturalization, reading English and learning about George Washington and Abraham Lincoln, would do the trick of assimilation.

The American faith in education meant that the school would become the chief agency for nationalizing our foreigners. The schools had long been performing an important function in introducing the children of immigrants to American culture, and through the children indirectly but effectively influencing adult assimilation in the immigrant home. They now took over a more conscious program including the following features:

First, provision was made for evening classes for adult foreigners in which English and history were stressed. These classes, as Frank V. Thompson remarks, were "hasty and makeshift" in character, providing "superficial instruction for non-English speaking aliens on a large scale" and aiming at "immediate results."[6] They were often taught by quite inadequately trained persons. There was no real appreciation of the need for special training and for specially picked personnel in this difficult field of adult education. These classes were patterned on day schools, attendance was irregular, and the work largely superficial.[7]

Second, laws were enacted in most states raising the upper age limits of compulsory education, making instruction in English mandatory in all elementary schools, insisting on the wiping out of illiteracy, especially in foreign-born and non-naturalized citizens, requiring formal school rituals to pledge loyalty to the country, and making more adequate provision for vocational education, partly motivated with the immigrant situation in mind.

Finally, private agencies were enlisted in the campaign. During the war many employers insisted that their workers become naturalized, and there was a rush of adults for first naturalization papers

[6]See Frank V. Thompson, *Schooling the Immigrant*, 1920, p. 377. This entire volume presents material on the situation during and just after the World War.
[7]*Ibid.*, pp. 381–82.

and for some semblance of acquaintance with the American tongue and with history. Classes were actually set up by some industrialists to aid their workers. Then organizations like the Y. M. C. A., Y. W. C. A., Knights of Columbus, Y. M. H. A., D. A. R., local women's clubs, churches, and no end of special groups were called upon to aid in the Americanization program. Thompson lists 30 types of organizations of private and semi-public sort, and 10 public agencies, which had direct bearing on this program during the World War and just after.[8]

It is not necessary to point out that many benefits came from this enthusiastic, even if badly managed, campaign. As the war hysteria subsided, as people no longer saw in every foreigner a potential if not an actual "red menace," the program took on a more healthy and normal aspect. Yet the negative results of this campaign must be noted, since they reveal some important matters in regard to assimilation.

First of all, there was a tendency to use coercion and force in the whole program. Second, there was too much attention to the externals of naturalization: reading English, knowledge of bits of history, and passage through the legal rituals. The husks of assimilation, the externals, were blown up, and the kernel of assimilation, the true inward change of ideas, attitudes, and habits was neglected. Third, the most serious mistake was the failure to realize that a program of adult education for making citizens is not something distinct from the larger problem of adult education and the improvement of all citizenship.[9]

The mistakes of formal Americanization are obvious. First, it tended to be too consciously planned and coercive and hence to take on the nature of accommodation. Second, it rested on the assumption that American culture is something already complete and easily defined which the newcomer can take over *in toto*. And only passing attention was paid to the reciprocal relations of assimilation; the contribution of immigrant culture in the process was treated superficially.

Immigrant Forces Fostering Assimilation. In spite of the retarding effects of spatial and cultural segregation or isolation, the immigrant community itself aids the process of assimilation. The foreign-born enter into American industry or other economic

[8] *Ibid.,* pp. 40 ff.
[9] See Donald Young, *op. cit.,* pp. 458–59, for a strong criticism of Americanization.

activities; the material culture is the first to be acquired. These contacts educate them to hundreds of new situations. The substitution of the wage system for peasant rural life is often a great crisis. So, too, unemployment, illness, accident, or death from industrial injuries, and other crises have their place in training the immigrant in American customs and laws.

Then, too, immigrant mutual aid organizations in their own communities have certain relations with American organizations: banks, social work agencies, and the police. In the same way parochial schools cannot avoid the implications of the American culture. Immigrant patriotic societies which agitate for democracy in the home land also favorably influence the foreigners toward American democracy. Even the foreign-language press, often associated with these nationality movements in Europe, aids assimilation. It includes news, editorials, and readers' correspondence on American events and personalities, which force the readers' attention upon the American scene willy nilly.

Since the rate of acquiring the new culture is important, the very isolation of the immigrant and the retention of his Old World culture are not without important bearing on the total result. This very retardation often prevents too rapid loss of the stabilizing features of the old culture before those of the new are secured. Community disorganization and personal demoralization of the immigrant constitute a loss, not a gain, in the matter of assimilation. W. I. Thomas and F. Znaniecki have made this clear in their monumental work on assimilation, *The Polish Peasant in Europe and America* (1918-20). If the shift from one culture to another be too rapid, the breakdown of ideas, attitudes, and habits of individuals may well make the acquirement of new ones more difficult, especially if in the meantime the demoralization has taken the trend toward criminal or psychopathic behavior. The incidence of crime and insanity among our immigrant peoples is not so much a mark of inferior biological stock or of inferior European culture as it is a measure of the disorder set up by the crisis of changing over to American culture norms.

The whole process of assimilation is not concerned ordinarily with only one generation, but stretches over two, three, and sometimes more. The adult who migrates from home is often largely accommodated but never assimilated in the new society and its culture. His children usually represent a much more definite step toward assimilation. As a rule the third generation is well assimilated. This extension of the process through time leads naturally to a discussion of the personality changes involved in assimilation.

PERSONALITY FACTORS IN ASSIMILATION

To alter the ideas, attitudes, and habits which touch the deepest features of cultural training may be difficult. Where changes may go on slowly and within the confines of primary groups, with all their supporting intimacy and sympathy, assimilation is simpler than where it involves a wide range of secondary contacts. This is the reason for saying that assimilation at its best goes on within the family, the play group, and the neighborhood. Even the importance of the school is slight if it does not reflect itself back into the family and neighborhood.

We shall discuss the personality changes in assimilation under three heads: (*1*) immigrant adult generation, (*2*) first generation American born, and (*3*) the second generation American born. That is, we shall deal with the foreign-born adults, with their American-born children,[10] and with their grandchildren. It must be recognized that biological mixture with native stock or with mixed foreign and native stock usually aids this process, just as strong immigrant community solidarity may retard it and extend the number of generations necessary to bring about complete assimilation. These limiting factors must not be forgotten, but our space prevents more than a generalized picture.

The Immigrant Generation. Motives for coming to America differ. Freedom from political oppression and wish for religious liberty doubtless have played a part, but the economic motive has been and still is the chief driving force to migration. During the nineteenth century the myth of America as the land of golden opportunity penetrated to the remotest corners of Europe. The idealization of America was often the outcome of rich fantasy rather than real knowledge. The picture conjured up in the migrant's mind was often shattered when he arrived. The "Promised Land" often turned out to be dirty, sordid, and full of difficulties.

---

[10] Ordinarily immigrant children who are born in foreign countries but come over before they reach school age are considered in the second group—not for census purposes, of course, but in regard to assimilation.

The alien newly arrived on our shores usually feels a distinct sense of inferiority. His job is often of a new character, to which he must become accustomed through mistakes and difficulties that bruise his self-feeling. His unfamiliarity with the language in most instances constitutes a distinctly isolating factor that keeps him from feeling a part of his American world. This in turn keeps him tied to his own immigrant neighborhood, where he feels that not all of the past is lost.

Age is an extremely important factor in these first adaptations. It may fairly be said that with few exceptions, the older the immigrant, the more difficulty he will have in adjusting himself to the new environment. The grandparents who are sometimes brought along seldom get beyond the first stages of accommodation to America.

The earliest identification of the immigrant concerns externals of behavior. Differences in dress, walk, manners, and daily routine of overt habits set up ridicule and resentment in others and a sense of inferiority in the immigrant. Unless handicapped by long-standing religious taboos, as in the case of the orthodox Jews, the newcomer tends to take on the dress and externals of the Americans. One immigrant has described her early experience thus:

"To my mother, in her perplexity over the cooking stove, the woman who showed her how to make the fire was an angel of deliverance. A fairy godmother to us children was she who led us to a wonderful country called 'uptown,' where, in a dazzlingly beautiful palace called a 'department store,' we exchanged our hateful homemade European costumes, which pointed us out as 'greenhorns' to the children on the street, for real American machine-made garments, and issued forth glorified in each other's eyes."[11]

In this early stage the function of the immigrant's own neighborhood or community is most apparent. We noted above that the accommodations which one's fellow countrymen have already made to the American scene prove of great use in helping the newcomer over the first difficulties. Friends and relatives assist him in interpreting and defining the new situations.

It is in the economic rôle and status, however, that the immigrant often suffers his most acute sense of inferiority. It is only the money wages and the hope of economic improvement that make

[11]Mary Antin, *The Promised Land*, 1912, p. 187.

up to him, often, the loss of self-regard when a skilled mechanic
has to become a garbage collector, or an intellectual rabbi takes to
selling notions on the street corner. M. E. Ravage in his autobiography *The Making of an American* (1917) relates how he met
his fellow townsmen in America, almost all of them at work of
decidedly inferior status to what they had had at home: "Jonah
Gershon, who had been the chairman of the hospital committee in
Vaslui and a prominent grain-merchant . . . was dispensing soda-
water and selling lollypops on the corner of Essex street. . . . I recognized young Layvis . . . who, after two years of training in medicine at the University of Bucharest, was enjoying the blessings
of American liberty by selling newspapers on the streets."[12] Although the adult immigrant may be an economic success, although
he may in time learn the language and be naturalized, his American
acquirements with few exceptions will be relatively superficial to
his earlier and deeper layer of habits, ideas, and attitudes. At best
he becomes accommodated to his new situation. In his children
we find the changes taking place in a more fundamental way.

Children of Immigrants. The first generation born in this
country has a distinct advantage over their parents. They are
born on American soil and are socially and legally "American
citizens" by birth. This very fact, borne in upon the growing
child's mind by his parents, relatives, and friends, must unconsciously influence him in the process of assimilation in spite of the
hangover of old-world customs in his home and neighborhood.

As a child goes to school and as he comes into contact with
Americans, he picks up many attitudes and ideas which stand in
sharp contrast to those fostered at home. Out of this situation we
get the first indications of the coming storm of conflict that often
breaks upon the immigrant home. Manner of dress, dietary habits,
notions of sanitation and personal hygiene which the girl or boy
learns from school or his playmates run counter to those of the
parents, and opposition is set up when the child must obey his
parents!

Other conflicts arise when the immigrant's child wishes to play

---

[12] M. E. Ravage, *The Making of an American*, 1917, p. 67. See Louis Bloch, "Occupations of Immigrants Before and After Coming to the United States," *Quarterly
Publication of the American Statistical Association*, 1920–21, vol. XVII, p. 760,
where he points out that in 16 skilled occupations which he examined, over 76 per
cent of the immigrants trained in these skills gave them up when they came to this
country.

instead of taking up serious work. When adolescent children of immigrants "want to play all day," as one Greek father put it, the parent is at a loss to know what to do. To him it seems that America is ruining his boy. Then, too, the moral conduct of young people in this country stands in sharp contrast to European standards in many matters: disrespect for parental authority and freedom in the choice of friends, as witnessed in the practice of young girls going about at night without chaperons, of "wasting" hours in commercial recreation, and spending hard-earned money on personal adornment; or in the case of the boys, their disobedience of parental authority, leaving home to go to work or play as they choose, and their freedom from parental supervision generally. Often opposition arises over education or choice of major occupation. If the foreign culture from which the immigrant comes puts a premium on book learning and education, the family may sacrifice much to educate the children. Very frequently the older brothers and sisters give up their own educational advancement in the interests of the higher education of their younger brothers and sisters. But often the immigrant's culture gives little place to education. Only after exposure to the American educational system will the children and grandchildren get the great American faith in higher education.

Sometimes the conflicts between parents and children are not serious. The former learn to tolerate the new and strange habits of the latter. Sometimes the former actually change many of their views, though it may be a painful ordeal.

The children of immigrants live literally in two worlds. In one sense they are more aware of the conflict of culture than their parents are or than their own children will be. There is the attraction of their parental culture, stimulated at every point by the intimate character of family affection. There is the pull in the other direction by their desire to improve both their economic and their social status as Americans. Sometimes the conflict is avoided by moving out of the immigrant neighborhood, but even so, speech and name may pursue one. The foreign-born sometimes changes his name, but more often his son and grandson will change theirs. Fetchke becomes Freda, Geert becomes George, Greenbaum becomes Green, Jan becomes John, and so on. This reaction is particularly significant. There is nothing more intimate than a name. Nothing reveals the nationality and sub-racial background so well. And nothing shows more surely that one wishes to lose this background than the desire to change the name.

The change of names is peculiarly effective in helping the individual "pass" from immigrant status to another, provided he moves to a new locality. This cultural passing is most evident among Jewish and mixed Jewish families who wish to give up their religion and distinctive culture to merge themselves more completely with the American life.

The children of immigrants as they grow up often remain tied to the immigrant community, and their assimilation is only slightly more advanced than that of some of the foreign-born themselves. Much depends on their own background, their occupation, and the force of family tradition. Marriage outside the nationality group, of course, is another evidence of the breakdown of the Old World patriarchal control and the assumption of attitudes and habits of American independence in mating. When an Italian boy proposes marrying a Bohemian or Polish girl, his own immigrant mother and father may oppose the plan, but it means for him an emancipation from the Italian culture. With the patriarchal sys-tem still strongly intrenched, the marriage of an immigrant daugh-ter to a man of another European nationality or to an American is frequently even a more serious crisis for the parents.

As we have noted, the rapidity with which the children of immigrants become thoroughly a part of the American society depends upon many cultural factors and upon personality traits which express themselves differently in the face of the new crisis. A shy, retiring, introverted individual may well prefer the protection of the transplanted immigrant culture to the rough battle with the American world around him. Some immigrants and some of their children remain tied to the Old World culture much more than others. These individual differences must be taken into account in any concrete study of assimilation. The rate of the process varies in every case.

The Grandchildren of Immigrants. With the grandchildren of the immigrants we find, ordinarily, such progress made toward becoming Americans that they often resent any implication that they are even a part of such a sociological process.[13] They have usually left the immigrant neighborhood for something better as

[13] See H. G. Duncan, "A Study in the Process of Assimilation," *Publications of the American Sociological Society*, 1929, vol. XXIII, p. 187.

they have risen in the economic and social scale. All traces of language background of their grandparents have disappeared. They wish, in fact, to forget the native tongue of their ancestors. Intermarriage with native American families of long standing often aids them to put further barriers between them and their ancestry. Their children constitute most of the native American stock of our present-day population. There are perhaps few American families of pure strains running back four generations without any inter-marriage with other strains of more recent immigration.

The Marginal Man. Between the third or fourth generation American and his foreign ancestors there stand, then, a number of "half-way" persons, who had to undergo the internal and external conflict of living in a dual world. R. E. Park has coined the apt expression for such a person, the *marginal man.* Sometimes this is the child of immigrant parents; sometimes it is the grandchild. Very occasionally with one who came to the new country at an early age, it might be an immigrant himself. We are not interested so much in discovering in which generation this sort of person falls, as in examining some of his psychological features, since it is through him that the process of assimilation passes.

The marginal man may be defined as any person who lives in two cultures that are in conflict, that is, where attitudes of superiority and inferiority, of prejudice and opposition are common. He is called on by the situation to participate in two divergent sets of ideas, attitudes, and habits. He must identify himself with both cultures in so far as he can. As Park puts it, "It is in the mind of the marginal man that the moral turmoil which new cultural contacts occasion manifests itself in the most obvious forms."[14] Everett V. Stonequist goes so far as to say that if the conflict of patterns continues long enough, such an individual becomes a "personality type" with somewhat distinctive traits.[15] Certainly by reason of his "two-way" identification he often takes on some of the characteristics of a dual personality.

As a rule the marginal man is not at first aware of his "double life." Born in one culture he gradually takes over another. Later these individuals come into situations in which the conflict becomes overt and apparent. To quote Stonequist:

[14] R. E. Park, "Human Migration and the Marginal Man," *American Journal of Sociology,* May, 1928, vol. XXXIII, p. 893.
[15] See Everett V. Stonequist, *The Marginal Man: A Study in the Subjective Aspects of Cultural Conflict,* Ph.D. thesis, University of Chicago, 1930, ms. p. 308.

"When they become conscious of the cultural cleavage which involves their personal destiny, this identification is shaken and thrown into consciousness. But the process of dissociating oneself from something which has formed the matrix of one's deepest personal characteristics can only be painful and incomplete. The making of a new racial or national identification is forced by the violent emotional reaction against the old. The old identification, however, though bruised and shattered, continues to exist and troubles the mind. . . . Meanwhile, a new racial identification cannot be formed by the mere willing of it. It must grow with time and experience. In the interval of transition the individual suffers from a divided loyalty—an ambivalent attitude." [16]

In some instances the ambivalent reactions result in a constant swing back and forth between the two groups and their cultures. The Negro or immigrant is proud when some one of his nationality or race accomplishes something of public acclaim. On the other hand, he is ashamed when another member does something to disgrace his nationality or race. He may have the same sort of fluctuating attitude toward the dominant group in which he participates at other times.

As a member, originally, of a group which is looked down upon, the marginal man easily develops a sense of inferiority. This leads to over-compensation. The Jew is labeled "greedy," "insolent," "too aggressive." The Negro who wants to improve his position is called an "upstart." "Dagoes" are told "to go back where they came from," that is, to the inferior rôle and status of "Little Italy," beyond the tracks.

Correlated with the sense of inferiority and compensatory actions which grow out of it is the hypersensitiveness of the marginal individual. His self-consciousness becomes exaggerated. He grows suspicious, sometimes almost to the point of paranoia.[17] He broods over slights to himself and to his race or nationality group.

This very hypersensitiveness has its merits. It makes the marginal man an effective critic of the hypocrisy of the native citizens. He may call their attention to their own over-superiority, to the hiatus between their professions of liberty, equality, and fair dealing and their actual behavior, which is often quite the

[16] *Op. cit.*, ms. pp. 124–25.
[17] A psychopathic trait characterized by undue suspicion of others, accusations of persecution by others, and heightened sense of being abused.

contrary. For example, he may criticize the American pacifist and internationalist who talk glibly of peace and good will among all men but neglect the problems of racial discrimination at home. The "Brahmans" of older American stock prate of equal educational advantages to all comers in our colleges and universities, but thereupon devise quota schemes to keep down the number of Jews who may be admitted to these schools. Gentile students in colleges refuse to admit Jews to their fraternities and clubs and then blame the Jews for crowding into the recreational buildings constructed for the use of all the students. The marginal man may well serve a valuable function in pointing out these inconsistencies. This may aid in making the "natives" realize that assimilation after all is a reciprocal interaction leading to complete identity on each side and not a plan for saying to the newcomer, "Thus far and no farther."

This dichotomy of ideas and attitudes leads to dual behavior, some of which is compensatory in nature. The marginal man tends to be unstable and contradictory. Sometimes his conflict expresses itself in criminal or even psychopathic behavior. In less severe cases, it may take the direction of rebellion against the dual culture and social system out of which he came. Thus many leaders of racial and cultural minorities fighting for their "rights" are made up of just such persons who have lived in two worlds, and finally throw their support against the very divergences which produced them. Others disillusioned about becoming assimilated to the dominant culture return to their former culture. One of the outstanding examples of this return to former culture is the instance of Ludwig Lewisohn, shown admirably in his *Upstream: An American Chronicle* (1922), in *Israel* (1925), and in *Mid-Channel: An American Chronicle* (1929). He traces the course of his own disillusionment and his acceptance, in the end, of his rôle and status as a Jew in an alien and somewhat unfriendly world.

It is not uncommon among Jews to find that their relatively complete assimilation in one national society may not be recognized in another, and they are thrown back upon a culture from which they had already escaped. The writer has known a number of English Jews who, having migrated to this country, found themselves classified by native Americans as Jews and more or less obliged by the situation to identify themselves with Zionism and Judaistic culture. This is a case in which migration forces a previous assimilation to be given up and a new accommodation to replace it.

With divergent culture groups possessing different racial stock, the rebellious behavior and the acceptance of the former culture are the two most common outlets. In the case of immigrant peoples, where these racial factors do not complicate matters, most marginal persons struggle along through life making compromises with themselves and their fellows and are seldom able to solve any of the more fundamental problems. The better-balanced individuals will recognize the situation for what it is and neither struggle against it nor give up. After all, living in a dual world is not impossible. Their children when brought up in one of the two conflicting cultures, however, are often quite different and more stable, unless unfortunately the parents have projected their own struggles upon them.

The marginal man, then, represents but one stage in the cycle of processes from conflict through accommodation to complete assimilation. For this very reason he is a particularly important object of careful analysis. As Park says, "It is in the mind of the marginal man—where the changes and fusions of culture are going on—that we can best study the processes of civilization and of progress."[18]

CLASS ASSIGNMENTS

A. Further reading assignment:
  1. K. Young, *Source Book for Sociology*, chap. XXV.
  2. E. T. Hiller, *Principles of Sociology*, chap. XXIV.
  3. R. E. Park and E. W. Burgess, *Introduction to the Science of Sociology*, chap. XI.

B. Questions and exercises:
  1. Define assimilation. How does it differ from accommodation?
  2. What factors in a community hinder and what enhance assimilation? Discuss the place of the school in this process; is it always a help?
  3. Illustrate by actual life stories the major differences between accommodation and assimilation.
  4. Discuss critically the Americanization programs which were developed during and just after the World War.
  5. Bring to class illustrations of prejudice which hinder assimilation of immigrants.
  6. Why do peoples of northwestern Europe become assimilated to American culture more readily than those of southern and eastern Europe? What aspect of the process does this illustrate?
  7. Define and illustrate the concept "marginal man." What is meant by saying that the "marginal man" lives in two worlds?

[18]R. E. Park, *op. cit.*, p. 893.

C. Topics for class reports or longer written papers:

1. Cite the agencies which aid assimilation in some selected community, preferably your own, and choose one of these for more detailed analysis of functions.

2. Special topics on immigrant assimilation in America. (Consult R. E. Park and E. W. Burgess, *Introduction to the Science of Sociology*, bibliography to chap. XI; R. E. Park and H. A. Miller, *Old World Traits Transplanted*, 1921; W. I. Thomas and F. Znaniecki, *The Polish Peasant in Europe and America*, 1927 ed.; Bessie B. Wessell, *An Ethnic Survey of Woonsocket, Rhode Island*, 1931; Pauline V. Young, *The Pilgrims of Russian Town*, 1932; Christine A. Golitzi, *A Study of Assimilation Among the Roumanians of the United States*, 1929; Donald Young, *American Minority Peoples*, 1932; Donald Young, *Research Memorandum on Minority Peoples in the Depression*, 1937; F. J. Brown and J. S. Roucek, editors, *Our Racial and National Minorities*, 1937; D. R. Taft, *Human Migration*, 1936.)

3. Analytical review in terms of conflict, accommodation, and assimilation of selected autobiographies of immigrants. (Among other references consult Mary Antin, *The Promised Land*, 1912; Horace J. Bridges, *On Becoming an American: Some Meditations of a Newly Naturalized Immigrant*, 1919; Rose Cohen, *Out of the Shadow*, 1918; Elizabeth Hasanovitz, *One of Them; Chapters from a Passionate Autobiography*, 1918; Ludwig Lewisohn, *Upstream: An American Chronicle*, 1929; Constantine M. Panunzio, *The Soul of an Immigrant*, 1921; Michael Pupin, *From Immigrant to Inventor*, 1925; M. E. Ravage, *An American in the Making*, 1917; Abraham M. Rihbiny, *A Far Journey*, 1914; Maurice Samuel, *I, the Jew*, 1927, and *You Gentiles*, 1924; E. G. Stern, *My Mother and I*, 1919; Andreas Ueland, *Recollections of an Immigrant*, 1929; Silvio Villa, *The Unbidden Guest*, 1923.)

4. The rôle of the marginal man in accommodation and assimilation. (Consult Everett V. Stonequist, *The Marginal Man*, 1937; Brown and Roucek, *op. cit.*)

PART FIVE

PHASES OF SOCIAL CONTROL

INTRODUCTION

PART FIVE deals with the manner in which society regulates or controls the behavior of groups and of individuals in the interests of stability and security. However, as W. I. Thomas remarks in the introduction to his *Source Book for Social Origins* (1909), from one point of view "All activity can be translated . . . or at least be related" to the concept of *control*. As he says further, "Control is not a social force, but is the object, realized or unrealized, of all purposive activity." In this sense culture may be considered the result of controlling or managing the environment— physical and social—in the interests of mankind. In the chapters which follow, however, we shall deal with control only in a more restricted and traditional sense. But it must not be forgotten that what we have to say is but a phase of the larger matter of culture and societal organization. In discussing societal organization and culture (Part Three), as well as in analyzing the social processes (Part Four), we have already presented certain aspects of social control in our narrower sense. This material we need not repeat.

In the first chapter of this division we shall deal more particularly with the forms and agencies of control in our society and then discuss in the two following chapters particular applications of such control to economic and professional life, and to the problem of personal demoralization. In the final chapter we shall present certain prospects for control and change in the modern world.

CHAPTER XXVI

SOCIAL CONTROL

Taking part in group life is like playing games in which one is the member of various teams: one team has to do with family matters, another with church, recreational, or artistic interests, and still others concern getting a living or participating as citizens in a political state. Just as all teams at play must have rules in order to carry on, so wherever men develop any sort of permanent groupings, they unconsciously or consciously develop rules of the social game. Thus in primitive society there may be regulations giving in detail the manner of dividing up the kill, or rules setting strict barriers on the contacts of age and sex classes. Or in our own society we have laws protecting private property, setting tariff rates, regulating sanitation, or we have customs which control sex expression or set down the rules of etiquette or furnish a code of ethics for medicine or law.

These rules of the game in society are usually discussed under the general term social control, which we propose to examine in this and the two following chapters.

THE NATURE AND PURPOSES OF SOCIAL CONTROL

In a broad sense, social control refers to any verbal or bodily action by which one person determines the response of another. But any response is determined not alone by the present stimulus, but by the cumulative effects of past stimuli and responses—in the form of habits, attitudes, and ideas. This conception of control is sound enough. In discussing expectancy of behavior in Chapter VI, we saw that by setting up anticipatory reactions in another, one may control that other person. Thus parents manage their children when they furnish ideals for them to follow; lovers exercise control when they identify themselves with each other; and one purpose of patriotic training is to build up attitudes and ideas which will control the behavior of the citizens in time of war. There is also the negative or restrictive sort of stimulus which people use. They deny or inhibit the responses of others. That is, they force some contrary response on the other persons. Taboos or negative orders are illustrations. These are the "Thou shalt nots" of every society.

Definition of Social Control. For our purpose we shall limit the term social control to a somewhat narrower field. We do not include those more intimate person-to-person influences which grow up in the sympathetic or antagonistic interactions of husband and wife, children and parents, members of a congeniality group, or among friends. We shall define *social control* as the use of coercion, force, restraint, suggestion, or persuasion of one group over another, or of a group over its members, or of persons over others to enforce the prescribed rules of the game. These rules may be set down by the members themselves, as in a professional code of ethics, or they may be those laid down by a larger, more inclusive group for the regulation of another smaller group, as in the state's regulation of monopoly. In our present-day society, social control is directed chiefly at individuals and at special interest groups whose purposes and practices run counter to the broader morals of the community or the legal codes of the political state. Failure to live up to the code leads or may lead to a penalty or an infliction of pain. That is, failure to do a required act, or indulgence in a forbidden act, leads to punishment or restriction of response in other areas of behavior. In other words, the power of coercion finds its overt expression in the threat to punish or the actual punishment of the offenders against the code. But even in these cases the more positive control by devices of suggestion or persuasion is not neglected.

J. M. Clark states in his book *The Social Control of Business* (1926), "In a broad sense, we may call it social control whenever the individual is forced or persuaded to act in the interest of any group of which he is a member, rather than in his own personal interest." But this definition neglects the fact that control may take the form of exploitation of one sub-group or person by another group or person. Social control covers a wide range of acts, some of which represent narrower interests of in-groups while others touch the wider community. Social control arises when an individual or group is forced or persuaded to act to the benefit of his own or other group. This may be seen in the domination by a special-interest group, accommodative arrangements of two competing or conflicting organizations, or the regulation by a professional association of its own members. But in a broader, ethical sense, it concerns regulative devices of the government or of other agencies of the community which aim to promote justice or to prevent undue exploitation of one sub-group by another, as well as to direct the behavior of the community members toward the welfare of the entire society. Exploitative control might include advertising or racketeering, working arrangements of control between opposing groups among competitors, or wage agreements between labor unions and employers. Professional codes of ethics illustrate in-group control of members. And government control covers not only general protection of life and property, but special regulation of corporations, employers' associations, trade unions, professions, churches, or any other sub-groups which may at times threaten the general welfare.

Purposes of Social Control. The aims of social control are: (*1*) to regulate behavior, that is, it makes for regularity of responses; and (*2*) to make possible three important features of social life—predictability, stability, and continuity.

Control means that it is possible to anticipate what an individual will do, or what will be the punishment if he fails to do it. This makes for reliability of social action. For example, a contract enables the parties thereto to know in advance what each will do and what to expect. There is no changing of intention from day to day, and the obligation is binding for the time set. Social control also furnishes equilibrium between warring factions or groups, by restraining individuals and groups from activities which might disrupt the whole society. So, too, the mechanisms of control make for continuity. They form a part of the culture which is carried down from generation to generation. They give each generation a pattern which keeps the social order running smoothly and without the friction which would arise if each generation had to develop its own codes. However, in a rapidly changing society like our own, this continuity is disturbed with the result that new codes have to be developed. New codes often fall into conflict with old ones.

Social control in a primary community is relatively direct, face to face, and rather informal in character. There is in such a society what E. A. Ross in his *Social Control* (1901) calls a "natural order" based on sympathy, sociability, sense of justice, and resentment against wrongdoing. In these cases, the society is usually homogeneous, the force of public gossip or ridicule is effective, and only in reference to the more serious offenses is the fundamental "ordering and forbidding technique" of control invoked by the community or neighborhood elders. Public opinion may be mobilized directly upon new issues when they arise, because the crises which arise are, as a rule, not difficult to understand.

As culture and peoples become heterogeneous and as secondary groups arise, the whole problem of social control changes in character. Not only is there increased differentiation and increased complexity of interaction, but the crosscurrents of warring factions are more and more apparent. Employers' associations get at odds with labor unions over hours of work, rates of pay, and conditions of labor. Racial groups conflict with each other for jobs and social status. Sectarian groups have long flung themselves at each others' throats in the frenzy of their enthusiasm over theological differences. Professional classes are in competition and conflict: physicians and surgeons against quacks, well-trained attorneys against the shysters, and the scientist against the fakir and magician. Out of this sort of situation arises a need to regulate and delimit the expression of these narrower interests. There is always a danger that strong special interest groups in conflict may disrupt the community and threaten the existence of all groups.

Occasionally some special interest group comes to dominate the entire community and tries to manipulate the wider social control to its own ends. This is seen in certain secret societies of west Africa, in the priestly caste of ancient Egypt, and partially, at least, in the church hierarchy during the Middle Ages. Sometimes it has been the intellectual élite, as the Brahman caste in India or the learned class of old China. Throughout Western society it has been the military, aristocratic classes and more especially the owners of property. As we noted in Chapter II, the capitalists have tended to determine the entire ethos of our Western society for several centuries. Since getting a living is the basic necessity of the members of every community, wherever a dominant economic class arises, their exploitation has played an important part in control, even where Brahman, priestly, or warrior classes have been ascendant. Any special interest group may exploit a community to its own ends unless stopped by contrary forces. Today it is control by the state which acts to offset such exploitation.

FORMS AND AGENCIES OF SOCIAL CONTROL

In the last analysis, the community, large or small, has the power of coercion, which is essential to social control. The expression of this authority or power, however, varies with the culture. Let us look at the forms which control may take.

Forms of Control. Social control may be classified into two types: informal and formal. The informal are illustrated by the mores and public opinion; the formal controls are those worked out by the state through law and administrative devices or those consciously developed within organizations themselves, or between or among organizations to regulate their relations.

Many of the early informal patterns of control were undoubtedly hit upon more or less by trial and error to meet particular situations and then gradually became fixed practices. They are often formulated unconsciously and are not always consistent with each other. Man is rather slow and late in arriving at any attempts to make his social order logical and consistent. Yet it would be a mistake to imagine that all folkways are the product of unconscious adaptation. Sometimes the informal controls are quite consciously set up, although perhaps in contradiction to others already in vogue.

The most important *informal controls* in a primary community are the moral codes and ideals, the religious convictions, and public opinion. The first are largely set down and carried on by the elders of the group whose offices are elective or hereditary. Gossip plays an important part in the actual operation of the moral code. The second, religious beliefs, are dominated by the priestly classes everywhere: medicine men, priests, pastors, or other church dignitaries. We have already noted in Chapter XIV on religion how belief in a god and in immortality influences conduct. In the same way we have presented certain features of social control in our discussion of the family, of education, of play life, art, and science. We need not repeat this material here, although the means by which such control operates will be discussed in a subsequent section. In more modern times public opinion, an outgrowth of discussion and gossip, has come to play an ever larger part in informal social control. It is highly important, and will receive attention.

Like other folkways the patterns of social control are slow to change. In the face of new situations there gradually develops a strain upon them because they do not change as fast as the other behavior patterns which they attempt to regulate. Moreover, in the secondary community, with its specialized groups, these simpler controls do not suffice, and doubtless the growing awareness of strain in the modes of control stimulates man to set up more consistent devices.

When standardized codes of conduct are set down to be managed by special groups and passed on from generation to generation by special agencies, we have the beginnings of *formal control*. The rise of the political state, with formal law-making, and the invention of writing, which made possible the keeping of records and the preservation of codes, were especially important. In a modern complex social-economic society we could not get along without these formalized controls, because the personal, intimate relations have largely been replaced by more impersonal and indirect contacts. Thus, in the primary group life of village economy, barter and direct dealing in produce were possible. Today, in an intricate economic organization such relations are possible only in a limited way, and all sorts of controls have been evolved to meet the needs of buyers and sellers, of producers and consumers, of merchants, bankers, shippers, manufacturers, farmers, and others who have a part in the complex web of economic life. We shall examine some aspects of this problem in the next chapter.

Kinds of Formal Control. In our own society, formal controls fall into two classes: those forms set down by the political state, and those codes which are developed among various groups to handle their interrelations or the regulations set up within a group itself to control its own members.

The political state is obviously the dominant organization in our present world. The state through its exercise of sovereignty is supreme in its power of coercion. The *law* is laid down in order to maintain or establish the rights, duties, and liberties of the members of the state. Rights imply a two-sided relationship in which one person owes the other a duty and the other person benefits thereby. A person has rights only in so far as others have duties toward him. When persons have no duties toward one another they are free. As J. M. Clark puts it, "Liberty begins where duty ends, and *vice versa.*" One's rights, in other words, set the boundaries upon other people's liberties.

Yet liberty implies more than mere absence of duty. If other people are free to interfere, a person's liberty may be useless. Liberty, to be of benefit, must be protected by rights to non-interference from others. The common man usually does not distinguish between "rights" and "liberties." In fact the protected liberties are what he means by rights—often called "natural rights."[1]

These "natural" or "inalienable" rights and liberties, therefore, rest upon consensus of others and upon their power to make them effective for us. The law tells people what they *must do* and what they *must not do*. This sets the limits of what they *may do*. It fixes the direction of behavior along stable and predictable lines, thus serving an essential purpose of social control.

In theory the law is general in its application. It is not supposed to play favorites. It is not a special act for the benefit or injury of one person or special group. Its functions are as follows: (*1*) to make known the will of the sovereign; (*2*) to enforce this will upon the citizens in the name of the whole state; (*3*) to punish infringements without regard to special interests of persons; and (*4*) to supplement with the aid of compulsion the informal controls of the community when needed.

In our own country the political state expresses itself in legal form in four basic channels: (*1*) constitutional law, which is the fundamental legal code of the nation and the states, upon which all other law is predicated, and from which there is no redress except (*a*) through change of the constitution itself by pre-established ways, (*b*) by judicial reinterpretation of the constitution, or (*c*) by revolutionary abolition of the constitution; (*2*) statute law, which covers all the formal enactments of national and state legislative bodies, and which law governs the country within the limitations set down by the constitution as it is interpreted by the proper courts; (*3*) court-made or case law, which is made by the judges, who in their decisions and interpretations of law and cases set the precedent for future decisions; (*4*) quasi-legal, administrative regulations based on the police power of the state, which are used to govern many of the newer special economic interests that have arisen since the formal codes were worked out—for example, public utilities and interstate commerce.

One of the most interesting developments in the field of control has been the rise of codes voluntarily developed between compet-

[1] For further discussion of this point see J. M. Clark, *Social Control of Business*, 1926, pp. 99–105.

ing or conflicting special interest groups which find it advantageous to devise and enforce among themselves regulations defining their relations. Illustrations are the trade associations, with their agreements among members; better business bureaus, with their attempts to regulate products and business practices; and all sorts of agreements between laborers and employers. Another development is the rise of codes within various businesses and professions themselves for the regulation of their own members. We shall examine the place of these in the next chapter.

These extra-legal devices, like the informal ones, simply mean that the state alone cannot handle all the problems of social control. This factor is often forgotten by well-meaning people who wish to force upon the political state the necessity and duty of attempting all forms of social control. This leads us naturally into the whole problem of the interrelations of morality, public opinion, the law, and the extra-legal codes of control.

The Function of Public Opinion in Social Control. The enforcement of the mores, at least in primary communities, is largely personal and direct. The law, in contrast, is assumed to be carried out only under fixed rules by stipulated authorities of the organized state. The extra-legal codes of groups themselves are but an extension of the idea of formal control working its way out among the various groups without recourse to interference by the state.

In the light of these facts we may ask just what place public opinion has in control? In order to answer this we must look briefly at the nature and function of public opinion.

Opinion refers to the verbalized convictions which people express in reference to some social object or situation. Opinion is related to the fundamental attitudes, myths, legends, and ideas of a group or community. The opinions of a group are their verbalized attitudes, but opinion is not identical with habits and attitudes. It merely gives them a certain interactional setting in terms of language.

Public opinion refers to the discussion or talk about common social objects by members of a community. In other words, it is opinion that is "published" or expressed in the marketplace, the forum, or wherever community members interact. Where opinion in a community wholeheartedly supports some particular value or object, we may, following E. A. Ross, speak of *preponderant* opinion. Thus, in European and American society monogamy is not only established in the law but rests firmly upon preponderant opinion.

Public opinion in democratic Western society refers rather to the discussion among members of a community concerning issues upon which there is difference as well as agreement. It comes into play where the mores and the law do not cover a critical social situation. So long as no crises arise around some practice or belief, preponderant opinion will support it. It is in a time of rapidly shifting habits and attitudes like the present that differences arise. Public opinion therefore refers to *the verbalization of these differences in anticipation of changes in attitudes and habits*. But it does not develop unless there is an accepted pattern in the culture which permits it. As we know it in Western society, it is linked with other culture traits, such as suffrage and representative government.

Public opinion really goes through a number of stages: (*1*) the rise of an issue, (*2*) the discussion of this issue with particular reference to various proposed solutions, and (*3*) the swing to one side or the other as evidenced by consensus and voting or other methods of registering decisions. Strictly speaking, active public opinion usually ceases when this third stage is completed. From then on the beliefs and convictions of people about an issue may easily become less aggressive. There remains a kind of passive, spectator reaction until an issue arises again.

An interesting case of the interplay of public opinion, the mores, and the law is afforded in the history of national prohibition of the liquor traffic in this country. The early agitation for temperance in drinking was followed by a more intensive campaign of ardent minorities everywhere against the evils of the saloon. Although drinking habits were rather deeply ingrained in the American culture, our people were eventually so aroused that the program of nation-wide prohibition which these militant groups had fostered was made into constitutional and statute law. It cannot be said that there was ever a completely preponderant opinion, but certainly the most powerful agencies were behind the movement, and there was widespread support.

From the day the prohibition law went into effect, however, in large sections of our country there began to develop negative attitudes toward its enforcement. Gradually the prohibition sentiment which had been built up began to wane, and within 14 years there was such a decided swing in the opposite direction that the Eighteenth Amendment was repealed. This was a case where the law did not correlate closely with the mores, and where public opinion in time reversed itself.

It is evident that whoever dominates the formation of beliefs and convictions can profoundly affect the changes in the law and the mores. Censorship and propaganda thus become the most powerful weapons in social control in any secondary community, characterized as it is by specialization of work, impersonal relations, rapid transportation, and indirect communication over long distances. At their best, censorship and propaganda operate together. During the World War the various governments censored certain news and deliberately manufactured other news in its place in order to keep up the morale at home and if possible to break it down among the enemy nations.

Although in democratic, capitalist societies, the monied groups often attempt to control the news and press interpretations, they seldom do so completely. But employers and employees alike have not hesitated to inflict upon the wider community propaganda directed to their own selfish aims.

In the recently founded communist and fascist states in Europe, censorship and propaganda are a part of the whole educational and promotional program of the national state. As we noted in Chapter XIII in discussing indoctrination in education, these devices become highly important in securing public support. Wherever such complete control comes into operation, we cannot speak of public opinion in the sense of discussion and changing consensus. In such a system all opinion once formed is, at least officially, preponderant opinion; there is no freedom of speech or of the press.

THE MEANS OF SOCIAL CONTROL

We have already noted some of the means of social control in discussing family institutions, education, recreation, art, religion, and the sciences. In this section we shall examine more systematically the psychology of the methods used in exercising social control.

E. A. Ross, whose book *Social Control: A Survey of the Foundations of Order* (1901) remains the classic work on the subject in

English, discusses the means of social control under 14 headings: public opinion, law, belief, social suggestion, education, custom, religion, personal ideals, ceremony, art, personality, enlightenment, illusion, and social valuations. F. E. Lumley in his more recent volume *Means of Social Control* (1925) also lists 14 topics: rewards, praise, flattery, persuasion, advertising, slogans, propaganda, gossip, satire, laughter, calling names, commands, threats, and punishment.

We may distinguish between those means of control which are negative and those which are positive. The former consist of all techniques of interaction which involve repression, that is, inhibition of the speech or action of others by restraint or counter conditioning. The infliction of pain in learning to avoid certain objects illustrates the method by which this sort of control is built up. The positive devices are those which elicit and facilitate response. There is stimulation to an action which, because it is pleasant and because others socially approve, is enjoyed and sought after.

Within this framework of negative or inhibitory and positive or evocative stimuli, we also note that some means of control are largely colored by emotions, while others depend much more on intellectual considerations. Of those means discussed by Ross, certainly religion, ceremony, art, and what he calls "personality" draw heavily upon emotional appeals, while education, enlightenment, illusion, and social valuations lean upon intellectual devices more particularly. Of Lumley's list, laughter, flattery, persuasion, advertising, and punishment employ the emotions, while praise, commands, threats, and satire rest more particularly on intellectual grounds. Obviously emotions and ideas are mixed in all these devices, just as they are mixed in all behavior and mental life. For this reason any classification of means of control as emotional or intellectual is open to question. Yet because man is dominated so much more completely by his emotions than by logical ideas this division is not wholly without merit.

A sounder classification is one which takes into account the social act or interaction, which always involves two or more persons. For convenience we may put them down under two headings: the language or verbal and gestural method,[2] and the overt action

---

[2] This includes gestures of face, hand, or body. After all, language proper is but a highly symbolic form of gesture. See K. Young, *Social Psychology*, Chap. X.

method. Informal control tends to use some; formal control others. Moreover these devices are used with different effects in different groups or in different problems of control.

Taking up the language method first, let us recall that a great bulk of all social interaction goes on at the verbal rather than at the bodily level of action. To realize this, one has only to recall how much time is spent in talking, reading, or writing, as contrasted with direct handling of persons. Furthermore the range of verbal interaction is clearly much greater and more flexible than the range of overt bodily action. At best one can push and shove another, or withdraw from him, or strike, bite, pinch, or kick him, or fondle, caress, and make love. But the range of intercourse possible through talk and writing is enormous. For this very reason verbal controls are effective since as stimuli they are much more flexible and cover a much wider area of meaning. The child soon learns that words are a substitute for overt management. In the field of social control, as we have limited it, children and adults also learn that verbal communication will turn the trick of group control without recourse to more direct coercive measures. Since words are conditioned to actions, it is easy enough in most cases to bring about the desired result in behavior by the verbal approach. Overt bodily action we reserve for the extreme cases.

So far as results go, the verbal method may be either negative and inhibitory, or positive and evocative. That is, some language appeals may be directed toward stopping oncoming or anticipated behavior. Other language stimuli may facilitate action in the desired direction.

From the standpoint of the recipient, those pleasant and positive verbal methods are chiefly praise, flattery, suggestion and persuasion, education, advertising, slogans, and propaganda.

Praise is a sort of reward in words, especially from upper to lower strata, and induces social amenability and conformity. In other words it carries its own authority. *Flattery* is undue, exaggerated, and somewhat false praise, usually set up for more ulterior purposes in dealing with others, especially those in an upper or superior social position. It appeals directly to the ego and is a particularly effective weapon in a culture dominated by individualism and desire for material goods. Yet flattery is effective in any society where there is a difference in status and where prestige plays a part in control. *Education, advertising,* and *propaganda,* though different theoretically in motive, all stimulate pleasant ideas and condition persons to act along lines which they like or imagine they like. Individuals come to want to do the acts suggested for them. In the case of *persuasion,* the suggestive appeals lead to the desired attitude or action. *Slogans* help to define situations and limit behavior along desirable lines. Slogans are the verbal sign-posts which guide a group to victory and success.

Closely associated with praise and flattery is the giving of badges, rewards, or other tangible objects drawn from a limited supply. *Rewards* often represent getting something for nothing. And rewards usually pass from those of superior status to those of inferior. *Badges* are but external symbols of authority conferred on officials or on members of a group to designate status as well as authority. They exercise a great influence upon the recipients and upon others with whom they come in contact. Other material symbols are *uniforms* or *insignia.* Thus the black shirt in Italy and the brown shirt in Germany became important marks of identification and reward.

Verbal controls of an unpleasant and negative sort are gossip, satire, laughter at others, calling names, commands, censorship, and threats. While some *gossip* may be innocuous, that which concerns social control is largely critical in tone. Gossip helps to make myths and legends and is effective in formulating public opinion. Gossip is the "voice of the herd" thundering in our ears, telling us that the goblins of ridicule, ostracism, and punishment will get us if we don't "behave!"

Satire, a curious combination of humor and critical logic put in a sarcastic way, is a highly intellectual and hence distinctly limited means of control. It is a method of exposing the foibles and weaknesses of persons and making them squirm under the verbal lash. It is unpleasant, although the more genial satire may not sting deeply. *Laughing at others* has doubtless been one of the oldest methods of control. It bespeaks superiority and is highly effective since it tends to mark off and isolate the individual from his fellows, a very effective means of control. If a person loses his sense of belonging to a group, of participating in common enterprises, even though he is not bodily removed, he feels lonesome, unattached, and insecure. Although usually only temporary, ridicule and laughter may have powerful effects. This sort of thing if continued often produces a lasting sense of inferiority.

Calling names or hurling epithets, especially at others whom one dislikes, is an old device of control. It is closely bound up with the still prevalent notion that words have some peculiar magical power of their own to do damage to those upon whom they are cast.[3] To call names is an aid in giving a person a lower social status. As Elsie Clews Parsons says in her book *Social Rule* (1916), " 'Calling names' partakes of the satisfaction of declassifying." A "wop" or a "red" is beneath us socially. A "moron" is stupid and a "Bohemian" is wild in his conduct. Calling names is common because it is easy to use. It is effective, since most of us have been conditioned to a peculiar reverence for words.

Commands are a direct verbal form of ordering and forbidding, the oldest techniques of negative control through words. The command may be a positive order to do something, or an inhibitory statement forbidding an action. Commands represent power in a direct way. They have much more the sense of exterior authority than do satire, laughter at others, or calling names. In our society the most effective commands in secondary groups are those issued by the church and state.

Closely related to commands is *censorship*. Censorship is complementary to propaganda. It represents taboo on expression of opinion, whereas propaganda suggests opinion and action along predetermined lines. As it works itself out, it is really a command of someone in authority, usually a representative of the state or the church, to restrain or ban expression of fact or opinion. It is often purely physical in method, as in burning tabooed books. For the individual whose work is forbidden, censorship has all the effects of restraint of bodily motion. It usually sets up unpleasant and antagonistic attitudes.

Threats are the most severe forms of verbal control, since to be effective they must be backed by physical force or the appearance of power to deny action. If the threat does not inhibit, then the person threatened must be made to suffer injury, pain, or punishment. Threats are distinctive carriers of emotion and accordingly have great potential power. Moreover, as Lumley says, the threat puts but two alternatives before the person threatened. He can either do this act or suffer the consequences if he refrains from doing it. There are only two ways out of the dilemma, and he must choose

[3]See K. Young, *Social Psychology*, chap. XVI, and *Social Attitudes*, ed. by K. Young, chap. V, for a review of the power of words over behavior.

between them. Moreover, the threat loads the dice for the choice in the direction desired by the threatener.

To these various methods of control others might be added, and in the interplay of individuals various combinations of these are used together. Some devices are more suited to informal, others to formal control. Certainly much of praise, flattery, persuasion, calling names, and gossip—used so much in informal areas of control—depend for their best effects on face-to-face contacts. They were developed in the primary group situations. At present they have become a part also of secondary group relations, although they are most effective still in the direct person-to-person contacts. On the other hand, advertising, censorship, and propaganda are more distinctly an outgrowth of secondary group organization. Commands and threats also developed in the primary group relations, but the former are highly developed in certain legal controls.

The method of *bodily* or *overt action* is the final expression of control when no other way remains open. Overt action as a means of control has up to the present been largely negative and restrictive. It means that if the individual does not do as he is told, pain, suffering, and even death may be brought upon him. Such action is just what it says, forced and not voluntary. The general term for this negative overt control is punishment. This includes fines, imprisonment, whipping, mutilation, torture, banishment, and death.[4]

Gross overt action may be used in both informal and formal types of control and appears in both primary and secondary communities, although the state more and more reserves the right to inflict severe punishment upon the individual. In the past, obedience to law has been enforced largely by the negative method of punishment. In fact, it is but the carrying out in conduct of the ordering and forbidding technique of the command and threat, the most primitive of the verbal methods. Punishment, moreover, is easy because it relieves the punishers of responsibility for a system which makes such control necessary.

The fact that punishment is so easy is no reason to believe it is socially very effective. There is a traditional belief that punishment reforms the criminal or recalcitrant person, and deters others who know of it from wrongdoing. Such an idea is so deeply

---

[4]Lumley adds war, but this complicates the whole problem by drawing upon a rather wide range of other factors; so we shall omit it, although true enough, warfare may be a method of punishing another nation.

embedded in our culture that it will take a long time to change it. There is considerable evidence, however, that the most effective method of reform is not punishment, but rather the treatment of the recalcitrant as a socially maladjusted or socially ill person who needs reconditioning along positive and pleasant lines. The whole development of propaganda, education, advertising, and other social methods of control runs counter to the "Thou-shalt-not" devices of punitive justice. The former are positive. They build up habits and attitudes along desirable lines. They make unnecessary the fear of wrongdoing, since one is reconditioned to actions which are required, and which by their nature prevent the expression of contrary or negative responses. (See Chapter XXVIII on social control and personal demoralization.)

CLASS ASSIGNMENTS

A. Further reading assignments:

1. K. Young, *Source Book of Sociology,* chap. XXVI.

2. E. B. Reuter and C. W. Hart, *Introduction to Sociology,* chaps. XV and XVI.

3. R. E. Park and E. W. Burgess, *An Introduction to the Science of Sociology,* chap. XII.

B. Questions and exercises:

1. Distinguish between formal and informal social control. Illustrate each.

2. Distinguish between the law and the mores. Illustrate each in relation to effectiveness of control.

3. What are the main differences in the rise and scope of public opinion in a primary and in a secondary community?

4. Why has propaganda become so important in modern society?

5. Distinguish between the means of social control as to effectiveness in various situations.

C. Topics for class reports or longer written papers:

1. A critical discussion of the treatment of social control by E. A. Ross and F. E. Lumley. (Consult Ross, *Social Control;* and Lumley, *Means of Social Control,* and his *The Propaganda Menace.*)

2. The present use of propaganda and censorship in communist Russia. (Consult S. N. Harper, *Civic Training in Soviet Russia,* 1929, and his *Making Bolsheviks,* 1931; W. Duranty, *Duranty Reports Russia,* 1934, and his *I Write as I Please,* 1935; W. H. Chamberlin, *Russia's Iron Age,* 1934; E. Lyons, *Assignment in Utopia,* 1937; H. L. Childs, ed., *Propaganda and Dictatorship,* 1936, chap. III by B. W. Maxwell; and current periodicals.)

3. The use of propaganda and censorship in fascist Germany. (Consult E. A. Mowrer, *Germany Puts the Clock Back,* 1933; C. B. Hoover, *Germany Enters the Third Reich,* 1933; F. L. Schuman, *The Nazi Dictatorship,* 2nd ed., 1936; Childs, *op. cit.,* chap. I by F. M. Marx; and current periodicals.)

CHAPTER XXVII

CONTROL IN ECONOMIC AND PROFESSIONAL RELATIONS

During the post-war years in the United States the business interests had a favorite expression, "less government in business and more business in government." It voiced their opposition to regulation of business by the state, which regulation they considered illegal, immoral, and dangerous. This was largely wishful thinking on the part of business men, a rationalization in defense of "rugged individualism." But the modern world has moved away from this ideology and the practice of unrestricted exploitation. Strictly speaking, there never was a self-operating society produced by the balance of "free competition" alone. We are now face to face with the fact that the organized community, especially the political state, finds it more and more necessary to control the special interest groups that would exploit the larger society.

THE CONTROL OF BUSINESS

The proponents of *laissez faire* and private initiative cannot imagine a society organized otherwise than in terms of private profits and the individual competitive system. But there have been and are societies built on other lines. The medieval period witnessed much regulation: the guilds controlled workmen's time, apprenticeship, compensation, and quality of goods; the church forbade usury, unjust prices, and other devices of exploitation; and the emerging national state threw many regulations around industry and commerce. Today Soviet Russia seems to be making a success of its socialistic economic system.

Cultural Background of Economic Individualism. Modern capitalism grew out of Protestantism and nationalism, which were accompanied by the breakdown of the feudal order, colonization, the loss of traditional religious sanctions, the rise of commerce and, later, industry fostered by inventions. These conspired to produce the period of economic individualism, which had for its major tenets free competition, free enterprise, and the private profit system—all leading to a self-regulating economic order of checks and balances. It was unnecessary for the state to interfere in any way with this free competitive scheme. The belief of Thomas Jefferson (1743–1826) that that country is best governed which is least governed is but a political tenet of the same idea applied in economics. As Adam Smith rationalized in his well-known exposition of the *laissez-faire* system, *An Inquiry into the Nature and Causes of the Wealth of Nations* (1776), "All systems either of preference or restraint, therefore, being thus completely taken away, the obvious and simple system of natural liberty established itself of its own accord." The "invisible hand" of competition, by directing capital and labor into the most fruitful channels of using materials and technical processes in production, ends finally in a method of distribution by the "magic of the price mechanism." (See Chapter XVII on competition.)

Linked with this competitive culture pattern are two important economic institutions, property and contract. *Property* is really a collection of rights and liberties. The rights are chiefly those to exclude other persons, and the liberties consist of general and somewhat vague freedom to use one's property in any way one wishes so long as it does not infringe on the rights or protected (*i.e.*, legally sanctioned) liberties of others. As we saw in defining rights and liberties in the previous chapter, these rest on consensus and legal formulas. Property, both real and intangible, is a social creation quite as much as the institutions of marriage, guardianship, or the sacraments of religion. The conceptions of property, moreover, are changing today under the pressure of new economic and political circumstances. *Contract* is a form of agreement for mutual exchange which binds both parties and makes them liable to a definite measure of enforcement. Limiting contracts to mutual exchange "for a consideration" is a form of control of highest importance in our economic order. By a contract an individual signs away some of his liberty, and the law, expressing concretely common beliefs and consensus, sees to it that he does not go back on his word. There is nothing sacred or holy about contracts, except as they are defined in the accepted law and custom, and recent changes in regard to "due process" of law indicate that the older conception of contract is disappearing.

The self-regulating nature of free competition and individualism is a snare and a delusion. Sociologically, the patterns of competition and individualism are the creation of social interaction and culture. There is nothing divine or inevitable in any given economic system, and the so-called "natural laws" of economics, except the most rudimentary ones resting on physical nature, are man made. To talk of "personal liberties" and of "inalienable rights" as if they existed in a vacuum is meaningless. Without some sort of societal protection, these "sacred" liberties and rights would be worthless. Certainly there is a general consensus demanding protection of life, maintenance of health, and provision for some equality of opportunity and education. These might be called the minima of inalienable rights as they are defined by contemporary society. But the list is growing, and it is increasingly clear, as J. M. Clark says, that "inalienable rights" are actually "a very complex structure of regulations, and that they are matters of degree, with shifting boundary lines between what can be alienated and what cannot."[1] It thus comes about that the larger community is concerned with economic duties, rights, and liberties, especially as our economic world becomes more complex.

In order to stop undue exploitation and prevent the disturbance of a balance of group interaction within the community or state, agencies of the latter have always stepped in. If the factory system, the impersonality of employer-employee relations, and the financial complexities of modern business lead to disorder and lack of balance in the total community, the state and public opinion will surely develop means to correct the abuses. Because the earlier law and the mores made no provision for the machine and modern business organization, this is no reason why contemporary society may not regulate them if they prove destructive of values which society believes fundamental. Throughout the last century or more society has developed such new controls.

Legal Control of Business. Aside from constitutional, statute, and case law, there have arisen in our society a large number of quasi-legal administrative commissions which regulate various phases of business and industry. The most striking changes in the legal control of economic life have come, in fact, through this field and through case law. Together with new legislation itself, these provide the growing end of the law. Through them public opinion

[1] J. M. Clark, *The Social Control of Business*, 1926, p. 107.

and the mores influence the law. These changing definitions of control rest, in our society, largely upon two concepts, "due process of law" and general "police power."

In our American jurisprudence all powers not delegated specifically to the federal government are reserved to the separate states and to the people. The Fifth Amendment provided that no person shall be "deprived of life, liberty, or property without due process of law," and the Fourteenth Amendment extended this to "nor shall any State deprive any person of life, liberty, or property without due process of law." Since property and liberty are but bundles of rights and privileges, any regulation is a form of deprivation of the same. The matter of regulation, therefore, comes down to the definition of "due process," and this, in turn, rests upon the rather vague, general concept of police power.

No one has given a satisfactory definition of "police power," but it covers an undefined residue of legislative power of a restrictive sort so far as it is permitted in the Bill of Rights. In actual practice it means whatever the courts decide to permit the states to do in limiting individual action and property rights. It is a flexible concept permitting changes in public opinion and the mores to encroach upon the slower moving law through legislation and through juridical precedent. These devices for correlating the wider public concern for "social legislation" with the older legal framework are basic to the interference of the state in private business and industry.

In the arena of economic production, the state has stepped in to define "unfair competition." It also protects labor from undue exploitation at the hands of employers in the face of older common law regulating freedom of contract and relations of master and servant, which grew up before the machine age. All sorts of statutes and administrative rules concerning hours of work, minimum wage rates, sanitation, ventilation, lighting, and more recently unemployment and old age insurance, indicate changes in property and contract made legal by governmental action.

Where labor unions have attempted on their own initiative to force better bargains from the employers and failing this have resorted to strikes and violence, the state has come in to protect property and to maintain peace and order in the community. The legal right to strike may not be recognized, but the state has gone far in some instances in permitting peaceful picketing and demonstrations of force on the part of labor. Likewise, the state, at times, has set up arbitration boards to settle labor-employer disputes. (See Chapter XXIII on accommodation.) In its legislation since 1933—fostering the rights of labor, providing social security, and regulating business—the United States went farther than ever before in controlling many relations that had for decades been left to the opposing factions to settle by themselves. As the political state shifts from mere referee or peace keeper to active regulator, the older concepts of property and contract must give way. It is too early to predict whether the citizenry of this country are ready for these newer flights into legal control.

On the purely economic side, the state has controlled competition, laid down rules for corporations, especially public utilities and insurance companies, regulated monopolies, and has concerned itself with monetary regulations, notably in times of periodic depressions, when inflationary or deflationary measures are used to bring about what appears to be more equitable distribution of wealth. And the farm legislation since 1933 with its crop-control program is clearly a further intrusion of government into the older rights of private property.

The state has also concerned itself with conservation of natural resources of timber, coal, oil, and water power as they have become public problems. The earlier theory of unlimited freedom of private exploitation of these resources has broken down in the face of a growing public recognition of general community rights to the benefits of these resources of nature—which men did not create with their own labor.

In the early period of congested urban life, sewage disposal, water supply, and police protection were left largely to individual discretion or to co-operation among various special interest groups. In time, these matters came under state control. Zoning laws were enacted to restrict industry to some sections, business to others, and residential dwellings to still others. In fire protection, water supply, sewage disposal, and the maintenance of roads, as in postal service, the state has established effective monopolies whenever it was thought essential for public welfare. It is easy to inquire why the state may not go on to other public utilities: electricity, transportation, and even milk supply. One wonders just where, in the end, the community may draw the line between private enterprise and state monopoly.

Exploitation does not stop at taking advantage of competitors or of workers. The "ultimate consumer" is after all the object of all production, for it is from him that profits must come. Under the *laissez-faire* theory, the consumer is supposed to exercise sound judgment in purchasing only those things that give the best quality at a given price. This assumes that the consumer knows his own interests best, that he will consider quality as well as price, and that he will act always in a rational, deliberate manner in the presence of the seller of goods. Actually, in a complex network of economic relations this simple picture of the intelligent bargainer does not hold. Producers put out merchandise "that looks as good" as articles of better quality and sell it to the unwary at a lower price. Quality as well as price is thus beaten down to ever new low levels in the hope that quantity production and quantity consumption will pay a profit. Because exploitation of purchasers arose from this sort of practice, the state now regulates a large number of matters which in theory should be left to the individual producer and consumer to settle themselves. There have long been regulations as to weights and measures to insure honest dealing. But when the consumer had no way of judging what has gone into a product, need of other regulations arose. Thus we began to enact pure food legislation, such as that relating to oleomargarine in 1886 and 1902, the Animal Contagious Disease and Animal Quarantine Acts of 1903 and 1905, and the Pure Food and Drug Acts of 1906 and later years. The sale of narcotics was regulated by the Narcotic Acts of 1909 and 1914, and from 1920 to 1933 the Eighteenth Amendment prohibited the manufacture and sale of alcoholic beverages. There are also many state laws regarding inspection of milk, meat, grain, and other foodstuffs, and regulation of dairies, markets, and quality of produce.

It is in the field of the public utilities that the government has stepped in most drastically to protect the consumer. The regulations began when cutthroat competition was still the vogue and was directed to the prevention of rate discrimination and of rebates, and to the elimination of extortion. In time, under the Interstate Commerce Act, rate fixing, control of issuance of securities, abandonment of old and construction of new lines, mergers, and standards of service have been taken over as regular functions of governmental control. The individual states have likewise regulated bus lines, electric and gas companies, and intrastate commerce.

Yet the government does not stop there. At one time or another our own government has also fixed prices and has promoted co-operative buying on the part of the public. In addition various governmental agencies have published cost-of-production facts, encouraged truth-in-advertising campaigns, and by tampering with the tariffs and taxes have attempted to alter the cost of living for the majority of consumers.

In general, the political order in this country accepted the ideology of competition, at the same time steering a curious course to avoid legal sanction to monopoly, except in restricted cases, and attempting to regulate the nature of competition itself only where its evils became self-evident. Yet in spite of the general acceptance of "free competition," the whole trend has recently been toward more regulation.

Regulations to protect the consumer have also been developed under the general police power through agencies such as the Bureau of Standards, the United States Public Health Service, the Bureau of Chemistry, the Bureau of Internal Revenue (control of narcotics), the Interstate Commerce Commission, the railroad Board of Mediation, the Steamboat Inspection Service, the Federal Trade Commission, the Federal Communications Commission, and others. The separate states, of course, have their various boards and commissions regulating public health, public utilities, and correctional and educational institutions.

Informal Controls in Business. Informal controls are a witness to the fact that the state is limited in what it can do. The law cannot cover all phases of control. After all, "most of the control in business must always be moral in character," as J. M. Clark puts it. Control by the state is largely external and directly or indirectly coercive. It is also complicated by the fact that the public is the final arbiter of what shall be done, and by the costs of control, which to be effective are often far beyond the values received, as witness the millions spent between 1920 and 1933 to enforce federal prohibition.

Free competition goes on only under very simple circumstances. In our own society competitors themselves have found out that the social process of co-operation is also essential to their success and have begun to develop controls of their own making. "Unfair competition," as it is called, is simply "unregulated competition." If the state does not step in to control, the competitors themselves in time work out some scheme to prevent such social and economic waste as arises from the much heralded *laissez-faire* competition. Examples appear to us on every hand. One grocery store closes at 6 p. m. The one across the street keeps open till 8 p. m. or even as late as any stray customer appears. When the two grocerymen get together and agree on a closing time, a trade agreement is born, and we are on the way to the evolution of some form of intra-group control which works without direct recourse to the state.

Controls which can grow up within the special interest groups have many desirable features. They will be truly effective if they rest on genuine belief of the members that the codes are right and proper. They become habitual and expected. If a member of a business group fully accepts a code, he is coerced by his own conscience as well as by any external pressure brought to bear upon him by his fellows.

As business has become more widespread, as advertising has become so powerful an adjunct to salesmanship, as large-scale operators have developed, as the indirect connection between producer and consumer has made possible new and more subtle forms of exploitation, there has arisen an increased need for agreements not unlike that of the two grocerymen about the closing time, but relating to much more complex situations.

Another sort of special interest control has grown up around what are known as "trade associations." In the 1929 edition of the bulletin *Commercial and Industrial Organizations* of the United States Chamber of Commerce are listed more than 1500 national and interstate trade associations. Joseph H. Foth defines a trade association as "a co-operative organization of business men engaged in a particular trade or industry for the purpose of protecting and promoting their mutual interests, and for the purpose of increasing the profits of its members, and of improving their service to the public."[2] These associations are not to be confused with broader, more general organizations of individuals and corporations, such as the National Manufacturers' Association, National Metal Trades Association, American Foreign Export Association, or chambers of commerce, boards of trade, or merchants' exchanges. Trade associations are concerned with the production and sale of particular trade or industrial products.

[2] Joseph Henry Foth, *Trade Associations: Their Services to Industry*, 1930, p. 3.

Such organizations, although selfish in purpose, have learned that the consumer cannot be ignored. This is why Foth includes the final, third phrase "of improving their service to the public" in his definition. In the old days of indifference to the rights of the public, such a rationalization would scarcely have been added.

The trade organizations aim to control the quality of the goods —a function which requires a certain amount of education, propaganda, and even discipline applied to member organizations. The means of doing this are many, such as agreements on grading of products and on standards of production, and insistence on honest labels and trademarks.

Commercial arbitration is another means of self-government by accommodation. First, there is purely voluntary formal arbitration, in which the associations legally agree to arbitrate their differences. These agreements are legally binding contracts. In New York State, for instance, if the proceedings of the arbitration have been in accordance with the law, the award may be secured, if necessary, through the judgment of the court.[3] Second, several associations, such as the American Spice Trade Association, Grain Dealers' National Association, Rice Millers' Association, and the Cacao Merchants' Association, provide for compulsory arbitration and the acceptance of the award. There are standard contracts which include an arbitration clause. Failure to comply with the finding of their boards leads to expulsion from the association. Third, there are various practices of informal arbitration. Many trade associations aim to avoid all formal arbitration or litigation. Joint arbitration committees or bureaus try to smooth out difficulties without formal action.

These methods simply represent efforts on the part of business itself to eliminate friction among competitors, to build up a sense of solidarity in the special interest group, and to try to convince the consumer that they are dealing fairly with him.

Another type of informal but effective control of business has arisen in some American cities through a linking up of powerful racketeers, corrupt politicians, and certain business interests. Organized criminal gangs have exploited the idea of the trade association. For example, for a fat fee these gangs use the tactics of threats and violence to protect dealers from outside competition.

[3]There is now a Federal Arbitration Law (1926), and moreover the credit laws of six states also embody these principles.

The cleaners' and dyers' organizations in Chicago have long faced the problem of ridding themselves of such exploitation. Incidentally, organized criminal gangs have also at times controlled labor unions in the same manner.

Aside from the more specific organizations designed to handle problems of control, a number of organizations of business men help to stimulate public good will toward business and hope to improve the conduct of business and professional men among themselves. The various associations of commerce do this. Moreover, the Rotary, Kiwanis, Lions, Optimists, Exchange, and like organizations, although primarily recreational in nature, also assist in fostering the business ethos.

As we have already noted, all control rests upon the consensus and acceptance by the masses of the rules of the game. The latent power of the masses to resist controls which they do not approve is a well-known story in history. Ordinarily in a more or less static, slowly changing society, the mores and law are thoroughly integrated to the situations demanding control. There is little public discussion of the mores or law. There is a strong consensus in favor of the traditional manner of meeting community problems. In a society in transition like our own, the old mores and the old laws do not fit the new cases, and critical public opinion and discussion come to be more and more important. New techniques of control are suggested and tried. Often chaos develops for a time because of the divergence of advice and practice. Special interest groups resent the wider community discussion of their economic behavior. Yet these very groups are in the end dependent upon the wider community to buy their goods. During the last quarter of the nineteenth century some public utility companies, especially the railroads, expressed the "public-be-damned" attitude, but in the end they have had to come to public control, and today many utilities are using every device of advertising, education, and propaganda to undo the antagonism set up in the public by their own earlier extreme individualistic practices.

It is evident that public opinion is a strong factor in controlling commercial activities. Not only the use of propaganda by business men themselves with a view to influencing favorable attitudes toward trade practices but also the creation of current heroes of business is important: the Morgans, the Rockefellers, the Carnegies, the Fords, the Chryslers, the Duponts, and others. This myth-making has its effects upon control, since favorable attitudes in regard to private enterprise may prevent legislation which may really be to the interest of the consumer.

CONTROL OF LABOR-EMPLOYER RELATIONS

In reference to labor-employer disputes, we have already noted that in the interests of the larger community the state has acted as arbitrator and as protector of property and peace. Especially where labor organizations themselves have attempted to coerce the whole community, as in revolutionary general strikes, the state has usually acted with great force to prevent disorder. Yet we also noted the growing legal regulations of hours of work, wages, and working conditions.

Recent Legal Controls. In this country an attempt has recently been made to help in the struggle of workers with employers through the National Labor Relations Act passed by Congress in July, 1935. This Act specifically grants the workers the right to bargain collectively with their employers through representatives of their own choosing. It also forbids the employers such practices as (*1*) any interference or coercion in the choice of worker representation; (*2*) any domination of, or interference with, any union; (*3*) discrimination against any worker-member because of his union activities; (*4*) discharge of, or discrimination against, any worker who under the provisions of this Act has filed charges, or given testimony, against an employer; and (*5*) refusal to bargain collectively with the proper representatives of the employees. The Act is administered by the National Labor Relations Board, which is not an arbitration or conciliation board in the usual sense. Another national law—the Wages and Hours Act of 1938, applying to industries whose products enter interstate commerce—now sets limits to the number of hours in the normal work-week, and stipulates minimum wages per hour. It remains to be seen whether the price-fixing of wages can be co-ordinated with traditional union ideology and practice. And since both of these laws represent considerable departure from our traditions, the whole issue of how far the government should go in fostering labor unions, and in improving the conditions of labor, may be a matter of much public discussion and further legislation.

Informal Control of Labor. A most effective control of labor over itself is found in the trade unions, which have developed codes of behavior providing for agreements with employers covering wage scales, standard hours, and conditions of labor. Various regulations as to membership, dues, "scabbing," breaking strikes, and the like are developed. In addition to these, all workers, union and non-union, tend to build up certain labor folkways, such as not working too hard on the job, soldiering, condemnation of the pace-setter, and many little "rights" and "privileges" which have clustered around certain occupations. When time-study experts who would further mechanize industry try to alter these folkways, they often encounter unexpected resistance on the part of the worker.

In more primary economic groups where the individual had rather direct control over his product, the right to work was never questioned. Today, where the cycles of bad times and good times interfere with employment, where others own the machines and market the product, an individual worker's "right" to a job is rather difficult to defend. For the most part, it cannot be protected except by a strike or other coercion, showing that it is not yet universally accepted, or protected by legal means.

All this means that labor would modify the thesis of free competition and the doctrine of commodity supply and demand as to wages. The worker is coming to look upon a good living wage as a moral right or privilege, which the community itself must help him to secure. While the legal sanction to this view has come but slowly, the force of public sentiment is in many places gradually being mobilized in favor of some arrangement which will prevent the social and individual losses which come from seasonal and other cyclical periods of unemployment.

The mores and public opinion of the wider community also effectively control the activities of labor in other ways. While laboring people may develop a great deal of sympathy for particular labor groups, there are many lines of cleavage among laborers themselves. Unskilled, unorganized laborers are the object of scorn on the part of union men. The higher wage groups generally look down upon those in the lower brackets of income. In this situation labor does not develop any class consciousness in the Marxian sense. As a result, there is not always the outside support by other workers of the strike, sabotage, or threat of coercion on the part of particular workers against their employers. Often other laborers turn against their fellows, sometimes going so far as to attempt to break the strike.   It is against these practices, in part, that industrial unionism organizes.

The great middle class in this country—the small shopkeepers, the salaried workers, and the farmers—while divided into cross-currents of opinion on various public questions, play an effective part through public opinion in determining the outcome of conflicts between industrial laborers and employers.   This is amply illustrated in the manner in which public sentiment stimulated by the owners helped to break the Pittsburgh steel strike of 1919.[4] This illustrates an important point in the relation of the wider secondary community to conflict between special interest groups. It is highly important that information and interpretation from both sides reach this wider public.   For this reason adequate community control needs a further control, that of seeing that the media of communication are free from domination by certain special interests at the expense of others.   (See Chapter XVIII on strikes.)

SOCIAL CONTROL OF THE PROFESSIONS

The professions are subject to state regulations, to many sets of rules laid down by themselves, and to forms of control determined by the wider community.   It will be well to distinguish between business and the professions. The professions are concerned primarily with furnishing personal services. The professional relations to other individuals are often intimate and personal. The latter are clientele rather than customers.   The professional man, moreover, has a long period of highly technical training and apprenticeship which gives a common discipline and a common standpoint, making for group solidarity.   For the most part private profit-making is not the impelling motive among large numbers of professional men.   As the medical code puts it, "A profession has for its prime object the service it can render to humanity; reward or financial gain should be a subordinate consideration."[5]   Business, in contrast, deals largely with goods. The relations of the business man and the individual are less personal and take on the nature of a purely monetary interaction.   The business man may serve long years of practical apprenticeship, but up to the present, technical

---

[4]See Interchurch World Movement, *Public Opinion and the Steel Strike*, 1921.
[5]*Principles of Medical Ethics*, American Medical Association, chap. I, sec. 1.   See *American Medical Directory*, 12th ed., 1931, p. 13.

training in business in the sense of specialization, as in medicine, law, in engineering, or even in teaching, is not common. Likewise in business the making of money is clearly the dominant motive. Business as an occupation is open to all comers. The professions are much more selective in terms of mental ability and special talents, and far fewer persons enter them.[6]

Legal Control of Professions. The state exercises a variety of control over the professions. One common method is that of licensing to practice. In the case of medicine and law, the state requires the candidates for licenses to pass comprehensive examinations. There is a constant pressure from the professions themselves to improve these legal standards. Since so much of the work of engineers has direct connections with private business and industry, the state is not likely to be so directly concerned with their qualifications. The legal pressure upon the engineering profession comes indirectly through legal regulations regarding construction of industrial projects, buildings, etc. The case of the teacher, again, is somewhat different. Gradually minimum standards have been set up for the elementary and secondary-school teachers. In most states teachers must be properly licensed by the state board of education before they may teach in the public schools. The qualifications of teachers in the colleges, universities, and professional schools are determined by the personnel of each institution, and hence come under the category of informal controls.

Informal Control of Professions. The professions have been much more successful in building up standards for their own members than have the various business groups. Ethical codes have been in existence in some professions for ages. Medicine, for example, points with pride to the oath of Hippocrates (c. 460–377 B. C.), which still sets a high standard before the young medical man.

Yet formally worked out codes are relatively recent in our history. The purpose of these rules is to raise the level of conduct of the profession. The need for regulations, like the need for a law or a set of mores, is *prima-facie* evidence that some conduct falls below the norms set down in it. Usually these codes are worked out

---

[6] There are about 170,000 lawyers in this country, of whom about 25,000 belong to the American Bar Association, and about the same number of doctors. There are, in contrast, well over 2,200,000 people in business.

by the dominant organization of the particular profession.   Ordinarily they contain three items: (*1*) things or acts one *must* do; (*2*) things or acts one *must not do;* and (*3*) things or acts which carry some positive merit, but which are not required.   Some of these have to do with relations to fellow members, some with relations to other groups or to the community.   Thus the present code of the American Medical Association is divided into three headings: duties of physicians (*1*) to their patients, (*2*) to other physicians and to the profession at large, and (*3*) to the public. In the code itself material on the second class of duties covers three times as much space as that of the other two combined.

The strength of the American Medical Association lies in the fact that the local county medical societies, which meet frequently, watch the pertinent relations of the public to their profession and attempt to foster the good of the profession on every hand.   The national organization, managed by a House of Delegates composed of 175 members, carries out wider policies originating within the smaller units, and tries to work out programs to govern the whole profession, as to practice, research, and medical education.   The relations to the patients cover matters of truthtelling, diagnosis, obligations to answer calls, and willingness to care for the indigent sick without fees.   The relations to other members of the profession deal with consultation practices, fee-splitting, and criticism of each other.   Relations with the public deal with matters of advertising and of personal conduct.

Since about 1930 there has arisen a sharp conflict between the American Medical Association and the advocates of plans to "socialize" medicine by such devices as regulating fees, providing for low-cost health insurance, and setting up public health medical clinics for people of low income.   The Association has recently begun to modify its age-long opposition to this sort of governmental control of its functions, and we may soon witness new forms of legal regulation of this profession.

The lawyers have no such strong sense of solidarity as have medical men.   Relative to their numbers, far fewer of them belong to the bar associations, local or national.   But they have attempted to set up codes covering such items as conduct of cases, currying favor with juries, suppressing facts, concealing witnesses favorable to a defendant whom an opposing lawyer is prosecuting, and indulging in intimidation, fraud, or chicanery.   Likewise the lawyer is not supposed to advertise or indulge in other commercial methods of stimulating his professional advancement. His relations with his fellow lawyers are assumed to be honest, straightforward, and direct. He is not to refuse to help clients even though fees are not forthcoming.

Both in medicine and law the problem, so far as fellow members go, is to steer such a course between undue rivalry and competition and undue solidarity as will not destroy individual initiative and ambition.

The slight professionalization of teachers and the weakness of their we-group solidarity have already been discussed. (See Chapter XIII.) The wide variety in quality of preparation, the close tie with the traditional community and family culture patterns, and the fact that teachers for the most part are civil servants has prevented the development of their own we-group ethics. They, like other "white-collar" workers, thoroughly identify themselves with their middle-class employers. Only gradually through teachers' unions are teachers identifying themselves with the skilled and unskilled workers.

One phase of professional ethics linked closely with advanced teaching must be mentioned. This pertains to the ethics of scientific research. The scientific search for facts and for truth is bound up so thoroughly with logical method that anything but the highest form of honesty is intolerable.

A grave ethical question arises, however, when we come to the matter of the application of scientific findings. Men in applying science have occasionally perverted the facts and the truth for gain, and have, thereby, brought disrepute upon themselves and their colleagues. For this reason there is a strong sentiment among research workers that the highest form of research must be carried on without any notion of application at the moment lest economic motives and the desire for personal prestige influence the facts, their interpretation, and their application.

It is in this connection that another problem of ethical conduct on the part of engineers, accountants, architects, and other technically trained persons may be raised. Since these men who are trained in science sell their services directly to business men for a fee, the whole matter of their integrity is at stake. Their honesty as to fact-finding may not be questioned, although their employers may suppress or pervert their findings as they will. But they do face the temptation to misinterpret facts for a consideration, or to be secretly employed by competitors, or to accept commissions from dealers in materials, or otherwise try to play both ends against the middle for their own gain.

It is this close connection of profit making and engineering which makes genuine professionalism of the latter difficult. Most engineers are so closely tied to private industry that they fail to see their more important relation to the whole social structure. They have allied themselves very directly with the spirit of competition and capitalism. This is admirably brought out by Thorstein Veblen in his book *The Engineers and the Price System* (1919).

Yet matters are improving. Various engineering societies have worked out codes of conduct for their members, and while rarely disciplining them, they sometimes handle the more flagrant cases. On the other hand, until recently engineering organizations have not advocated state licensing of engineers, but during the last few decades state boards for examining the credentials of engineers have been established. Nevertheless, so far as the public is concerned the social status of the engineer, the architect, and the accountant rests upon a semi-professional basis. They are not looked upon as fundamentally concerned with service first and fees secondly, but rather as adjuncts of the business system.[7]

There is occasional discussion about other occupations rising to the level of professions. Journalism is often referred to as a profession, but it has not as yet developed either its codes or its organization. While codes have been proposed by teachers of journalism, and formally adopted by organizations advocating professionalization, the rank and file of newspaper personnel have little interest in the matter, nor have the owners and managers. Newspaper men, real-estate dealers, and undertakers cannot hope merely by adopting impressive names to raise themselves from the status of profit-making business men to professional men. It takes more than a change in title from newspaper man to journalist, from real-estate agent to realtor, from undertaker to mortician to do so. These attempts are, in part, deliberate efforts to capitalize on public respect for the professions. It is a grave question whether any business can arrive at the status of a

[7]See Carl F. Taeusch, *Professional and Business Ethics,* 1926; Also F. H. Newell, *Annals of American Academy of Political and Social Science,* May, 1922, vol. CI, p. 79.

profession in view of the impersonal nature of its transactions and the strong motives of profit-making.

The general mores and public opinion influence the professions just as they affect business and labor groups. The doctrines of professional service are pretty thoroughly imbedded in the mores, and when evidence accumulates that the doctor, the lawyer, the teacher, or scientist goes in for money profits ahead of professional contributions, negative criticism may well have a deterrent effect on others in the profession, if not on the person criticized.

There remains the question of how to control the controls. Behind the law and behind the business and professional codes of the special interest groups there remains always the wider community. Education and religion are two powerful agencies setting the standards of formal and especially of informal controls. Education may foster group prejudices, may throw its weight on the side of special interest groups, producing rationalizations for exploitation, or it may free the individual from too great attachment to any given special group, so that he can see the relation of the economic or other narrow organization to the wider good of the entire community. The problem of indoctrination *versus* freedom of intellectual growth, which we dealt with in discussing education, is implied here. (See Chapter XIII.) If we indoctrinate the individual with narrow class interests, we may lay the foundation for a very different sort of control than if we try to free him to see the whole society in an ethical framework.

Religion gives a sanction to various social practices and opposes others. In our capitalistic society it has tended for the most part to support private business and the economic competitive system, and business men's clubs often hear the remark that Jesus was the first Rotarian, or that God would approve of the purposes of this business organization or that. On the other hand, some more divergent Christian sects have opposed exploitation and have stood out against the special interests of economic groups.

In the end, social control itself is affected by various groups and institutions within the larger social framework. It is especially susceptible to education, formal and informal, to religious ideology, and today to the growing use of press, radio, and motion picture by the dominant business interests or by the political state, which, as in communist Russia or fascist countries, may foster the view of the dominant party in power. In the light of this latent power over public opinion one may raise some doubts as to how effective the control of the wider community may be unless the latter sees to it—by legal or informal means—that the media of public opinion be untrammeled by special interest groups, be they economic, political, or religious in character.

CLASS ASSIGNMENTS

A. Further reading assignment:

1. K. Young, *Source Book for Sociology,* chap. XXVII.

2. *Encyclopedia of the Social Sciences:* J. M. Clark, "Government Regulation of Industry," vol. VII, pp. 122–29; C. F. Taeusch, "Business Ethics," vol. III, pp. 111–13; George Soule, "Consumer Protection," vol. IV, pp. 282–85; C. F. Taeusch, "Professional Ethics," vol. XII, pp. 473–75.

B. Questions and exercises:

1. Cite some recent forms of legal control of business which run counter to the older notions of *laissez-faire* economics and rugged individualism.

2. Upon what situations do private businesses build up their own codes?

3. Illustrate how public sentiment and the mores in time influence (a) legal controls of business, and (b) the codes of business itself.

4. Discuss, pro and con, the distinction drawn in this chapter between business and profession. Is it valid?

5. Why have lawyers not developed such a closely knit professional code as the medical men?

6. What are some impending changes in the public control of medicine?

7. What are the principal handicaps to the professionalization (a) of teachers, (b) of engineers, accountants, and other technical experts?

C. Topics for class reports or longer written papers:

1. Government regulation of industry. (Consult J. M. Clark, "Government Regulation of Industry," *Encyclopedia of the Social Sciences,* vol. VII, pp. 122–29, and bibliography.)

2. Protection to the consumer. (Consult George Soule, "Consumer Protection," *Encyclopedia of the Social Sciences,* vol. IV, pp. 282–85.)

3. The rise and function of trade associations. (Consult Joseph H. Foth, *Trade Associations: Their Services to Industry,* 1930; *Trade Associations,* a report of the National Industrial Conference Board, 1927; and United States Department of Commerce report, "Trade Association Activities," *Domestic Commerce* Series, No. 20, 1927.)

4. Social control of business, industry, labor, and agriculture under the so-called "New Deal," following 1933. (Consult among others C. A. Beard and George H. E. Smith, *The Future Comes: A Study of the New Deal,* 1934; William MacDonald, *The Menace of Recovery: What the New Deal Means,* 1933; H. A. Wallace, *New Frontiers,* 1934; J. A. Ryan, *A Better Economic Order,* 1935; A. B. Adams, *National Economic Security,* 1936; Twentieth Century Fund, Inc., *Labor and Government, An Investigation of the Rôle of the Government in Labor Relations,* 1935; and files of current newspapers and magazines.)

CHAPTER XXVIII

SOCIAL CONTROL AND PERSONAL DEMORALIZATION

No society, except in the imagination of Utopian dreamers, exists in perfect equilibrium or in absolute harmony. Even where isolation and a strong reverence for the old ways make for a relatively static culture, there remain persons, groups, and institutions which are not perfectly adapted to other persons, groups, or institutions. There are the criminals, the insane, the chronically ill, the cripples, the aged. There are, in addition, often small groups that attempt to exploit individuals and other groups to their own ends. There are institutions, in turn, which are not completely co-ordinated with others. The very existence of social control gives evidence of dis-equilibrium and lack of complete adjustment. In a time like our own where change, especially of a technological sort, is in the cultural atmosphere, the whole society is marked by evidences of disorganization in groups, institutions, and personalities.

SOCIAL DISORGANIZATION AND SOCIAL PATHOLOGY

In sociology, disorganization has been discussed principally with reference to what are called "social problems." These deal especially with individuals and groups in relation to the norms of the primary or secondary community. Such matters as physical health, feeblemindedness, insanity, poverty, crime and delinquency, prostitution, drug addiction, alcoholism, and illegitimacy are the usual topics discussed in social pathology. It is clear that disorganization may well apply to conditions of dis-equilibrium set up among various groups and their institutions, but we shall confine our attention chiefly to the individual in reference to community standards.

No attempt will be made to review the vast literature in this field.[1] Attention will be chiefly focused on the individual and cul-

[1] Among other books the interested reader may consult Stuart A. Queen and Delbert M. Mann, *Social Pathology*, 1925; George B. Mangold, *Social Pathology*,

tural backgrounds of social pathology, with brief reference to the major problems and to the chief institutions which our own society has built up to handle and control these problems. The chapter will close with a discussion of the psychology of the variant personality who is labeled "pathological."

A word may be said about the use of terms. There is no sound objection to the term *social pathology,* although the broader term *disorganization* may be preferable. But since disorganization really covers the whole field of society and culture, we shall make no mistake in using the expression "social pathology" for our more limited discussion.

Normal and Pathological. It must not be imagined that either organization or disorganization is "normal." Normality depends on relative balances struck between diverging forces within society and within the person. The norms of behavior in the community are those laid down in the mores and the law. There may exist, however, other norms in small groups such as the family or clan, or in any of the secondary groups, economic, professional, or religious. In every society the norms of these subgroups may and often do differ from those of the larger community. The problem of larger societal and cultural disorganization as well as personal demoralization lies in the conflict of norms, themselves socially predetermined.

John L. Gillin delimits the field of social pathology as "the study of man's failure to adjust himself and his institutions to the necessities of existence to the end that he may survive and meet fairly well the felt needs of his nature."[2] Yet the "felt needs of his nature" are themselves not unrelated to personal-social and cultural conditioning. These are originally everywhere determined, true enough, by his basic biological and psychological needs, but the "felt needs" of man in society are always colored by social interaction itself.

So far as the individual is concerned, it is a matter of the rôle and status of the variant person in certain social situations. And the rôle and status depend not purely upon biological differences, but upon differences set up in terms of norms of conduct.

1932; John L. Gillin, *Social Pathology,* 1933; Mabel A. Elliott and Francis E. Merrill, *Social Disorganization,* 1934; John M. Gillette and James M. Reinhardt, *Current Social Problems,* 1937; and Harold A. Phelps, *Contemporary Social Problems,* rev. ed., 1938.

[2] See his *Social Pathology,* p. 4.

Crises and Divergent Behavior. Since disorganization and pathology depend on social norms or on definition of situations, we might use a normal probability curve to illustrate normality, subnormality, and supernormality in society. This is illustrated in Figure 15, in which the great mass of the population would be thought to cluster around the median line symbolizing group agreement as to cultural norms, deviating perhaps in some particulars from this norm, but in general adhering to it. At the right end of the curve would be those individuals whose conduct is superior to that demanded by the norm. At the left would be those who for some reason or other do not come up to the norm: criminals, physical and mental defectives, dependents, and others. Such a norm would vary with time and place, for conduct approved in one culture is obviously not always approved in another.

FIGURE 15

SHOWING DISTRIBUTION OF POPULATION AROUND AN AVERAGE OF THE CULTURAL NORMS THOUGHT OF AS MEAN OR MEDIAN, WITH THE VARIANTS AT EITHER END—THE CULTURALLY SUPERIORS AT THE ONE, THE CULTURALLY INFERIORS, DEFECTIVES, ANTI-SOCIALS, ETC., AT THE OTHER.

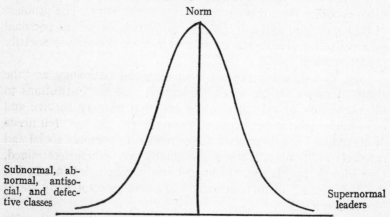

The curve tends to be steep in form, since the clustering of the mass of population, ordinarily, is within rather narrow range.

Any change in cultural pattern constitutes a crisis, that is, a difficult and novel situation around which the individual and the group have to develop new habits. In an age of rapid and widespread change, these crises may threaten the foundations of the culture and society. Among these are (*1*) the effects of speciali-

zation and mechanization of labor; (*2*) concentration of population in urban communities; (*3*) the marked mobility of modern
populations, including migration from nation to nation, from
rural to urban centers, and from city to city, and also the diurnal
movement of people to and from work and for purposes of recreation and worship; (*4*) the changing rôle of persons in relation to
secondary contacts, leading to the reforming of norms of behavior;
(*5*) the decided increase of impersonal relations in terms of money,
which greatly influences the forms of interaction; and (*6*) the
partial or segmental integration of persons around groups and
culture patterns that are not co-ordinated in the total society. Man
lived, perhaps, for over 100,000 years under the impress of primary
group organization and its related culture. Today, in less than
150 years he has become highly mobile, has extended the range of
indirect and impersonal interaction mediated through rapid transit
and rapid communication, and has built himself a world of material devices that on every hand affect the economic order, the
family, the state, religion, education, art, science, and his whole
system of social values.

There is little wonder, then, that individuals who might in more
static societies and less changeable cultures find it no great hardship to adapt themselves to an acceptable rôle and status find it
increasingly difficult to adjust in a society where in the words of
Aristophanes, the ancient Greek dramatist, "Whirl is king."

The manner in which the person meets a crisis varies with all
sorts of factors: its intensity; its relation to other critical situations, that is, whether the crisis is single or multiple; and fundamental flexibilities within the personality itself. Some persons are
more able to handle new situations than others, not only because
of social-cultural conditioning, but perhaps also on account of
deeper biological differences in energy expenditure, temperamental
balance, and the possible changes within the organism arising
from maturation, over which the external environment may have
had little influence. A new situation which may greatly disturb one
person may be for another an added stimulus to socially efficient behavior. A situation which may in one person lead to psychopathic,
fantasy thinking and acting may in another lead to creative activity or in still another to criminal action.

Figure 16 illustrates the directions in which behavior may go in
the face of a crisis: toward psychopathic, criminalistic, or other

inadequate behavior, toward adherence to old norms, or toward some behavior that enters into a new norm. If enough people in any given situation should choose what to others seem psychopathic, criminal, or otherwise ineffectual reactions, this behavior itself might easily constitute the core of the new norm. For example, socialism or communism would appear pathological to a reactionary capitalist, or usury might be a practice thought antisocial by a religious group. It must be remembered that "normality" is relative to the group-accepted definition of the situation.

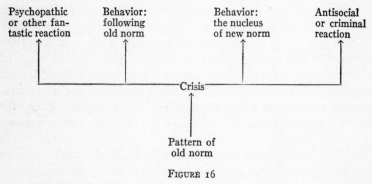

FIGURE 16

SHOWING DIRECTION WHICH BEHAVIOR MAY TAKE IN THE FACE OF A CRISIS

Personal demoralization and group and cultural disorganization usually go together, but as W. I. Thomas and Florian Znaniecki maintain in their monograph *The Polish Peasant in Europe and America* (1918–1920), personal pathology may arise without the whole social structure falling apart.[3] As they point out, the group-accepted norms never quite correspond to the individual's interpretation of the same. Actual behavior is not identical with the concept of normality laid down by the mores and the law. The concept is always an idealization. When rapid changes take place, such

---

[3] Mabel A. Elliott and Francis E. Merrill, in *Social Disorganization*, 1934, do not accept the interpretation of Thomas and Znaniecki. They say that "individual disorganization is . . . merely a particular aspect of social disorganization." And again, "There could be . . . no individual life organization or concomitant disorganization without the reciprocal influence of the group. The two are logically co-extensive and mutually interchangeable." (*Op. cit.*, p. 21.) This view, it seems to me, is misleading, since it fails to take into account the fundamental point of Thomas and Znaniecki that the idealized concept of normality is never identical with individual behavior. This divergence of the individual's conduct from the cultural norm, even in a relatively static society, is made clear in B. Malinowski, *Crime and Custom in Savage Society* (1926).

as the modern world is witnessing, personal demoralization is rather clearly related to the broader societal and cultural break-up. The whole problem of social control becomes doubly important in such a period, since the old norms give way before new ones are built up. As W. I. Thomas and Dorothy Swaine Thomas say in their introduction to *The Child in America* (1930):

"As the result of rapid communication in space, movements of population (concentration in cities, immigration), changes in the industrial order, the decline of community and family life, the weakening of religion, the universality of reading, the commercialization of pleasure, and for whatever other reasons there may be, we are now witnessing a far-reaching modification of the moral norms and behavior practices of all classes of society. Activities have evolved more rapidly than social structures, personalities more rapidly than social norms. This unstabilization of society and of behavior is probably no more than a stage of disorganization preceding a modified type of reorganization. When old habits break down, when they are no longer adequate, there is always a period of confusion until new habits are established; and this is true of both the individual and society."[4]

In the face of these striking changes, Western capitalistic society is making constant efforts to handle its problems within the framework of its basic economic, political, educational, and religious structure. Whether the strain of change and speed may prove too great and the whole foundation give way, no one knows. The influence of Russia on the capitalist nationalistic countries in the next few decades may be of tremendous significance, either as the way out, or as a horrible example of mistaken ideology and practice. For our purposes, we shall limit our discussion to the conditions within capitalistic society and culture.

Types of Problems. Any classification of the field of social pathology is open to question, because the categories are not clear cut. In a broad sense, however, we may distinguish between those which are organically founded, either from heredity or from accidents of birth or later life; and those which arise more especially from the social-cultural environment. In the first class fall the biological or organic cases, such as the blind, the deaf, the cripples, the low-grade feebleminded, the organic psychotics, and those who as a result of infectious or other diseases fail to adapt themselves to their particular society and culture. In the second fall those who

[4] P. xiii.

are "problems" as a result more particularly of cultural dishar-monies. Such are the poverty group; those who fail to adapt them-selves to the legal and moral codes, the delinquents, criminals, prostitutes, drug addicts, and perverts; and finally those whose domestic relations have broken down—widows, divorced persons, orphans, the illegitimates, and the homeless.

There are also many people suffering from mild nervous dis-orders—the neurotics whose adjustment to the societal order is inadequate but not sufficiently serious to warrant special care un-less the condition be associated with some of these other conditions. Many paupers and economic incompetents are really neurotics, as are also many prostitutes, homeless transients, drug addicts, and certain sorts of delinquents and criminals.

AGENCIES FOR CARE AND TREATMENT

In the earlier primary communities many individuals who today would be cared for by special agencies were left to shift for them-selves or were cared for by the family. Doubtless, too, many of the weak and crippled, and individuals of low-grade mentality died in early years from exposure. The psychopathic persons were often feared or treated with awe. They were frequently assumed to be possessors of supernatural power. Neurotics whom we would put in mental hospitals, in many primitive societies had a definite place in the religious-magic patterns of behavior—dreaming dreams, seeing visions, elaborating magical formulae which were accepted by their fellows as authentic. The problems of crime in these so-cieties were handled by family revenge, by clan regulations, or by tribal authorities. Poverty was handled by various devices. In many native societies a certain attitude of collective welfare saw to it that no one starved while others had plenty.

Our means of dealing with these conditions stand in sharp con-trast to many of these primitive practices. It is evident that culture determines the manner in which these variant individuals will be treated. One cannot speak of an instinct of sympathy to account for certain primitive kindnesses nor of an original instinct of com-munism, simply because among the Eskimo and other peoples we find a conception of the use of food and shelter divergent from that among ourselves. Nor can we be too certain of a peculiar inhu-manity by natives, when we learn of abortions, infanticide, and exposure of the weak, in circumstances that would shock us. Many pre-literate peoples whom we consider in a savage state of culture would be shocked by present-day bad housing, poor working conditions, and low pay, with their attendant social ills, and especially by wholesale slaughter in war.

Background of Modern Treatment. The historical treatment of personal demoralization in our Western society rests principally upon two fundamentals: Christian charity and humanitarianism, and the doctrines of *laissez faire* and individual responsibility.

The earliest Christians were earnest bands of religious zealots looking forward to a sudden and imminent end of the world, who were for the most part in humble circumstances and often "had all things common." As the Church grew in numbers, especially among the submerged classes, and rudimentary communism disappeared, the care of the sick, the aged, the defectives, and the poverty-stricken became a responsibility of the local religious communities. Nothing like organized charity was practiced.

When we consider the medieval period, say from the fifth to the fifteenth centuries, we find that the Christian Church played a large part in almsgiving and care of the sick. It is a mistake, however, to assume that the political order of the time did not contribute its part. The church was not the only channel of charity. The feudal lords had their almoners who gave aid to the poor. So, too, as wealth increased in the later centuries of the Middle Ages, there were large gifts from the rich; lay brotherhoods were organized to assist, and in time the guilds and cities played a part in the care of the poorer classes.[5]

The ascetic idealization of poverty had taken strong hold on medieval Christianity; and the poor, the defectives, and the inadequates were objects of solicitude and care. There was, of course, a strong class pattern. There was no notion of improving the economic and physical condition of these people. The biblical comment "Ye have the poor always with you" was resignedly accepted. Associated with this idealization of poverty was the notion that it was more blessed to give than to receive, and almsgiving was a form of penance. The medieval Christian practices were humanitarian in purpose within the limits of the prevalent conceptions.

[5] For an excellent and well-balanced account of the history of early European philanthropy see Lynn Thorndike, "The Historical Background" in the symposium, *Intelligent Philanthropy* (ed. by Ellsworth Faris, Ferris Laune and A. J. Todd), 1930.

More serious antisocial acts were punished, either by political or ecclesiastical authority, depending upon jurisdiction and upon the nature of the criminal act. Although Christianity did little at first to prevent a cruel punitive justice, the theory of reformation of criminals grew up in the canonical courts and was carried later into secular law.

When we enter into the fuller period of capitalistic exploitation with its emphasis on individualism and *laissez faire,* we find in many quarters an effort to repress mendicity, to force the poor into workhouses, and to put the defectives into inadequately supported establishments of one sort or another.

The Industrial Revolution brought about a marked dislocation of occupation, stimulated a rapid increase in population, and produced a host of new problems of poverty, crime, sickness, and defectiveness, which the older folkways and laws were not designed to handle. The belief in individual responsibility, that the person who suffered from social inadequacies had only himself to blame, became common. And although the various factory acts of the second quarter of the nineteenth century did improve working conditions, it was not until the last quarter of that century and the first decade of the present that what we now call "social legislation" —old-age insurance and old-age pensions, workmen's compensation laws, and social insurance—came into existence to prevent or offset economic hardships. Similar legislation under Count Bismarck in Germany and elsewhere since that time became the order of the day in capitalistic countries. All of these methods of preventing economic dislocation within the capitalistic system were developed without any idea of changing the fundamental system of private profits. Along with social legislation has gone better provision for defectives, mental and physical—for the criminal, the delinquents, dependents, and other social derelicts.

Present Methods. The situation in the United States will serve as a good example of the present practices of handling these problems. We have a dual system of treatment—one supported by the state, the other by private philanthropy. The private organizations for the most part reflect the whole religious and humanitarian background. The state institutions have, of course, long provided for criminals, insane, certain physical defectives, and for the more indigent classes. These are usually called "public agencies" to distinguish them from the former, called "private agencies."

In relation to present forms of social control four factors should be noted: the increasing number of agencies, with additional budgets, the professionalization of personnel, the shift in focus of control, and certain changes in diagnosis and care of personal demoralization. The latter will be discussed in the final section of this chapter.

Increases in number and cost of all phases of this work are apparent. The National Conference of Social Work, founded in 1874, represents a nation-wide organization with nearly 450 affiliated special agencies. This national organization today (1938) has divided its work into five major sections: social case work, social group work, community organization, social action, and public welfare administration. These include such specific items as child care, delinquency and correction, health, family life, industrial and economic problems, neighborhood and community life, the immigrant, mental hygiene, the administration of public and private social work, professional standards and education, publicity, and the support of social legislation. In 1937 at the Indianapolis meeting of the National Conference there were 53 affiliated national or regional organizations in session, chiefly from private organizations.

Costs of private agencies are not easy to discover, because of different methods of accounting and because doubtless only a fraction of this sort of work is reported. One measure of the increase in funds raised by private philanthropy is obtainable through income-tax reports. In 1917, there were reported 245 millions in gifts (not including bequests); in 1929, 529 millions were reported as gifts and an additional 223 millions were reported as bequests.

Mention should also be made in this connection of the various privately endowed foundations which support, in part, certain aspects of social welfare work. There were in 1931 over 350 known foundations in this country. Sydnor H. Walker lists the 20 outstanding foundations with total assets of over 858 million dollars. Although not all these bodies support welfare work, there is little doubt that the foundations are a direct descendant of the "charitable trust," which has existed for many centuries. For the most part, these organizations foster research, education, and certain sorts of investigation into the broader problems of social pathology.

Public expenditures for welfare were five times as great in 1928 as they were in 1903. In the earlier year these expenditures made up 17 per cent of the total public budget; in 1928 they constituted but 10 per cent. The burden of these atypical classes is growing. Since 1933 our governments have spent colossal amounts on direct relief, on public works, and on various types of welfare service, including recreational and educational programs.

The relation of the private to the public agencies will be discussed below, but there is no doubt that this increase in number of agencies and in costs is reflected also in professionalization of the work and in the applications of science which go with it. As the public realizes its problems, there has grown up a class of persons specially trained to take over this work.

Professional training for social work began with private agencies. Only during the past few years have the public organizations been affected by this change. Appointment under the political spoils system rather than by merit is still common in public welfare work.

The American Association of Social Workers, a national body founded in 1921 with standards based on specialized preparation and experience, numbered in 1933 approximately 6,000 members. Yet this number included only about one fourth of the total number of paid social workers in this country in 1930.[6] Formerly most social workers received their training largely "on the job." Later, apprentice periods were introduced. Today there is an increasing number of students entering the 28 professional schools of our country—all but four of which are connected with colleges or universities. In spite of these trends, Sydnor H. Walker remarks that "the schools of social work are not today supplying any large proportion of the personnel of social agencies."

The social worker does not appear to have even as good a community status as the elementary or high-school teacher. This is reflected in the median annual salaries of the two groups. For cities of more than 100,000 population, but excluding New York City, the median for social workers was $860 in 1914 and $1,517 in 1925; for elementary teachers the corresponding figures were $807 and $1,844; and for high-school teachers, $1,325 and

[6]See Sydnor H. Walker, "Privately Supported Social Work," chap. XXIII in *Recent Social Trends*, p. 1190. During the depression years following 1930 there was a large increase in the number of social workers employed by the various governmental units: federal, state, county, and city. Most of these were untrained or only partially trained.

$2,434.[7] Salaries for social work have sagged further below those of the teachers since 1925. There seems little economic inducement at present for professional training, but the increase of executive opportunities and improvements in methods with the application of science may stimulate this professional training in the next few years.

The shift in attitude toward welfare problems is evident in the fact that the state is taking over more and more of the functions formerly left to private agencies. This in turn reflects the change in emphasis from individualism and private enterprise toward some form of collective policy for the support and control of these welfare cases. Private agencies usually represent the spirit of private capitalism and individual initiative, both as to support and as to fundamental purposes. The rich and the better able citizens are indoctrinated with a certain sense of responsibility for the unfortunates. There still remains a good deal of the Christian ideal of charity as a benefit to the giver rather than to the recipient. There has developed in this country a certain standpoint among some of our wealthy persons that it is one's "Christian duty to make all the money one can, save all the money one can, and give all the money one can."[8] This ideology is born of Protestantism and capitalism. (See Chapter XIV.) Furthermore, private philanthropy has been rationalized as a protective device to keep the dependents and the masses from developing revolutionary tendencies. It is cheaper to feed them than to fight them.

Yet there is a growing belief that it is the function of the state to take over all welfare obligations, as concerns both care of the social pathological cases and the more positive character-building agencies which help prevent these conditions. In our country the state and federal governments are constantly assuming control in this field, just as they are in economic and other areas of public behavior. This is a growing socialistic conception within the older framework of individualistic capitalist enterprise. We cannot foresee the future, but doubtless the depression years following 1930 gave much impetus to this newer view in this country, as similar economic conditions had already done in many capitalist countries of western Europe. This gradual shift in viewpoint obviously

[7] Ralph G. Hurlin, *Social Work Salaries*, Russell Sage Foundation Pamphlet, 1926, Quoted *op. cit.*, p. 1191.
[8] Lynn Thorndike, *op. cit.*, p. 31.

bespeaks the increasing complexity of modern culture, especially as it concerns social control.

CULTURE AND THE MODERN TREATMENT OF PERSONAL DEMORALIZATION

There remain two matters which need attention, one regarding the culture patterns of demoralization themselves, the other concerning recent changes in the diagnosis and treatment of persons who are classified as demoralized or pathological.

Culture Patterns of Demoralization. The conception of individual responsibility so evident throughout recent centuries in our society has made us forget that some forms of demoralization, at least, develop distinctive culture patterns of their own. This is particularly true of the types of pathology which grow out of larger cultural situations, like poverty and crime.

Although illness or other physical defects may bring on extended loss of work, the most widespread poverty arises largely from low rates of pay or from unemployment brought on by conditions—business cycles, technical changes in industry, or other matters—over which the wage-earner has little or no personal control.

In our society, where the individual wage-earner is assumed to be economically self-supporting and responsible for his own care and that of his family, a steady job affords status and self-respect. Continued unemployment or low income which reduces the family budget below the subsistence level is a major tragedy. As a rule it is only after every other resource—such as loans from relatives, friends, or "personal loan" corporations, large accounts at stores, and sale of furniture and personal property—has been exhausted that the poverty-stricken family comes to the public or private agency, seeking relief. In a society in which the individual is held responsible for his acts, it is a great emotional strain to ask for charity. Long periods without wages, discouragement in seeking employment, certain conflicts of personalities at home, and acute need drive the wage-earner finally to ask for help from organized charity.

If the period of economic distress be not too extended or intense, the agency may secure the man some work, help him and his wife to manage a family budget, and assist them with advice to recover their sense of security and mutual respect. If, however, the period of unemployment is long extended, if such crises recur with only short interludes of work between, the whole attitude and idea of these families may change. Ambition to work, sense of responsibility, and pride in family economic independence may give way to an actual anticipation of economic support from outside. The individual and the family sink to the level of the pauper, one absolutely dependent on society for maintenance. These families, moreover, then may come to accept pauperism as "normal." Their new status is that of absolute dependents who throw the major responsibilities of life on others.

From this experience these individuals and families develop a new pattern of ideas, attitudes, and habits, or, put in sociological terms, new culture patterns. Usually such families are crowded together with others like them, or with families on the margin of subsistence, who are themselves likely to drop to this pauper level. Thus whole neighborhoods often possess a culture of pauperization.

Families of paupers intermarry, and we not infrequently find several generations of persons who have lived off public and private charity most of their lives. Such individuals, families, and even neighborhoods come in time not only to expect outside help and care, but also actually to devise means to exploit charity at every possible point. Sentimental persons, churches, lodges, and poorly manned public and private social agencies are often victimized for years by such people.

The poverty-stricken, therefore, suffer from a sense of inadequacy and dependency only so long as they do not accept fully the culture of pauperism. In a time of prolonged unemployment, the wage-earner faces an intense emotional crisis, largely because his traditional rôle and status are lost and he is not yet prepared to take on any other. Unless the community provides both adequate material and psychological relief in the way of work and status, he is fairly certain in time to sink to the infantile level of pauper and dependent, in which his inferiority becomes the badge of his new-found status.

This development of a culture pattern of poverty is frequently not recognized by social work agencies, and certainly is seldom realized by the makers of public policy. It is a factor, however, of importance; and any period of extended economic distress always sees an increased pauperization of families who find refuge in this culture of complete dependence which provides them subsistence without individual responsibility.

Again, the correlation of larger economic and political disorganization and personal demoralization is evident. Until recurrent economic depressions can be controlled or eliminated, we are likely to see repeated the periodic stimulation of these divergent cultures of pauperism within our larger society.

Like poverty, crime must be studied in its societal and cultural framework. A criminal act is "antisocial" only because it is so defined by society, which disapproves of it. All crimes, even those against property, are, strictly speaking, social acts. Crimes of violence against persons are set up by strain in the interaction of two or more people. Crimes against property are sometimes distinctly motivated from a desire not so much for gain but for personal revenge.

Crime, like any repeated act, easily becomes a habit; and once it is set up, the seeds are planted for the development of a culture of criminality. Furthermore, whole patterns of how to steal, to break jail, and to dispose of enemies or stolen property are built up among criminals and passed on from generation to generation. One cannot read the recent interesting autobiographies of criminals without realizing that crime, as a form of behavior, itself has a rich cultural content.[9]

Not only are such acts as thievery, burglary, embezzlement, and picking pockets found in the culture of criminal classes, but also organized crime has been developed in many societies. The Mafia of Italy were notorious for their long depredations as organized banditti, not without a certain status of respect in the wider community. Recently in our own country we have seen a rapid growth of organized crime, concerned principally with illicit liquor traffic in the years of prohibition, with racketeering in various legitimate businesses, like cleaning and dyeing or transport work, and in the control of prostitution, gambling, and kidnaping. Organized crime combines the tactics of modern business with those of the medieval robber barons, while the link-up of organized crime and politics is almost inevitable. Without assistance from corrupted police, attorneys, and judges, organized crime could not thrive in spite of the modern advantages of impersonality of control, mobil-

[9] See Jack Black, *You Can't Win*, 1925; Ernest Booth, *Stealing Through Life*, 1929; Clifford R. Shaw, *The Jack-Roller*, 1930.

ity, fighting tactics, and the overlapping of political units that fail to centralize authority.

The lag in governmental organization, leaving the ancient state, county, and city controls in the form of primary group organizations, has made it possible in many of our American cities to erect a super-government of corrupt political cliques and criminal gangs that have taken over many functions of social control. One has but to recall the use of gangster "militia" to protect labor unions, to wipe out rival gangs, to protect convoys of bootleg liquor, and to serve as bodyguards for the "big shots" of crime. Organized crime has engaged in price fixing in businesses, both illicit and legal, and in interference in the processes of criminal and civil justice.[10]

Crime, therefore, like poverty, develops its own culture patterns, and in organized form it takes on institutional and control functions, which reach into the political and economic order at many vulnerable points. Again, the interplay of the culture and the personality must be taken into account. When an individual is fully identified with the criminal culture, his own personality organization is likely to be well integrated. It is a grave mistake for reformers to assume that habitual delinquents and criminals yearn to become respectable members of the accepted community. Once these persons are full participants, they build their own personality patterns around the goals of criminal behavior. It is only the half-hearted criminals who still have a spark of the larger moral conscience in them, who "suffer" within themselves for their antisocial acts. Since the "hardened" criminal accepts his status and rôle in the cultural group of crime, it is doubly difficult to reform his habits and values.

Devices for Diagnosis and Treatment. The care of those variants in our society whom we classify as pathological or demoralized depends upon the viewpoint as to the nature and cause of their difficulties. In the case of those whose social handicaps rest upon organic difficulties—the blind, the deaf, the cripples, the feebleminded, and the physically or mentally diseased—they may be exposed to natural forces or otherwise disposed of, they may be tolerated, pitied, and given whatever care seems adequate at the time, or they may be treated as problems for which the society and culture has a larger responsibility. So, too, the variants who

[10] For accounts of the problem see John Landesco, "Organized Crime in Chicago," Part III of the *Illinois Crime Survey*, 1929, pp. 815–1087.

arise more especially out of social circumstances giving rise to poverty, crime, prostitution, and so on are handled in various ways depending on how such behavior is defined in the culture. Where the doctrine of *laissez faire* and individual responsibility is accepted, these persons will be treated quite differently than they will in a society which emphasizes heredity, or in one where collective social obligations are recognized.

Curiously enough, when the individual thesis of responsibility was long dominant, treatment took on group methods where prisoners, paupers, insane, feebleminded, or other defectives were herded together in special housing units under a severe régime and highly conventionalized control. There was little notion of education. Reform was piously talked about but seldom accomplished. Today, when we have departed from the older notions of personal responsibility to a view which holds that biological and especially social-cultural forces—over which the individual has no direct control—are largely responsible for these pathological variants, the treatment is much more highly individualized. That is, today the person is treated, not as a unit independent of social and cultural background, but as a person whose problems must be solved in terms of his social and cultural milieu. The cottage plan of housing orphans, the insane, delinquents, and even criminals, illustrates the newer practice. But more significant, perhaps, is the application of modern science to the diagnosis of cases and the planning of their care.

Biochemistry, psychiatry, and sociology are proving of great benefit in diagnosis. The first gives us a clue to the physical makeup of the individual with particular reference to disease, to endocrine balance—so important in temperament—and to general organic soundness. The second affords a theory and technique for dealing not only with the more serious cases of mental deficiency and mental pathology, but also for handling the personality problems of criminals, delinquents, dependents, and the whole group of physical defectives such as the blind, deaf, and cripples. Various statistical tests of intelligence, emotions, and attitudes are coupled with case study methods in the analysis of the individual's difficulties. The case method, especially, gives us tools and a standpoint for diagnosing the cultural background of these individuals in terms of the family, neighborhood, education, religion, and community, in regard to their economic condition, and in respect to their rôle and status in the various groups in which they have been members.

On the basis of combined diagnosis, then, the intelligent administrator of a private or public welfare agency attempts to make provision for his charges. In delinquency, systems of re-education, foster homes, and probation are common. With criminals the indeterminate sentence, probation, and parole are used. Increased importance of vocational and other types of education for prisoners is recognized. All of these devices are aimed at restoring the person to a normal place in society.

With the physically defective, especially the cripples, education for at least partial self-support is now recognized as desirable. The blind, deaf, and a large percentage of cripples, if of normal mentality, are capable of earning their own living when properly trained.

The pathological variants all represent some form of isolation (see Chapter IV), in which a sense of difference leads to feelings of inferiority or to resentment against society. Even those who have developed group life and a culture are cut off, as a group, from the wider community. The blind, deaf-mutes, and cripples are not mutually bound together in any such close-knit we-group as are some criminals or paupers, because their particular handicap prevents adequate group co-operation.

Infantile attitudes coupled with a sense of inferiority make these cases difficult to handle. These persons often come to accept their dependence and like the paupers "give up trying." They are likely to overindulge in daydreaming, which serves as a substitute for their felt inadequacy.[11]

These physical defectives are often also the victims of over-sentimentalism. Their treatment by parents, teachers, and the general public may not stimulate the growth of normal healthy-mindedness. Ill persons quite easily fall into infantile and helpless attitudes, and when the physical defect is of permanent character, these attitudes are fixed upon the personality during their entire lives.

The persons who may be classified as high-grade feebleminded and of borderline intelligence constitute a special problem in a

[11] Thomas D. Cutsforth in his book *The Blind in School and Society,* 1933, has dealt admirably with the psychological problems of the blind. Much that he has to say applies equally well to deaf-mutes and cripples.

complex society like ours. The majority of these individuals get along very well in simpler primary communities, but confronted with the secondary community and its problems they may fail to adapt themselves and may drift into crime or dependency or fall victims to types of exploitation like vice or prostitution. This challenge still stands; it has not been adequately answered by education and formal social control.

When certain antisocial cases get beyond any reasonable hope of restoration, there is a growing belief that society might dispose of them once and for all. In Soviet Russia, for example, a criminal has a number of "chances" at reformation, but if he fails to make good, he is quietly put out of the way—no matter what his crime is. So far as thousands of hopeless incurables among the insane and other thousands of idiots and imbeciles are concerned, we may come in time to take the view that society might eliminate them as the Russians now dispose of "incurable" criminals.

There is a growing recognition in Western society that reform and re-education are far more expensive and time consuming than prevention. Proper medical care will prevent a large percentage of blindness and the conditions making for deafness. A large percentage of our crippled children may be restored to normal activity by proper treatment. While the elimination of the mentally deficient by control of human reproduction is difficult because we do not know how to eliminate recessive strains and because the problem is complicated by social and cultural factors which we cannot yet control, there is no doubt that the discovery of borderline and high-grade feebleminded persons in the early school years would give us an opportunity to train them to useful citizenship.

The prevention of poverty is largely a matter of economic and political organization, and so long as we tolerate a society given to periodic dislocation of employment, this problem will continue to disturb us. Crime, too, has many of its roots in the economic soil. Those phases of crime that grow out of the economic order, therefore, are, like poverty, not to be eliminated until the economic order itself is modified.

There remain, of course, all sorts of antisocial acts which are not directly related to the economic order. Many of these have their roots in poorly integrated personality. Mental hygiene and far-sighted training in emotional-social habits, especially, will go far toward reducing this sort of conduct. It is a mistake to imagine that a socialistic or communistic society would have no problems of personal demoralization.

As a matter of fact, the whole program of so-called character-building agencies is aimed at turning out normal citizens. The agencies which provide supervised recreation and leisure-time activities will do much to prevent delinquency, psychopathic ideas and habits, and various forms of adolescent conduct which later may lead the individuals into more serious divergence from the social norms.

In these educational programs we see again that positive controls which facilitate sound habits, attitudes, and ideas are infinitely superior to those forms of control which rest upon inhibition and repression. Yet only as the larger societal order makes provision for education and training, can any society hope to eliminate many of its pathological problems. Not that all can be eliminated, but certainly their extent and intensity may be reduced.

CLASS ASSIGNMENTS

A. Further reading assignment:
  1. K. Young, *Source Book for Sociology,* chap. XXVIII.

B. Questions and exercises:
  1. Define social disorganization, social pathology, personal demoralization.
  2. Discuss, pro and con, the relation of wider social disorganization and personal demoralization. Are the two always closely correlated? If so, what about such cases as blind, deaf-mutes, cripples, etc.? Are they the result of social disorganization or of personal demoralization?
  3. What relation has crisis to divergent behavior? Illustrate.
  4. Discuss, pro and con, the idea that "normality" is a social-cultural definition. Illustrate from the fields of poverty, crime, feeblemindedness, and psychopathy.
  5. Is the increased cost of care of cases of demoralization evidence of increase in wider social disorganization?
  6. Has governmental aid through direct relief and through public works programs tended to pauperize large sections of our American population? Discuss, pro and con.
  7. What are the principal handicaps holding back the development of scientific social work?
  8. Discuss the integration of personality among the pathological population. Does it follow because the wider community labels a person demoralized or pathological that his own definition of his behavior will follow theirs?

C. Topics for class reports or longer written papers:
  1. The history of philanthropy and charity as an illustration of cultural changes. (Consult *Intelligent Philanthropy,* ed. by Ellsworth Faris, Ferris

Laune, and A. J. Todd, especially papers by Lynn Thorndike, Mordecai M. Kaplan, William J. Kerby, and Shailer Mathews; and pertinent articles in *Encyclopedia of the Social Sciences.*)

2. The relation of social disorganization to personal demoralization. (Consult W. I. Thomas and F. Znaniecki, *The Polish Peasant in Europe and America,* vol. II especially; Mabel A. Elliott and Francis E. Merrill, *Social Disorganization,* 1934; Stuart A. Queen and Delbert M. Mann, *Social Pathology,* 1925.)

3. Recent trends in public and private social work. (Consult *Recent Social Trends,* chaps. XXII, XXIII, XXIV, and footnote references therein; *Social Work Year Book, 1937,* earlier issues, and bibliographies; R. C. and M. K. White, *Research Memorandum on Social Aspects of Relief Policies in the Depression,* 1937, Bulletin No. 38, Social Science Research Council; F. S. Chapin and S. A. Queen, *Research Memorandum on Social Work in the Depression,* 1937, Bulletin No. 39, *ibid.*)

4. The culture patterns of poverty. (Consult Charles Booth, *Life and Labour in London,* 1889; S. B. Rowntree, *Poverty: A Study of York,* 1901; J. L. Gillin, *Poverty and Dependency,* 1926, and bibliography; J. L. Gillin, *Social Pathology,* 1933, and bibliography.)

5. The culture patterns of crime. (Consult B. Malinowski, *Crime and Custom in Savage Society,* 1926; J. L. Gillin, *Criminology and Penology,* rev. ed., 1935, and bibliography; Clifford R. Shaw, *The Jack-Roller,* 1930, and *The Natural History of a Delinquent Career,* 1931; *The Illinois Crime Survey,* 1929; Edwin H. Sutherland, *Principles of Criminology,* 1934; T. Sellin, *Culture Conflict and Crime,* 1938, Bulletin No. 41, Social Science Research Council.)

6. The disorganizing effects of economic depression upon personality. (Consult P. Eisenberg and P. F. Lazarsfeld, "The Psychological Effects of Unemployment," *Psychological Bulletin,* June, 1938, vol. XXXV, pp. 358–90, and bibliography therein; S. A. Stouffer and P. F. Lazarsfeld, *Research Memorandum on the Family in the Depression,* 1937, Bulletin No. 29, Social Science Research Council; and like bulletins by the Whites and by Chapin and Queen, *ibid.;* Ruth S. Cavan and K. H. Ranck, *The Family and the Depression,* 1938.)

CHAPTER XXIX

Prospects of Change and Control

From our survey of sociology in the previous chapters, the student should now have at hand many of the essential facts and interpretations about the nature of society and culture. The relation of the individual to the community and the relation of the subgroups to the larger society have been studied in terms of societal organization, culture, and the basic processes of interaction. In the previous three chapters we have also discussed various phases of these relationships from the point of view of social control. In the present chapter we shall briefly outline certain broad aspects of change and control that are faced by the modern world, especially in the light of contemporary interest in social and economic planning. Today men everywhere are taking thought of how they may improve society. This belief in the possibility of consciously directing the betterment of social life, in turn, touches on the matter of social progress, and on the rate and kind of change which we desire. And finally, a planned society raises the question of the influence of societal organization upon the development of personality, or the old problem of society and the individual.

THE DOCTRINE OF PROGRESSIVE CHANGE

In discussing cultural change in Chapter III, we traced the rise of the doctrine of progress and its connection with the theories of cultural evolution. In the last two centuries men have been impressed by the development of commerce, by the loosening of the control of the church, by extensive migration and colonization, by the appearance of nationalism and then of political democracy, by the amazing advances of science and invention and their attendant influence upon the rise of the factory system and upon the growth of population. In the face of these tremendous changes it was only natural that the notions of a fixed society should give way to belief in a dynamic, changing one. The Christian doctrine of perfection was brought down out of the sky to the mundane world of everyday affairs. Men came to believe that if the changes in material culture could be controlled in advance, then the larger societal organization—familial, political, educational, and religious —could also be directed and controlled. This optimism found expression in what has been called the "doctrine of progress."

Progress implies improvement or betterment as measured against some standard. Change can be demonstrated, but whether this marks moral advancement depends naturally upon one's definition of terms. The standard will of necessity be man made, and men differ as to what is better or worse, as to what is improvement or decay. In short, the concept of progress is a matter of faith or belief rather than a symbol of some objective, tangible object.

Writers of a romantic turn of mind make the doctrine of progress over into some mystical principle which governs the universe. In doing so they lay themselves open to criticisms from people who see and examine the social world in its concrete everyday aspects and who become skeptical about any such eternal principle of progress.

On the other hand, there are many students of society who see in the course of history evidences of improvement—improvement measurable by what seem to be reasonable standards. In other words, they lay down certain criteria which they believe give them a basis for detecting differences in various societies and for measuring improvement over a period of time. If there are evidences of advancement from unplanned evolution of society, we may well ask if deliberate and rational programs may not speed up the rate of progress itself. We cannot examine here the many standards or criteria of progress, but we shall note some samples.

Criteria of Progress. The particular standards of improvement reflect the bias of the writers who produce them. For example, Walter F. Willcox some years ago laid out "a statistician's idea of progress" under the following six items: (*1*) increase in population; (*2*) increase in the length of life; (*3*) uniformity of population; (*4*) racial homogeneity; (*5*) literacy; and (*6*) decrease of the divorce rate.[1] In contrast Alfredo Niceforo, an Italian criminologist, lists several indices of progress, as follows: (*1*) increase

[1] Walter F. Willcox, "A Statistician's Idea of Progress," *International Journal of Ethics,* 1913, vol. XVIII, pp. 275-98.

in wealth and in the consumption of goods; (*2*) decline in the mortality rate; (*3*) increase in intellectual superiority, as measured by the diffusion of culture and by the increased accomplishment of our men of genius; (*4*) moral advancement, measured by decrease in crime; (*5*) changes in the societal order, measured by the increase in individual liberty.[2]

The criteria of Willcox and Niceforo, like those of many other writers, lend themselves for the most part to numerical measurement. Other writers have combined both statistical and qualitative criteria. Thus Clarence M. Case lists the following three standards: (*1*) utilization of the physical environment, under which are included various techniques for managing this environment: mental and physical health, scientific knowledge, and industrial organization; (*2*) distribution, not narrowly economic, but broadly societal, including equalization of opportunities, freedom from class strain, and the whole matter of democratic participation of individuals in social life and its benefits; and (*3*) appreciation, that is, the estimation of things or events from "the standpoint of excellence, preciousness, and relative significance."[3]

There have been many other criteria suggested. The reader may consult with profit the excellent review and discussion in Arthur J. Todd's *Theories of Social Progress* (1918) and the more recent book, *Social Progress: A Theoretical Survey and Analysis* (1928), by J. O. Hertzler. The latter author has put together under 11 major headings, 190 detailed criteria which seem to him fairly objective tests of progress: (*1*) moral, (*2*) economic, (*3*) political, (*4*) biological, (*5*) educational, (*6*) religious, (*7*) domestic, (*8*) aesthetic, (*9*) intellectual, (*10*) recreational, and (*11*) racial.

Even a cursory examination of the various criteria or tests of progress reveals not only the personal bias of the writers but also their own culture and society. Such criteria always reflect both their analysis of the past and their projection of their interpretation of the past into the future. A religious leader, for example, is rather likely to emphasize the spiritual values, and a man who believes in the totalitarian state might not agree with a person indoctrinated with democratic ideas and beliefs.

[2]See R. E. Park and E. W. Burgess, *Introduction to the Science of Sociology*, 1924 ed., p. 1003, for a review of Niceforo's thesis.
[3]Clarence M. Case, "What is Social Progress?" *Journal of Applied Sociology*, 1925, vol. X, pp. 109–19; reprinted in part in E. S. Bogardus, *Contemporary Sociology*, 1931, pp. 397–402.

Although strictly scientific "tests" of progress may be hard to find, except by the method of consensus of experts in any given time and place, there is no good reason for ignoring two important facts: first, that faith in progress itself may act as an incentive to the changing of conditions; and second, that the criteria, reflecting as they do a society and culture of a time and place, may well furnish a blueprint for the planning and controlling of social change for that particular society.

The faith in progress is a form of social myth, but as we have seen throughout our volume, social myths are highly important parts of culture. Men act largely on the basis of such beliefs, and without faith there can be no works of importance. The strength of the contention of John Dewey and his followers that we begin training our citizens in their childhood to use scientific tools for managing their world bespeaks a great faith in science and produces an attitude toward progress which takes it out of its self-perpetuating, mystical realm and brings it down to earth in terms of concrete situations which we must face as individuals and groups. (See Chapter XIII on education.) In this way the social myth of progress becomes a genuine tool for planning and not an abstract principle.

If, therefore, we have made a sufficiently careful analysis of past cultural change and have interpreted it in terms of a direction which seems desirable, that is, in the light of our conception of progress, we may be in a position to use this analysis as the basis for testing the next steps in change. This standpoint again is practical and does not necessarily imply any fantastic view of cosmic progress. Thus the standpoint of Dewey and the use of analysis of past changes as a basis for anticipating the future puts the whole matter directly into man's own hands. Man himself is to determine the course of his future social life. If we are, then, to plan for the future, we must look next to the rates of change and the kinds of change which lie before us.

VARIABLE RATES OF CHANGE

In discussing the rate of cultural change in Chapter III, we described as evolutionary the slow and almost imperceptible modifications and additions. Those which were more sudden, rapid, and perhaps marked by violent conflict we termed revolutionary. We also noted the fact that some features of culture are modified much more rapidly than others of related sort and that out of the resulting cultural lag, conflict may arise which disrupts the societal order for the time. We need not repeat the material on evolution and revolution, but clearly most of cultural change in the past has been unplanned and rather haphazard. Here we are concerned with a planned society in relation to the rate of change.

Rates of Change. Only in recent decades has man conceived of a planned society. The idea itself is an outgrowth of the application of material sciences. From the fact that plans may be laid in advance for an industrial or commercial change has gradually emerged the idea that, if we care to do so, we may consciously lay down a program for the evolution of an entire society, touching every important phase of life.

But a planned society demands a concentration of power into certain hands. The engineer constructing a bridge or an industrial plant must have complete control of his materials and his techniques if he is to be successful. In somewhat analogous fashion a planned society implies a form of control by experts, who, although they may follow the ideas or beliefs of the masses, nevertheless possess the requisite power to put their program into action. This concentration of power in a few hands raises a difficult problem as to how it should be expressed.

There is a struggle now going on in nearly every Western country among various advocates of organized social change. Some hold for slower, more gradual, and peaceful accumulation of political power, through which they hope in time to take over the state and remake it. This view is held by the liberals and socialists in our own country. Others, like the communist and fascist parties, hold outright for violent seizure of political power and the use of revolutionary tactics in order to bring about the desired changes. In any serious consideration of programs for organized and controlled social change, the revolutionary ideology must not be neglected.

Yet for those of us brought up on notions of more peaceable and unconscious modifications, any suggestion for the use of revolution as a method of improvement, even in times of great crisis, may come as a shock. Although most Americans are highly sentimental about our own armed revolt against England, nevertheless we have been timid about the prospect of armed seizure of power in the present situation. Certainly most Americans would disclaim Thomas Jefferson's contention that a country requires a revolution about every generation in order to keep alive the spirit of liberty. The domination of the middle-class ideology has been so pronounced that even the mild suggestions of the socialists in this country have been frowned upon as highly dangerous and subversive.

Yet with the evidence of revolutionary programs actually under way in Russia, China, Italy, Spain, and Germany, we can no longer deny the likelihood that other regions of the world may consider favorably revolutionary tactics as a means of bringing about deliberate social change. Such tactics usually mean the rise of militant minorities who can produce a program which in time will catch the fancy of a sufficient number of people to enable this minority to execute a *coup d'état*, the seizure of the power of the state. And once a revolutionary minority has taken over the state, the rate of change may be greatly accelerated. The possibility of indoctrinating the masses by control of the press, the radio, the motion picture, and the public platform, through all the devices of mass suggestion or propaganda as well as by control of the educational system, gives those in power an opportunity for securing support little dreamed of by our ancestors. (See Chapter XIII on education.)

KINDS OF CHANGE

We have repeatedly pointed out in the previous chapters that nineteenth-century extreme individualism and simple notions of democracy do not fit in the modern world of secondary group organization. *Laissez-faire* economics and *laissez-faire* political practices—and the two grew up together—belonged to a world of a character different from that of our own present complex one.

Change and Crisis. The changes in our present economic and political order are related, among others, to the following matters. (*1*) The day of easy exploitation of natural resources for raw materials and of new markets for disposal of goods has gone. (*2*) The modern complex industrial and financial order does not correspond to the older competitive self-operating conception of the eighteenth and early nineteenth centuries. (*3*) Monopoly and corporate practices have superseded "free" competition, individual initiative, and the risks of the individual entrepreneur. (*4*) The ownership of capital and of production plants is diffused into many hands through stockholders, and the former close relation of the employer-owner and worker has disappeared. Managers and technical workers with special training, although they tend to accept the private profit motive, are not essentially bound to the present system. (5) There is a growing interdependence of the parts of the economic structure and a consequent realization of the need for regulation of these parts in the interest of the whole community. (6) This is especially evident when we consider the growing severity of the business cycle, with its attendant periods of unemployment, hunger and suffering, and demoralization of the masses.

Yet in spite of critical times for the capitalistic order and for its associated political democracy, in spite of the disappearance of many of the features of earlier *laissez faire*, it is amazing how the ideology of individualism hangs on in our non-material culture as well as in business. For the masses, in this country at least, there still remain among other beliefs the following. (1) Faith in the individual's capacity to rise in the social scale. The open class system remains an incentive to personal ambition. (2) The faith in popular education reflects this in another way. People are thoroughly convinced that knowledge and skill assist one up the economic and social ladder to success. Connected with this is the profound belief in the literacy and knowledge of the masses as an aid to the functioning of representative democracy. The advocates here contend that we need but educate the individual, only "train him to think for himself," and we shall be on the high road to a satisfactory societal order. (3) Speaking of Americans, most amazing of all is the toleration by the masses of their recent sufferings, based, doubtless, upon their deep-seated faith in the fundamental correctness of the present economic and political system. The slight amount of violence through several years of intense economic hardship is considerable evidence of the continued strength in the foundations of the established order.

Yet as times do not improve, as the panaceas of politicians and economists do not work out successfully, the masses are likely to develop feelings of disgust and despair, and to become ready to turn to other devices as the means of getting out of their difficulties. The crisis in European countries since the World War has been much more serious than in the United States, and it is there that the revolutionary changes are most evident. But the American society may witness a loss of faith in the old order and a shift to new political and economic devices.

Rise of Dictatorship. As representative democracy and the competitive system of economics break down, men turn easily to those forms of power and domination that appear to offer security, safety, and a stable world. We have noted in other connections how crises are resolved by leadership which crystallizes the vague hopes and fears of the masses into some tangible program of action. (See Chapter XXII.) As the capitalist democratic countries drift somewhat aimlessly along, tinkering with this device and that to improve conditions, the masses in time may grow weary and more restless. It is then that the prophets of change with their more radical programs make their appeal. In the modern world the shift in belief has taken the direction of political and economic dictatorship. It is a mistake to imagine that men in a time of economic and political disorder and of mental or moral distress will not follow new expressions of power. In a time of crisis concentration of power in the hands of a clique, a party, a new élite, seems to solve the difficulties. To be effective, such a minority must have a forceful and dynamic leadership, must satisfy through the symbols of appeal or identification the wishes of the masses, especially in having a definite plan of action, and must be in a position to take over political and economic functions by force if necessary.

This is precisely what has happened in Russia, Turkey, Italy, Hungary, Spain, and Germany. It may even happen in France, in Great Britain, and in the United States.

In Russia the change has taken the form of state socialism under a so-called "dictatorship of the proletariat," which is, according to the theories of Marx and Lenin, but a transitional stage toward a classless society of true communism. Communism abolishes the motives of the market, which are the foundation of the system of private profits. The instruments of production are taken out of the hands of private owners and given over to the workers. Private property in the form of land and capital goods is abolished and under the present transitional system becomes the property of the state.

Under communism the incentives for economic action are transferred from an individual to a collective view. The social myth of personal aggrandizement gives way to a faith in the soviet or the community, and personal ambition is integrated to the aims of group or collective welfare. This sort of program does not appeal to most English-speaking peoples, but it has taken root in Russia and elsewhere, and without doubt the continuance of the Soviet regime through more than twenty difficult years is some evidence that the system has possibilities, although there is as yet no reason to believe that it will become common elsewhere.

Dictatorship in Italy, and more recently in Germany and Spain, which goes under the name of fascism, is of a different character. Fascism links the economics of monopoly capitalism with the functions of the political state. Under this system labor groups and capitalists are theoretically dominated by the state as representative of the wider national community. In other words, the economics of fascism, often called "national socialism," is not based on free competition but upon monopoly and upon regulated competition in which the government plays the rôle of determiner of policy or arbitrator of differences between private owners of capital and the laborers. As it has developed in Europe, it is largely a mass movement of petty bourgeois classes, on the one hand, and the peasants and farmers on the other, supported by the large capitalist interests. The latter see in it a device for preventing a movement toward communism, which is more likely to be the program of the industrial workers of the cities.

So far as social control is concerned, fascism, like Russian communism, means a concentration of power in the hands of a minority. It implies the death of representative democracy and political liberalism, which themselves grew up in the era of free competition in economics. Fascism, at least in Germany, is attempting to remake the entire societal order and culture in favor of a totalitarian state which, though nominally accepting capitalism, apparently aims to control practically every phase of individual and group life.

This is not the place to attempt an evaluation of these two movements of reform. And so far as American society is involved, no one can foretell the direction which change will take. From present trends, however, it seems rather clear that if it moves in the direction of a dictatorship, it is much more likely to be of fascist than of communist sort. The United States is still a pioneer country so far as industrialization and exploitation are concerned.

The ideology of individual initiative and capitalism is deeply entrenched, and although we have seen since 1933 an attempt at governmental regulation of the capitalist system of private profits, one cannot at present predict how thoroughly the American public will accept such added regulation. If the present lack of balance in world trade continues and if the varied attempts at control of industry and business at home fail to bring expected results and economic distress continues, we may possibly see a swing to some American brand of fascism. This may not mean a violent revolution but a rapid shift in acceptance by the masses of a strong minority rule with a definite program.

But rather than attempt to foretell future events, we may well ask how divergent societal organizations affect the individual.

SOCIETAL ORGANIZATION AND THE INDIVIDUAL

The crux of the problem of controlled cultural change and a planned societal order concerns the relation of such a planned society to the individual. Can a societal order produce any pattern of personality it wishes? Or put the statement otherwise, what are the limits, if any, to the complete correlation of the societal organization and the culture, on the one hand, with the personality on the other?

Correlation of Societal Organization and Personality. If we make even a cursory examination of the vast literature of anthropology and history, we become impressed by the fact that there is scarcely any imaginable form of behavior which has not been found in actual practice at some time or other among the world's peoples. The plasticity or adaptability of the individual in the presence of such a variety of stimuli is striking indeed. From this evidence one might almost be ready to conclude that mankind is capable of any sort of cultural and social conditioning.

On the basis of this flexibility of man in the presence of a variety of cultures, none of which was the result of deliberate planning, is there any reason to doubt that a planned and controlled society might not be devised to which the individual would make an adequate adjustment? What, on the contrary, one asks, are we to do about individual differences? Are we to assume that individual initiative might be wiped out in the perfect society, where all activity is regulated? The whole matter comes down largely to the question of collectivism, on the one hand, and individualism, of one sort or another, on the other.

These are challenging questions of sociological theory. In the present state of our knowledge one may only approximate the correct answers. Certainly so far as universal, abstract principles are concerned, they are not at hand to give us an adequate answer. Yet in a more concrete way these are the very problems which contemporary society faces. If we assume, as we may, that representative democracy and capitalism, fascism and national socialism, and communism represent the three directions in which modern society is likely to move in the next decades, what are some of the problems of planned societal order that we are likely to face?

The communistic philosophy calls for a classless society as the ultimate goal and the elimination of the political state as we now know it. The basic philosophy of communism is not unlike that of anarchism. It holds that man is by nature co-operative, kindly, and capable of self-control; social evils result largely from a faulty economic system. It contends that once we eliminate the selfish motives of private property and private gain, class stratification will disappear, and with the disappearance of classes there will be little or no place for the political state. The standpoint of communistic ideology is expressed by John Strachey in his *The Coming Struggle for Power* (1933) in these words, "Remove class conflict in the only way in which it can be removed, namely, by the abolition of classes, and nine tenths of the present activities of the State become redundant."

Yet, as we noted in discussing stratification (Chapter XXIV), while economic conditions in the past have doubtless played a part in the formation of class lines, there is no reason to assume that stratification may not arise from non-economic activities. The communists, like some sociologists, assume that stratification is the result of conflict of classes. But stratification is also the result of differentiation of social function, or put otherwise, of the division of social labor. Certainly there is no reason to believe that differentiation of function will be eliminated in a planned society, whether it be communist or some form of capitalist-fascist régime or a planned capitalism under democracy. In any case, a complex societal order demands differentiation.

Differentiation, in turn, depends on individual variation in ability, and once we have this division, is there any reason to believe that some sorts of social labor may not acquire more prestige than other sorts? In a machine culture, whether communist or capitalist in ownership, no one would doubt that a research chemist or inventive engineer was more important for the success of the society than a machine tender or an unskilled workman. If the money motive be removed, other forms of prestige will obtain. And once differences in prestige are born, we have the beginning of class differences or stratification. Certainly in Soviet Russia today, there has arisen a new élite—the leading men of the Communist Party—who control the destinies of that nation. There is also clear evidence, too, of discrimination in favor of the members of the Communist Party and of their children in matters of education and occupational opportunities. And though the communist theorists tell us that present Russia is but a transition to a classless, equalitarian society, have we any reason to believe that those families, cliques, or factions which have acquired prestige and power are going to relinquish them without a struggle? In the light of the history of other societal orders, there seems to be little prospect that they will.

But a thoroughly planned communist society raises another problem. When the planned society touches every major phase of culture—economic, political, familial, artistic, recreational, and all the others—what freedom of choice is left for the individual? Is he to be set to a task or activity as a mere automaton, or is he to have some choice? A thoroughly planned societal order means in effect a limited or foreordained range of stimuli and responses. Under such a system what becomes of individual initiative? As a matter of fact, the major limitations on the individual in Russia seem to concern acceptance of communist economic practices, following the patterns of the soviet political order, restrictions upon freedom of speech and writing, and upon religious activities in so far as they are imagined to be subversive of the plans of the state itself. There remains, so we are told, much freedom of choice in matters of love, play, and artistic creation—although the framework of expression in these fields of behavior is also set down by communist ideology.

Obviously there is no reason to believe that men's habits and attitudes in regard to economic functions and political organization must follow the traditional patterns of Western capitalism. And it is also possible that individual initiative in various non-economic and non-political activities will satisfy many of the creative trends of people which would otherwise find their expression in business or politics in our own society.

Nevertheless, in the first decades of a great revolutionary movement such as we are witnessing in Russia there is a great enthusiasm and a burst of energy not unlike that of a vigorous pioneer people in other periods of history. Once the economic and political order is fully developed, will this enthusiasm and initiative continue? As the culture becomes crystallized will it not by its very nature as a planned order limit initiative? Again, one cannot answer because we have little basis for inference or judgment, but we must be cautious and not confuse present pioneer enthusiasm and exploitation with the ideology of control and restriction. We cannot be certain whether in Soviet Russia the early successes are not like the initial success of religious revivalism and the foundation of new denominations. But once the new order gets under way and becomes stabilized, some of this first flush of enthusiasm may disappear. What will then happen to individual ambition and interest, no one knows.

Although in Nazi Germany much of the ideology and practice of capitalism remains, it is evident that the totalitarian state is to be just what it says: a complete coverage of more or less every aspect of life, including the economic, at points where life in any way touches the state and community interests. (Moreover, "state" interests are interpreted to include a vast number of details of personal, family, and other relations which under democracy are not considered as any concern of the state. See below.) A revolutionary minority party, having seized the government, has by propaganda, education, and practical devices proceeded to integrate the country into an impressive unity. One of the most significant sociological features of the political organization under Hitler has been the development of a few basic ideals of primary-group character. The appeal to the masses in terms of a social myth of a unifying blood or racial ancestry, under the name of Aryanism, and the appeal in terms of land and resources —the twin symbols of *Blut und Boden*—have been highly effective in reviving the morale of that country. Thus the National Socialists under Hitler have imposed upon a highly complex industrialized society a few simple but fundamental features of the primary group: (*1*) kinship, through blood, (*2*) locus and subsistence through emphasis upon land and resources, and (*3*) the appeal of a closely knit country headed by a Führer, a guide and friend and director—much in the manner of a kind yet stern father—who will look after the wants of his people. This integration of the masses into a proud national community is witnessed not only in the unification of Germany through removal of former separate state functions, and the expansion to include the Austrian and Sudeten Germans, but it also reaches into the schools, into the Nazi Party clubs and organizations even down to the smallest unit or group—all of them co-ordinated together into one solidified folk. The fanfare, the Party festivals, the marching and countermarching, the public work programs to give the unemployed something to do, the rejuvenation of a great military force—these and other items make for amazingly unified sense of power. The ideology and practice of totalitarianism, of course, also look to national economic self-sufficiency, and great progress has been made in that direction, but Germany still lacks many resources, not only foodstuffs but raw materials for manufacture. She may acquire some of these by conquest, but whether she could exist for any extended period in any adequate and satisfactory way without international trade and at least a certain modicum of international co-operation, remains to be seen. As noted above in regard to Soviet Russia, once the expansive spirit of revolution and recently restored political power in the world have passed and the population settles down to a routinized life, some of the enthusiasm may fade, and new crises of their own may arise to disturb the power of the ruling class.

Certainly so far as the individual is concerned, totalitarian theory implies regimentation and complete submission of personal and sub-group wishes to the purposes of the state. It puts its essential emphasis upon the collectivity, upon some mystic group unity of higher and more sacred value than is to be found in the individual. And it is here—in spite of many likenesses in overt practice in recent years—that the ideology of Soviet Russia and of Nazi Germany diverge sharply. In Marxist theory at least, the ultimate goal of revolution is the abolition of the political state and of any class organization of society. The aspiration is for a happy society of free people without a state or class. Totalitarianism stands for quite the opposite: it exalts the state above the individual, and the state's success in turn is predicated

upon a hierarchy of classes. In the one theory, progress looks
to the further emancipation of the individual through freeing him
for an ever wider range of choices in his social contacts and functions in terms of his wishes, talents, and interests. The other
theory assumes that the individual will secure his greatest fulfill-
ment in his complete identification with the aims of his national
state. Here the emphasis is on close-knit integration and not on
personal differences and wide variation of life organization, either
in person or in sub-groups existing within the larger framework
of the political state.

Conditions in fascist Italy, as is well known, have been much
like those in Nazi Germany. In fact, the governments of both
nations are often called *fascist,* as the dictators in both have
similar ambitions and have followed more or less the same totalitarian theory, calling for a close-knit integration of the people.
Mussolini has built up a social myth of expansive imperialism—
using among others the appeals of the glory of the Roman Empire—which has enhanced the morale and the political and economic ambitions of his followers.

In the face of such highly integrated programs for societal and
individual welfare, offering such dynamic appeals to integration
of personal life, one may well ask what have the countries of
democratic custom and tradition to offer the individual or any
sub-group within the national community in the way of security,
ideals, or integrating principles? Is there only a choice between
communistic and fascist dictatorship?

On the economic side, there are two drifts in democratic countries which may prove suggestive. The first of these is the spread
in Europe, especially in Finland, Scandinavia, and England, of
both consumers' and producers' co-operatives. In the United
States the diffusion of these patterns has been slow but the movement is gaining considerable momentum. The success of such
ventures within the framework of essentially capitalistic countries may provide some hope and even practical devices as to how
to modify the extremes of the system of private enterprise in
such a way as to enable us to retain many of its benefits without
suffering from its mistakes and foolishness. Along with co-operation doubtless will go further regulation and reduction of the excessive exploitative activities of capitalistic business so common
in the previous century.

A second hope lies in the continued adoption of schemes for social-economic planning—something of course common to fascism and communism as well. In this country various units of government have increasingly co-ordinated their efforts to conserve our soil, our water, our timber, our minerals and oil, and other natural resources. So, too, there is a growing recognition of the place of planning in reference to industrial and business expansion, these in turn being related to resources and movements of population. We are even beginning to see the need to plan for a population which is rapidly approaching a stationary condition—bringing with it a period in which profound changes in economics, education, family and community life will be apparent. And in this connection we are increasingly aware of the huge possibilities of greatly enhancing our capacity to produce and consume more goods, and to do so without using up or destroying the fundamental sources of these products too rapidly or wastefully.

A planned society, however, demands experts; it requires executive orders and a certain regimentation and coercion, at least on the side of economic activities. And herein lies a certain danger and challenge. Can a political democracy retain its representative character, determine its fundamental policies and programs through recourse to the masses, and yet turn over the execution of the work itself to experts? It is an old familiar dilemma of the expert versus the common man. It is partially an old struggle between the impersonal ideas and facts of logic and science, and the warm and intimate personal feelings, emotionalized attitudes, and beliefs of the man in the street. Under dictatorship the masses are fed their daily propaganda dished up to them in highly emotionalized tones and terms which serve to keep them thrilled, and alert and happy to do the daily bidding of the experts, who in turn are dominated by the political cliques at the top.

In order to preserve the democratic process certain limitations have been set up. In representative democracy the state is not coterminous in power and function with the national community; it is the servant, not the master, of the people. Quite to the contrary under totalitarianism the state is co-extensive with the nation and is the master, not the servant, of the people. Under such circumstances, as the political philosopher von Treitschke said long ago, "Der Staat ist Macht" (The state is the power) in a very real and complete sense.

But so long as the citizens in a democracy do not abandon their safeguards to liberty and their participation in communal life, they will be able to keep some rein on the expert and on the politician, and planning will not prove dangerous to their welfare. Such safeguards include the use of the secret ballot, the continuance of the party system, the trial by jury, and protection of the rights of minorities. Then, too, the provisions in the First Amendment to the Constitution itself, including the rights to free assembly, free speech, and free religious choice, are highly significant. A real threat to the continuation of representative democracy lies in the growing belief that such matters are not important when people have got a certain modicum of economic security. But democracy implies more than individualism in economic and political life. It represents the basic ethos or value of a whole culture.

Moreover, in spite of the mistakes of capitalist democratic society, there is much to be said in defense of the stimulation it affords to individuals and for the relative freedom of thought and action which has grown up within its framework. Research in the social sciences in Russia, Italy, and Germany, except along lines acceptable to those in power, has practically ceased. And one may well ask whether research in the natural sciences will not be retarded by the general atmosphere of censorship and of deliberate planning of the major activities of the society. While the traditional *laissez-faire* individualism in economics has been largely dissipated in capitalist countries, the spirit of free inquiry, of tolerance, and of initiative remains. Whether these values are more important than others, such as more equal distribution of material goods, must be decided by the particular society, but the fact remains that representative democracy and its correlated capitalistic order have produced many important human values which must not be overlooked in the contemporary criticisms of this order.

In conclusion, we must realize that social control symbolizes or expresses the utilitarian purposes of men in society, especially those looking to material and political security, order, and continuity. So long as these are vouchsafed, one may reasonably ask if individual liberty of choice and action may not be considered one of the most important values which man has developed for himself in the face of centuries of a rather repressive societal order and a somewhat inflexible culture. Whether planned communism or fascism, or a planned capitalism within a political democracy will give the most satisfactory balance of societal controls and individual wishes, only the future can show.

CLASS ASSIGNMENTS

A. Further reading assignment:

1. K. Young, *Source Book for Sociology*, chap. XXIX.

2. *Encyclopedia of the Social Sciences*, the following articles: A. D. Lindsay, "Individualism," vol. VII, pp. 674–80; Walton H. Hamilton, "Collectivism," vol. III, pp. 633–37; Harold J. Laski, "Democracy," vol. V, pp. 76–85; Max Beer, "Communism," vol. IV, pp. 81–86; and Erwin von Beckerath, "Fascism," vol. VI, pp. 133–39.

B. Questions and exercises:

1. Does the fact that the doctrine of progress is a social myth make it any the less important as a rallying point around which a planned society may be built? Discuss pro and con.

2. What place, if any, may the masses play in determining the nature and direction of a planned society? Have they anything to say about these matters in modern Russia, Italy, or Germany?

3. What are the major features of a national crisis which lead the masses to feelings of despair and the consequent willingness to follow those who seize power and who have a plan for stabilizing society again?

4. W. I. Thomas and Florian Znaniecki in the "Methodological Note" to their monograph, *The Polish Peasant in Europe and America*, 1927 ed., vol. I, p. 86, put this question: "Is there one perfect form of organization that would unify the widest individualism and the strongest social cohesion, that would exclude any abnormality by making use of all human tendencies, that would harmonize the highest efficiency with the greatest happiness?" Discuss this question pro and con.

5. Discuss, pro and con, the respective merits of totalitarianism, communism, and democracy.

C. Topics for class reports or longer written papers:

1. The theories of social progress. (Consult A. J. Todd, *Theories of Social Progress*, 1918, and bibliography; Ulysses G. Weatherley, *Social Progress*, 1926; J. O. Hertzler, *Social Progress*, 1928, and bibliography; Hornell Hart, *The Technique of Social Progress*, 1931, and bibliography; P. A. Sorokin, *Social and Cultural Dynamics*, 3 vols., 1937.)

2. Critical analysis of Russian communism. (Consult Maurice Hindus, *Humanity Uprooted*, 1929, his *Red Bread*, 1931, and his *The Great Offensive*, 1933; W. H. Chamberlin, *Soviet Russia*, 1931; Calvin B. Hoover, *The Economic Life of Soviet Russia*, 1932; Louis Fischer, *Machines and Men in Russia*, 1932; and Harry F. Ward, *In Place of Profit*, 1933; John

Dewey, *Impressions of Soviet Russia,* 1929; Jerome Davis, editor, *The New Russia,* 1933; Frankwood E. Williams, *Russia, Youth, and the Present-day World,* 1934; Ella Winter, *Red Virtue,* 1933; Bertram W. Maxwell, *The Soviet State,* 1934; Sherwood Eddy, *The Challenge of Russia,* 1931, and *Russia Today,* 1934; Sidney and Beatrice Webb, *Soviet Communism: A New Civilization?,* 2 vols., 1936; Eugene Lyons, *Assignment in Utopia,* 1937; E. Heiman, *Communism, Fascism, or Democracy,* 1938.)

3. Critical study of Italian fascism. (Consult H. W. Schneider and S. B. Clough, *Making Fascists,* 1929; H. W. Schneider, *The Making of the Fascist State,* 1928, and bibliography; Carmen Haider, *Capital and Labor under Fascism,* 1930, and bibliography; Erwin von Beckerath, "Fascism," *Encyclopedia of the Social Sciences,* vol. VI, pp. 133-38, and bibliography; G. Salvemini, *Under the Axe of Fascism,* 1936; R. A. Brady, *The Spirit and Structure of Fascism,* 1937.)

4. The end of *laissez faire.* (Consult Sidney and Beatrice Webb, *The Decay of Capitalist Civilization,* 1923; R. H. Tawney, *The Acquisitive Society,* 1920; Thorstein Veblen, *The Theory of Business Enterprise,* 1904; John A. Hobson, *Free-thought in the Social Sciences,* 1926; J. M. Keynes, *The End of Laissez-Faire,* 1926; G. D. H. Cole, "Laissez Faire," *Encyclopedia of the Social Sciences,* vol. IX, pp. 15-20, and bibliography; John Strachey, *The Coming Struggle for Power,* 1933, and his *The Nature of the Capitalist Crisis,* 1935; Reinhold Niebuhr, *Reflections on the End of an Era,* 1934; W. E. Rappard, *The Crisis of Democracy,* 1938.)

5. A planned society. (Consult G. D. H. Cole, *A Planned Society,* 1932; Stuart Chase, *A New Deal,* 1932; C. A. Beard, editor, *America Faces the Future,* 1932; J. George Frederick, *Readings in Economic Planning,* 1932; Hugo von Haan, compiler, *American Planning in the Words of its Promoters,* 1932; Emil Lederer, "National Economic Planning," *Encyclopedia of the Social Sciences,* vol. XI, pp. 197-205, and bibliography; and the files of current newspapers and periodicals.)

6. National, regional, and state planning in the United States. (Consult H. W. Odum and H. E. Moore, *American Regionalism,* 1938; H. W. Odum, *Southern Regions of the United States,* 1936; and appropriate reports of National Resources Committee, and of special federal departments, and of various state planning boards. For general background, see, for example, the following from the National Resources Committee: *Regional Factors in National Planning,* Dec., 1935; *State Planning, Review of Activities and Progress,* June, 1935; *State Planning, Programs and Accomplishments,* Dec., 1936. Sample surveys of national importance are found in: *Public Works Planning,* Dec., 1936; *Drainage Basin Problems and Programs,* Dec., 1936; *Technological Trends and National Policy,* June, 1937; *Our Cities, Their Rôle in the National Economy,* June, 1937; *The Problems of a Changing Population,* May, 1938. See also J. M. Clark, *Economics of Planning Public Works,* 1935, a report for the National Planning Board, later merged with National Resources Committee.)

GLOSSARY

ACCOMMODATION, A form of social adjustment between groups, growing out of conflict in which certain working arrangements or functional relations are adopted as a means of getting on together. Common forms of accommodation are domination, compromise, arbitration, conciliation, and conversion. Accommodation is sometimes used to describe the state or condition which follows these processes of inter-group adjustment.

AMALGAMATION, The biological union of previously distinct racial or subracial groups.

AMBIVALENCE, The simultaneous attractiveness and repulsiveness of an object, person, or action.

AMBIVERSION, Equally strong tendency to turn to introversion or extroversion.

ANTICIPATORY BEHAVIOR, Behavior in a cycle of activity which is preparatory to (or anticipatory of) the final, overt responses.

ASSIMILATION, The fusion of divergent habits, attitudes, and ideas of two or more groups into a common set of habits, attitudes, and ideas. The process usually takes place within the framework of the national state.

ASSOCIATION, A general term to describe a group of interacting persons, sometimes used synonymously with a consciously formed group, usually of secondary sort.

ASTHENIC TYPE OF PHYSIQUE, Physical form of body marked by lean, narrow build, angular face, long, thin arms and legs, thin chest, flat stomach, poor circulation, and poor secretion through the skin.

ATHLETIC TYPE OF PHYSIQUE, Physical form of body marked by strong muscular and skeletal development, broad shoulders, thick chest, tapering trunk, strong arms and legs, firm face, prominent jaw, and tendency to short nose form.

ATTITUDE, Incipient overt response or the determining behavior tendency toward some stimulus or situation; often accompanied by feelings and emotions.

BEHAVIOR PATTERN, A configuration or organization of actions or habits into a larger whole directed toward some object or purpose.

CASTE, A group resulting from stratification in which rank or status is definitely fixed by birth and from which the individual is ordinarily not permitted to depart.

CENSORSHIP, Taboo on, or prohibition of, writing, speaking, or overt action in terms of group-accepted codes.

COMMUNITY, A group living in one locality or region under the same culture and having some common geographical focus for their major activities.

COMPENSATION, Making up in one trait or activity for a loss in another. Substitutive behavior where responses are built up around some new object or some new situation in order to offset some actual or imagined weakness or inefficiency.

COMPETITION, The act of striving for some object that is sought for by others at the same time; a contention of two or more persons or groups for the same object or for superiority; in economics the independent effort of two or more persons or groups to obtain the business patronage of a third person or group by offering more advantageous terms as an inducement to secure trade.

CONDITIONED RESPONSE, A learned reaction built up by association or connection of native or learned stimulus and response with a new or artificial stimulus or response.

CONFLICT, Direct and open antagonistic struggle of persons or groups for some object or end. The aim of conflict is defeat, annihilation, or subjection of the other person or group.

CONSUMMATORY RESPONSE, Final, overt response which concludes any given cycle of activity.

CO-OPERATION, Joint action or working together for a common object or end; mutual aid.

COVERT BEHAVIOR, Behavioristic term which embraces memory images, imagination, and feelings.

CRISIS, A novel or unexpected situation or set of stimuli for which the individual (or group) is not prepared by reflex, habit, or intellectual training.

CROWD, A temporary interacting aggregation of persons in the presence of a common stimulus or situation.

CULTURAL CONDITIONING, Learning which is predetermined by the culture patterns of the group or society.

CULTURAL EVOLUTION, Changes in culture. The term does not necessarily imply any universal stages of change or progress.

CULTURAL LAG, A condition arising out of unequal or uneven change in culture patterns.

CULTURE, Forms of habitual behavior common to a group, community, or society. It is made up of material and non-material traits.

CULTURE PATTERNS, Separate units or traits of culture organized into some more or less constant form or configuration.

CULTURE TRAIT, The single unit or feature of a culture pattern.

CYCLE OF ACTIVITY, Course of behavior through which the organism passes from tension or need to release of tension by satisfaction of the stimulus which set up the tension in the first instance.

CYCLOTHYMIC TYPE OF PERSONALITY, Characterized by tendencies to periodic or cyclic fluctuations of mood, or extremes of emotions and feelings, essentially the pattern of behavior found in the manic-depressive personalities. Akin to INTROVERT.

DIFFUSION, The spread or extension in space of culture traits or patterns.

DISORGANIZATION, The state or process of disintegration or breakdown of culture patterns or of individual habits, ideas, and attitudes when measured against a norm of culture or behavior.

ÉLITE, The dominant, prestige-receiving minority within a larger group.

EMOTION, An aroused or agitated state of mind accompanied by increased physiological activity and strong feelings directed to some definite object: for example, fear, anger, love, joy, and sorrow.

ETHNOCENTRISM, Belief that one's race or society is superior to all others.

ETHOS, Predominant characteristic of a whole culture or society.

EXTROVERSION, Turning one's interests to the external world.

EXTROVERT, A type of person whose activities are chiefly determined by external stimulation.

FANTASY THINKING, Process of wishful thinking which follows personal desires undirected by logic.

FEELING, Pleasant or unpleasant state of the organism. Connected closely with emotional reactions.

FOLKWAYS, Culturalized habits common to a group or community. Includes both moral and non-moral habits. Often used as a synonym for CULTURE.

GROUP, Two or more people in a state of social interaction.

HEREDITY, Transmission of physical and psychical traits from parents to offspring through biological mechanisms.

HUMAN NATURE, The acquired patterns of behavior or habits, attitudes, and ideas which people learn in social life. Often confused with ORIGINAL NATURE.

IDENTIFICATION, Method of putting oneself in the place of another in imagination or activity, the process often going so far as to result in a sense of oneness with the other person.

INFERIORITY, Feeling a sense of inadequacy or insufficiency in regard to some act or situation.

INSTITUTION, Culturalized, more or less standardized, set of habits and associated attitudes and ideas centering around primary or derived wants or needs of individuals, such as survival, sustenance, sex, childbearing and care, transmission of culture, etc.

INTEGRATION, Building up units of response by co-ordination into a larger pattern or a totality.

INTERACTION, Action between individuals involving reciprocal stimulation and response. Relationship set up between two or more people in regard to each other or in regard to some common object or situation.

INTROVERSION, Withdrawal of interest from the external world and its concentration upon one's own self and the products of one's imagination.

INTROVERT, One who indulges in excessive daydreaming, fantasy thinking, and habits of introversion.

INVENTION, The construction or origination of some new device or idea, or the discovery of some previously unknown fact in nature or society.

ISOLATION, State of separation, segregation, or detachment. May be geographic, cultural, or psychological.

LEADERSHIP, A position of dominance and prestige acquired by ability to lead or to set the pattern of behavior for others.

MORES, Folkways which have moral meaning, by which right or wrong, in terms of welfare of the group, is determined.

NATIVE, An inhabitant in the country of his birth; sometimes used as a synonym for PRIMITIVE.

OBJECTIVE THINKING, Thinking directed by correct and logically verifiable associations. Contrasted with FANTASY THINKING.

OPINION, Conviction about some person or object which falls short of positive knowledge.

ORIGINAL NATURE, The organic structure and corresponding functions which the individual possesses at birth. Often confused with human nature.

OVERT BEHAVIOR, Behavior marked by responses of the larger skeletal musculature, involving the adjustment of the organism to external environment.

PARANOIA, A psychopathic condition characterized by undue suspicion of others, by accusations of persecution by others, and by a heightened sense of being abused.

PARTICIPATION, Social interaction within a group directed to some common end or sharing social activities with others.

PERSONAL-SOCIAL CONDITIONING, Learning from social interaction which is not predetermined by culturalized habits and attitudes but which grows out of more or less natural interactions of persons. (See CULTURAL CONDITIONING.)

PERSONALITY, Totality of habits, attitudes, ideas, and characteristics of an individual which grow out of his rôle and status in the various groups of which he is a member.

PREJUDICE, Culturally predetermined attitude or idea of a person or group toward another person, group, or idea.

PRESTIGE, High social-cultural status given to a leader or to a group by others.

PRIMARY GROUP, Fundamental social group in terms of intimate face-to-face contacts. The source of the early personal or cultural training which the individual receives from others: for example, in the family, neighborhood, and play group.

PRIMITIVE CULTURE or PRIMITIVE SOCIETY, Used in the sense of preliterate tribes or native peoples whose culture is simpler and often divergent from our own. Primitive peoples have sometimes been called our contemporaneous ancestors, since their culture is thought to represent the earlier stages of society.

PROJECTION, Thrusting qualities upon others which arise from one's own experience. Referring to another one's repressed attitudes and feelings.

PROPAGANDA, Suggestions meant to promote or to secure acceptance of attitudes, ideas, or acts. In the most effective propaganda the true purpose is not apparent to the receiver.

PUBLIC, A non-contiguous aggregation of persons with more or less common interest.

PYKNIC TYPE OF PHYSIQUE, Type of physical form characterized by rounded figure, fatness about trunk, deep chest, round, soft arms, shoulders usually rounded and pushed slightly forward.

RACE, A main biological division of the human species, the members of which have several physical traits in common. There are usually a number of sub-races with somewhat distinctive physical characteristics within the larger categories. Race is often confused with SOCIETY.

RATIONALIZATION, Alleging some socially justifiable reason for an act really performed from some other motive.

Rôle, The function or action of a person in a particular group, usually directed to some end acceptable to other members of the group, *e.g.*, wage-earner, parent, pastor, teacher, citizen, etc.

Schizophrenia, Splitting of personality, especially the dissociation of emotional from ideational processes, and often both from overt responses. Also called dementia praecox.

Schizothyme, Normal person possessing schizophrenic characteristics. Akin to Introvert.

Secondary Group, Group or association founded on conscious common interest, not necessarily dependent on face-to-face relations. Many institutions grow out of secondary groups, *e.g.*, the state, the church, and education.

Social Class, A group resulting from stratification in which the status or rank, while determined at birth or during early life, is not so thoroughly or irrevocably fixed as is caste.

Social Control, Control or power over members of a group in terms of group-accepted codes, or power over a smaller group by a larger, more inclusive group.

Social Distance, Term to express the idea that one's own group and its values are superior to those of another group; measured by the degree of acceptance and intimacy of contact.

Social Heritage, Synonym for folkways or culture patterns which are passed on from generation to generation by means of education, formal or informal, and by diffusion. Not an altogether satisfactory term because of its possible confusion with biological Heredity.

Social Interaction. (See Interaction.)

Social Process, Mode of action, operation, or movement among individuals or groups that come into contact.

Social Reality, Beliefs, ideas, values, and attitudes around any number of objects built up by social interaction.

Social Status, Position in the social scale. (See Status.)

Social Value, Objects around which meanings grow up in the course of social interaction, the meanings coming in time to be accepted by the group.

Societal Organization, More or less conventional or standard form or structure of group life which grows out of repeated and common social interaction.

Society, The general term for men living in social relations. More specifically, the largest social group or aggregate in which more or less common culture patterns are found, covering the fundamental institutions.

Status, Relative position, rank, or standing of a person in a group, or of a group in reference to some larger grouping.

Stereotype, Group-accepted image or idea, usually expressed in verbal form, with which is often associated a strong feeling-emotional tone.

Stratification, The process of forming caste, class, or other status-giving groups, or of determining level or plane of status for the individual within a group, community, or society.

Sublimation, Form of substitute response which is socially or ethically acceptable.

Tᴀʙᴏᴏ, The forbidding of an act or word by virtue of custom or tradition.

Tᴏᴛᴀʟɪᴛᴀʀɪᴀɴɪsᴍ, A political practice and philosophy which holds that the state or government shall dominate and control all the important phases of personal and public life.

Wᴇ-Gʀᴏᴜᴘ (Iɴ-Gʀᴏᴜᴘ), Any group toward which an individual has a strong sense of belonging, of identification, of common ends. The opposite of others-group (out-group).

INDEX OF NAMES

(For Index of Subjects, see pp. 609–622)

Abelard, Peter, 329
Adams, Abigail, 428
Adams, A. B., 553
Adams, John, 428
Adams, John Couch, 328
Adler, Alfred, 134, 446
Allport, F. H., xviii, 110, 134
Ammon, Otto, 485
Anastasi, A., 436, 451
Anderson, E. L., 494
Anderson, H. D., 494
Angell, R. C., xviii, 256, 493
Antin, Mary, 508, 516
Aquinas, Thomas, 337, 341, 343, 344
Archimedes, 329
Aristophanes, 557
Aristotle, 30, 337
Arnold, T. W., 114
Arnot, Robert P., 152
Atkins, W. E., 382
Atkinson, C. F., 33
Augustine, Saint, 298, 336

Babson, Roger W., 299
Baker, Jacob, 415
Baker, Paul E., 472
Baker-Crothers, Hayes, 428, 429, 436
Ballard, L. V., xviii
Barnes, Harry Elmer, xviii, xix, 128, 144, 184, 230
Barrows, H. H., 152
Barzun, J., 166
Bawden, H. H., 110
Beard, Charles A., 70, 382, 383, 553, 593
Becker, Howard, xviii, xxii
Beer, Max, 592
Beethoven, Ludwig von, 323
Bell, H. W., 283
Benedict, Ruth, 301, 303, 443
Bernard de Clairvaux, Saint, 313
Bertholet, Alfred, 303
Bertillon, Jacques, 195
Bhattacharya, J. N., 494
Binkley, F. W., 256
Binkley, R. C., 256
Bismarck, Prince, 422, 499
Black, Jack, 568
Blackmar, F. W., xix
Bloch, Louis, 509
Blumenthal, Albert, xviii, 303
Blumenthal, F. H., 152
Boas, Franz, xviii, 35, 166
Bodenhafer, W. B., xxi

Boettiger, Louis A., xviii
Bogardus, E. S., 118, 129, 374, 453, 577
Bonaparte, Napoleon, 447, 455
Booth, Charles, 574
Booth, Ernest, 568
Boothe, Viva B., 382
Borgia, Lucrezia, 427
Borsodi, Ralph, 73
Bousquet, G. H., 492
Bowers, Anna Mae, 134
Brady, R. A., 593
Brailsford, H. N., 87
Breckinridge, Sophonisba P., xviii
Bridges, Horace J., 516
Briffault, R., 436
Brigham, A. P., 152
Brinkmann, Carl, 55
Brinton, C., 56
Brissenden, Paul F., 399
Bronner, Augusta F., 134
Brown, F. J., 472, 516
Bruere, Robert, 152
Bruner, F. G., 160
Brunhes, Jean, 143
Brunner, Edmund de S., xviii, xx, 62, 64, 88, 292, 303
Bryan, William J., 84
Buck, Pearl, 421
Buddha, 290
Bunting, W. L., 152
Bunzel, Ruth L., 322
Burdge, H. C., 485
Burgess, E. W., xxi, 17, 58, 65, 66, 70, 126–27, 251, 256, 364, 367, 382, 398, 399, 401, 415, 440, 472, 495, 496, 515, 516, 534, 577
Burke, Edmund, 457
Burke, Kenneth, xviii
Burks, Barbara, 104
Burnham, W. H., 60
Burns, C. Delisle, 325
Bushee, Frederick A., 394
Butterfield, Kenyon L., 7
Byron, Lord, 342

Calverton, V. F., 217
Calvin, John, 313, 340, 341
Campbell, J. C., 59
Carmichael, Leonard, 107
Carpenter, J. E., 297
Carpenter, Niles, xviii, 68, 69, 88
Carr, L. J., xviii, 493
Carr-Saunders, A. M., xviii, 185, 415
Case, Clarence M., 577

Castle, W. E., 99
Catherine II, The Great, 427
Catherine de' Medici, 427
Cavan, Ruth S., xviii, 574
Chamberlain, Houston Stewart, 159
Chamberlin, William Henry, 534, 592
Chapin, F. S., 51, 56, 59, 574
Charters, W. W., 276
Chase, Stuart, 29, 309, 593
Child, C. M., 101, 108
Childs, H. L., 166, 534
Clark, John Maurice, 520, 524, 525, 537,
    541, 553, 593
Clark, L. Pierce, 201-02
Clay, Henry, 356, 437, 450
Clemenceau, Georges, 422
Cleopatra, 427
Clough, Shepard B., 79, 593
Coghill, G. E., 108
Cohen, Rose, 516
Colby, C. C., 152, 185
Cole, G. D. H., 593
Coleridge, Samuel Taylor, 342
Collins, S. D., xxiv
Compton, Arthur H., 391
Comte, Auguste, 32, 439
Condorcet, Marquis de, 32, 169
Confucius, 290
Conklin, E. G., 96, 211
Cook, L. A., 283
Cooley, C. H., xviii, 118, 148, 360, 361,
    362, 365, 402, 475, 476, 477, 490,
    491, 493, 494
Copernicus, 329, 337
Counts, George S., 279, 280, 283
Cowdrey, E. V., xviii
Cressey, Paul G., xviii
Crowther, Samuel, 88
Cutsforth, Thomas D., 571

Dahlberg, Arthur O., 210
Dale, Edgar, 311
Dante, 337
Darwin, Charles, 31, 91, 330, 342, 349,
    350, 401
Dashiell, J. F., 112
Daugherty, C. R., 472
Davenport, C. B., 97, 99
Davidson, P. E., 494
Davie, Maurice R., xviii, xxii, 88
Davies, G. R., 108
Davies, John Langdon, 256
Davies, Stanley P., xviii
da Vinci, Leonardo, 36
Davis, Allison, 154
Davis, Jerome, xviii, xix, 83, 144, 184,
    415, 593
Dawson, C. A., xix, 399
Dawson, W. H., 405
Dayton, Neil A., 202

Dedrick, C. L., 67
de Gobineau, Arthur Comte, 159
Delaisi, Francis, 152, 431
de Laplace, Marquis, 342
de la Tramerye, Pierre l'Espagnol, 152
Dell, B. N., 185
Demosthenes, 122
de Sakhnoffsky, Alexis, 319
Descartes, René, 337
de Vries, Hugo, 91, 92
Dewey, John, xix, 271, 277, 281, 283,
    327, 341, 578, 593
Dexter, E. G., 151
Dickens, Charles, 49-50
Doering, Carl R., 202
Dolan, Helen H., 202
Dollard, John, xix, 472
Donham, W. B., 88
Doob, L., xxiv, 349, 411, 415
Dorn, Harold F., 205-06
Douglass, H. Paul, 293, 303
Drachsler, Julius, 497
Draper, John W., 345
Dublin, Louis I., 197, 200, 201, 484
Duffus, R. L., xx
Dummer, Ethel S., 108
Duncan, H. G., xix, 511
Duranty, Walter, 534
Durkheim, Emile, 128, 440

East, E. M., 176, 185
Ebert, Friedrich, 486
Eckel, E. C., 152
Eddington, A. S., 339
Eddy, Sherwood, 593
Eden, Karl Arvid, 196
Edison, Thomas A., 37-38, 331
Edman, Irwin, 324, 325, 345
Edwards, Lyford P., xix, 46, 48, 56
Einstein, Albert, 447
Eisenberg, P., 574
Elderton, E. M., 102
Elizabeth, Queen, 427
Elliott, Mabel A., xix, 555, 558, 574
Ellis, Havelock, 216, 325, 399
Ellis, Robert S., 436, 451
Ellwood, C. A., xix, 33
Emeny, B., 472
Emerson, Ralph Waldo, 342, 447
Emmich, 422
Empedocles, 30
Engels, Friedrich, 387, 389, 399, 427
Ertz, Susan, 230
Eubank, E. E., xix

Fairgrieve, James, 152
Faris, Ellsworth, 561, 573
Farrand, Max, 78
Febvre, Lucien, 151
Feinsinger, N. P., 252

Feldman, Herman, 382
Field, J. A., 185
Fielding, Henry, 340
Finney, Ross L., 279
Fischer, Louis, 152, 592
Fleming, G. W. T. H., 442
Florence, P. S., 415
Foch, Ferdinand, 422
Folsom, Joseph K., xix, 134, 256
Foth, Joseph H., 542, 543, 553
Fowler, B. B., 415
Fox, George, 340
Frank, Jerome, 88
Frank, Lawrence K., 236
Frazer, George C., 303
Frazier, E. Franklin, xix
Fredrick, J. George, 593
Freeman, Frank N., 104, 108
French, John D. P., 422
Freud, Sigmund, 301
Freyd, Max, 442
Froebel, Friedrich, 341
Fry, C. Luther, xix, 293, 303
Furness, J. W., 152

Galileo, 329, 337
Galle, John G., 328
Galpin, C. J., xxii
Galton, Sir Francis, 91, 108, 161, 206
Garrison, William Lloyd, 450
Garth, Thomas R., 165, 166
Geisler, Walter, 148
George, Henry, 171
Gerard, Jane E., 59, 461
Gettys, W. E., xix, 399
Gilfillan, S. C., 51, 55
Gillette, J. M., xix, 256, 555
Gillin, J. L., xix, 67, 555, 574
Ginsberg, Morris, 399, 493
Gist, Noel P., xix, 69–70, 88
Gitterman, John W., 377
Glück, Elsie, 415
Goddard, H. H., 97, 98, 108
Godwin, William, 169
Goethe, Johann Wolfgang von, 70, 341
Goldenweiser, Alexander, xix, 32, 55, 56, 166, 229, 230, 421
Goldschmidt, R., 108
Golitzi, Christine A., 516
Goodrich, Carter, 472
Goodsell, Willystine, xix, 229, 256
Gordon, Hugh, 106
Gosnell, Harold F., 382
Gowin, E. B., 389, 444
Grant, Madison, 159, 161
Greco, el, 321
Grey, Sir Edward, 422
Griffin, H. C., 212
Grimké, Angelina Emily, 428
Grimké, Sarah Moore, 428

Groos, Karl, 305
Groves, Ernest R., xix, 230
Gudernatsch, J. F., 103
Guillebaud, G. W., 472
Gundlach, R. H., 125

Hadley, A. T., 352
Haider, Carmen, 593
Haig, Douglas, 422
Halbert, L. A., xix, 69–70, 88
Haldane, J. B. S., 390
Hall, G. Stanley, 436
Hambly, W. D., 283
Hamilton, Walton H., 355, 365, 592
Hammurabi, 481
Hankins, Frank H., xx, 151, 166
Hansen, Alvin H., 88
Harper, E. B., xxi
Harper, Samuel N., 79, 534
Harrison, Jane, 320, 325
Hart, C. W., xxi, 471, 534
Hart, Hornell, 332, 592
Hartley, David, 338
Hartshorne, Hugh, 245
Hasanovitz, Elizabeth, 516
Hauser, Kaspar, 57, 58
Havemeyer, Loomis, 152
Hayes, Carlton J. H., 79
Healy, William, 134
Hegel, G. W. Friedrich, 342
Heiman, E., 593
Helmer, Velma, 162, 163
Hemming, Doris, 299
Hemming, H. H., 299
Heraclitus, 30
Herschel, Sir Frederick William, 327
Hertzler, Joyce O., 169, 577, 592
Hervé, Gustave, 380
Hilferty, Margaret M., 202
Hiller, E. T., xx, 369, 382, 415, 515
Hindenburg, Paul von, 422
Hindus, Maurice, 592
Hippocrates, 548
Hirsch, N. D. M., 104
Hitler, Adolf, 56, 159, 389, 447, 456, 486, 587
Hobhouse, Leonard T., 21, 223
Hobson, John A., 487, 593
Hogben, L., xx, 154, 177, 211
Holcombe, Arthur N., 382
Holzinger, Karl, 104, 108
Hooton, E. A., 153, 154, 155, 166
Hoover, Calvin B., 56, 534, 592
Hoover, Guy, 263
Hoover, Herbert, xxiii, 450
Hoyt, W. D., 101–102
Huberman, L., 382
Hudnut, Ruth Allison, 428, 429, 436
Hudson, Manley O., 84
Hughes, E. R., 29

Hunter, Walter, 98
Huntington, Ellsworth, 141, 144, 151
Hurd, Richard M., 146-47
Hurlin, Ralph G., 565

Israel, Henry, 291

Jacks, L. P., 325
Jaederholm, G., 99
James, William, xx, 120, 124, 300, 447
Jeans, Sir James, 339
Jefferson, Mark, 65
Jefferson, Thomas, 383, 536, 580
Jennings, H. S., 100, 207, 211
Jensen, Friedrich, 134, 451
Jesus, 290, 291, 320
Joerg, W. L. G., 88
Joffre, 422
Johnson, Alvin, xxiii
Johnson, Charles S., xx, 382, 472
Johnson, G. B., 88
Johnson, R. H., 211
Jones, L. M., 152
Joyce, James, 321
Judd, Charles H., 259
Junek, O. W., 59, 88
Jung, Carl G., 124, 134, 451

Kant, Immanuel, 340
Kaplan, Mordecai M., 574
Karpinos, B. D., 211
Keith, Sir Arthur, 166
Keller, A. G., xxii, 17
Kelley, Abigail, 428
Kellogg, L. A., 17
Kellogg, W. N., 17
Kelly, Fred J., 279, 280-81
Kent, Frank R., 382
Kepler, Johannes, 337
Keppel, F. P., xx
Kerby, William J., 574
Kerr, Charles H., 387, 399
Key, Cora B., 106, 108, 162
Keynes, J. M., 365, 593
Kilpatrick, W. H., 271, 278, 283
Kincheloe, S. C., 303
Kipling, Rudyard, 80
Kitchener, Lord, 422
Klineberg, Otto, 163, 164, 166
Kneeland, Hildegard, 237
Knibbs, Sir George Handley, 176, 185
Knight, M. M., 223
Knox, J. H. M., 203
Köhler, Wolfgang, 3-4, 17
Kolb, J. H., xviii, xx, 62, 64, 88, 292
Kosok, Paul, 79
Kretschmer, Emil, 125, 451
Kroeber, A. L., xx, 55, 56, 155, 162, 165, 493, 494
Kropotkin, P. A., 415

Kuczynski, R. R., 177, 185
Kuroki, Count Tamemoto, 422

Landesco, John, 569
Landis, Benson Y., 291
Landtman, Gunnar, 494
LaPiere, R. T., 17
Laski, Harold J., 592
Lasswell, Harold D., xx, 247, 380, 382, 397, 399, 449, 450, 451
Laune, Ferris, 561, 573-74
Lawton, George, 436
Lazarsfeld, P. F., xxiv, 212, 256, 574
Le Bon, Gustave, 128
Lederer, Emil, 593
Leese, C. Leonard, 152
Lehman, H., 325
Leith, C. K., 146, 152
Lenin, Nikolai, 391, 399, 447, 450, 486, 582
Letourneau, Charles, 425
Leverrier, Jean Joseph, 328
Levine, Louis, 399
Lewisohn, Ludwig, 514, 516
Lichtenberger, J. P., xx
Lincoln, Abraham, 447, 504
Lindley, E. K., 283
Lindsay, A. D., 365, 592
Lindsey, Ben, 223
Linn, W. A., 230
Linnaeus, Carl, 31
Linton, Ralph, xx, 29, 134, 166, 230, 322
Lippmann, Walter, 375-76
Lissauer, Ernst, 397
Lloyd George, David, 422
Loeb, E. M., 217
Loria, Achille, 209
Lorimer, Frank, xx, 211
Lorwin, Lewis L., 399
Low, Sidney, 480
Lowie, R. H., xx, 151, 166, 216, 221, 223, 225, 226, 230, 235, 377, 436, 494
Lucretius, 31
Lumley, F. E., xx, 529, 532, 533, 534
Luther, Martin, 258, 340, 386
Luthringer, G. F., 185
Lyell, Sir Charles, 31, 342
Lynd, Helen M., xx, 238, 239, 256, 303, 307, 324, 325
Lynd, Robert S., xx, 238, 239, 256, 303, 307, 324, 325
Lyons, E., 534, 593

McAdoo, William G., 39
McCourtie, William B., 269
MacDonald, Lois, 382, 472
MacDonald, William, 553
McDougall, William, 160
Macfadden, Bernarr, 314
McGee, W. J., 401

McGregor, J. H., 166
Macintosh, W. A., 88
MacIver, R. M., xx, 17, 197
Mackaye, Percy, 59
McKenzie, F. A., 499
McKenzie, R. D., xx, 66, 76, 235
Mackinder, H. J., 151
Maher, Helen C., 202
Malinowski, Bronislaw, 216, 217, 218–19, 220, 230, 241, 558, 574
Malthus, Thomas R., 169, 171, 184, 350
Mangold, George B., 554
Mann, Delbert M., 554, 574
Mann, Horace, 341
Mannheim, Karl, xx
March, Lucien, 179, 204
Marett, R. R., 285
Marx, F. M., 534
Marx, Karl, 171, 342, 386, 387, 389, 399, 438, 450, 490, 582
Masaryk, Thomas G., 450, 486
Mathews, Shailer, 574
Maxwell, Bertram W., 534, 593
May, H. L., 325
May, Mark A., xxiv, 245, 349, 411, 415
Mead, Margaret, xx, 162, 227, 230, 283, 306, 349, 415, 419, 434
Mearns, Hughes, 283, 325
Mendel, Johann, 91, 92, 93
Merriam, Charles E., 79, 382
Merrill, Francis E., xix, 555, 558, 574
Meusel, Alfred, 55
Michelangelo, 337
Michels, Robert, 382
Mill, John Stuart, 365
Miller, H. A., 29, 48, 81, 516
Mohammed, 290
Mohr, G. J., 125
Mombert, Paul, 493
Moon, Parker T., 88
Moore, H. E., 88, 593
Morgan, Christine M., 422, 436
Morgan, E. L., 7
Morgan, Lewis Henry, 33, 56
Morgan, T. H., 95, 96, 100
Morse, M. N., 303
Mott, Lucretia, 428
Mowrer, Edgar Ansel, 56, 534
Mowrer, Ernest R., xx, xxi, 256
Mowrer, H. R., xxi, 256
Muir, Ramsay, 88
Müller, H. J., 104
Muntz, E. E., xxi, 88
Murphy, Gardner, xxi, 112, 134, 451
Murphy, Lois B., xxi, 134
Mussolini, Benito, 389, 447, 456, 486, 589
Mustafa, Kemal (Pasha), 486
Myers, Charles S., 160
Myres, John L., 19

Neumeyer, Martin, xxi
Newcomb, T., xxi, 134
Newell, F. H., 551
Newman, H. H., 104–06, 108
Newsholme, Sir Arthur, 195
Newton, Sir Isaac, 37, 338, 339, 342, 343
Niceforo, Alfredo, 576, 577
Nieboer, H. J., 455
Niebuhr, Reinhold, 593
Nodzu, Marquis Michitsura, 422
Nogi, Count Maresuke, 422
North, C. C., xxi, 417, 418, 424, 436, 450, 477
Northrop, F. S. C., 108
Notestein, Frank W., 196, 212
Noyes, John Humphrey, 405

Odum, H. W., 88, 593
Ogburn, W. F., xix, xxi, 38, 51, 53, 55, 56, 233, 234, 237, 251, 256
O'Hara, E. V., 291
Oppenheimer, Franz, 377
Orth, Samuel P., 382
Osborn, Frederick, xx, 211
Osborn, Loran D., xxi
Owen, Robert, 404, 405
Oxley, H. W., 283
Oyama, Prince Iwao, 422

Panunzio, Constantine M., 516
Pareto, Vilfredo, 492
Park, Robert E., xxi, 17, 58, 75, 364, 367, 381, 382, 398, 399, 401, 415, 440, 466, 470, 471, 472, 495, 496, 498, 512, 515, 516, 534, 577
Parmalee, Maurice F., 29
Parsons, Elsie Clews, 532
Parsons, Talcott, 298
Parten, Mildred, 233
Pascal, Blaise, 337
Patterson, J. T., 101
Paul, Saint, 290
Paul, Cedar, 382, 399
Paul, Eden, 382, 399
Pavlov, L., 111
Pearl, Raymond, 102, 201, 211
Pearson, Karl, 99, 102
Peck, Gustav, xxiii
Peers, R., 415
Perrott, G. St. J., 212
Pershing, John J., 422
Pestalozzi, Johann Heinrich, 341
Petgie, D., 325
Petrie, Sir W. M. Flinders, 33
Pettit, Walter W., xxi
Phelps, Harold A., 555
Pigors, Paul, 451
Pinkevitch, A. P., 280
Pius XI, Pope, 294

Plato, 320, 335, 336
Popenoe, Paul, 211
Powdermaker, Hortense, 230
Powers, Grover F., 203
Pratt, J. B., xxi
Pressey, S. L., 162
Proust, Marcel, 323
Pruette, Lorine, 436
Pupin, Michael, 516

Queen, Stuart A., xxi, 554, 574

Raikes, Robert, 294
Rainey, H. P., 283
Ranck, K. H., 574
Randall, John Herman, Jr., xxi, 338, 345, 365
Randall, John Herman, Sr., 87
Rappard, W. E., 593
Ravage, M. E., 509, 516
Read, Carveth, 303
Reckless, Walter C., xxi
Reinhardt, J. M., xix, 256, 555
Reuter, E. B., xxi, 177, 178, 211, 255, 256, 382, 471, 534
Rice, S. A., xxi, xxii, 345
Richardson, Samuel, 340
Riddle, Oscar, 103–04
Ribbiny, Abraham M., 516
Risley, H. H., 494
Roberts, Stephen H., 56
Robinson, J. H., xxi
Rockne, Knute, 310
Rogers, A. K., 340
Rolland, Romain, 392
Roosevelt, Franklin D., 390
Roosevelt, Theodore, 172, 447
Ross, E. A., xxi, 59, 151, 171, 185, 360, 367, 375, 388, 392, 415, 460, 461, 491, 521, 526, 528, 534
Rouceck, J. S., 472, 516
Rousseau, Jean Jacques, 278, 313, 339, 340, 341, 343, 427
Rowntree, S. B., 574
Ruch, F. L., 112
Rubinow, I. M., 436
Rugg, H. O., 283
Runner, Jessie R., xxi, 255, 256
Ryan, J. A., 553

Sait, Una B., xxi, 256
Samuel, Maurice, 516
Salvemini, G., 593
Sanderson, D., xxiv, 88
Santayana, George, 325, 336
Savonarola, Girolamo, 313
Sayles, Mary B., 256
Schiller, Friedrich, 305, 341
Schmalhausen, S. D., 217
Schmoller, Gustav, 490, 491

Schneider, Herbert W., 79, 593
Schreiner, Olive, 59
Schrieke, B., 472
Schuman, F. L., 56, 472, 534
Schwarz, O. L., 448
Schwesinger, Gladys C., xxi, 107, 108, 451
Scopes, John Thomas, 268
Seligman, E. R. A., xxiii, 352, 353
Sellin, T., xxiv, 574
Semple, Ellen C., 151
Shakespeare, William, 321
Shaw, Clifford R., 127, 568, 574
Shelley, Percy Bysshe, 342
Sherman, Mandel, 106, 107, 108, 162
Shumaker, Ann, 283
Siegfried, André, 299
Simmel, Georg, 465, 466, 467
Simonds, F. H., 472
Sims, N. L., 88
Skinner, C. E., 112
Small, Albion W., 400, 465, 490
Small, M. H., 60
Smith, Adam, 338, 536
Smith, G. Elliot, 43
Smith, George H. E., 553
Smith, George O., 152
Smith, Mapheus, xxi
Socrates, 335
Sorokin, P. A., xxi, xxii, 56, 483, 484, 485, 494, 592
Soule, George, 553
Spranger, Eduard, 127, 450
Spencer, Herbert, 19, 31, 32, 56, 305
Spender, J. A., 466
Spengler, Oswald, 33
Spinoza, Baruch, 338
Spykman, N. J., 399, 472
Squires, B. M., 472
Stagner, R., 134
Stalin, Joseph V., 486
Stanton, Elizabeth Cady, 428
Stein, Gertrude, 321
Stein, Leo, 324
Steiner, Jesse F., xxii, xxiv, 71–72, 293, 308, 310, 325
Stern, B. J., 256
Stern, E. G., 516
Sterne, Lawrence, 340
Stevenson, T. H. C., 195
Stockard, C. R., 101, 102
Stoddard, Lothrop, 159, 161
Stonequist, Everett V., 512, 516
Stouffer, S. A., xxiv, 198, 212, 256, 574
Stowell, W. L., 201–02
Strachey, John, 585, 593
Stravinsky, Igor, 322
Sumner, William G., xxii, 15, 17, 26, 214, 330, 377
Sutherland, Edwin H., xxii, 574

Sutherland, R. L., xxii
Sydenstricker, Edgar, xxii, 199, 201, 203, 212
Symonds, P. M., 134

Taeusch, Carl F., 551, 553
Taft, D. R., xxii, 472, 516
Taussig, F. W., 443
Tawney, R. H., xxii, 298, 299, 365, 593
Taylor, C. C., 88
Tennyson, Alfred, Lord, 58
Terman, L. M., 104
Thom, W. T., 152
Thomas, Dorothy Swaine, 559
Thomas, Franklin, 137
Thomas, J. B., 162
Thomas, Olive J., 152
Thomas, W. I., xxii, 8, 113, 125, 138, 246, 283, 354, 425, 426, 432, 435, 436, 499, 506, 516, 518, 558, 559, 574, 592
Thompson, Frank V., 504
Thompson, Warren S., xxii, 171, 175–76, 179, 182, 184, 185, 192, 193, 198, 200, 211
Thompson, William Hale, 268
Thomson, J. Arthur, 90
Thoreau, Henry David, 342
Thorndike, Lynn, 303, 561, 565, 574
Thrasher, Frederic M., xxii
Tibbitts, C., xxiv
Todd, A. J., xxii, 561, 574, 577, 588
Tolstoy, Count Leo, 321, 325
Tower, Walter S., 145
Toynbee, Arnold J., 86
Tozzer, Alfred M., 223, 416
Trotsky, Leon, 485
Turner, Frederick J., 78
Tylor, Edward B., 19, 225

Ueland, Andreas, 516

Van Dyke, G. E., 271
Vane, R. J., 484
Van Hise, Charles R., 152
Van Waters, Miriam, 253, 256
Veblen, Thorstein, xxii, 488, 551, 593
Villa, Silvio, 516
Vinacke, H. M., 29, 472
Vincent, Melvin J., 453, 472
Visher, Stephan S., 445
Voltaire, 338, 341
von Baer, K. E., 31
von Beckerath, Erwin, 592, 593
von Haan, Hugo, 593
von Kluck, Alexander H. R., 422
von Moltke, Helmuth J. L., 422
von Tirpitz, Alfred, 422
von Treitschke, 590
von Wiese, Leopold, xxii
Voskuil, Walter H., 152

Wagner, Richard, 322
Walker, F. A., 351, 352
Walker, Sydnor H., 563, 564
Wallace, H. A., 553
Wallace, W. K., 85
Wallas, Graham, xxii, 65
Waller, Willard, xxii, 252, 256, 282, 283
Wallis, Wilson D., 108
Walsh, J. R., 382
Wang, P. L., 203
Waples, Douglas, 325
Ward, Harry F., 592
Ward, Lester F., 108
Washburne, C. W., 283
Washington, George, 447, 504
Waterman, T. T., xx
Watson, John, 340
Watson, John B., 90
Watson, Maude E., 256
Weatherley, Ulysses G., 592
Webb, Beatrice, 593
Webb, Sidney, 593
Weber, Max, 298
Weinstein, A., 108
Werner, M. R., 230
Wesley, John, 341
Wessell, Bessie B., 516
Westermarck, Edward, xxii, 220, 230, 417
Whelpton, P. K., xxii, 192, 193, 196, 200
Whitbeck, R. H., 152
White, Andrew D., 329, 345
White, M. K., xxiv, 574
White, R. C., xxiv, 574
Whitman, Walt, 342
Wiechel, 65
Wiggam, Albert E., 89, 161
Wilhelm II, Kaiser, 422
Willcox, Walter F., 65, 168, 576, 577
Willey, M. M., xxii
Williams, Frankwood E., 593
Williams, J. M., xxiii, 270, 408, 412
Wilson, L. R., 325
Wilson, Woodrow, 39, 84
Winslow, C. E. A., 203
Winter, Ella, 593
Wirth, Louis, xxiii, 70
Wissler, Clark, xxiii, 29, 377
Witmer, Lightner, 60
Witty, P. L., 325
Wolfe, A. B., 185, 449
Wollstonecraft, Mary, 427
Wolman, Leo, xxiii
Wood, Arthur Evans, xxiii
Wood, Margaret M., xxiii
Wooddy, C. H., xxiii
Woods, A. W., 97
Woodward, J. L., xxii
Woodworth, R. S., 112, 160

Woofter, T. J., Jr., xxiii, 497
Woolley, Helen B. Thompson, 431, 432, 433
Woolston, Howard B., xxiii, 88
Wordsworth, William, 342
Wright, Frances, 428
Wright, Frank Lloyd, 319
Wrightstone, J. W., 283

Yamagata, Prince Aritomo, 422
Yerkes, A. W., 17, 161
Yerkes, Robert M., 17, 161

Yoder, Dale, 55
Young, Donald, xxiv, 499, 505, 516
Young, K., xxiii, 17, 23, 29, 67, 108, 110, 111, 112, 114, 134, 252, 303, 322, 331, 401, 448, 449, 451, 529, 532
Young, Pauline V., 59, 516

Zimmerman, Carle C., xxii, xxiii
Znaniecki, Florian, xxii, 125, 506, 516, 558, 574, 592
Zorbaugh, Harvey, xxiii
Zuckerman, S., 17

INDEX OF SUBJECTS

(For Index of Names of persons, see pp. 601-608)

Accommodation, 452-72; arbitration as, 458; assimilation, amalgamation, and, 496-97; as universal culture pattern, 26; balancing of opposition by, 453-54; coercion and domination, 455-57; compromise as, 457-59; conciliation as, 459-60; conversion as, 464-65; devices of, in informal control in business, 543; dictatorship as form of, 455-56; domination and submission in, 465-69; forms of, 454-65; nature of, 452-54; opposition and, 452-54; personality and, 465-71; slavery as, 455; social distance and, 453; stratification and, 473; subjective conflicts and personal, 469-71; toleration and participation as, 460-64

Adolescence, differentiation and, 418-19

Adult education, 274-75

Adulthood, differentiation and, 419-20

Aesthetics, See Art

Ainu sub-race, characteristics and distribution of, 156

Alpine sub-race, characteristics and distribution of, 155

Altitude, influence of, on man, 142

Amalgamation, 497; accommodation, assimilation, and, 496-97; of Negro, 462

Ambivalence, 119; emotional, through conflict, 396-98; group participation, personality, and, 131; identification and, 119; of co-operation and conflict, 400, 401, 414; socialization and moralization affected by, 131-32; we-group versus others-group, 395-98

Ambivert, 125, 126

American family, changes in economic functions in, 236-39; changes in, in size, 233-35; community differences in, 233-35; divorces in, 250-51; size and composition of, 232-35; size of housing units and, 234-35

American Indian, a sub-race, characteristics of, 157

American Medical Association, function of, in social control, 548-49

Americanization, 503-05; ineffectual features of, 504-05

Amusement, definition of, 305; relation to play, 305

Animism, 286

Anticipatory behavior, 111-12; attitudes, 112; intelligence, 112

Apes, social life among, 3-5

Arbitration, as accommodation, 458-59; industrial, 458; means of self-regulation in business, 543

Armenoid sub-race, characteristics and distribution of, 155

Art, as universal culture pattern, 24; foundations of, 317-18; material culture and, 318-20; morality and, 320-21; place of, in society and culture, 317-25; rationalization and standards of, 323; relation to fantasy, 317; relation to play, 317; religion and, 320; standards of, and culture, 321-24

Aryanism, a social myth in Nazi Germany, 153, 159

Aspiration and achievement, levels of, 364

Assimilation, 495-516; accommodation, amalgamation, and, 496-97; as universal cultural pattern, 26; definition of, 495; disintegration of personality and, 133; factors helping, 502-07; factors influencing rate of, 497-98; factors in immigrant, 500-01; immigrant aids to, 505-07; large percentage of foreign-born influences, 189; marginal man, importance in, 512-15; nationality, segregation, and, 498-99; nature of, 495-98; of immigrant, 463; of Negro, 462; place of recreation in, 502-03; primary groups and, 496; rôle of immigrant children in, 502; school and, 266; situations hindering, 498-501; time element in, 506-07; variations in rate of, 497-98

Association, depends on contact, 3

Athletics, 309-10; commercialization of college, 310; education and, 310

Attitudes, as phase of anticipatory behavior, 112; ideas and emotions and, 112

Audience, as impermanent primary group, 11-12

Birth control, difficulty in applying in order to breed superior stocks, 209-10; negative eugenics and, 207-08; world population pressure and, 183

Birth rate, community and religious differences and, 198; crude and specific, 176-77; differentials in, 195-98; social status and occupation and, 195-97; world, 176-77

Business, informal controls of, 541–45; legal control of, 537–41; social control of, 535–45

Capitalism, effect of Protestantism on, 298–99; form of culture compared with others, 586–92; open class system and, 482–83, 487–89; relation to cultural change, 55
Caste, divisions within Hindu, 479; factors in breakdown of Hindu, 480–81; foundation of Hindu, 478–79; Hindu, 478–81; in ancient Mediterranean societies, 481–82; in primitive societies, 477–78; not always formed by economic differences, 474; regulations in Hindu, 479–80; societal organization and, 477–82
Catharsis, play life and, 316
Censorship, as phase of social control, 528; mass impression and, 277; under communism, 528; under fascism, 528
Ceremony, in religion, 287
Child, differentiation in parental care of, 423–24
Childhood, differentiation and, 417
Child-parent relations, psychology of, 245–49
Children, culture and training of, 243–44; divorce and, 250, 251, 253–55; economic activities of, in home, 244; education of, in home, 245; effects of remarriage on, 254; religious and moral training of, in home, 244–45; training of, in family, 243–49
Christianity, attitudes of early, toward personal demoralization, 561; Western family affected by, 231–32
Chromosomes, 92; and sex, 95, 96
Church, community and, 291–93; competition with state, 358–59; definition of, 288; liberalism versus conservatism in, 292–93; sect and, 288–89; urban and rural, 292–93
Cities, direction of growth in, 148–50; influence of trade and transportation on growth of, 148; location of, factors in, 146–47; man-made topography in, 147–49
City, decentralization of, 72–73; dominance of culture of, 71–73; mob-mindedness in, 71; urban community, 65–73
Civilization, as phase of culture, 20
Clan, relation of individual to, 217
Class and caste systems, 477–82; in ancient Mediterranean culture, 481–82
Clubs, place of in play, 307, 308
Coercion, accommodation and, 455–57; disintegrative effects of, 456

Commensalism, 401
Communism, accommodation and dictatorship under, 456; class conflict and, 386–88; classless society aim of, 585; co-operation and, 413; incentives under, 582–83; rôle of individual initiative under, 586; Russia, and planning under, 179; social control under, 552–53; stratification under, 493; suppression of freedom of research under, 587; theory of society under, 582–83
Community, church and, 291–93; definition of, 5–6; distinct from neighborhood, 7; factors in, aiding immigrant assimilation, 502–03; personality influenced by, 123; place of teacher in, 267–69; population differences in types of, 187–92; primary and secondary, 6; type of, and leadership, 445; urban, 65–73; variations in attitudes toward divorce, 253; variations in divorce rates in, 251; variations in family size and composition in types of, 233–35
Community centers, assimilation and, 503; educational and recreational functions of, 309
Community church, 293
"Companionate" marriage, 219, 222–23
Compensation, 121–22; among school children, 263; inferiority feelings and, 121–22; leadership and, 446–47; marginal man and, 513, 514
Competition, 17, 349–65; always related to other social processes, 356; as universal cultural pattern, 25, 26; co-operation and, 356; economic, 351–54; economic, and laissez faire, in primary groups, 354–55; economic, not a self-regulating mechanism, 537; economic, societal organization, and, 354–56; form of opposition, 349–50; forms of, 351–60; forms of economic, 352–53; ideology of, 541; in missionary work, 357; in religion, 357; institutional, 358–60; intensity of personal, 361–62; laissez faire and, 353, 542; native, with machine products, 357; personality and, 360–64; political, 358; population growth and nationalism in, 180–81; racial and cultural, 356–58; relation to conflict, 366; restlessness and personal, 362–63; selection in personal, 361–62; success motive and personal, 363–64; widens range of stimulation and response, 363–64
Compromise, as accommodation, 457–59; political, 457–58; religious, 457;

usefulness of, 459; weakness in philosophy of, 458–59
Comradeship, as primary group, 8; between parents and children, 246; need of, between husband and wife, 240–41
Conciliation, as accommodation, 459–60; deliberation and, 460; religious, 459
Concubinage, 227
Conflict, 17, 366–99; as universal cultural pattern, 25, 26; between public and parochial schools, 294–95; biracial, in United States, 461–64; characteristics of, 366–67; class, 386–88; communism aims to abolish class, 585; communism and class, 386–88; culture patterns of, 392–93; culture, societal order, and, 392–95; distinction of, from competition, 366; emotional appeal of, 395, 397–98; employer-laborer and social control, 547; form of opposition, 366; impersonal ideas and revolutionary, 391–92; industrial, 367–71, 458, 459; intensity of, and range of, 394; integration of person in, 395–98; intercommunity, 383–85; intermittent nature of, 366, 394–95; intra-class, 388; intra-community, 385–86; may arise from imposition of alien ethos, 27; nature of, 366–67; of impersonal ideas, 390–92; personality and, 395–98; population changes and age, 389–90; population factors fostering, 180–81; population pressure on resources and, 175–76; racial, 371–73; religious, 373–75; resolution of subjective, 469–71; rural against urban, 64–65, 383–85; sex, 388–89; societal organization and, 393–95; solution of Negro-white, 462–63; solution of sex, by toleration, 463–64; strike as a form of, 368–71; sublimation in, 394; types of, 367–92; war as a form of, 376–81; we-group versus others-group attitudes in, 396–98
Congeniality group as primary group, 8; rôle in play, 307
Consummatory response, 115–16; pleasant feelings and, 115–16
Contact, See Interaction
Continuity of culture, 18–19; essential to social life, 29
Contract, 353, 536
Conversion, as accommodation, 464–65; not confined to religion, 464–65
Co-operation, 400–15; ambivalence with conflict, 414; among churches, 293; as universal cultural pattern, 25, 26; church and religious, 409; communistic ideology and, 413; consumers'

economic, 405–07; economic, 403–08, 589; forms of, 403–11; in human society, 402–03; in political behavior, 408–09; international aspects of economic, 572; international political, 408–09; lack of basic philosophy in economic types of, 407; limitations of economic, 407–08; most effective within community sub-groups, 414; nature of, 400–03; necessary to business, 541; personality and, 411–14; producers' economic, 403–04; psychology of, 411–14; range of, 402–03; related to we-group, 411–12; relation of, to culture, 403; restrains individual, 412–13; rural primary groups and, 61; science, art, and, 409–11; sympathetic reactions necessary to, 411
Co-operatives, 403–08, 589
Crime, culture patterns of, 568–69; economic roots of much, 572
Crises, divergent behavior and, 556; individual variations in meeting, 557–58; leadership and, 444–45; number of, in modern society, 555–56; recent changes producing, 580–81
Crowd, as impermanent primary group, 11–12
Cultural anthropology, field of, xiv; relation to other social sciences, xiv
Cultural change, 30–56; controlled and planned, 281–82; cumulative effects of, 51–52; education in planned, 282; integration of traits in, 52; see Social change
Cultural evolution, 32–34; unilinear theories of, 33
Cultural growth, 30–56; diffusion in, 39–42; factors in, 34–44; invention in, 35–39; stages in, 30, 32
Cultural lag, expressed in disorganization, 53–54; nature of, 53; various effects of, 54
Culture, art standards reflect, 321–24; attitudes towards divorce affected by, 253–55; commercial and machine, and urban life, 66–69; conflict patterns in, 392–93; content of, 20–27; crime as a pattern of, 568–69; definition of, xiii, 18–20; dominance of city, 71–79; factors in growth of, 34–44; fundamental factors in, 20; geography and, 137–52; growth and change of, 30–56; influences of race, geography, and historical events, 34; nature of, 18–29; pauperism as a pattern of, 567–68; personality and participation in, in relation to, 116–24; philosophy and, 334–45; population, food sup-

ply, and, 172; progress and change, 30–34; science and, 326–34; theories of growth of, 30–34; transmission of, 27–29

Culture complex, see Culture pattern

Culture pattern, 21; material, 21–22; non-material, 22; universal, 21–26

Culture trait, 20

Cycles of activity, 110–11

Death rate, 177–80; decline in, and economic and social status, 179–80; decline in, and medical care, 180; density and, 206; differentials in, 198–206; disease and, 198–200; factors in decline of, 178–79; longevity and, 200–02; occupation and, 204–05; race, nativity, and, 202–03; rapid decline of, in Western countries, 178–80; reduction in infant, 200; sex and marital status, and, 203–04; trends in reduction of, in the United States, 199–200; urban-rural differences in, 205–06; variation in, according to mentality, 201–02; vitality and, 199–200

Definition of the situation, 118; crises, divergent behavior, and, 556–59; group effect on, 120; hedonistic, 131; utilitarian, 131

Degeneration, Christian form of as part of plan of salvation, 31; classic idea of, 30

Democracy, political, capitalism and Protestantism, 298–99; contrast with totalitarianism, 587; possible factors favoring survival of, 589–91; theory of equality in, and education, 263

Dictatorship, as accommodation, 455–56; in Soviet Russia, 582–83; rise of in modern world, 582–84; totalitarian, 587–89; under fascism, 583, 589

Differentiation, 416–51; adult, 419–20; age, 417–22; arises in complex society everywhere, 585–86; conflict and age, 389–90; conflict and sex, 388–89; culture and adolescent, 418–19; division of labor, 437–43; in adolescence, 418–19; in infancy and childhood, 417; leadership and, 443–50; old age and, 420–23; sex, 423–35; sex and economic, 425–27; sex and political activity, 427–30; stratification and, 473, 474

Diffusion, Christianity and, 82–83; controversy over theories of, 42–44, 56; definition of, 39–40; diffusionist school and, 43; direct and indirect methods of, 40–41; factors in rate of, 42; historical school and, 43–44; invention less important than, in build-ing culture, 41; modification of other traits in relation to, 41–42; rates of, 41; taboo and, 42; theories of, 42–44; war and conquest a factor in, 40–41

Division of labor, 61; economic, 437–39; interdependence, and, 438–39; makes for stratification in complex society, 492–93; sexual, reflected in household, 235–39; social implications of economic, 439–40

Divorce, 249–53; adjustments following, 252–53; children and, 253–55; community differences in rates of, 251; difficulties following remarriage, 252; economic factors in, 250; grounds for, 250, 251; in Soviet Russia, 255; influence of children on incidence of, 250, 251; legal grounds for, not real ones, 251–52; mores and public opinion influence, 251–52

Dominance, law of, in heredity, 92–93; recessiveness and, 93

Domination, accommodation and, 455–57

Drama, as form of play life, 310

Economic order, religion and, 297–99

Economics, field of, xiv

Education, 257–83; adult, 274–75; competition in, 359–60; competitors of formal, 275–77; correspondence courses and, 272; costs of, in the United States, 259; extension, 272; a family function, 295; for organized labor, 273; formal, related to complex culture, 257–58; indoctrination in, 279–81; in industry and business, 273; in Soviet Russia, 260; interaction, instruction, and, 262–63; interactional patterns of formal, 260–61; international contacts, and, 82–83; modern society and, 258–70; new trends in, 270–75; nursery, 270–71; outside formal institutions, 272–75; popular faith in, 581; population influences, 186; primitive, purposes of, 257; provision for emotional and conduct problems in, 271; pupil-to-pupil relations and, 263–64; rapid expansion of formal, 258–60; recent trends in formal, 270–72; religion and, 293–95; scientific attitudes fostered by, 332; social rituals in, 263–64; students engaged in, in United States, 259; teacher-pupil relations in, 261–64; theory of equality and, 263; training to think in, 277–79; vocational, 271–72

Elite, circulation of, 492; social control and, 492

Emotions, 110; attitudes and, 112; in conflict, 395; war and, 397–98

Endocrines, affected by genes, 103; development affected by, 102–04

Endogamy, 223

Environment, definition of, 90; effect of, on organic development, 101–02; interrelated with, not antagonistic to heredity, 106–08; original nature, heredity, and, 89–108; types of, 19

Esthetics, See Art

Ethnocentrism, 13; basic to group conflict and prejudice, 13–15

Ethos, as societal character, 26–27; business, 544; capitalistic, 55; features of American, 26; features of Oriental, 26–27

Eugenics, negative, 206–08; positive, 208–10

Euthenics, 206

Evolution, relation to philosophy, 342–43; theories of social evolution and progress, and biological, 31

Evolutionary change, relation to revolution, 54–55

Exogamy, 223

Exploitation, by organized gangs, 543–44; dictatorship and, 456; fostered by cultural lag, 54; in economic life, 537, 540; more subtle forms of, 542; regulations to prevent, 540–41

Extrovert, 124, 126; as personality type, 124; leader as, 448–50; occupational choice of, 442–43

Family, 6–7, 215–56; backgrounds of Western, 231–32; basic primary group, 215; basis of societal order, 216–17; bilateral, 218; changed relations of husband and wife in, 239–43; changes in child care in modern, 243–44; child training in, 243–49; Christianity and, 231–32; composition of American, 232–35; definition of, 215; dissolution of, 249–55; divorce and, 249–55; economic functions in, 235–39; functions of, vary with culture, 215; Industrial Revolution and, 232; influence of population changes on, 194; influence of population distribution on, 188; inheritance systems and, 235–36; institutions for control of, 24; institutions of, 215–30; "joint," 215; lines of descent in, 217–18; male and female position in, 228–29; "marriage group" and, 215; matriarchal, 228; modern, 231–56; patriarchal, 228–29; psychology of husband-wife relations in, 240–43; romanticism and, 232; sex relations in, 218–27

Fantasy thinking, 113–14; art and, 317; daydreams, dreams, and free associations as, 113; legends and, 114; magic and, 113–14; myths and, 114; natural and essential to man, 114; relation to play life, 316–17

Fascism (and Nazism), accommodation and dictatorship under, 455–56; family relations and divorce under, 255; indoctrination through education under, 280; planned social change under, 580, 587–89; social control under, 552–53; state planning and, 179, 579; stratification under, 493; suppression of freedom of research under, 587, 591; theory of society and control under, 583, 587–89

Fecundity, 176

Feebleminded, colonization of, 207; sterilization of, 207

Feelings, 110

Feral men, 57–58, 60

Fertility, 176; affected by social status, standards of living, etc., 195–98

Folkways, as culture, 18–19

Food, culture, and population in relation to, 172–74; population pressure and synthetic, 183; population pressure on, 167–74

Foreign-born, population changes among, in the United States, 190–91

Gambling, as form of play life, 311–12; culture patterns of, 312; definition of, 311

Gang, childhood, as primary group, 8

Genes, as chemical substances, 92, 100; not a mystic force, 99

Genetic theory of heredity, 96–97

Geographic influences, various sorts of, 137

Geography, climate, land surfaces, minerals, and, 140–46; culture and, 137–52; culture, not geography, determines behavior, 138–39; migration and settlement in regard to, 146–50; principal influences of, 140–46; theories of determinism in, 137–40

Great man theory of history, and invention, 37–38

Group, definition of, xiii; definition of situation affected by, 120; impermanent types of, 9–12; rôle in, 120; status in, 121–22

Group attitudes, personality and, 128–29

Group-life, participation and integration in, 16–17

"Group marriage," nowhere found, 216, 219

Habits, continuity of social, 5

Heredity, defective strains in human, 97–99; definition of, 90; due to complex factors, 99–100; human, 97–101; incorrectly used to explain genius, crime, defectiveness, etc., 89; interrelated with, not antagonistic to, environment, 106–08; law of ancestral inheritance and, 91; law of dominance and, 92–93; law of filial regression and, 91; law of linkage and, 95–96; law of segregation and, 94–95; mechanisms of, 91–96; Mendelian laws of, 92–96; mutations and, 100–01; nature of, 89–97; original nature and, 89–91; original nature, environment, and, 89–108; particulate theory of, 96–97; racial mental differences not explained by, 164–65; sex determination and, 95–96

Historical school of anthropology, controversy with diffusionists, 42–44, 56; unilinear theories and, 33–34

History, field of, xiv–xv; relation to sociology, xiv

Household, changes in size and function in American, 236–39

Human groups, 5–17

Human nature, socially acquired, 89

Husband, sense of comfort and assurance through wife, 241–42

Ideas, as phase of thought, 112; attitudes, emotions, and, 112

Identification, 117–18; ambivalence and, 119; nationalistic and internationalistic attitudes and, 85–87; of teachers with bourgeois classes, 270; personality development and, 117–18; projection and, 119–20; rôle and, 120–21; with outside power in religious experience, 301

Illegitimacy, seldom given group sanction, 217

Immigrant, assimilation of, 495–516; changes in personality of children of, 509–11; grandchildren of, 511; heritages of, 499; nationalist sentiments of, 500; native-language press and, 500; personality changes in, 507–09; reaction of native-born to, 501; segregation of, 500–01

Individual, influenced by philosophy, 343–45

Individual differences, crises affect persons in terms of, 557–58; leadership and, 443–44

Individualism, advantages of, in open class system, 493; ambition complex and, 488–89; background of economic,

535–37; economic competition and, 353; education, competitive spirit, and, 263–64; freedom under system of, 586–89; laissez faire, 535–37; laissez faire, industrial conflict, and, 367; open class system and, 482–83, 487–89; personal competition fosters, 362–64; personal demoralization and doctrine of, 562; philosophy affects, 338–39; Protestantism fosters, 298; social change in a world marked by, 580–82; theory of responsibility for demoralization under, 570; traditional among American farmers, 64; unique religious experience and, 300; Western family life and, 231, 232

Indoctrination, and formal transmission of culture, 28; and mass impression, 281; conscious control of, under communism and fascism, 279–80; ethos of a society rests on, 279; of rich to support poor, 565–66; through planned or unplanned means, 277; use of art for, 321

Industrial Revolution, competition and, 364; population and, 168; social problems growing out of, 562; urbanization related to, 67; Western family and, 232

Infancy, differentiation and, 417

Inferiority feelings, immigrant and, 508–09; in family relations, 246; in poverty classes, 567; leadership sometimes a compensation for, 446–47; of marginal man, 513; of teacher in community, 267–68; produced by school situations, 263; produced in children by divorce of their parents, 253; stratification and, 475–76

In-group, see We-group

Instincts, 110; no social, 111

Institutions, as universal culture patterns, 23–24, 25–26; educational, 257–83; family, 215–30; stratification and, 475

Integration, in cultural change, 52; in group life, 17; personality and, 129–30; we-group and others-group attitudes in personality, 130

Intelligence, as phase of anticipatory behavior, 112; various definitions of, 98

Intelligence tests, see Mental tests

Interaction, economic expansion, world contact, and, 81–87; expanding world of, 57–88; isolation and, 57–87; leadership and, 446–48; masses and leader in, 447; national state as area of, 78–80; primary community and, 60–65; region as it affects, 73–78; secondary community and, 65–73

Internationalism, economic expansion and, 81–82; nationalism versus, 85–86; organizations fostering, 84–85; a phase of secondary community, 80–87; political contacts and, 83–85; population growth and, 180–84

Introvert, 124, 126; as personality type, 124–25; leader as, 448–50; occupational choice of, 442–43

Invention, as a factor in growth of culture, 35–39; dependence of, on culture, 37–38; diffusionist school and, 43; discovery and, 35; duplication of, 38; empirical, 36; great man theory of history and, 37–38; historical school and, 43–44; list of duplications in, 38; mental ability in relation to, 37; planned, 39; psychology of, 37; science and planned, 39; stimulus to, 36–38; theories of, 42–44

Isolation, 57–60; American farmer's individualism and, 64; breakdown of, 71–72; cultural aspects of, 88–89; factors fostering, 57–60; geographic, 146; language differences foster, 58–59; of defective, delinquent, and dependent classes, 571; of immigrant, 498–501, 506; of teachers from community, 270; personality and, 60; primary community and, 60–61; rural primary groups and, 61–62; scientist and intellectual, 331; undue wishful thinking produces, 113; we-group versus others-group feeling and, 58–59

Jew, as marginal man, 513, 514

"Joint" family, 215, 217

Kallikak family, 97–98

Kinship, family in relation to, 216–18

Labor, control of, 545–47

Laissez faire, breakdown of economic, 355–56; co-operation and, 404; economic competition and, 351–55; social change under, 580–81

Land, conflict over, to relieve population pressure, 183–84; "destructive occupation" of, 143; influences of, on man and culture, 142–44

Language, and thought, 22–23; as cultural pattern, 22; thought in relation to, 112–13

Laughter, place of, in play, 316; social control by, 531

Law, 24; business control by, 537–41; function as social control, 524–25; mores and, in business, 544; public opinion, mores, and, 24, 527–28

Leaders, classifications of, 448–50; symbols of power for masses, 447–48; types of, 448–50

Leadership, 443–50; competition fosters rise of, 364; crises and rise of, 444–45; cultural and situational factors in, 444–46; in church, 299; in revolution, 47; individual differences and, 443–44; masses and, 447–48; occupation and, 445; old age and, 421–22; scientists given, by masses, 331–32; social interaction and, 446–48; submission to, and accommodation, 466; type of community and, 445

League of Nations, 84–85, 87

Learning, configurations of stimuli in, 111–12; nature of, 111–12

Legal profession, social control of, 548, 549–50

Legend, as universal cultural pattern, 24–25, 26; fantasy in, 114; used in informal transmission of culture, 28; war fostered by, 377–81

Leisure, definition of, 305; relation to play, 305

Levirate, 225

Lodge, fraternal, and play life, 308

Logic as cultural pattern, 25, 26

Logical thinking, contrasted with fantasy, 113–14

Magic, as universal cultural pattern, 24; relation of, to fantasy of insane, 113–14; religion and, 285–86

Male, changing attitudes toward women, 430; dominance of, in family, 424; early attitude toward woman suffrage, 428–29

Malthusian doctrine of population, 169–71; kinds of checks on reproduction, 170–71

Marginal man, 133; important in assimilation, 512–15; personality of, 512–15

Marriage, cross-cousin, 225; dissolution of, 249–53; forms of, 219–23; levirate form of, 226; nature of, 218–19; preparation for, 226–27; prohibitions against, 223–24; religious sanctions not universal, 219; romantic pattern of, 239–40; sex relations not to be confused with, 218–19; sororate form of, 225; symbolism in, 219; wife-purchase and, 225

Mass impression, conflict of formal versus informal, 277

Masses, rôle of, in revolution, 49

Material culture, 22; art and, 318–20

Matrilineal descent, 218

Matrilocal system, 222

Mediation, 458

Mediterranean sub-race, characteristics and distribution of, 156
Melanesians, a Negroid sub-race, 157
Mendelian laws of heredity, 92–96
Mental differences, among races, 158–65; in occupations, 440–43; in sex, 432–36; individual and racial, 165
Mental hygiene, aid to dealing with personal demoralization, 572–73
Mental tests, applied to races and sub-races, 160–64; cultural factors in, 161–64; innate ability of race and, 164–65; motivation in, 163–64
Metropolis, region and, 75–78
Migration, geographical factors in, 146
Mineral resources, importance to industrial culture, 144–46; limitation of, and culture, 150–51
Minority group, place in political revolution, 47
Missionary enterprises, competition in, 357–58
Mob, as impermanent primary group, 11–12
Mobility, as factor of cultural lag, 54; cityward, 67; increases in daily, 67–68; occupational, 483–86; population, in cities, 66–69; residential, 67–68; rural-urban backgrounds to occupational, 485; various sorts of, in cities, 66–69
Mobmindedness, city and, 71
Mongoloid race, 157–58
Mongols, a sub-race, characteristics and distribution of, 157
Monogamy, 219–20
Morality, in words and in action, 132–33; nationalistic and internationalistic features of, 86–87; play important for training in, 314; play life and, 312–15; relation of success to, 363
Moralization, myths, legends, and stereotypes in, 131–32; socialization and, 130–32
Mores, and professions, 552; belief in future reward or punishment supports, 297; belief in God supports, 296; definition of, 24; divergence in sex, 425; law and, in business, 544; public opinion and, regarding rights of labor, 546; public opinion, law, and, 527–28; religion and, 295–97
Mortality, see Death rate
Motion picture, and mass impression, 276–77; as form of play life, 310–11; competitor of formal education, 275–77; rôle of, in picturing war, 378
Motives, anticipatory behavior and acquired, 114–15; rationalization hides real, 122–23

Motor organs, 109
Mutations, 100–01; X-ray treatment and germ cells and, 101
Mutual aid, among immigrants, 500; in human society, 401–03; in nature, 400–01
Mysticism, 340–41
Myth, as universal cultural pattern, 24–25, 26; fantasy thinking in, 114; Nordic, 159–60; use in conscious indoctrination, 279; use in transmission of informal culture, 28; use of in political revolution, 47–48; war fostered by, 377–81

Nationalism, 60; education and, 258; factors in, 80–81; internationalism versus, 85–86; relation to capitalism, 298; stimulation to, 79
Nationality minorities, 498–99
Nativity, survival, and, 202–03
Natural selection, culture and society prevent, in man, 209–10
Nazi Germany, dictatorship in, 456, 587–89; See also Fascism
Negritos, a Negroid sub-race, characteristics and distribution of, 156
Negro, accommodation of white man and, 461–63; amalgamation of, slow, 462; as marginal man, 513; competition of, and higher education, 357; difficulty in assimilating, 462; mental tests of, 160–61; survival rates among, 202–03
Negroid race, 154, 156–57
Negro sub-race, characteristics and distribution of, 156
Negro-white conflict, 372–73; accommodation and, 373, 461–63
Neighborhood, as primary group, 7; distinct from community, 7
Neo-Malthusianism, 171–72
Nervous system, autonomic, 110; central, 109–10; structure of, 109–10
Newspaper, circulation of, as criterion of region, 75–76; competition of formal education, 275; influence of, on masses, 275
Nordic myth, 159–60
Nordic sub-race, characteristics and distribution of, 155
Norms of behavior, culture sets, 556; set by mores, law, and public opinion, 555

Occupation, family size in relation to, 234; mental differences and, 440–43
Occupations, descent in scale of, 485–86; mobility in, 483–86; rise in scale of, 483–85

Old age, differentiation and, 420–22; rôle of, in leadership, 422; rôle of, in primitive societies, 421

Open class system, 482–89; advantages of, in stratification, 493; occupational mobility in, 483–86; perpetuation of, 487–89; political and religious mobility in, 486–87; relation to individualism and *laissez faire*, 482–83; rise of, 482–83; social change and, 581

Opposition, 17, 349–51

Organic drives or tendencies, 110–11

Original nature, heredity and environment and, 89–108

Others-group, definition of, 13; distinction from we-group, 13–15; interrelations with various we-groups, 14–16; personality integrated toward, 129–30

Out-group, See Others-group

Parent-child relations, authority in, 246–47; companionship in, 246; maturation in emotions and intelligence in reference to, 395–97; over-domination of parents in, 247; psychology of, 245–49; sense of independence and responsibility in, 247; sense of security in, 245–46; vocational attitudes in reference to, 249

Parenthood, basis of family, 216–18; child care in differentiation in, 423–24; kinship, social structure, and, 216–18

Parent-Teacher Association, 266–67

Participation, in accommodation, 460–64; in group life, 16; personality and culture in relation to, 116–24

Particularism, dangers of, 138

Patriarchal family, 228–29, 236

Patrilineal descent, 218

Pauperization, culture patterns developed in, 567–68; from long unemployment, 566–67

Personal demoralization, agencies for care and treatment, 560–66; and social control, 554–74; backgrounds of, treatment of, 561–62; culture determines type of care and treatment of, 560–61; culture patterns of, 566–69; mental hygiene and, 572–73; modern diagnosis and treatment of, 569–73; not always correlated with social disorganization, 558; present-day methods of treatment of, 562–66; types of, 559–60

Personality, 109–34; accommodation and, 465–71; ambivalence of attitudes in, toward we-group and others-group, 128–29; assimilation and, 507–15; changes in, in children of immi-

grants, 509–11; changes in, in grandchildren of immigrants, 511–12; changes in, in immigrant generation, 507–09; conflict and, 395–98; definition of, xiii, 116; disintegration of, 133–34; effects of division of labor on, 438–39; factors in rise of, 116–24; group attitudes and, 128–29; group participation and, 128–36; influence of city on, 69–71; integration and balance of, 129–30, 570–71; leadership and, 446–48; mother's importance in rise of, 116–17; participation and culture in relation to, 116–24; personal-social and cultural factors in rise of, 117; personality growth and societal organization, 584–93; play as balancing factor in, 315–17; play, moral conduct, and, 312–17; psychological foundations of, 109–16; rationalization and resolution of conflicts, 470; religion and, 300; resolution of conflicts within, 469–71; selection and resolution of conflicts, 469; sensory experience in rise of, 116–17; social types of, in city, 69–70; we-group versus others-group attitudes in conflict, and, 395–98

Personality type, 124–27; extrovert as, 124; introvert as, 124–25; relation to physique, 125–26; relation to social type, 125–27

Personal-social learning, 19; distinction from cultural learning, 20

Philosophy, and balanced world view, 344–45; and everyday life, 343–44; art and religion in, 344–45; and individual, 343–45; Christian, 337; culture and, 334–45; Deistic, 338; effect on education, 341; fields of, 334–35; formal, 334–36; how culture affects, 336–42; individualistic, 338–39; mystical, 340–41; nature and growth of formal, 334–36; reflected in literature, 341–42; romantic, 339–40

Play, as balancing factor in personality, 315–17; athletics and sports as form of, 309–10; catharsis through, 316; definition of, 304–05; forms of, 306–12; general features of, 304–06; hunting pattern in, 315–16; personality, moral conduct, and, 312–17; primary-group forms of, 307–09; Puritan restrictions on, 312–13; relation to recreation, amusement, etc., 304–05; theories of origin of, 305–06; work and, 305

Playgrounds, 308–09

Political conflict, 375–81; party form of, 375–76

Political party, cliques within the, 376; place of, in political conflict, 375–76

Political power, mobility in, in reference to classes, 486

Political revolution, background factors of, 45–48; consolidation of new power in, 50; factors in, 48–50; ideology of, 46–47; rationalizations in defense of, 50; rôle of masses in, 49; terrorism in, 49–50

Political science, field of, xiii–xiv

Polyandry, 219, 222

Polygyny, 219, 220–22, 235

Population, 167–211; affected by family life, community, etc., 188; age changes of, in the United States, 191–94; birth control and, 183; colonization and emigration only temporary solutions of problem of, 181; cultural factors in, 182–84; danger spots in, 175–76, 181; decline of births affecting distribution of, 192; density in cities, 65–66; density of, and pressure of, 175–76; differentials in, 186–211; differentials in birth and death rates and, 194–206; doctrine of progress and, 171–72; education affected by, 186; food supply, culture, and, 172–74; geographical influences on, 151; growth affected by preventive and positive checks, 170–71; growth and differential rates among nations, 174–84; nationalism and internationalism and, 180–84; pressure of, a matter of attitudes as well as food and other resources, 182–83; pressure of, and fascist nationalism, 197; pressure of, factors producing, 175–76, 180–81; pressure of, on food supply, 167–74; relation of density to culture, 65; resources and, 174; rural and urban differences in, 189–90; selection and quality of, 206–10; sex and age distributions in, 186–94; sex and age distributions of, in various communities, 187–91; societal order and culture related to, 167; solutions offered to problems of, 181–84; theories of: optimistic and pessimistic, 170–72; variations in density of, 174–76; world problems of, 167–84

Preferential mating, 224–25

Prehuman social life, 3–5

Prejudice, applied to Negro, 372–73; nature of, 372; Nordic myth and, 159–60; racial, 158–60

Press, and creation of myths, legends, and stereotypes, 276; competitor of formal education, 275–76; influence on masses, 275–76; in strikes, 370–71

Prestige, factor in stratification, 474; scientist and, 331–32; wealth, open class system, and, 488

Primary community, 60–65; isolation and, 60–61; recent changes in, 62–65

Primary group, 6–12; childhood gang as, 8; comradeship as, 8; congeniality group as, 8; family as, 6–7; neighborhood as, 7; permanence of, 9–12; play group as, 7; rôle determined at outset in, 120; rural, 61; social control in, 521–22

Principle of legitimacy, family based on, 216–17, 241

Professions, codes of, 549–50; competition stimulates merit in, 363; informal control of, 548–53; legal control of, 548; not created by mere names, 551–52; social control of, 547–53

Profit-making, incentive to economic competition, 353–54

Progress, criteria of, 576–77; doctrine of, 575–78; doctrine of, and population, 171–72; education as an instrument of, 278; influence of faith in, 576; stages in, 32; tests of, 578; theories of, 31–32

"Progressive" education, 264, 277; as training to think, 277–79

Projection, 119–20; attitudes toward others-group rest on, 129; identification and, 119–20; parental, on children, 249

Propaganda, and formal transmission of culture, 29; and mass impression, 277; as phase of social control, 528; competitor of formal education, 276; education and, 258

Property, 536; as cultural pattern, 23–24; private, and competition, 353

Prostitution, 227–28

Protestantism, relation to capitalism and political democracy, 298–99

Psychic unity, doctrine of, 34–35

Public, as impermanent secondary group, 11–12

Public opinion, 24; influence of, on professions, 552; labor, social control, and, 546, 547; mores, law, and, 527–28; nature of, 526; not same as preponderant opinion, 526–27; place of, in social control, 526–28; place of, in strikes, 370–71; stages in development of, 527

Pupil-to-pupil relations, 264–65

Race, a biological term, 5; blood tests of, 154; a classificatory term, 158; criteria of, 153–54; definition of, 153; innate ability of, 164–65; nationality and language groups often called, 153; nature and distribution of, 153–58; popular misunderstanding of, 153; sub-race often called, 153; survival and, 202–03

Races, major groups of, 155–58; mental differences among, 158–65; prejudices regarding, 158–59; probably no pure, 158; various mixed, 157–58

Racial conflict, 371–73; causes of, 371; culture and, 373

Radicalism, tabooed in schools, 268–69

Radio, and mass impression, 276–77; as phase of play life, 311; competitor of formal education, 276–77

Rainfall, influence of, on man, 141–42

Rationalization, 122–23; art standards and taste and, 323–24; a defense mechanism, 123; place of, in morality, 132; preservation of ego by, 122–23; real motives hidden by, 122–23; used to defend revolutionary changes, 50

Recessiveness, in heredity, 93

Recreation, aids assimilation of immigrants, 502–03; as universal cultural pattern, 24; church and, 295; definition of, 304; loss of, in home, 245; nature of, in city, 69; relation of play life to, 304–05; religion and, 295

Reformation, 60; education affected by, 258; family affected by, 232

Region, 73–78; economic basis of, 75–76; Federal Reserve districts as, 75–76; metropolitan center of, 76–78; newspaper circulation in, 75–76; wholesale trade areas as, 75–76; zones of influence in, 77

Religion, 284–303; animism in, 286; art and, 320; as balancing factor in personality, 300–01; as universal cultural pattern, 24; ceremony and ritual in, 287; children's training in, at home, 244–45, 249; church and, 288; competition of, 357; creed and, 288; culture and, 284–91; denomination and, 288, 289; divorce affected by, 251; economic order and, 297–99; education and, 262, 293–95; international contacts fostered by, 82–83; magic and, 285–86; mores and, 295–97; personality and, 300–03; primitive, 284–87; recreation and, 295; sacred objects and buildings, 288; science and, 332–34; secondary group life and, 292–93; sect and, 288–89; symbolism in, 287–88; teachers and conformity to, 268; theology and, 288; variation in expression of, 301–03

Religious conflict, 373–75; factors making for, 374

Religious experience, integrated to culture, 301; levels of, 301–03; psychology of, 300–03; reality of, 301

Religious organizations, as focus of varied activities, 295; community churches as, 293; relation to other organizations, 291–99

Religious power, mobility among classes in, 487

Renaissance, 60, 232; education affected by, 258

Revolution, change and, 44–50; evolution closely linked to, 44, 54–55; factors in outbreak of political, 48–50; relation to slow or evolutionary change, 54–55; social change and, 580; use of myths in, 47–48; various uses of term, 44–45

Rights and liberties, nature of, 536, 538

Ritual, in religion, 287

Rôle, definitions of situation and, 120; differentiation and adult, 419–20; differentiation and types of, 437–51; identification and, 120–21; primary group effect on, 120; pupil types of, 265; rural types of, 61; teacher types of, 262–63; traditional, of husband, 241; traditional, of wife, 241; urban types of, 69–70

Romantic love, 240

Romanticism, doctrine of progress and, 32; effect on education, 341; in literature, 341–42; philosophy of, 339–40; Western family and, 232

School, assimilation and, 266; family routine affected by, 265–66; institutional features of, 261; purposes of, 261; social rituals in, 263–64

Schoolhouses, persistence of one- and two-room, 63

Schools, for workers, 273; in industrial plants, 273; night schools, 272; private schools, 272–73; vocational schools, 271–72

Science, and culture, 326–34; as a cultural pattern, 25, 26, 27; based on logical thinking, 328–29; conflict of ideas in, 390–91; dangers of "orthodoxy" in, 330; definition of, 326; factors hindering and fostering, 329–30; growing interest in, 332; individual and, 330–34; invention and, 39; masses look to, as authority, 333; method of, 327–28; nature of, 327–30; religion, morality, and, 332–34

Scientist, intellectual isolation of, 331; motives of, 330; prestige of, 331–32

Secondary community, internationalism and, 80–87; state as, 78–80

Secondary group, 9–12; characteristics of, 9; impermanent forms of, 11; modern family affected by, 236–39, 241; permanence of, 9–12; social control in, 522

Sect, nature of, 288–89

Sectionalism, 78

Segregation, law of, in heredity, 94–95

Self-image, authority and, 118–20; dual imagery regarding parents and, 119

Sense of security, competition often destroys, 362–63

Sense organs, 109

Sex differences, 423–35; conflict and, 388, 463; culture and, 423–35; mental features of, 432–35; physical features of, 430–32; social rôle and, 423–30; survival rate and, 203–04

Sex relations, outside family, 226–28

Sexual hospitality, restrictions on, 228

Slavery, as accommodation, 455

Social change, control of, 579–80; crisis and, 580–82; kinds of, 580–84; planned, 579; prospects of control and, 575–89; rates of, 578–80; revolutionary programs of, 579–80; stratification varies with, 477; under communism, 580; under fascism, 580, 587–89; see also Cultural change

Social control, 519–93; accommodation and, 469; advertising as means of, 530–31; art and, 320–21; calling names as means of, 532; censorship as means of, 528, 532; commands as means of, 532; control of, 552–53; definition of, 520–21; education as means of, 530–31; ethics of medical profession and, 548–49; expresses utilitarian purposes in society, 587–92; extra-legal devices of, 526; flattery as means of, 530; forms and agencies of, 523–28; function of state in, 524; general features of, 519–34; gossip as means of, 523, 531; in business and industry, 535–47; informal, in business, 541–45; in labor relations, 545–47; in professions, 547–53; indoctrination and, 279–80, 552; kinds of formal, 524–26; laughter as means of, 531; law as, 524–25; legal forms of, for business, 537–41; means of, 528–34; nature and purpose of, 519–22; nature of formal, 524; nature of informal, 523–24; negative and positive means of, 529; of labor, 545–47; of professions, 547–53; overt action as means of, 533; personal demoralization and, 554–74; persuasion as

means of, 531; place of feelings and emotions in, 533–34; play and, 312–15; praise as means of, 530; primary group and, 522; professionalization and, 548–51; propaganda and, 528, 530–31; prospects of social change and, 575–89; public opinion and, 526–28; rewards and badges as a means of, 531; satire as a means of, 531; slogans as a means of, 531; threats as a means of, 532; under communism, 528, 552–53; under fascism, 528, 552–53; use of language in, 530

Social disorganization, affected by cultural lag, 53–54; factors in modern society producing, 555–56; not always correlated with personal demoralization, 558; social pathology and, 554–60

Social distance, 129, 453

Social-economic planning, 590–91

Social evolution, factors in, 50–55; theories of, 30–34; unilinear theories of, 33

Social expectancy, 120–21; family rôles and, 242; in marital relations, 242

Social heritage, 27; see Culture

Social inventions, effects of, 52; interrelation of social and mechanical, 52–53

Social pathology, culture and, 555, 556; social disorganization, 554–60

Social processes, 349–516; as universal culture patterns, xiii, 25, 26

Social psychology, xv; relation to sociology, xv

Social ritual, in education, 263–64; in religion, 287

Social self, see Personality

Social service organizations, aid of in assimilation, 503

Social service work, increasing costs of, 563–64; professional training for, 564–65

Social solidarity, reflected in social attitudes, 128

Social type, relation to personality type, 125–27; see Rôle

Social types, in family, 241; in religious organizations, 289–91; in rural communities, 61; in urban communities, 69–70; introverts and extroverts among, 289; leaders as, 448–50; primary group effects on, 120; pupils develop, 265; teachers develop, 262–63

Social worker, low status of, 564–65; professional training of, 564

Socialization, ambivalence in, 130–31; moralization and, 130–32

Societal organization, and culture, 215–345; conflict and, 393–95; economic